Hopkin's History
The Football League

Volume One
1888-1946

Series Editor: Clive Leatherdale

ROGER HOPKIN

Desert Island Books

First Published in 2009

DESERT ISLAND BOOKS LIMITED
7 Clarence Road, Southend-on-Sea, Essex SS1 1AN
United Kingdom
www.desertislandbooks.com

© 2009 Roger Hopkin

The right of Roger Hopkin to be identified as author
of this work has been asserted under
The Copyright Designs and Patents Act 1988

British Library Cataloguing-in-Publication Data:
A catalogue record for this book
is available from the British Library

ISBN:978-1-905328-70-3

*All rights reserved. No part of this book may be reproduced
or utilised in any form or by any means, electronic
or mechanical, including photocopying, recording
or by any information storage and retrieval system,
without prior permission in writing from the Publisher*

Printed in Great Britain by
4edge Ltd, Hockley. www.4edge.co.uk

INTRODUCTION

The fascinating history of the Football League, part of our nation's heritage, is well worth preserving. That is a key part of the reason why this particular interpretation has been written. I became hooked on the game in the late 1950s, thanks to my late father, who one day brought home a copy of '60 seasons of League Football' by R. C. Churchill. Loving the book, I was disappointed only by what it missed out – something which that excellent work has in common with subsequent publications.

I have never discovered a single volume, no matter how packed with information, that covered everything I hoped to find. The specific gap I noted, and now hope to fill, is how and when titles have been won and other issues settled. That omission provides the other major reason for this book.

All pages in this history have two columns – to maximise data. For seasons 1888-1915 and 1919-1929, the focus is on champions clubs, named at the head of the pages. Short paragraphs outline how the campaign progressed in two halves, up to the point when the title was decided in each division. All the champions' results are provided, with opponents' names in capitals when the champions played at home. Halfway league tables and final league tables are also presented in abbreviated form, giving games played, goals for and against, and points. The bottom figure in each column is the computerised tally of the column in question, to minimise errors.

Coverage of seasons 1929-1939 focuses on both the top and bottom of each division (in which the interim tables are not tabulated). Once again descriptions are given to cover 'how' and 'when' issues were settled. Champions' results are provided, together with a tabulated final table, plus a summary of outcomes for each section. Clubs elected, re-elected or losing League status are displayed in italics for Division 3.

At intervals throughout the book I provide pages of 'other information', including things like the F.A. Cup, crowds, goal-scoring, club colours, grounds, nicknames and rule changes. These pages also include a variety of miscellaneous items.

This history also offers short sections on wartime football, 1915-1919 and 1939-1946, when the Football League was suspended. Outcomes of regional competitions are shown, together with brief explanations of how soccer in this country was organised in wartime. Tabulated final tables are included within this.

ACKNOWLEDGEMENTS

I would like to thank football enthusiast Mike Mahon for encouraging me to seek to have this work published and long-time friend Derek Megginson for proof-reading and checking. I am also grateful to Clive Leatherdale at Desert Island Books for providing the chance for this work to reach a wider audience. Most of all, I wish to dedicate the book to my late father, Norman Hopkin, who inspired my interest in 'the beautiful game' in the first place.

This is for you, Dad.

1888-1889 – FOOTBALL LEAGUE

PRESTON NORTH END

The First Half

The first Football League season was almost all about Preston North End. The Deepdale club, packed with talented Scots, won their opening 6 matches, averaging more than 4 goals per game. North End claimed to have scored the first-ever league goal – Jack Gordon's opener against Burnley. Preston's game started 45 minutes late, however, and there was a counter-claim from Bolton, whose right-winger Kenyon Davenport notched the first of the Trotters' 3 goals in the opening 10 minutes against Derby County.

There was, however, no disputing Preston's superiority. Their 4-0 win at Wolves' Dudley Road ground on September 15th put North End top of the table, ahead of Everton on goal average. Victory over Bolton a week later saw the club go a point clear. After that, Preston remained leaders. In second place by the end of September were Aston Villa, who became only the second side to take a point off North End when drawing with the pace-setters on November 10th. As it turned out, this was the only home game Preston failed to win. Villa could claim a 'moral victory', but little else.

Preston North End's '1st half' record

September	08	BURNLEY	5-2
	15	Wolves	4-0
	22	BOLTON WANDERERS	3-1
	29	Derby County	3-2
October	06	STOKE	7-0
	13	WEST BROMWICH ALBION	3-0
	20	Accrington	0-0
	27	WOLVES	5-2
November	03	Notts County	7-0
	10	ASTON VILLA	1-1
	12	Stoke	3-0

Table at November 12th, 1888

1	PRESTON NORTH END	11	41	8	20
2	Aston Villa	10	32	14	15
3	Blackburn Rovers	9	34	23	12
4	Wolves	10	26	22	12
5	Everton	10	22	21	12
6	West Bromwich Albion	10	22	24	11
7	Accrington	10	29	25	10
8	Bolton Wanderers	10	26	29	6
9	Notts County	9	19	33	6
10	Burnley	10	21	38	6
11	Stoke	10	14	32	5
12	Derby County	9	17	34	3
		118	303	303	118

Attendances 1888-1889

The total number of spectators at the 132 Football League matches is said to have been 605,550 – an average of 4,588 per game.

F.A. CUP FINAL - *30th March, 1889*

Preston North End beat Wolverhampton Wanderers 3-0 at the Kennington Oval. Scorers were Gordon, Goodall and Thompson. 25,000 are said to have watched the game.

The Second Half

When Villa crashed 1-5 at Blackburn Rovers on November 17th, Preston stretched their lead to 7 points. The Midlands club kept up their vain pursuit of North End until January 5th. No other club could step in to put pressure on North End. Preston extended their unbeaten record in the league to nineteen matches by seeing off the challenge of lowly Notts County. On the same afternoon, Aston Villa, excellent at home but vulnerable away, slumped to a 0-4 reverse at Burnley. The first Football League trophy was now definitely on its way to Deepdale.

Preston North End completed the cup and league 'double' by winning the F.A. Cup Final, on March 30th, 3-0, against Wolves. A crowd of 25,000 were present at the game, which was played at The Oval, with Major Marindin, the F.A. President, refereeing. The only thing Preston North End failed to win in the 1888-89 season was the 'honour' of being the League's best-supported club. The average crowd for league games at Deepdale was 6,275. Everton, whose 7,400 average was over 1,000 more, were able to claim the largest following.

Preston North End's '2nd half' record

November	17	ACCRINGTON	2-0
	24	Bolton Wanderers	5-2
December	08	DERBY COUNTY	5-0
	15	Burnley	2-2
	22	EVERTON	3-0
	26	West Bromwich Albion	5-0
	29	BLACKBURN ROVERS	1-0
January	05	NOTTS COUNTY	4-1
	12	Blackburn Rovers	2-2
	19	Everton	2-0
February	09	Aston Villa	2-0

Final Football League Table 1889

1	PRESTON NORTH END	22	74	15	40
2	Aston Villa	22	61	43	29
3	Wolves	22	50	37	28
4	Blackburn Rovers	22	66	45	26
5	Bolton Wanderers	22	63	59	22
6	West Bromwich Albion	22	40	46	22
7	Accrington	22	48	48	20
8	Everton	22	35	46	20
9	Burnley	22	42	62	17
10	Derby County	22	41	61	16
11	Notts County	22	40	73	12
12	Stoke	22	26	51	12
		264	586	586	264

Goals 1888-1889

A total of 586 goals were scored in the 132 games – an average of 4.44 goals per game. The leading goal-scorer was John Goodall (Preston North End) with 21 goals.

ELECTION/RE-ELECTION

All 4 re-election applicants were successful in 1889. Stoke polled 10 votes, Burnley 9, Derby County 8 and Notts County 7. Clubs failing to gain election were Mitchell St. George's of Birmingham (5), Sheffield Wednesday (4), Bootle (2) Sunderland (2), Newton Heath (1), Grimsby Town, South Shore, Sunderland Albion and Walsall Town Swifts (all 0).

1889-1890 – FOOTBALL LEAGUE

PRESTON NORTH END

The First Half

Now nicknamed the 'Old Invincibles', as well as the 'Lilywhites', Preston began their defence of the title on the season's second Saturday. Their 10-0 demolition of Stoke at Deepdale must have sent shudders round the rest of the League. A week later though, North End were well beaten at Aston Villa and, after 3 wins, lost the next two. The last of these defeats was at the hands of the league leaders Wolves, but the latter's 1-2 loss at Villa, while the earlier table-toppers, Everton, buried Stoke 8-0, meant the Anfield Road side reclaimed pole position.

Preston's return to form at the beginning of November led to North End winning three in a row, which left them in second place, tucked in a point behind Everton. The two clubs met at Anfield on 16th November, in a game of huge significance. Everton's Frank Geary led the goal-scoring charts before the match, with 13. With one less to his name, Jimmy Ross was Preston's leading hit-man. Both men scored in the match, but Ross had more to be pleased about, as Preston won 5-1. The win took North End to the top of the table for the first time in the 1889-90 campaign.

Preston North End's '1st half' record

September	14	STOKE	10-0
	21	Aston Villa	3-5
	28	Burnley	3-0
October	05	WEST BROMWICH ALBION	5-0
	12	Bolton Wanderers	6-2
	19	Derby County	1-2
	26	WOLVES	0-2
November	02	Blackburn Rovers	4-3
	09	ACCRINGTON	3-1
	11	Stoke	2-1
	16	Everton	5-1

Table at November 16th, 1889

1	PRESTON NORTH END	11	42	17	16
2	Everton	12	32	23	15
3	Wolves	11	22	15	14
4	Aston Villa	11	25	23	13
5	Derby County	10	19	24	12
6	Blackburn Rovers	9	40	19	11
7	Notts County	11	24	23	11
8	West Bromwich Albion	10	20	22	10
9	Accrington	9	21	24	8
10	Bolton Wanderers	9	16	29	6
11	Burnley	10	13	29	4
12	Stoke	11	9	35	4
		124	283	283	124

Attendances 1888-1889

The total number of spectators at the 132 Football League matches is said to have been 712,910 – an average of 5,401 per game.

F.A. CUP FINAL - 29th March, 1890

Blackburn Rovers hammered non-league Sheffield Wednesday 6-1. Townley scored three for Rovers, with Lofthouse, J. Southworth and Walton hitting the others. Wednesday's reply came from Bennett. The game, played at the Kennington Oval, was attended by 20,000.

The Second Half

By the end of December, it was clear that the only club capable of sustaining a real challenge to Preston North End was Everton. Both stunned and embarrassed by the result of November 16th, the Toffees redoubled their efforts. With wins at both Preston and Blackburn in late December, Everton ended the year a point behind North End, having played one game fewer. If North End were to win the Football League championship this time, it would be a much harder job than a year earlier. More than anything, 'the force' seemed to be Everton's.

After 6 wins on the bounce, Everton lost 3-5 at Accrington on February 22nd. This swung the pendulum in Preston's favour, but it was not over yet. By the end of March 15th, the rivals were level on points, with one match each left to play. An exciting end to the season loomed. What in fact happened was far from exciting. A week later, on March 22nd, Everton lost at West Bromwich Albion, 1-4. If they could avoid defeat by 16 goals at Notts County on March 27th, North End would be League champions again. The 'Lilywhites' won the match 1-0.

Preston North End's '2nd half' record

November	23	BOLTON WANDERERS	3-1
	30	BURNLEY	6-0
December	07	BLACKBURN ROVERS	1-1
	21	EVERTON	1-2
	25	ASTON VILLA	3-2
	26	West Bromwich Albion	2-2
January	04	Wolves	1-0
	11	DERBY COUNTY	5-0
March	01	NOTTS COUNTY	4-3
	15	Accrington	2-2
	27	Notts County	1-0

Final Football League Table 1890

1	PRESTON NORTH END	22	71	30	33
2	Everton	22	65	40	31
3	Blackburn Rovers	22	78	41	27
4	Wolves	22	51	38	25
5	West Bromwich Albion	22	47	50	25
6	Accrington	22	53	56	24
7	Derby County	22	43	55	21
8	Aston Villa	22	43	51	19
9	Bolton Wanderers	22	54	65	19
10	Notts County	22	43	51	17
11	Burnley	22	36	65	13
12	Stoke	22	27	69	10
		264	611	611	264

Goals 1888-1889

A total of 611 goals were scored in the 132 games – an average of 4.63 goals per game. The leading goal-scorer was Jimmy Ross (Preston North End) with 24 goals.

ELECTION/RE-ELECTION

In 1890, only 3 clubs faced re-election as Bolton claimed that they had lost to Notts County 0-3 not 0-4 on October 26th. If they were right then it would mean the club would have finished above Aston Villa on goal average, not below them. So, neither Bolton nor Villa were put through the vote. In fact, the voting details are, mysteriously, unknown for 1890. Notts County and Burnley were re-elected, but Stoke lost their place to Sunderland. Bootle, Darwen, Grimsby Town, Newton Heath and Sunderland Albion were all unsuccessful.

1890-1891 – FOOTBALL LEAGUE

EVERTON

The First Half

Everton began the 1890-91 season like an express train, charging to the top of the Football League table through a string of both exhilarating and entertaining performances.

The only team to come close to the Toffees in their first 5 matches was Accrington and even they were beaten, in front of their own Peel Park crowd.

With three more points from the next two games, Everton looked well capable of 'doing a Preston'. It was not to be though and 3 defeats in a row both dented confidence and allowed Wolves to take over at the top and a number of others to move to within striking distance.

When Sunderland were beaten at Anfield 1-0 on November 15th, Everton clambered back to the top. Importantly, however, the club's leading striker, Frank Geary, failed to score for the fourth time in five games. All was not well. The team had lost its fluency and self-belief.

Everton's '1st half' record

September	06	West Bromwich Albion	4-1
	13	WOLVES	5-0
	20	Bolton Wanderers	5-0
	27	Accrington	2-1
October	04	DERBY COUNTY	7-0
	11	Aston Villa	2-2
	18	BOLTON WANDERERS	2-0
	25	WEST BROMWICH ALBION	2-3
November	01	Notts County	1-3
	08	Blackburn Rovers	1-2
	15	SUNDERLAND	1-0

Table at November 15th, 1890

1	EVERTON	11	32	12	15
2	Wolves	11	25	23	15
3	Blackburn Rovers	10	24	20	13
4	Notts County	12	25	19	13
5	Preston North End	10	17	8	12
6	Bolton Wanderers	12	21	23	12
7	Burnley	11	27	28	11
8	Aston Villa	11	25	26	10
9	West Bromwich Albion	11	17	26	8
10	Accrington	11	14	22	8
11	Sunderland*	10	25	20	7
12	Derby County	10	18	43	4
		130	270	270	128

*Sunderland docked 2 points for fielding unregistered player (Ted Doig) at West Bromwich, 20/09/1890.

Attendances 1888-1889

The total number of spectators at the 132 Football League matches is said to have been 833,525 – an average of 6,315 per game.

F.A. CUP FINAL

21st March, 1891

Blackburn Rovers retained the Cup by defeating Notts County 3-1. Southworth, Dewar and Townley scored for the winners, with Oswald on target for the runners-up. The attendance at the Oval was 23,000.

The Second Half

Everton's defeat at Preston on November 22nd had led to Wolves moving into first place again and forced the Anfield boss, Dick Molyneux, into a key decision. David Jardine replaced Jack Angus in goal for the next game – at home to Blackburn – which Everton won 3-1. Jardine, signed from Bootle, inspired confidence in others. Victory at Wolves a week later enabled the Toffees to reclaim top spot and they won 5 of the next 6 to pull clear.

One major worry remained though – Preston North End had enough games in hand to catch them. On January 10th, Preston won at Anfield and Evertonians feared the worst. Having played all but one of their fixtures, Everton had to sit and watch Preston eat away at their lead. By March 14th, when both clubs faced their final league fixture, Everton had a 2 points lead and a fractionally better goal average. After a 2-3 loss at Turf Moor, Burnley Everton were left dreading the news of a North End win at Sunderland, but when it was learned that the Wearsiders had won 3-0, the Merseyside party could begin.

Everton's '2nd half' record

November	22	Preston North End	0-2
	29	BLACKBURN ROVERS	3-1
December	06	Wolves	1-0
	13	Derby County	6-2
	20	Sunderland	0-1
	26	ACCRINGTON	3-2
	27	BURNLEY	7-3
January	01	ASTON VILLA	5-0
	03	NOTTS COUNTY	4-2
	10	PRESTON NORTH END	0-1
March	14	Burnley	2-3

Final Football League Table 1891

1	EVERTON	22	63	29	29
2	Preston North End	22	44	23	27
3	Notts County	22	52	35	26
4	Wolves	22	39	50	26
5	Bolton Wanderers	22	47	34	25
6	Blackburn Rovers	22	52	43	24
7	Sunderland*	22	51	31	23
8	Burnley	22	52	63	21
9	Aston Villa	22	45	58	18
10	Accrington	22	28	50	16
11	Derby County	22	47	81	15
12	West Bromwich Albion	22	34	57	12
		264	554	554	262

*Sunderland deducted 2 points.

Goals 1888-1889

A total of 554 goals were scored in the 132 games – an average of 4.2 goals per game. The leading goal-scorer was Jack Southworth (Blackburn Rovers) with 26 goals.

ELECTION/RE-ELECTION

Aston Villa and Accrington (8 votes each) + Derby County and West Bromwich Albion (6 votes apiece) were re-elected in 1891. Joining them in the League would be Stoke and Darwen, both of whom got 7 votes. Ardwick led the 'losers' with 4 votes, while Nottingham Forest (1), Sunderland Albion (1) and Newton Heath (0) also failed.

1891-1892 – FOOTBALL LEAGUE

SUNDERLAND

The First Half

The fourth Football League campaign got off to a surprising start. Champions Everton went down 0-4 at re-elected West Bromwich on the opening day, Preston lost 4 of their six opening games and Sunderland, a club many expected to do well, won only one of their opening 4 matches and occupied bottom spot at the end of September, with a goals aggregate of 12-14.

At the top, re-elected Aston Villa won their first 4 games to lead the table at the start of October, but suffered a 2-4 defeat at Derby County, which allowed the re-elected Rams to go top. A week later, with Derby not in action, Bolton Wanderers took over at the head of the table after winning 2-1 at Aston Villa.

While Everton continued to struggle, both Preston and Sunderland put together good runs in October and November to move up the table. Bolton clung on to the top spot, however, despite 0-4 drubbings at both Blackburn Rovers and Preston in late November.

Sunderland's '1st half' record

September	05	WOLVES	5-2
	12	Preston North End	1-3
	19	Bolton Wanderers	3-4
	28	Aston Villa	3-5
October	03	EVERTON	2-1
	17	West Bromwich Albion	5-2
	24	WEST BROMWICH ALBION	4-0
	31	ACCRINGTON	4-1
November	07	Blackburn Rovers	1-3
	14	DERBY COUNTY	7-1
	21	BURNLEY	2-1
	28	Stoke	3-1
December	05	NOTTS COUNTY	4-0

Table at December 5th, 1891

1	Bolton Wanderers	16	31	22	23
2	Preston North End	15	31	17	21
3	Aston Villa	14	45	26	20
4	SUNDERLAND	13	44	24	18
5	Blackburn Rovers	15	36	40	15
6	Notts County	14	33	26	13
7	Wolves	16	34	32	13
8	Everton	14	27	31	13
9	Derby County	12	28	24	13
10	Burnley	13	21	27	12
11	Darwen	14	31	44	10
12	Accrington	14	18	41	10
13	Stoke	14	24	33	9
14	West Bromwich Albion	14	24	40	8
		198	427	427	198

Attendances 1891-1892

The total number of spectators at the 182 Football League matches is said to have been 1,079,975 – an average of 5,934 per game.

F.A. CUP FINAL - 12th March, 1892

25,000 watched West Bromwich Albion record a 3-0 win over Aston Villa at the Oval. Albion's scorers were Nicholls, Geddes and Reynolds.

The Second Half

Normality appeared to have returned on January 2nd when, with an 11th win in a row, at Accrington, Preston went top of the League. By the middle of February, North End had a 3-point lead over Bolton and looked well capable of staying ahead of these rivals. In third place, however, were Sunderland – 7 points adrift, with 4 games in hand.

On March 12th, Sunderland beat Preston by 4-1 at Newcastle Road. A fortnight later, a 2-1 victory over Villa lifted the North-Eastern club above North End. Although a couple of scary moments were still to come, the Wearside club held the lead from now on, reaching the middle of April as champions-elect.

The decisive date proved to be April 16th. Preston lost 1-3 at Villa, while Sunderland crushed the barely interested Blackburn Rovers 6-1, with leading scorer Johnny Campbell hitting four. The Newcastle Road club were champions of the Football League.

Sunderland's '2nd half' record

December	12	DARWEN	7-0
	25	Everton	4-0
	26	Wolves	3-1
March	01	BOLTON WANDERERS	4-1
	05	Accrington	5-3
	12	PRESTON NORTH END	4-1
	19	Derby County	1-0
	26	ASTON VILLA	2-1
April	02	STOKE	4-1
	09	Notts County	0-1
	16	BLACKBURN ROVERS	6-1
	23	Darwen	7-1
	30	Burnley	2-1

Final Football League Table 1892

1	SUNDERLAND	26	93	36	42
2	Preston North End	26	61	31	37
3	Bolton Wanderers	26	51	37	36
4	Aston Villa	26	89	56	30
5	Everton	26	49	49	28
6	Wolves	26	59	46	26
7	Burnley	26	49	45	26
8	Notts County	26	55	51	26
9	Blackburn Rovers	26	58	65	26
10	Derby County	26	46	52	24
11	Accrington	26	40	78	20
12	West Bromwich Albion	26	51	58	18
13	Stoke	26	38	61	14
14	Darwen	26	38	112	11
		364	777	777	364

Goals 1891-1892

A total of 777 goals were scored in the 182 games – an average of 4.3 goals per game. The leading goal-scorer was John Campbell (Sunderland) with 28 goals.

ELECTION/RE-ELECTION

In 1892, West Bromwich Albion, having won the F.A. Cup, were re-elected without any need for voting. Accrington (7 votes) and Stoke (6) did enough to join the new 16-club First Division, but Darwen (4) missed out. The 3 remaining places in the top flight went to Sheffield Wednesday (10), Nottingham Forest (9) and Newton Heath (6). Sheffield United (5) just missed out, with Burton Swifts, Newcastle East End and a joint bid, from Teesside's Middlesbrough and Middlesbrough Ironopolis, each getting just 1 vote. Liverpool Caledonians were given no votes and Liverpool were rejected before the ballot.

OTHER INFORMATION   1888-1892

Elections 1888

There was keen interest in joining the new Football League from the start. No details survive on exactly how the original twelve clubs were chosen, but we know that there were 15 who 'showed a strong interest'. A chance remark about finances by one of its committee seems to have cost Sheffield Wednesday a place in the starting line-up, while, from Nottingham, Notts County were preferred to city rivals Forest and Halliwell lost out to neighbours Bolton Wanderers in the final shake-up.

Football League homes

Accrington	Peel Park
Aston Villa	Perry Barr
Blackburn Rovers	Leamington Street
	Ewood Park (1890)
Burnley	Turf Moor
Darwen	Barley Bank
Derby County	The Racecourse
Everton	Anfield
Notts County	Trent Bridge
	Castle Ground (occasionally)
Preston North End	Deepdale
Stoke	Victoria Ground
Sunderland	Newcastle Road
West Bromwich Albion	Stoney Lane
Wolves	Dudley Road
	Molineux (1889)

Football League Attendances

Although the professional clubs relied on gate money to fund them in the early years of the Football League, accurate details on crowds do not seem to have been recorded. Different sources give differing information. The figures below are based on Brian Tabner's research, as shown in his publication 'Through the Turnstiles … again' (2002).

Best and least supported clubs

Everton were the best supported Football League club in each of the first 4 seasons. Attendances at Anfield rose from c. 7,400 average 1888-89 to over 10,000 for 1889-90 and to 11,250+ for 1890-91 when the Toffees were League champions. Despite a much less successful campaign 1891-92, an average home crowd of around 10,000 turned out to watch Everton.

Derby County's average attendances of about 3,000 for the 1888-89 and 1890-91 seasons left the Rams at the bottom of the 'home crowds' pile twice. The wooden spoon for crowds went to Accrington in both the other campaigns, with average home crowds of c. 2,900 for 1889-90 and around 3,350 for 1891-92.

A surprising eviction

There was a major upheaval on Merseyside in 1892 when Everton's landlord raised the rent on the Anfield Road Ground. The club refused to pay more and moved out. They crossed Stanley Park and built a new home at Goodison. Mr. Houlding, meanwhile, set up his own football club – Liverpool F.C. – and applied for the new Division Two.

Goal scoring

Three clubs hit double figures in the early years of the Football League. Preston North End hammered Stoke 10-0 on September 14th, 1889. Aston Villa later demolished Accrington 12-2 on March 12th, 1892 and, less than a month later, West Bromwich Albion crushed the hapless Darwen team 12-0 on April 4th, 1892.

A very cold day

On Saturday, December 12th, 1891, bitterly cold weather and blizzards caused havoc with league games. The Accrington-Aston Villa match lasted 7 minutes before both sides ran off the pitch, while, at Preston, the Notts County team finished the match with only five players after the rest refused to play on because it was too cold. At Turf Moor, only Blackburn 'keeper, Herbie Arthur, stayed on to face Burnley, though this was linked to another incident over the sending off of a man from each team – the earliest record of dismissals uncovered to date.

Good and Bad Runs

Preston North End's unbeaten season 1888-1889 and their victory in the first game of the following campaign set 23 games as the record for going unbeaten in the Football League. The nearest anyone came to this in the period up to 1892 was when the same club went 15 games without losing between October 3rd, 1891 and March 5th, 1892. Sunderland's run of 13 successive wins between November 14th, 1891 and April 2nd, 1892 was the next best unbeaten sequence. The record would fall eventually.

Derby County went 10 matches without a win from September 15th to December 8th in 1888, but this record was beaten 1889-1890 by Burnley, who failed to win any of their opening 17 league matches. This unenviable record was not beaten in the next two seasons, but West Bromwich Albion (10 games, 1890-91) and Darwen (13 games, 1891-92) also had fruitless experiences.

Other leagues

The success of the Football League led quickly to similar competitions being set up all over the North and Midlands. Only in the South was there resistance to the idea as it was thought that leagues would lead to increased professionalism. This is rather strange as the highly popular F.A. Cup Final was played in London – usually between professional Football League clubs.

The strongest competition outside the Football League was the 12-club Football Alliance, which began in September 1889. The first champions were Sheffield Wednesday, with Merseyside's then second team, Bootle, finishing runners-up. Stoke pipped Sunderland Albion for the Alliance crown in 1891 and the final winners of the competition were Nottingham Forest, with Newton Heath (Manchester) second.

Other competitions included the Midland Counties League, the Northern League, the Lancashire League and The Combination, which drew most of its members from the area south of the River Mersey. All these leagues would supply new members of the Football League over the next few years.

North of the border, the Scots also gave league soccer a chance, beginning in 1890. The Scottish League was an amateur competition because professionalism was still very much frowned upon – officially, that is.

1892-1893 – LEAGUE DIVISION 1

SUNDERLAND

The First Half

By the end of September, Preston led the 1st Division table, having played and won their opening 5 matches. Sunderland held second place with three wins and a draw, a remarkable goals aggregate of 19-3, and a game in hand on the leaders.

By mid-November, with striker John Campbell's personal goal haul up to 17, the Wearside club were 2 points behind Preston, having played 2 fewer games.

After Sunderland beat the table-toppers at Newcastle Road on December 17th, North End's lead was again 2 points, but the North-East club now had a 3 match deficit to make up. The 3-1 win at West Bromwich Albion on Christmas Eve carried Sunderland to the top for the first time in the campaign.

Sunderland's '1st half' record

September	03	Accrington	6-0
	10	NOTTS COUNTY	2-2
	17	Aston Villa	6-1
	24	BLACKBURN ROVERS	5-0
October	01	STOKE	3-1
	18	Everton	4-1
	15	ACCRINGTON	4-2
	22	WEST BROMWICH ALBION	8-1
	29	Sheffield Wednesday	2-3
November	05	BURNLEY	2-0
	19	NOTTINGHAM FOREST	1-0
	26	Notts County	1-3
December	03	Nottingham Forest	5-0
	17	PRESTON NORTH END	2-0
	24	West Bromwich Albion	3-1

Table at December 24th, 1892

1	SUNDERLAND	15	54	15	25
2	Preston North End	17	34	19	25
3	Sheffield Wednesday	18	41	34	22
4	Aston Villa	20	44	43	21
5	Stoke	18	34	30	19
6	Bolton Wanderers	18	35	30	18
7	Notts County	18	38	33	17
8	Wolves	17	33	38	17
9	Everton	17	35	40	16
10	Blackburn Rovers	17	29	35	16
11	West Bromwich Albion	17	33	43	16
12	Derby County	16	30	36	15
13	Accrington	16	36	47	14
14	Nottingham Forest	19	28	38	14
15	Burnley	19	20	30	14
16	Newton Heath	18	33	46	11
		280	557	557	280

Attendances 1892-1893

The total number of spectators at the 240 Football League matches is said to have been 1,663,125 – an average of 6,930 per game.

Goals 1892-1893

A total of 936 goals were scored in the 240 games – an average of 3.9 goals per game.

The leading goal-scorer was John Campbell (Sunderland) with 30 goals.

The Second Half

Preston were back in first place by New Year, but Sunderland's two wins in early January knocked North End off the First Division summit. The 2-1 Sunderland victory at Deepdale on January 7th carried the North-East club clear. The lead was stretched to 5 points by mid-February.

By this stage both the top two had 8 matches left. By March 31st, Sunderland boss Tom Watson was able to look at a 10-point lead and the need for just 3 points from the last 4 games to make the Newcastle Road men champions once again. The April 1st loss at Bolton merely delayed the inevitable, as North End also lost. On April 3rd, Sunderland took the title without even playing, because Preston failed to beat Accrington at Deepdale. A day later, the Wearside team celebrated by crushing bottom club Newton Heath 6-0.

Sunderland's '2nd half' record

December	26	Wolves	0-2
January	02	WOLVES	5-2
	03	EVERTON	4-3
	07	Preston North End	2-1
	14	ASTON VILLA	6-0
	28	SHEFFIELD WEDNESDAY	4-2
February	14	BOLTON WANDERERS	3-3
March	04	Newton Heath	5-0
	11	DERBY COUNTY	3-1
	18	Stoke	1-0
	31	Blackburn Rovers	2-2
April	01	Bolton Wanderers	1-2
	04	NEWTON HEATH	6-0
	08	Derby County	1-1
	15	Burnley	3-2

Final League Division 1 Table 1893

1	SUNDERLAND	30	100	36	48
2	Preston North End	30	57	39	37
3	Everton	30	74	51	36
4	Aston Villa	30	73	62	35
5	Bolton Wanderers	30	56	55	32
6	Burnley	30	51	44	30
7	Stoke	30	58	48	29
8	West Bromwich Albion	30	58	69	29
9	Blackburn Rovers	30	47	56	29
10	Nottingham Forest	30	48	52	28
11	Wolves	30	47	68	28
12	Sheffield Wednesday	30	55	65	27
13	Derby County	30	52	64	27
14	Notts County	30	53	61	24
15	Accrington	30	57	81	23
16	Newton Heath	30	50	85	18
		480	936	936	480

The F.A. Cup

Despite the creation of the League in 1888 and its growth in popularity and size over the next five years, clubs and supporters seem to have still seen the F.A. Cup as the most important football competition in England.

The Final - 25th March, 1893

A huge crowd for the times (45,000) turned up to see Wolves take the trophy. Centre half Allen hit the only goal of the game to beat Everton. The match, at Fallowfield in Manchester, had referee C.J. Hughes of Northwich in charge and the gate receipts grossed an amazing £2,559.

1892-1893 – LEAGUE DIVISION 2

SMALL HEATH

The First Half

For most of the new 2nd Division clubs, there was a sense of déjà vu as the new season got under way. Of the 12 teams involved, 8 had played in the Football Alliance in the previous campaign, while a ninth, Darwen, were previous Alliance members. For 3 clubs though, the fixture list had a wholly new look to it. Burslem Port Vale had played previously in the Midland League, Northwich Victoria came from The Combination, and Sheffield United were a Northern League side.

Ardwick started best of the pack, winning their first 4 games, then taking 3 points from the next two. A draw and 2 defeats in the Manchester club's next 4 games though allowed both Small Heath and Darwen to pass the Hyde Road club at the top. By mid-November, it was clear that the leading two were likely to be involved in the shake-up for the top three placings and the possibility of promotion. Other things were not quite so clear. As the league table at November 12th shows, there was considerable difference in the fixture-completion rates of the clubs.

Small Heath's '1st half' record

September	03	BURSLEM PORT VALE	5-1
	10	Walsall Town Swifts	3-1
	17	Sheffield United	0-2
	24	LINCOLN CITY	4-1
October	01	Grimsby Town	2-3
	03	Burton Swifts	3-2
	08	CREWE ALEXANDRA	6-0
	22	Ardwick	2-2
	29	DARWEN	3-2
November	05	Bootle	4-1
	12	BURTON SWIFTS	3-2

Table at November 12th, 1892

1	SMALL HEATH	11	35	17	17
2	Darwen	11	27	14	15
3	Ardwick	10	24	11	14
4	Burton Swifts	8	22	13	10
5	Sheffield United	6	10	5	8
6	Grimsby Town	8	11	10	8
7	Burslem Port Vale	10	15	22	8
8	Walsall Town Swifts	8	15	23	6
9	Northwich Victoria	7	11	15	5
10	Crewe Alexandra	8	15	33	4
11	Bootle	9	7	23	4
12	Lincoln City	6	9	15	3
		102	201	201	102

Promotion and Relegation 1893

The system of automatic promotion from and relegation to the 2nd Division lay some years in the future in 1893. It was agreed that the bottom 3 in Division 1 would play one-off deciders, on neutral grounds, with the top 3 in Division 2 to decide on any changes in status. The games took place on April 22nd, 1893. Small Heath drew 1-1 with Newton Heath at Stoke's Victoria Ground. A replay was arranged for 5 days later. In the other 2 matches, Sheffield United won 1-0 against Accrington at Forest's Town Ground and Darwen beat Notts County 3-2 at Hyde Road, home of Ardwick, after the 1st Division side led 2-1 at half-time. The replayed game, at Olive Grove, home of Sheffield Wednesday, was 1-1 at the interval. Newton Heath then stepped up a gear and ran out 5-2 winners. Small Heath remained in the 2nd Division and are still the only 2nd Division champions to fail to win promotion.

Attendances 1892-1893 – 292,600 attended 132 matches, an average of 2,217. **Goals** – 591 goals were scored in the 132 games, an average of 4.77 per game. With 25 goals, Small Heath's Freddie Wheldon was the top marksman for Division 2.

The Second Half

Darwen moved to the top of Division Two at the start of December after a 7-3 win over Crewe Alexandra at Barley Bank. When Small Heath were beaten a week later, on December 10th, the Lancashire club took a 3-point lead at the top. Meanwhile, a Football League record was being set further south which still stands today. On a snow-bound Cobridge pitch in Burslem, visitors Sheffield United were destroying the home side, Port Vale, 10-0. *This is still the biggest Football League away win.* The Blades' record-setting win was their 3rd match unbeaten – a run which grew to fifteen games without defeat by the end of the season.

This was still not enough to secure the club the 2nd Division title because Small Heath put in a run of 9 straight wins to finish the season on. The championship was not finally decided until April 15th. Small Heath's total of 36 points was to remain within Sheffield United's reach until the Blades failed to beat Walsall Town Swifts at The Chuckery in their last game. The 1-1 draw left United on 35 points and the title on its way to Coventry Road, Birmingham.

Small Heath's '2nd half' record

December	03	SHEFFIELD UNITED	1-1
	10	Darwen	3-4
	17	WALSALL TOWN SWIFTS	12-0
	24	Northwich Victoria	6-0
	31	Crewe Alexandra	3-1
January	07	Lincoln City	4-3
	14	NORTHWICH VICTORIA	6-2
February	18	BOOTLE	6-2
	25	GRIMSBY TOWN	8-3
March	25	Burslem Port Vale	3-0
April	01	ARDWICK	3-2

Final League Division 2 Table 1893

1	SMALL HEATH	22	90	35	36
2	Sheffield United	22	62	19	35
3	Darwen	22	60	36	30
4	Grimsby Town	22	42	41	23
5	Ardwick	22	45	40	21
6	Burton Swifts	22	47	47	20
7	Northwich Victoria	22	42	58	20
8	Bootle	22	49	63	19
9	Lincoln City	22	45	51	17
10	Crewe Alexandra	22	42	69	15
11	Burslem Port Vale	22	30	57	15
12	Walsall Town Swifts	22	37	75	13
		264	591	591	264

Election time 1893

The 4 bottom clubs in Division 2 were all re-elected at the Football League A.G.M.. It was decided to increase the size of the competition to 16 clubs, but, before any voting on this could be considered, both Accrington and Notts County refused to commit themselves to playing in the 2nd Division. Two clubs were elected – Rotherham Town and Newcastle United, while 2 others were rejected – Loughborough Town and Doncaster Rovers. No details of the voting are available. Final decisions on League membership were postponed while the 2 relegated clubs decided what they were going to do. *It is not totally clear what happened after this.*

Notts County opted to take part in the 2nd Division and new clubs, Liverpool and Woolwich Arsenal, were added to the line-up for the 1893-94 season. The Accrington club seem to have indicated that they wished to remain in the Football League, but then either they changed their minds or the League refused to have them. In any case, Middlesbrough Ironopolis were offered Accrington's place and accepted it. The chaos wasn't quite over yet, however, because, just before the season started, Bootle resigned, leaving Division Two with 15 clubs.

1893-1894 – LEAGUE DIVISION 1 — ASTON VILLA

The First Half

Champions Sunderland made a poor start to the '93-'94 season, winning only one of their first six games. By the end of September, the table was headed by West Bromwich Albion, a point up on both Aston Villa and newly-promoted Sheffield United.

United took over as Division 1 leaders by beating Aston Villa 3-0, on October 2nd, at Bramall Lane. The Blades stayed in front until October 28th when defeat by West Bromwich Albion, combined with Villa's 4-0 sorting of Burnley, enabled the Perry Barr men to pass them.

When Aston Villa made it six games without defeat by hammering Sheffield United 4-0 on October 30th, a 3-point gap opened up at the top. This became 4 points after Villa edged out Sunderland on November 11th.

Aston Villa's '1st half' record

September	02	WEST BROMWICH ALBION	3-2
	09	Sunderland	1-1
	11	STOKE	5-1
	16	Everton	2-4
	23	EVERTON	3-1
	30	DERBY COUNTY	1-1
October	02	Sheffield United	0-3
	07	Nottingham Forest	2-1
	14	Darwen	1-1
	16	Stoke	3-3
	21	West Bromwich Albion	6-3
	28	BURNLEY	4-0
	30	SHEFFIELD UNITED	4-0
November	04	Blackburn Rovers	0-2
	11	SUNDERLAND	2-1

Table at November 11th, 1893

1	ASTON VILLA	15	37	24	20
2	West Bromwich Albion	13	32	27	16
3	Blackburn Rovers	11	25	17	15
4	Burnley	12	29	23	15
5	Sheffield United	12	21	19	15
6	Derby County	12	22	26	12
7	Sunderland	11	26	19	11
8	Nottingham Forest	12	23	19	11
9	Stoke	13	24	35	11
10	Wolves	12	16	27	11
11	Everton	12	36	27	10
12	Preston North End	10	15	13	10
13	Bolton Wanderers	12	17	20	10
14	Sheffield Wednesday	13	21	28	9
15	Darwen	13	16	31	9
16	Newton Heath	11	12	17	9
		194	372	372	194

Attendances 1893-1894

The total number of spectators at the 240 Division 1 matches is said to have been 1,663,125 – an average of 6,930 per game.

Goals 1893-1894

A total of 939 goals were scored in the 240 games – an average of 3.91 goals per game.

The leading goal-scorer was Jack Southworth (Everton) with 27 goals.

The Second Half

With six wins in a row between November 11th and December 16th, Villa continued to boss things. By mid-February, with the F.A. Cup disrupting League matters, the leaders were 7 points clear of Blackburn, although Rovers had 2 games in hand.

Villa's 2-3 defeat at Bolton Wanderers on March 3rd presented the chasing pack with something of a slim chance, however. Neither Blackburn Rovers nor Burnley proved able to profit, but, with three wins, Sunderland moved to within 3 points of the top by March 17th.

At this point, the Wearsiders faltered, losing 0-2 at Stoke. Villa travelled to Burnley on April 7th needing only a draw to become champions. A spectacular performance produced a 6-3 win and the club took the Football League title for the first time.

Aston Villa's '2nd half' record

November	18	Bolton Wanderers	1-0
	25	PRESTON NORTH END	2-0
December	02	Derby County	3-0
	09	SHEFFIELD WEDNESDAY	3-0
	16	Newton Heath	3-1
	23	Wolves	0-3
	26	DARWEN	9-0
January	06	Sheffield Wednesday	2-2
	18	Preston North End	5-2
February	03	NEWTON HEATH	5-1
March	03	BOLTON WANDERERS	2-3
	24	BLACKBURN ROVERS	2-1
	26	WOLVES	1-1
April	07	Burnley	6-3
	14	NOTTINGHAM FOREST	3-1

Final League Division 1 Table 1894

1	ASTON VILLA	30	84	42	44
2	Sunderland	30	72	44	38
3	Derby County	30	73	62	36
4	Blackburn Rovers	30	69	53	34
5	Burnley	30	61	51	34
6	Everton	30	90	57	33
7	Nottingham Forest	30	57	48	32
8	West Bromwich Albion	30	66	59	32
9	Wolves	30	52	63	31
10	Sheffield United	30	47	61	31
11	Stoke	30	65	79	29
12	Sheffield Wednesday	30	48	57	26
13	Bolton Wanderers	30	38	52	24
14	Preston North End	30	44	56	23
15	Darwen	30	37	83	19
16	Newton Heath	30	36	72	14
		480	939	939	480

F.A. CUP FINAL - 31st March, 1894

Second Division Notts County confounded the odds to hammer Bolton Wanderers 4-1 in front of a 37,000 crowd at Goodison Park, Liverpool.

TEST MATCHES

On April 28th, the bottom two clubs in Division 1, Darwen and Newton Heath, lost their Test Matches against Small Heath (1-3) and Liverpool (0-2) respectively, and were relegated to Division Two. In the third game, former League champions Preston North End brushed aside F.A. Cup winners, Notts County, 4-0 at Olive Grove, Sheffield.

1893-1894 – LEAGUE DIVISION 2

LIVERPOOL

The First Half

With seven September wins, re-elected Burslem Port Vale swept ahead of the rest. Small Heath lay 4 points behind, with newcomers Liverpool and relegated Notts County one point further back, both unbeaten.

Amazingly, the leaders crashed 1-8 in their next game, at Ardwick. Vale then lost both their next 2 games. By October 21st, Small Heath and Liverpool had caught up with the Burslem club, while Notts County eased past everyone on October 26th, smashing the out-of-sorts Valiants 6-1.

Superior goal average saw Liverpool go top two days later and the Anfield club pulled clear by drawing at Walsall on 11th November. 5 points from the next three matches ensured Liverpool stayed ahead.

The Second Half

From here, 'Pool simply marched towards the 2nd Division title. The goal let in against Rotherham Town on January 6th was the first conceded in 7 games. Liverpool were simply streets ahead of the rest.

Nine wins in a row by March 2nd lifted the Anfield club to 40 points and needing four more from their remaining six matches to guarantee them the Division 2 crown.

The title was eventually won at Anfield on 24th March, Easter Saturday, when goals from Douglas Dick and Hugh McQueen saw Crewe Alexandra beaten 2-0. The battle for second place was settled a fortnight later when Small Heath defeated Notts County 3-0 at Coventry Road.

Liverpool's '1st half' record

September	02	Middlesbrough Ironopolis	2-0
	09	LINCOLN CITY	4-0
	16	Ardwick	1-0
	23	SMALL HEATH	3-1
	30	Notts County	1-1
October	07	MIDDLESBROUGH IRONOPOLIS	6-0
	14	Small Heath	4-3
	21	Burton Swifts	1-1
	28	Woolwich Arsenal	5-0
November	04	NEWCASTLE UNITED	5-1
	11	Walsall Town Swifts	1-1
	18	NOTTS COUNTY	2-1
	25	Newcastle United	0-0
December	02	ARDWICK	3-0

Liverpool's '2nd half' record

December	09	WALSALL TOWN SWIFTS	3-0
	28	Crewe Alexandra	5-0
	30	GRIMSBY TOWN	2-0
January	01	WOOLWICH ARSENAL	2-0
	06	Rotherham Town	4-1
	13	ROTHERHAM TOWN	5-1
February	03	NORTHWICH VICTORIA	4-0
March	03	BURTON SWIFTS	3-1
	17	Lincoln City	1-1
	24	CREWE ALEXANDRA	2-0
	28	Northwich Victoria	3-2
	31	Grimsby Town	1-0
April	07	Burslem Port Vale	2-2
	14	BURSLEM PORT VALE	2-1

Table at December 2nd, 1893

1	LIVERPOOL	14	38	9	24
2	Notts County	16	40	18	22
3	Small Heath	14	46	25	20
4	Burslem Port Vale	13	36	28	18
5	Burton Swifts	13	41	27	17
6	Grimsby Town	12	39	27	14
7	Lincoln City	10	25	20	12
8	Woolwich Arsenal	10	18	27	9
9	Crewe Alexandra	9	16	16	8
10	Walsall Town Swifts	12	14	28	8
11	Ardwick	13	22	26	7
12	Newcastle United	10	18	24	6
13	Middlesbrough Ironopolis	11	10	34	6
14	Rotherham Town	11	16	36	5
15	Northwich Victoria	12	14	48	4
		180	393	393	180

Final League Division 2 Table 1894

1	LIVERPOOL	28	77	18	50
2	Small Heath	28	103	44	42
3	Notts County	28	70	31	39
4	Newcastle United	28	66	39	36
5	Grimsby Town	28	71	58	32
6	Burton Swifts	28	79	61	31
7	Burslem Port Vale	28	66	64	30
8	Lincoln City	28	59	58	28
9	Woolwich Arsenal	28	52	55	28
10	Walsall Town Swifts	28	51	61	23
11	Middlesbrough Ironopolis	28	37	72	20
12	Crewe Alexandra	28	42	73	19
13	Ardwick	28	47	71	18
14	Rotherham Town	28	44	91	15
15	Northwich Victoria	28	30	98	9
		420	894	894	420

Attendances 1893-1894

The total number of spectators at the 210 Division 2 games is said to have been 611,450 – an average of 2,912 per game.

Goals 1893-1894

A total of 834 goals were scored in the 210 games – an average of 3.97 goals per game.

The leading goal-scorer was Frank Mobley (Small Heath) with 24 goals.

ELECTION/RE-ELECTION

Only the bottom three faced re-election in 1894 as there was already a vacancy because of Bootle's resignation just before the season had started. However, Northwich Victoria did not apply and, crippled by financial troubles, Middlesbrough Ironopolis resigned. This left 5 places up for grabs and, not surprisingly, Ardwick (now reformed as Manchester City) and Rotherham Town were voted back in, with 20 and 15 votes respectively. Three new clubs were elected – Leicester Fosse (20 votes), Burton Wanderers (17) and Bury (17). Accrington (7), Blackpool (8), Loughborough Town (8) and Rossendale (0) were unsuccessful.

1894-1895 – LEAGUE DIVISION 1   SUNDERLAND

The First Half

Everton made a sprint start to the '94-'95 season, winning their eight opening matches to go well clear at the top by mid-October.

Defeat for the Toffees at Blackburn Rovers on October 20th and three successive draws allowed Sunderland to get within a single point of the lead by November 17th.

The leading two both won their next 4 matches, with Everton staying ahead of their North-East rivals and at the head of the 1st Division over the next 5 weeks.

The pair were joined in the battle at the top by champions Aston Villa, whose 4th win in a row, at Blackburn Rovers on December 8th, moved the Midlands club into 2nd place.

When Villa thumped Wolves 4-0 and Stoke 6-0 either side of Christmas Day, Everton dropped to second, on goal average, but had at least some consolation of several games in hand entering the New Year.

Sunderland's '1st half' record

September	01	DERBY COUNTY	8-0
	08	BURNLEY	3-0
	15	Aston Villa	2-1
	22	WEST BROMWICH ALBION	3-0
	29	Bolton Wanderers	1-4
October	06	STOKE	3-1
	13	Derby County	2-1
	27	Everton	2-2
November	03	WOLVES	2-0
	10	Blackburn Rovers	1-1
	17	BOLTON WANDERERS	4-0
	24	LIVERPOOL	3-2
December	08	SMALL HEATH	7-1
	15	BLACKBURN ROVERS	3-2
	26	West Bromwich Albion	2-0

Table at December 26th, 1894

1	Aston Villa	20	54	23	27
2	Everton	16	52	23	27
3	SUNDERLAND	15	46	15	26
4	Blackburn Rovers	19	36	32	21
5	Preston North End	19	32	29	20
6	Burnley	18	31	25	19
7	Sheffield Wednesday	16	28	25	19
8	Sheffield United	20	36	42	19
9	Nottingham Forest	16	29	30	18
10	Small Heath	19	36	50	16
11	West Bromwich Albion	18	32	38	15
12	Wolves	19	26	44	14
13	Bolton Wanderers	19	30	38	13
14	Derby County	16	26	35	12
15	Liverpool	19	26	46	11
16	Stoke	17	20	45	9
		286	540	540	286

Attendances 1894-1895

The total number of spectators at the 240 Division 1 matches is said to have been 1,804,500 – an average of 7,519 per game.

Goals 1894-1895

A total of 917 goals were scored in the 240 games – an average of 3.82 goals per game.

The leading goal-scorer was Sunderland's John Campbell with 22 goals.

The Second Half

Sunderland, having played 5 matches fewer than Villa, began the second half of their campaign by losing twice, after which they drew twice in 3 games. This could have proved fatal to their title hopes, but Everton also stumbled to 2 reverses in early January and then beat Villa 4-2 on the 17th to dent the Perry Barr bid to retain the title. By beating Stoke 5-2 on January 26th, Sunderland moved to the top of Division 1 on goal average.

A point from the visit to Small Heath on February 9th put the club one clear of Villa and 2 ahead of Everton, who had one match in hand, but an inferior goals count. Villa faded, but the threat from Everton loomed large until April 13th, when 2 results changed the entire picture. Everton lost at home to Derby County, while Sunderland won 3-0 at Burnley. On April 20th, Sunderland played host to Everton at Newcastle Road needing to avoid defeat to regain the First Division title. The home side's 2-1 win proved more than enough. Top scorer John Campbell struck the winner.

Sunderland's '2nd half' record

December	27	Nottingham Forest	1-2
	29	Preston North End	0-1
January	01	PRESTON NORTH END	2-0
	02	ASTON VILLA	4-4
	05	NOTTINGHAM FOREST	2-2
	12	Wolves	4-1
	26	Stoke	5-2
February	09	Small Heath	1-1
	23	SHEFFIELD UNITED	2-0
	26	SHEFFIELD WEDNESDAY	3-1
March	09	Sheffield United	0-4
	23	Sheffield Wednesday	2-1
	25	Liverpool	3-2
April	13	Burnley	3-0
	20	EVERTON	2-1

Final League Division 1 Table 1895

1	SUNDERLAND	30	80	37	47
2	Everton	30	82	50	42
3	Aston Villa	30	82	43	39
4	Preston North End	30	62	46	35
5	Blackburn Rovers	30	59	49	32
6	Sheffield United	30	57	55	32
7	Nottingham Forest	30	50	56	31
8	Sheffield Wednesday	30	50	55	28
9	Burnley	30	44	56	26
10	Bolton Wanderers	30	61	62	25
11	Wolves	30	43	63	25
12	Small Heath	30	50	74	25
13	West Bromwich Albion	30	51	66	24
14	Stoke	30	50	67	24
15	Derby County	30	45	68	23
16	Liverpool	30	51	70	22
		480	917	917	480

F.A. CUP FINAL - 20th April, 1895

In a new move to make the F.A. Cup Final the closing game in the season and to reintroduce the event into the London sporting calendar, the 1895 Final was staged at Crystal Palace. 42,560 saw Aston Villa's Jack Devey score the only goal of the game against West Bromwich Albion.

TEST MATCHES

On April 27th, the bottom three clubs in Division 1 faced the top three from Division 2, to determine which level each club would play at 1895-96. While Derby County beat Notts County 2-1 and Stoke eased past Newton Heath 3-0, 1st Division wooden spoonists, Liverpool, were beaten 0-1 by Bury, who replaced the Anfield club in the top flight.

1894-1895 – LEAGUE DIVISION 2   BURY

The First Half

Newly-elected Bury were quick to emerge as the team to beat in Division II, opening their season with 4 wins. The other sides to start well were Grimsby Town, who topped the table on goal average at the end of September, and Notts County, who took seven points from their 4 games in the first month of the season.

Beaten at Notts County and Bury in the first week of October, Grimsby Town slipped to third by mid-November and were left with little more than a chasing role thereafter.

Bury set a terrific pace at the top, winning eight matches in a row by November 17th and losing, for only the second time, a week later at Notts County. The effort of beating the leaders clearly took a lot out of the Magpies as they failed to win any of their next four fixtures.

Bury's '1st half' record

September	01	MANCHESTER CITY	4-2
	08	CREWE ALEXANDRA	4-1
	15	Burslem Port Vale	2-1
	18	ROTHERHAM TOWN	2-1
	22	Woolwich Arsenal	2-4
	29	DARWEN	1-0
October	06	GRIMSBY TOWN	5-1
	20	Crewe Alexandra	5-1
	27	Walsall Town Swifts	3-0
November	03	NEWCASTLE UNITED	4-1
	06	Rotherham Town	3-2
	10	BURSLEM PORT VALE	4-0
	17	Burton Wanderers	2-1
	24	Notts County	1-2
December	01	BURTON SWIFTS	2-0

Table at December 1st, 1894

1	BURY	15	44	17	26
2	Grimsby Town	14	47	26	20
3	Notts County	13	30	20	18
4	Darwen	13	30	12	16
5	Newton Heath	12	29	18	16
6	Burton Swifts	13	26	21	15
7	Woolwich Arsenal	12	30	30	14
8	Newcastle United	14	34	43	13
9	Walsall Town Swifts	12	19	29	10
10	Leicester Fosse	11	25	26	9
11	Manchester City	13	33	37	9
12	Burton Wanderers	11	16	20	9
13	Rotherham Town	14	28	35	8
14	Lincoln City	10	20	33	8
15	Burslem Port Vale	11	8	25	5
16	Crewe Alexandra	10	10	37	2
		198	429	429	198

Attendances 1894-1895

The total number of spectators at the 240 Division 2 games is said to have been 864,750 – an average of 3,603 per game.

Goals 1894-1895

A total of 1,023 goals were scored in the 240 games – an average of 4.26 goals per game.

The leading goal-scorer was David Skea (Leicester Fosse) with 23 goals.

The Second Half

Bury continued to dictate matters in Division Two, dropping only one point in six December games and ending the year a massive ten points clear of second-placed Newton Heath at the top. The Shakers remained well ahead throughout January, February and March, despite losing twice, albeit by the odd goal, in the five matches played.

By the start of April, with 5 games to play, Bury needed 4 points to become champions of the 2nd Division. This requirement was then halved with a 4-1 win over Walsall on April 2nd.

The job was completed four days later, on April 6th, when right full-back Billy Barbour's goal was enough to secure 2 points and the Division 2 title at Burton Swifts. Barbour started the last 3 games of the season at centre-forward. He scored once more.

Bury's '2nd half' record

December	08	Manchester City	3-3
	15	Darwen	1-0
	22	BURTON WANDERERS	4-0
	25	LEICESTER FOSSE	4-1
	26	Lincoln City	3-1
January	01	NOTTS COUNTY	2-1
	05	Grimsby Town	2-3
	12	LINCOLN CITY	4-1
March	02	WOOLWICH ARSENAL	2-0
	16	Newcastle United	0-1
April	02	WALSALL TOWN SWIFTS	4-1
	06	Burton Swifts	1-0
	12	Newton Heath	2-2
	15	NEWTON HEATH	2-1
	20	Leicester Fosse	0-1

Final League Division 2 Table 1895

1	BURY	30	78	33	48
2	Notts County	30	75	45	39
3	Newton Heath	30	78	44	38
4	Leicester Fosse	30	72	53	38
5	Grimsby Town	30	79	52	37
6	Darwen	30	74	43	36
7	Burton Wanderers	30	67	39	35
8	Woolwich Arsenal	30	75	58	34
9	Manchester City	30	82	72	31
10	Newcastle United	30	72	84	27
11	Burton Swifts	30	52	74	25
12	Rotherham Town	30	55	62	24
13	Lincoln City	30	52	92	20
14	Walsall Town Swifts	30	47	92	20
15	Burslem Port Vale	30	39	77	18
16	Crewe Alexandra	30	26	103	10
		480	1023	1023	480

ELECTION/RE-ELECTION

The bottom four 2nd Division clubs had to apply for re-election in 1895. Three were successful, with Lincoln City and Burslem Port Vale topping the poll with 22 votes apiece. Crewe Alexandra completed the returning trio, having 18 votes – the same as newcomers Loughborough Town. Walsall Town Swifts were therefore voted out of the Football League, by virtue of what seems to be a harsh decision. The number of votes the club were given in the poll was not recorded, as was also the case with the other unsuccessful clubs – Blackpool, Buxton and Fairfield, champions of the Lancashire League, which had provided the last two Second Division winners.

OTHER INFORMATION 1892-1895

New Football League homes

By 1895, a number of other grounds had hosted Football League matches. These, of course, included Everton's new home at Goodison Park.

Other new venues were :

Burslem Port Vale	Cobridge (The Athletic Ground)
Burton Swifts	Peel Croft
Burton Wanderers	Derby Turn
Bury	Gigg Lane
Crewe Alexandra	Alexandra Ground
Grimsby Town	Abbey Park
Leicester Fosse	Walnut Street
Lincoln City	John O'Gaunt's
Manchester City	Hyde Road
Middlesbrough Ironopolis	Paradise Ground
Newcastle United	St. James' Park
Newton Heath	Bank Street (Clayton)
Northwich Victoria	Drill Field
Nottingham Forest	Town Ground
Rotherham Town	Clifton Grove
Sheffield United	Bramall Lane
Sheffield Wednesday	Olive Grove
Small Heath	Coventry Road
Walsall Town Swifts	West Bromwich Road
Woolwich Arsenal	Manor Ground (Plumstead)

Other leagues and competitions

The success and popularity of league-based football continued to grow, with the Sheffield League, the Birmingham League, the Shropshire League, the Kent League, the Bristol & District League and the Lancashire Combination among the new competitions established. In Scotland, a second division was added to the Scottish League in 1893 and professionalism was introduced in an attempt to stem the flow of Scottish talent out of the country and into the English game.

In 1894, after much discussion among leading clubs in the South-East, the 2-division Southern League was begun. The first champions were Millwall Athletic, whose team consisted largely of Scotsmen working at a preserves factory in the East End. With the number of professional and semi-professional clubs growing, the London-based Football Association decided to introduce an F.A. Amateur Cup in 1893. The first winners were Old Carthusians, who beat Casuals 2-1 in the Final. Twelve months later, the Old Carthusians reached the Final for a second time, but were beaten 1-2 this time by Middlesbrough from the Northern League.

Football League Attendances

Crowds continued to grow at Football League grounds. Everton led the way, attracting well over 13,000 on average 1893-94 and 16,000+ per game 1894-95, when the club's gates topped the pile for the 7th season running. In Division 2, Woolwich Arsenal pulled in the biggest crowds, averaging more than 6,000 at their home games in both 1893-94 and 1894-95, despite fairly moderate seasons on the pitch. This is not really surprising as the Gunners were the only professional club in London at the time. Less successful were Middlesbrough Ironopolis, whose average of 1,300 for games at the club's Paradise Ground was not enough to keep the Nops alive.

End of an era

At the close of the '94-'95 season, Charles W. Alcock stepped down from his role as Secretary of the Football Association after 25 years' great service to the game. He had only been paid since 1887 for the many hours of work he put in. Sir Frederick Wall took over, serving until 1934.

The F.A. Cup

The F.A. Cup remained the country's premier football competition, but the growing status of the Football League is reflected in Sunderland's fixture list for the 1894-95 season shown previously. League games are shown as being played fairly consistently after early January.

Where's the Cup?

On returning to Birmingham in April 1895, Villa agreed to allow the F.A. Cup to be put on display at W.Shillcock, Boot & Shoe Manufacturer's shop in the city. The trophy was stolen from the shop and, apparently, melted down to make half-crowns (12·5 pence coins).

Goal scoring 1892-1895

Division 1

Despite having an otherwise appalling season, Newton Heath demolished Wolves on October 15th, 1892, winning 10-1. On Boxing Day, 1893, League leaders Aston Villa thrashed lowly Darwen 9-0 at Perry Barr. West Bromwich Albion recorded an 8-0 away win at Wolves on December 27th, 1894. Less than 2 weeks later Blackburn Rovers registered the highest top flight score of the season by crushing Small Heath 9-1 at Ewood Park on January 5th.

Division 2

Sheffield United's 10-0 away win at Burslem Port Vale on December 10th, 1892 has never been bettered in the Football League. A week later, Small Heath buried Walsall Town Swifts 12-0 at Coventry Road. Lincoln City won 8-2 at Rotherham Town on 2nd December, 1893. Notts County went one better on 17th February, 1894 by beating Crewe Alexandra 9-1. One month later, Small Heath sank their visitors Ardwick by 10-2. During the 1894-95 season, Leicester Fosse thumped Walsall Town Swifts 9-1 on January 5th and there were 9-0 victories for both Newton Heath (v. Walsall Town Swifts, 3rd April) and League debutants Burton Wanderers (v. Newcastle United, 15th April). Notts County recorded a 10-0 home win over Burslem Port Vale on February 26th and the highest score honour went to Manchester City, who beat their visitors, Lincoln City, 11-3 on March 23rd.

The Amateur-Professional Gap

Professionalism in English soccer was 10 years old by 1895. The gap in standards between amateur and professional teams and players had widened greatly. The International Trial Match between Amateurs and Professionals on March 28th resulted in a 7-0 win for the Pros. An England team made up only of professional players beat Ireland 9-0, whereas a purely amateur XI could only manage a 1-1 draw with Wales. Scotland were beaten 3-0 by an England side containing just two amateur players.

Almost crippled by financial troubles, 2nd Division Crewe Alexandra played the 1894-95 season as an amateur club. Having won their F.A. Cup First Qualifying Round tie at Newtown 3-1, Alexandra were dumped out of the competition by Fairfield, 3-6 on their own ground, in the next round. In the new Amateur Cup, Crewe reached the last 8 before losing 0-1 to holders Old Carthusians. In Division Two, the Railwaymen used 36 players in their 30 matches. Only 3 games were won, with the side failing to score in 13 matches and never hitting more than 2 goals in a game. Having lost the first 3 of their fixtures, Crewe defeated Rotherham Town 2-1 on September 22nd. They then failed to win any of the next 14 games and had to wait until February 9th for their next victory – over Grimsby Town. Taking just 1 point from their last 7 games, Alexandra collected the League wooden spoon and proved the Football League was no place for amateurs.

1895-1896 – LEAGUE DIVISION 1

ASTON VILLA

The First Half

Sunderland began with two wins, then went 5 games without victory. By the time the defending champions lost 1-2 at Villa, it was the Midlanders who led the table from Everton and Bolton.

After an odd goal reverse at Sheffield United on September 14th, the Claret & Blues went eight matches without defeat, six of these being won, up to and including November 2nd. New signing from Celtic, Johnny Campbell had hit 9 goals by this stage, with Jack Devey adding a further 7 of the 33 scored. Bolton stayed closest to Aston Villa from mid-October to the early part of November, before losing four times in five to drop right out of contention. It was Everton who now took up the mantle of leading pursuers.

Villa's charge at the top stalled rather with a 1-2 defeat at Sunderland and a home draw against Sheffield United, enabling Everton to draw level on points on the final Saturday of November. The Goodison Park club then went two points clear on December 7th by winning 3-0 at Small Heath, while Villa lost 3-4 at Preston North End.

Aston Villa's '1st half' record

September	02	WEST BROMWICH ALBION	1-0
	07	SMALL HEATH	7-3
	14	Sheffield United	1-2
	21	DERBY COUNTY	4-1
	28	Blackburn Rovers	1-1
	30	EVERTON	4-3
October	05	SUNDERLAND	2-1
	12	West Bromwich Albion	1-1
	19	BLACKBURN ROVERS	3-1
	26	Small Heath	4-1
November	02	BURNLEY	5-1
	09	Sunderland	1-2
	16	SHEFFIELD UNITED	2-2
	23	Burnley	4-2
December	07	Preston North End	3-4

Table at December 7th, 1895

1	Everton	17	39	23	23
2	Derby County	14	42	19	21
3	ASTON VILLA	15	43	26	21
4	Stoke	17	33	20	20
5	Bolton Wanderers	15	25	20	18
6	Blackburn Rovers	13	23	16	17
7	Sunderland	14	20	18	16
8	Sheffield Wednesday	13	26	25	16
9	Preston North End	15	25	33	16
10	Wolves	14	29	30	11
11	Sheffield United	14	17	28	11
12	Nottingham Forest	15	23	30	10
13	Bury	13	22	27	9
14	Burnley	15	17	29	9
15	West Bromwich Albion	15	17	31	8
16	Small Heath	13	20	46	6
		232	421	421	232

Attendances 1895-1896

The total number of spectators at the 240 Division 1 matches is said to have been 1,857,000 – an average of 7,738 per game.

F.A. CUP FINAL - 18th April, 1896

Sheffield Wednesday beat Wolves 2-1 at Crystal Palace in front of 48,836 spectators, who paid a total of £1,824. Fred Spiksley scored Wednesday's goals, with Black replying for the losers.

The Second Half

Defeat at Everton on December 21st left Villa 4 points off the lead. More worrying perhaps was the fact that the club was now third, having also been passed by Derby County.

In Steve Bloomer, who had hit 18 goals in 15 matches, the Rams, who also had a game in hand, had a prolific marksman who might just make the key difference. From Boxing Day, however, Villa went on a 10-match unbeaten run, dropping only two points in the process. One of the drawn games was at Derby, on February 8th – a result crucial to the Villains' title aspirations in the final reckoning. At the start of April, Villa led the table by 5 points with 2 matches left.

Derby and Everton both had 2 games in hand, but had to face each other twice. To Villa's delight, their rivals drew on April 3rd, 2-2, while the leaders won at Forest – it was indeed a very Good Friday. Everton's title challenge was now ended. 24 hours later it was all over. Derby, without Bloomer, were held at Burnley on April 4th and, without playing, Aston Villa were League champions again.

Aston Villa's '2nd half' record

December	14	BOLTON WANDERERS	2-0
	21	Everton	0-2
	26	Wolves	2-1
	28	BURY	2-0
January	04	Stoke	2-1
	11	PRESTON NORTH END	1-0
	18	Sheffield Wednesday	3-1
	25	NOTTINGHAM FOREST	3-1
February	08	Derby County	2-2
	22	STOKE	5-2
March	07	Bolton Wanderers	2-2
	14	SHEFFIELD WEDNESDAY	2-2
	21	Bury	3-5
April	03	Nottingham Forest	2-0
	06	WOLVES	4-1

Final League Division 1 Table 1896

1	ASTON VILLA	30	78	45	45
2	Derby County	30	68	35	41
3	Everton	30	66	43	39
4	Bolton Wanderers	30	49	37	37
5	Sunderland	30	52	41	37
6	Stoke	30	56	47	30
7	Sheffield Wednesday	30	44	53	29
8	Blackburn Rovers	30	40	50	29
9	Preston North End	30	44	48	28
10	Burnley	30	48	44	27
11	Bury	30	50	54	27
12	Sheffield United	30	40	50	26
13	Nottingham Forest	30	42	57	25
14	Wolves	30	61	65	21
15	Small Heath	30	39	79	20
16	West Bromwich Albion	30	30	59	19
		480	807	807	480

Goals 1895-1896

A total of 807 goals were scored in the 240 games – an average of 3.36 goals per game. The leading goal-scorer was Steve Bloomer (Derby County) with 22 goals.

TEST MATCHES

In a new move, these end-of-season games involved only the bottom 2 from Division 1 and the top 2 from the 2nd Division. A mini-league saw each club play the 2 clubs from 'the other division', home and away. The 'top 2' would win the right to play in Division 1. In 1896, success went to Liverpool and West Bromwich Albion.

1895-1896 – LEAGUE DIVISION 2 — LIVERPOOL

The First Half

Back in Division II after only one season in the top flight, Liverpool opened up with 5 straight wins. The last of these was a 4-1 drubbing of closest rivals, Burton Wanderers, victors in their opening 4 matches. 'Pool now stood clear at the top.

Four defeats in the next 7 outings changed the nature of things, however, and Liverpool were knocked off the top of the division by Manchester City, on November 2nd, when the Hyde Road men won 3-2 at Darwen. Two days later, City repeated the score in beating Rotherham Town to head the table by 3 points.

Liverpool closed the gap to one point five days after this, by defeating Leicester Fosse 3-1, then reclaimed the leadership by securing a pleasing 2-0 win at Woolwich Arsenal, while City slipped up at Burton Wanderers. The Anfield club stayed at the Division II summit after their draw with Darwen could not be bettered by their chief rivals.

Liverpool's '1st half' record.

September	07	Notts County	3-2
	14	NEWCASTLE UNITED	5-1
	21	Loughborough Town	4-2
	28	BURSLEM PORT VALE	5-1
	30	BURTON WANDERERS	4-1
October	05	Newcastle United	0-1
	07	CREWE ALEXANDRA	6-1
	12	NEWTON HEATH	7-1
	19	Grimsby Town	0-1
	21	Burslem Port Vale	4-5
	26	NOTTS COUNTY	3-0
November	02	Newton Heath	2-5
	09	LEICESTER FOSSE	3-1
	16	Woolwich Arsenal	2-0
	23	DARWEN	0-0

Table at November 23rd, 1895

1	LIVERPOOL	15	48	22	21
2	Manchester City	13	23	17	20
3	Burton Wanderers	13	24	14	19
4	Woolwich Arsenal	12	27	13	15
5	Newton Heath	12	33	23	15
6	Newcastle United	9	25	16	12
7	Burton Swifts	11	19	20	12
8	Grimsby Town	11	29	22	11
9	Darwen	12	31	36	10
10	Notts County	12	23	31	8
11	Leicester Fosse	9	16	17	7
12	Rotherham Town	11	14	22	7
13	Burslem Port Vale	9	17	31	7
14	Loughborough Town	9	13	25	6
15	Lincoln City	10	15	31	4
16	Crewe Alexandra	10	11	28	4
		178	368	368	178

Attendances 1895-1896

The total number of spectators at the 240 Division 2 games is said to have been 982,875 – an average of 4,095 per game.

Goals 1895-1896

A total of 942 goals were scored in the 240 games – an average of 3.93 goals per game.

The leading goal-scorer was George Allan (Liverpool) with 25 goals.

The Second Half

Liverpool's better goal average kept them ahead of Burton Wanderers before Christmas, but a third successive, decisive win, on December 28th, took Burton top. Manchester City were still a threat, 3 points behind 'Pool, with 4 games in hand. Vitally, City were beaten 3-1 at Anfield on January 1st. This was Liverpool's fourth win in a row.

Six more victories in January/February stretched the run to ten games and lifted the points haul to 41 from 26 matches by the start of March. Burton Wanderers now lay 7 points behind, while Manchester City were still 3 points adrift, with 2 matches in hand.

When Liverpool lost at Burton on March 7th, things seemed to swing in City's favour, but, on March 21st, the Citizens lost 1-4 at Newcastle, while 'Pool won 6-1 at Burton Swifts. On April 3rd, the two leaders met at Hyde Road and drew 1-1. Liverpool's goal average was so much better that City needed 60 goals+ in their last 2 matches. Game over.

Liverpool's '2nd half' record

November	30	Leicester Fosse	0-2
December	07	LOUGHBOROUGH TOWN	1-0
	14	Darwen	4-0
	21	Lincoln City	1-0
January	01	MANCHESTER CITY	3-1
	04	Rotherham Town	5-0
	11	WOOLWICH ARSENAL	3-0
	25	LINCOLN CITY	6-1
February	18	ROTHERHAM TOWN	10-1
	22	GRIMSBY TOWN	3-1
	29	Burton Swifts	7-0
March	07	Burton Wanderers	1-2
	21	BURTON SWIFTS	6-1
	28	Crewe Alexandra	7-0
April	03	Manchester City	1-1

Final League Division 2 Table 1896

1	LIVERPOOL	30	106	32	46
2	Manchester City	30	63	38	46
3	Grimsby Town	30	82	38	42
4	Burton Wanderers	30	69	40	42
5	Newcastle United	30	73	50	34
6	Newton Heath	30	66	57	33
7	Woolwich Arsenal	30	59	42	32
8	Leicester Fosse	30	57	44	32
9	Darwen	30	72	67	30
10	Notts County	30	57	54	26
11	Burton Swifts	30	39	69	24
12	Loughborough Town	30	40	67	23
13	Lincoln City	30	53	75	22
14	Burslem Port Vale	30	43	78	18
15	Rotherham Town	30	34	97	17
16	Crewe Alexandra	30	30	95	13
		480	943	943	480

ELECTION/RE-ELECTION

In another new move, only the bottom 3 clubs faced re-election in 1896. Rotherham Town opted not to continue, leaving 1 definite space for a new club. Burslem (10 votes) and Crewe (4) both failed to be re-elected. The successful clubs were Blackpool (19), Gainsborough Trinity (15) and Walsall (16). Those missing out were Luton Town (10), Fairfield and Glossop North End (3 each), Macclesfield and Tottenham Hotspur (2 each).

1896-1897 – LEAGUE DIVISION 1

ASTON VILLA

The First Half

The opening exchanges in the '96-'97 First Division season suggested that the race for the title would be a close one. How far from the truth this turned out to be! Bolton Wanderers began well, and, by the end of September, headed the table by one point from promoted Liverpool. Newly-installed at Burnden Park, the Trotters remained undefeated until losing at Blackburn Rovers, 0-1, on October 17th. Bolton continued to lead the 1st Division table at mid-November, though their seventeen points total was now matched by both Liverpool and Aston Villa.

The defending champions had enjoyed a seven-match unbeaten run, from October 3rd. The Villa continued to impress, taking advantage of Bolton not having a game to go top, in style, hammering Blackburn 5-1 at Ewood Park on November 28th. Wanderers returned to the head of the table on December 7th by beating Everton 3-0, but, when West Bromwich Albion held the Burnden Park men to a draw on December 19th, Villa reclaimed top spot with victory at Nottingham Forest.

Aston Villa's '1st half' record

September	02	STOKE	2-1
	05	West Bromwich Albion	1-3
	12	SHEFFIELD UNITED	2-2
	19	Everton	3-2
	26	EVERTON	1-2
October	03	Sheffield United	0-0
	10	WEST BROMWICH ALBION	2-0
	17	Derby County	3-1
	24	DERBY COUNTY	2-1
	31	Stoke	2-0
November	07	BURY	1-1
	14	Sheffield Wednesday	3-1
	21	SHEFFIELD WEDNESDAY	4-0
	28	Blackburn Rovers	5-1
December	19	NOTTINGHAM FOREST	3-2

Table at December 19th, 1896

1	ASTON VILLA	15	34	17	23
2	Bolton Wanderers	15	28	14	22
3	Liverpool	18	28	19	20
4	Preston North End	15	33	22	19
5	Derby County	16	38	29	17
6	West Bromwich Albion	17	16	18	17
7	Sheffield United	13	19	13	16
8	Sheffield Wednesday	16	22	24	16
9	Everton	15	25	22	15
10	Nottingham Forest	16	27	28	15
11	Blackburn Rovers	16	16	29	15
12	Wolves	15	19	17	12
13	Bury	14	18	25	12
14	Stoke	17	26	43	12
15	Sunderland	16	12	26	9
16	Burnley	14	17	32	8
		248	378	378	248

Attendances 1896-1897

The total number of spectators at the 240 Division 1 matches is said to have been 1,880,625 – an average of 7,836 per game.

Goals 1896-1897

A total of 751 goals were scored in the 240 games – an average of 3.13 goals per game.

The leading goal-scorer was Steve Bloomer (Derby County) with 24 goals.

The Second Half

Villa moved further ahead by New Year, helped greatly by Bolton Wanderers losing twice. The leaders then faced their own crisis by suffering 2 defeats, which allowed Derby County, with five successive wins, to move to within a point of the top. Digging deep, Villa recovered their form, won 3 in a row and reached mid-February with a 3-point advantage and a game in hand. With four wins and a draw to follow, the champions reached the end of March needing only two points from three remaining fixtures to retain the title.

Derby County, the only club left to pose any kind of threat to Villa's championship intentions, won 3-2 at Burnley on April 5th to prolong the agony a little further. The Rams were still 7 points behind Villa though and faced the next 3 matches away. On April 10th, Derby lost 0-1 at Bury. This handed the title to Villa, who became Football League champions, again without playing on the key day. By winning their last three games, Villa equalled Preston's 11-points winning margin.

Aston Villa's '2nd half' record

December	25	Liverpool	3-3
	26	Wolves	2-1
January	02	BURNLEY	0-3
	09	Sunderland	2-4
	16	SUNDERLAND	2-1
February	06	Bury	2-0
	08	Burnley	4-3
	22	PRESTON NORTH END	3-1
March	06	Nottingham Forest	4-2
	13	LIVERPOOL	0-0
	22	BOLTON WANDERERS	6-2
	27	Bolton Wanderers	2-1
April	17	BLACKBURN ROVERS	3-0
	19	WOLVES	5-0
	26	Preston North End	1-0

Final League Division 1 Table 1897

1	ASTON VILLA	30	73	38	47
2	Sheffield United	30	42	29	36
3	Derby County	30	70	50	36
4	Preston North End	30	55	40	34
5	Liverpool	30	46	38	33
6	Sheffield Wednesday	30	42	37	31
7	Everton	30	62	57	31
8	Bolton Wanderers	30	40	43	30
9	Bury	30	39	44	30
10	Wolves	30	45	41	28
11	Nottingham Forest	30	44	49	26
12	West Bromwich Albion	30	33	56	26
13	Stoke	30	48	59	25
14	Blackburn Rovers	30	35	62	25
15	Sunderland	30	34	47	23
16	Burnley	30	43	61	19
		480	751	751	480

F.A. CUP FINAL - 10th April, 1897

A Cup Final record attendance of 65,891 paid £2,162 to see Aston Villa complete 'the Double' by beating Everton 3-2 at Crystal Palace. All the goals came in the first half. For the winning Villa combination, Devey, Campbell and Crabtree scored, with Bell and Hartley netting for Everton.

TEST MATCHES The 4-club mini-league approach used a year earlier was employed again in 1897. Notts County were the most successful team, with Sunderland second. Burnley were therefore relegated, Notts County promoted

- 18 -

1896-1897 – LEAGUE DIVISION 2

NOTTS COUNTY

The First Half

Notts County proved to be the class act in the 2nd Division. Winning their first 4 games, they ended September second in the table, trailing Newton Heath by 4 points. The Bank Street club had played 7 games in a month, however, and such high activity was almost certain to take its toll.

So it proved and Newton Heath failed to win in their next 4 outings. By October 17th, Notts lay just a point behind their rivals and went top 2 weeks later with a 4-1 success at Manchester City. By mid-November County's lead was up to 3 points and they had gone 7 matches unbeaten.

Two defeats failed to disturb their advantage as, not for the last time, others near the top of the Second Division could not put together a decent run when it really mattered. The Notts County side reached their half-way stage with a solid 5-point lead over the others.

Notts County's '1st half' record

September	05	LOUGHBOROUGH TOWN	3-1
	12	Leicester Fosse	3-2
	19	NEWCASTLE UNITED	3-1
	26	Woolwich Arsenal	3-2
October	01	GRIMSBY TOWN	1-3
	03	Burton Wanderers	3-0
	10	MANCHESTER CITY	3-3
	17	LEICESTER FOSSE	6-0
	24	Loughborough Town	1-0
	31	Manchester City	4-1
November	07	WOOLWICH ARSENAL	7-4
	14	WALSALL	5-2
	21	Grimsby Town	1-3
	28	Blackpool	2-3
December	05	BURTON SWIFTS	6-1

Table at December 5th, 1896

1	NOTTS COUNTY	15	51	26	23
2	Newton Heath	14	29	18	18
3	Grimsby Town	15	36	28	18
4	Newcastle United	12	27	20	16
5	Manchester City	14	28	24	15
6	Woolwich Arsenal	12	34	27	14
7	Walsall	14	29	32	14
8	Small Heath	13	29	20	13
9	Gainsborough Trinity	12	15	16	13
10	Blackpool	10	26	20	12
11	Leicester Fosse	11	25	25	12
12	Burton Swifts	12	21	28	12
13	Darwen	12	22	27	10
14	Lincoln City	10	12	25	4
15	Burton Wanderers	12	8	28	4
16	Loughborough Town	14	10	38	4
		202	402	402	202

Attendances 1896-1897

The total number of spectators at the 240 Division 2 games is said to have been 1,013,625 – an average of 4,223 per game.

Goals 1896-1897

A total of 908 goals were scored in the 240 games – an average of 3.78 goals per game.

The joint leading goal-scorers were Notts County duo Tom Boucher and John Murphy with 22 goals each.

The Second Half

Newton Heath were beaten 3-0 on December 19th and the Trent Bridge men went into the New Year holding a 4-point lead over Grimsby Town and Newton Heath. By mid-February, with their winning run extended to 6 games, County held a 7-point advantage over their nearest rivals.

Perhaps this led to complacency, because Notts suffered unexpected reverses at Darwen and Gainsborough Trinity. Grimsby Town, with a draw at Blackpool and wins over Walsall and Darwen, closed the gap at the top and moved to within 2 points of the leaders.

County's players heard the wake-up call. Burton Wanderers felt their reaction to this on March 13th. A week later, Grimsby and Newcastle both lost, while Notts beat Blackpool. A 1-1 draw on March 27th at Newton Heath meant Notts needed only a point to become champions. This was collected at Lincoln on March 31st.

Notts County's '2nd half' record

December	12	Newcastle United	2-2
	19	NEWTON HEATH	3-0
January	02	Burton Swifts	4-1
	09	GAINSBOROUGH TRINITY	2-0
	16	Walsall	3-1
	23	LINCOLN CITY	8-0
February	06	DARWEN	4-0
	27	Darwen	1-2
March	06	Gainsborough Trinity	2-3
	13	BURTON WANDERERS	5-0
	20	BLACKPOOL	3-1
	27	Newton Heath	1-1
	31	Lincoln City	1-1
April	03	SMALL HEATH	1-2
	10	Small Heath	1-3

Final League Division 2 Table 1897

1	NOTTS COUNTY	30	92	43	42
2	Newton Heath	30	56	34	39
3	Grimsby Town	30	66	45	38
4	Small Heath	30	69	47	37
5	Newcastle United	30	56	52	35
6	Manchester City	30	58	50	32
7	Gainsborough Trinity	30	50	47	31
8	Blackpool	30	59	56	31
9	Leicester Fosse	30	59	56	30
10	Woolwich Arsenal	30	68	70	30
11	Darwen	30	67	61	28
12	Walsall	30	53	69	26
13	Loughborough Town	30	50	64	25
14	Burton Swifts	30	46	61	24
15	Burton Wanderers	30	31	67	20
16	Lincoln City	30	27	85	12
		480	907	907	480

ELECTION/RE-ELECTION

Applying for re-election for the 3rd year running, Lincoln City topped the poll with 21 votes. Burton Swifts were also re-elected with 15 and Luton Town joined Division Two, having finished 3rd with 13 backers. Burton Wanderers (9) were out, with Burslem Port Vale (11), Nelson (7), Glossop North End (5), Fairfield (3), Crewe Alexandra (2) and Millwall Athletic (1) also unsuccessful.

1897-1898 – LEAGUE DIVISION 1   SHEFFIELD UNITED

The First Half

Aston Villa, winners of 'the Double' the previous season, began their pursuit of a third successive League title with an emphatic 5-2 win, at their new home Villa Park, over Sheffield Wednesday, on September 1st. Three wins later, Villa led the First Division by a point. On September 25th, however, the reigning champions were beaten 3-4 at Blackburn Rovers and Sheffield United moved above them on goal average. Not as fashionable as Villa, United had assembled a hard-working squad, including giant 'keeper William Foulke, England captain Ernest Needham and goal poacher Walter Bennett.

Going unbeaten in their opening 14 games, the Blades eventually lost for the first time at Stoke on December 11th. Villa's 5-1 demolition of Blackburn on the same day brought the champions level on points with the leaders. With their considerably better defensive record, however, United had a superior goal average and stayed at the top.

The Second Half

With United taking only 1 point from their next two games, Villa moved top on December 27th, after drawing at Wolves, who, along with neighbours West Bromwich Albion, tucked in a point behind the Blades.

The Bramall Lane men went into the New Year without having won in six games, but ended their drought at Notts County on January 1st. Two wins over Aston Villa followed and, with a further three victories, United reached mid-February 7 points clear at the top of Division One. With the League title coming into sight, the Blades stalled, getting 1 goal and 1 point in their next 4 games. By March 31st, United held a one point lead over their next visitors, Sunderland, who had a game in hand. The 1-0 win, on April 2nd, gave the Blades control over their own destiny and six days later, on Good Friday, April 8th, Ernest Needham's goal, at Bolton, gave United the title, as Sunderland lost 0-1 at Bury.

Sheffield United's '1st half' record

September	01	DERBY COUNTY	2-1
	04	Preston North End	3-1
	11	STOKE	4-3
	18	Nottingham Forest	1-1
	25	BURY	1-1
October	02	Wolves	1-1
	04	BLACKBURN ROVERS	5-2
	09	Bury	5-2
	16	Sheffield Wednesday	1-0
	23	PRESTON NORTH END	2-1
	30	Everton	4-1
November	13	Derby County	1-1
	20	Blackburn Rovers	1-1
December	04	NOTTINGHAM FOREST	1-1
	11	Stoke	1-2

Sheffield United's '2nd half' record

December	27	SHEFFIELD WEDNESDAY	1-1
	29	LIVERPOOL	1-2
January	01	Notts County	3-1
	08	ASTON VILLA	1-0
	15	Aston Villa	2-1
	22	WOLVES	2-1
February	05	Liverpool	4-0
	07	BOLTON WANDERERS	4-0
	19	NOTTS COUNTY	0-1
	22	EVERTON	0-0
March	05	Sunderland	1-3
	26	West Bromwich Albion	0-2
April	02	SUNDERLAND	1-0
	08	Bolton Wanderers	1-0
	11	WEST BROMWICH ALBION	2-0

Table at December 11th, 1897

1	SHEFFIELD UNITED	15	33	19	22
2	Aston Villa	16	42	30	22
3	Wolves	16	29	20	19
4	Sheffield Wednesday	15	28	17	18
5	West Bromwich Albion	15	27	23	18
6	Everton	14	26	23	17
7	Bolton Wanderers	15	18	18	17
8	Nottingham Forest	15	23	21	15
9	Derby County	16	32	30	15
10	Liverpool	14	24	24	13
	Sunderland	13	19	19	13
12	Bury	12	16	22	11
13	Preston North End	17	16	27	11
14	Blackburn Rovers	14	21	33	10
15	Stoke	16	17	35	10
16	Notts County	15	15	25	7
		238	386	386	238

Final League Division 1 Table 1898

1	SHEFFIELD UNITED	30	56	31	42
2	Sunderland	30	43	30	37
3	Wolves	30	57	41	35
4	Everton	30	48	39	35
5	Sheffield Wednesday	30	51	42	33
6	Aston Villa	30	61	51	33
7	West Bromwich Albion	30	44	45	32
8	Nottingham Forest	30	47	49	31
9	Liverpool	30	48	45	28
10	Derby County	30	57	61	28
11	Bolton Wanderers	30	28	41	26
12	Preston North End	30	35	43	24
13	Notts County	30	36	46	24
14	Bury	30	39	51	24
15	Blackburn Rovers	30	39	54	24
16	Stoke	30	35	55	24
		480	724	724	480

F.A CUP FINAL - 16th April, 1898

Former Burton Wanderers front-man Capes hit two goals for Nottingham Forest as they defeated Derby County 3-1 in front of 62,017 watchers. The great Steve Bloomer scored for the Rams, while Forest's other goal came from McPherson.

Attendances 1897-1898

The total number of spectators at the 240 Division 1 matches is said to have been 2,260,875 – an average of 9,420 per game.

Goals 1897-1898

A total of 724 goals were scored in the 240 games – an average of 3.02 goals per game.

The leading goal-scorer was Freddie Wheldon (Aston Villa) with 23 goals.

A TITANIC STRUGGLE

While Sheffield United eased their way to the title, there was a tense and ever-changing battle at the foot of the section to escape from the bottom 2 places and the Test Matches. Stoke, Notts County and Preston all won their last games on April 9th, and awaited news of the bottom two, Blackburn Rovers and Bury. Blackburn moved up to 14th on April 14th by winning at Bolton and needed to avoid defeat at Bury on April 16th to go safe. Bury had to win and a tight contest went the Gigg Lane men's way, 1-0, so that the Shakers slipped above Rovers who joined Stoke in the Test Match shake down.

PROMOTION/RELEGATION DETAILS 1898

These appear 2 pages further on because of the 'interesting situation' which developed in the Test Matches.

1897-1898 – LEAGUE DIVISION 2   BURNLEY

The First Half

Burnley quickly established themselves as one of two leading teams, going unbeaten in their eight opening games, with only 1 point dropped. With a similar run of good form, Manchester City were equal to this, however. City led the table by a point up to October 16th, when their 'derby' draw at Newton Heath gave Burnley the chance to pull level, with exactly the same goals aggregate, by beating Burton Swifts. City went clear again a week later, by thrashing Darwen 5-0, while Burnley lost at Grimsby Town. This set up an interesting situation as Manchester City's next fixture was at Burnley.

When the two leaders met at Turf Moor on 30th October, it was the home eleven who ran out winners. With City not in action a week later, Burnley went to the top by winning at Darwen and then moved 6 points clear by the end of the month, though City had three matches in hand. The situation remained the same by the time Burnley reached the half-way stage in their league programme.

Burnley's '1st half' record

September	04	BLACKPOOL	5-1	
	06	WOOLWICH ARSENAL	5-0	
	11	Blackpool	1-1	
	18	WALSALL	4-1	
	25	Walsall	2-1	
October	02	NEWCASTLE UNITED	3-0	
	09	Leicester Fosse	1-0	
	16	BURTON SWIFTS	2-0	
	23	Grimsby Town	1-2	
	30	MANCHESTER CITY	3-1	
November	06	Darwen	1-0	
	13	LUTON TOWN	4-0	
	20	Manchester City	1-1	
	27	DARWEN	6-1	
December	11	GRIMSBY TOWN	6-0	

Table at December 11th, 1897

1	BURNLEY	15	45	9	26
2	Manchester City	12	32	9	20
3	Newcastle United	12	25	12	19
4	Small Heath	12	25	19	17
5	Grimsby Town	16	30	29	16
6	Newton Heath	14	25	12	15
7	Leicester Fosse	13	20	15	14
8	Woolwich Arsenal	14	26	25	14
9	Walsall	15	25	37	10
10	Darwen	12	15	33	10
11	Luton Town	11	16	22	9
12	Loughborough Town	12	13	27	9
13	Lincoln City	12	21	33	8
14	Gainsborough Trinity	11	20	28	7
15	Burton Swifts	11	14	26	5
16	Blackpool	12	13	29	5
		204	365	365	204

Attendances 1897-1898

The total number of spectators at the 240 Division 2 games is said to have been 1,084,500 – an average of 4,519 per game.

Goals 1897-1898

A total of 860 goals were scored in the 240 games – an average of 3.58 goals per game.

The leading goal-scorer was Jimmy Ross (Burnley) with 23 goals.

The Second Half

Burnley kept up the pressure after Christmas, reaching 10 games unbeaten by drawing 0-0 at Newton Heath on January 12th. City's moderate return of 6 points in 6 matches between Christmas and mid-January left them trailing the leaders. By mid-February, the Turf Moor outfit led by 7 points and City were coming under pressure for second place from Newcastle United. Burnley stretched their unbeaten sequence to 16 games with a draw at home to Gainsborough Trinity on March 12th, maintaining their 7-point advantage at the top. By now though, their leading pursuers were Newcastle.

The Geordies cut the gap to 5 by beating City on March 16th. Burnley's loss at Luton 3 days later implied things might get tighter than expected. Newcastle then beat Grimsby 4-0 on March 26th. The pressure on Turf Moor was eased though with a 9-3 crushing of Loughborough Town. April 9th proved decisive. Newcastle reached 43 points, with 2 to play, by drawing at Leicester. Burnley drew 0-0 draw at Gainsborough to go to 48 points and out of their rivals' reach.

Burnley's '2nd half' record

December	27	Newcastle United	1-0	
January	01	LINCOLN CITY	2-1	
	08	Small Heath	2-2	
	12	Newton Heath	0-0	
	15	LEICESTER FOSSE	4-0	
	22	Loughborough Town	2-0	
February	05	SMALL HEATH	4-1	
March	05	Burton Swifts	2-0	
	07	NEWTON HEATH	6-3	
	12	GAINSBOROUGH TRINITY	1-1	
	19	Luton Town	0-2	
	28	LOUGHBOROUGH TOWN	9-3	
April	02	Woolwich Arsenal	1-1	
	08	Lincoln City	1-1	
	09	Gainsborough Trinity	0-0	

Final League Division 2 Table 1898

1	BURNLEY	30	80	24	48
2	Newcastle United	30	64	32	45
3	Manchester City	30	66	36	39
4	Newton Heath	30	64	35	38
5	Woolwich Arsenal	30	69	49	37
6	Small Heath	30	58	50	36
7	Leicester Fosse	30	46	35	33
8	Luton Town	30	68	50	30
9	Gainsborough Trinity	30	50	54	30
10	Walsall	30	58	58	29
11	Blackpool	30	49	61	25
12	Grimsby Town	30	52	62	24
13	Burton Swifts	30	38	69	21
14	Lincoln City	30	43	82	17
15	Darwen	30	31	76	14
16	Loughborough Town	30	24	87	14
		480	860	860	480

ELECTION/RE-ELECTION 1898

These appear on the next page because of the 'interesting situation' which developed in the Test Matches.

OTHER INFORMATION   1895-1898

Promotion and Relegation 1898

The furore which erupted after the completion of the Test Matches in 1898 led to a major change in the system of promotion and relegation within the Football League. The Test Matches were held towards the end of April, with Burnley beating Blackburn Rovers twice while Stoke and Newcastle United each won one of their games. Stoke then won at Burnley 2-0 and Blackburn beat Newcastle 4-3 at Ewood Park. The results created a problem. Burnley and Stoke each had 4 points, Blackburn and Newcastle had 2. The 2 leaders met on April 28th, both needing a draw to earn the right to play in Division One. The game was notable for its lack of threat on goal and ended 0-0.

The result and reports of the match set off huge protests from Newcastle United, who had beaten Blackburn 4-0. Rovers then joined in. Allegations of collusion between Burnley and Stoke were made and formal complaints forwarded to both the F.A. and the Football League. The Football League A.G.M. was almost certain to be eventful.

Election time 1898

There were 3 sets of elections at the Football League A.G.M. in 1898, the need for the second and third votes being directly linked to the Test Match controversy noted above. The first election focussed on Division Two. The bottom three clubs faced opposition from four clubs seeking election to the Football League. Once again, Lincoln City topped the poll with 21 votes and, with Loughborough Town (16), were re-elected. Burslem Port Vale (18) came second in the voting and therefore replaced Darwen (15) in Division Two. New Brighton Tower (13), Nelson (3) and Bristol City (1) were the other unsuccessful applicants.

It was then announced that the League was to be extended, with 2 more clubs joining each division. In the vote to decide who should join the 1st Division, Blackburn (27) and Newcastle (18) were, not surprisingly, chosen, finishing well ahead of Manchester City (10), Small Heath (4), Newton Heath (3) and Woolwich Arsenal (2). The final election saw Darwen restored to the 2nd Division, with New Brighton Tower, Glossop North End and Barnsley being added to the League's second tier. There does not appear to have been any voting, which is rather strange, which cannot have pleased Nelson or Bristol City much.

Goal scoring 1895-1898

The number of goals per game 1895-1898 fell in each successive season in the Football League. By the 1897-1898 campaign, 1st Division games were producing an average of just over three goals, while there was also a significant drop in the mean in matches in Division Two. This probably reflects two things. Firstly, coaching improved and sides began to defend better. Secondly, the number of genuinely weak teams in each section of the League fell. Although there continued to be 2nd Division sides who were out of their depth for a while longer, there was a definite improvement in overall standards.

High scores – Division 1

Derby County beat Small Heath 8-0 on November 30th, 1895 and Sheffield United won their home game against Bury equally convincingly on April 6th, 1896. On Xmas Day, 1896, Derby County thrashed West Bromwich Albion 8-1 - the top Division 1 score. The highest score achieved in the 1897-98 season was 6 – by Everton v. West Bromwich (6-1), November 27th and by Forest at Sheffield Wednesday (6-3) on New Year's Day.

High scores – Division 2

During the 1895-96 campaign, Rotherham Town conceded 10 goals in each of two away fixtures, crashing 2-10 at Darwen on 13th January and 1-10 at Liverpool on February 18th. Loughborough hammered Woolwich Arsenal 8-0 on 12th December, 1896. Two weeks later Darwen enjoyed a 12-0 Boxing Day romp against Walsall. In the following December, Luton Town had a 9-3 win over Lincoln City on the 18th and this was matched by champions-to-be Burnley on March 28th against Loughborough. On April 16th, Manchester City crushed Burton Swifts 9-0.

The F.A. Cup 1896-98

The Football League had increased in popularity since its foundation and the prominence of the F.A. Cup had been eroded as a result. In moving the Final to mid-April, the F.A. recognised this. Football League clubs continued to dominate the country's premier knock-out competition, 1896 to 1898, but the appearance in the 1898 semi-finals of one of the top Southern League clubs, Southampton, acted as a reminder that the Cup had something the League lacked - a national basis.

The F.A. Amateur Cup 1896-98

The knock-out competition for amateur clubs grew in popularity also. This too had a national basis and often pitted a top Home Counties side against a leading North-Eastern club in the latter stages of the Cup. This was the case in all three finals played 1896-1898.

In 1896 Bishop Auckland beat Royal Artillery (Portsmouth) 1-0 at Leicester Fosse's Walnut Street ground.

In 1897 in a replayed Final-tie at Darlington's Feethams ground, Old Carthusians cruised to a 4-1 victory over Stockton.

In 1898 Middlesbrough beat Uxbridge in front of a crowd of 2,000 at Crystal Palace.

Football League Attendances

Everton remained the best supported club in the Football League, their average gate over 17,500 in the 1897-98 season. The Goodison Park club were 1 of 3 to attract a mean which was in excess of 10,000 for 1896-97. This number rose to 6 pulling 5-figure average crowds a season later, including Newcastle United of Division II. Meanwhile, at the other end of the scale, small town clubs rarely averaged 3,000 for their games. Gainsborough Trinity managed a mean attendance of 3,325 during their first League campaign.

While new and/or better facilities provided part of the reason why crowds rose, it was also down to the more competitive nature of football in both divisions, as is reflected in the number of goals which were scored per game shown towards the foot of the last few pages. In 1898, the overall aggregate for the Football League passed 3 million for the first time, with over a million attending Division Two games for the second season running.

Attendance figures continued to be the stuff of estimates for 1896-98. The clubs were not asked too many questions about accounts and, although gate receipts were the main source of income, the best way to describe attendance figures is perhaps 'reliable to a point'. The biggest crowds any club attracted in the 1890s were for 'local derbies' and when one of the top three or four teams visited.

1898-1899 – LEAGUE DIVISION 1

ASTON VILLA

The First Half

Sheffield United went 11 games unbeaten at the start of the season, but, with 8 of these drawn, the Blades never got away from the pack. Defeat at Liverpool on October 29th saw the leaders caught by Aston Villa and Everton, on 14 points. Villa moved two points clear at the top on November 12th, the 1-0 win over West Bromwich being their ninth game in a row without defeat. Everton lost at Sunderland, but remained in second because Sheffield United crashed 0-3 at Bolton.

Both the top 2 won their next game and it was not until December 10th that Everton crept closer, with a 2-0 win at Stoke, while Villa drew with Wolves. Goodison hopes were shattered a week later when Villa beat the Toffees 3-0. To make things worse, Burnley beat Wolves 4-2 to nip into 2nd place, returning here, when Everton had no game, on Boxing Day. Villa returned to winning ways the same day, having dipped at Notts County on Christmas Eve.

Aston Villa's '1st half' record

September	03	STOKE	3-1
	10	Bury	1-2
	17	Burnley	4-2
	24	SHEFFIELD UNITED	1-1
October	01	Newcastle United	1-1
	08	PRESTON NORTH END	4-2
	15	Liverpool	3-0
	22	NOTTINGHAM FOREST	3-0
	29	BOLTON WANDERERS	2-1
November	05	DERBY COUNTY	7-1
	12	West Bromwich Albion	1-0
	19	BLACKBURN ROVERS	3-1
December	03	SUNDERLAND	2-0
	10	WOLVES	1-1
	17	EVERTON	3-0
	24	Notts County	0-1
	26	NEWCASTLE UNITED	1-0

Table at December 26th, 1898

1	ASTON VILLA	17	40	14	27
2	Burnley	19	33	24	25
3	Everton	19	29	20	24
4	Sheffield United	20	27	29	22
5	Notts County	17	28	20	21
6	Bury	18	28	26	21
7	Liverpool	18	25	21	20
8	West Bromwich Albion	19	26	23	18
9	Blackburn Rovers	19	32	32	18
10	Wolves	18	27	27	17
11	Derby County	18	30	36	17
12	Preston North End	21	28	34	17
13	Stoke	20	27	37	17
14	Sunderland	17	24	26	16
15	Nottingham Forest	19	20	28	14
16	Sheffield Wednesday	17	19	29	14
17	Newcastle United	19	27	33	13
18	Bolton Wanderers	17	17	28	11
		332	487	487	332

Attendances 1898-1899

The total number of spectators at the 306 Division 1 matches is said to have been 3,047,675 – an average of 9,960 per game.

Goals 1898-1899

A total of 868 goals were scored in the 306 games – an average of 2.82 goals per game.

The leading goal-scorer was Steve Bloomer (Derby County) with 24 goals.

The Second Half

Despite losing at Stoke, Villa entered the New Year as 1st Division leaders, reinforcing their status with three January wins. Burnley and Everton both lost twice in the month, but a new challenge was emerging in the shape of Liverpool, whose win over Everton was a 9th game unbeaten. Villa's next 5 games produced only 2 points, from draws. Then, having beaten Sheffield Wednesday on March 25th, the Villains lost 2 and drew 2. By April 17th, George Ramsay, the Villa boss, was faced with a league table showing Villa level on points and games with Liverpool, but behind on goal average.

What happened next was remarkable. Liverpool won 2 games, not conceding while scoring 3 and so having a 2·13 goal average. Villa's destructions of Notts County and West Bromwich improved the club's goal average to 2·2, i.e. better than their rivals'. Liverpool came to Villa Park within one win of the title on April 29th, but this went to Villa, with a stunning 5-0 success.

Aston Villa's '2nd half' record

December	31	Stoke	0-3
January	07	BURY	3-2
	14	BURNLEY	4-0
	21	Sheffield United	3-1
February	04	Preston North End	0-2
	18	Nottingham Forest	0-1
March	04	Derby County	1-1
	13	Sheffield Wednesday	1-4
	18	Blackburn Rovers	0-0
	25	SHEFFIELD WEDNESDAY	3-1
April	01	Sunderland	2-4
	03	Wolves	0-4
	15	Everton	1-1
	17	Bolton Wanderers	0-0
	22	NOTTS COUNTY	6-1
	24	WEST BROMWICH ALBION	7-1
	29	LIVERPOOL	5-0

Final Football League Table 1899

1	ASTON VILLA	34	76	40	45
2	Liverpool	34	49	33	43
3	Burnley	34	45	47	39
4	Everton	34	48	41	38
5	Notts County	34	47	51	37
6	Blackburn Rovers	34	60	52	36
7	Sunderland	34	41	41	36
8	Wolves	34	54	48	35
9	Derby County	34	62	57	35
10	Bury	34	48	49	35
11	Nottingham Forest	34	42	42	33
12	Stoke	34	47	52	33
13	Newcastle United	34	49	48	30
14	West Bromwich Albion	34	42	57	30
15	Preston North End	34	44	47	29
16	Sheffield United	34	45	51	29
17	Bolton Wanderers	34	37	51	25
18	Sheffield Wednesday	34	32	61	24
		612	868	868	612

Bolton Wanderers and Sheffield Wednesday relegated.

F.A. CUP FINAL - 15th April, 1899

Sheffield United came back from a goal down at half-time to beat Derby County 4-1. Boag had given the Rams the lead, but goals from Bennett, Beer, Almond and Priest saw United take the trophy. The crowd of 73,833 was a new record. The referee was Mr. A. Scragg of Crewe.

1898-1899 – LEAGUE DIVISION 2   MANCHESTER CITY

The First Half

Burslem Port Vale began the season with 6 wins and a 16-1 goals aggregate, leaving the Potteries club 4 points clear by October 1st and looking at an unlikely promotion bid. The Cobridge outfit managed just 3 points in their next 5 games and reached the middle of November sharing the 2nd Division lead, on 15 points, with Newton Heath.

By inflicting a first defeat of the season on New Brighton Tower, Newton Heath went top on November 19th and stayed there until crashing 1-5 at Woolwich Arsenal. Manchester City beat Port Vale 3-1 on the same day, taking their unbeaten run to 9 and going top on goal average.

City's 4-0 hammering of their Manchester rivals on Boxing Day opened up a 4-point gap at the top, though clubs just below Newton Heath all had matches in hand, and somebody was almost certain to reduce the leaders' advantage.

Manchester City's '1st half' record

September	03	GRIMSBY TOWN	7-2
	10	Newton Heath	0-3
	17	NEW BRIGHTON TOWER	1-1
	24	Lincoln City	1-3
October	01	WOOLWICH ARSENAL	3-1
	08	Luton Town	3-0
	15	LEICESTER FOSSE	3-1
	22	Darwen	2-0
November	05	Barnsley	1-1
	12	Glossop North End	2-1
	19	WALSALL	2-0
	26	Burton Swifts	3-3
December	03	BURSLEM PORT VALE	3-1
	10	Loughborough Town	3-1
	17	LOUGHBOROUGH TOWN	5-0
	24	Blackpool	4-2
	26	NEWTON HEATH	4-0

Table at December 26th, 1898

1	MANCHESTER CITY	17	47	20	27
2	Newton Heath	17	38	25	23
3	New Brighton Tower	15	35	17	22
4	Leicester Fosse	16	30	20	22
5	Small Heath	15	46	19	20
6	Burslem Port Vale	15	26	12	20
7	Walsall	16	34	18	18
8	Woolwich Arsenal	15	31	22	17
9	Glossop	14	33	21	15
10	Burton Swifts	15	32	29	15
11	Lincoln City	15	25	23	15
12	Barnsley	14	19	21	13
13	Luton Town	15	25	36	12
14	Grimsby Town	14	17	29	10
15	Gainsborough Trinity	16	27	34	9
16	Loughborough Town	14	7	42	6
17	Blackpool	14	14	46	4
18	Darwen	15	8	60	4
		272	494	494	272

Attendances 1898-1899

The total number of spectators at the 306 Division 2 games is said to have been 1,179,375 – an average of 3,845 per game.

Goals 1898-1899

A total of 1,103 goals were scored in the 306 games – an average of 3.60 goals per game.

The leading goal-scorer was Walter Abbott (Small Heath) with 34 goals.

The Second Half

By New Year, New Brighton, Leicester and Small Heath had all won twice to move closer. None of these proved able to benefit from the leaders' defeat at Glossop on January 2nd though. City then struck a crucial blow, on January 14th, by beating New Brighton Tower 1-0. The Hyde Road men reached mid-February still ahead of the rest.

Five wins and a draw in the next 7 games took City 4 points clear with 5 to play by March 31st. Importantly, the Hyde Road club's remaining fixtures did not involve games against any of their closest rivals. Leicester Fosse and New Brighton Tower had, however, to play each other.

April 8th was the date on which City won both promotion and the 2nd Division title. A brace of goals from Fred Williams was enough to beat Small Heath, while the last remaining threat, New Brighton Tower, sank 0-4 at Woolwich Arsenal.

Manchester City's '2nd half' record

December	27	Small Heath	1-4
January	02	GLOSSOP NORTH END	0-2
	14	New Brighton Tower	1-0
February	04	LUTON TOWN	2-0
	11	Leicester Fosse	1-1
	18	DARWEN	10-0
	22	LINCOLN CITY	3-1
	25	Gainsborough Trinity	1-3
March	04	BARNSLEY	5-0
	18	Walsall	1-1
	25	BURTON SWIFTS	6-0
	31	GAINSBOROUGH TRINITY	4-0
April	01	Burslem Port Vale	1-1
	03	Woolwich Arsenal	1-0
	08	SMALL HEATH	2-0
	11	Grimsby Town	2-1
	22	BLACKPOOL	4-1

Final League Division 2 Table 1899

1	MANCHESTER CITY	34	92	35	52
2	Glossop	34	76	38	46
3	Leicester Fosse	34	64	42	45
4	Newton Heath	34	67	43	43
5	New Brighton Tower	34	71	52	43
6	Walsall	34	79	36	42
7	Woolwich Arsenal	34	72	41	41
8	Small Heath	34	85	50	41
9	Burslem Port Vale	34	56	34	39
10	Grimsby Town	34	71	60	35
11	Barnsley	34	52	56	31
12	Lincoln City	34	51	56	31
13	Burton Swifts	34	51	70	28
14	Gainsborough Trinity	34	56	72	25
15	Luton Town	34	51	95	23
16	Blackpool	34	49	90	20
17	Loughborough Town	34	38	92	18
18	Darwen	34	22	141	9
		612	1103	1103	612

Manchester City and Glossop promoted. Chesterfield and Middlesbrough were elected in place of Blackpool and Darwen.

1899-1900 – LEAGUE DIVISION 1 — ASTON VILLA

The First Half

By winning their first 5 games, Sheffield United were top by the end of September. 2 points behind were Sunderland and Aston Villa, the Roker Park club having lost once and the champions having suffered 2 defeats.

Villa moved up to second on October 21st, when Sunderland had no game, with a 2-1 win over Manchester City, staying there despite defeat at Bramall Lane, because Sunderland lost at West Bromwich Albion.

Although the champions continued to chase the leaders, going 7 matches unbeaten, the half-way mark was reached for both clubs with the Villa still 4 points adrift. Sheffield United had gone a stunning 17 league games without losing, leaking well under a goal per game in the process.

The Second Half

United opened the second half of their season with 2 draws, but Villa's surprise defeat at Glossop meant no advantage was taken. Both the top 2 had 2 good wins to end the year on. United were 6 points up on Villa, who were 6 ahead of Wolves. Between January 1st and March 10th, Sheffield United played 5, failing to win any of these. Villa managed 10 points from 8 games. Their best performance in this spell came on February 17th, with a 6-2 smashing of Notts County. The points won carried Villa above United for the first time. Three wins in three took the Claret & Blues three points ahead by March 31st, but, with 2 games in hand, United still threatened. Villa ended their programme on Easter Monday, 4 points ahead. United won at Wolves the next day and went to Burnley needing an 8-0 win on April 23rd. A 0-1 defeat for the Sheffield men meant Aston Villa retained the title.

Aston Villa's '1st half' record

September	02	Sunderland	1-0
	04	GLOSSOP	9-0
	09	WEST BROMWICH ALBION	0-2
	16	Everton	2-1
	23	BLACKBURN ROVERS	3-1
	30	Derby County	0-2
October	07	BURY	2-1
	14	Notts County	4-1
	21	MANCHESTER CITY	2-1
	28	Sheffield United	1-2
November	04	NEWCASTLE UNITED	2-1
	11	WOLVES	0-0
	13	Stoke	2-0
	18	Liverpool	3-3
	25	BURNLEY	2-0
December	02	Preston North End	5-0
	09	NOTTINGHAM FOREST	2-2

Aston Villa's '2nd half' record

December	16	Glossop	0-1
	23	STOKE	4-1
	30	SUNDERLAND	4-2
January	01	Bury	0-2
	06	West Bromwich Albion	2-0
	13	EVERTON	1-1
	20	Blackburn Rovers	4-0
February	03	DERBY COUNTY	3-2
	17	NOTTS COUNTY	6-2
March	03	SHEFFIELD UNITED	1-1
	10	Newcastle United	2-3
	19	Manchester City	2-0
	24	LIVERPOOL	1-0
	31	Burnley	2-1
April	07	PRESTON NORTH END	3-1
	14	Nottingham Forest	1-1
	16	Wolves	1-0

Table at December 9th, 1899

1	Sheffield United	17	35	12	29
2	ASTON VILLA	17	40	17	25
3	Sunderland	14	22	10	19
4	Bury	14	24	19	18
5	Stoke	16	20	19	18
6	Wolves	14	21	15	17
7	Nottingham Forest	14	25	22	16
8	Manchester City	14	28	19	15
9	Newcastle United	14	20	12	14
10	West Bromwich Albion	15	18	24	14
11	Derby County	13	16	17	12
12	Burnley	15	14	25	12
13	Everton	14	17	22	11
14	Blackburn Rovers	13	20	25	10
15	Liverpool	16	18	27	10
16	Notts County	16	21	40	9
17	Glossop	13	13	29	8
18	Preston North End	15	9	27	7
		264	381	381	264

Final League Division 2 Table 1900

1	ASTON VILLA	34	77	35	50
2	Sheffield United	34	63	33	48
3	Sunderland	34	50	35	41
4	Wolves	34	48	37	39
5	Newcastle United	34	53	43	36
6	Derby County	34	45	43	36
7	Manchester City	34	50	44	34
8	Nottingham Forest	34	56	55	34
9	Stoke	34	37	45	34
10	Liverpool	34	49	45	33
11	Everton	34	47	49	33
12	Bury	34	40	44	32
13	West Bromwich Albion	34	43	51	30
14	Blackburn Rovers	34	49	61	30
15	Notts County	34	46	60	29
16	Preston North End	34	38	48	28
17	Burnley	34	34	54	27
18	Glossop	34	31	74	18
		612	856	856	612

Burnley and Glossop relegated.

Attendances 1899-1900

The total number of spectators at the 306 Division 1 matches is said to have been 2,891,275 – an average of 9,449 per game.

Goals 1899-1900

A total of 856 goals were scored in the 306 games – an average of 2.80 goals per game.

The leading goal-scorer was Bill Garratty (Aston Villa) with 27 goals.

F.A. CUP FINAL - 21st April, 1900

Attended by 68,945, the F.A. Cup Final matched Southern League Southampton with 1st Division Bury. The Gigg Lane club overran the Saints, winning 4-0. The Shakers' goals came from McLuckie (2), Wood and Plant. Receipts for the match were £2,587 and the man in charge was Mr. A.G. Kingscott of Derby.

1899-1900 – LEAGUE DIVISION 2 — SHEFFIELD WEDNESDAY

The First Half

Three clubs dropped only a point in September, which meant Leicester Fosse topped the end of the month rankings, with Sheffield Wednesday and Small Heath 2 points behind, having played a game less. Despite crashing 0-4 at Owlerton on October 21st, Small Heath headed the table at mid-November on 18 points from 11 games. This gave the Blues a one point lead from unbeaten rivals, Leicester and Wednesday. A 0-0 draw between these two saw both ease above Small Heath on November 25th, as the Birmingham side crashed at Woolwich.

The Owls went top in style on December 2nd when, with Leicester losing for the first time, they destroyed visitors Luton Town 6-0. The Foxes came back though and led the table by 31st December after Chesterfield Town had ended Wednesday's 14-match unbeaten run. Two days later, Bolton Wanderers went top with a thumping 5-0 win over Burslem Port Vale.

Sheffield Wednesday's '1st half' record

September	02	CHESTERFIELD TOWN	5-1
	09	Gainsborough Trinity	2-0
	16	BOLTON WANDERERS	2-1
	23	Loughborough Town	0-0
	30	NEWTON HEATH	2-1
October	07	Burton Swifts	5-0
	14	Lincoln City	2-1
	21	SMALL HEATH	4-0
November	11	Woolwich Arsenal	2-1
	25	Leicester Fosse	0-0
December	02	LUTON TOWN	6-0
	16	WALSALL	2-0
	23	Middlesbrough	2-1
	25	New Brighton Tower	2-2
	30	Chesterfield Town	0-1
January	01	GRIMSBY TOWN	2-1
	06	GAINSBOROUGH TRINITY	5-1

Table at January 6th, 1900

1	Bolton Wanderers	19	51	18	30
2	SHEFFIELD WEDNESDAY	17	43	11	29
3	Leicester Fosse	18	30	10	28
4	Small Heath	17	41	22	24
5	Newton Heath	17	29	13	21
6	Lincoln City	19	32	28	21
7	Burslem Port Vale	18	26	23	21
8	Grimsby Town	17	35	32	18
9	Walsall	19	31	33	18
10	Chesterfield	16	32	38	17
11	Woolwich Arsenal	16	19	21	16
12	New Brighton Tower	17	27	23	15
13	Middlesbrough	18	24	32	13
14	Gainsborough Trinity	17	23	38	10
15	Burton Swifts	17	22	43	9
16	Luton Town	17	18	38	8
17	Barnsley	17	15	46	8
18	Loughborough Town	16	11	40	6
		312	509	509	312

Attendances 1899-1900

The total number of spectators at the 306 Division 2 games is said to have been 1,124,975 – an average of 3,676 per game.

Goals 1899-1900

A total of 984 goals were scored in the 306 games – an average of 3.22 goals per game.

The leading goal-scorer was John Wright (Sheffield Wednesday) with 26 goals.

The Second Half

When Wednesday lost at Burnden Park on 13th January, the Owls' season looked to be in grave danger of turning sour. Bolton were 3 points clear and had gone 17 games without losing. Small Heath and Leicester Fosse were also still around. With 2 wins in 3, Owls scrambled back to the top by mid-February, benefiting from all their 3 main rivals dropping more points than them. Five wins in the next 7 games upped the pressure at the top and Wednesday reached March 31st 3 points ahead of Bolton and Small Heath, whose 2 dropped points in draws ended their challenge.

Wanderers were still a threat though. Their 3 wins by mid-April could have been serious, but the Owls matched this. Bolton's defeat at New Brighton on April 16th enabled Wednesday to go 5 points up by winning the next day. Wanderers cut this to two, but the Owls still faced Middlesbrough on April 28th needing only 1 point for the title. In fact they won 3-0, taking 2 points and the title.

Sheffield Wednesday's '2nd half' record

January	13	Bolton Wanderers	0-1
	20	LOUGHBOROUGH TOWN	5-0
February	03	Newton Heath	0-1
	12	Burslem Port Vale	3-0
	24	Small Heath	1-4
	27	BARNSLEY	5-1
March	03	NEW BRIGHTON TOWER	4-0
	12	BURTON SWIFTS	6-0
	17	WOOLWICH ARSENAL	3-1
	24	Barnsley	0-1
	31	LEICESTER FOSSE	2-0
April	07	Luton Town	1-0
	13	Grimsby Town	2-1
	14	BURSLEM PORT VALE	4-0
	17	LINCOLN CITY	1-0
	21	Walsall	1-1
	28	MIDDLESBROUGH	3-0

Final League Division 2 Table 1900

1	SHEFFIELD WEDNESDAY	34	84	22	54
2	Bolton Wanderers	34	79	25	52
3	Small Heath	34	78	38	46
4	Newton Heath	34	63	27	44
5	Leicester Fosse	34	53	36	43
6	Grimsby Town	34	67	46	40
7	Chesterfield Town	34	65	60	38
8	Woolwich Arsenal	34	61	43	36
9	Lincoln City	34	46	43	36
10	New Brighton Tower	34	66	58	35
11	Burslem Port Vale	34	39	49	34
12	Walsall	34	50	55	32
13	Gainsborough Trinity	34	47	75	25
14	Middlesbrough	34	39	69	24
15	Burton Swifts	34	43	84	24
16	Barnsley	34	46	79	23
17	Luton Town	34	40	75	18
18	Loughborough Town	34	18	100	8
		612	984	984	612

Sheffield Wednesday and Bolton Wanderers promoted. Blackpool and Stockport County were elected in place of Luton Town, who did not seek re-election, and Loughborough Town.

THE DEPARTURE LOUNGE   1899-1900

Four teams left the Football League 1899-1900. Two of these never returned – Loughborough Town and Darwen. Both had catastrophic final campaigns.

In terms of the bare facts, Darwen finished at the foot of Division Two in 1899 with 9 points from 34 games. The Lancashire club resigned from the Football League. Loughborough, who finished a place higher, were re-elected to Division II with 28 votes, 1 more than one elected club, Chesterfield Town, and 11 up on the other Middlesbrough. In 4th came Blackpool, who thus lost their League place, with 15. Other unsuccessful teams were Stockport County (11), Chorley (7), Wigan County (7), and Coventry City and Ashton North End, neither of whom received support from anyone.

A year later, Loughborough finished bottom of the League, but they did apply for re-election, unlike Luton Town. The Luffs came fifth in the poll with just 3 votes, behind re-elected Barnsley (29), Stockport County (28) (elected), Blackpool (24) (elected), and Doncaster Rovers (5). At least they beat Kettering (2) and Stalybridge Rovers (1), but the club's Football League career was over.

It is worth looking a bit more closely at the demise of Darwen and Loughborough, purely out of a macabre sort of interest. What players, officials and supporters of these two unfortunate clubs must have gone through, one can only guess.

Darwen

The writing was on the wall for Darwen during the 1897-98 season. Having taken 8 points from their first eight matches, the team mustered only six more points from the next 22 games. The last 11 fixtures all ended in defeat, meaning a total of 22 Second Division games (73%) were lost out of 30. Darwen only survived because the League was extended. The wisdom of the club being re-admitted to the 2nd Division has to be questioned.

During the 1898-99 season, the average number of players used by the other 17 2nd Division clubs was 23·7. Darwen used 45 players. Only three of these appeared in more than half the games and 22 men played 5 matches or fewer. Thomas Woolfall, who later played for both Burnley and Bolton, topped the appearance charts with 30.

Darwen played three games with fewer than 11 men. In one of these, at Newton Heath on 24th December, only nine started for the Darreners. The team went 27 matches without winning, 8th October to 8th April; suffered 17 consecutive defeats, 12th November to 18th March; and had two runs of seven games without scoring. Top marksman was O. Pilkington with 4 goals.

Away from home, Darwen won one point – at Gainsborough Trinity on October 15th when they drew 2-2. In 13 of their 17 away fixtures, Darwen failed to score.

The team ended with a goals aggregate from games on their travels of 6-109. This meant they conceded an average of 6·4 goals per away game. In seven of these, Darwen let in eight goals or more, including 0-10 reverses at Newton Heath, Walsall and Loughborough.

However, two home matches were won. Leicester Fosse were beaten 3-0 on October 1st and Luton Town were thumped 4-1 on April 11th. With crowds at Barley Bank averaging just 900 (the lowest ever for a Football League club), it is no wonder the club called it a day.

Loughborough Town

Loughborough might have read the signs better in the 1897-98 campaign, during which 11 away games were lost in a row and the team failed to score in 18 of its 30 games, including 11 of the last 14.

During the 1898-99 season, the team went 15 without winning, December 12th to March 4th, and failed to score in 16 of their 34 fixtures. With only 10 goals in their first 24 games, the Luffs somehow turned things round over their last ten outings to hit 28 goals and gather ten points, more than doubling their total.

Maybe their end to the '98-'99 season fooled everyone. Loughborough failed to win any of their first 15 games '99-'00, putting an even worse run of 18 without winning together after their one victory of the season, 2-1 against Burton Swifts, on January 6th. Thirteen consecutive defeats were suffered from January 13th to April 13th.

The Luffs lost all their away games, 6-74 being the goals aggregate. The worst defeat was a 0-12 at Woolwich Arsenal on March 12th. In all, 27 of the 34 matches (79%) were lost. The team failed to score in 21 of its games, managing two goals in a match just five times. With only eight starting the fixture at Barnsley on March 10th, it is hardly a shock that Loughborough did not score on that occasion.

Seven of the squad played more than 25 league games during the 1899-1900 season. Top of the appearance charts was the goalkeeper Frank L. Stubbs, who seems to have missed only 1 game. He was signed by Sheffield Wednesday during the summer of 1900 and played for the Owls 18 times the following season in Division One. Harry Parker (32), Walter Rose (31), James Tebbs (30), W. Hardy (28), F. H. Bailey and William Hodgkin (27) make up the list of Athletic Ground 'regulars'.

1900-1901 – LEAGUE DIVISION 1

LIVERPOOL

The First Half

When Villa opened their season with 4 wins in the first ten days without conceding, the rest of the 1st Division dreaded a 'one-horse race' developing. Everton's 2-1 win at Villa Park, however, put the brakes on the champions a little, on September 15th. By the month's end, Villa led an unbeaten Newcastle United by 3 points, but the Tyneside club had three games in hand.

Nottingham Forest, with a run of 6 games without defeat took the top flight lead on goal average on October 13th, after the leaders lost 3 matches in five. Newcastle also passed the out-of-sorts champions on November 3rd, when Villa lost at Sheffield Wednesday. Liverpool's 5-1 blasting of the Birmingham side saw the Anfield club do the same on November 10th. 'Pool then fell away, not winning again until December 8th. Despite a better spell, the club reached its half-way mark in 5th place, 4 points off the lead after drawing with top outfit, Forest, in the last pre-Christmas fixture.

Liverpool's '1st half' record

September	01	BLACKBURN ROVERS	3-0
	08	Stoke	2-1
	15	WEST BROMWICH ALBION	5-0
	22	Everton	1-1
	29	SUNDERLAND	1-2
October	06	Derby County	3-2
	13	BOLTON WANDERERS	2-1
	20	Notts County	0-3
	27	PRESTON NORTH END	3-2
November	03	Wolves	1-2
	10	ASTON VILLA	5-1
	17	Sheffield Wednesday	2-3
	24	Newcastle United	1-1
December	01	SHEFFIELD UNITED	1-2
	08	Manchester City	4-3
	15	BURY	1-0
	22	Nottingham Forest	0-0

Table at December 22nd, 1900

1	Nottingham Forest	17	31	11	25
2	Newcastle United	17	22	16	22
3	Aston Villa	20	36	28	22
4	Bury	17	30	15	21
5	LIVERPOOL	17	35	24	21
6	Notts County	19	27	30	20
7	Sunderland	15	23	12	19
8	Manchester City	17	26	29	18
9	Sheffield United	17	21	27	18
10	Everton	16	20	14	17
11	Derby County	17	33	26	15
12	Sheffield Wednesday	16	22	22	15
13	Wolves	17	27	35	15
14	West Bromwich Albion	19	20	36	14
15	Bolton Wanderers	16	15	25	13
16	Blackburn Rovers	18	18	31	13
17	Stoke	17	17	27	11
18	Preston North End	18	20	35	11
		310	443	443	310

Attendances 1900-1901

The total number of spectators at the 306 Division 1 matches is said to have been 3,387,250 – an average of 11,069 per game.

Goals 1900-1901

A total of 855 goals were scored in the 306 games – an average of 2.79 goals per game.

The leading goal-scorer was Steve Bloomer (Derby County) with 24 goals.

The Second Half

Liverpool's failure to improve on an unbeaten 4-game run saw them lose 3 of 4 after the holiday programme and slip down to eighth in the table. However, eight matches without losing, with only two points dropped, lifted the Anfield club right back into title contention. By mid-April, the club lay third, behind leaders Sunderland and Notts County, with games in hand.

When Liverpool drew 0-0 at Bury on April 20th, while Forest beat Villa 3-1, the Anfield club fell to fourth on goal average. Things were so close, however, that, 2 days later, a 2-0 win at Sheffield United lifted the Reds level on points with leaders Sunderland. Roker hopes were revived when the Wearsiders won 2-0 at Newcastle on April 24th. On Saturday, April 27th, Liverpool caught up once again by beating Forest 2-0. 'Pool travelled to bottom club, West Bromwich Albion on Monday, April 29th, needing a draw to take the title. A 1-0 victory secured Liverpool's first 1st Division crown.

Liverpool's '2nd half' record

December	25	DERBY COUNTY	0-0
	29	Blackburn Rovers	1-3
January	01	STOKE	3-1
	19	EVERTON	1-2
February	16	Bolton Wanderers	0-1
	23	Sunderland	1-0
March	02	Preston North End	2-2
	09	WOLVES	1-0
	16	Aston Villa	2-0
	23	SHEFFIELD WEDNESDAY	1-1
	30	NEWCASTLE UNITED	3-0
April	08	NOTTS COUNTY	1-0
	13	MANCHESTER CITY	3-1
	20	Bury	0-0
	22	Sheffield United	2-0
	27	NOTTINGHAM FOREST	2-0
	29	West Bromwich Albion	1-0

Final League Division 1 Table 1901

1	LIVERPOOL	34	59	35	45
2	Sunderland	34	57	26	43
3	Notts County	34	54	46	40
4	Nottingham Forest	34	53	36	39
5	Bury	34	53	37	39
6	Newcastle United	34	42	37	38
7	Everton	34	55	42	37
8	Sheffield Wednesday	34	52	42	36
9	Blackburn Rovers	34	39	47	33
10	Bolton Wanderers	34	39	55	33
11	Manchester City	34	48	58	32
12	Derby County	34	55	42	31
13	Wolves	34	39	55	31
14	Sheffield United	34	35	52	31
15	Aston Villa	34	45	51	30
16	Stoke	34	46	57	27
17	Preston North End	34	49	75	25
18	West Bromwich Albion	34	35	62	22
		612	855	855	612

Preston North End and West Bromwich Albion were relegated to Division 2 at the end of the season.

F.A CUP FINAL - 27th April, 1898

After a 2-2 draw, watched by 114,815, at Crystal Palace, seven days earlier, Tottenham Hotspur fought back from a goal down at the interval to beat Sheffield United 3-1 at Burnden Park, Bolton. Priest had put United one up, but goals from Cameron, Smith and Brown won Spurs the Cup. Only 20,470 watched the game, which, like the first encounter, was refereed by Mr. Kingscott. Blades' captain, Ernest 'Nudger' Needham, said, after the match, "We felt we had let the North down and vowed to make amends." No sign of a North-South divide there then!

1900-1901 – LEAGUE DIVISION 2   GRIMSBY TOWN

The First Half

Burnley and Blackpool made the early running to lead the table by the end of September, with Grimsby Town, Leicester Fosse and Small Heath among the teams just behind.

Going a further six games unbeaten, the Mariners had joined Burnley and Blackpool at the head of the rankings by mid-November, with Small Heath, not having lost yet, well-placed just a single point behind.

The Coventry Road side went top on December 15th by winning 1-0 at Middlesbrough, while the leaders, Grimsby, were being held to a draw at Glossop. A week later though, the Blues lost at home to Burnley and the Mariners reached the half-way stage in top spot, having beaten Boro 2-0, at Blundell Park. Burnley, meanwhile, were now second.

Grimsby Town's '1st half' record

September	01	Burnley	0-3
	08	BURSLEM PORT VALE	6-1
	15	Leicester Fosse	0-4
	22	NEW BRIGHTON TOWER	5-2
	29	Gainsborough Trinity	1-0
October	06	WALSALL	0-0
	13	Burton Swifts	2-1
	20	BARNSLEY	1-0
	27	Woolwich Arsenal	1-1
November	03	Burslem Port Vale	0-0
	10	STOCKPORT COUNTY	5-1
	17	SMALL HEATH	1-1
	24	CHESTERFIELD TOWN	5-2
December	01	LINCOLN CITY	4-0
	08	NEWTON HEATH	2-0
	15	Glossop	0-0
	22	MIDDLESBROUGH	2-0

Table at December 22nd, 1900

1	GRIMSBY TOWN	17	35	16	25
2	Burnley	17	24	12	24
3	Small Heath	16	22	8	23
4	Woolwich Arsenal	17	21	16	21
5	Leicester Fosse	17	18	14	18
6	Blackpool	15	13	12	18
7	New Brighton Tower	16	26	19	17
8	Burslem Port Vale	18	19	29	16
9	Walsall	15	23	25	15
10	Gainsborough Trinity	15	23	29	15
11	Glossop	14	17	10	14
12	Middlesbrough	14	17	18	13
13	Stockport County	16	18	37	12
14	Newton Heath	15	18	16	11
15	Lincoln City	14	16	22	11
16	Burton Swifts	17	22	32	11
17	Chesterfield	14	19	27	9
18	Barnsley	13	16	25	7
		280	367	367	280

Attendances 1900-1901

The total number of spectators at the 306 Division 2 games is said to have been 1,160,675 – an average of 3,793 per game.

Goals 1900-1901

A total of 819 goals were scored in the 306 games – an average of 2.68 goals per game.

The leading goal-scorer was Harry Swann (Barnsley) with 18 goals.

The Second Half

The top 3 pulled away from the rest over the next 6 weeks. Although Burnley lost at Grimsby on 29th December, the Turf Moor men took advantage of slips by Town to head them at mid-February. Five wins and a draw by the end of March took Grimsby 6 points clear, however. Burnley and Small Heath had both had bad patches, each hitting a 3-match winless run. The Blues had the consolation of having 3 games in hand on the leaders. By April 15th, Grimsby and Small Heath shared the lead on 46 points. Burnley, with 2 games left, had 42 points and defeat at Stockport on April 20th meant their hopes had gone. Small Heath lost at Woolwich on April 22nd, leaving the top 2, with one match each to play, level on points.

Heath lost again on April 27th, at Burnley. Grimsby took a point, and the title, by drawing at Boro 0-0.

Grimsby Town '2nd half' record

December	25	Lincoln City	1-0
	29	BURNLEY	2-1
January	12	LEICESTER FOSSE	4-1
	19	New Brighton Tower	0-5
	26	BLACKPOOL	2-0
February	09	Walsall	0-0
	16	BURTON SWIFTS	5-2
	23	Barnsley	3-2
March	02	WOOLWICH ARSENAL	1-0
	09	Blackpool	1-0
	16	Stockport County	1-0
	30	Chesterfield Town	3-3
April	01	Small Heath	1-2
	05	GAINSBOROUGH TRINITY	0-0
	13	Newton Heath	0-1
	20	GLOSSOP	1-0
	27	Middlesbrough	0-0

Final League Division 2 Table 1901

1	GRIMSBY TOWN	34	60	33	49
2	Small Heath	34	57	24	48
3	Burnley	34	53	29	44
4	New Brighton Tower	34	57	38	42
5	Glossop	34	51	33	38
6	Middlesbrough	34	50	40	37
7	Woolwich Arsenal	34	39	35	36
8	Lincoln City	34	43	39	33
9	BUrselm Port Vale	34	45	47	33
10	Newton Heath	34	42	38	32
11	Leicester City	34	39	37	32
12	Blackpool	34	33	58	31
13	Gainsborough Trinity	34	45	60	30
14	Chesterfield Town	34	46	58	28
15	Barnsley	34	47	60	27
16	Walsall	34	40	56	27
17	Stockport County	34	38	68	25
18	Burton Swifts	34	34	66	20
		612	819	819	612

Grimsby Town and Small Heath promoted.

Burton Swifts merged with ex-League club Burton Wanderers as Burton United. The Burton United combination (23 votes) and Stockport County (16) were re-elected. Walsall (7) were not re-elected and were replaced by Bristol City (23). New Brighton Tower then resigned and Doncaster Rovers, having lost out to Stockport (13-21) in a second ballot, were elected in their place. Clubs missing out were Stalybridge Rovers (7), Crewe Alexandra (5), Darwen (0) and Southport Central (0).

- 29 -

1901-1902 – LEAGUE DIVISION 1

With Everton the only team who opened the season with two wins, there were early signs that the 1901-02 title campaign might be a highly competitive and interesting affair. The Toffees drew their next three matches to reach 7 points by the end of September and headed the top flight, on goal average, from Sunderland and Wolves.

Sunderland moved to the top of the table on October 12th after Everton crashed 0-4 at Nottingham Forest. The Roker Park men remained in pole position over the next month, despite successive away defeats, with Wolves their closest challengers, until the Everton team rediscovered their form to beat both Stoke and Grimsby Town in early November.

This brought the Merseysiders to within a point of Sunderland. The belief that the title race would be interesting, seemed to be confirmed as fixtures for November 16th included Everton travelling up to Wearside for a 'Clash of the Titans'. Everton won the match 4-2 to reclaim first place, where they stayed by winning four of their next five games, reaching December 21st three points clear of Sunderland. One point and one place behind were Aston Villa, who had lost only once in seven outings. On Christmas Day, Villa won 3-2 at Goodison Park. Boxing Day saw Everton lose again, while Sunderland and Aston Villa both won to close the gap at the top.

Sunderland's '1st half' record

September	02	SHEFFIELD UNITED	3-1
	07	MANCHESTER CITY	1-0
	14	Wolves	2-4
	21	LIVERPOOL	1-1
	28	Newcastle United	1-0
October	05	ASTON VILLA	1-0
	12	Sheffield United	1-0
	19	NOTTINGHAM FOREST	4-0
	26	Bury	0-1
November	02	BLACKBURN ROVERS	3-2
	09	Stoke	0-3
	16	EVERTON	2-3
	23	Grimsby Town	3-3
	30	Small Heath	3-2
December	14	Sheffield Wednesday	1-1
	21	NOTTS COUNTY	2-1
	26	Liverpool	1-0

Table at December 26th, 1901

1	Everton	19	36	24	24
2	SUNDERLAND	17	29	23	23
3	Aston Villa	18	25	13	22
4	Derby County	16	19	14	20
5	Nottingham Forest	17	24	20	19
6	Blackburn Rovers	17	24	22	19
7	Sheffield Wednesday	16	26	27	19
8	Wolves	19	24	31	19
9	Bury	16	24	18	18
10	Stoke	17	27	25	18
11	Newcastle United	16	27	12	17
12	Sheffield United	17	28	25	15
13	Liverpool	16	20	20	14
14	Small Heath	16	22	21	13
15	Bolton Wanderers	15	19	25	12
16	Notts County	19	22	38	12
17	Grimsby Town	16	14	35	10
18	Manchester City	15	13	30	8
		302	423	423	302

Goals 1900-1901

A total of 840 goals were scored in the 306 games – an average of 2.745 goals per game. The joint leading goal-scorers were James Settle (Everton) and Fred Priest (Sheffield United) with 18 goals.

- 30 -

SUNDERLAND

With Everton not in action on December 28th, Villa moved smoothly to the 1st Division summit with a 3-0 defeat of Nottingham Forest. However, the Midlands club's astonishing 0-6 collapse at Sheffield United on New Year's Day enabled Sunderland to take over as leaders, after Jackson's goal proved enough to sink Derby County.

By the time Everton played again, on January 11th, Sunderland were 4 points clear of the Merseysiders and Villa's 0-4 crash at Blackburn on the same day meant the Rokerites held the same advantage over the Birmingham club. Any hopes Villa had of staging a recovery were dashed on February 1st, when the leaders won 1-0 at Villa Park.

As Villa faded, only Everton offered any challenge to Sunderland. However, despite beating the North-Easterners 2-0 on March 15th, the Goodison Park club dropped too many points in their other matches to threaten seriously. By March 31st, Everton were just two points behind, but had played two games more – and fixtures were starting to run out. Home defeat by Notts County on April 12th meant Everton missed the chance to go top and four days later, on Wednesday April 16th, the destination of the 1st Division title was decided when Sunderland's 3-0 defeat of mid-table Bury lifted the Roker club three points clear of Everton, who had only one game left.

Sunderland's '2nd half' record

December	28	Bolton Wanderers	0-0
January	01	DERBY COUNTY	1-0
	04	Manchester City	3-0
	11	WOLVES	2-0
February	01	Aston Villa	1-0
	15	Nottingham Forest	1-2
March	01	Blackburn Rovers	1-0
	08	STOKE	2-0
	15	Everton	0-2
	22	GRIMSBY TOWN	3-1
	29	SMALL HEATH	1-1
	31	NEWCASTLE UNITED	0-0
April	05	Derby County	0-1
	12	SHEFFIELD WEDNESDAY	1-2
	16	BURY	3-0
	19	Notts County	0-2
	26	BOLTON WANDERERS	2-1

Final League Division 1 Table 1902

1	SUNDERLAND	34	50	35	44
2	Everton	34	53	35	41
3	Newcastle United	34	48	34	37
4	Blackburn Rovers	34	52	48	36
5	Nottingham Forest	34	43	43	35
6	Derby County	34	39	41	35
7	Bury	34	44	38	34
8	Aston Villa	34	42	40	34
9	Sheffield Wednesday	34	48	52	34
10	Sheffield United	34	53	48	33
11	Liverpool	34	42	38	32
12	Bolton Wanderers	34	51	56	32
13	Notts County	34	51	57	32
14	Wolves	34	46	57	32
15	Grimsby Town	34	44	60	32
16	Stoke	34	45	55	31
17	Small Heath	34	47	45	30
18	Manchester City	34	42	58	28
		612	840	840	612

Small Heath and Manchester City relegated.

Attendances 1900-1901

The total number of spectators at the 306 Division 1 matches is said to have been 3,435,700 – an average of 11,228 per game.

1901-1902 – LEAGUE DIVISION 2

The three games which marked the start of the 2nd Division season, on Monday, September 2nd, saw home wins for Lincoln City and Woolwich Arsenal, together with a surprise success for Glossop at West Bromwich. By September 14th, however, Albion had reached the top of the table, with five points from four games, helped by the fact that both Glossop and Woolwich lost, while Lincoln did not play. Two further September wins kept the Throstles at the head of things, two points up on Lincoln, who had played two matches fewer. The Red Imps' challenge weakened in October, however, as the capable West Bromwich team extended their unbeaten run to nine games, with six of these matches having been won and only three points dropped.

By mid-November, Middlesbrough had moved into second, courtesy of a 2-1 win over Preston, but two defeats for Boro, at The Hawthorns on December 14th and Bristol City a week later, enabled North End to claim the mantle of 'main challengers' to West Brom, who continued to set an impressive pace at the top of the table.

West Bromwich Albion's '1st half' record

September	02	GLOSSOP	0-1
	07	PRESTON NORTH END	3-1
	09	CHESTERFIELD TOWN	4-0
	14	Burnley	0-0
	21	BURSLEM PORT VALE	3-1
	28	Chesterfield Town	3-0
October	05	GAINSBOROUGH TRINITY	7-0
	12	Middlesbrough	2-1
	19	BRISTOL CITY	2-2
	26	Blackpool	2-2
November	09	Newton Heath	2-1
	23	Doncaster Rovers	0-2
December	07	Burton United	3-1
	09	LINCOLN CITY	4-1
	14	MIDDLESBROUGH	2-0
	21	BARNSLEY	3-1
	26	STOCKPORT COUNTY	3-0

Table at December 26th, 1901

1	WEST BROMWICH ALBION	17	43	14	27
2	Preston North End	15	39	10	23
3	Woolwich Arsenal	17	23	13	22
4	Middlesbrough	16	33	14	20
5	Lincoln City	15	25	12	20
6	Glossop	14	16	11	16
7	Bristol City	14	20	18	16
8	Manchester United	15	23	24	15
9	Burnley	15	14	15	15
10	Leicester Fosse	15	21	24	15
11	Doncaster Rovers	15	15	25	12
12	Stockport County	15	17	26	11
13	Barnsley	16	19	31	11
14	Burton United	13	14	23	11
15	Blackpool	13	16	23	10
16	Burslem Port Vale	14	18	27	9
17	Chesterfield Town	15	12	33	8
18	Gainsborough Trinity	14	13	38	7
		268	381	381	268

Attendances 1900-1901

The total number of spectators at the 306 Division 2 matches is said to have been 1,173,425 – an average of 3,835 per game.

Goals 1900-1901

A total of 885 goals were scored in the 306 games – an average of 2.892 goals per game. The leading goal-scorer was Chippy Simmons (West Bromwich Albion) with 23 goals.

WEST BROMWICH ALBION

Any hopes the chasing group had that Albion would suffer a post-holiday season slump were quickly to be dispelled. The leaders simply pressed on, stacking up 11 more points in 6 games played by mid-February. Preston North End thumped well-placed Lincoln City 8-0 on December 28th, won at Newton Heath on New Year's Day, then failed to win any of their next four games. West Bromwich's lead grew to 9 points.

Over the next 6 weeks, Albion's form remained first-class and the club went into the Easter programme in need of 1 win from its remaining 5 matches to be sure of promotion. Although successive defeats were suffered, at Lincoln and Woolwich, West Bromwich were promoted on March 31st, when Preston slipped to a 0-1 reverse at Leicester Fosse. Middlesbrough won 2-1 at Newton Heath on April 7th to move to within 4 points of Albion, with a game in hand. The Hawthorns' club were not to be denied, however, and, with goals from Simmons and Lee, took the title on April 12th by beating the visiting Woolwich Arsenal 2-1, while Middlesbrough went down 2-3 at Burton United.

West Bromwich Albion's '2nd half' record

December	28	Leicester Fosse	3-0
January	04	Preston North End	2-1
	06	LEICESTER FOSSE	1-0
	11	BURNLEY	3-0
	18	Burslem Port Vale	3-2
February	01	Gainsborough Trinity	1-1
	15	Bristol City	2-1
	22	BLACKPOOL	7-2
March	01	Stockport County	2-0
	08	NEWTON HEATH	4-0
	15	Glossop	2-1
	22	DONCASTER ROVERS	2-2
	29	Lincoln City	0-1
	31	Woolwich Arsenal	1-2
April	05	BURTON UNITED	2-1
	12	WOOLWICH ARSENAL	2-1
	19	Barnsley	2-0

Final League Division 2 Table 1902

1	WEST BROMWICH ALBION	34	82	29	55
2	Middlesbrough	34	90	24	51
3	Preston North End	34	71	32	42
4	Woolwich Arsenal	34	50	26	42
5	Lincoln City	34	45	35	41
6	Bristol City	34	52	35	40
7	Doncaster Rovers	34	49	58	34
8	Glossop	34	36	40	32
9	Burnley	34	41	45	30
10	Burton United	34	46	54	30
11	Barnsley	34	51	63	30
12	Burslem Port Vale	34	43	59	29
13	Blackpool	34	40	56	29
14	Leicester Fosse	34	38	56	29
15	Newton Heath	34	38	53	28
16	Chesterfield Town	34	47	68	28
17	Stockport County	34	36	72	23
18	Gainsborough Trinity	34	30	80	19
		612	885	885	612

West Bromwich Albion and Middlesbrough were promoted to Division 1. Chesterfield Town (33 votes), Gainsborough Trinity (31) and Stockport County (29) were all re-elected. Only one other club (Walsall) applied to join Division 2 and their votes were not recorded. Newton Heath, who only escaped from the re-election positions by winning their final match, against Chesterfield Town, on the last day of the season, went bust during the close season. Re-formed as Manchester United, the club was re-admitted to Division 2 without, it seems, any question.

OTHER INFORMATION   1898-1902

Football League Attendances

Aston Villa took over from Everton as the best-supported club, averaging 20,675 for the 1898-99 campaign, and stayed at the head of the list for the next three seasons. In Division Two, highest home crowds were attracted by the champions '98-'99 and '99-'00, i.e. Manchester City and Sheffield Wednesday, though Middlesbrough, with 8,375, headed the rankings '00-'01 and retained their 'top position' in the promotion season which followed.

With the number of clubs and therefore games rising from 240 to 306 in each division, 1898-99, the aggregates rose to new record levels. The fact that the average mean also went up for top flight matches, however, is the key indication of the continuing 'popularity boom', which league soccer was experiencing.

The figures show that attendances fell in the 1899-1900 season. In Division 1, crowds at Bury, Derby County, Glossop and West Bromwich Albion rose, but dropped everywhere else. In Division Two, Grimsby Town and Lincoln City improved their attendances, while Barnsley maintained the 3,000 average of the previous campaign. For all others, gates were down.

The overall trend had nothing to do with football. In 1899, the Boer War started and, with hundreds signing up to fight in South Africa, it is not really surprising that there were fewer men around to watch English League football. Figures for the 1900-01 season saw an upturn in attendance figures with a further rise 1901-02 when the average Football League attendance was 7,531.

High scoring matches 1898-1902

Division 1

Derby County thrashed Sheffield Wednesday 9-0 on January 21st, 1899, while on the following September 4th, Aston Villa took promoted Glossop apart at Villa Park, winning 9-0. In the 1900-01 season the highest score achieved was 7 – by three clubs. Aston Villa beat Manchester City 7-1 on December 1st. A week later West Bromwich Albion defeated Bolton Wanderers 7-2 and, on January 12th, Sunderland matched this against Wolves at Roker Park. On January 6th, 1902, Liverpool crushed Stoke 7-0 at Anfield to make the season's high score.

Division 2

In the 1898-99 campaign Darwen lost 3 matches 0-10. On February 18th, the Darreners crashed at Manchester City, following this with the same experience on 4th March at Walsall. Finally, the Barley Bank men were humbled at Loughborough Town on All Fools' Day, April 1st. On March 12th, 1900, Woolwich Arsenal hammered Loughborough 12-0 on March 12th and a year less 10 days later Blackpool sank 1-10 at Small Heath while Middlesbrough ran up a 9-2 win over Gainsborough Trinity. In the 1901-02 season, in a bottom of the table battle on April 19th, Chesterfield Town demolished fellow strugglers Stockport County 8-1.

The number of goals per game 1898-1901 fell in each successive season in the Football League. By the 1900-1901 campaign, matches in both divisions were producing an average of fewer than 3 goals.

It is fair to say though that the goals per game figures in previous seasons were probably inflated by the presence of 'weak teams'. Things were different by 1901.

In Division 1 1901-02 there was a rise in the number of goals scored, but not in Division 2 where the fall in goals scored continued. In the season 23.53% of the League games produced either no goals or one goal.

The death of Queen Victoria

After 64 years on the throne, Queen Victoria died on January 22nd, 1901. According to a number of sources, places of public entertainment were shut during a week of national mourning and Football League matches were called off. However, on 26th January there was one First Division fixture played – at the Victoria Ground, Stoke, where Manchester City were beaten 2-1. The ground name link might explain why this match went ahead, but why 2nd Division fixtures at Burnley, Grimsby Town and Lincoln City were played is a mystery.

The F.A. Cup 1899-1902

Finals continued to be played in April, though the date moved into the second half of the month in this period. Attendances at Crystal Palace were, as usual, higher than for league matches and the same pattern of a dip in the 1899-1900 season is evident, with the country at war.

Perhaps the most significant footballing change lies in the success of Southern League clubs. In the 1899-1900 competition, four teams reached the last sixteen, compared with one club from the Second Division, and Southampton made it all the way to the Final.

A year later, three teams from the Southern League were in the draw for the round before the ¼-Finals and the eventual winners of the trophy were Tottenham Hotspur, the last club from outside the Football League to win the F.A. Cup. Southampton were finalists in 1902.

F.A. CUP FINAL 1902 - 19th April

Sheffield United drew 1-1 with Southern League Southampton in front of 76,914 spectators. In a match refereed by T. Kirkham, United's goal was scored by Common and Wood was on target for Saints. The Blades won the replay a week later with goals from Hedley and Barnes, who had not featured in the first match. Brown replied for Southampton. Only 33,068 turned up to watch the game, which Mr. Kirkham again refereed.

The F.A. Amateur Cup 1899-1902

The knock-out competition for amateur clubs was dominated by clubs from the North-East as the 19th century gave way to the 20th. The three finals all matched clubs from County Durham against teams from East Anglia. In all three cases, it was Northern League sides who triumphed.

In 1899 Stockton defeated Harwich & Parkeston 1-0 at Ayresome Park, Middlesbrough, on March 25th. Fairbairn hit the Stockton winner in a match which was watched by a crowd of 7,000.

In 1900, on March 31st, Bishop Auckland beat Lowestoft Town 5-1. Marshall scored three for the victors, with for James and Pennington also on target.

In 1901 Crook Town won the trophy for the first time when beating King's Lynn 3-0, in a replay, at Portman Road, Ipswich, in front of 1,500. Hamill hit two for Crook, whose other came from Rippon. A week earlier, on April 6th, the teams had drawn 1-1 at Dovercourt, watched by 4,000. Iley had given Crook a half-time lead, but Macdonald had equalised for the Linnets in the second period.

In 1902 Old Malvernians restored some Southern pride when they crushed Bishop Auckland 5-1 in the Final, which was played at Elland Road, Leeds.

Club colours 1888-1902

It used to be thought that football clubs' colours had rarely changed since the early days. Over recent years, it has emerged that this is far from the truth in many cases. The most recent work done on this 'area' is 'a work in progress' by Dave Moor. Between June 2006 and the present, Mr. Moor has built up a website 'Historical football kits' which provides a fascinating insight into club colours in the past.

Below are details of the colours used by Football League clubs in the period 1888-1902 – as far as it is possible to tell. Although the term 'shorts' is used, it is fair to say that these were, in fact, more like 'longs'.

Accrington played in Red shirts with Blue shorts in their 5 seasons in the League, but may have worn White shorts at the start.

Aston Villa began with shirts which had thin Claret and Blue stripes and White shorts. Villa used the well-known Claret shirts with Blue sleeves for most of the period 1888-1902, but had Claret and Blue halves 1892-93 and a Chocolate and Blue halved shirt at times before 1893-94.

Barnsley wore Blue and White striped shirts with Dark Blue shorts.

Blackburn Rovers wore Light Blue and White halved shirts, with White shorts 1888-1891 and 1894-95. From 1891-92 the normal kit was Royal Blue and White Halves, with Dark Blue shorts.

Blackpool wore Thin Blue and White striped shirts, with Dark Blue shorts.

Bolton Wanderers used White shirts and Dark Blue shorts for the majority of the period 1888-1902. For the 1890-91 season, they seem to have played in Royal Blue and White striped tops and Dark Blue shorts.

Bootle's shirts were Royal Blue and White striped and the accompanying shorts were Dark Blue.

Bristol City's strip consisted of Red shirts with White shorts.

Burnley began League life wearing Dark Blue and White striped shirts and Dark Blue shorts. An all Dark Blue kit was being used by January 1889, but the stripes, now thin, returned to the shirts 1889-90. For 1891-93 broad Claret and Amber stripes were worn, which gave way to striped shirts in Black & Yellow 1893-94. These returned in 1895 after the team had worn Pink and White striped tops, with Blue shorts for the 1894-95 campaign. Next, for the 1897-98 season, the team wore Red shirts and Black shorts changing these to Blue a year later. Finally, in 1900, a kit of Green shirts and White shorts was adopted.

Burslem Port Vale played in Red shirts with Black shorts 1892-95, adopting Black and Yellow stripes for shirts in 1896. In 1898, a Red and White top came into use, with Blue shorts.

Burton Swifts wore Blue shirts and White shorts 1892-95, changing to Claret and Amber halves for 1895-97. During 1897-98, Red and White halved tops were used, with Dark Blue shorts.

Burton Wanderers' colours were Blue and White halved shirts, with White shorts.

Bury, Chesterfield Town and Crewe Alexandra all played in a simple, uncomplicated kit of White Shirts and Blue shorts.

Darwen used Salmon shirts and Dark Blue shorts 1891-92, changing to White shorts for 1892-93. Black and White striped tops, with Blue shorts, were worn 1894-95, with White shirts with Blue shorts being used from 1896. During their final League season the Darreners played in Black and White striped tops, with Blue shorts.

Derby County wore Chocolate and Yellow halved shirts with Light Blue sleeves 1888-89, switching to an altogether different All Black strip in 1890. Red and White halved shirts with Black shorts were sported in 1893, with stripes in those 3 colours on the shirts for 1894-96. White shirts were first used 1896-97, with Blue shorts for that season and Black shorts after that.

Doncaster Rovers played in Red and White striped shirts with Navy Blue shorts.

Everton used Light Blue and White halved shirts 1888-90, before using a kit of Salmon tops with Blue shorts 1890-91. From 1891 to 1895, the team wore Dark Red shirts with Blue shorts, and finally adopted the Blue shirts and White Shorts strip in 1895.

Gainsborough Trinity wore Royal Blue shirts and Dark Blue shorts.

Glossop (North End)'s uniform consisted of Black and White halved tops, with Black shorts.

Grimsby Town's shirts 1892-97 were Claret and Light Blue halved. For 1897-98 the Mariners wore White shirts with Dark Blue shorts. The Blundell Park club then wore a kit of Chocolate and Light Blue halved shirts and White shorts.

Leicester Fosse had a kit of White shirts and Dark Blue shorts. Switching to Blue shirts and White shorts in 1899, the Foxes adopted Light Blue tops with Dark Blue shorts in 1900.

Lincoln City used Red and White striped shirts, with Black shorts up to 1897, then changed to a kit of Green shirts with Black shorts. The striped tops were back in use in 1900, with White shorts being worn.

Liverpool played in halved shirts of Light Blue and White, with Dark Blue shorts, 1892-94. The club then changed to Red shirts and White shorts. It is probable that this change was made in order to distinguish the club more clearly from rivals and near-neighbours, Everton.

Loughborough Town had broad Black and White striped shirts and Dark Blue shorts.

Luton Town played in Pink, Black and White striped tops and Dark Blue shorts.

Manchester City replaced the 'Ardwick kit' of White shirts with Dark Blue shorts worn 1892-94 with a strip of Light Blue shirts and White shorts.

Middlesbrough began their League career using a kit of White shirts and Blue shorts, but switched in November 1899 to Red shirts and White shorts.

Middlesbrough Ironopolis wore Pink and White striped shirts with White shorts.

Club colours (continued)

New Brighton Tower wore a different outfit in each of their three years in the Football League. Starting with Blue and White quarters and White shorts in 1898, the club colours became White shirts with Dark Blue shorts in 1899 and a Salmon top, with Black trim, and White shorts in 1900.

Newcastle United used Black and White striped shirts from the time they entered the League. At first it seems Dark Grey shorts were worn, but these were soon replaced by Black ones.

Newton Heath began their League career in a kit of Green and Yellow halved shirts and Dark Blue shorts. At some point the tops were changed to ones of Red and White Quarters. Green shirts, with a Yellow trim, and White shorts were used 1894-95, with a uniform of White shirts and Dark Blue shorts first worn in 1896.

Northwich Victoria and Nottingham Forest both wore Red shirts and Blue shorts. Forest changed to using White shorts in 1899.

Notts County wore Chocolate and Light Blue halved shirts and White shorts 1888-90, then changed to Black and White striped tops and Black shorts.

Preston North End's kit was White shirts with Blue shorts.

Rotherham Town played in Red shirts with Dark Blue shorts.

Sheffield United had Red and White shirts and Blue shorts.

Sheffield Wednesday wore Royal Blue and White striped shirts and Dark Blue shorts. In 1900, the Owls switched to wearing Black shorts.

Small Heath sported Royal Blue tops with White shorts 1892-93, using Light Blue shirts with Dark Blue trim 1893 onwards.

Stockport County wore Red and White striped shirts, with Dark Blue shorts.

Stoke colours were thin Red and White striped shirts and White shorts 1888-90. A kit of thin Black and Yellow striped shirts with Black shorts was used 1891-92, which was replaced by Red and Dark Blue striped tops and Black shorts 1892-93. For 1893-94 the team wore White shirts and Blue shorts, returning to the '92-'93 strip 1894-97. In 1897 another uniform, of Claret shirts and White shorts, was adopted. For their next campaign, the Potters changed to using Dark Blue shorts.

Sunderland used Red and White striped shirts. Black shorts made up the kit 1890-97, with Dark Blue shorts being introduced 1897-98.

Walsall Town Swifts had Red and White halved shirts 1892-94 and Red and Blue halved ones for 1894-95. Shorts were Dark Blue. Returning to the League as 'Walsall' in 1896, the club played in White shirts with Dark Blue shorts, with Black shorts being adopted for 1897-98.

West Bromwich Albion played in Blue and White striped shirts with White shorts for most of the period. A kit of broad Light Blue and Dark Red striped tops with Black shorts appears to have been used in 1889.

Wolves' first League uniform consisted of shirts in thin Red and White stripes and White shorts. By 1891 the club was playing Old Gold and Black diagonally halved tops and Black shorts, with a switch to thin stripes for shirts, in the same colours, by 1896.

Woolwich Arsenal wore Red shirts and Dark Blue shorts 1893-95 and 1896-98. During the 1895-96 season, shirts had thin Light Blue and Dark Red stripes, with Dark Blue shorts still being used. In 1899, the Gunners began to wear White shorts.

MISCELLANEOUS MATTERS

Goals aggregates

Between 1888 and 1902, the champions were usually highest-scoring in each Football League division. Exceptions were Blackburn (1889-90), Everton and Small Heath (1893-94), Everton and Aston Villa in Division 1 and Manchester City in Division 2 (1894-95), and Aston Villa (1897-98). With goals aggregates, it was different. Tables below show teams with the highest (GA) goals aggregates, together with the total matches played (P.) and the resulting mean (Mn.) achieved.

Football League

Season	P.	Club	GA	Mn.
1888-89	22	Bolton Wanderers	122	5.55
1889-90	22	Blackburn Rovers	119	5.41
		Bolton Wanderers	119	5.41
1890-91	22	Burnley	115	5.23
1891-92	26	Darwen	150	5.77

Division One

Season	P.	Club	GA	Mn.
1892-93	30	Accrington	138	4.60
1893-94	30	Everton	147	4.90
1894-95	30	Everton	132	4.40
1895-96	30	Wolves	126	4.20
1896-97	30	Derby County	120	4.00
1897-98	30	Derby County	118	3.93
1898-99	34	Derby County	119	3.50
1899-00	34	Aston Villa	112	3.29
1900-01	34	Preston North End	124	3.65
1901-02	34	Notts County	108	3.18

Division Two

Season	P.	Club	GA	Mn.
1892-93	22	Small Heath	125	5.68
1893-94	28	Small Heath	147	5.25
1894-95	30	Newcastle United	156	5.20
1895-96	30	Liverpool	148	4.93
1896-97	30	Woolwich Arsenal	138	4.60
1897-98	30	Lincoln City	126	4.20
1898-99	34	Darwen	163	4.79
1899-00	34	Burton Swifts	127	3.74
1900-01	34	Barnsley	107	3.15
1901-02	34	Barnsley	114	3.35
		Middlesbrough	114	3.35

While there are exceptions to this, the trend in the goals aggregate means is downwards until the very end of the period for Division 2, which is a reflection of the evening out of standards, better defensive coaching and a gradual removal of weaker teams from the Football League. Twice, it appears, Darwen, with exceptionally awful seasons, caused a blip in the general pattern. Preston's over-generous defence was responsible for the other 'out of place' figure' 1900-1901, when North End conceded 13 more goals than any other team in Division One.

If you were a neutral and it was goal action you wanted, Everton (1893-95) and Derby County (1896-99) were worth watching in the First Division. Champions' appearances are rare in these tables. Only Aston Villa (1899-1900) make the 1st Division table with just two 2nd Division title winners, Small Heath (1892-93) and Liverpool (1895-96), listed.

1902 - A 'watershed' for the Football League?

There had been changes in the game since 1888, including a referee being solely in charge rather than two umpires, the penalty kick, and games which were abandoned replayed in full. The last year of 'Victorian football' saw 3 major new rules introduced, however.

To put an end to 'poaching', a maximum wage was set of £4 a week, with signing on fees limited to a maximum of £10 + 'match bonuses' banned. The penalty area and 6-yard box were given their basic present-day shape, so the 'area' no longer went across the width of the pitch. 'Keepers, though still not confined to their line for penalties, could only be charged when holding the ball, not when simply playing it.

The 1901-02 season ended with no changes being made either to the rules or to the pitch or the membership of the Football League. After repeated change over the past few years, this was itself a change.

There would, however, be a new name on the 2nd Division fixture lists for the 1902-1903 campaign in the shape of Manchester United, who emerged from the ashes of the bankrupt Newton Heath club.

1902-1903 – LEAGUE DIVISION 1 # SHEFFIELD WEDNESDAY

With victories in their opening three games, Sheffield Wednesday became the early leaders of Division One, but the team then faltered in its next two outings. By the end of September, the Owls had been overhauled by Notts County, free-scoring Derby and promoted West Bromwich Albion.

Wednesday went top again by winning 3-0 at Notts County on October 3rd, but lost at Liverpool a day later, enabling West Bromwich to move above them on goal average. A week later, Albion lost 1-2 away to Liverpool, so Derby County, 3-2 winners against Middlesbrough took over as leaders, remaining at the 1st Division helm for the next fortnight, thanks to their 4-2 success at Blackburn Rovers.

The Rams were held at home by Newcastle United on October 25th, while West Bromwich won at home to Grimsby Town and moved a point clear at the top. By mid-November, the Throstles' lead was up to 3 points and five points from their next three games kept the Albion men in top spot going into December.

Just when it seemed the leaders might pull away from the rest, however, they were pegged back, losing at Everton and against Sheffield Wednesday in the last pre-Christmas fixture on December 20th. Extending their unbeaten run to 10 games by beating Everton by 2-0, Notts County claimed second spot. A cluster of clubs lay just behind the Magpies.

In a fascinating last week of 1902, Derby County beat West Bromwich Albion, Notts County lost at Sheffield Wednesday, and Sheffield United leapfrogged into first place, on goal average, after a 7-1 thumping of Bolton and a 2-2 draw at Nottingham Forest. Four sides shared the points lead, with 24 each.

Four consecutive wins in the New Year put West Bromwich Albion back in charge, with only Sheffield Wednesday staying in touch. Albion then lost at Newcastle United on January 24th and could only manage to produce draws in their next two games at The Hawthorns. Wednesday fared slightly better, but trailed the leaders by 2 points at mid-February, having played one game more.

Both the top two were by now aware of Sunderland, whose unbeaten 12-match run had carried the Roker Park men into third place. As defending champions, Sunderland had the pedigree to thwart the ambitions of the leading pair. West Bromwich cracked under the pressure, losing their next 8 games in a row. Having gone top on February 28th, Wednesday won a key match at Sunderland on March 21st and ended the month 3 points up on their rivals, who had 2 games in hand. Both teams wobbled in early April. Wednesday finished their games on the 18th, leaving Sunderland needing a draw at Newcastle a week later to retain the title. When the Rokerites lost, 0-1, Wednesday became English soccer's new champions.

Sheffield Wednesday's '1st half' record

September	01	Sheffield United		3-2
	06	Bolton Wanderers		2-0
	13	MIDDLESBROUGH		2-0
	20	Newcastle United		0-3
	27	WOLVES		1-1
October	03	Notts County		3-0
	04	Liverpool		2-4
	11	SHEFFIELD UNITED		0-1
	18	Grimsby Town		1-0
November	01	Nottingham Forest		4-1
	08	BURY		2-0
	15	Blackburn Rovers		1-2
	22	SUNDERLAND		1-0
	29	Stoke		0-4
December	06	EVERTON		4-1
	13	DERBY COUNTY		0-1
	20	West Bromwich Albion		3-2

Table at December 20th, 1902

1	West Bromwich Albion	17	35	22	24
2	Notts County	17	21	18	23
3	Derby County	17	33	23	22
4	SHEFFIELD WEDNESDAY	17	29	22	21
5	Sheffield United	17	23	18	21
6	Liverpool	16	40	24	20
7	Stoke	16	24	18	20
8	Nottingham Forest	18	21	23	18
9	Sunderland	16	23	21	17
10	Bury	15	22	16	16
11	Wolves	17	25	29	16
12	Everton	18	27	28	15
13	Newcastle United	16	22	25	15
14	Aston Villa	15	26	21	14
15	Middlesbrough	16	16	25	13
16	Blackburn Rovers	16	21	36	10
17	Grimsby Town	16	22	36	8
18	Bolton Wanderers	16	15	40	3
		296	445	445	296

Attendances
Total   3,584,875 – 306 games
Average   11,715 per game
Goals
Total   885 – 306 games
Average   2.892 per game
Top scorer Alec Raybould (Liverpool) 31

Sheffield Wednesday's '2nd half' record

December	26	Aston Villa		0-1
	27	NOTTS COUNTY		2-0
January	01	ASTON VILLA		4-0
	03	BOLTON WANDERERS		3-0
	10	Middlesbrough		1-2
	17	NEWCASTLE UNITED		3-0
	24	Wolves		1-2
	31	LIVERPOOL		3-1
February	14	GRIMSBY TOWN		1-1
	28	NOTTINGHAM FOREST		1-0
March	14	BLACKBURN ROVERS		0-0
	21	Sunderland		1-0
	28	STOKE		1-0
April	04	Everton		1-1
	06	Bury		0-4
	11	Derby County		0-1
	18	WEST BROMWICH ALBION		3-1

Final League Division 1 Table 1903

1	SHEFFIELD WEDNESDAY	34	54	36	42
2	Aston Villa	34	61	40	41
3	Sunderland	34	51	36	41
4	Sheffield United	34	58	44	39
5	Liverpool	34	68	49	38
6	Stoke	34	46	38	37
7	West Bromwich Albion	34	54	53	36
8	Bury	34	54	43	35
9	Derby County	34	50	47	35
10	Nottingham Forest	34	49	47	35
11	Wolves	34	48	57	33
12	Everton	34	45	47	32
13	Middlesbrough	34	41	50	32
14	Newcastle United	34	41	51	32
15	Notts County	34	41	49	31
16	Blackburn Rovers	34	44	63	29
17	Grimsby Town	34	43	62	25
18	Bolton Wanderers	34	37	73	19
		612	885	885	612

Grimsby Town and Bolton Wanderers relegated.

1902-1903 – LEAGUE DIVISION 2

MANCHESTER CITY

The opening exchanges of the 2nd Division campaign saw Bristol City top of the table by September 30th, with maximum points from four games. Also on 8 points were Lincoln City, who slipped past Bristol on October 11th after beating Gainsborough Trinity, while the Cherries lost at Woolwich Arsenal.

Bristol City were back at the top a week later on goal average and moved clear at the start of November, reaching the mid-point of the month a point ahead of Woolwich and Small Heath, with Manchester City, 2-3 losers at Bristol's St. John's Lane ground on November 15th, tucked in behind these two.

Victory over Barnsley on November 24th took the Manchester club a point clear at the top, but wins for their 3 closest rivals the following Saturday returned the Hyde Road men to fourth spot. Gillespie's 13th goal of the season then helped the Citizens demolish neighbours Stockport County 5-0 on December 6th and defeats for both Bristol City and Woolwich Arsenal, at Small Heath, saw Manchester City move into second place. When Small Heath lost at Doncaster Rovers a week later, Manchester City eased into first place by beating Blackpool and the club went into the holiday period at the 2nd Division summit after a 5th successive win – by 4-1 against Woolwich – on December 20th.

By New Year, Manchester City were 3 points clear at the top. Small Heath, in second place, had a game in hand, while Bristol City, in third, had played 2 games fewer. The early pace-setters were, however, seven points behind the leaders, who seemed to be taking control of things. Three points were dropped by City in their January visits to Lincoln and Leicester Fosse, enabling Small Heath to nudge closer by January 17th. A week later, however, the Birmingham side dipped 1-2 at Preston, while City began a 'goalfest period', which produced 17 'hits' in their next three outings.

By mid-February, Manchester City held a 4-point lead over Small Heath. This was a comfortable advantage, even though the dogged Midlanders had two games in hand. The two clubs clashed at Hyde Road on 23rd February. 'Welsh Wizard' Billy Meredith opened the scoring and City went on to overrun their visitors and main rivals 4-0.

By the end of March, Manchester City were on the verge of promotion and this was secured on April 4th with the 2-0 success at Stockport. Easter followed and victory over Blackpool on April 11th left 2 points needed to guarantee the title, it seemed. When Small Heath lost 0-3 at Barnsley on Easter Monday, April 13th, however, City took the 2nd Division crown.

Manchester City's '1st half' record

September	06	LINCOLN CITY	3-1
	13	Small Heath	0-4
	20	LEICESTER FOSSE	3-1
	27	Chesterfield Town	1-0
October	04	Burnley	1-1
	11	PRESTON NORTH END	1-0
	18	Burslem Port Vale	4-1
	22	Gainsborough Trinity	3-0
November	01	Woolwich Arsenal	0-1
	08	BURTON UNITED	2-0
	15	Bristol City	2-3
	22	GLOSSOP	5-2
	24	BARNSLEY	3-2
December	06	STOCKPORT COUNTY	5-0
	13	Blackpool	3-0
	20	WOOLWICH ARSENAL	4-1
	25	Manchester United	1-1

Table at December 25th, 1902

1	MANCHESTER CITY	17	41	18	26
2	Small Heath	16	30	12	24
3	Bristol City	16	27	20	21
4	Woolwich Arsenal	16	27	18	20
5	Chesterfield Town	15	29	15	17
6	Manchester United	13	16	12	16
7	Lincoln City	15	24	21	16
8	Burslem Port Vale	16	25	27	15
9	Preston North End	14	25	16	14
10	Burton United	13	17	19	13
11	Leicester Fosse	13	19	23	13
12	Blackpool	13	20	18	12
13	Doncaster Rovers	15	20	28	12
14	Glossop	14	17	25	11
15	Burnley	16	14	30	11
16	Gainsborough Trinity	12	12	22	9
17	Barnsley	13	17	24	8
18	Stockport County	15	11	43	4
		262	391	391	262

Attendances
Total   1,606,500 – 306 games
Average   5,250 per game

Goals
Total   940 – 306 games
Average   3.072 per game
Top scorer   Billy Gillespie (Manchester City) 30

Manchester City's '2nd half' record

December	26	Preston North End	2-0
	27	Doncaster Rovers	2-1
January	01	DONCASTER ROVERS	4-1
	03	Lincoln City	0-1
	17	Leicester Fosse	1-1
	24	CHESTERFIELD TOWN	4-2
	31	BURNLEY	6-0
February	14	BURSLEM PORT VALE	7-1
	23	SMALL HEATH	4-0
	28	GAINSBOROUGH TRINITY	9-0
March	07	Burton United	5-0
	14	BRISTOL CITY	2-2
	21	Gainsborough Trinity	1-0
April	04	Stockport County	2-0
	10	MANCHESTER UNITED	0-2
	11	BLACKPOOL	1-0
	14	Barnsley	3-0

Final League Division 2 Table 1903

1	MANCHESTER CITY	34	95	29	54
2	Small Heath	34	74	36	51
3	Woolwich Arsenal	34	66	30	48
4	Bristol City	34	59	38	42
5	Manchester United	34	53	38	38
6	Chesterfield Town	34	67	40	37
7	Preston North End	34	56	40	36
8	Barnsley	34	55	51	34
9	Burslem Port Vale	34	57	62	34
10	Lincoln City	34	46	53	30
11	Glossop	34	43	58	29
12	Gainsborough Trinity	34	41	59	29
13	Burton United	34	39	59	29
14	Blackpool	34	44	59	28
15	Leicester Fosse	34	41	65	28
16	Doncaster Rovers	34	35	72	25
17	Stockport County	34	39	74	20
18	Burnley	34	30	77	20
		612	940	940	612

Manchester City and Small Heath promoted. Stockport County (20 votes) and Burnley (19) were re-elected, but Bradford City (30) replaced Doncaster Rovers (14). Four other clubs were unsuccessful - Crewe Alexandra and West Hartlepool (7), Southport Central (4) and Willington Athletic (1). Doncaster Rovers seem to have been very unlucky – Bradford City were a new club and had yet to play a game!

1903-1904 – LEAGUE DIVISION 1

September 1903 saw strong starts to the season by four clubs – Manchester City, Sunderland and the two Sheffield teams, United and Wednesday. Ten goals were scored by Sunderland in their opening 2 fixtures and the Wearsiders went clear at the top following a 4th win in a row on September 19th.

Defeat at Bury a week later saw the Roker Park club slip to third place, on goal average, with promoted Manchester City and reigning champions Sheffield Wednesday taking the top two places. Joining the leading trio on eight points were Sheffield United, who secured a 3-2 win over Derby County – their fourth success in a row.

United extended their winning start to eight games at Newcastle United on October 24th. Despite losses at Aston Villa and Middlesbrough, which enabled city rivals Wednesday to pass them, the Blades again headed the table at mid-November after beating Liverpool.

Manchester City emerged as the leading contenders for the leadership of the top flight over the next few weeks, going to the top of the 1st Division standings on 19th December after winning 3-0 at Small Heath. When the Hyde Road outfit lost at home to Everton on Boxing Day, however, Sheffield United returned to the top by beating West Bromwich Albion 4-0 at Bramall Lane.

Sheffield Wednesday's '1st half' record

September	02	West Bromwich Albion	1-0
	05	MIDDLESBROUGH	4-1
	12	Liverpool	3-1
	19	BURY	1-1
	26	Blackburn Rovers	0-0
October	03	NOTTINGHAM FOREST	2-1
	10	Wolves	1-2
	17	Sunderland	1-0
	24	WEST BROMWICH ALBION	1-0
	31	Small Heath	0-0
November	07	EVERTON	1-0
	14	Stoke	1-3
	21	DERBY COUNTY	1-0
	28	Manchester City	1-1
December	12	Sheffield United	1-1
	19	NEWCASTLE UNITED	1-1
	26	Aston Villa	1-2

Table at December 26th, 1903

1	Sheffield United	18	40	25	26
2	Manchester City	17	34	22	24
3	Aston Villa	18	40	28	23
4	SHEFFIELD WEDNESDAY	17	21	14	22
5	Sunderland	18	36	28	22
6	Everton	18	33	22	21
7	Newcastle United	19	30	30	21
8	Blackburn Rovers	19	28	26	20
9	Wolves	17	23	31	20
10	Notts County	19	22	34	18
11	Nottingham Forest	19	35	35	17
12	Middlesbrough	16	29	23	16
13	Stoke	19	40	37	15
14	Derby County	18	33	32	15
15	Bury	18	24	31	13
16	West Bromwich Albion	18	14	30	12
17	Liverpool	18	26	39	10
18	Small Heath	18	16	37	9
		324	524	524	324

Attendances
Total 3,892,150 – 306 games
Average 12,719 per game

Goals
Total 939 – 306 games
Average 3.069 per game
Top scorer Steve Bloomer (Derby County) 20

SHEFFIELD WEDNESDAY

A 5-3 win over City at Bramall Lane on December 28th gave United a 4-point lead at the head of the 1st Division. Aston Villa moved into second, on goal average, following a draw at Derby County, and Sheffield Wednesday lay fourth, behind Manchester City, 6 points off the lead with 2 games in hand. Things turned around significantly during January. Sheffield United took 4 points from 4 games, which enabled all their rivals to close the gap by the 23rd. With the Blades not in action on the 30th, Sheffield Wednesday, who completed their 5th win of the month, at Nottingham Forest, joined United on 32 points, going ahead of their rivals on goal average.

United lost four of their next five and disappeared from the title reckoning, but Wednesday pressed on, following a 0-0 draw against Sunderland with four wins on the bounce. The last of these was against chief pursuers Manchester City and meant the Owls took a 4-point lead into April 1904. Both the top two lost 2 of their next 3 games, but the Manchester club then picked up 3 points while Wednesday did not play, meaning the Owls had a lead of 1 point. City's 4-0 win over Small Heath on April 16th took them to the top, but Wednesday bounced back from defeat at Newcastle to reclaim the lead by beating Aston Villa a week later. Two days later, on April 25th, City lost 0-1 at Everton and it was all over – Wednesday were champions again.

Sheffield Wednesday's '2nd half' record

January	01	WOLVES	4-0
	02	Middlesbrough	1-0
	09	LIVERPOOL	2-1
	16	Bury	0-1
	23	BLACKBURN ROVERS	3-1
	30	Nottingham Forest	1-0
February	13	SUNDERLAND	0-0
	22	NOTTS COUNTY	2-0
	27	SMALL HEATH	3-2
March	12	STOKE	1-0
	26	MANCHESTER CITY	1-0
April	02	Notts County	0-1
	04	Everton	0-2
	09	SHEFFIELD UNITED	3-0
	16	Newcastle United	0-4
	23	ASTON VILLA	4-2
	30	Derby County	2-0

Final League Division 1 Table 1904

1	SHEFFIELD WEDNESDAY	34	48	28	47
2	Manchester City	34	71	45	44
3	Everton	34	59	32	43
4	Newcastle United	34	58	45	42
5	Aston Villa	34	70	48	41
6	Sunderland	34	63	49	39
7	Sheffield United	34	62	57	38
8	Wolves	34	44	66	36
9	Nottingham Forest	34	57	57	31
10	Middlesbrough	34	46	47	30
11	Small Heath	34	39	52	30
12	Bury	34	40	53	29
13	Notts County	34	37	61	29
14	Derby County	34	58	60	28
15	Blackburn Rovers	34	48	60	28
16	Stoke	34	54	57	27
17	Liverpool	34	49	62	26
18	West Bromwich Albion	34	36	60	24
		612	939	939	612

Liverpool and West Bromwich Albion relegated.

1903-1904 – LEAGUE DIVISION 2

The 2nd Division title race 1903-04 was dominated throughout by two teams – Preston North End and Woolwich Arsenal. These two clubs were clear of the rest by mid-September and each won its opening five games.

Woolwich Arsenal did not concede a goal until 10th October and the Londoners remained at the top of the table until October 31st, when they lost 1-2 at Barnsley. Preston's victory over Grimsby Town on the same afternoon carried the Lancashire side a point clear.

North End's first reverse of the season was also suffered at Barnsley, on December 19th, by which time Woolwich had lost a second fixture, at Bolton Wanderers. The Plumstead-based club were getting used to second place in the rankings. By the time Preston closed their programme for December with a 0-0 draw at Burton United, their main rivals lay 4 points behind them. Woolwich, in turn, held a four-point advantage over 3rd-placed Bolton Wanderers, with three games in hand on the Trotters.

Preston North End's '1st half' record

September	05	Stockport County	5-1	
	12	CHESTERFIELD TOWN	2-1	
	19	Bolton Wanderers	2-0	
	26	BURNLEY	2-0	
October	03	BURSLEM PORT VALE	3-1	
	10	Grimsby Town	1-1	
	17	LEICESTER FOSSE	4-3	
	24	Blackpool	3-0	
	31	GRIMSBY TOWN	2-0	
November	14	BRISTOL CITY	3-0	
	21	Manchester United	2-0	
	28	GLOSSOP	3-0	
December	05	Bradford City	1-1	
	19	Barnsley	0-1	
	25	GAINSBOROUGH TRINITY	2-0	
	26	LINCOLN CITY	2-1	
	28	Burton United	0-0	

Table at December 28th, 1903

1	PRESTON NORTH END	17	37	10	29
2	Woolwich Arsenal	15	56	9	25
3	Bolton Wanderers	18	37	20	21
4	Bristol City	15	35	20	17
5	Burnley	15	18	25	17
6	Manchester United	14	26	18	16
7	Barnsley	15	18	23	16
8	Lincoln City	17	17	28	16
9	Burslem Port Vale	15	26	22	15
10	Bradford City	15	23	26	14
11	Grimsby Town	14	18	21	14
12	Chesterfield Town	15	17	24	13
13	Burton United	15	17	27	12
14	Leicester Fosse	15	15	29	12
15	Glossop	16	20	35	10
16	Gainsborough Trinity	13	15	23	9
17	Blackpool	14	16	29	9
18	Stockport County	16	17	39	9
		274	428	428	274

Attendances
Total   1,779,050 – 306 games
Average   5,814 per game

Goals
Total   942 – 306 games
Average   3.078 per game
Top scorer   Tommy Shanks (Woolwich Arsenal)
                     + Percy Smith (Preston North End) 24

PRESTON NORTH END

Early January results suggested there would be little change. Preston added 5 points to their tally in 3 games, the last of these involving a 3-1 defeat of Bolton. Woolwich, meanwhile, drew twice before thrashing Gainsborough Trinity 6-0 on January 9th. When the Gunners lost successive matches at Burton United and Manchester United, Bolton pulled level with the London club.

By mid-February, improving Burnley had almost caught up also. Woolwich had 5 games in hand on Bolton, however, and two games in hand on the Turf Moor men. Six consecutive wins then saw Woolwich pull clear of any challengers and, with Preston North End winning only one in five, the end of March was reached with the Deepdale club a point ahead of the Gunners, having played a game more. The leading duo met and drew twice in the next 9 days. Importantly though, Woolwich lost 0-1 at Burnley in between. Although the Londoners ended their programme on April 23rd a point ahead, P.J. Smith's winner for Preston on April 30th, against Blackpool, meant the title went to Deepdale.

Preston North End's '1st half' record

January	02	STOCKPORT COUNTY	1-1	
	09	Chesterfield Town	1-0	
	16	BOLTON WANDERERS	3-1	
	23	Burnley	1-2	
	30	Burslem Port Vale	1-0	
February	13	Leicester Fosse	4-1	
	27	Gainsborough Trinity	0-2	
March	05	BURTON UNITED	4-0	
	12	Bristol City	1-3	
	19	MANCHESTER UNITED	1-1	
	26	Glossop	2-2	
April	01	WOOLWICH ARSENAL	0-0	
	02	BRADFORD CITY	4-0	
	09	Woolwich Arsenal	0-0	
	16	BARNSLEY	1-1	
	23	Lincoln City	0-0	
	30	BLACKPOOL	1-0	

Final League Division 2 Table 1904

1	PRESTON NORTH END	34	62	24	50
2	Woolwich Arsenal	34	91	22	49
3	Manchester United	34	65	33	48
4	Bristol City	34	73	41	42
5	Burnley	34	50	55	39
6	Grimsby Town	34	50	49	36
7	Bolton Wanderers	34	59	41	34
8	Barnsley	34	38	57	32
9	Gainsborough Trinity	34	53	60	31
10	Bradford City	34	45	59	31
11	Chesterfield Town	34	37	45	30
12	Lincoln City	34	41	58	30
13	Burslem Port Vale	34	54	52	29
14	Burton United	34	45	61	29
15	Blackpool	34	40	67	27
16	Stockport County	34	40	72	27
17	Glossop	34	57	64	26
18	Leicester Fosse	34	42	82	22
		612	942	942	612

Preston North End and Woolwich Arsenal promoted to Division 1. Leicester Fosse (33 votes) and Glossop (27) were re-elected, but Stockport County (11) were replaced by Doncaster Rovers (21). Crewe Alexandra (10) were also unsuccessful. Stockport could consider themselves unlucky, having finished third from bottom – then again it was the club's fourth successive re-election bid. Also, there was some sympathy for Doncaster, who had been voted out a year before, despite finishing third from bottom.

1904-1905 – LEAGUE DIVISION 1 NEWCASTLE UNITED

There were to be many twists and turns during the 1904-05 season, which began on September 1st with Preston winning at Aston Villa and Derby County 2-1 victors at Stoke. North End headed the table until September 24th when their defeat by Everton enabled Sheffield Wednesday to take over.

Wednesday won all opening seven games and looked set to walk away with the title by mid-October. The Owls' visit to Sunderland on October 22nd resulted, however, in a 3-0 win for the home side and began an 11-match run for the losers in which only 5 points were picked up.

Sunderland were top of Division 1 by mid-November, having gone eight games unbeaten. Preston clung on in second place, with Everton sharing third spot with fading Wednesday, following a 5-5 draw between the two clubs at Owlerton.

After beating Everton 1-0 on November 19th, the Rokerites also faded, however, and Newcastle United swept into the top slot on the back of seven straight wins. Though this run ended on December 24th, the Geordies went into Christmas two points clear at the head of the 1st Division.

Fog had denied Everton second place because their 26th November game at Woolwich Arsenal had been halted after 78 minutes, with the Toffees 3-1 up.

By New Year the top flight had new leaders. Three wins in 6 days after Christmas enabled Sheffield United to go top. Everton, with similar success in this period, were 2nd – a point behind the Blades, with a game in hand. Newcastle returned to first place on January 2nd, however, by beating Notts County. Sheffield United beat Everton on January 7th, but then lost two out of three by the end of January.

With Newcastle losing three in a row, Everton assumed the League leadership, reaching mid-February a point ahead of new challengers Small Heath, whose 4-1 win over Wolves on February 11th was their 8th unbeaten. Just as with earlier 'new contenders', Small Heath fell away, losing three of their next five. Manchester City now put in a good run, however, and were third, on goal average, by the end of March. Everton led by 2 points from Newcastle, who had a game in hand.

Things tightened greatly on April 21st, when City beat Everton 2-0 and, with Newcastle, moved to within a point of the lead. A day later, the Toffees lost 1-2 at Arsenal in the game rearranged from November 26th. Despite victory at Forest on April 24th, Everton knew their fog-damaged fate lay in others' hands. News that Aston Villa had beaten Manchester City 3-2 raised Evertonians' spirits briefly. Newcastle's win at Middlesbrough on the same day shattered Goodison hopes, however, and the title went to Tyneside.

Newcastle United's '1st half' record

September	03	WOOLWICH ARSENAL	3-0
	10	Derby County	1-1
	17	EVERTON	3-2
	24	Small Heath	1-2
October	01	MANCHESTER CITY	2-0
	08	Notts County	3-0
	15	SHEFFIELD UNITED	1-1
	22	Stoke	0-1
	29	Preston North End	0-1
November	05	MIDDLESBROUGH	3-0
	12	Wolves	3-1
	19	BURY	3-1
	26	Aston Villa	1-0
December	03	BLACKBURN ROVERS	1-0
	10	Nottingham Forest	3-1
	17	SHEFFIELD WEDNESDAY	6-2
	24	Sunderland	1-3

Newcastle United's '2nd half' record

December	31	Woolwich Arsenal	2-0
January	02	NOTTS COUNTY	1-0
	07	DERBY COUNTY	2-0
	14	Everton	1-2
	21	SMALL HEATH	0-1
	28	Manchester City	2-3
February	11	Sheffield United	3-1
	25	PRESTON NORTH END	1-0
March	11	WOLVES	3-0
	18	Bury	4-2
April	01	Blackburn Rovers	0-2
	05	ASTON VILLA	2-0
	08	NOTTINGHAM FOREST	5-1
	21	STOKE	4-1
	22	SUNDERLAND	1-3
	26	Sheffield Wednesday	3-1
	29	Middlesbrough	3-0

Table at December 24th, 1904

1	NEWCASTLE UNITED	17	35	16	24
2	Sheffield United	18	31	29	22
3	Everton	17	30	20	21
4	Sunderland	17	32	23	21
5	Derby County	18	23	24	21
6	Manchester City	17	36	20	20
7	Preston North End	18	23	22	20
8	Small Heath	16	29	20	19
9	Woolwich Arsenal	16	18	13	19
10	Aston Villa	19	29	26	19
11	Sheffield Wednesday	16	33	30	18
12	Blackburn Rovers	17	27	23	15
13	Wolves	18	28	40	14
14	Stoke	17	16	33	13
15	Nottingham Forest	18	24	33	12
16	Middlesbrough	17	17	28	12
17	Bury	17	26	39	10
18	Notts County	17	18	36	10
		310	475	475	310

Attendances
Total   4,081,700 – 306 games
Average   13,339 per game

Goals
Total   904 – 306 games
Average   2.954 per game
Top scorer Arthur Brown (Sheffield United) 23

Final League Division 1 Table 1905

1	NEWCASTLE UNITED	34	72	33	48
2	Everton	34	63	36	47
3	Manchester City	34	66	37	46
4	Aston Villa	34	63	43	42
5	Sunderland	34	60	44	40
6	Sheffield United	34	64	56	40
7	Small Heath	34	54	38	39
8	Preston North End	34	42	37	36
9	Sheffield Wednesday	34	61	57	33
10	Woolwich Arsenal	34	36	40	33
11	Derby County	34	37	48	32
12	Stoke	34	40	58	30
13	Blackburn Rovers	34	40	51	27
14	Wolves	34	47	73	26
15	Middlesbrough	34	36	56	26
16	Nottingham Forest	34	40	61	25
17	Bury	34	47	67	24
18	Notts County	34	36	69	18
		612	904	904	612

Bury and Notts County escaped relegation because of the decision of the Football League to increase the size of each of the two divisions to 20 clubs. In the elections for the two 1st Division places, Bury polled 33 votes and Notts County 32. Manchester United (13), Bristol City (9) and West Bromwich Albion (3) were all unsuccessful.

1904-1905 – LEAGUE DIVISION 2

LIVERPOOL

Bolton Wanderers topped the 2nd Division at the end of September, with maximum points from their first four matches. A fraction of a goal (0·05) separated the Burnden Park men from second-placed Liverpool, while the leading pair were three points clear of their nearest rivals, the most prominent of whom were West Bromwich Albion and Manchester United.

Wanderers won the next two games, but slipped to a 0-1 loss at Chesterfield on October 15th, which allowed title favourites Liverpool to step in and take over at the top. By mid-November, the Anfield club led the table by four points, with Bolton second. Manchester United and Bristol City shared third position with 16 points each.

Liverpool, surprisingly relegated at the end of the previous season, stretched their unbeaten start to the campaign to 13 matches by winning at Gainsborough Trinity on November 19th. The next five weeks were to see dramatic changes, however. 'Pool's defeat at Bolton Wanderers on December 3rd, coupled with the Trotters' 4-0 win at lowly Doncaster Rovers a week later, saw the League leadership switch from Anfield to Burnden Park. A 1-3 reverse at Bank Street two weeks after this saw Liverpool slip to third, with their conquerors, Manchester United, going second on goal average.

By the middle of February, Bolton's lead was up to 6 points, despite their having suffered a 2-4 home loss against Manchester United on January 3rd. The Red Devils had themselves suffered a setback on February 11th, losing 0-3 at Lincoln. Liverpool were able to go 2nd again, on goal average, by winning at West Bromwich on the same day. The next phase of the campaign proved crucial in determining the destination of the 2nd Division crown. Both Bolton's pursuers had 3 games in hand – but these had to be won. By March 11th, Liverpool had made up the deficit in matches and points, taking top spot on goal average for good measure. Meanwhile, United dropped 3 points in 4 games.

The Manchester club closed to within a point on March 25th, when the leading pair both lost, and pulled level with a 6-0 crushing of Doncaster Rovers on April 1st while Bolton drew at Anfield. By mid-April, however, Liverpool and Wanderers were again a point ahead. Both leaders were promoted on Easter Saturday when Manchester United were thrashed 4-0 at Liverpool, while Bolton Wanderers won 1-0 at West Bromwich Albion. The Trotters now relaxed and lost their last match 1-2 at Barnsley. Liverpool, needing only to avoid heavy defeat by Burnley on April 29th, became 2nd Division champions in style with a 3-0 triumph.

Liverpool's '1st half' record

September	01	BURTON UNITED	2-0
	03	GLOSSOP	2-2
	10	Chesterfield Town	1-1
	17	BRADFORD CITY	4-1
	24	Lincoln City	2-0
October	01	LEICESTER FOSSE	4-0
	08	Barnsley	2-0
	15	WEST BROMWICH ALBION	3-2
	22	Burnley	2-0
	29	GRIMSBY TOWN	5-0
November	05	Blackpool	3-0
	12	Burslem Port Vale	2-1
	19	Gainsborough Trinity	2-1
December	03	Bolton Wanderers	0-2
	17	BRISTOL CITY	3-1
	24	Manchester United	1-3
	26	BARNSLEY	2-1

Liverpool's '2nd half' record

December	31	Glossop	2-0
January	07	CHESTERFIELD TOWN	6-1
	21	LINCOLN CITY	1-1
	28	Leicester Fosse	3-0
February	11	West Bromwich Albion	2-0
	25	Grimsby Town	1-0
March	04	BLACKPOOL	5-0
	07	Bradford City	4-2
	11	Doncaster Rovers	4-1
	18	GAINSBOROUGH TRINITY	6-1
	25	Burton United	1-2
April	01	BOLTON WANDERERS	1-1
	08	BURSLEM PORT VALE	8-1
	15	Bristol City	1-0
	21	DONCASTER ROVERS	1-0
	22	MANCHESTER UNITED	4-0
	29	BURNLEY	3-0

Table at December 26th, 1904

1	Bolton Wanderers	17	50	14	30
2	Manchester United	16	36	11	28
3	LIVERPOOL	17	40	15	28
4	Bristol City	17	45	25	24
5	Chesterfield Town	17	19	18	19
6	Gainsborough Trinity	16	32	29	18
7	Lincoln City	17	18	20	16
8	Barnsley	17	15	24	16
9	Burnley	19	22	32	15
10	Grimsby Town	16	14	29	14
11	West Bromwich Albion	17	32	29	13
12	Burslem Port Vale	16	21	25	13
13	Blackpool	16	17	23	13
14	Bradford City	15	21	24	12
15	Leicester Fosse	15	18	24	12
16	Glossop	14	14	21	11
17	Burton United	17	17	39	10
18	Doncaster Rovers	17	11	40	4
		296	442	442	296

Final League Division 2 Table 1905

1	LIVERPOOL	34	93	25	58
2	Bolton Wanderers	34	87	32	56
3	Manchester United	34	81	30	53
4	Bristol City	34	66	45	42
5	Chesterfield Town	34	44	35	39
6	Gainsborough Trinity	34	61	58	36
7	Barnsley	34	38	56	33
8	Bradford City	34	45	49	32
9	Lincoln City	34	42	40	31
10	West Bromwich Albion	34	56	48	30
11	Burnley	34	43	52	30
12	Glossop	34	37	46	30
13	Grimsby Town	34	33	46	30
14	Leicester Fosse	34	40	55	29
15	Blackpool	34	36	48	28
16	Burslem Port Vale	34	47	72	27
17	Burton United	34	30	84	20
18	Doncaster Rovers	34	23	81	8
		612	902	902	612

Attendances
Total   1,744,200 – 306 games
Average   5,700 per game

Goals
Total   902 – 306 games
Average   2.948 per game
Top scorer Sam Marsh (Bolton Wanderers) 26

Liverpool and Bolton Wanderers promoted to Division 1. Burslem Port Vale (21 votes) were re-elected, but Burton United (10) and Doncaster Rovers (4) were replaced by Leeds City (25) and Chelsea (20). Other unsuccessful applicants were Hull City (18), Crewe Alexandra (10), Stockport County (3) and Clapton Orient (1). A 2nd vote was held after it was decided to increase Division 2 to 20 clubs. Burton United (36 votes), Hull City (36), Clapton Orient (26) and Stockport County (26) were elected, while Doncaster Rovers (20) were unsuccessful.

OTHER INFORMATION

1902-1905

F.A. Cup 1902-1905

All F.A. Cup Finals 1903-1905 were staged at Crystal Palace in London. All the finalists were from the Football League.

Details of F.A. Cup Finals 1902-03 to 1904-05

18th April, 1903

Mr. J. Adams took charge of the match between Bury and Derby County which was watched by 63,102. Ross scored to give the Shakers a half-time lead. Derby County collapsed in the second period and Bury ran riot, adding a further five goals to create a record for the winning margin in a Final. Sagar, Leeming (2), Wood and Plant hit the second half goals.

23rd April, 1904

Manchester City beat Bolton Wanderers by 1-0 in an all-Lancashire affair which was attended by a crowd of 61,374. City wingman, Billy Meredith, hit the only goal of the game in the first half. The referee was Mr. A.J. Barker.

15th April, 1905

A massive crowd of 101,117 packed into Crystal Palace for the clash between Aston Villa and title-chasing Newcastle United. Villa adapted better to the atmosphere and led at half-time through Hampton. The same player went on to score again in the second half. There were no further goals and, when P.R. Harrower blew the final whistle, Aston Villa were Cup winners by 2-0.

Pitch/Rule changes

In 1902 the 'basic' modern goal and penalty areas were introduced, with the penalty spot set at 12 yards from goal. It was not until 1911, however, that the rule restricting goalkeepers' handling of the ball to the penalty area was brought in.

Attendances 1902-03 to 1904-05

Aston Villa received the largest support for seasons 1902-1904, with champions Newcastle United having the highest home following during their first title-winning campaign 1904-1905.

In the 2nd Division, Manchester City attracted the top home crowds during their promotion season, with Manchester United drawing the highest average number of spectators to their Bank Street home for the two years after that.

While top flight attendances continued to grow throughout the period, numbers watching 2nd Division games rose as far as 1904 and then fell back by an average of over 100. This can be largely explained by the collapse of support for West Bromwich Albion, whose relegation in 1904 cost them more than 8,500 spectators per game at The Hawthorns.

The overall trend, for the Football League as a whole, was consistently upwards.

The average attendance for a Football League fixture 1901-02 was 7,531. In the 1904-05 season the average was 9,519 – a mean rise of 1,988.

A World Game?

F.I.F.A. was set up at a meeting in Paris on May 21st, 1904. Representatives from 7 countries were present – Belgium, Denmark, France, Holland, Spain, Sweden and Switzerland. There was nobody at the meeting from Britain, the 'home unions' feeling far superior to their European counterparts.

Goal scoring 1902-1905

High scores in League matches had gradually become less common, but there were still some 'goalfests' around 1902-1905.

Division 1

1902-03
Liverpool hit the top score for the season by beating Grimsby Town 9-2 on December 6th.
1903-04
Sheffield United thrashed Wolves 7-2 on October 17th. This score was matched by Derby County against Sunderland on November 28th.
1904-05
Gigg Lane saw the highest individual club score on November 12th, when hosts Bury hammered Sheffield United 7-1.

Division 2

1902-03
Two sides racked up double figures in high-scoring wins. Chesterfield Town beat Glossop 10-0, but were outdone on April 11th when Small Heath swept aside Doncaster Rovers 12-0.
1903-04
Woolwich Arsenal ran up two 8-0 wins, beating Burton United on September 19th and Leicester Fosse on October 26th.
1904-05
On April 8th, championship-chasing Liverpool buried Burslem Port Vale 8-1.

The number of goals scored in both divisions rose 1902-1904, dropping during the following campaign. This trend was matched exactly by the pattern of percentage of Football League games with more than one goal scored.

The % of Football League matches in which more than 1 goal was scored were :

1902-03	78·26%
1903-04	78·59%
1904-05	77·94%

Transfer troubles

There was a major outcry in February 1905 when Middlesbrough, deep in relegation trouble, paid £1,000 to sign England international Alf Common from Sunderland. Middlesbrough's 'plan' worked and the club avoided relegation. Average transfer fees for top players at the time were around £400, though Sunderland had paid £500 when signing Common from Sheffield United.

New Rules

From 1903 goals could be scored direct from a free-kick awarded for 'intentional foul play'. The referee was also allowed to 'play advantage' at his own discretion. A year later, the F.A. passed a rule insisting that shorts 'must cover the knee'. In 1905, the laws on 'charging' were changed to curb 'violent and dangerous use of the practice'. Charging had to be of the 'good, honest type'.

FOOTBALL LEAGUE GROUNDS — 1902 - 1915

Eight League clubs moved during the period 1902-1915, raising the number of changes of address since the Football League began to 18.

The majority of teams listed have not moved since.

The lists below give the name of the ground each club was playing at in either 1915 or for its last season in the Football League. The date at which the club moved to this location is shown in brackets after the name of the ground.

Aston Villa	Villa Park (1897)
Barnsley	Oakwell (1888)
Birmingham*	St. Andrew's (December 1906)
Blackburn Rovers	Ewood Park (1890)
Blackpool	Bloomfield Road (1900)
Bolton Wanderers	Burnden Park (1895)
Bradford City	Valley Parade (1903)
Bradford Park Avenue	Park Avenue (1907)
Bristol City	Ashton Gate (April 1904)
Burnley	Turf Moor (1883)
Burslem Port Vale	Cobridge Athletic Ground (1886)
Burton United	Peel Croft (1890)
Bury	Gigg Lane (1885)
Chelsea	Stamford Bridge (1905)
Chesterfield Town	Recreation Ground (1887)
Clapton Orient	Millfields Road (1896)
Derby County	The Baseball Ground (1895)
Doncaster Rovers	Intake Ground (1885)
Everton	Goodison Park (1892)
Fulham	Craven Cottage (1894)
Gainsborough Trinity	Northolme (1884)
Glossop	North Road (1898)
Grimsby Town	Blundell Park (1899)
Huddersfield Town	Leeds Road (1907)
Hull City	Anlaby Road (March 1906)
Leeds City	Elland Road (1904)
Leicester Fosse	Walnut Street (1891)
Lincoln City	Sincil Bank (1895)
Liverpool	Anfield (1892)
Manchester City	Hyde Road (1887)
Manchester United**	Old Trafford (1910)
Middlesbrough	Ayresome Park (1903)
Newcastle United	St. James' Park (1892)
Nottingham Forest	City Ground (1898)
Notts County	Meadow Lane (1910)
Oldham Athletic	Boundary Park (1906)
Preston North End	Deepdale (1875)
Sheffield United	Bramall Lane (1889)
Sheffield Wednesday	Owlerton (1899)
Stockport County	Edgeley Park (1902)
Stoke	Victoria Ground (1883)
Sunderland	Roker Park (1898)
The Arsenal***	Manor Ground (1913)
Tottenham Hotspur	White Hart Lane (1899)
West Bromwich Albion	The Hawthorns (1900)
Wolverhampton Wanderers	Molineux (1889)

*   Birmingham also played as 'Small Heath'.
** Manchester United also played as 'Newton Heath'
***The Arsenal also played as 'Woolwich Arsenal'

1905-1906 – LEAGUE DIVISION 1

LIVERPOOL

With a 4-match, 100% start, Stoke were the unlikely 1st Division leaders by September 16th, marginally ahead of unbeaten Sheffield Wednesday. Both clubs won again a week later, swapping places because of the relative victory margins. The month ended with the Owls a point clear after a draw with Newcastle. Stoke moved down to third by losing at Blackburn while Derby beat Aston Villa to join the Potters on 10 points, but pass them on goal average. During the following 6 weeks, Newcastle showed the best form, winning 5 in a row, including an 8-0 rout of Wolves on November 11th. It was, however, Aston Villa who moved to the top by taking 11 points from 7 games, their 5 wins including a 3-0 defeat of Sheffield Wednesday, who were pushed into second place on November 13th by the Villains' 1-0 win at Stoke.

Over the next 2 weeks, Villa and Wednesday changed places a couple of times, both winning and losing a game each. With this form matched exactly by mid-November's third- and fourth-placed clubs, Derby County and Newcastle United, there was a chance for any mid-table side able to string a few wins together to enter the title reckoning. Liverpool did just this, their 4th successive victory, at Sheffield United on December 16th, taking the Anfield club a point clear at the top, an advantage doubled on Christmas Day through a draw with Bolton Wanderers.

Defeat at Stoke on Boxing Day proved only a slight setback and seven points from the next four games carried Liverpool four points clear as the close of January approached. Defeat at Birmingham provided a useful wake-up call for the Reds, however, and, by the middle of February, the leaders held a 3-point lead over Manchester City, with Preston North End and Sheffield Wednesday a point further behind in berths three and four.

Despite losing at home to Manchester City on March 3rd, Liverpool continued to dominate. Three March losses for City and victory over Preston on the 24th enabled the Reds to reach April with the 3-point advantage still in place. There were only six matches left to play and F.A. Cup semi-final defeat on March 31st increased Anfield determination for League success.

'Pool were a further point clear by the start of Easter. Even better was the fact that City were now 8 points adrift, having lost at Arsenal on April 8th. It seemed that only Preston now stood between Liverpool and the title. Defeat for North End at Stoke on April 14th left the North Lancashire side with a mountain to climb. When the Deepdale men lost again, at Sunderland, on Easter Monday, it was all over. Despite their April 16th reverse at Bolton, Liverpool became the new champions.

Liverpool's '1st half' record

September	02	Woolwich Arsenal	1-3
	09	BLACKBURN ROVERS	1-3
	11	Aston Villa	0-5
	16	Sunderland	2-1
	23	BIRMINGHAM	2-0
	30	Everton	2-4
October	07	DERBY COUNTY	4-1
	14	Sheffield Wednesday	2-3
	21	NOTTINGHAM FOREST	4-1
	28	Manchester City	1-0
November	04	BURY	3-1
	11	Middlesbrough	5-1
	18	PRESTON NORTH END	1-1
	25	Newcastle United	3-2
December	02	ASTON VILLA	3-0
	09	WOLVES	4-0
	16	Sheffield United	2-1
	23	NOTTS COUNTY	2-0
	25	BOLTON WANDERERS	2-2

Table at December 25th, 1905

1	LIVERPOOL	19	44	29	26
2	Aston Villa	19	39	20	24
3	Sheffield Wednesday	19	27	22	23
4	Preston North End	20	28	23	23
5	Birmingham	18	29	22	22
6	Manchester City	18	38	20	21
7	Blackburn Rovers	18	30	20	21
8	Newcastle United	19	41	29	21
9	Derby County	18	22	21	21
10	Stoke	20	23	25	20
11	Everton	18	42	34	19
12	Sheffield United	18	28	30	17
13	Notts County	19	29	41	17
14	Nottingham Forest	19	31	45	17
15	Bolton Wanderers	18	36	30	15
16	Woolwich Arsenal	19	26	34	15
17	Sunderland	18	25	34	14
18	Middlesbrough	18	28	39	14
19	Bury	19	28	45	12
20	Wolves	20	22	53	12
		374	616	616	374

Attendances
Total   5,055,245   Average   13,304
Goals
Total   1,242   Average   3.268
Top scorer   Albert Shepherd (Newcastle United) 26
380 games

Liverpool's '2nd half' record

December	26	Stoke	1-2
	30	WOOLWICH ARSENAL	3-0
January	01	STOKE	3-1
	06	Blackburn Rovers	0-0
	20	SUNDERLAND	2-0
	27	Birmingham	0-1
February	10	Derby County	3-0
	17	SHEFFIELD WEDNESDAY	2-1
March	03	MANCHESTER CITY	0-1
	14	Nottingham Forest	2-1
	17	MIDDLESBROUGH	6-1
	21	Notts County	0-3
	24	Preston North End	2-1
April	02	Bury	0-0
	09	NEWCASTLE UNITED	3-0
	13	EVERTON	1-1
	14	Wolves	2-0
	16	Bolton Wanderers	2-3
	21	SHEFFIELD UNITED	3-1

Final League Division 1 Table 1906

1	LIVERPOOL	38	79	46	51
2	Preston North End	38	54	39	47
3	Sheffield Wednesday	38	63	52	44
4	Newcastle United	38	74	48	43
5	Manchester City	38	73	54	43
6	Bolton Wanderers	38	81	67	41
7	Birmingham	38	65	59	41
8	Aston Villa	38	72	56	40
9	Blackburn Rovers	38	54	52	40
10	Stoke	38	54	55	39
11	Everton	38	70	66	37
12	Woolwich Arsenal	38	62	64	37
13	Sheffield United	38	57	62	36
14	Sunderland	38	61	70	35
15	Derby County	38	39	58	35
16	Notts County	38	55	71	34
17	Bury	38	57	74	32
18	Middlesbrough	38	56	71	31
19	Nottingham Forest	38	58	79	31
20	Wolves	38	58	99	23
		760	1242	1242	760

Nottingham Forest and Wolverhampton Wanderers were relegated. Although it is hard to tell whether this took place in December, in January or before the season, the Small Heath club was renamed as 'Birmingham'.

1905-1906 – LEAGUE DIVISION 2

BRISTOL CITY

Greatly disappointed by their late dip in form the previous season, which cost the club promotion, Manchester United began the season in style by thumping first-day visitors Bristol City 5-1. Five more September wins meant the Red Devils headed the 2nd Division table at the end of the month. Their closest rivals, perhaps surprisingly, were Bristol City, who had gone 100% since the debacle at Bank Street.

City leapfrogged to the top on October 14th when their 7th consecutive win carried them past United, who lost at West Bromwich. Both sides ended the month on 18 points, with United's superior goal average, which was due to that opening day score-line, meaning the Mancunians occupied first place.

When the Manchester team lost at Chesterfield on November 11th, the Robins returned to the top with an 11th straight win. The new leaders then ploughed on, reaching the half-way point in their season, on Boxing Day, with a 3-point lead over United, whose own form since mid-November had been excellent, with 5 wins, one draw and only 1 goal against in six matches played. Remarkably, Chelsea and West Bromwich Albion were still in touch with the two leaders, neither of whom could afford to relax despite exceptionally good first halves.

With honours even when the two sides met at Ashton Gate on December 30th, Bristol City and Manchester United continued to press the promotion pedal in the New Year. Both Chelsea and West Bromwich faltered in early February and, although United had dipped against Leeds City on January 15th and Bristol went down 1-2 to Leicester Fosse on February 17th, there seemed every chance that a gap might open up.

However, the third and fourth clubs each played 7 times between mid-February and March 31st, both picking up 12 points. Manchester United took 9 points from 6 games in this period and came under pressure in second place, unlike Bristol City, who won for the 25th time on March 31st and were now 6 points clear.

City were promoted on Easter Saturday, April 14th. By beating visitors Leeds City at Ashton Gate, the Robins moved onto 60 points and were out of third-placed Chelsea's reach. Top scorer Maxwell hit the first in the 2-0 win over Grimsby Town, three days later, which gave City a record number of Football League wins for a season with 28. On the following Saturday, April 21st, the 1-0 win at Burton United ensured that the 2nd Division trophy was lifted, with Manchester United no longer able to match City's total.

Bristol City's '1st half' record

September	02	Manchester United	1-5
	09	GLOSSOP	2-1
	16	Stockport County	3-2
	20	BRADFORD CITY	1-0
	23	BLACKPOOL	2-1
	30	Bradford City	2-1
October	07	WEST BROMWICH ALBION	1-0
	14	Leicester Fosse	2-1
	21	HULL CITY	2-1
	28	Lincoln City	3-0
November	04	CHESTERFIELD TOWN	3-1
	11	Burslem Port Vale	1-0
	18	BARNSLEY	3-0
	25	Clapton Orient	2-0
December	02	BURNLEY	2-0
	09	Leeds City	1-1
	16	BURTON UNITED	4-0
	23	Chelsea	0-0
	26	Gainsborough Trinity	3-1

Table at December 26th, 1905

1	BRISTOL CITY	19	38	15	34
2	Manchester United	19	37	12	31
3	Chelsea	19	36	10	28
4	West Bromwich Albion	18	39	13	27
5	Hull City	19	37	24	23
6	Leicester Fosse	20	28	22	23
7	Bradford City	20	26	26	22
8	Chesterfield Town	20	27	31	20
9	Burnley	19	20	22	19
10	Stockport County	18	25	26	17
11	Grimsby Town	17	18	19	17
12	Burton United	20	13	26	17
13	Leeds City	15	19	19	16
14	Barnsley	18	24	35	13
15	Blackpool	18	17	27	13
16	Glossop	19	24	37	12
17	Port Vale	19	23	41	12
18	Lincoln City	20	29	45	11
19	Gainsborough Trinity	19	21	33	10
20	Clapton Orient	18	16	34	9
		374	517	517	374

Attendances
Total 2,283,325   Average 6,009
Goals
Total 1,116   Average 2.937
Top scorer   Billy Maxwell (Bristol City) 25
380 games

Bristol City's '2nd half' record

December	27	Grimsby Town	1-1
	30	MANCHESTER UNITED	1-1
January	06	Glossop	5-1
	20	STOCKPORT COUNTY	7-0
	27	Blackpool	3-1
February	10	West Bromwich Albion	3-1
	17	LEICESTER FOSSE	1-2
	24	Hull City	3-0
March	03	LINCOLN CITY	1-0
	10	Chesterfield Town	2-1
	17	BURSLEM PORT VALE	4-0
	24	Barnsley	2-2
	31	CLAPTON ORIENT	1-0
April	07	Burnley	2-2
	13	GAINSBOROUGH TRINITY	2-0
	14	LEEDS CITY	2-0
	17	GRIMSBY TOWN	2-0
	21	Burton United	1-0
	28	CHELSEA	2-1

Final League Division 2 Table 1906

1	BRISTOL CITY	38	83	28	66
2	Manchester United	38	90	28	62
3	Chelsea	38	90	37	53
4	West Bromwich Albion	38	79	36	52
5	Hull City	38	67	54	44
6	Leeds City	38	59	47	43
7	Leicester Fosse	38	53	48	42
8	Grimsby Town	38	46	46	40
9	Burnley	38	42	53	38
10	Stockport County	38	44	56	35
11	Bradford City	38	46	60	34
12	Barnsley	38	60	62	33
13	Lincoln City	38	69	72	30
14	Blackpool	38	37	62	29
15	Gainsborough Trinity	38	44	57	28
16	Glossop	38	49	71	28
17	Burslem Port Vale	38	49	82	28
18	Chesterfield Town	38	40	72	28
19	Burton United	38	34	67	26
20	Clapton Orient	38	35	78	21
		760	1116	1116	760

Bristol City and Manchester United promoted to Division 1. Chesterfield Town (36 votes), Burton United (32) and Clapton Orient (21) were all re-elected. Oldham Athletic (20) missed out narrowly, while Wigan Town (5) were also unsuccessful.

- 45 -

1906-1907 – LEAGUE DIVISION 1 — NEWCASTLE UNITED

Five wins in their first six games enabled Aston Villa to go clear at the top of the 1st Division before the end of September. Woolwich Arsenal moved into second by beating Newcastle United on September 22nd and the Gunners' draw at Villa a week later suggested that the South had at last produced a team which could mount a serious bid for Football League honours. In third place, Newcastle United had also started well. A week later, things got even better for the Manor Ground men. Having beaten Liverpool 2-1, Arsenal ended October 6th in first place, on goal average, because Villa lost at Sheffield Wednesday. Wins over Bristol City and Notts County kept Woolwich at the top over the next fortnight, but, on October 27th, they lost 2-4 at Sheffield United and were passed by Everton, whose 3-1 success at Bolton Wanderers was their fifth win on the bounce.

Between the end of October and Christmas, four teams vied for the League leadership. Successive defeats for both Sheffield Wednesday and Woolwich Arsenal in December meant, however, that Everton and Newcastle United occupied the top two spots. The Toffees went clear on Christmas Day with a 2-1 win at Bury, while Newcastle finished well-beaten at Blackburn Rovers.

The battle for honours turned into a private contest between the top two in the New Year, with Everton going 3 points clear on January 19th by beating the Geordies 3-0 at Goodison Park. The Tyneside men quickly turned the tables, however, taking advantage of successive reverses for Everton at Villa and Bristol City to take a 3-point lead by winning three in a row by February 9th. By the end of March, Newcastle's lead was up to 6 points. Everton's preoccupation with the F.A. Cup meant the Geordies played 3 more League games than their rivals in this period, picking up 10 points to the Goodison club's 7. Two points behind Everton were Aston Villa and Bristol City, but neither of these was seen as a major threat. As if to confirm this, Newcastle beat the Robins easily at St. James' Park on March 30th.

Duffy, Appleyard and Speedie were on target as Newcastle reached 50 points by beating Blackburn Rovers 3-1 on April 1st. Everton lost at Birmingham and Blackburn during the next week, but beat the fading Woolwich Arsenal on April 10th to prolong matters. Newcastle United secured the point needed to become champions for the second time on April 13th, with a 0-0 draw against Sheffield United.

Newcastle United's '1st half' record

Month	Date	Opponent	Score
September	01	SUNDERLAND	4-2
	03	Sheffield Wednesday	2-2
	08	Birmingham	4-2
	15	EVERTON	1-0
	22	Woolwich Arsenal	0-2
	29	SHEFFIELD WEDNESDAY	5-1
October	06	Bury	2-3
	13	MANCHESTER CITY	2-0
	20	Middlesbrough	3-0
	27	PRESTON NORTH END	2-1
November	03	Derby County	0-0
	10	Aston Villa	0-0
	17	LIVERPOOL	2-0
	24	Bristol City	1-2
December	01	NOTTS COUNTY	4-3
	08	Sheffield United	0-0
	15	BOLTON WANDERERS	4-0
	22	Manchester United	3-1
	25	Blackburn Rovers	0-4

Newcastle United's '2nd half' record

Month	Date	Opponent	Score
December	26	Stoke	2-1
January	01	DERBY COUNTY	2-0
	05	BIRMINGHAM	2-0
	19	Everton	0-3
	26	WOOLWICH ARSENAL	1-0
February	02	MANCHESTER UNITED	5-0
	09	BURY	3-2
	16	Manchester City	1-1
	23	MIDDLESBROUGH	4-0
March	02	Preston North End	2-2
	16	ASTON VILLA	3-2
	20	Sunderland	0-2
	23	Liverpool	1-4
	29	STOKE	1-0
	30	BRISTOL CITY	3-0
April	01	BLACKBURN ROVERS	3-1
	06	Notts County	0-1
	13	SHEFFIELD UNITED	0-0
	20	Bolton Wanderers	2-4

Table at December 25th, 1906

1	Everton	20	42	19	28
2	NEWCASTLE UNITED	19	39	23	26
3	Aston Villa	20	41	30	25
4	Sheffield Wednesday	19	33	25	24
5	Woolwich Arsenal	18	33	26	23
6	Bristol City	19	36	28	22
7	Sheffield United	18	31	29	21
8	Birmingham	19	29	28	20
9	Preston North End	18	27	28	20
10	Liverpool	19	36	28	19
11	Sunderland	18	25	25	19
12	Bolton Wanderers	18	25	29	18
13	Manchester United	19	23	34	17
14	Blackburn Rovers	19	31	31	16
15	Derby County	20	20	26	16
16	Manchester City	19	25	40	15
17	Bury	20	33	41	14
18	Stoke	21	22	34	14
19	Middlesbrough	18	23	34	12
20	Notts County	19	15	31	11
		380	589	589	380

Attendances
Total 5,836,325 Average 15,359
Goals
Total 1,148 Average 3.021
Top scorer Alec Young (Everton) 28
380 games

Final League Division 1 Table 1907

1	NEWCASTLE UNITED	38	74	46	51
2	Bristol City	38	66	47	48
3	Everton	38	70	46	45
4	Sheffield United	38	57	55	45
5	Aston Villa	38	78	52	44
6	Bolton Wanderers	38	59	47	44
7	Woolwich Arsenal	38	66	59	44
8	Manchester United	38	53	56	42
9	Birmingham	38	52	52	38
10	Sunderland	38	65	66	37
11	Middlesbrough	38	56	63	36
12	Blackburn Rovers	38	56	59	35
13	Sheffield Wednesday	38	49	60	35
14	Preston North End	38	44	57	35
15	Liverpool	38	64	65	33
16	Bury	38	58	68	32
17	Manchester City	38	53	77	32
18	Notts County	38	46	50	31
19	Derby County	38	41	59	27
20	Stoke	38	41	64	26
		760	1148	1148	760

Derby County and Stoke relegated.

English soccer was rocked before the start of the season by the suspension of 6 Manchester City players pending investigations into allegations of illegal payments. Top players resented the maximum wage rules and there were moves to start a Players' Union, with City's suspended Billy Meredith a leading figure.

1906-1907 – LEAGUE DIVISION 2

NOTTINGHAM FOREST

Chelsea and Leicester Fosse made bright starts to their campaigns, leading the table at September 30th, with 9 points each. Tucked in behind them, one point worse off, were Hull City and West Bromwich. Albion enjoyed an excellent October, with 3 wins and a draw to go top, 2 points ahead of Chelsea, Leicester and improving Nottingham Forest, whose 6 wins in 7 matches had made up for a disappointing opening in which only 1 point had been won in the first 3 games.

When West Bromwich Albion lost 1-2 at Blackpool on November 10th, Forest pulled level on points with the Throstles, but had to settle for second place due to their inferior goal average. That is how things stayed until December 1st, when Albion crashed 0-3 away to Leicester Fosse, enabling Nottingham Forest to go clear by beating Bradford City. A week later, West Bromwich beat the City Ground men to reclaim top spot, but dipped 1-2 at Lincoln City on December 15th, which let Forest in again after a fine 2-1 victory over Leicester. Things remained close at the top though.

By New Year, things had changed. Forest played and lost once, Chelsea won their one game and Leicester and West Bromwich picked up 4 points from 2 wins. The Reds were now fourth, 3 points off the lead. By the time Forest won 2-0 at Stamford Bridge on the 9th of February the picture had changed again. Victory took the Reds second, pegging back the threatened Chelsea breakaway. West Bromwich and Leicester, in contrast, had both failed to win since December 29th.

By the end of March, the leading pair had opened up a 6-point gap between themselves and 3rd place. Chelsea, having played 2 games more, led on goal average. The Blues' 3 defeats – at Grimsby, Bradford and Barnsley – had enabled Forest to pull level, on 49 points, with a 3-0 win at Blackpool on March 30th. By April 2nd, Forest led by 3 points. On April 6th, Shearman's brace secured the points at Bradford and guaranteed Forest's promotion. Victory at Leicester on April 20th ensured the club of the Division 2 title. Fittingly the key goals were scored by top two marksmen, Grenville Morris and Enoch West.

Nottingham Forest's '1st half' record

September	01	Grimsby Town	1-3
	08	BURSLEM PORT VALE	2-2
	15	Burnley	1-2
	22	LEEDS CITY	3-0
	29	Barnsley	1-0
October	04	CHESTERFIELD TOWN	3-1
	06	CHELSEA	3-1
	13	Wolves	0-2
	20	CLAPTON ORIENT	4-0
	27	Gainsborough Trinity	3-2
November	03	STOCKPORT COUNTY	2-1
	10	Hull City	2-1
	17	GLOSSOP	2-0
	24	Blackpool	2-1
December	01	BRADFORD CITY	3-0
	08	West Bromwich Albion	1-3
	15	LEICESTER FOSSE	2-1
	22	Chesterfield Town	1-1
	25	BURTON UNITED	2-0

Nottingham Forest's '2nd half' record

December	29	GRIMSBY TOWN	0-3
January	05	Burslem Port Vale	2-4
	19	BURNLEY	2-0
	26	Leeds City	4-1
February	09	Chelsea	2-0
	16	WOLVES	1-0
	23	Clapton Orient	1-0
March	02	GAINSBOROUGH TRINITY	3-1
	09	Stockport County	0-0
	16	HULL CITY	2-1
	23	Glossop	2-0
	29	Lincoln City	2-1
	30	BLACKPOOL	3-0
April	01	Burton United	2-0
	02	BARNSLEY	0-0
	06	Bradford City	2-1
	13	WEST BROMWICH ALBION	3-1
	20	Leicester Fosse	2-1
	24	LINCOLN CITY	3-1

Table at December 25th, 1906

1	NOTTINGHAM FOREST	19	38	21	28
2	West Bromwich Albion	19	52	20	27
3	Chelsea	18	34	15	27
4	Leicester Fosse	19	35	15	26
5	Bradford City	19	27	24	23
6	Hull City	18	30	18	22
7	Burnley	19	30	19	21
8	Gainsborough Trinity	20	25	31	21
9	Wolves	19	30	28	20
10	Stockport County	18	22	24	20
11	Port Vale	18	36	40	17
12	Clapton Orient	17	24	29	15
13	Lincoln City	19	21	31	15
14	Barnsley	18	30	23	14
15	Leeds City	19	24	32	14
16	Blackpool	19	15	28	13
17	Glossop	17	23	48	13
18	Grimsby Town	18	20	33	12
19	Chesterfield Town	19	18	30	12
20	Burton United	18	14	39	10
		370	548	548	370

Final League Division 2 Table 1907

1	NOTTINGHAM FOREST	38	74	36	60
2	Chelsea	38	80	34	57
3	Leicester Fosse	38	62	39	48
4	West Bromwich Albion	38	83	45	47
5	Bradford City	38	70	53	47
6	Wolves	38	66	53	41
7	Burnley	38	62	47	40
8	Barnsley	38	73	55	38
9	Hull City	38	65	57	37
10	Leeds City	38	55	63	36
11	Grimsby Town	38	57	62	35
12	Stockport County	38	42	52	35
13	Blackpool	38	33	51	33
14	Gainsborough Trinity	38	45	72	33
15	Glossop	38	53	79	32
16	Burslem Port Vale	38	60	83	31
17	Clapton Orient	38	45	67	30
18	Chesterfield Town	38	50	66	29
19	Lincoln City	38	46	73	28
20	Burton United	38	34	68	23
		760	1155	1155	760

Attendances
Total 2,536,025   Average 6,674
Goals
Total 1,155   Average 3.039
Top scorer   Fred Shinton (West Bromwich Albion) 28
380 games

Nottingham Forest and Chelsea promoted to Division 1. Lincoln City (28 votes) and Chesterfield Town (23) were re-elected, but Burton United (7) were replaced by Fulham (28). Unsuccessful clubs were Oldham Athletic (17), Bradford Park Avenue (11), Rotherham Town (0), Salford United (0) and Wigan Town (0). Burslem Port Vale then resigned from the Football League. Burton United applied to replace Vale, but the vacant place was given instead to Oldham Athletic.

1907-1908 – LEAGUE DIVISION 1

For the neutral, September 1907 proved to be the most interesting month of the 1st Division season. Manchester United opened with 3 wins, but lost at Middlesbrough on September 14th. Two days later, the Red Devils were replaced at the top of the table by Bury, who completed a second 1-0 win in 3 days over an already struggling Birmingham. United were back at the summit on 21st September, after Bury crashed 1-6 at Everton and Sheffield United had been beaten.

The leaders were, however, passed again, on September 23rd, by The Wednesday, who beat Bristol City 5-3 at Owlerton. 5 days later, the Owls lost at Manchester City, while United strolled to their fifth campaign win at Chelsea and regained the league lead.

From then on, the Bank Street club cruised ahead. By November 16th, following a further 7 successive wins, United led by 5 points from Wednesday. Defeat at the Owls' ground on November 30th was a mere blip in the Red Devils' progress. The leaders completed the half-way stage in their fixture list 9 points ahead of Sheffield Wednesday and Newcastle United.

Manchester United's '1st half' record

September	02	Aston Villa	4-1
	07	LIVERPOOL	4-0
	09	MIDDLESBROUGH	2-1
	14	Middlesbrough	1-2
	21	SHEFFIELD UNITED	2-1
	28	Chelsea	4-1
October	05	NOTTINGHAM FOREST	4-0
	12	Newcastle United	6-1
	19	Blackburn Rovers	5-1
	26	BOLTON WANDERERS	2-1
November	02	Birmingham	4-3
	09	EVERTON	4-3
	16	Sunderland	2-1
	23	WOOLWICH ARSENAL	4-2
	30	Sheffield Wednesday	0-2
December	07	BRISTOL CITY	2-1
	14	Notts County	1-1
	21	MANCHESTER CITY	3-1
	25	BURY	2-1

Table at December 25th, 1907

1	MANCHESTER UNITED	19	56	24	33
2	Newcastle United	19	41	26	24
3	Sheffield Wednesday	18	39	26	24
4	Bury	20	36	32	23
5	Bristol City	19	38	36	21
6	Everton	18	37	31	19
7	Aston Villa	19	35	36	19
8	Notts County	20	22	28	19
9	Manchester City	17	33	30	18
10	Preston North End	19	29	31	18
11	Woolwich Arsenal	19	26	30	18
12	Liverpool	18	35	32	16
13	Blackburn Rovers	18	24	32	16
14	Chelsea	19	30	41	16
15	Middlesbrough	19	19	26	16
16	Sheffield United	17	28	30	15
17	Bolton Wanderers	17	25	33	15
18	Nottingham Forest	18	28	37	14
19	Sunderland	19	33	39	13
20	Birmingham	18	21	35	13
		370	635	635	370

Attendances
Total 6,170,725   Average 16,239
Goals
Total 1,176   Average 3.095
Top scorer   Enoch West (Nottingham Forest) 26
380 games

MANCHESTER UNITED

Crucial to Manchester United's success were four former Manchester City stars – Bannister, Burgess, Meredith and Turnbull, all signed on January 1st, 1907, after their suspensions over alleged illegal payments were lifted. United were not upset by Meredith's role in setting up the Players' Union on December 2nd and supported his lead in challenging the maximum wage. The other major issue in English soccer at the time concerned transfers. In January 1908, the F.A. set a limit of £350 on transfer fees and capped any monies paid to transferred players. Leading clubs like United wanted nothing to do with such arrangements and worked with the Players' Union to undermine these rules, which were abolished in April, having failed to work.

By the start of April, Manchester United were well on their way to the title, despite 4 defeats, including a bizarre 4-7 reverse at Liverpool. Second-placed Newcastle United lay 7 points adrift, having played a game more and went out of contention by losing 3 times by April 8th. Defeats for both Manchester City and Sheffield Wednesday on April 11th sealed things.

Manchester United's '2nd half' record

December	28	Preston North End	0-0
January	01	Bury	1-0
	18	Sheffield United	0-2
	25	CHELSEA	1-0
February	08	NEWCASTLE UNITED	1-1
	15	BLACKBURN ROVERS	1-2
	29	BIRMINGHAM	1-0
March	14	SUNDERLAND	3-0
	21	Woolwich Arsenal	0-1
	25	Liverpool	4-7
	28	SHEFFIELD WEDNESDAY	4-1
April	04	Bristol City	1-1
	08	Everton	3-1
	11	NOTTS COUNTY	0-1
	17	Nottingham Forest	0-2
	18	Manchester City	0-0
	20	ASTON VILLA	1-2
	22	Bolton Wanderers	2-2
	25	PRESTON NORTH END	2-1

Final League Division 1 Table 1908

1	MANCHESTER UNITED	38	81	48	52
2	Aston Villa	38	77	59	43
3	Manchester City	38	62	54	43
4	Newcastle United	38	65	54	42
5	Sheffield Wednesday	38	73	64	42
6	Middlesbrough	38	54	45	41
7	Bury	38	58	61	39
8	Liverpool	38	68	61	38
9	Nottingham Forest	38	59	62	37
10	Bristol City	38	58	61	36
11	Everton	38	58	64	36
12	Preston North End	38	47	53	36
13	Chelsea	38	53	62	36
14	Blackburn Rovers	38	51	63	36
	Woolwich Arsenal	38	51	63	36
16	Sunderland	38	78	75	35
17	Sheffield United	38	52	58	35
18	Notts County	38	39	51	34
19	Bolton Wanderers	38	52	58	33
20	Birmingham	38	40	60	30
		760	1176	1176	760

Bolton Wanderers and Birmingham relegated.

1907-1908 – LEAGUE DIVISION 2

The struggle to become champions of Division 2 proved to be a tough and interesting contest all through. The League table at the end of September showed Hull City one point up on Leeds City, with Stockport County and Gainsborough Trinity sitting in the next two places. None of these sides was to play a major part in the battle for the title. Hull City remained in contention by mid-November, trailing Oldham Athletic on goal average, with West Bromwich Albion and Leicester Fosse beginning to show the sort of form which had made them promotion contenders a year earlier.

Although Leicester drifted off the pace by losing three of their next four games, the other three clubs moved neck-and-neck to the end of 1907. Joining the top trio by December were Bradford City and Derby County, whose run of eight wins in 10 games from November 16th saw them top of the pile as the New Year was reached. With just six points covering the top eight teams, however, it was clear that there would be plenty to play for in 1908.

Bradford City's '1st half' record

September	07	CHESTERFIELD TOWN	8-1
	14	Burnley	1-2
	21	OLDHAM ATHLETIC	1-0
	28	Clapton Orient	3-0
October	05	LEEDS CITY	5-0
	12	Wolves	0-0
	19	GAINSBOROUGH TRINITY	7-1
	26	Stockport County	1-1
November	02	GLOSSOP	2-1
	09	Leicester Fosse	1-2
	16	BLACKPOOL	3-0
	23	Stoke	0-3
	30	WEST BROMWICH ALBION	0-0
December	07	Grimsby Town	1-0
	14	Hull City	2-0
	21	DERBY COUNTY	3-1
	25	BARNSLEY	2-0
	26	FULHAM	1-3
	28	Lincoln City	4-2

Table at December 28th, 1907

1	Derby County	20	49	19	29
2	West Bromwich Albion	21	37	18	28
3	Oldham Athletic	19	37	21	28
4	Hull City	22	39	31	28
5	BRADFORD CITY	19	45	17	27
6	Fulham	20	44	28	25
7	Burnley	21	39	30	25
8	Leicester Fosse	20	36	28	23
9	Stoke	21	35	25	22
10	Stockport County	20	25	26	21
11	Wolves	21	21	21	20
12	Clapton Orient	20	26	36	19
13	Leeds City	19	33	41	18
14	Barnsley	19	29	28	16
15	Gainsborough Trinity	21	26	45	16
16	Glossop	17	27	35	14
17	Grimsby Town	21	23	46	12
18	Chesterfield Town	19	22	51	12
19	Blackpool	20	29	42	10
20	Lincoln City	20	25	59	7
		400	647	647	400

Attendances
Total 2,942,625   Average   7,744
Goals
Total 1,187   Average   3.124
Top scorer   Jack Smith (Hull City) 31
380 games

BRADFORD CITY

The Rams continued to impress throughout the first few weeks of 1908, reaching St. Valentine's Day ahead of Bradford on goal average and 2 points up on Oldham Athletic. Fulham, having gone 7 matches unbeaten, were now 4th. Hull City and West Bromwich Albion had both dropped 4 points in 4 games, but were still in touch at this stage. None of the top six looked particularly convincing over the next few weeks. At the end of March, Bradford City headed Oldham on goal average, with Derby County in third, a point behind with a game in hand.

On the same 42-point mark as the Rams were Leicester Fosse, whose 11-match unbeaten run had forced them back into the reckoning. By mid-April, the top 3 all had 46 points to Leicester's 44. Derby lost at Lincoln on Good Friday and fell 4 points behind Bradford the next day, April 18th, by losing at home to their rivals. Other Easter scores went City's way. Promotion on April 20th was followed by the club becoming champions, after beating the bottom club, Lincoln City, 2-0 on the 25th.

Bradford City's '2nd half' record

January	01	Barnsley	2-1
	04	Chesterfield Town	1-1
	18	Oldham Athletic	0-4
	25	CLAPTON ORIENT	1-0
February	01	Leeds City	1-0
	08	WOLVES	6-2
	15	Gainsborough Trinity	5-1
	22	STOCKPORT COUNTY	5-0
	29	Glossop	2-2
March	07	LEICESTER FOSSE	1-5
	14	Blackpool	1-2
	21	STOKE	6-0
	28	West Bromwich Albion	2-3
April	04	GRIMSBY TOWN	1-1
	11	HULL CITY	2-1
	17	Fulham	2-0
	18	Derby County	3-2
	20	BURNLEY	2-0
	25	LINCOLN CITY	2-0

Final League Division 2 Table 1908

1	BRADFORD CITY	38	90	42	54
2	Leicester Fosse	38	72	47	52
3	Oldham Athletic	38	76	42	50
4	Fulham	38	82	49	49
5	West Bromwich Albion	38	61	39	47
6	Derby County	38	77	45	46
7	Burnley	38	67	50	46
8	Hull City	38	73	62	46
9	Wolves	38	50	45	37
10	Stoke	38	57	52	37
11	Gainsborough Trinity	38	47	71	35
12	Leeds City	38	53	65	32
13	Stockport County	38	48	67	32
14	Clapton Orient	38	40	65	32
15	Blackpool	38	51	58	31
16	Barnsley	38	54	68	30
17	Glossop	38	54	74	30
18	Grimsby Town	38	43	71	30
19	Chesterfield Town	38	46	92	23
20	Lincoln City	38	46	83	21
		760	1187	1187	760

Bradford City and Leicester Fosse promoted to Division 1. Grimsby Town (32 votes) and Chesterfield Town (23) were both re-elected, but Lincoln City (18) were replaced by Bradford Park Avenue (20). Tottenham Hotspur (14) and Burton United (1) were unsuccessful. Cash-strapped Stoke later resigned, in the close season, but then tried to give back word on this. At a Special General Meeting, Tottenham and Lincoln City tied 20-20 twice, with Stoke a poor third, with 6 votes, in the first ballot. Hotspur were then elected 5-3 by the Management Committee.

- 49 -

1908-1909 – LEAGUE DIVISION 1

The season got off to its almost inevitably disjointed start on Tuesday, September 1st, with five matches. Two more games were played the day after, leaving 6 teams not launching their campaigns until September 5th, the first Saturday of the 1908-09 season. Newcastle's 5 straight wins saw the Magpies top at September 19th, but defeat at Sheffield Wednesday a week later let in reigning champions Manchester United, whose 3-2 defeat of Liverpool took them top, on goal average, where they stayed until October 17th. Defeat for United at Villa meant that Everton, 5-1 winners at Sheffield United, went into first place.

By mid-November Everton held a 2-point lead from Newcastle. Everton stretched their lead to 4 points on December 5th with a 3-2 win over United, while 2nd-placed Newcastle crashed bizarrely at home to Sunderland. Eight goals in 28 crazy second-half minutes saw the Roker men triumph 9-1. Quite how manager Frank Watt lifted the Geordies remains a mystery, but the deficit at the top was cut to 2 points by the end of Christmas Day.

NEWCASTLE UNITED

Newcastle lost at Manchester United on Boxing Day, but then embarked on a 12-game unbeaten run, which burned off all their rivals. First to fall in this sequence were Everton, on January 2nd, Jimmy Howie's winner slashing the Toffees' lead to 1 point. When Everton were held at home by Middlesbrough on January 23rd, the Geordies eased into top spot with a 4-0 demolition of Notts County. Albert Shepherd hit all four. From then on it was cruise control time as Newcastle pulled away at the head of Division 1.

A 4-point lead at mid-February had become a six-point advantage by the end of March. Everton lost at home to Bradford City on April 3rd, but hammered neighbours Liverpool 5-0 on Good Friday, before drawing 2-2 at Manchester United a day later, April 10th. Newcastle lost at Sunderland that same afternoon and still needed two points to take the title. Two days later, on April 12th, Everton visited Tyneside for an Easter Monday fixture. McCracken opened the scoring, Stewart added two more, and Newcastle won 3-0 to take the title for the third time in 5 years.

Newcastle United's '1st half' record

September	02	BRADFORD CITY	1-0
	05	LEICESTER FOSSE	2-0
	09	BRISTOL CITY	2-1
	12	Woolwich Arsenal	2-1
	19	NOTTS COUNTY	1-0
	26	Sheffield Wednesday	0-2
October	03	Bristol City	3-3
	10	PRESTON NORTH END	2-0
	17	Middlesbrough	0-0
	24	MANCHESTER CITY	2-0
	31	Liverpool	1-2
November	07	BURY	3-1
	14	Sheffield United	1-1
	21	ASTON VILLA	0-2
	28	Nottingham Forest	4-0
December	05	SUNDERLAND	1-9
	12	Chelsea	2-1
	19	BLACKBURN ROVERS	2-0
	25	MANCHESTER UNITED	2-1

Newcastle United's '2nd half' record

December	26	Manchester United	0-1
January	01	Everton	1-0
	02	Leicester Fosse	4-0
	09	WOOLWICH ARSENAL	3-1
	23	Notts County	4-0
	30	SHEFFIELD WEDNESDAY	1-0
February	13	Preston North End	1-0
	27	Manchester City	2-0
March	13	Bury	1-1
	20	SHEFFIELD UNITED	4-0
	23	Bradford City	2-1
	31	MIDDLESBROUGH	1-0
April	03	NOTTINGHAM FOREST	1-1
	10	Sunderland	1-3
	12	EVERTON	3-0
	17	CHELSEA	1-3
	24	Blackburn Rovers	4-2
	26	Aston Villa	0-3
	30	LIVERPOOL	0-1

Table at December 25th, 1908

1	Everton	19	48	23	29
2	NEWCASTLE UNITED	19	31	24	27
3	Manchester United	18	40	31	24
4	Sheffield Wednesday	18	31	24	23
5	Bristol City	19	23	24	22
6	Liverpool	20	32	32	20
7	Notts County	17	22	16	19
8	Aston Villa	18	24	23	19
9	Blackburn Rovers	18	23	23	19
10	Sunderland	18	38	25	18
11	Manchester City	18	32	33	17
12	Middlesbrough	18	27	27	16
13	Woolwich Arsenal	19	23	27	16
14	Sheffield United	19	25	30	16
15	Chelsea	20	26	37	16
16	Preston North End	18	21	22	15
17	Bury	19	31	47	15
18	Nottingham Forest	19	28	34	14
19	Leicester Fosse	18	23	38	13
20	Bradford City	18	17	25	12
		370	565	565	370

Attendances
Total 5,973,125   Average   15,719
Goals
Total 1,185   Average   3.118
Top scorer   Bert Freeman (Everton) 36
380 games

Final League Division 1 Table 1909

1	NEWCASTLE UNITED	38	65	41	53
2	Everton	38	82	57	46
3	Sunderland	38	78	63	44
4	Blackburn Rovers	38	61	50	41
5	Sheffield Wednesday	38	67	61	40
6	Woolwich Arsenal	38	52	49	38
7	Aston Villa	38	58	56	38
8	Bristol City	38	45	58	38
9	Middlesbrough	38	59	53	37
10	Preston North End	38	48	44	37
11	Chelsea	38	56	61	37
12	Sheffield United	38	51	59	37
13	Manchester United	38	58	68	37
14	Nottingham Forest	38	66	57	36
15	Notts County	38	51	48	36
16	Liverpool	38	57	65	36
17	Bury	38	63	77	36
18	Bradford City	38	47	47	34
19	Manchester City	38	67	69	34
20	Leicester Fosse	38	54	102	25
		760	1185	1185	760

Manchester City and Leicester Fosse relegated. An investigation into Leicester Fosse's 0-12 dip at Forest on April 21st revealed that the losing side were feeling the effects of celebrating the marriage of a team-mate. Already relegated, the Fosse team had not been bribed. Manchester City were not impressed as the result meant they went down.

1908-1909 – LEAGUE DIVISION 2

BOLTON WANDERERS

Dropping only one point in their opening six games, Birmingham led the 2nd Division table at the end of September, two points ahead of second-placed Bolton Wanderers, who had played a game more. Derby County occupied third place, with Blackpool fourth. Having drawn three and lost one of their opening matches, West Bromwich Albion emerged as one of the form teams in the next phase of the action as most of the leading teams experienced problems. Albion's 3-0 win over Tottenham Hotspur enabled manager Fred Everiss' men to push past rivals Birmingham, on goal average, on November 7th.

When the Blues folded 0-4 at White Hart Lane a week later, the Throstles' draw at Hull City took them a point clear. As Birmingham faded, Tottenham Hotspur and Bolton Wanderers became the main challengers to West Bromwich Albion. Four wins for The Hawthorns club by December 19th carried the leaders into the Christmas holiday period with a three-point advantage at the top of the table, however, and they were looking ominously strong.

Albion were four points clear by New Year and a 7-0 drubbing of Grimsby Town on January 2nd suggested the leaders were going to be hard to knock off the top. Bolton and Spurs could only hope for a dip in the front runners' form. This came soon enough, with Albion failing to score in their next 4 games and dropping 6 points. Wanderers failed to profit from this, losing 3 in a row, and it was Spurs who went second, beating Bolton on January 23rd in the process. The Burnden Park men then recovered, stringing together 6 consecutive wins to end March level with West Bromwich on 43 points, 2 more than Hotspur.

Defeat at West Bromwich Albion on April 12th left Bolton third, however, 2 points off the lead. After the games played on April 24th, Albion had 51 points, with Spurs and Bolton on 50. All 3 clubs had 1 match left, with, strangely, Derby County being the opponent. On April 26th, the Rams beat Albion, then drew with Spurs 2 days later. Wanderers visited The Baseball Ground on April 30th. Billy Hughes' goal gave Bolton victory and a remarkable last-gasp title win.

Bolton Wanderers' '1st half' record

September	02	Birmingham	0-2
	05	Barnsley	1-0
	12	GAINSBOROUGH TRINITY	4-0
	14	HULL CITY	1-0
	15	WEST BROMWICH ALBION	1-1
	19	Tottenham Hotspur	1-2
	26	GRIMSBY TOWN	2-0
October	03	Hull City	0-2
	10	FULHAM	0-0
	17	Derby County	0-1
	24	BURNLEY	2-1
	31	Blackpool	2-1
November	07	BRADFORD PARK AVENUE	0-1
	14	Chesterfield Town	2-0
	21	WOLVES	1-1
	28	Glossop	2-0
December	05	OLDHAM ATHLETIC	3-0
	12	Stockport County	0-1
	19	CLAPTON ORIENT	2-0

Bolton Wanderers' '2nd half' record

December	25	LEEDS CITY	2-0
	26	Leeds City	2-1
January	01	BIRMINGHAM	2-1
	02	BARNSLEY	3-0
	09	Gainsborough Trinity	1-2
	23	TOTTENHAM HOTSPUR	0-1
	30	Grimsby Town	0-1
February	13	Fulham	2-1
	20	CHESTERFIELD TOWN	4-0
	27	Burnley	2-1
March	06	BLACKPOOL	3-1
	13	Bradford Park Avenue	2-1
	27	Wolves	2-1
April	03	GLOSSOP	2-0
	10	Oldham Athletic	1-1
	12	West Bromwich Albion	0-2
	17	STOCKPORT COUNTY	4-1
	24	Clapton Orient	2-0
	30	DERBY COUNTY	1-0

Table at December 19th, 1908

1	West Bromwich Albion	18	28	12	27
2	Tottenham Hotspur	17	32	12	24
3	BOLTON WANDERERS	19	24	13	23
4	Stockport County	17	21	24	22
5	Derby County	18	24	18	21
6	Birmingham	18	28	26	21
7	Hull City	18	25	16	20
8	Leeds City	17	24	22	20
9	Fulham	17	31	23	19
10	Glossop	17	25	22	19
11	Oldham Athletic	16	32	20	17
12	Wolves	19	28	28	16
13	Burnley	18	28	35	15
14	Chesterfield Town	17	18	27	15
15	Blackpool	17	19	26	14
16	Grimsby Town	17	18	27	13
17	Clapton Orient	17	14	22	13
18	Gainsborough Trinity	16	18	38	11
19	Barnsley	18	18	29	10
20	Bradford Park Avenue	17	15	30	8
		348	470	470	348

Attendances
Total 3,559,650   Average 9,638
Goals
Total 1,026   Average 2.7
Top scorer   Alf Bentley (Derby County) 27
380 games

Final League Division 2 Table 1909

1	BOLTON WANDERERS	38	59	28	52
2	Tottenham Hotspur	38	67	32	51
3	West Bromwich Albion	38	56	27	51
4	Hull City	38	63	39	44
5	Derby County	38	55	41	43
6	Oldham Athletic	38	55	43	40
7	Wolves	38	56	48	39
8	Glossop	38	57	53	38
9	Gainsborough Trinity	38	49	70	38
10	Fulham	38	58	48	37
11	Birmingham	38	58	61	37
12	Leeds City	38	43	53	35
13	Grimsby Town	38	41	54	35
14	Burnley	38	51	58	33
15	Clapton Orient	38	37	49	33
16	Bradford Park Avenue	38	51	59	32
17	Barnsley	38	48	57	32
18	Stockport County	38	39	71	31
19	Chesterfield Town	38	37	67	30
20	Blackpool	38	46	68	29
		760	1026	1026	760

Bolton Wanderers and Tottenham Hotspur promoted to Division 1. Only the bottom two had to apply for re-election. Blackpool (27 votes) were successful, but Chesterfield Town (21) lost out to Lincoln City (24). Stoke (6) and Rotherham Town (0) were also unsuccessful.

1909-1910 – LEAGUE DIVISION 1

ASTON VILLA

Despite a humbling 1-4 defeat by Newcastle United at Goodison Park on September 6th, Everton were three points clear at the top of Division 1 by the end of the month, having won 5 of their 7 matches, including a 2-1 revenge success at St. James' Park on September 30th.

Four losses in a row saw the Toffees displaced at the head of things, however, and it was Blackburn Rovers, with a 7-game unbeaten run, and Manchester United, with 5 wins in a row, who led the top flight by mid-November, each with 19 points. Sheffield United lay third and Liverpool were fourth. Both had 17 points.

Blackburn Rovers beat Manchester United 3-2 on 20th November to go clear, but then failed to win in their next 3 matches. United fared even worse. The Bank Street club lost five times in six games and tumbled swiftly into mid-table. This opened the door for other teams. Bradford City, Sheffield United, Aston Villa, Notts County and Liverpool all mounted a challenge, with the Manningham Lane outfit leading the First Division into 1910 after thumping Middlesbrough 7-3 and 4-1 over the holiday period.

City could not keep this up, however. Defeat at Manchester United on New Year's Day was followed by eight games without a win stretching into mid-March. The form of Blackburn Rovers and Sheffield United also wavered, leaving Aston Villa and Notts County to rise above the rest by February 12th. County then stumbled dramatically, winning only 1 of their next 8, leaving Villa to ease ahead at the top. Victory at Bury on March 26th was the lead club's 15th match unbeaten in a sequence stretching back to mid-December. Despite losing at lowly Middlesbrough 2 days later, Villa ended March seven points clear.

A routine 3-0 success against mid-table Preston North End lifted Aston Villa to the threshold of their first title in 10 years. The champions-elect could even afford a 0-1 reverse at struggling Woolwich Arsenal, such was their lead. Goals from club top scorer Harry Hampton, Charlie Wallace and Edmund Eyre helped Villa to a 3-2 win over Notts County on April 16th. This sealed championship success for Aston Villa, who, 11 days later, were able to celebrate in front of their own supporters with an emphatic 4-0 win over Newcastle United.

Aston Villa's '1st half' record

September	01	WOOLWICH ARSENAL	5-1
	04	Bolton Wanderers	2-1
	11	CHELSEA	4-1
	18	Blackburn Rovers	2-3
	25	NOTTINGHAM FOREST	0-0
October	02	Sunderland	1-1
	09	EVERTON	3-1
	16	Manchester United	0-2
	23	BRADFORD CITY	3-1
	30	Sheffield Wednesday	2-3
November	06	BRISTOL CITY	1-0
	13	Bury	2-0
	20	TOTTENHAM HOTSPUR	3-2
	27	Preston North End	0-1
December	04	NOTTS COUNTY	1-1
	11	Newcastle United	0-1
	18	LIVERPOOL	3-1
	25	Sheffield United	1-0
	27	SHEFFIELD UNITED	2-1

Aston Villa's '2nd half' record

January	01	Nottingham Forest	4-1
	08	BOLTON WANDERERS	3-1
	22	Chelsea	0-0
	29	BLACKBURN ROVERS	4-3
February	12	SUNDERLAND	3-2
	26	MANCHESTER UNITED	7-1
March	05	Bradford City	2-1
	12	SHEFFIELD WEDNESDAY	5-0
	14	Everton	0-0
	19	Bristol City	0-0
	25	MIDDLESBROUGH	4-2
	26	BURY	4-1
	28	Middlesbrough	2-3
April	02	Tottenham Hotspur	1-1
	09	PRESTON NORTH END	3-0
	11	Woolwich Arsenal	0-1
	16	Notts County	3-2
	27	NEWCASTLE UNITED	4-0
	30	Liverpool	0-2

Table at December 27th, 1909

1	Bradford City	19	43	22	27
2	Blackburn Rovers	19	44	24	26
3	Sheffield United	20	39	22	25
4	ASTON VILLA	19	35	21	25
5	Notts County	21	40	30	25
6	Liverpool	19	39	30	25
7	Newcastle United	21	35	32	23
8	Nottingham Forest	20	32	31	22
9	Sunderland	19	36	26	21
10	Everton	20	28	28	21
11	Manchester United	19	29	33	21
12	Sheffield Wednesday	19	35	35	20
13	Bristol City	20	24	33	16
14	Chelsea	20	27	39	16
15	Bury	20	33	40	15
16	Preston North End	20	30	38	15
17	Woolwich Arsenal	20	22	49	14
18	Tottenham Hotspur	19	24	37	13
19	Middlesbrough	19	29	40	12
20	Bolton Wanderers	19	22	36	10
		392	646	646	392

Final League Division 1 Table 1910

1	ASTON VILLA	38	84	42	53
2	Liverpool	38	78	57	48
3	Blackburn Rovers	38	73	55	45
4	Newcastle United	38	70	56	45
5	Manchester United	38	69	61	45
6	Sheffield United	38	62	41	42
7	Bradford City	38	64	47	42
8	Sunderland	38	66	51	41
9	Notts County	38	67	59	40
10	Everton	38	51	56	40
11	Sheffield Wednesday	38	60	63	39
12	Preston North End	38	52	58	35
13	Bury	38	62	66	33
14	Nottingham Forest	38	54	72	33
15	Tottenham Hotspur	38	53	69	32
16	Bristol City	38	45	60	32
17	Middlesbrough	38	56	73	31
18	Woolwich Arsenal	38	37	67	31
19	Chelsea	38	47	70	29
20	Bolton Wanderers	38	44	71	24
		760	1194	1194	760

Attendances
Total 5,774,575 Average 15,196
Goals
Total 1,195 Average 3.142
Top scorer John Parkinson (Liverpool) 30
380 games

Chelsea and Bolton Wanderers relegated.

1909-1910 – LEAGUE DIVISION 2

Smarting from their relegation at the end of the previous campaign, Manchester City made a hit-and-miss start to the season, ending September seven points behind leaders West Bromwich Albion, whose six victories gave them a one-point lead over Hull City.

One win in five October outings torpedoed Albion's bid to push on and ten points in six games in this period brought Manchester City into the leading group, along with Leicester Fosse, the other club demoted from the top flight earlier in the year. At the top of Division Two by this time, however, were the unfashionable Glossop club, with just one defeat in their first 10 games.

The North Road men continued to head the table through November, amassing 23 points from their 14 matches before losing, for only the second time, at Derby County on December 4th. Glossop's progress was not damaged by this, however, as Christmas victories over Birmingham (4-1) and Oldham Athletic (6-2) proved. The Derbyshire side held a 3-point lead going into New Year.

Manchester City's '1st half' record

September	02	BLACKPOOL	1-2
	04	Leicester Fosse	3-1
	11	LINCOLN CITY	6-2
	18	Clapton Orient	2-3
	25	Blackpool	0-0
October	02	Hull City	2-1
	09	DERBY COUNTY	2-1
	16	Stockport County	2-1
	23	GLOSSOP	3-3
	27	Gainsborough Trinity	3-1
	30	Birmingham	1-1
November	06	WEST BROMWICH ALBION	3-2
	13	Oldham Athletic	0-1
	27	Fulham	1-1
December	04	BURNLEY	4-0
	11	Leeds City	3-1
	18	WOLVES	6-0
	25	Bradford Park Avenue	0-2
	27	GRIMSBY TOWN	2-0

Table at December 27th, 1909

1	Glossop	19	44	21	30
2	Derby County	18	45	20	27
3	MANCHESTER CITY	19	44	23	26
4	Leicester Fosse	19	48	27	26
5	Hull City	21	40	26	26
6	Fulham	20	31	19	24
7	Wolves	21	40	42	22
8	Barnsley	18	38	21	21
9	Blackpool	21	24	29	21
10	West Bromwich Albion	20	33	29	20
11	Burnley	19	30	28	19
12	Oldham Athletic	17	21	25	17
13	Bradford Park Avenue	18	27	30	16
14	Stockport County	20	19	24	16
15	Clapton Orient	20	22	32	15
16	Leeds City	19	25	45	14
17	Gainsborough Trinity	20	21	49	13
18	Lincoln City	17	20	34	12
19	Birmingham	19	24	45	11
20	Grimsby Town	19	16	43	8
		384	612	612	384

Attendances
Total   3,126,925   Average   8,229
Goals
Total   1,166   Average   3.068
Top scorer   Jack Smith (Hull City) 32
380 games

MANCHESTER CITY

A 0-1 loss at Oldham on January 1st was the first of 3 defeats in the month for Glossop. Their poor start to the year continued, the club slipping down to fourth by mid-February and into a run of 14 matches which produced only 2 wins. The bigger clubs took over. Derby County and Manchester City headed the front-runners through to the end of March. The Rams led until February 26th when City went top by beating Stockport County, while County dipped 0-6 away at Leicester. Derby led again after a win over Lincoln City on March 5th and pulled 3 points clear by beating Manchester City 11 days later. City had reversed this by April 16th, with 8 points from 5 games. In this period, Derby played only twice and lost one of these.

By April 23rd, City, with 1 game left, had 54 points. On 53 from 37 were Hull, with Derby on 51 from 35 and Oldham Athletic on 49 from 36. In a frantic finale, the Rams crashed 0-4 at Oldham, then drew at Glossop and West Bromwich, finishing on 53 points. Oldham beat Hull 3-0 on April 30th to head their rivals, on goal average, on 53 also. Manchester City, last day losers at Wolves, emerged from the chaos as champions

Manchester City's '2nd half' record

January	01	BRADFORD PARK AVENUE	3-1
	08	LEICESTER FOSSE	2-0
	22	Lincoln City	2-0
February	12	HULL CITY	3-0
	26	STOCKPORT COUNTY	2-1
March	09	BARNSLEY	0-0
	12	BIRMINGHAM	3-0
	16	Derby County	1-3
	19	West Bromwich Albion	0-0
	25	Grimsby Town	1-0
	26	OLDHAM ATHLETIC	0-2
	28	GAINSBOROUGH TRINITY	3-1
April	02	Barnsley	1-1
	06	Glossop	3-0
	09	FULHAM	3-1
	13	CLAPTON ORIENT	2-1
	16	Burnley	3-3
	23	LEEDS CITY	3-0
	30	Wolves	2-3

Final League Division 2 Table 1910

1	MANCHESTER CITY	38	81	40	54
2	Oldham Athletic	38	79	39	53
3	Hull City	38	80	46	53
4	Derby County	38	72	47	53
5	Leicester Fosse	38	79	58	44
6	Glossop	38	64	57	43
7	Fulham	38	51	43	41
8	Wolves	38	64	63	40
9	Barnsley	38	62	59	39
10	Bradford Park Avenue	38	64	59	38
11	West Bromwich Albion	38	58	56	37
12	Blackpool	38	50	52	36
13	Stockport County	38	50	47	34
14	Burnley	38	62	61	34
15	Lincoln City	38	42	69	31
16	Clapton Orient	38	37	60	30
17	Leeds City	38	46	80	27
18	Gainsborough Trinity	38	33	75	26
19	Grimsby Town	38	50	77	24
20	Birmingham	38	42	78	23
		760	1166	1166	760

Manchester City and Oldham Athletic were promoted. Birmingham (30 votes) were re-elected, but Grimsby Town (12) were replaced by Huddersfield Town (26). Darlington (7), Chesterfield Town (6), Stoke (3), Hartlepools United (1) and Rochdale (1) were also unsuccessful.

OTHER INFORMATION   1905-1910

F.A. Cup 1905-1910

The five F.A. Cup Finals played 1906-1910 were again staged at Crystal Palace in London. When the 1910 Final ended in a draw, however, it was decided to have the replay at a northern venue to see if this would prop up the attendance.

Details of F.A. Cup Finals 1905-06 to 1909-10

21st April, 1906
A crowd of 75,609 saw Newcastle United lose a second successive F.A. Cup Final, with Young's 2nd half goal for Everton taking the trophy back to Goodison Park. F. Kirkham officiated.

20th April, 1907
Stewart for Sheffield Wednesday and Sharp for holders Everton were the first-half scorers. After the interval, Owls' Simpson added the final goal of the game and Wednesday won 2-1. The man in charge was N. Whittaker and 84,584 paid to watch.

25th April, 1908
Newcastle United arrived for their third F.A. Cup Final in four years as red-hot favourites. Once again, however, the Geordies froze in front of the 74,967 crowd and it was 2nd Division Wolves who took the trophy despite having far less possession. Scorers for the 3-1 winners were Hunt, Hedley and Harrison, with Newcastle's solitary reply coming from Howey. The match was refereed by T.P. Campbell.

24th April, 1909
Played in front of the lowest crowd for five years (71,401), the 1909 Final was won by Manchester United thanks to Sandy Turnbull's first-half goal. Bristol City were unable to find a way back into the game, though United supporters were glad to hear J. Mason blow the final whistle.

23rd April, 1910
Newcastle United returned to Crystal Palace in 1910 determined not to lose another Final. By half-time Second Division Barnsley had the lead through Tufnell and it was much to the relief of the North-East fans in the 77,747 crowd when Rutherford forced a replay in the second-half. J.T. Ibbotson again took charge as the two sides met five days later at Goodison Park, watched by 69,000. Two second-half goals from Shepherd, the second a penalty, meant, at last, the Cup went back to Tyneside.

More Transfer Troubles

Middlesbrough avoided relegation again in 1906 after signing Billy Brawn from Aston Villa and Steve Bloomer from Derby County late on in the season. In January 1908, a maximum transfer fee of £350 was introduced, but clubs found ways round this scheme and the lid was lifted in April. In April 1910, Chelsea tried the 'Teesside trick', signing 4 players, but went down anyway. Tired of clubs trying to buy their way out of trouble, Football League officials responded by introducing the mid-March transfer deadline.

Attendances 1905-1910

Newcastle United twice produced the highest average home gates in this period – these being when the club won the Football League title. None of the other 'chart-toppers' managed to win the championship. Aston Villa were the best supported club at home 1905-06, with promoted London clubs, Chelsea (1907-08) and Tottenham Hotspur (1909-10) receiving the largest home backing in the other seasons.

Attendances 1905-1910 (continued)

The numbers of people attracted to Football League matches grew for the first 4 seasons in this phase, but attendances fell back for the 1st Division 1908-09 and then significantly for the whole League during the 1909-10 campaign. There may have been an economic side to the reasons for this, but it seems more likely that the winter weather was the major factor in keeping crowds down. The 1908-09 winter was bitterly cold in some areas, with temperatures of -25° C. recorded in several areas in Lancashire. This does not explain, however, why crowds at 2nd Division games continued to grow.

Heavy snowfall in Lancashire in November 1909 is said to have stopped trams running and to have covered the ground in some parts to waist level. Met. Office records pick out the winter of 1909-10 as the coldest of the 20th century. We know also that January, February and March 1910 were all wet months in the North Midlands from figures taken at the Sheffield Weather Centre. The combination of these pieces of information seems to form a fairly sound basis for the belief that bad weather 1909-10 caused average attendances to fall.

The average attendance for a Football League fixture 1909-1910 was still a healthy 11,713.

High scoring 1905-1910

Division 1

On November 11th, 1905, Newcastle United thrashed Wolves 8-0 at St. James' Park. On 3rd September, 1906, Everton sounded out a warning to all others by pasting Manchester City 9-1, while in 1907 Newcastle enjoyed another November 'goalfest', crushing Birmingham 8-0 on the 23rd. A little over a year later, Sunderland sprang a major surprise by winning 9-1 at Newcastle on December 5th, 1908, but this was overshadowed by Nottingham Forest's April 21st, 1909, 12-0 romp against bottom club Leicester Fosse. During the 1909-10 season Aston Villa, Blackburn Rovers, Liverpool and Bradford City (away) all won matches in which they scored 7 goals.

Division 2

On January 20th, 1906, Barnsley thumped Chesterfield Town 8-1. Later in the year Chelsea opened their second League campaign with a 9-2 destruction of Glossop. Next, it was the turn of Bradford City to put unlucky Chesterfield Town to the sword, the Bantams winning 8-1 on September 7th, 1907. West Bromwich Albion began the New Year in style with a 7-0 demolition of Grimsby Town in 1909, while at the other end of the calendar, on December 27th, Leicester Fosse gave their supporters a slightly late Christmas present, battering Gainsborough Trinity 9-1.

Goal-scoring issues

The number of goals scored in Division 1 rose to an average of more than 3 per game during the 1905-06 season and remained there over the next four seasons. In the 2nd Division, the mean number also reached more than 3 per game, but not until the following campaign, dropping back again below three 1908-09 for one season. The percentage of Football League games with more than 1 goal scored was fairly consistent 1905-10, with the 1908-09 campaign being the single exception to this.

```
1905-06 = 79·48%
1906-07 = 79·47%
1907-08 = 79·34%
1908-09 = 78·42%
1909-10 = 79·08%
```

OTHER INFORMATION 1910-1915

F.A. Cup 1910-1915

The four F.A. Cup Finals played 1911-1914 took place at Crystal Palace in London, but, because of the Great War, the 1915 Final was played at Old Trafford in Manchester. The first two games in this sequence ended in draws, with replays being staged at the grounds of northern clubs. After the 1912 tie ended all square, the decision was taken to play extra time of 15 minutes each way if things remained undecided at the end of 90 minutes. Of course, once this proviso had been set up, it proved to be unnecessary, in this period at least.

Details of F.A. Cup Finals 1910-11 to 1914-15

22nd April, 1911

Back at Crystal Palace for the fifth time in seven years, Cup holders Newcastle United failed to break their duck at this venue, drawing 0-0 with Bradford City in a game run by J.H. Pearson. A goal from Speirs in the Old Trafford replay took the Cup to Valley Parade on April 26th. The crowd for the first game was 69,098, with an estimated 58,000 present for the re-match.

20th April, 1912

J.R. Schumacher officiated for the Barnsley v. West Bromwich Albion clash, which ended 0-0, in front of just 54,556. In the replay, at Bramall Lane four days later, the 2nd Division side won the trophy thanks to Tufnell's first half goal, with 38,555 in attendance.

19th April, 1913

The biggest crowd to date for a Final (120,081) saw Aston Villa defeat Sunderland 1-0. The goal came in the second half from Barber. A. Adams was the referee.

25th April, 1914

A single goal settled the F.A. Cup final again, this time being scored by Burnley's Freeman against Liverpool. The man in charge of the game was H.S. Bamlett and there were 72,778 present to watch another closely-contested Final.

24th April, 1915

The 'Khaki Final', so called because of the high number of men in military uniform in the crowd of 49,557, saw Sheffield United stroll to a 3-0 win against Chelsea. H.H. Taylor refereed the game, which saw Simmons give the Blades a half-time lead. Goals from Masterman and Kitchen in the second period put the game beyond the London club's reach.

Attendances 1910-1915

The 'honour' of attracting the highest home attendances was taken by Manchester City for the first and last season in the period, with Chelsea leading the way for the 3 campaigns in between, despite spending 1911-1912 in the 2nd Division. Newcastle United, Tottenham Hotspur and Aston Villa were usually among the top five in terms of home crowds throughout the period.

Top flight crowds grew 1911-1914, but there was a significant drop 1914-1915 because of the effects of the 1st World War. In Division Two, the numbers rose 1910-1912, but dipped the following season after Chelsea's promotion.

In the following campaign, 2nd Division crowds rose again, the average topping 10,000 for the first time ever. However, as happened with the 1st Division, there was a sharp fall 1914-1915, with the Football League's 2nd tier attendances dropping by around 40%.

Attendances 1910-1915 (continued)

Average attendances for the Football League were up each season from 1909-10 to 1913-14. With many men volunteering to fight in the war against Germany in 1914, the average crowd for a Football League fixture 1914-1915 fell below 10,000 for the first time since 1905-1906.

Average crowds for the Football League 1910-15 were:
1910-11	12,406
1911-12	12,889
1912-13	13,573
1913-14	16,179
1914-15	9,824

High scoring 1910-1915

Division 1

Blackburn Rovers (twice), Newcastle United (twice) and Tottenham Hotspur all won matches in which they scored six times in the 1910-11 season. On Boxing Day 1911, Sheffield Wednesday overran Sunderland to win 8-0, but were on the receiving end on October 5th, 1912, when crushed 0-10 at Aston Villa. In the 1913-14 campaign Blackburn Rovers (twice), Bolton Wanderers (twice) and Aston Villa (at Manchester United) all won games in which they hit 6 goals and in the last season before League soccer was suspended due to the Great War four teams won games in which they scored 7 goals – Middlesbrough, Liverpool, Bolton Wanderers and Sheffield Wednesday.

Division 2

1910-11
Barnsley, Chelsea and Huddersfield Town were all '7 scoring', home winners 1910-11, while Wolves sank Hull City 8-0 on November 4th, 1911. On January 8th, 1913, Stockport County lost 2-7 at Bristol City and on March 8th crashed 0-7 at Fulham. On November 29th in the same year, Leeds City demolished Nottingham Forest 8-0 and on January 23rd, 1915 Birmingham overran demoralised Glossop, running out victors by 11-1.

Goal-scoring trends

The number of goals scored in Division 1 fell sharply in the 1910-11 season and remained below three per game until the 1914-15 season. In Division 2, the mean number also dipped below 3 per game 1910-11. Although the average rose again 1912-13, there was another fall during the following campaign. The percentage of Football League games with more than one goal scored dropped to under 75% by the 1911-12 season, rising for the next campaign, before falling back again during the season after this. For 1914-15, there was an upward movement in the figure.

The percentages of Football League matches in which more than 1 goal was scored were:
1910-11	75·53%
1911-12	74·08%
1912-13	78·95%
1913-14	74·74%
1914-15	77·63%

Transfer Troubles ... again

Despite all the efforts of the football authorities to control transfer fees, the record amount paid by clubs for players continued to rise. The first £2,000 fee was paid in December 1912 when Blackburn Rovers bought Danny O'Shea from West Ham United. Manchester City then set a new high by paying £2,500 for Horace Barnes of Derby County in May 1914.

1910-1911 – LEAGUE DIVISION 1

Sunderland enjoyed the best start to the season, with 4 odd-goal victories and a draw, on September 24th, taking the Roker Park club in front of the rest by the start of October. The Wearsiders remained unbeaten throughout the second month of the campaign, winning two and drawing three of their 5 games.

This run of matches without defeat continued in November, with a 4-0 success against Tottenham Hotspur on the 26th, the Rokerites' 14th outing without losing. Despite this, Sunderland went into the last month of the year only 2 points clear of Manchester United and Aston Villa. The Villains' threat loomed larger at this point, following 7 straight victories.

Villa's 3-1 win over Notts County on December 10th lifted the club above Sunderland, who had lost a week earlier at Middlesbrough and who now could only draw with Preston North End. A fortnight later, Manchester United, having beaten both their main rivals, got their noses in front and thrashed Woolwich Arsenal 5-0 on Boxing Day to underline their right to lead the division.

Manchester United's '1st half' record

September	01	Woolwich Arsenal	2-1
	03	BLACKBURN ROVERS	3-2
	10	Nottingham Forest	1-2
	17	MANCHESTER CITY	2-1
	24	Everton	1-0
October	01	SHEFFIELD WEDNESDAY	3-2
	08	Bristol City	1-0
	15	NEWCASTLE UNITED	2-0
	22	Tottenham Hotspur	2-2
	29	MIDDLESBROUGH	1-2
November	05	Preston North End	2-0
	12	NOTTS COUNTY	0-0
	19	Oldham Athletic	3-1
	26	Liverpool	2-3
December	03	BURY	3-2
	10	Sheffield United	0-2
	17	ASTON VILLA	2-0
	24	Sunderland	2-1
	26	WOOLWICH ARSENAL	5-0

Table at December 26th, 1910

1	MANCHESTER UNITED	19	37	21	28
2	Aston Villa	18	37	21	27
3	Sunderland	19	34	20	26
4	Everton	19	27	17	24
5	Middlesbrough	18	29	24	24
6	Bradford City	18	31	25	23
7	Newcastle United	19	33	23	20
8	Nottingham Forest	20	40	37	20
9	Sheffield United	19	28	20	18
10	Oldham Athletic	18	21	24	18
11	Notts County	19	19	24	18
12	Blackburn Rovers	19	35	34	17
13	Tottenham Hotspur	19	25	34	15
14	Bury	19	28	40	15
15	Preston North End	20	20	31	15
16	Sheffield Wednesday	18	24	31	14
17	Liverpool	19	26	34	14
18	Woolwich Arsenal	19	16	32	14
19	Manchester City	19	23	31	13
20	Bristol City	18	21	31	13
		376	554	554	376

Attendances
Total 5,918,975   Average   15,576
Goals
Total 1,028   Average   2.705
Top scorer   Albert Shepherd (Newcastle United) 25
380 games

MANCHESTER UNITED

None of the leading trio won again before New Year and Everton nipped into third on December 31st by beating Middlesbrough 2-0 at Goodison. A 1-5 dip at home to Newcastle on January 2nd saw the Blues back to fourth, however, with Sunderland's 4-0 defeat of Liverpool adding to Mersey misery. United were up by 2 points by mid-February, though Villa had 2 games in hand, plus a better goal average. Sunderland and Everton were 2 points off second place.

The leaders stayed ahead, stretching their unbeaten run to 9 games by March 15th. When United did lose, on March 18th, Villa also fell, 0-1 at Newcastle, while neither Sunderland nor Everton could win at this time. The Manchester club reached mid-April a point ahead of Aston Villa. The clubs met on April 22nd, the Fates seeming to favour Villa, who won 4-2 and moved top. After drawing at Blackburn on the 26th, the Villains went into the season's last game seemingly in control. It was United's nerve which held better. Villa lost at Liverpool. United, meanwhile, destroyed Sunderland 5-1, moving back to the top and to the title.

Manchester United's '2nd half' record

December	27	Bradford City	0-1
	31	Blackburn Rovers	0-1
January	02	BRADFORD CITY	1-0
	07	NOTTINGHAM FOREST	4-2
	21	Manchester City	1-1
	28	EVERTON	2-2
February	11	BRISTOL CITY	3-1
	18	Newcastle United	1-0
March	04	Middlesbrough	2-2
	11	PRESTON NORTH END	5-0
	15	TOTTENHAM HOTSPUR	3-2
	18	Notts County	0-1
	25	OLDHAM ATHLETIC	0-0
April	01	LIVERPOOL	2-0
	08	Bury	3-0
	15	SHEFFIELD UNITED	1-1
	17	Sheffield Wednesday	0-0
	22	Aston Villa	2-4
	29	SUNDERLAND	5-1

Final League Division 1 Table 1911

1	MANCHESTER UNITED	38	72	40	52
2	Aston Villa	38	69	41	51
3	Sunderland	38	67	48	45
4	Everton	38	50	36	45
5	Bradford City	38	51	42	45
6	Sheffield Wednesday	38	47	48	42
7	Oldham Athletic	38	44	41	41
8	Newcastle United	38	61	43	40
9	Sheffield United	38	49	43	38
10	Woolwich Arsenal	38	41	49	38
11	Notts County	38	37	45	38
12	Blackburn Rovers	38	62	54	37
13	Liverpool	38	53	53	37
14	Preston North End	38	40	49	35
15	Tottenham Hotspur	38	52	63	32
16	Middlesbrough	38	49	63	32
17	Manchester City	38	43	58	31
18	Bury	38	43	71	29
19	Bristol City	38	43	66	27
20	Nottingham Forest	38	55	75	25
		760	1028	1028	760

Bristol City and Nottingham Forest were relegated.

- 56 -

1910-1911 – LEAGUE DIVISION 2

To the surprise of many in football, Clapton Orient headed the 2nd Division table by September 30th. The unfashionable Millfields Road men won their opening 4 games and stood a point clear of Blackpool, Lincoln City and Bolton Wanderers as October dawned. With only 3 points from their next 4 games, Orient could not keep the lead, however, and a third 0-0 draw, against Lincoln City on November 5th, showed both the strength and weakness of the team. It also let in West Bromwich Albion, who moved to top spot, with Orient second with a goals aggregate of 16-4 in 11 games.

Defying all the odds, however, Orient pushed back into first place on November 19th by beating Birmingham 1-0, while Albion slipped up at home to Chelsea. The lead was held until Christmas Eve, when Burnley won 2-0 at Millfields Road. West Bromwich Albion won at Huddersfield, while Bolton thrashed Birmingham at Burnden Park. Both winning teams moved onto 24 points, one more than Orient. The top two then met at The Hawthorns on Boxing Day, Albion taking the honours with goals from Bowser and Lloyd.

West Bromwich Albion's '1st half' record

September	03	Hull City	1-1
	05	Bolton Wanderers	1-3
	10	FULHAM	2-1
	17	Bradford Park Avenue	3-3
	24	BURNLEY	2-1
October	01	Gainsborough Trinity	1-1
	08	LEEDS CITY	2-0
	15	Stockport County	1-0
	22	DERBY COUNTY	1-1
	29	Barnsley	1-1
November	05	LEICESTER FOSSE	5-1
	12	Wolves	3-2
	19	CHELSEA	1-3
	26	Clapton Orient	0-0
December	03	Blackpool	0-1
	10	Glossop	2-0
	17	LINCOLN CITY	3-0
	24	Huddersfield Town	2-0
	26	BOLTON WANDERERS	2-0

Table at December 26th, 1910

1	WEST BROMWICH ALBION	19	33	19	26
2	Bolton Wanderers	20	34	26	26
3	Clapton Orient	18	21	10	25
4	Chelsea	17	37	13	23
5	Blackpool	17	28	16	23
6	Wolves	19	34	22	23
7	Burnley	19	26	21	23
8	Hull City	18	34	22	22
9	Derby County	19	39	27	21
10	Leicester Fosse	18	29	24	20
11	Fulham	18	26	24	19
12	Glossop	19	23	37	17
13	Bradford Park Avenue	19	30	29	16
14	Barnsley	17	25	28	12
15	Leeds City	18	27	35	12
16	Stockport County	17	21	37	12
17	Birmingham	18	17	34	12
18	Huddersfield Town	16	18	28	10
19	Lincoln City	17	11	40	10
20	Gainsborough Trinity	17	13	34	8
		360	526	526	360

Attendances
Total 3,509,300 Average 9,235
Goals
Total 1,050 Average 2.763
Top scorer Bob Whittingham (Chelsea) 30
380 games

WEST BROMWICH ALBION

By New Year, after Albion stumbled, Bolton were top and Chelsea second. Both the leaders then took 6 points from 5 games, while West Bromwich and Orient hit problems, enabling Derby County and Blackpool to pass them. Almost immediately, however, the 'new contenders' faltered and, by the end of March, Albion and Orient were back in slots three and four. Bolton headed the table going into April, two points up on Chelsea, but with three more matches played. West Bromwich Albion were four points behind the leaders, but had two matches in hand at this stage.

By mid-April, Chelsea had made up their games on Bolton and led Division 2 by a point from Wanderers. There were 4 games left. West Bromwich were third, a point behind Bolton. Three wins in 6 days, however, swept Albion to the top. As matters moved to a head, Bolton Wanderers beat Chelsea 2-0, on April 26th, to take a goal average lead over West Bromwich, with Chelsea 2 points back. Final day action, on April 29th, saw Bolton lose away at Birmingham, while Albion beat Huddersfield Town 1-0 to become champions

West Bromwich Albion's '2nd half' record

December	27	Birmingham	1-1
	31	HULL CITY	0-2
January	07	Fulham	1-0
	21	BRADFORD PARK AVENUE	3-0
	28	Burnley	0-2
February	11	Leeds City	1-3
	18	STOCKPORT COUNTY	4-2
March	01	Derby County	3-1
	04	BARNSLEY	3-3
	11	Leicester Fosse	3-2
	18	WOLVES	2-1
	29	Chelsea	1-2
April	01	CLAPTON ORIENT	3-0
	08	Blackpool	0-0
	15	GLOSSOP	3-1
	17	BIRMINGHAM	1-0
	18	GAINSBOROUGH TRINITY	2-1
	22	Lincoln City	2-1
	29	HUDDERSFIELD TOWN	1-0

Final League Division 2 Table 1911

1	WEST BROMWICH ALBION	38	67	41	53
2	Bolton Wanderers	38	69	40	51
3	Chelsea	38	71	35	49
4	Clapton Orient	38	44	35	45
5	Hull City	38	55	39	44
6	Derby County	38	73	52	42
7	Blackpool	38	49	38	42
8	Burnley	38	45	45	41
9	Wolves	38	51	52	38
10	Fulham	38	52	48	37
11	Leeds City	38	58	56	37
12	Bradford Park Avenue	38	53	55	37
13	Huddersfield Town	38	57	58	34
14	Glossop	38	48	62	34
15	Leicester Fosse	38	52	62	33
16	Birmingham	38	42	64	32
17	Stockport County	38	47	79	30
18	Gainsborough Trinity	38	37	55	29
19	Barnsley	38	52	62	28
20	Lincoln City	38	28	72	24
		760	1050	1050	760

West Bromwich Albion and Bolton Wanderers were promoted.

Barnsley (28 votes) were re-elected, but Lincoln City (17) were replaced by Grimsby Town (18). Darlington (7), Chesterfield Town (6), Hartlepools United (1) and Rochdale (1) were all unsuccessful.

1911-1912 – LEAGUE DIVISION 1

There was an unusual look to the top of Division 1 by the close of September, with West Bromwich Albion leading, followed by Bolton Wanderers, Bradford City and Notts County. None of the top four places was occupied by a team which had won the title before. Albion, Wanderers and County all faded in October, however, producing only one win between them.

Although Bradford City managed 4 points from 5 games in the month and opened November with a 4-1 success over West Bromwich, they too were overhauled by Blackburn Rovers and Newcastle United by the middle of the season's third month. City then beat Rovers to claim second spot, only to falter again and miss the chance to push for top place.

Newcastle won 2-1 at Tottenham on November 25th to stretch their unbeaten run to eight games. The Magpies were looking ominously strong, but home defeat by Manchester United pegged them back a little on December 2nd. Despite a 6-2 win over Aston Villa and a Christmas Day 4-2 breeze at Oldham, the Geordies lead was limited to 3 points. Only 2 points covered the eight chasing clubs.

BLACKBURN ROVERS

Newcastle ended the year by thumping Bolton 5-2, entering 1912 with a 4-point lead over Blackburn and Everton. This advantage had gone by January 6th, because Rovers won twice, while Newcastle lost at Sheffield Wednesday. Two weeks later, United lost at home to Woolwich Arsenal, while Blackburn won at Notts County and took over the Division 1 lead.

By mid-February Newcastle United were down to third as their wretched form continued. Blackburn Rovers led Everton by 2 points, though the Goodison club had a game in hand. Despite playing fewer matches than their rivals over the next few weeks, Rovers were still top at March 31st and by mid-April, having lost only 1 of 17 games, the Ewood Park men held a 3 point lead.

Defeats for Newcastle and Bolton on April 20th left only Everton, winners at Sheffield Wednesday, able to catch the leaders. With the title beckoning, Blackburn were struck by stage-fright and fell 1-5 at Arsenal on the 22nd. Everton closed to within a point by beating West Bromwich. Albion visited Ewood Park 3 days later. Rovers were up for it this time and won 4-1 to become the 10th club to win the Football league title.

Blackburn Rovers' '1st half' record

September	02	BURY	2-0
	06	Sunderland	0-3
	09	Middlesbrough	1-2
	16	NOTTS COUNTY	0-0
	23	Tottenham Hotspur	2-0
	30	MANCHESTER UNITED	2-2
October	07	Liverpool	2-1
	14	ASTON VILLA	3-1
	21	Newcastle United	2-4
	28	SHEFFIELD UNITED	1-0
November	04	Oldham Athletic	1-0
	11	BOLTON WANDERERS	2-0
	18	Bradford City	0-1
	25	WOOLWICH ARSENAL	4-0
December	02	Manchester City	0-3
	09	EVERTON	2-1
	16	West Bromwich Albion	0-2
	23	SUNDERLAND	2-2
	25	SHEFFIELD WEDNESDAY	0-0

Table at December 25th, 1911

1	Newcastle United	19	36	25	26
2	Bradford City	19	27	22	23
3	Middlesbrough	18	30	21	22
4	Tottenham Hotspur	19	37	27	22
5	BLACKBURN ROVERS	19	26	22	22
6	Manchester United	18	28	22	21
7	Notts County	18	26	22	21
8	Sunderland	19	31	27	21
9	Everton	19	20	20	21
10	Bolton Wanderers	19	29	24	20
11	Aston Villa	18	36	32	19
12	West Bromwich Albion	18	23	22	19
13	Sheffield Wednesday	19	31	27	18
14	Preston North End	17	18	25	16
15	Woolwich Arsenal	18	24	34	15
16	Liverpool	19	24	34	14
17	Oldham Athletic	18	25	31	13
18	Sheffield United	17	15	23	13
19	Manchester City	18	21	33	13
20	Bury	17	13	27	7
		366	520	520	366

Goals
Total 1,057 Average 2.782
Top scorers Harry Hampton (Aston Villa),
Dave McLean (Sheffield Wednesday), and
George Holley (Sunderland) 25

Blackburn Rovers' '2nd half' record

December	26	Preston North End	2-2
	30	Bury	2-1
January	01	PRESTON NORTH END	3-0
	06	MIDDLESBROUGH	2-1
	20	Notts County	3-1
	27	TOTTENHAM HOTSPUR	0-0
February	10	LIVERPOOL	1-0
	17	Aston Villa	3-0
March	02	Sheffield United	1-1
	16	Bolton Wanderers	0-2
	23	BRADFORD CITY	3-1
April	06	MANCHESTER CITY	2-0
	08	Sheffield Wednesday	1-1
	13	Everton	3-1
	15	OLDHAM ATHLETIC	1-0
	22	Woolwich Arsenal	1-5
	25	WEST BROMWICH ALBION	4-1
	27	NEWCASTLE UNITED	1-1
	29	Manchester United	1-3

Final League Division 1 Table 1912

1	BLACKBURN ROVERS	38	60	43	49
2	Everton	38	46	42	46
3	Newcastle United	38	64	50	44
4	Bolton Wanderers	38	54	43	43
5	Sheffield Wednesday	38	69	49	41
6	Aston Villa	38	76	63	41
7	Middlesbrough	38	56	45	40
8	Sunderland	38	58	51	39
9	West Bromwich Albion	38	43	47	39
10	Woolwich Arsenal	38	55	59	38
11	Bradford City	38	46	50	38
12	Tottenham Hotspur	38	53	53	37
13	Manchester United	38	45	60	37
14	Sheffield United	38	63	56	36
15	Manchester City	38	56	58	35
16	Notts County	38	46	63	35
17	Liverpool	38	49	55	34
18	Oldham Athletic	38	46	54	34
19	Preston North End	38	40	57	33
20	Bury	38	32	59	21
		760	1057	1057	760

Preston North End and Bury were relegated.

Attendances
Total 6,185,925 Average 16,279
380 games

1911-1912 – LEAGUE DIVISION 2

DERBY COUNTY

With wins in their first 4 games, Burnley soon headed Division 2, holding that position despite failing to win 3 further September matches. Clapton Orient started well again to occupy second spot, with big-guns Chelsea, Hull City and Forest tucked in behind the Os. The only leading club to maintain their form through October was Hull, with 8 points from 5 games. The Tigers clawed their way to the front of the pack and set off for Wolves on November 4th in confident mood. The Molineux club were enjoying a good run, having gone 5 unbeaten, but their 8-0 drubbing of the 2nd Division leaders can only be described as a shock.

A week later Wolves lost at Barnsley and Hull, 4-1 winners over Leicester Fosse, were back at the top. Heavy December defeats at Clapton and Birmingham December cost the Tigers dearly, however, and by Boxing Day they were down to fourth. A run of 13 matches unbeaten had carried Derby County to the 2nd Division summit by this time, the Rams having been boosted by 13 goals from Steve Bloomer, now back at the Baseball Ground after a spell on Teesside.

County closed 1911 by crushing Clapton Orient 5-1, but the next 6 games produced only 2 points and by February 21st the Rams looked in danger of sliding out of the promotion race, trailing second-placed Chelsea by 4 points and leaders Burnley by five. Quite why a team suddenly goes from being sinners to winners is one of football's great mysteries. Nine points from five unbeaten games brought Derby to within reach of Chelsea by the end of March. The Rams pressed on, with a further eight points being gathered in the next five matches, which were played by mid-April.

Chelsea had been passed when beaten on the 8th, Easter Monday, and a stumbling Burnley were then replaced at the head of Division 2 after County held Fulham to a 0-0 draw at Craven Cottage on April 15th. Derby County finished their fixtures on April 22nd and then waited. Both Burnley and Chelsea could match the Rams' points total, but needed record wins to beat their 2·643 goal average. Neither club managed to do this, in their final games, on April 27th, and Derby County therefore became champions.

Derby County's '1st half' record

September	02	Clapton Orient	0-3
	09	BRISTOL CITY	3-0
	11	Chelsea	0-1
	16	Birmingham	4-0
	23	HUDDERSFIELD TOWN	4-2
	30	Blackpool	0-1
October	07	GLOSSOP	5-0
	14	Hull City	0-0
	21	BARNSLEY	0-0
	28	Bradford Park Avenue	1-0
November	04	FULHAM	6-1
	25	LEEDS CITY	5-2
December	02	Wolves	1-0
	06	BURNLEY	2-0
	09	LEICESTER FOSSE	5-0
	16	Gainsborough Trinity	1-1
	23	GRIMSBY TOWN	3-0
	25	Grimsby Town	2-1
	26	Nottingham Forest	3-1

Table at December 26th, 1911

1	DERBY COUNTY	19	45	13	29
2	Burnley	20	40	25	28
3	Chelsea	20	30	15	27
4	Hull City	19	35	25	27
5	Wolves	20	34	16	25
6	Barnsley	20	30	18	25
7	Clapton Orient	19	30	19	23
8	Bradford Park Avenue	19	26	24	20
9	Nottingham Forest	19	23	22	20
10	Fulham	19	34	26	19
11	Grimsby Town	20	23	25	19
12	Huddersfield Town	18	28	29	18
13	Blackpool	19	20	26	18
14	Bristol City	20	20	37	15
15	Leicester Fosse	21	18	40	15
16	Birmingham	20	26	38	14
17	Leeds City	20	25	43	13
18	Stockport County	17	16	25	11
19	Gainsborough Trinity	19	14	34	11
20	Glossop	18	13	30	9
		386	530	530	386

Attendances
Total   3,610,000   Average   9,500
Goals
Total   1,032   Average   2.716
Top scorer   Bert Freeman (Burnley) 32
380 games

Derby County's '2nd half' record

December	30	CLAPTON ORIENT	5-1
January	01	Stockport County	0-4
	06	Bristol City	1-1
	27	Huddersfield Town	0-0
February	10	Glossop	1-3
	17	HULL CITY	2-3
	21	BIRMINGHAM	0-1
	24	BLACKPOOL	5-1
March	02	BRADFORD PARK AVENUE	1-0
	16	Burnley	0-0
	23	STOCKPORT COUNTY	2-0
	30	Leeds City	1-0
April	06	WOLVES	1-1
	08	CHELSEA	2-0
	09	NOTTINGHAM FOREST	1-0
	13	Leicester Fosse	1-0
	15	Fulham	0-0
	20	GAINSBOROUGH TRINITY	4-0
	22	Barnsley	2-0

Final League Division 2 Table 1912

1	DERBY COUNTY	38	74	28	54
2	Chelsea	38	64	34	54
3	Burnley	38	77	41	52
4	Clapton Orient	38	61	44	45
5	Wolves	38	57	33	42
6	Barnsley	38	45	42	42
7	Hull City	38	54	51	42
8	Fulham	38	66	58	39
9	Grimsby Town	38	48	55	39
10	Leicester Fosse	38	49	66	37
11	Bradford Park Avenue	38	44	45	35
12	Birmingham	38	55	59	34
13	Bristol City	38	41	60	34
14	Blackpool	38	32	52	34
15	Nottingham Forest	38	46	48	33
16	Stockport County	38	47	54	33
17	Huddersfield Town	38	50	64	32
18	Glossop	38	42	56	28
19	Leeds City	38	50	78	28
20	Gainsborough Trinity	38	30	64	23
		760	1032	1032	760

Derby County and Chelsea were promoted. Leeds City (33 votes) were re-elected, but the season's wooden spoonists, Gainsborough Trinity (9), were replaced by Lincoln City (27). Other unsuccessful clubs were Chesterfield Town (6), Cardiff City (1), Darlington (1), Newcastle City (1) and Doncaster Rovers, who received no support.

1912-1913 – LEAGUE DIVISION 1

SUNDERLAND

Manchester City and Sheffield Wednesday made the best starts to the season, both clubs going through September unbeaten. Wednesday's 3-3 draw with Manchester United on the 28th meant, however, that they ended the month in third place, a point behind City and reigning champions Blackburn Rovers, who had 10 points from 7 games.

With only 2 points from 6 games, Sunderland lay 17th and looked more likely to face a relegation struggle than anything else. The best hope for the North-East seemed to be Newcastle United, who lay third by mid-November, behind Aston Villa and Blackburn, with Manchester City now fourth.

The Geordies faded, however, sliding to mid-table by Christmas, being passed by Sunderland, with 10 wins in 12 games, and a host of other clubs, including the recovering Manchester City and Sheffield Wednesday, West Bromwich Albion, Oldham Athletic and Derby County. In what was developing into a nip-and-tuck situation at the top, only 2 points separated leaders Manchester City from Derby County in eighth.

West Bromwich Albion went into the New Year as leaders, on goal average, from Sheffield Wednesday. Albion then picked up only 3 points from their next 6 games and tumbled down the table. With none of the top sides able to produce a decisive, telling run, things stayed tight at the head of the Football League. By mid-February the title race was too close to call. Sheffield Wednesday held a 1 point advantage over Oldham Athletic, with Villa and improving Sunderland just a point behind the Latics. Wednesday clung onto the lead over the next few weeks, staying marginally ahead of the chasing group. By March 31st the Owls had 44 points to Sunderland's 43 and Aston Villa's 42.

Three successive wins in the first half of April saw Sunderland leapfrog over Wednesday, whose 1-2 home defeat by Newcastle United, on April 14th, proved to be a crucial setback. The Owls rallied to pull level on points at the top by beating West Bromwich, but Sunderland's draw with Villa on the 23rd took them clear again. A 3-1 victory at Bolton Wanderers on April 26th secured Sunderland's first title since 1902.

Sunderland's '1st half' record

September	07	Newcastle United	1-1
	09	Blackburn Rovers	0-4
	14	DERBY COUNTY	0-2
	18	BLACKBURN ROVERS	2-4
	21	Oldham Athletic	0-3
	28	TOTTENHAM HOTSPUR	2-2
October	05	Chelsea	0-2
	12	MIDDLESBROUGH	4-0
	19	Woolwich Arsenal	3-1
	26	NOTTS COUNTY	4-0
November	02	Bradford City	5-1
	09	MANCHESTER UNITED	3-1
	16	Manchester City	0-1
	23	ASTON VILLA	3-1
	30	West Bromwich Albion	1-3
December	07	LIVERPOOL	7-0
	14	Everton	4-0
	21	BOLTON WANDERERS	2-1
	25	Sheffield Wednesday	2-1

Sunderland's '2nd half' record

December	26	SHEFFIELD WEDNESDAY	0-2
	28	NEWCASTLE UNITED	2-0
January	01	WOOLWICH ARSENAL	4-1
	18	OLDHAM ATHLETIC	1-1
	25	Tottenham Hotspur	2-1
February	08	CHELSEA	4-0
	15	Middlesbrough	2-0
	26	Derby County	3-0
March	01	Notts County	1-2
	15	Manchester United	3-1
	21	SHEFFIELD UNITED	1-0
	22	MANCHESTER CITY	1-0
	24	Sheffield United	3-1
April	05	WEST BROMWICH ALBION	3-1
	09	EVERTON	3-1
	12	Liverpool	5-2
	23	Aston Villa	1-1
	26	Bolton Wanderers	3-1
	30	BRADFORD CITY	1-0

Table at December 25th, 1912

1	Manchester City	18	25	14	24
2	West Bromwich Albion	18	36	23	24
3	Aston Villa	19	49	28	23
4	Oldham Athletic	17	27	18	23
5	Sheffield Wednesday	18	31	27	23
6	Blackburn Rovers	19	41	24	22
7	SUNDERLAND	19	43	28	22
8	Derby County	18	36	30	22
9	Bolton Wanderers	18	25	25	21
10	Manchester United	18	33	24	20
11	Newcastle United	19	28	25	20
12	Everton	19	23	30	18
13	Liverpool	19	30	37	17
14	Middlesbrough	17	28	33	16
15	Sheffield United	18	30	36	16
16	Bradford City	16	22	27	14
17	Tottenham Hotspur	18	21	41	12
18	Chelsea	19	18	32	11
19	Notts County	18	10	28	9
20	Woolwich Arsenal	19	9	35	7
		364	565	565	364

Attendances
Total 6,987,725 Average 18,389
Goals
Total 1,153 Average 2.987
Top scorer Dave McLean (Sheffield Wednesday) 30
380 games

Final League Division 1 Table 1913

1	SUNDERLAND	38	86	43	54
2	Aston Villa	38	86	52	50
3	Sheffield Wednesday	38	75	55	49
4	Manchester United	38	69	43	46
5	Blackburn Rovers	38	79	43	45
6	Manchester City	38	53	37	44
7	Derby County	38	69	66	42
8	Bolton Wanderers	38	62	63	42
9	Oldham Athletic	38	50	55	42
10	West Bromwich Albion	38	57	50	38
11	Everton	38	48	54	37
12	Liverpool	38	61	71	37
13	Bradford City	38	50	60	35
14	Newcastle United	38	47	47	34
15	Sheffield United	38	56	70	34
16	Middlesbrough	38	55	69	32
17	Tottenham Hotspur	38	45	72	30
18	Chelsea	38	51	73	28
19	Notts County	38	28	56	23
20	Woolwich Arsenal	38	26	74	18
		760	1153	1153	760

Notts County and Woolwich Arsenal were relegated.

Woolwich Arsenal changed their name to 'The Arsenal'.

1912-1913 – LEAGUE DIVISION 2

There were good openings to the 1912-13 season from Hull City and Clapton Orient, these two topping the table by September 30th. Bristol City's mean defence helped the Ashton Gate club to third place, with Birmingham, with a similar record of 2 wins and 3 draws, in fourth. Matches ending all square proved common in Division 2 at this time. Preston North End, for example, tied 5 of their six September fixtures. None of the top three prospered in October and Birmingham, with 9 points from 6 games by mid-November, were able to go to the front.

Also going well in this phase were Nottingham Forest, Lincoln City and Wolves, while Preston North End had got over their indifferent start and, despite losing 1-3 at Fulham on November 9th, looked likely to force their way into the mix. With 7 games unbeaten between November 16th and Christmas, North End pulled up to third place, just behind Birmingham on goal average. Burnley, with seven straight wins, which produced a stunning 26-3 goals aggregate, had, however, taken top spot and were 2 points clear.

Preston North End's '1st half' record

September	02	STOCKPORT COUNTY		1-1
	07	CLAPTON ORIENT		0-1
	14	Lincoln City		0-0
	16	Burnley		2-2
	21	NOTTINGHAM FOREST		1-1
	28	Bristol City		1-1
October	05	BIRMINGHAM		1-0
	12	Huddersfield Town		1-1
	19	LEEDS CITY		3-2
	26	Grimsby Town		0-0
November	02	BURY		2-0
	09	Fulham		1-3
	16	BARNSLEY		4-0
	23	Bradford Park Avenue		0-0
	30	WOLVES		1-1
December	07	Leicester Fosse		3-0
	14	BRADFORD PARK AVENUE		4-2
	21	Blackpool		1-0
	25	GLOSSOP		2-0

Table at December 25th, 1912

1	Burnley	20	45	23	27
2	Birmingham	18	30	16	25
3	PRESTON NORTH END	19	28	15	25
4	Wolves	19	25	18	23
5	Nottingham Forest	19	29	23	23
6	Lincoln City	17	26	22	21
7	Clapton Orient	18	22	19	20
8	Huddersfield Town	19	26	21	19
9	Barnsley	18	23	25	19
10	Bristol City	18	16	19	19
11	Hull City	19	29	27	18
12	Leeds City	17	28	31	17
13	Grimsby Town	18	23	27	16
14	Leicester Fosse	19	21	31	16
15	Fulham	18	24	24	15
16	Bradford Park Avenue	18	17	23	15
17	Bury	18	20	31	14
18	Blackpool	19	15	30	12
19	Stockport County	18	18	28	11
20	Glossop	15	14	26	9
		364	479	479	364

Attendances
Total 3,327,375 Average 8,756
Goals
Total 1,123 Average 2.955
Top scorer Bert Freeman (Burnley) 31
380 games

PRESTON NORTH END

The Deepdale men joined Burnley on points after beating Hull City on Boxing Day and then moved ahead of their Lancashire rivals with a 3-2 victory at struggling Glossop on New Year's Day. An excellent sequence of results over the next few weeks saw Preston stretch their lead over Burnley to 4 points by mid-February. Birmingham, in third, were now seven points adrift of the leaders. North End's 1-5 slump at Leeds City proved to be a temporary setback only and an unbeaten run in March lifted the leaders' points total to 47 from 33 games.

Birmingham trailed Preston by 5 points, while Burnley were 6 points behind with a game in hand. Despite losing to Wolves on April 5th, Preston reached mid-April 4 points ahead of Burnley, having drawn with their chief rivals on April 10th. It seemed likely that the battle for the title might go to the final day of the season after Burnley won 3-2 at Leicester Fosse on April 19th, while Preston could only draw at lowly Stockport County. However, on April 23rd, Barnsley won 1-0 at Turf Moor and Preston could no longer be caught by Burnley.

Preston North End's '2nd half' record

December	26	HULL CITY		1-0
	28	Clapton Orient		2-1
January	01	Glossop		3-2
	04	LINCOLN CITY		0-0
	25	BRISTOL CITY		5-1
February	05	Nottingham Forest		2-0
	08	Birmingham		1-0
	15	HUDDERSFIELD TOWN		2-1
	22	Leeds City		1-5
March	01	GRIMSBY TOWN		2-0
	08	Bury		0-0
	15	FULHAM		1-0
	22	Barnsley		1-1
	24	Hull City		2-2
April	05	Wolves		0-2
	10	BURNLEY		1-1
	12	LEICESTER FOSSE		1-0
	19	Stockport County		1-1
	26	BLACKPOOL		2-1

Final League Division 2 Table 1913

1	PRESTON NORTH END	38	56	33	53
2	Burnley	38	88	53	50
3	Birmingham	38	59	44	46
4	Barnsley	38	57	47	45
5	Huddersfield Town	38	66	40	43
6	Leeds City	38	70	64	40
7	Grimsby Town	38	51	50	40
8	Lincoln City	38	50	52	40
9	Fulham	38	65	55	39
10	Wolves	38	56	54	38
11	Bury	38	53	57	38
12	Hull City	38	60	56	36
13	Bradford Park Avenue	38	60	60	36
14	Clapton Orient	38	34	47	34
15	Leicester Fosse	38	50	65	33
16	Bristol City	38	46	72	33
17	Nottingham Forest	38	58	59	32
18	Glossop	38	49	68	32
19	Stockport County	38	56	78	26
20	Blackpool	38	39	69	26
		760	1123	1123	760

Preston North End and Burnley were promoted. Blackpool (32 votes) and Stockport County (22) were both re-elected. The unsuccessful applicants were Chesterfield Town (10), Stalybridge Celtic (6), Darlington and Gainsborough Trinity (4 each) and South Shields, who received no support.

1913-1914 – LEAGUE DIVISION 1

Two clubs went unbeaten during the first month of the season – Blackburn Rovers and West Bromwich. However, Albion drew 3 of their 5 games, whereas the 1911-12 champions dropped only one point in their 6 matches. Rovers therefore headed the table at 30th September, two points clear of Tottenham Hotspur, with Manchester United a further point behind in third. United proved the strongest of the leading teams over the next few weeks, winning all four matches during October. When the Red Devils extended their winning run to seven games by beating Liverpool 3-0 at Old Trafford, the club slipped into first place following Blackburn's defeat at Sunderland.

However, a week later Rovers regained the League leadership by a 6-0 crushing of Everton, while United lost 1-3 at Aston Villa. Blackburn stayed clear at the top of the table until December 20th, when Manchester United won 1-0 at Ewood Park to pull level on 24 points. Rovers went clear again five days later, crushing Preston North End 5-0 on Christmas Day while United lost at Everton. By winning 1-0 at Burnley, Sunderland went second.

Blackburn Rovers' '1st half' record

September	01	NEWCASTLE UNITED	3-0
	06	LIVERPOOL	6-2
	08	Burnley	2-1
	13	Aston Villa	3-1
	20	MIDDLESBROUGH	6-0
	27	Sheffield United	1-1
October	04	DERBY COUNTY	3-1
	11	Manchester City	2-1
	18	BRADFORD CITY	0-0
	25	Tottenham Hotspur	3-3
November	01	Sunderland	1-2
	08	EVERTON	6-0
	15	West Bromwich Albion	0-2
	22	SHEFFIELD WEDNESDAY	3-2
	29	Bolton Wanderers	0-1
December	06	CHELSEA	3-1
	13	Oldham Athletic	1-1
	20	MANCHESTER UNITED	0-1
	25	PRESTON NORTH END	5-0

Table at December 25th, 1913

1	BLACKBURN ROVERS	19	48	20	26
2	Sunderland	19	36	22	25
3	Manchester United	18	32	17	24
4	Bolton Wanderers	17	32	22	21
5	West Bromwich Albion	18	21	17	21
6	Oldham Athletic	18	27	24	21
7	Bradford City	18	20	17	19
8	Tottenham Hotspur	18	33	31	19
9	Burnley	19	29	22	18
10	Sheffield United	19	31	30	18
11	Aston Villa	18	26	29	18
12	Liverpool	18	21	32	18
13	Chelsea	18	26	31	17
14	Everton	18	21	29	17
15	Derby County	19	31	38	16
16	Sheffield Wednesday	19	25	34	16
17	Newcastle United	18	16	23	16
18	Middlesbrough	18	28	36	14
19	Manchester City	18	20	30	12
20	Preston North End	19	14	33	10
		366	537	537	366

Attendances
Total   8,229, 200   Average   21,840
Goals
Total   1,103   Average   2.903
Top scorer   George Elliott (Middlesbrough) 31
380 games

BLACKBURN ROVERS

By New Year, Blackburn had opened up a 3-point lead, thanks to both their main challengers losing games. Although Rovers failed to score in their first three games of 1914, neither Manchester United nor Sunderland proved able to take advantage and three wins in a row for the leaders saw them five points clear by mid-February.

As Sunderland joined Manchester United in falling away over the next phase of the campaign, Bolton Wanderers, Aston Villa and West Bromwich Albion emerged as the leaders of the chasing group. Rovers kept the pressure on, going 8 games unbeaten by March 23rd. Despite losing at Sheffield Wednesday on the last Saturday of the month, Blackburn started April with a six point lead over Bolton at the top of the 1st Division.

With victory over second-placed Wanderers on April 4th, Rovers struck what proved to be a killer blow in the title race. When Bolton lost 0-3 at Tottenham and Aston Villa fell 1-3 at Manchester City on Good Friday, April 4th, Blackburn's 0-0 draw at Newcastle became enough to take the championship back to Ewood Park.

Blackburn Rovers' '2nd half' record

December	26	Preston North End	5-1
	27	Liverpool	3-3
January	01	BURNLEY	0-0
	03	ASTON VILLA	0-0
	17	Middlesbrough	0-3
	24	SHEFFIELD UNITED	3-2
February	07	Derby County	3-2
	14	MANCHESTER CITY	2-1
	25	Bradford City	2-0
	28	TOTTENHAM HOTSPUR	1-1
March	14	Everton	0-0
	21	WEST BROMWICH ALBION	2-0
	23	SUNDERLAND	3-1
	28	Sheffield Wednesday	1-3
April	04	BOLTON WANDERERS	3-2
	10	Newcastle United	0-0
	11	Chelsea	0-2
	18	OLDHAM ATHLETIC	2-1
	25	Manchester United	0-0

Final League Division 1 Table 1914

1	BLACKBURN ROVERS	38	78	42	51
2	Aston Villa	38	65	50	44
3	Middlesbrough	38	77	60	43
4	Oldham Athletic	38	55	45	43
5	West Bromwich Albion	38	46	42	43
6	Bolton Wanderers	38	65	52	42
7	Sunderland	38	63	52	40
8	Chelsea	38	46	55	39
9	Bradford City	38	40	40	38
10	Sheffield United	38	63	60	37
11	Newcastle United	38	39	48	37
12	Burnley	38	61	53	36
13	Manchester City	38	51	53	36
14	Manchester United	38	52	62	36
15	Everton	38	46	55	35
16	Liverpool	38	46	62	35
17	Tottenham Hotspur	38	50	62	34
18	Sheffield Wednesday	38	53	70	34
19	Preston North End	38	52	69	30
20	Derby County	38	55	71	27
		760	1103	1103	760

Preston North End and Derby County were relegated.

1913-1914 – LEAGUE DIVISION 2   NOTTS COUNTY

Four sides shared the 2nd Division lead at the end of September – Leicester Fosse, Bury, Notts County and Bradford Park Avenue. All this quartet had 8 points, though the two northern sides had each played one game less than their rivals. Bury remained prominent during October, but then lost their way and slipped to fourth by mid-November. Leicester were beaten 4 times in six outings to drop away too.

Despite suffering setbacks themselves, Notts County and Bradford managed to continue to grind out points to lead the table, with Leeds City moving into third. As the campaign wound on into December, Hull City and The Arsenal also made progress. By December 20th, when leaders Notts County reached the half-way point in their league fixtures, only 3 points separated the Trent Bridge club from fifth place. Importantly, all the chasing teams had games in hand on the front-runners.

By the New Year, Hull City had gone top, on goal average, with 28 points – the same as both Notts County and The Arsenal. With Leeds City on 27 points, things were tight at the head of Division Two and a real dog-fight for the title was anticipated. Notts County, it seems, had different ideas. Crucial January wins over The Arsenal, on the 1st, and Leeds City, on the 24th, helped the Magpies to establish a three-point lead by mid-February.

The Nottingham outfit were helped by the fact that none of the other clubs in contention at the top could match their five wins in six matches. The pattern continued into March and a 4-1 victory over fading Hull City on the 28th carried Notts County 8 points clear, with Bradford Park Avenue now back in second. The leaders were promoted on April 11th when they beat Bury 2-0 and The Arsenal drew with Leeds. Two days later, Bradford lost at Nottingham Forest and Notts County were champions.

Notts County's '1st half' record

September	06	Grimsby Town	0-0
	13	BIRMINGHAM	5-1
	15	The Arsenal	0-3
	20	Bristol City	1-1
	24	BLACKPOOL	2-0
	27	LEEDS CITY	4-0
October	02	LINCOLN CITY	2-1
	04	Clapton Orient	0-1
	11	GLOSSOP	2-2
	18	Stockport County	2-1
	25	BRADFORD PARK AVENUE	2-3
November	01	FULHAM	4-0
	08	Leicester Fosse	2-0
	15	WOLVES	2-0
	22	Hull City	0-2
	29	BARNSLEY	3-1
December	06	Bury	3-3
	13	HUDDERSFIELD TOWN	3-0
	20	Lincoln City	0-0

Notts County's '2nd half' record

December	25	NOTTINGHAM FOREST	2-2
	26	Nottingham Forest	0-1
	27	GRIMSBY TOWN	4-0
January	01	THE ARSENAL	1-0
	03	Birmingham	1-2
	17	BRISTOL CITY	4-0
	24	Leeds City	4-2
February	07	CLAPTON ORIENT	3-0
	14	Glossop	1-0
	21	STOCKPORT COUNTY	2-1
	28	Bradford Park Avenue	3-0
March	07	Fulham	2-1
	14	LEICESTER FOSSE	4-1
	21	Wolves	1-4
	28	HULL CITY	4-1
April	04	Barnsley	1-0
	11	BURY	2-0
	13	Blackpool	0-0
	18	Huddersfield Town	1-2

Table at December 20th, 1913

1	NOTTS COUNTY	19	37	19	25
2	Bradford Park Avenue	17	31	22	24
3	Hull City	17	31	13	23
4	Leeds City	16	39	18	22
5	The Arsenal	17	23	17	22
6	Fulham	17	25	17	20
7	Wolves	18	19	21	20
8	Bury	17	20	19	19
9	Clapton Orient	16	13	10	18
10	Grimsby Town	17	21	25	18
11	Barnsley	16	20	19	17
12	Leicester Fosse	18	28	27	17
13	Bristol City	17	23	23	15
14	Stockport County	17	21	25	15
15	Birmingham	17	18	28	15
16	Huddersfield Town	17	16	19	12
17	Blackpool	17	14	24	12
18	Glossop	16	15	28	10
19	Lincoln City	18	12	29	10
20	Nottingham Forest	18	17	40	8
		342	443	443	342

Final League Division 2 Table 1914

1	NOTTS COUNTY	38	77	36	53
2	Bradford Park Avenue	38	71	47	49
3	The Arsenal	38	54	38	49
4	Leeds City	38	76	46	47
5	Barnsley	38	51	45	45
6	Clapton Orient	38	47	35	43
7	Hull City	38	53	37	41
8	Bristol City	38	52	50	41
9	Wolves	38	51	52	41
10	Bury	38	39	40	40
11	Fulham	38	46	43	38
12	Stockport County	38	55	57	36
13	Huddersfield Town	38	47	53	34
14	Birmingham	38	48	60	34
15	Grimsby Town	38	42	58	34
16	Blackpool	38	33	44	32
17	Glossop	38	51	67	28
18	Leicester Fosse	38	45	61	26
19	Lincoln City	38	36	66	26
20	Nottingham Forest	38	37	76	23
		760	1011	1011	760

Attendances
Total 3,996,650   Average 10,518
Goals
Total 1,011   Average 2.661
Top scorers Sammy Stevens (Hull City)
and
Jack Peart (Notts County) 28
380 games

Notts County and Bradford Park Avenue were promoted.

Nottingham Forest (34 votes) and Lincoln City (24) were both re-elected. The unsuccessful clubs included Stoke (16), Darlington (2), and Chesterfield Town and South Shields (1). Gainsborough Trinity and South Liverpool received no support.

- 63 -

1914-1915 – LEAGUE DIVISION 1   EVERTON

Sheffield Wednesday were the first club to show in September 1914, with 7 points from their opening 4 games. When the Owls lost away at Liverpool on 19th September, Manchester City eased to the top on goal average. Although City won again against Tottenham a week later, Wednesday reclaimed pole position by crushing Bradford Park Avenue 6-0 at Owlerton.

A point behind the leading pair were Oldham Athletic, but the Lancashire club moved second by trouncing Wednesday 5-2 at Boundary Park on October 3rd. The Latics went unbeaten through October and after a 4-1 win over Tottenham on November 14th went into top spot, after leaders Manchester City were toppled at Wednesday's Owlerton ground.

Two further victories before the end of the month kept Oldham clear of City, with Sheffield Wednesday slipping back and Everton joining Blackburn Rovers at the head of the group of clubs below the leading duo. Despite a 0-3 slip at Sheffield United, the Boundary Park club reached Christmas with a 2-point lead over Wednesday, who had played one game more than the Latics.

Oldham's advantage remained intact at year's end, but, when the next 6 games produced only 1 win and 4 points, the pressure tightened at the top. By mid-February, Athletic still led the 1st Division, but only one point separated them from Manchester City and Sheffield Wednesday, neither of whom had been particularly convincing over the previous few weeks.

With only 6 points from their next six games, Oldham were fortunate to stay in touch with the new top flight leaders Manchester City. The Hyde Road club's own stumbles in this phase allowed the more consistent Blackburn Rovers to assume the league leadership, on goal average, by the end of March. Had the reigning champions come good at the right time? Six or seven teams were still in title contention as the final month of the season began. By the middle of April, Oldham Athletic had gone back to the summit, a point up on Everton and Manchester City. As Destiny beckoned, Oldham faltered. Everton beat Manchester City on April 17th while Athletic drew at Villa. Both the Latics and City then lost their last 2 games, the losses on April 24th presenting Everton with the title.

Everton's '1st half' record

September	02	Tottenham Hotspur	3-1
	05	Newcastle United	1-0
	07	Burnley	0-1
	12	MIDDLESBROUGH	2-3
	19	Sheffield United	0-1
	26	ASTON VILLA	0-0
October	03	Liverpool	5-0
	10	BRADFORD PARK AVENUE	4-1
	17	Oldham Athletic	1-1
	24	MANCHESTER UNITED	4-2
	31	Bolton Wanderers	0-0
November	07	BLACKBURN ROVERS	1-3
	14	Notts County	0-0
	21	SUNDERLAND	7-1
	28	Sheffield Wednesday	4-1
December	05	WEST BROMWICH ALBION	2-1
	12	MANCHESTER CITY	4-1
	19	Chelsea	0-2
	25	BRADFORD CITY	1-1

Everton's '2nd half' record

December	26	Bradford City	1-0
January	01	TOTTENHAM HOTSPUR	1-1
	02	NEWCASTLE UNITED	3-0
	16	Middlesbrough	1-5
	23	SHEFFIELD UNITED	0-0
February	06	LIVERPOOL	1-3
	10	Aston Villa	5-1
	27	Manchester United	2-1
March	13	Blackburn Rovers	1-2
	17	OLDHAM ATHLETIC	3-4
	20	NOTTS COUNTY	4-0
	22	BURNLEY	5-3
April	02	BOLTON WANDERERS	0-2
	03	SHEFFIELD WEDNESDAY	0-1
	06	Sunderland	3-0
	10	West Bromwich Albion	2-1
	14	Bradford Park Avenue	2-1
	17	Manchester City	1-0
	26	CHELSEA	2-2

Table at December 25th, 1914

1	Oldham Athletic	18	42	27	27
2	Sheffield Wednesday	19	38	26	25
3	Manchester City	18	24	16	24
4	EVERTON	19	39	20	23
5	Blackburn Rovers	19	44	28	23
6	Bradford City	19	39	26	23
7	Aston Villa	18	33	32	21
8	West Bromwich Albion	19	27	21	20
9	Bradford Park Avenue	18	28	33	20
10	Sunderland	18	38	38	19
11	Middlesbrough	18	24	31	18
12	Sheffield United	17	22	20	17
13	Burnley	18	28	27	16
14	Newcastle United	19	24	26	15
15	Chelsea	18	23	29	15
16	Liverpool	19	29	42	15
17	Bolton Wanderers	20	37	48	14
18	Tottenham Hotspur	19	26	50	12
19	Manchester United	17	20	31	11
20	Notts County	18	16	30	10
		368	601	601	368

Attendances
Total   5,088,675   Average   13,391
Goals
Total   1,203   Average   3.166
Top scorer   Bobby Parker (Everton) 36
380 games

Final League Division 1 Table 1915

1	EVERTON	38	76	47	46
2	Oldham Athletic	38	70	56	45
3	Blackburn Rovers	38	83	61	43
4	Burnley	38	61	47	43
5	Manchester City	38	49	39	43
6	Sheffield United	38	49	41	43
7	Sheffield Wednesday	38	61	54	43
8	Sunderland	38	81	72	41
9	Bradford Park Avenue	38	69	65	41
10	West Bromwich Albion	38	51	43	40
11	Bradford City	38	55	51	40
12	Middlesbrough	38	62	74	38
13	Liverpool	38	65	75	37
14	Aston Villa	38	62	72	37
15	Newcastle United	38	46	48	32
16	Notts County	38	41	57	31
17	Bolton Wanderers	38	68	84	30
18	Manchester United	38	46	62	30
19	Chelsea	38	51	65	29
20	Tottenham Hotspur	38	57	90	28
		760	1203	1203	760

Competition suspended due to outbreak of Great War.

1914-1915 – LEAGUE DIVISION 2

DERBY COUNTY

Despite losing their second fixture, at Wolves, The Arsenal headed Division 2 at the close of September, on goal average, from Huddersfield Town. One point behind the leading pair were Bristol City and Fulham, who each had eight points. Huddersfield then outshone all their rivals over the next six weeks, dropping only 1 point from 12 and threatening to break away.

Defeat at Clapton Orient on November 14th put the brakes on the Leeds Road club, however, limiting their advantage to three points. The Arsenal held second place, with Derby County, five games without conceding a goal, in third spot and looking to be in exceptionally good form. The Rams' excellent run continued and their 1-0 win against the leaders narrowed the gap at the top to two points. Huddersfield lost their next two games, against Lincoln City and Birmingham, by the same score and, with two defeats for The Arsenal, Derby County moved to the front of the pack. By Boxing Day, with a further five points from three games, the Baseball Ground men had established a 3-point lead.

A 6-0 thrashing of Leicester Fosse at Walnut Street on December 28th enabled the Rams to lead by 5 points going into 1915. Despite a surprise loss at Stockport on January 30th, County had pulled further ahead by the middle of February, though things might have been different if Birmingham had been able to play between January 6th and February 13th. Understandably perhaps, the Derby men took their foot off the accelerator. They reached the end of March with a reduced advantage of 4 points over second-placed Preston, who were unbeaten in eleven games, having won the last eight. With both clubs having 6 to play, the title race was clearly not over.

By April 3rd, Preston had won twice and went into Easter Monday a single point behind the Rams. Derby then reopened the gap, but lost at Bury on the 17th, while Preston beat Arsenal 3-0 and moved within a point of County once again. The title was therefore decided when the top two met head on at the Baseball Ground on April 24th. Grimes and Leonard scored as Derby won to become 2nd Division champions.

Derby County's '1st half' record

September	02	BARNSLEY	7-0
	05	Glossop	1-1
	12	WOLVES	3-1
	19	Fulham	0-2
	26	STOCKPORT COUNTY	1-0
October	03	Hull City	0-1
	10	LEEDS CITY	1-2
	17	Clapton Orient	1-0
	24	THE ARSENAL	4-0
	31	BLACKPOOL	5-0
November	07	Lincoln City	0-0
	14	BIRMINGHAM	1-0
	21	Grimsby Town	2-1
	28	HUDDERSFIELD TOWN	1-0
December	05	Bristol City	3-2
	12	BURY	2-1
	19	Preston North End	3-1
	25	Nottingham Forest	2-2
	26	NOTTINGHAM FOREST	1-0

Derby County's '2nd half' record

December	28	Leicester Fosse	6-0
January	02	GLOSSOP	1-1
	16	Wolves	1-0
	23	FULHAM	1-1
	30	Stockport County	2-3
February	06	HULL CITY	4-1
	13	Leeds City	5-3
	20	CLAPTON ORIENT	0-3
	27	The Arsenal	2-1
March	06	Blackpool	1-2
	13	LINCOLN CITY	3-0
	20	Birmingham	2-0
	27	GRIMSBY TOWN	1-1
April	02	Barnsley	0-1
	03	Huddersfield Town	0-0
	05	LEICESTER FOSSE	1-0
	10	BRISTOL CITY	1-0
	17	Bury	0-2
	24	PRESTON NORTH END	2-0

Table at December 26th, 1914

1	DERBY COUNTY	19	38	14	29
2	Huddersfield Town	19	34	16	26
3	The Arsenal	20	42	24	24
4	Birmingham	19	33	19	24
5	Bristol City	19	41	27	22
6	Preston North End	20	25	25	22
7	Barnsley	19	23	27	22
8	Hull City	18	30	23	21
9	Fulham	19	30	23	21
10	Wolves	20	33	29	19
11	Bury	19	33	35	19
12	Lincoln City	20	24	28	19
13	Leeds City	20	36	29	18
14	Clapton Orient	19	23	23	18
15	Grimsby Town	20	20	41	17
16	Stockport County	19	20	26	16
17	Nottingham Forest	20	26	35	16
18	Blackpool	19	21	35	14
19	Leicester Fosse	19	18	48	10
20	Glossop	19	16	39	9
		386	566	566	386

Attendances
Total 2,377,850   Average 6,258
Goals
Total 1,135   Average 2.987
Top scorer   Joe Lane (Blackpool) 28
380 games

Final League Division 2 Table 1915

1	DERBY COUNTY	38	71	33	53
2	Preston North End	38	61	42	50
3	Barnsley	38	51	51	47
4	Wolves	38	77	52	45
5	The Arsenal	38	69	41	43
6	Birmingham	38	62	39	43
7	Hull City	38	65	54	43
8	Huddersfield Town	38	61	42	42
9	Clapton Orient	38	50	48	41
10	Blackpool	38	58	57	39
11	Bury	38	61	56	38
12	Fulham	38	53	47	37
13	Bristol City	38	62	56	37
14	Stockport County	38	54	60	37
15	Leeds City	38	65	64	32
16	Lincoln City	38	46	65	31
17	Grimsby Town	38	48	76	31
18	Nottingham Forest	38	43	77	29
19	Leicester Fosse	38	47	88	24
20	Glossop	38	31	87	18
		760	1135	1135	760

Competition suspended due to Great War.

The re-election vote was held despite the suspension of the League. Leicester Fosse (33 votes) were successful, but Glossop (1) were not and their place went to Stoke, who polled 21 votes, beating South Shields (11), Chesterfield Town (8) and Darlington (4).

Club colours   1902-1915

20 Football League clubs played in the same basic colours during the period 1902-1915, or that part of the period they were in the League.

Red shirts and White shorts were worn by five teams - **The Arsenal (Woolwich Arsenal), Barnsley, Bristol City, Liverpool, and Nottingham Forest.**

Three clubs used a combination of Light Blue shirts and White shorts – **Birmingham (Small Heath), Chelsea, and Manchester City.**

Three others sported a kit comprising White shirts and Navy Blue shorts - **Bury, Preston North End, Tottenham Hotspur. Fulham** also appeared in White shirts, but the Craven Cottage team had Black shorts.

Aston Villa played in Claret shirts with Light Blue Sleeves and White shorts, while Stoke wore a similar kit, but without the use of Light Blue for the sleeves.

Seven Football League clubs made a minor, but significant change to their colours during the period 1902-1915.

Clapton Orient played in White Shirts and Navy Blue Shorts, adding a Red 'V' to their shirts for the 1914-1915 season.

Middlesbrough added White Shoulders to their kit of Red Shirts with White Shorts in 1912.

While the Black and White Striped Shirts were retained throughout, **Newcastle United** used Navy Blue Shorts 1903-04 and 1905-12, with Black Shorts worn in the other years.

9 clubs made at least one major change to their colours in the period. None of the clubs listed in this section can be described as 'multiple changers'.

Blackburn Rovers changed from Light Blue and White halved shirts with Navy Blue shorts to Royal Blue and White halved shirts with White shorts in 1905.

Bolton Wanderers began and ended the period wearing White shirts and Navy Blue shorts. For 1908-1912, Black shorts were used and, for 1912-13, the club played in Red shirts with White shorts.

Bradford City used a kit of Claret shirts, with an Amber trim, and White shorts up to 1909, when Amber Shoulders were introduced for the shirts.

Bradford Park Avenue had hooped shirts and White Shorts. At first the shirt colours were Amber, Black & Red, but Green and White were adopted in 1911.

Burnley played in Green shirts with White shorts until 1910, when a switch was made to Claret & Blue tops.

Royal Blue Shirts and White shorts was the kit choice of **Everton.**

Royal Blue and White were also the colours used by **Oldham Athletic, Sheffield Wednesday and West Bromwich Albion**, all three wearing striped shirts. The Latics' stripes were, however, broad ones and Wednesday played in Black shorts whereas the others used White.

Lincoln City, Notts County and Wolves all had striped shirts and Black shorts. The Imps wore Red and White, County's colours were Black and White, and the Molineux men turned out in a Black and Amber combination.

Sheffield United wore Red and White Striped Shirts all through the 1901-1915 period, but changed the colour of shorts used from Navy Blue to Black in 1904.

Sunderland's kit saw the same change made in 1910. **Doncaster Rovers** also made this switch for the 1904-05 season during their brief appearances in the League.

Gainsborough Trinity wore Royal Blue Shirts, changing the colour of players' shorts from Navy Blue to White in 1909.

Burslem Port Vale changed from Red/White striped shirts with Navy Blue shorts to Claret/Blue striped shirts and White shorts in 1902.

Chesterfield Town's kit comprised Green and White striped shirts with Navy Blue shorts up to 1906, when a plainer outfit of White shirts and Navy Blue shorts was introduced.

Derby County used White shirts and Black shorts up to 1904 and again from 1907. In between, at least one campaign (1904-05) was played using White and Black striped shirts.

Huddersfield Town used White shirts with Light Blue Shoulders and White shorts 1910-13, changing to Light Blue and White striped tops and White shorts.

As Newton Heath, **Manchester United** had worn White shirts with Navy Blue shorts for the 1901-02 season. With the new name came new colours – Red shirts with White shorts.

Club colours   1902-1915   (continued)

The eight other Football League clubs which were involved between 1902 and 1915 can be described as 'multiple changers' with colours and kits being altered on a number of occasions.

Blackpool switched from Red/ White halved shirts with Black shorts to an All White strip in 1902. This was altered to Red shirts with Black shorts two years later, with White shorts being adopted in 1908.

The **Burton United** club seemed unable to settle on a kit. Light Blue and White quartered shirts with Navy Blue shorts gave way to a simpler Maroon shirts/Black shorts combination 1902-03. Red shirts with Black shorts were used 1903-04, followed by Dark Green tops and White shorts the next season. In 1905, the club reverted to earlier colours of Chocolate and Light Blue quartered shirts, though the White shorts were retained.

Glossop changed from Black & White halved shirts with Black shorts to Thin Black and White Hoops and Black shorts in 1904. The team wore an all White strip 1907-1910, with a Purple 'V' being added to the shirts 1910-1914. In their final League season, Glossop did without the 'V' and changed to using Navy Blue shorts.

Grimsby Town wore Chocolate and Light Blue halved tops and White shorts 1901-02, switching to the use of quartered shirts 1902-04. After using Salmon shirts with Black shorts 1904-06, the Mariners wore White shirts with Red shorts 1906-08, before reverting to the earlier quartered kit 1908-10. On returning to the League after a 1-year absence the team appeared in Black and White striped shirts with Black shorts.

The **Hull City** team began their league career wearing Black and Amber striped shirts with Black shorts. An All Black was adopted for the 1909-10 season, but the striped kit was back for the next campaign and was used until 1914 when the club changed to an outfit of Black shirts with White shorts.

Leeds City wore Dark Blue shirts, with Gold trim, and White shorts 1905-08. A kit of Dark Blue and Thin Gold striped tops and White shorts was worn 1908-09, with the stripes reversed on the shirts used in the following season. Returning to the original kit in 1910, City added a Gold Hoop to the shirts in 1913, replacing this with a Gold 'V' a year later.

Leicester Fosse had Dark Blue shirts with Light Blue sleeves 1901-03, before playing for one season in Red shirts with White shorts. Dark Blue shirts and White shorts were sported 1904-11, only for the team to have a different kit of Red and White striped shirts with Black shorts 1911-12. In 1912 an outfit of Royal Blue shirts and White shorts was introduced.

Stockport County spent 1901-05 playing in Red and White striped shirts, with Navy Blue shorts. Blue and White striped tops and White shorts were then used 1905-06, after which the stripes went back to being Red and White, though the shorts remained White. A kit of All White, with Blue Shoulders to the shirts was worn 1913-14, these shirts being replaced by ones comprising broad Blue and White stripes for the 1914-15 campaign.

MISCELLANEOUS MATTERS

A Third Division?

In 1907, the Southern League proposed the setting up of a new, 3-division National League in which it would combine with the Football League. This was rejected by Football League clubs. A year later, a proposal to form a 20-club 3rd Division, including 18 clubs from the Southern League, was also rejected.

The 1908 proposal was made again in 1909, receiving 27 votes in support, with 13 against. Despite this, no progress could be made because any restructuring of the Football League required a three-quarters majority.

A further proposal to set up a Third Division was put forward in 1911, coming this time mainly from clubs in the North. In the vote on this, there were 11 votes in favour and 27 against, with one abstention.

2 up, 2 down

Despite proposals for 3 up, 3 down in 1905 and a more radical 4 up, 4 down system of promotion and relegation in 1912, the existing 2 up, 2 down scheme remained in place.

Rules

In 1906 a new law was passed stating that the outer casing of the ball must be made of leather. A 1909 rule decreed that goalkeepers had to wear a different coloured top from the rest of their team. The '10-yard rule' replaced the '6-yard rule' at free-kicks in 1912, this being extended to corner kicks in 1913.

The root of all evil ?

In 1906, Manchester City were fined £250 for offering bonuses to their players which breached League rules. The club secretary and chairman were banned from football for life and 17 players were suspended until January 1907, banned from playing for the club again and auctioned off.

On Good Friday, 1915, Manchester United defeated Liverpool 2-0, a result with odds of 7-1 before the match. After an investigation, 4 players from each side were found guilty of 'match-fixing' and banned from football for life. The seven who survived the Great War later had the bans lifted.

THE WAR YEARS 1915-1919

Although the Football League did not operate in the years 1915-1919, there were 'regional leagues'. The main competitions were in Lancashire, London and the Midlands, with 'principal' leagues and 'subsidiary' competitions. The records are on the sparse side and it has been impossible to get a full picture. For example, we don't know what happened in the North-East pre-1918, nor in the South-West post-1916. Below are the final tables from all the 'principal' leagues it has been possible to find, with the 'goals per game' averages shown as 'GPG ='. Tables for the 'subsidiary' competitions are provided for 1915-1916, with details of 'section' winners only for the other seasons. The leagues were made up of Football League clubs, with some non-league clubs, depending on which part of the country the competition was being played in.

There were some changes in league membership. During the 1915-1916 season a number of League clubs did not take part, as far as we know - Aston Villa, Birmingham, Blackburn Rovers, Middlesbrough, Newcastle United, Sunderland, West Bromwich Albion and Wolverhampton Wanderers. Birmingham and Blackburn appeared in the 1916-1917 season, but Derby County did not. For other changes, it is probably best to look at the tables below.

1915-1916

LANCASHIRE SECTION - *Principal Competition* - GPG = 3.69

1	Manchester City	26	61	35	35
2	Burnley	26	71	43	33
3	Blackpool	26	54	41	31
4	Everton	25	59	42	30
5	Stockport County	26	47	43	29
6	Liverpool	26	48	42	29
7	Oldham Athletic	25	52	44	29
8	Stoke	26	43	46	27
9	Southport Central	26	41	41	24
10	Bury	26	46	52	23
11	Manchester United	26	41	51	22
12	Bolton Wanderers	26	48	65	21
13	Rochdale	26	34	56	19
14	Preston North End	26	23	67	10
		362	668	668	362

Unplayed - Everton v. Oldham Athletic

Northern Subsidiary Competition – GPG = 4.00

1	Burnley	10	29	12	16
2	Blackpool	10	24	13	16
3	Preston North End	10	22	19	10
4	Bolton Wanderers	10	16	22	9
5	Bury	10	17	26	6
6	Southport Central	10	12	28	3
		60	120	120	60

Southern Subsidiary Competition – GPG = 3.70

1	Manchester City	10	23	19	13
2	Everton	10	19	13	13
3	Liverpool	10	21	13	10
4	Oldham Athletic	10	17	21	10
5	Stockport County	10	19	18	9
6	Manchester United	10	12	27	5
		60	111	111	60

SOUTH-WESTERN SECTION – GPG = 3.34

1	Portsmouth	12	29	11	18
2	Southampton	12	37	19	17
3	Cardiff City	12	21	18	14
4	Bristol Rovers	12	17	20	13
5	Bristol City	12	13	16	11
6	Swindon Town	11	12	17	6
7	Newport County	11	8	36	3
		82	137	137	82

Not played - Swindon Town v. Newport County

LONDON SECTION - *Principal Competition* – GPG = 3.57

1	Chelsea	22	71	18	37
2	Millwall Athletic	22	46	24	30
3	The Arsenal	22	43	46	25
4	West Ham United	22	47	35	24
5	Fulham	22	45	37	24
6	Tottenham Hotspur	22	38	35	24
7	Brentford	22	36	40	20
8	Queen's Park Rangers	22	27	41	19
9	Crystal Palace	22	35	55	19
10	Watford	22	37	46	17
11	Clapton Orient	22	22	44	14
12	Croydon Common	22	24	50	11
		264	471	471	264

Supplementary Competition – GPG = 4.14

1	Chelsea	14	50	15	21
2	West Ham United	14	32	16	20
3	Tottenham Hotspur	14	32	22	19
4	Fulham	14	38	19	18
5	Millwall Athletic	14	30	22	18
6	Crystal Palace	14	41	29	18
7	Watford	14	22	20	13
8	Brentford	14	29	33	12
9	Croydon Common	14	28	27	11
10	Clapton Orient	14	17	27	10
11	The Arsenal	14	19	31	10
12	Luton Town	14	31	44	9
13	Queen's Park Rangers	14	14	37	9
14	Reading	14	23	64	8
		196	406	406	196

MIDLAND SECTION - *Principal Competition* – GPG = 3.40

1	Nottingham Forest	26	48	25	35
2	Sheffield United	26	51	36	31
3	Huddersfield Town	26	43	36	29
4	Bradford City	26	52	32	28
5	Barnsley	26	47	55	28
6	Leicester Fosse	26	42	34	28
7	Sheffield Wednesday	26	46	44	27
8	Notts County	26	39	36	26
9	Lincoln City	26	54	54	26
10	Leeds City	26	39	43	25
11	Hull City	26	42	58	23
12	Bradford Park Avenue	26	46	46	22
13	Grimsby Town	26	31	46	20
14	Derby County	26	39	74	16
		364	619	619	364

Northern Subsidiary Competition – GPG = 3.77

1	Leeds City	10	21	13	15
2	Bradford Park Avenue	10	27	17	12
3	Huddersfield Town	10	19	15	11
4	Bradford City	10	18	20	9
5	Rochdale	10	15	21	9
6	Barnsley	10	13	27	4
		60	113	113	60

Central Subsidiary Competition – GPG = 3.57

1	Grimsby Town	10	25	10	14
2	Sheffield United	10	17	11	11
3	Rotherham County	10	20	24	11
4	Sheffield Wednesday	10	10	13	9
5	Hull City	10	18	27	8
6	Lincoln City	10	17	22	7
		60	107	107	60

Southern Subsidiary Competition – GPG = 3.93

1	Nottingham Forest	10	28	12	14
2	Notts County	10	16	12	13
3	Leicester Fosse	10	15	19	9
4	Stoke	10	21	18	8
5	Derby County	10	23	28	8
6	Chesterfield	10	15	29	8
		60	118	118	60

1916-1917

LANCASHIRE SECTION - *Principal Competition* –
GPG = 3.48

1	Liverpool	30	62	26	46
2	Stockport County	30	61	31	43
3	Stoke	30	64	36	39
4	Manchester City	30	49	29	37
5	Everton	30	62	41	37
6	Burnley	30	73	56	34
7	Manchester United	30	48	54	32
8	Rochdale	30	47	54	29
9	Southport Central	30	40	43	28
10	Bolton Wanderers	30	59	65	24
11	Blackburn Rovers	30	52	66	24
12	Preston North End	30	47	65	23
13	Bury	30	40	63	22
14	Oldham Athletic	30	36	65	22
15	Port Vale	30	50	60	21
16	Blackpool	30	44	80	19
		480	834	834	480

In the Subsidiary Competition each team played 6 matches. **Rochdale** came out top with 11 points.

LONDON SECTION – GPG = 3.86

1	West Ham United	40	110	45	65
2	Millwall Athletic	40	85	48	58
3	Chelsea	40	93	48	53
4	Tottenham Hotspur	40	112	64	53
5	The Arsenal	40	62	47	48
6	Fulham	40	102	63	45
7	Luton Town	39	101	82	43
8	Crystal Palace	38	68	72	35
9	Southampton	39	57	80	34
10	Queen's Park Rangers	39	48	86	29
11	Watford	39	69	115	25
12	Brentford	40	56	99	25
13	Portsmouth	40	58	117	22
14	Clapton Orient	40	49	104	19
		554	1070	1070	554

Unplayed - Crystal Palace v. Luton Town, Queen's Park Rangers v. Watford, Southampton v. Crystal Palace. Portsmouth took over Reading's fixtures in October.

MIDLAND SECTION - *Principal Competition* – GPG = 3.16

1	Leeds City	30	68	29	46
2	Barnsley	30	65	41	38
3	Birmingham	30	56	38	37
4	Huddersfield Town	30	41	31	36
5	Bradford Park Avenue	30	51	32	34
6	Nottingham Forest	30	57	39	33
7	Notts County	30	47	52	32
8	Bradford City	30	41	41	31
9	Rotherham County	30	53	52	30
10	Sheffield United	30	43	47	29
11	Hull City	30	36	57	27
12	Chesterfield	30	59	62	26
13	Sheffield Wednesday	30	36	48	24
14	Grimsby Town	30	38	71	22
15	Leicester Fosse	30	29	53	19
16	Lincoln City	30	38	65	16
		480	758	758	480

In the Subsidiary Competition each team played 6 matches. 5 teams won 8 points, but **Bradford Park Avenue** came out top with the best goal average.

1917-1918

LANCASHIRE SECTION - *Principal Competition* –
GPG = 3.80

1	Stoke	30	109	27	48
2	Liverpool	30	101	26	48
3	Everton	30	92	36	44
4	Rochdale	30	78	47	39
5	Manchester City	30	57	28	38
6	Stockport County	30	59	32	37
7	Bolton Wanderers	30	68	70	30
8	Manchester United	30	45	49	30
9	Oldham Athletic	30	50	59	28
10	Preston North End	30	38	53	27
11	Port Vale	30	47	58	26
12	Blackpool	30	38	67	24
13	Southport Central	30	33	69	22
14	Bury	30	46	64	21
15	Burnley	30	29	100	13
16	Blackburn Rovers	30	22	127	5
		480	912	912	480

In the Subsidiary Competition each team played 6 matches. Both Everton and **Liverpool** won 10 points, but the Reds had the better goal average.

LONDON SECTION – GPG = 3.83

1	Chelsea	36	82	39	50
2	West Ham United	36	103	51	49
3	Fulham	36	75	60	47
4	Tottenham Hotspur	36	86	56	46
5	The Arsenal	36	76	56	37
6	Brentford	36	81	94	35
7	Crystal Palace	36	54	83	30
8	Queen's Park Rangers	36	48	73	30
9	Millwall Athletic	36	51	74	28
10	Clapton Orient	36	34	104	8
		360	690	690	360

MIDLAND SECTION - *Principal Competition* - GPG = 3.34

1	Leeds City	28	75	23	47
2	Sheffield United	28	66	27	41
3	Birmingham	28	59	38	34
4	Hull City	28	67	50	34
5	Nottingham Forest	28	41	28	30
6	Bradford Park Avenue	28	40	29	30
7	Leicester Fosse	28	52	43	29
8	Huddersfield Town	28	49	46	26
9	Rotherham County	28	42	52	25
10	Notts County	28	43	54	23
11	Sheffield Wednesday	28	45	59	23
12	Grimsby Town	28	24	62	21
13	Bradford City	28	34	55	20
14	Lincoln City	28	25	62	19
15	Barnsley	28	40	74	18
		420	702	702	420

In the Subsidiary Competition each team played 6 matches. **Grimsby Town** came out top with 9 points.

1918-1919

LANCASHIRE SECTION - *Principal Competition*

1	Everton	30	108	26	56
2	Stoke	30	84	36	43
3	Liverpool	30	82	33	42
4	Bolton Wanderers	30	58	58	36
5	Manchester City	30	57	36	33
6	Southport Vulcan	30	49	53	33
7	Preston North End	30	41	51	30
8	Stockport County	30	48	52	29
9	Manchester United	30	51	50	27
10	Rochdale	30	56	61	27
11	Blackpool	30	45	61	25
12	Port Vale	30	39	77	24
13	Burnley	30	54	76	23
14	Bury	30	27	58	20
15	Oldham Athletic	30	39	62	18
16	Blackburn Rovers	30	35	83	14
		480	873	873	480

Goals per game = 3·64

In the Subsidiary Competition the 16 teams were divided into 4 sections, each team playing 6 matches. Section winners were : A - **Blackpool** (8 points), B - **Oldham Athletic** (10 points + superior goal average), C - **Manchester City** (11 points), and D - **Liverpool** (10 points).

LONDON SECTION

1	Brentford	36	94	46	49
2	The Arsenal	36	85	56	45
3	West Ham United	36	65	51	41
4	Fulham	36	70	55	40
5	Queen's Park Rangers	36	69	60	39
6	Chelsea	36	70	53	37
7	Crystal Palace	36	66	73	34
8	Tottenham Hotspur	36	52	72	34
9	Millwall Athletic	36	50	67	29
10	Clapton Orient	36	35	123	12
		360	656	656	360

Goals per game = 3·64

MIDLAND SECTION - *Principal Competition*

1	Nottingham Forest	30	59	31	42
2	Birmingham	30	72	36	41
3	Notts County	30	65	38	41
4	Leeds City	30	53	38	38
5	Bradford Park Avenue	30	53	41	37
6	Huddersfield Town	30	45	45	34
7	Hull City	30	48	42	31
8	Sheffield United	30	56	47	30
9	Coventry City	30	55	59	30
10	Leicester Fosse	30	53	53	29
11	Sheffield Wednesday	30	49	49	28
12	Lincoln City	30	38	59	24
13	Bradford City	30	48	56	22
14	Barnsley	30	45	79	21
15	Grimsby Town	30	40	69	20
16	Rotherham County	30	23	60	12
		480	802	802	480

Goals per game = 3·34

In the Subsidiary Competition the 16 teams were divided into 4 sections, each team playing 6 matches. Section winners were : A - **Sheffield United** (11 points), B - **Birmingham** (10 points), C - **Bradford Park Avenue** (8 points), and D - **Hull City** (8 points + superior goal average).

MIDLAND VICTORY SECTION

1	West Bromwich Albion	6	12	5	7
2	Derby County	6	11	9	7
3	Wolves	6	9	9	7
4	Aston Villa	6	9	18	3
		24	41	41	24

Goals per game = 3·42

NORTHERN VICTORY SECTION

1	Middlesbrough	14	29	12	21
2	Sunderland	14	32	20	18
3	South Shields	14	27	25	15
4	Scotswood	14	29	24	14
5	Newcastle United	14	21	23	14
6	Darlington Forge	14	15	27	12
7	Hartlepools United	14	34	34	11
8	Durham City	14	8	30	7
		112	195	195	112

Goals per game = 3·48

1919 – A YEAR OF ...   ... GREAT CONTROVERSY

TOTTENHAM HOTSPUR and THE ARSENAL

In 1919, the Football League decided to increase the size of both divisions from 20 to 22 clubs. Twice before, the First Division had been increased by two clubs, in 1898 and in 1905. On both occasions, the top two in Division Two had been promoted and there had been no relegation from the top flight.

Why things were done very differently in 1919 is open to question. Sure enough, the winners and runners-up of the 1914-1915 Second Division season, Derby County and Preston North End, were promoted. Chelsea, second from bottom in the First Division in 1915 were reprieved. The fact that the F.A. wanted to use Stamford Bridge for the Cup Final in 1920 is a fact which some claimed was a factor in this.

This left, anyway, one First Division place and Tottenham Hotspur had every right to believe this should have been given to them. The Football League had other ideas, however, and there is a powerful suspicion that this was the result of behind-the-scenes activity involving the President of the Football League, John McKenna, and Sir Henry Norris, Chairman of The Arsenal.

It was announced that the twenty-second club to play in the First Division 1919-1920 would be elected and clubs were invited to apply. Tottenham and Arsenal were among the seven hopeful applicants, who also included Barnsley and Wolverhampton Wanderers, who had finished in third and fourth positions in the Second Division in 1915, i.e. ahead of Arsenal in the final table.

One version of the story says that the League was actually keen to have a second London club in the top level of English soccer, making the contest effectively a two-horse race. Another version tells, however, how League President McKenna did the rounds pushing the Arsenal case and saying it would be better to vote for the Gunners because they had played in the Football League for longer than Tottenham.

Quite how this argument fitted in with the fact that founder members of the Football League, Wolves, were among the applicants is unclear. With Wolves and Barnsley having finished above Arsenal in 1915, the argument looks even more spurious. Whatever really went on, Arsenal were elected to the First Division, their 18 votes being ten more than Tottenham's and over three times as many as Barnsley's five.

In the 1980s, I worked with a Tykes' supporter named Tony Gill, who inherited his family's traditional resentment of the events of 1919, and spoke passionately of 'the red mist descending' whenever the name of 'Arsenal' was mentioned in the South Yorkshire coal-field. In 1919, Spurs' players, officials and fans may have felt something similar.

FOR THE RECORD

The clubs elected to the 2nd Division for the 1919-1920 season were Coventry City (35 votes), West Ham United (32), Rotherham County (28) and South Shields (28). Port Vale just missed out, with 27 supporters, while Rochdale (7), Southport (7) and Chesterfield Town (0) were also rejected.

LEEDS CITY and PORT VALE

In the time which had elapsed since the 1914-15 season, there had been friendlies and regional competitions. How well-organised the running of Leeds City was during these confused years is open to question, but it seems likely that things were no worse at Elland Road than elsewhere and, probably, matters were handled better than at many clubs. City manager, Herbert Chapman, had effectively left the club in the War, to work in a West Yorkshire munitions factory. His former role at Elland Road was shared by George Cripps and Leeds City Chairman, Joseph Connor. These two fell out amid Connor's allegations of Cripps' incompetence and, following his demotion within the club, Cripps making accusations that illegal payments had been made to players.

Added to this were the issues surrounding one Charlie Copeland, a full-back signed in 1912, who was angered by the reserve team contract offered in 1919. The player threatened to report the club to the F.A. and the Football League, for making illegal payments to players during the war, if he was not offered better terms. City turned him down and Copeland duly 'spilled the beans' in July 1919. With George Cripps' accusations being common knowledge by this time and a sealed box of evidence to support his claims allegedly in the hands of solicitors, matters moved to a head. A joint Football League/ Football Association meeting was held in Manchester on September 26th, 1919. Leeds City were charged with 'financial irregularities' and were ordered to present records of the club's accounts.

The club refused to present its books by the October 6th deadline. As a result, Leeds City were expelled from the Football League and disbanded. The club's fixtures were taken over by Port Vale, whose role in events has been questioned, given the swiftness and the severity of the punishment, plus the ease with which the Valiants were able to slot into the vacancy created by the expulsion of the Leeds club.

City officials, including Herbert Chapman, were banned from football for life, though Chapman's ban was lifted when he made the Football Authorities realise that he was not involved with the club when the alleged irregularities took place and could prove that he was employed, in the war effort, in a munitions factory. Leeds City players were auctioned off on October 17th at the Metropole Hotel in the city centre. Around £10,000 was raised for the 22 men. The 'lots' included 4 future English internationals, Billy Kirton, the scorer of the winning goal in the next FA Cup Final, and City's top striker over several pre-war seasons, Billy McLeod.

A fortnight later, football was back at Elland Road, largely thanks to Leeds solicitor Alfred Masser, who led efforts to form a new club, Leeds United. Active life for the the new Leeds began on October 31st in the Midland League, the club having taken over the fixtures of Leeds City Reserves. Competing with such giants of soccer as Worksop Town, Mexborough, Castleford Town and Silverwood Colliery, Leeds United finished 12th of 18. In spite of this, the Elland Road team were elected to the 2nd Division at the 1920 Football League A.G.M., finishing easily ahead of all their rivals in the poll. This perhaps reflected what League clubs thought of the events of the previous October.

The new club had been taken over by the chairman of West Yorkshire rivals, Huddersfield Town, Hilton Crowther, who gave United his full support. It was through him that Town's manager, Arthur Fairclough, was brought to Elland Road late in February 1920.

1919-1920 – LEAGUE DIVISION 1

With four extra fixtures to be fitted in, the season kicked off in August, for the first time in the Football League's history. Somebody had had the bright idea of clubs, for the most part, playing each other home and away on successive match dates. The 'new practice' lasted for five years before being abandoned.

With the effects of the Great War on soccer impossible to judge, interest centred on whether the pre-1914 giants would continue to dominate the game or if there would be changes at the top. Early indications suggested the latter, with West Bromwich Albion leading the table at September 30th, with Burnley, Middlesbrough and Bradford Park Avenue in close order behind them.

Three defeats in their next six outings saw Albion overtaken in November, with Newcastle United and Burnley sitting a point ahead of the Throstles by November 15th. After losing their game at Sheffield Wednesday a week later, however, West Bromwich won six in a row, resumed the Division 1 leadership, on goal average on Boxing Day, and ended December 27th a point clear of Burnley at the head of the table. The two leaders had pulled away from the rest.

West Bromwich Albion's '1st half' record

August	30	OLDHAM ATHLETIC	3-1
September	03	Newcastle United	2-0
	06	Oldham Athletic	1-2
	08	NEWCASTLE UNITED	3-0
	13	EVERTON	4-3
	20	Everton	5-2
	27	BRADFORD CITY	4-1
October	04	Bradford City	0-3
	11	BOLTON WANDERERS	4-1
	18	Bolton Wanderers	2-1
	25	NOTTS COUNTY	8-0
November	01	Notts County	0-2
	10	ASTON VILLA	1-2
	15	Aston Villa	4-2
	22	SHEFFIELD WEDNESDAY	1-3
	29	Sheffield Wednesday	3-0
December	06	Manchester City	3-2
	13	MANCHESTER CITY	2-0
	20	Derby County	4-0
	26	SUNDERLAND	4-0
	27	DERBY COUNTY	3-0

Table at December 27th, 1919

1	WEST BROMWICH ALBION	21	61	25	32
2	Burnley	23	37	30	31
3	Newcastle United	22	29	20	27
4	Sunderland	22	38	31	26
5	Chelsea	22	33	27	25
6	Bolton Wanderers	23	42	35	25
7	The Arsenal	22	35	33	24
8	Aston Villa	21	42	37	23
9	Bradford Park Avenue	22	37	33	23
10	Everton	22	42	38	22
11	Liverpool	22	29	29	22
12	Notts County	21	41	43	22
13	Manchester United	20	31	24	21
14	Manchester City	22	45	43	21
15	Sheffield United	23	37	38	21
16	Middlesbrough	22	29	37	20
17	Derby County	23	22	35	19
18	Bradford City	23	37	46	18
19	Blackburn Rovers	22	29	44	18
20	Preston North End	22	31	50	17
21	Sheffield Wednesday	22	17	35	13
22	Oldham Athletic	20	23	34	12
		482	767	767	482

WEST BROMWICH ALBION

Albion remained clear despite dipping at Roker Park on New Year's Day, as Burnley crashed 0-4 at Middlesbrough. The Turf Moor men then drew 2 and lost 2 of their next 4, which allowed the Throstles to go 5 points clear. This gap was reduced to 3 points on February 14th after Burnley's win at Manchester City, becoming 2 points by the end of the month. With the renewed challenges of Liverpool and Sunderland having petered out, the top two clubs clashed head on at the start of March. After an honours even meeting at Turf Moor, the March 14th return at The Hawthorns produced an easy win for West Bromwich, Morris scoring twice in the 4-1 victory. Burnley fell again, 0-3 at Sunderland, a fortnight later and West Bromwich moved 6 points clear with 2 games in hand.

Flagging Claret hopes flickered briefly over Easter. Burnley beat Newcastle United 1-0 on Good Friday, defeating The Arsenal 2-1 a day later. Although Albion had a comfortable win at Bradford the same day, they lost at Highbury on Easter Monday. On April 6th, West Bromwich beat The Arsenal 1-0, however, reopening the 6 points gap. On April 10th, Albion became champions. Bradford were beaten 3-1 at The Hawthorns while Burnley lost 0-2 at Highbury.

West Bromwich Albion's '2nd half' record

January	01	Sunderland	1-4
	03	Blackburn Rovers	5-1
	17	BLACKBURN ROVERS	5-2
	24	MANCHESTER UNITED	2-1
February	07	SHEFFIELD UNITED	0-2
	14	Sheffield United	0-1
	21	MIDDLESBROUGH	4-1
	25	Manchester United	2-1
	28	Middlesbrough	0-0
March	06	Burnley	2-2
	13	BURNLEY	4-1
	20	Preston North End	1-0
	27	PRESTON NORTH END	4-1
April	03	Bradford Park Avenue	4-0
	05	The Arsenal	0-1
	06	THE ARSENAL	1-0
	10	BRADFORD PARK AVENUE	3-1
	17	Liverpool	0-0
	24	LIVERPOOL	1-1
	26	Chelsea	0-2
May	01	CHELSEA	4-0

Final League Division 1 Table 1920

1	WEST BROMWICH ALBION	42	104	47	60
2	Burnley	42	65	59	51
3	Chelsea	42	56	51	49
4	Liverpool	42	59	44	48
5	Sunderland	42	72	59	48
6	Bolton Wanderers	42	72	65	47
7	Manchester City	42	71	62	45
8	Newcastle United	42	44	39	43
9	Aston Villa	42	75	73	42
10	The Arsenal	42	56	58	42
11	Bradford Park Avenue	42	60	63	42
12	Manchester United	42	54	50	40
13	Middlesbrough	42	61	65	40
14	Sheffield United	42	59	69	40
15	Bradford City	42	54	63	39
16	Everton	42	69	68	38
17	Oldham Athletic	42	49	52	38
18	Derby County	42	47	57	38
19	Preston North End	42	57	73	38
20	Blackburn Rovers	42	64	77	37
21	Notts County	42	56	74	36
22	Sheffield Wednesday	42	28	64	23
		924	1332	1332	924

Notts County and Sheffield Wednesday were relegated.

1919-1920 – LEAGUE DIVISION 2

TOTTENHAM HOTSPUR

After the club controversially lost out to The Arsenal in the vote for the last place in Division 1, Tottenham Hotspur had something to prove to the rest of English football. Spurs' early opponents felt the sharp edge of this as the White Hart Lane men swept to 7 wins in their opening seven games, scoring 28 goals against four and opening up a three point lead at the head of the 2nd Division by September 30th.

No other club could match the consistency of or the pace set by the Hotspur. Having dropped only one point out of 24, the Tottenham team finally lost. This was in their thirteenth league fixture, 1-2 at Bury. A return to winning ways a week later against the same opposition saw Spurs top the Division 2 table by five points at mid-November, with Birmingham, Blackpool and Hull City leading the rest.

The leaders pressed on into December, winning five of their next seven games. Birmingham, who had managed to close the gap at the 2nd Division summit to a mere three points by December 20th, with a 3-0 win over Grimsby Town, lost twice to lowly Leicester City over Christmas. This allowed a new contender, in the form of improving Huddersfield Town, now being guided by the great Herbert Chapman, to nose ahead of the out-of-sorts Midlanders, on goal average.

In what was becoming more of a procession than a race for the Division 2 championship, Tottenham continued to apply pressure at the front. The six games which opened the second half of Spurs' league programme produced four more wins and ten additional points. When Huddersfield Town were defeated on February 16th, the gap between Tottenham and their closest rivals stretched to 10 points.

A further nine points had been gathered by the end of the next month. Birmingham followed 8-0 and 7-0 thrashings of Nottingham Forest and Lincoln City in the opening part of March with three defeats in a row to slip 12 points off the lead. This left only Huddersfield Town, 10 points down, but with a game in hand, for even the most pessimistic Spurs' follower to worry about.

Easter results failed to confirm Tottenham as title winners, in spite of their season-long dominance. Three more wins lifted Spurs' points total to 63, but Huddersfield Town with a draw at Barnsley and a double over Stoke, clung on tenaciously, to deny Spurs an early celebration, reaching 52 points with 6 games still to play. On April 10th, however, the title went to White Hart Lane as Spurs beat Stoke for a second time to establish an unassailable points advantage.

Tottenham Hotspur's '1st half' record

August	30	Coventry City	5-0
September	01	LEICESTER CITY	4-0
	06	COVENTRY CITY	4-1
	11	Leicester City	4-2
	13	SOUTH SHIELDS	2-0
	20	South Shields	3-0
	27	LINCOLN CITY	6-1
October	04	Lincoln City	1-1
	11	Clapton Orient	2-1
	18	CLAPTON ORIENT	4-0
	27	Port Vale	1-0
November	01	PORT VALE	2-0
	08	Bury	1-2
	15	BURY	2-1
	22	Nottingham Forest	1-1
	29	NOTTINGHAM FOREST	5-2
December	06	Fulham	4-1
	13	FULHAM	4-0
	20	Barnsley	0-3
	25	HULL CITY	4-0
	26	Hull City	3-1

Table at December 26th, 1919

1	TOTTENHAM HOTSPUR	21	62	17	36
2	Huddersfield Town	21	47	17	29
3	Birmingham	21	40	18	29
4	Blackpool	21	40	22	28
5	Barnsley	21	43	21	25
6	Stockport County	21	35	22	25
7	Stoke	21	39	28	25
8	West Ham United	21	21	21	25
9	Bristol City	21	24	19	24
10	Hull City	22	43	39	24
11	Fulham	20	28	26	22
12	Bury	20	27	25	21
13	South Shields	20	16	20	19
14	Port Vale*	20	27	26	18
15	Nottingham Forest	21	24	32	18
16	Leicester City	21	18	35	17
17	Clapton Orient	22	23	35	16
18	Wolves	20	28	34	15
19	Rotherham County	21	21	45	15
20	Grimsby Town	20	15	41	10
21	Lincoln City	21	17	56	10
22	Coventry City	21	8	47	7
		458	646	646	458

*Record includes 8 games played by Leeds City, prior to their expulsion from the League, October 1919.

Tottenham Hotspur's '2nd half' record

December	27	BARNSLEY	4-0
January	03	Stockport County	2-1
	17	STOCKPORT COUNTY	2-0
	24	Huddersfield Town	1-1
February	07	Blackpool	1-0
	14	BLACKPOOL	2-2
	16	HUDDERSFIELD TOWN	2-0
	25	Bristol City	2-1
	28	BRISTOL CITY	2-0
March	13	West Ham United	1-2
	20	ROTHERHAM COUNTY	2-0
	22	WEST HAM UNITED	2-0
	27	Rotherham County	1-1
April	02	Wolves	4-2
	03	STOKE	2-0
	05	WOLVES	3-1
	10	Stoke	3-1
	17	GRIMSBY TOWN	3-1
	24	Grimsby Town	0-2
	26	BIRMINGHAM	0-0
May	01	Birmingham	1-0

Final League Division 2 Table 1920

1	TOTTENHAM HOTSPUR	42	102	32	70
2	Huddersfield Town	42	97	38	64
3	Birmingham	42	85	34	56
4	Blackpool	42	65	47	52
5	Bury	42	60	44	48
6	Fulham	42	61	50	47
7	West Ham United	42	47	40	47
8	Bristol City	42	46	43	43
9	South Shields	42	58	48	42
10	Stoke	42	60	54	42
11	Hull City	42	78	72	42
12	Barnsley	42	61	55	40
13	Port Vale*	42	59	62	40
14	Leicester City	42	41	61	40
15	Clapton Orient	42	51	59	38
16	Stockport County	42	52	61	37
17	Rotherham County	42	51	83	34
18	Nottingham Forest	42	43	73	31
19	Wolves	42	55	80	30
20	Coventry City	42	35	73	29
21	Lincoln City	42	44	101	27
22	Grimsby Town	42	34	75	25
		924	1285	1285	924

*Record includes 8 games played by Leeds City, prior to their expulsion from the League, October 1919.

Tottenham Hotspur and Huddersfield Town were promoted. Lincoln City (7 votes) and Grimsby Town (20) both failed to gain re-election, being replaced by Leeds United (31) and Cardiff City (23). Walsall (3) were unsuccessful.

- 73 -

1920-1921 – LEAGUE DIVISION 1   BURNLEY

Several clubs made sound starts to the season, including promoted Huddersfield Town, who began with three 1-0 wins. Everton and Bolton Wanderers were also prominent in the early exchanges, but it was Aston Villa who headed the table at the end of September with six wins in their opening 8 games.

Villa crashed 1-6 at Preston North End on October 16th. This allowed Everton to go a point clear at the top, but the blue half of Merseyside then lost twice to Liverpool. The Anfield club shared the lead, at the end of October, with Villa and Newcastle United.

However, the Geordies suffered a double reverse against Burnley, who eased into top spot by drawing at Oldham on November 20th while Liverpool lost at Newcastle. The Clarets went clear a week later by thumping the Latics 7-1. By the time the Turf Moor club completed its 'first half', two days after Christmas, an unbeaten run of 18 league games had carried Burnley 4 points clear at the 1st Division summit. For a team which had lost its first 3 games this was quite remarkable. Since the opening day debacle against Bradford City, Burnley had gone 100% at home for 10 games in a row.

In many previous campaigns, the New Year leaders had faltered in January. Not Burnley. Three wins in the first month of 1921 were followed by a 7-1 demolition of Villa in which Joe Anderson scored five times. By mid-February, Burnley held a lead of 7 points over Newcastle, with Bolton and Liverpool a point further behind. On March 25th, the Clarets reached 30 games without defeat. Despite losing their next game, at Manchester City, the 1st Division front-runners won again on Easter Monday, ending March with a 9-point advantage over three clubs tied on 44 points – Liverpool, Newcastle United and Bolton Wanderers.

With one hand already on the title trophy, Burnley travelled to West Bromwich Albion on April 9th to play the reigning champions on their home turf. Albion were in mid-table, but, lifted by pride, produced an above average show to win 2-0. The return, a week later, ended all square, leaving the Turf Moor men still needing a point to become champions. This was duly gathered at Everton on April 23rd, with Benny Cross scoring in the 1-1 draw. With their first Football League title safely won, Burnley relaxed, taking just 2 points from their 3 closing fixtures. Their superiority in 1921 is shown by the fact that they still finished 5 points clear.

Burnley's '1st half' record

August 28	28	BRADFORD CITY	1-4
	30	Huddersfield Town	0-1
September	04	Bradford City	0-2
	06	HUDDERSFIELD TOWN	3-0
	11	MIDDLESBROUGH	2-1
	18	Middlesbrough	0-0
	25	CHELSEA	4-0
October	02	Chelsea	1-1
	09	Bradford Park Avenue	3-1
	16	BRADFORD PARK AVENUE	1-0
	23	Tottenham Hotspur	2-1
	30	TOTTENHAM HOTSPUR	2-0
November	06	Newcastle United	2-1
	13	NEWCASTLE UNITED	3-1
	20	Oldham Athletic	2-2
	27	OLDHAM ATHLETIC	7-1
December	04	Liverpool	0-0
	11	LIVERPOOL	1-0
	18	PRESTON NORTH END	2-0
	25	SHEFFIELD UNITED	6-0
	27	Sheffield United	1-1

Table at December 27th, 1920

1	BURNLEY	21	43	17	31
2	Bolton Wanderers	22	44	28	27
3	Liverpool	21	38	21	26
4	Newcastle United	21	36	22	26
5	Manchester City	21	35	27	26
6	Middlesbrough	21	33	27	26
7	Everton	23	35	32	26
8	Tottenham Hotspur	21	49	30	24
9	The Arsenal	21	32	27	24
10	Manchester United	21	36	31	24
11	Aston Villa	22	39	37	24
12	Blackburn Rovers	21	32	28	21
13	Preston North End	21	34	30	20
14	West Bromwich Albion	20	25	31	20
15	Sunderland	21	26	34	19
16	Chelsea	21	22	34	19
17	Bradford City	20	29	28	18
18	Huddersfield Town	21	17	26	17
19	Oldham Athletic	21	23	54	13
20	Sheffield United	23	17	44	13
21	Bradford Park Avenue	21	25	46	11
22	Derby County	21	14	30	11
		466	684	684	466

Burnley's '2nd half' record

January	01	Preston North End	3-0
	15	BLACKBURN ROVERS	4-1
	22	Blackburn Rovers	3-1
February	05	ASTON VILLA	7-1
	09	Aston Villa	0-0
	12	DERBY COUNTY	2-1
	23	Derby County	0-0
	26	BOLTON WANDERERS	3-1
March	05	Bolton Wanderers	1-1
	12	THE ARSENAL	1-0
	19	The Arsenal	1-1
	25	MANCHESTER UNITED	1-0
	26	Manchester City	0-3
	28	Manchester United	3-0
April	02	MANCHESTER CITY	2-1
	09	West Bromwich Albion	0-2
	16	WEST BROMWICH ALBION	1-1
	23	Everton	1-1
	30	EVERTON	1-1
May	02	Sunderland	0-1
	07	SUNDERLAND	2-2

Final League Division 1 Table 1921

1	BURNLEY	42	79	36	59
2	Manchester City	42	70	50	54
3	Bolton Wanderers	42	77	53	52
4	Liverpool	42	63	35	51
5	Newcastle United	42	66	45	50
6	Tottenham Hotspur	42	70	48	47
7	Everton	42	66	55	47
8	Middlesbrough	42	53	53	46
9	The Arsenal	42	59	63	44
10	Aston Villa	42	63	70	43
11	Blackburn Rovers	42	57	59	41
12	Sunderland	42	57	60	41
13	Manchester United	42	64	68	40
14	West Bromwich Albion	42	54	58	40
15	Bradford City	42	61	63	39
16	Preston North End	42	61	65	39
17	Huddersfield Town	42	42	49	39
18	Chelsea	42	48	58	39
19	Oldham Athletic	42	49	86	33
20	Sheffield United	42	42	68	30
21	Derby County	42	32	58	26
22	Bradford Park Avenue	42	43	76	24
		924	1276	1276	924

Derby County and Bradford Park Avenue were relegated

1920-1921 – LEAGUE DIVISION 2

BIRMINGHAM

With five wins and two draws, South Shields swept into a three point lead by the last week of September, seven of their 14 goals coming from Arthur Hawes. Newcomers Cardiff City were second, leading West Ham United and Blackpool on goal average. Birmingham, who had been long-time promotion contenders the previous season, lay 19th in the Division Two table, having scraped together just 4 points from their opening seven matches.

The leaders continued to hold onto pole position through October and November. It was not until December 4th, when Shields fell at home to Wolves, that the way was opened up for Bristol City and Cardiff City to move into the promotion spots. Birmingham's winning run of eight games in a row had, however, brought the St. Andrew's club right into contention. Cardiff went two points clear at the top on December 18th by beating Bury. With Bristol City not in action that afternoon, Birmingham moved into second, on goal average, having beaten Leeds United 1-0 through centre half Alex McClure's goal. City reclaimed 'Berth 2' with victory at Port Vale on Christmas Day, while the Blues were held at West Ham.

With Cardiff losing at home to Coventry City on December 27th, the Ashton Gate men then went top by beating Vale again. Birmingham, unbeaten for 2½ months, were 1 point behind the leading pair. In 12 matches since last losing, the Blues had only let in more than 1 goal on one occasion.

All the top three lost their games on New Year's Day and, with F.A. Cup 3rd Round action occupying all 1st and 2nd Division clubs a week later, there was no change at the top of the table until January 15th. Bristol City were held at home by Cardiff on that date, which let in Birmingham, who hit the top for the first time in the 1920-21 campaign after winning at Stockport County. By the middle of February, the Blues still led the 2nd Division, albeit on goal average. With Cardiff City involved in a run to the F.A. Cup Semi-Final and Bristol City hitting a barren run of five games without scoring, Birmingham were able to pull clear at the head of the table during March.

The Blues ended the month 2 points ahead of Blackpool, who had won nine of their 14 matches since Christmas. One point further back were Cardiff City, with 2 games in hand. Cardiff made up these games in early April. With a draw and four wins, City were catapulted into top slot by April 16th - a real test of Birmingham's mettle lay ahead, it seemed. When the Welsh club produced successive below-par performances against Hull City, the Blues managed to pull level again, on 54 points, with two games each to play. Goal average seemed likely to prove crucial and Birmingham held the advantage here – by 0·179 of a goal.

The Bluebirds did what they could, beating Wolves twice. It was not quite enough. The title went to Birmingham, on May 7th, when they completed the double over Port Vale.

Birmingham's '1st half' record

August	28	28	South Shields	0-3
		30	HULL CITY	5-1
September		04	SOUTH SHIELDS	1-1
		06	Hull City	0-1
		11	Cardiff City	1-2
		18	CARDIFF CITY	1-1
		25	Leicester City	0-3
October		02	LEICESTER CITY	5-0
		09	Blackpool	0-3
		16	BLACKPOOL	3-0
		23	Sheffield Wednesday	2-1
		30	SHEFFIELD WEDNESDAY	4-0
November		06	Wolves	3-0
		13	WOLVES	4-1
		20	Stoke	2-1
		27	STOKE	3-0
December		04	COVENTRY CITY	3-2
		11	Coventry City	4-0
		18	LEEDS UNITED	1-0
		25	West Ham United	1-1
		27	WEST HAM UNITED	2-1

Birmingham's '2nd half' record

January	01	Leeds United	0-1
	15	Stockport County	3-0
	22	STOCKPORT COUNTY	5-0
February	05	NOTTS COUNTY	2-1
	12	Clapton Orient	1-1
	16	Notts County	0-0
	19	CLAPTON ORIENT	0-0
	26	Bury	1-0
March	05	BURY	4-0
	12	Bristol City	1-0
	19	BRISTOL CITY	0-0
	25	Fulham	0-5
	26	BARNSLEY	1-3
	29	FULHAM	1-0
April	02	Barnsley	1-1
	09	NOTTINGHAM FOREST	3-0
	16	Nottingham Forest	1-1
	23	ROTHERHAM COUNTY	3-2
	30	Rotherham County	1-1
May	02	PORT VALE	4-0
	07	Port Vale	2-0

Table at December 27th, 1920

1	Bristol City	21	28	12	30
2	Cardiff City	21	35	17	30
3	BIRMINGHAM	21	45	22	29
4	Blackpool	22	28	21	27
5	South Shields	21	37	21	26
6	Clapton Orient	21	26	22	24
7	Notts County	21	29	22	23
8	West Ham United	21	23	15	22
9	Nottingham Forest	21	30	26	22
10	Leeds United	21	24	22	21
11	Wolves	21	27	29	21
12	Bury	21	28	29	20
13	Leicester City	21	22	29	20
14	Rotherham County	22	19	32	20
15	Port Vale	20	28	28	19
16	Fulham	21	19	26	19
17	Stoke	21	27	25	18
18	Hull City	21	19	27	18
19	Barnsley	21	22	23	17
20	Sheffield Wednesday	22	17	32	15
21	Coventry City	21	17	42	13
22	Stockport County	21	20	48	10
		464	570	570	464

Final League Division 2 Table 1921

1	BIRMINGHAM	42	79	38	58
2	Cardiff City	42	59	32	58
3	Bristol City	42	49	29	51
4	Blackpool	42	54	42	50
5	West Ham United	42	51	30	48
6	Notts County	42	55	40	47
7	Clapton Orient	42	43	42	45
8	South Shields	42	61	46	44
9	Fulham	42	43	47	42
10	Sheffield Wednesday	42	48	48	41
11	Bury	42	45	49	40
12	Leicester City	42	39	46	40
13	Hull City	42	43	53	40
14	Leeds United	42	40	45	38
15	Wolves	42	49	66	38
16	Barnsley	42	48	50	36
17	Port Vale	42	43	49	36
18	Nottingham Forest	42	48	55	36
19	Rotherham County	42	37	53	36
20	Stoke	42	46	56	35
21	Coventry City	42	39	70	35
22	Stockport County	42	42	75	30
		924	1061	1061	924

Birmingham and Cardiff City were promoted. Stockport County were relegated to the new Division 3 (North).

1920-1921 – LEAGUE DIVISION 3

With 5 wins apiece, Crystal Palace and Southampton shared the lead of the new 3rd Division after seven games, although Palace were placed first on goal average. Other five-times winners, Watford and Swindon Town, were a point behind the two leaders. Despite a 9-1 opening day romp against Luton Town, Swindon's goal average was inferior to that of Watford. It looked as if the scrap for the one promotion place might turn into a tight affair.

Four draws in six October outings weakened Swindon Town's challenge, while Watford lost twice at the start of the month to slip off the pace. Palace also lost twice in the month, so Southampton were able to go top by beating Swansea Town 3-0 on October 9th and, remaining unbeaten over the next 5 weeks, to hold the 'Number 1 spot' at mid-November. Crystal Palace lay second, with Millwall Athletic having moved third. The run up to Christmas saw a surge from Watford produce 4 consecutive victories, which carried the Brewers into second place, while both Southampton and Crystal Palace made rather stuttering progress. Both clubs lost two games and were having difficulty scoring regularly. Queen's Park Rangers, with 3 wins in a row, and Merthyr Town, unbeaten in 5, moved closer to the leaders.

Crystal Palace's '1st half' record

August	28	Merthyr Town	1-2
September	01	PLYMOUTH ARGYLE	0-0
	04	MERTHYR TOWN	3-0
	08	Plymouth Argyle	1-0
	11	Norwich City	1-0
	18	NORWICH CITY	1-0
	25	Brentford	4-0
October	02	BRENTFORD	4-2
	09	Bristol Rovers	1-2
	16	BRISTOL ROVERS	3-0
	23	Reading	0-1
	30	READING	2-0
November	03	SOUTHEND UNITED	2-3
	06	Luton Town	2-2
	13	LUTON TOWN	2-1
	20	Exeter City	1-1
	27	EXETER CITY	2-1
December	04	Swansea Town	0-0
	11	SWANSEA TOWN	0-1
	18	Queen's Park Rangers	0-3
	25	Brighton & Hove Albion	2-0

Table at December 25th, 1920

1	Southampton	20	36	14	28
2	Watford	19	35	18	26
3	CRYSTAL PALACE	21	32	19	26
4	Queen's Park Rangers	20	35	16	24
5	Merthyr Town	19	26	16	24
6	Swindon Town	19	40	25	24
7	Millwall Athletic	20	24	16	24
8	Luton Town	19	30	33	21
9	Northampton Town	20	28	35	20
10	Swansea Town	20	22	28	20
11	Plymouth Argyle	20	19	14	19
12	Exeter City	20	23	18	19
13	Grimsby Town	20	25	32	18
14	Bristol Rovers	19	25	32	17
15	Southend United	21	20	29	17
16	Newport County	20	21	34	17
17	Brighton & Hove Albion	20	20	33	17
18	Norwich City	20	17	24	16
19	Brentford	20	17	32	16
20	Portsmouth	19	20	19	15
21	Reading	20	23	31	14
22	Gillingham	18	16	36	12
		434	554	554	434

Crystal Palace were promoted to Division 2. Brentford and Gillingham were re-elected without a vote being taken, due to changes being made to the League structure. The 3rd Division became the 3rd Division (South) with a parallel 3rd Division (North) of 20 clubs being introduced. Grimsby Town were transferred to the new competition, joining Stockport County (relegated from Division 2) and 14 northern clubs automatically elected to Division 3 (North).

CRYSTAL PALACE

While Southampton's problems continued after Christmas, seeing the club slip to third by mid-February, Palace took nine points from 6 games and established a 3-point lead at the top. Swindon Town, with five wins in 6 games, now lay second, with a potentially useful trio of matches in hand on the league leaders. The Robins won their next two games, at Brentford and against Norwich City, to put the pressure onto Palace. At the start of March, however, Swindon lost their return match with the Canaries and then lost twice in their matches with Crystal Palace.

This effectively put an end to Swindon's challenge. When Palace and resurgent Southampton drew 1-1 twice during the Easter programme, the leaders were able to ease into April with a 5 points lead over their nearest rivals and looking odds-on favourites to lift the title. Draws in their next 3 games made Palace vulnerable. News that Southampton had gone down 0-1 at Exeter City on April 16th was a major boost, however, and Swindon's third failure to win in a row confirmed the Wiltshire club's 'also-rans' fate. Palace took the 3rd Division title on April 30th. Jack Conner's brace at Northampton earned the point which meant Crystal Palace could no longer be caught and were champions.

Crystal Palace's '2nd half' record

December	27	BRIGHTON & HOVE ALBION	3-2
January	01	QUEEN'S PARK RANGERS	0-0
	15	Millwall Athletic	1-0
	22	MILLWALL ATHLETIC	3-2
February	05	Grimsby Town	0-1
	09	GRIMSBY TOWN	2-0
	12	Newport County	1-0
	19	NEWPORT COUNTY	2-0
	26	Gillingham	1-0
March	05	GILLINGHAM	4-1
	12	Swindon Town	3-1
	19	SWINDON TOWN	1-0
	26	PORTSMOUTH	3-0
	28	Southampton	1-1
	29	SOUTHAMPTON	1-1
April	02	Portsmouth	0-0
	09	WATFORD	2-2
	16	Watford	1-1
	23	NORTHAMPTON TOWN	5-1
	30	Northampton Town	2-2
May	07	Southend United	2-1

Final League Division 3 Table 1921

1	CRYSTAL PALACE	42	70	34	59
2	Southampton	42	64	28	54
3	Queen's Park Rangers	42	61	32	53
4	Swindon Town	42	73	49	52
5	Swansea Town	42	56	45	51
6	Watford	42	59	44	48
7	Millwall Athletic	42	42	30	47
8	Merthyr Town	42	60	49	45
9	Luton Town	42	61	56	44
10	Bristol Rovers	42	68	57	43
11	Plymouth Argyle	42	35	34	43
12	Portsmouth	42	46	48	39
13	Grimsby Town	42	49	59	39
14	Northampton Town	42	59	75	38
15	Newport County	42	43	64	37
16	Norwich City	42	44	53	36
17	Southend United	42	44	61	36
18	Brighton & Hove Albion	42	42	61	36
19	Exeter City	42	39	54	35
20	Reading	42	42	59	31
21	Brentford	42	42	67	30
22	Gillingham	42	34	74	28
		924	1133	1133	924

This left 2 places vacant in Division 3 (South) and 4 vacant in Division 3 (North). Voting was held. Aberdare Athletic (38 votes) and Charlton Athletic (30) beat Bath City (12), Pontypridd (5), Abertillery Town (4) and Barry (1) in the southern voting. The successful clubs in the northern poll were Wigan Borough (34) + Halifax Town, Southport and Stalybridge Celtic (all 25 votes).

OTHER INFORMATION 1919-1921

Attendances 1919-1921

1st Division
(Total for year is followed by average per game)

1919-20	11,115,720	24,060
1920-21	13,580,805	29,396

2nd Division
(Total for year is followed by average per game)

1919-20	5,892,201	12,754
1920-21	7,718,340	16,706

3rd Division
(Total for year is followed by average per game)

1920-21	4,953,795	10,723

There were 462 games played in the season.

Football League

(The total for season is followed by the average per game, with the last column showing the number of league games played altogether)

1919-20	17,007,921	18,407	924
1920-21	26,252,940	18,942	1,386

Lowest attendance of all

On May 7th, 1921, the lowest-ever attendance for a Football League match was recorded for the Second Division encounter between already relegation-doomed Stockport County and Leicester City. With the Hatters' Edgeley Park ground closed following suspension, the game took place at Old Trafford. A 'crowd' of 13 were present to witness a 0-0 draw.

F.A. Cup 1919-1921

The two F.A. Cup Finals were played at Stamford Bridge, home of Chelsea. Crowds were good, but attendances were lower than had been common at Crystal Palace before 1914.

Details of F.A. Cup Finals 1920-1921

24th April, 1920

J.T. Howcroft ran the first post-war Cup Final, which went into extra time. With 50,018 in attendance, the game was decided by a goal scored in the 100th minute by Aston Villa's Billy Kirton. The runners-up were Huddersfield Town.

23rd April, 1921

Record receipts of £13,400 were paid by the 72,805 who turned out in the pouring rain to see Tottenham Hotspur beat 2nd Division Wolves 1-0. Spurs' goal came from Jimmy Dimmock after 53 minutes. The referee was J. Davies.

The Northern vote 1921

The creation of a 3rd Division (North) in 1921 moved the Football League closer to becoming a truly national competition. Not all the applicants joined the League in either 1921 or later. Some might have done better if they had applied twenty years earlier.

Unsuccessful clubs were Castleford Town (18), Rotherham Town (13), Blyth Spartans (9), Gainsborough Trinity (8), Doncaster Rovers and West Stanley (6 each), Wakefield City (4), Lancaster Town and Scunthorpe & Lindsey United (3 each), and South Liverpool (1).

Goal scoring 1919-1921

The leading marksmen for each season were :

Division 1

1919-20 37 – Fred Morris (West Bromwich)
1920-21 38 – Joe Smith (Bolton Wanderers)

Division 2

1919-20 35 – Sam Taylor (Huddersfield Town)
1920-21 29 – Syd Puddefoot (West Ham United)

Division 3

1920-21 29 – John Conner (Crystal Palace)
             Ernie Simms (Luton Town)

There continued to be some high-scoring games in the Football League in the years after the Great War.

Division 1

On October 25th, 1919, League leaders West Bromwich Albion crushed Notts County 8-0. A couple of weeks later Manchester City hammered Blackburn Rovers 8-2. On February 5th, 1921, champions-elect Burnley thrashed Aston Villa 7-1.

Division 2

Birmingham handed out an 8-0 caning to Nottingham Forest on March 10th, 1920, while, during the following season, West Ham United destroyed New Year's Day visitors, Coventry City, in a 7-0 romp.

Division 3

Swindon Town overran Luton Town 9-1 on August 28th, 1920 - the first day of the season.

The number of goals scored in Football League matches after World War I fell between 1919-20 and 1920-21. This downward trend was to continue over the next few campaigns, with 1/3rd of a goal per game 'lost', on average, by the end of the 1923-24 season.

1st Division
(Total for year is followed by average per game)

1919-20	1,332	2·88
1920-21	1,276	2·76

There were 462 games played in each season.

2nd Division
(Total for year is followed by average per game)

1919-20	1,285	2·78
1920-21	1,061	2·30

There were 462 games played in each season.

3rd Division
(Total for year is followed by average per game)

1920-21	1,133	2·45

NICKNAMES OF LEAGUE CLUBS 1919 - 1929

ABERDARE ATHLETIC	DARIANS/DARE	LUTON TOWN	HATTERS
ACCRINGTON STANLEY	REDS	MANCHESTER CITY	CITIZENS
ARSENAL	GUNNERS	MANCHESTER UNITED	RED DEVILS
ASHINGTON	COLLIERS	MERTHYR TOWN	MARTYRS
ASTON VILLA	VILLAINS	MIDDLESBROUGH	BORO
BARNSLEY	COLLIERS	MILLWALL (ATHLETIC)	LIONS
BARROW	BLUEBIRDS	NELSON	SEEDHILLITES
BIRMINGHAM	BLUES	NEW BRIGHTON	RAKERS
BLACKBURN ROVERS	BLUE & WHITES	NEWCASTLE UNITED	MAGPIES
BLACKPOOL	SEASIDERS	NEWPORT COUNTY	IRONSIDES
BOLTON WANDERERS	TROTTERS	NORTHAMPTON TOWN	COBBLERS
BOURNEMOUTH & B.A.	CHERRIES	NORWICH CITY	CANARIES
BRADFORD CITY	BANTAMS/PARADERS	NOTTINGHAM FOREST	REDS
BRADFORD PARK AVENUE	AVENUE	NOTTS COUNTY	MAGPIES
BRENTFORD	BEES	OLDHAM ATHLETIC	LATICS
BRIGHTON & H.A.	DOLPHINS	PLYMOUTH ARGYLE	PILGRIMS
BRISTOL CITY	ROBINS	PORT VALE	VALIANTS
BRISTOL ROVERS	PIRATES	PORTSMOUTH	POMPEY
BURNLEY	CLARETS	PRESTON NORTH END	LILYWHITES
BURY	SHAKERS	QUEEN'S PARK RANGERS	Rs
CARDIFF CITY	BLUEBIRDS	READING	BISCUITMEN
CARLISLE UNITED	CUMBRIANS	ROCHDALE	VALLIANS/'DALE
CHARLTON ATHLETIC	HADDICKS	ROTHERHAM	(MERRY) MILLERS
CHELSEA	BLUES/PENSIONERS	SHEFFIELD UNITED	BLADES
CHESTERFIELD	BLUES/SPIREITES	SHEFFIELD WEDNESDAY	OWLS
CLAPTON ORIENT	Os	SOUTH SHIELDS	LAIDES
COVENTRY CITY	BANTAMS/SKY BLUES	SOUTHAMPTON	SAINTS
CREWE ALEXANDRA	RAILWAYMEN	SOUTHEND UNITED	SHRIMPERS
CRYSTAL PALACE	GLAZIERS	SOUTHPORT	SANDGROUNDERS
DARLINGTON	QUAKERS	STALYBRIDGE CELTIC	CELTIC
DERBY COUNTY	RAMS	STOCKPORT COUNTY	HATTERS
DONCASTER ROVERS	ROVERS	STOKE (CITY)	POTTERS
DURHAM CITY	CITIZENS	SUNDERLAND	ROKERITES
EVERTON	TOFFEES	SWANSEA TOWN	SWANS
EXETER CITY	GRECIANS	SWINDON TOWN	ROBINS
FULHAM	COTTAGERS	TORQUAY UNITED	GULLS
GILLINGHAM	GILLS	TOTTENHAM HOTSPUR	SPURS
GRIMSBY TOWN	MARINERS	TRANMERE ROVERS	ROVERS
HALIFAX TOWN	SHAYMEN	WALSALL	SADDLERS
HARTLEPOOLS UNITED	POOLS	WATFORD	BREWERS
HUDDERSFIELD TOWN	TERRIERS	WEST BROMWICH ALBION	THROSTLES/BAGGIES
HULL CITY	TIGERS	WEST HAM UNITED	HAMMERS
LEEDS CITY	PEACOCKS	WIGAN BOROUGH	BOROUGH
LEEDS UNITED	PEACOCKS	WOLVERHAMPTON WANDERERS	WOLVES
LEICESTER CITY	FOXES/FILBERTS		
LINCOLN CITY	(RED) IMPS	WREXHAM	RED DRAGONS
LIVERPOOL	REDS		

NEW LEAGUE GROUNDS ...   ... AFTER WORLD WAR I

ABERDARE ATHLETIC	ATHLETIC GROUND	NELSON	PARK GROUND
ACCRINGTON STANLEY	PEEL PARK	NEW BRIGHTON	SANDHEYS PARK
ASHINGTON	PORTLAND PARK	NEWPORT COUNTY	SOMERTON PARK
BARROW	HOLKER STREET	NORTHAMPTON TOWN	THE COUNTY GROUND
BOURNEMOUTH & B.A.	DEAN COURT	NORWICH CITY	THE NEST
BRENTFORD	GRIFFIN PARK	PLYMOUTH ARGYLE	HOME PARK
BRIGHTON & H.A.	GOLDSTONE GROUND	PORT VALE	OLD RECREATION GROUND
BRISTOL ROVERS	EASTVILLE		
CARDIFF CITY	NINIAN PARK	PORTSMOUTH	FRATTON PARK
CARLISLE UNITED	BRUNTON PARK	QUEEN'S PARK RANGERS	LOFTUS ROAD
CHARLTON ATHLETIC	THE VALLEY	READING	ELM PARK
CHESTERFIELD	RECREATION GROUND	ROCHDALE	SPOTLAND
COVENTRY CITY	HIGHFIELD ROAD	ROTHERHAM	MILLMOOR
CREWE ALEXANDRA	GRESTY ROAD	SOUTH SHIELDS	HORSLEY HILL ROAD
CRYSTAL PALACE	THE NEST/SELHURST PARK	SOUTHAMPTON	THE DELL
DARLINGTON	THE FEETHAMS	SOUTHEND UNITED	ROOTS HALL
DONCASTER ROVERS	BELLE VUE	SOUTHPORT	HAIG AVENUE
DURHAM CITY	KEPIER HAUGHS + HOLIDAY PARK 1923	STALYBRIDGE CELTIC	BOWER FOLD
		STOKE (CITY)	VICTORIA GROUND
EXETER CITY	ST. JAMES' PARK	SWANSEA TOWN	THE VETCH FIELD
GILLINGHAM	PRIESTFIELD STADIUM	SWINDON TOWN	THE COUNTY GROUND
HALIFAX TOWN	THE SHAY	TORQUAY UNITED	PLAINMOOR
HARTLEPOOLS UNITED	VICTORIA GROUND	TRANMERE ROVERS	PRENTON PARK
LEEDS UNITED	ELLAND ROAD	WALSALL	FELLOWS PARK
LUTON TOWN	KENILWORTH ROAD	WATFORD	VICARAGE ROAD
MANCHESTER CITY	HYDE ROAD + MAINE ROAD 1923	WEST HAM UNITED	BOLEYN GROUND
		WIGAN BOROUGH	SPRINGFIELD PARK
MERTHYR TOWN	PENYDARREN PARK	WREXHAM	RACECOURSE GROUND
MILLWALL (ATHLETIC)	THE DEN		

1921-1922 – LEAGUE DIVISION 1   LIVERPOOL

Despite losing 2 of their first 7 games, defending champions, Burnley, assumed the role of front-runners in early season. Five weeks into the new campaign, the Clarets headed the table, on goal average, from Liverpool, both clubs having 10 points. In 3rd slot were Aston Villa, on 9 points, with the top flight's North-East trio, Middlesbrough, Newcastle United and Sunderland, also well-placed. Burnley kicked on in October, established a two-point lead over Liverpool by October 8th and held this by winning their next 2 games. The champions crashed at Chelsea, however, on the last Saturday of the month, after which three points were dropped against Preston North End. Sunderland drew level with the leaders on November 5th and Liverpool, having secured a 7th 1-1 draw, on November 12th, joined both clubs on 19 points.

Liverpool took temporary lead of Division 1 after thumping Middlesbrough 4-0 on November 19th, while their rivals both drew. However, Burnley beat Tottenham Hotspur 1-0 on November 26th to pass the Reds, who lost at Ayresome Park. As Sunderland lost their way, Liverpool and Burnley slugged it out in the run-up to Christmas. The Anfield club got their noses in front on 17th December by defeating Manchester United while Burnley fell 1-4 at Middlesbrough. The Reds remained clear by the completion of the Boxing Day fixtures.

Although things were all square at the top by New Year, this changed dramatically over the next phase of the season. Burnley lost 3 out of 4, picking up only one point, by mid-February. With 4 wins and a draw in the same period, Liverpool pulled away at the top. Aston Villa, Bolton and Cardiff all passed Burnley, but the gap between first and second was now 5 points.

Burnley reclaimed second place and moved to within 3 points of Liverpool by winning four in a row, by March 4th, when they won 1-0 at Oldham. Form deserted the Turf Moor men again at this juncture, their next three matches producing only a single point. Despite suffering 2 defeats in the month, Liverpool reached the end of March with a six-point lead over Burnley, with Aston Villa and improving Tottenham Hotspur in third and fourth places.

By mid-April, with 4 games to play, Spurs had gone second, with Liverpool's lead standing at 5 points. Easter Monday, April 17th, dawned as a potentially decisive day, with Burnley playing at Anfield. Harry Chambers and Dick Forshaw were on target as the Merseysiders won 2-1, in front of a bumper crowd of 60,000. With Tottenham losing 0-1 at relegation-haunted Oldham Athletic, Liverpool were champions. The day therefore ended with Anfield able to celebrate its first title for 16 years.

Liverpool's '1st half' record

August	27	Sunderland	0-3
	31	MANCHESTER CITY	3-2
September	03	SUNDERLAND	2-1
	07	Manchester City	1-1
	10	Sheffield United	1-0
	17	SHEFFIELD UNITED	1-1
	24	Chelsea	1-0
October	01	CHELSEA	1-1
	08	Preston North End	1-1
	15	PRESTON NORTH END	4-0
	22	Tottenham Hotspur	1-0
	29	TOTTENHAM HOTSPUR	1-1
November	05	Everton	1-1
	12	EVERTON	1-1
	19	MIDDLESBROUGH	4-0
	26	Middlesbrough	1-3
December	03	Aston Villa	1-1
	10	ASTON VILLA	2-0
	17	MANCHESTER UNITED	2-1
	24	Manchester United	0-0
	26	NEWCASTLE UNITED	1-0

Liverpool's '2nd half' record

December	27	HUDDERSFIELD TOWN	2-0
	31	Bradford City	0-0
January	02	Newcastle United	1-1
	14	BRADFORD CITY	2-1
	21	Huddersfield Town	1-0
February	04	Birmingham	2-0
	11	BIRMINGHAM	1-0
	25	THE ARSENAL	4-0
March	04	Blackburn Rovers	0-0
	11	BLACKBURN ROVERS	2-0
	18	BOLTON WANDERERS	0-2
	22	The Arsenal	0-1
	25	Bolton Wanderers	3-1
April	01	OLDHAM ATHLETIC	2-0
	08	Oldham Athletic	0-4
	14	Burnley	1-1
	15	CARDIFF CITY	5-1
	17	BURNLEY	2-1
	22	Cardiff City	0-2
	29	WEST BROMWICH ALBION	1-2
May	06	West Bromwich Albion	4-1

Table at December 26th, 1921

1	LIVERPOOL	21	30	18	29
2	Burnley	21	42	25	28
3	Aston Villa	22	43	29	26
4	Bolton Wanderers	21	36	28	26
5	Huddersfield Town	21	28	18	25
6	Sunderland	21	39	27	25
7	Middlesbrough	21	36	30	24
8	Preston North End	21	29	31	23
9	Manchester City	21	33	35	22
10	Tottenham Hotspur	21	28	22	21
11	Birmingham	21	29	28	21
12	Newcastle United	21	23	27	20
13	Oldham Athletic	21	17	23	20
14	Cardiff City	21	21	28	19
15	Chelsea	21	16	25	19
16	Blackburn Rovers	22	27	29	18
17	West Bromwich Albion	21	20	33	18
18	Everton	21	28	29	17
19	Sheffield United	21	26	27	17
20	Bradford City	21	24	39	17
21	Manchester United	21	23	37	15
22	The Arsenal	21	19	29	14
		464	617	617	464

Final League Division 1 Table 1922

1	LIVERPOOL	42	63	36	57
2	Tottenham Hotspur	42	65	39	51
3	Burnley	42	72	54	49
4	Cardiff City	42	61	53	48
5	Aston Villa	42	74	55	47
6	Bolton Wanderers	42	68	59	47
7	Newcastle United	42	59	45	46
8	Middlesbrough	42	79	69	46
9	Chelsea	42	40	43	46
10	Manchester City	42	65	70	45
11	Sheffield United	42	59	54	40
12	Sunderland	42	60	62	40
13	West Bromwich Albion	42	51	63	40
14	Huddersfield Town	42	53	54	39
15	Blackburn Rovers	42	54	57	38
16	Preston North End	42	42	65	38
17	The Arsenal	42	47	56	37
18	Birmingham	42	48	60	37
19	Oldham Athletic	42	38	50	37
20	Everton	42	57	55	36
21	Bradford City	42	48	72	32
22	Manchester United	42	41	73	28
		924	1244	1244	924

Bradford City and Manchester United were relegated.

1921-1922 – LEAGUE DIVISION 2

Clubs from West Yorkshire and the East Midlands led the way in the 2nd Division in August and September. After 7 games, Leeds United, Barnsley and Nottingham Forest all had twelve points from their fixtures to date, with Notts County in fourth place with 10. Leeds, the only club unbeaten of these four, led on goal average, having conceded only two goals in their opening run. Barnsley were second.

None of the leaders looked particularly convincing over the next six weeks. Barnsley began October well and won four out of five, only to dip at Derby County on the 29th and fail to score in this and the three succeeding games. The Oakwell men led the table at mid-November, however, which is a fair measure of the performance of the other clubs. Nottingham Forest, with 8 points from seven games, fared best and held second place, with Leeds United down to third. Moving up the table at this stage were London pair, Fulham and West Ham United.

Forest passed Barnsley, on goal average, on November 26th. The West Yorkshire club dropped three points to West Ham United, while the new leaders took 3 points from lowly Port Vale. A fortnight later, Fulham went second, after a sixth successive victory, while Barnsley lost 0-1 at home to Rotherham County. Despite losing at Clapton Orient, the Craven Cottage men held second spot after the Boxing Day programme, 3 points behind Forest, who had gone 6 games without conceding a goal.

NOTTINGHAM FOREST

In spite of losing at home to Bury on January 14th, Forest extended their lead at the top to 5 points by the middle of February. Fulham and West Ham United, with four draws each in six games, and Barnsley, with three defeats in five outings, were overhauled by in-form Stoke, whose twelve points from seven matches put them clear in second place, without, it seemed, threatening Forest as yet.

The Potters continued their good run, however, going six further games without losing to extend their unbeaten run to 13 games and to catch up with the leaders on March 25th. As well as their own good form, Stoke benefited from the problems being experienced by the front-runners. Forest's six games in this period saw only one win and odd goal defeats at two of the strugglers, Blackpool and Bradford Park Avenue. With reviving West Ham United and Barnsley not far away in third and fourth, there was cause for concern at the City Ground as the season entered April 1922.

Over the next 4 games, the clubs immediately below Forest all broke even, while the leaders earned 5 points. Crucially, the Reds had both Barnsley and Stoke to play at home. This worked out very well. Barnsley were held and the Potters were beaten. With West Ham United falling apart under the pressure, Forest faced Leeds United on April 29th already promoted. The Reds also knew that a win would make them champions. Noah Burton's goal won the game … and the 2nd Division title.

Nottingham Forest's '1st half' record

August	27	Crystal Palace	1-4
	31	HULL CITY	3-2
September	03	CRYSTAL PALACE	2-1
	05	Hull City	1-0
	10	Coventry City	1-0
	17	COVENTRY CITY	1-0
	24	Derby County	2-1
October	01	DERBY COUNTY	3-0
	08	Leicester City	2-2
	15	LEICESTER CITY	0-0
	22	West Ham United	0-1
	29	WEST HAM UNITED	2-0
November	05	Notts County	1-1
	14	NOTTS COUNTY	0-0
	19	PORT VALE	1-1
	26	Port Vale	2-0
December	03	South Shields	0-0
	10	SOUTH SHIELDS	1-0
	17	BRISTOL CITY	1-0
	24	Bristol City	1-0
	26	WOLVES	0-0

Nottingham Forest's '2nd half' record

December	27	Wolves	0-0
	31	Bury	2-1
January	14	BURY	1-2
	21	ROTHERHAM COUNTY	1-0
February	04	Sheffield Wednesday	4-0
	08	Rotherham County	1-0
	11	SHEFFIELD WEDNESDAY	2-0
	25	FULHAM	0-0
	28	Fulham	0-2
March	04	Blackpool	1-2
	11	BLACKPOOL	0-0
	18	BRADFORD PARK AVENUE	4-1
	25	Bradford Park Avenue	0-1
April	01	CLAPTON ORIENT	2-0
	08	Clapton Orient	2-1
	14	Barnsley	0-2
	15	Stoke	1-1
	17	BARNSLEY	1-1
	22	STOKE	3-1
	29	LEEDS UNITED	1-0
May	06	Leeds United	0-0

Table at December 26th, 1921

1	NOTTINGHAM FOREST	21	25	13	31
2	Fulham	21	43	21	28
3	Barnsley	22	31	23	28
4	West Ham United	21	30	17	26
5	Hull City	21	29	20	25
6	Leicester City	21	18	14	24
7	Stoke	21	25	21	24
8	Notts County	22	27	23	24
9	Leeds United	21	24	21	24
10	Crystal Palace	21	24	23	22
11	Bury	21	30	27	21
12	Derby County	21	29	28	21
13	Wolves	21	24	26	21
14	Sheffield Wednesday	20	24	25	20
15	Rotherham County	21	16	25	20
16	South Shields	21	15	17	19
17	Clapton Orient	21	20	26	18
18	Bradford Park Avenue	21	23	32	15
19	Coventry City	20	19	25	14
20	Port Vale	21	25	35	14
21	Bristol City	21	15	37	12
22	Blackpool	21	16	33	11
		462	532	532	462

Final League Division 2 Table 1922

1	NOTTINGHAM FOREST	42	51	30	56
2	Stoke	42	60	44	52
3	Barnsley	42	67	52	52
4	West Ham United	42	52	39	48
5	Hull City	42	51	41	48
6	South Shields	42	43	38	46
7	Fulham	42	57	38	45
8	Leeds United	42	48	38	45
9	Leicester City	42	39	34	45
10	Sheffield Wednesday	42	47	50	44
11	Bury	42	54	55	40
12	Derby County	42	60	64	39
13	Notts County	42	47	51	39
14	Crystal Palace	42	45	51	39
15	Clapton Orient	42	43	50	39
16	Rotherham County	42	32	43	39
17	Wolves	42	44	49	37
18	Port Vale	42	43	57	36
19	Blackpool	42	44	57	35
20	Coventry City	42	51	60	34
21	Bradford Park Avenue	42	46	62	33
22	Bristol City	42	37	58	33
		924	1061	1061	924

Nottingham Forest and Stoke were promoted. Bradford Park Avenue (3 North) and Bristol City (3 South) were relegated.

1921-1922 – DIVISION 3 (North)   STOCKPORT COUNTY

Stockport County reached the end of September without conceding a goal. Nine points from the 5 games played gave the Hatters the lead in the Football League's new division, with unbeaten Durham City and Nelson having matched the top team's points total, but not their impeccable defensive record. Stalybridge Celtic lay fourth, having won 3 home games, without letting a goal in, and drawn one away.

The Durham and Nelson clubs slipped back over the next few weeks, both dropping points to the two sides who replaced them as 'pack leaders' in the pursuit of Stockport County – Accrington Stanley and Darlington. The front runners' form also dipped at the start of November and they were beaten twice by Grimsby Town. This enabled Darlington to draw level at the top, by the middle of the month, with a double over Barrow. Stockport's strength was defence, whereas their chief rivals' was attack, with 37 goals hit in 12 games. It was an interesting contrast.

The Quakers went top on November 19th by beating Lincoln City 4-2. Remarkably, Darlington did not play another league fixture until Christmas Eve. By this time, Stockport County had regained the leadership of the division. By New Year, Darlington were in fourth place, but, with crushing 5-0 wins over both Walsall and Ashington, the Feethams men swept back to the top by January 3rd. In their next match though, Darlington slipped to a 0-1 reverse at Accrington Stanley. This let Stockport County back in, on goal average, on January 14th, when the Hatters completed a 4-0 double over Stalybridge.

A real battle for pole position developed as both Stockport and Darlington scored eight times in winning their next three games. County failed to beat Wrexham on February 11th though and the Quakers' 1-0 victory at Tranmere Rovers carried them a point clear. A week later, this advantage was doubled as Darlington beat Stalybridge Celtic 3-0, while the Hatters were held to another draw, at Nelson.

Stockport County then defeated Nelson to return to the head of the division when, on February 25th, Darlington produced a lacklustre performance and went down to a 0-1 reverse at Stalybridge Celtic's Bower Fold ground. Both clubs recorded a win next time out, but Stockport then moved ahead with 6 points from four games by the end of March, compared with Darlington's 3 successive draws, against Hartlepools United, home and away, and Wigan Borough. The Feethams' men's game in hand was not enough with only a quarter of the season remaining.

Darlington then lost three in four, including a 3-7 debacle at Crewe Alexandra, and, despite beating Stockport County 1-0 on April 15th, trailed by 3 points with four games left to play. Narrow wins for the top two meant that the gap was exactly the same when they met again for the do-or-die return clash, at Edgeley Park, on April 22nd. An estimated 17,000 crowd turned up for the game – 5,000 more than Stockport's best previous attendance for the season. Charlie Jones' goal killed off the Quakers' lingering hopes and, with Grimsby Town losing at Accrington Stanley, Stockport County became the first-ever champions of the 3rd Division (North).

Stockport County's '1st half' record

August	27	Barrow	2-0
September	10	Wigan Borough	1-0
	17	WIGAN BOROUGH	3-0
	19	BARROW	2-0
	24	Hartlepools United	0-0
October	01	HARTLEPOOLS UNITED	1-0
	08	Southport	1-2
	15	SOUTHPORT	2-1
	22	Rochdale	1-0
	29	ROCHDALE	3-0
November	05	GRIMSBY TOWN	0-1
	12	Grimsby Town	1-2
	26	WALSALL	3-1
December	17	Tranmere Rovers	2-0
	24	TRANMERE ROVERS	0-0
	26	HALIFAX TOWN	0-0
	27	Halifax Town	0-1
	31	Stalybridge Celtic	4-0
January	14	STALYBRIDGE CELTIC	4-0

Table at January 14th, 1922

1	STOCKPORT COUNTY	19	30	8	27
2	Darlington	19	51	17	27
3	Accrington Stanley	22	41	28	26
4	Grimsby Town	21	38	29	25
5	Southport	21	38	23	24
6	Durham City	20	38	34	24
7	Crewe Alexandra	22	29	33	24
8	Stalybridge Celtic	21	33	33	23
9	Wrexham	21	32	35	22
10	Hartlepools United	21	20	21	20
11	Walsall	20	34	39	20
12	Wigan Borough	20	26	33	20
13	Ashington	19	24	34	19
14	Nelson	20	28	31	18
15	Tranmere Rovers	20	30	29	17
16	Lincoln City	20	22	33	16
17	Chesterfield	21	28	43	16
18	Barrow	20	19	28	15
19	Halifax Town	21	29	44	13
20	Rochdale	20	29	44	12
		408	619	619	408

Stockport County's '2nd half' record

January	16	Walsall	2-0
	21	Durham City	2-0
	28	DURHAM CITY	4-0
February	11	WREXHAM	0-0
	18	Nelson	2-2
	25	NELSON	3-0
March	04	Chesterfield	1-0
	08	Wrexham	0-0
	11	CHESTERFIELD	2-1
	18	CREWE ALEXANDRA	1-1
	25	Crewe Alexandra	1-0
April	01	ACCRINGTON STANLEY	2-1
	08	Accrington Stanley	3-1
	14	Ashington	0-2
	15	Darlington	0-1
	17	ASHINGTON	3-2
	22	DARLINGTON	1-0
	29	LINCOLN CITY	2-2
May	06	Lincoln City	1-0

Final League Division 3 (North) Table 1922

1	STOCKPORT COUNTY	38	60	21	56
2	Darlington	38	81	37	50
3	Grimsby Town	38	72	47	50
4	Hartlepools United	38	52	39	42
5	Accrington Stanley	38	73	57	41
6	Crewe Alexandra	38	60	56	41
7	Stalybridge Celtic	38	62	63	41
8	Walsall	38	66	65	39
9	Southport	38	55	44	38
10	Ashington	38	59	66	38
11	Durham City	38	68	67	37
12	Wrexham	38	51	56	37
13	Chesterfield	38	48	67	35
14	Lincoln City	38	48	59	34
15	Barrow	38	42	54	33
16	Nelson	38	48	66	33
17	Wigan Borough	38	46	72	31
18	Tranmere Rovers	38	51	61	29
19	Halifax Town	38	56	76	29
20	Rochdale	38	52	77	26
		760	1150	1150	760

Stockport County were promoted to Division 2. Halifax Town (42 votes) and Rochdale (31) were both re-elected. Unsuccessful applicants were Doncaster Rovers (9), New Brighton (7), York City (1) and Castleford (0).

1921-1922 – DIVISION 3 (South)   SOUTHAMPTON

After a season in which their promotion push had faded in the early months of 1921, Southampton were once again among the leaders of the division at the end of September, with 11 points from 7 games. Just above the ambitious Saints, on goal average, were Millwall Athletic, who had played a game more. Both clubs trailed leaders Luton Town and newcomers to the Football League, Welsh club Aberdare Athletic, by a point.

With one win between them, the two Athletics Aberdare and Millwall slipped off the pace during October. With Luton Town faltering also, Southampton took over the lead on October 1st by winning at Brighton & Hove Albion, but the point dropped a week later, at Norwich City, cost the Saints the top spot. This was because improving Plymouth Argyle won 1-0 at Reading. This meant the Pilgrims pulled level on points with Southampton, but the Devon men's superior goal average put them ahead.

The clubs ended November equal on points, with 26 from 18 games. Southampton then pulled clear by winning away at Millwall, increasing this to a 3-point advantage a week later, when Argyle lost at Portsmouth, while the Saints overcame a dogged Bristol Rovers 1-0 at The Dell. Although Plymouth added 5 points from their next four games, Southampton took four from their 3 fixtures to end the Christmas period still ahead.

None of the leading clubs managed to stamp its authority on the 3rd Division (South) over the next few weeks. The net effect of the results up to the middle of February was that Southampton and Plymouth Argyle pulled away from the rest a little, with Saints holding a one-point lead over their rivals with 2 games in hand. It was still an open race and, after what had happened at this stage of the previous season, Southampton supporters were glad to still be in contention. By the end of March, however, The Dell faithful had begun to worry. Saints had lost just once in six, but had only won twice. Plymouth, on the other hand, had collected 10 points in the same period and had gone 2 points clear. In 4 games played in March, Argyle had kept four 'clean sheets'. It was starting to look as if the Pilgrims had peaked at just the right time. It was also beginning to appear as if, for the second year running, Southampton would be cast in the role of 'also-rans'.

On April 15th, a crowd of about 24,000 watched as Plymouth Argyle beat Southampton 1-0 at Home Park, to go 7 points clear. Saints' 3 games in hand looked almost worthless. The gap was down to 2 points, however, by the time May 6th, the last day of the season, arrived. Southampton beat Newport County 5-0, then waited. Amazingly, Plymouth lost 0-2 at Q.P.R. – the Pilgrims' first reverse in 17 games. Southampton, with their better goal average, were champions!

Southampton's '1st half' record

August	27	GILLINGHAM	2-0
	29	Luton Town	0-0
September	03	Gillingham	0-2
	05	LUTON TOWN	2-1
	10	SWINDON TOWN	3-1
	17	Swindon Town	3-2
	24	BRIGHTON & HOVE ALBION	3-0
October	01	Brighton & Hove Albion	1-0
	08	Norwich City	2-2
	15	NORWICH CITY	2-0
	22	Watford	1-1
	29	WATFORD	2-0
November	05	Reading	1-0
	12	READING	0-0
	19	CHARLTON ATHLETIC	6-0
	28	Charlton Athletic	2-1
December	03	Millwall Athletic	1-0
	10	BRISTOL ROVERS	1-0
	24	NORTHAMPTON TOWN	8-0
	26	Queen's Park Rangers	2-2
	27	QUEEN'S PARK RANGERS	1-1

Southampton's '2nd half' record

December	31	BRENTFORD	0-0
January	14	Brentford	0-1
	21	MILLWALL ATHLETIC	4-2
February	04	EXETER CITY	2-0
	11	Exeter City	0-0
	20	SWANSEA TOWN	1-1
	25	Swansea Town	0-1
March	04	SOUTHEND UNITED	5-0
	11	Southend United	0-0
	18	Portsmouth	2-0
	25	PORTSMOUTH	1-1
April	08	MERTHYR TOWN	1-1
	14	Bristol Rovers	0-0
	15	Plymouth Argyle	0-1
	17	ABERDARE ATHLETIC	1-0
	18	Aberdare Athletic	1-0
	22	PLYMOUTH ARGYLE	0-0
	24	Northampton Town	0-0
	29	Newport County	1-0
May	01	Merthyr Town	1-0
	06	NEWPORT COUNTY	5-0

Table at December 27th, 1921

1	SOUTHAMPTON	21	43	13	34
2	Plymouth Argyle	22	28	10	32
3	Luton Town	22	34	14	32
4	Portsmouth	21	39	20	29
5	Queen's Park Rangers	22	28	27	24
6	Aberdare Athletic	21	32	27	23
7	Millwall Athletic	23	19	17	23
8	Merthyr Town	21	25	32	23
9	Brentford	21	24	21	22
10	Bristol Rovers	20	28	26	20
11	Swansea Town	21	23	22	20
12	Swindon Town	21	32	32	20
13	Charlton Athletic	21	24	33	20
14	Brighton & Hove Albion	21	27	25	19
15	Newport County	21	24	28	18
16	Northampton Town	19	24	39	18
17	Watford	21	18	24	17
18	Gillingham	20	20	29	14
19	Reading	20	16	25	14
20	Southend United	22	15	34	14
21	Norwich City	20	20	26	13
22	Exeter City	21	15	34	13
		462	558	558	462

Final League Division 3 (South) Table 1922

1	SOUTHAMPTON	42	68	21	61
2	Plymouth Argyle	42	63	24	61
3	Portsmouth	42	62	39	53
4	Luton Town	42	64	35	52
5	Queen's Park Rangers	42	53	44	49
6	Swindon Town	42	72	60	45
7	Watford	42	54	48	44
8	Aberdare Athletic	42	57	51	44
9	Brentford	42	52	43	43
10	Swansea Town	42	50	47	41
11	Merthyr Town	42	45	56	40
12	Millwall Athletic	42	38	42	38
13	Reading	42	40	47	38
14	Bristol Rovers	42	52	67	38
15	Norwich City	42	50	62	37
16	Charlton Athletic	42	43	56	37
17	Northampton Town	42	47	71	37
18	Gillingham	42	47	60	36
19	Brighton & Hove Albion	42	45	51	35
20	Newport County	42	44	61	34
21	Exeter City	42	38	59	34
22	Southend United	42	34	74	27
		924	1118	1118	924

Southampton were promoted to Division 2. Southend United (36 votes) and Exeter City (32) were re-elected. Unsuccessful applicants were Pontypridd (21), Bath City (1) and, with no votes, Llanelli.

1922-1923 – LEAGUE DIVISION 1

LIVERPOOL

In an otherwise even start to the season, Chelsea produced the best opening sequence to top the 1st Division after five games. However, the Blues' 1-2 defeat at Middlesbrough on September 16th allowed champions Liverpool to draw level, with a third 5-goals home show, against Preston North End. 'Pool and Chelsea moved onto 10 points a week later with comprehensive victories, but both lost on September 30th and were joined by Middlesbrough, who drew with Villa.

Liverpool moved clear by winning their next 3 games and, despite defeat at Cardiff City on October 28th, headed the table at mid-November. Chelsea had fallen away rather dramatically by this time, home defeat by Sunderland on October 21st having started a run of 11 games without a win. With Charles Buchan scoring in 6 successive games, the Roker Park club rose to second in the division, passing Boro on November 11th by beating Newcastle United 2-0. Burnley had moved up to third.

The leaders turned up the pressure over the next 6 weeks, winning six of their 7 matches. The leaders' defeat at home to Newcastle on December 2nd offered hope to others, but proved to be no more than an 'off day', as 'Pool reached 31 points by winning 2-0 at Oldham Athletic on Christmas Day. Sunderland went 6 matches unbeaten in this period, but drew three, to go 4 points behind the Reds. Middlesbrough and Burnley stayed in touch, but all the top sides were mindful of the progress of Huddersfield Town, who ended December 25th unbeaten in 8 games.

Liverpool showed no signs of easing up and took 12 points from their next seven games, in which only one goal was let in by Elisha Scott, the Reds' net minder. Sunderland fought gamely to stay within sight of the leaders, extending their unbeaten run to 14 matches by mid-February. Importantly, the Roker men had taken three points off Huddersfield Town late in January and were now 6 points clear of the third-placed club.

Sunderland's run ended on March 3rd, when they lost 1-3 at Sheffield United. This seemed to dent Roker confidence and only one point was taken from two games with Preston North End. It was the worst time possible for the Wearsiders' form to dip, because Liverpool were beaten twice in mid-March. By the end of the month, 'Pool had recovered and led their chief rivals by 5 points. It seemed as if Sunderland's chance to close the gap and put real pressure on the Anfield club had been missed.

Strange things happened in early April. Both the top two lost to Sheffield United and Liverpool began to draw games they expected to win. Sunderland closed to within 3 points. As Liverpool's 'draw sequence' continued at Bolton on April 18th, however, Sunderland lost 0-2 at Middlesbrough and fell 4 points behind with 3 games to go. The destination of the 1st Division title was settled on April 21st. Sunderland lost 0-2 at Burnley. Liverpool drew against Huddersfield 1-1 at home, the point guaranteeing retention of the title. Harry Chambers scored the championship-winning goal.

Liverpool's '1st half' record

August	26	THE ARSENAL	5-2
	30	Sunderland	0-1
September	02	The Arsenal	0-1
	06	SUNDERLAND	5-1
	09	Preston North End	3-1
	16	PRESTON NORTH END	5-2
	23	BURNLEY	3-0
	30	Burnley	0-2
October	07	EVERTON	5-1
	14	Everton	1-0
	21	CARDIFF CITY	3-1
	28	Cardiff City	0-3
November	04	Tottenham Hotspur	4-2
	11	TOTTENHAM HOTSPUR	0-0
	18	ASTON VILLA	3-0
	25	Aston Villa	1-0
December	02	NEWCASTLE UNITED	0-2
	09	Newcastle United	1-0
	16	NOTTINGHAM FOREST	2-1
	23	Nottingham Forest	3-1
	25	Oldham Athletic	2-0

Table at December 25th, 1922

1	LIVERPOOL	21	46	21	31
2	Sunderland	20	39	28	27
3	Middlesbrough	21	36	28	26
4	Burnley	21	37	22	25
5	Huddersfield Town	21	27	18	25
6	Manchester City	21	28	26	24
7	Newcastle United	21	23	18	23
8	Bolton Wanderers	22	32	28	23
9	Sheffield United	22	30	29	23
10	Tottenham Hotspur	20	27	27	22
11	Birmingham	22	20	20	21
12	West Bromwich Albion	20	31	25	20
13	Blackburn Rovers	20	25	25	20
14	Aston Villa	21	25	29	20
15	Everton	20	25	30	20
16	Nottingham Forest	22	23	34	18
17	Preston North End	21	30	36	17
18	Chelsea	21	22	28	17
19	Cardiff City	20	30	35	15
20	Oldham Athletic	21	22	39	15
21	Stoke	20	24	31	14
22	The Arsenal	22	27	52	14
		460	629	629	460

Liverpool's '2nd half' record

December	26	OLDHAM ATHLETIC	2-1
	30	Chelsea	0-0
January	06	CHELSEA	1-0
	20	Middlesbrough	2-0
	27	MIDDLESBROUGH	2-0
February	07	WEST BROMWICH ALBION	2-0
	10	West Bromwich Albion	0-0
	17	BLACKBURN ROVERS	3-0
March	03	BOLTON WANDERERS	3-0
	12	Blackburn Rovers	0-1
	17	Manchester City	0-1
	24	MANCHESTER CITY	2-0
	30	SHEFFIELD UNITED	2-1
	31	Birmingham	1-0
April	02	Sheffield United	1-4
	07	BIRMINGHAM	0-0
	14	Huddersfield Town	0-0
	18	Bolton Wanderers	1-1
	21	HUDDERSFIELD TOWN	1-1
	28	Stoke	0-0
May	05	STOKE	1-0

Final League Division 1 Table 1923

1	LIVERPOOL	42	70	31	60
2	Sunderland	42	72	54	54
3	Huddersfield Town	42	60	32	53
4	Newcastle United	42	45	37	48
5	Everton	42	63	59	47
6	Aston Villa	42	64	51	46
7	West Bromwich Albion	42	58	49	45
8	Manchester City	42	50	49	45
9	Cardiff City	42	73	59	43
10	Sheffield United	42	68	64	42
11	The Arsenal	42	61	62	42
12	Tottenham Hotspur	42	50	50	41
13	Bolton Wanderers	42	50	58	40
14	Blackburn Rovers	42	47	62	40
15	Burnley	42	58	59	38
16	Preston North End	42	60	64	37
17	Birmingham	42	41	57	37
18	Middlesbrough	42	57	63	36
19	Chelsea	42	45	53	36
20	Nottingham Forest	42	41	70	34
21	Stoke	42	47	67	30
22	Oldham Athletic	42	35	65	30
		924	1215	1215	924

Stoke and Oldham Athletic were relegated.

1922-1923 – LEAGUE DIVISION 2

NOTTS COUNTY

In a hectic opening to the season, Barnsley, Leicester City and Notts County all won their first three games. The Foxes then drew at Rotherham County on September 4th, while County lost at South Shields and the Oakwell men had no game. Despite losing at Bury two days later, Barnsley replaced Leicester at the Division 2 summit on September 9th by beating Southampton 3-0, while City lost 0-2 at Clapton Orient. The two leaders were back on level terms a week later and remained in tandem to the end of the month. Having beaten Notts County 1-0 on October 7th, Barnsley hit a rocky patch, losing 3 of their next 5. With Bury merely breaking even over 6 games up to mid-November, Leicester took advantage to move away at the top, but defeat by Hull City pegged the Filbert Street men back as Notts County joined them on 19 points by beating Blackpool 2-0.

Victory at Hull a week later restored City to top spot, however, after County were held 1-1 on the Lancashire coast. The Foxes took 5 points from their next 3 games to treble their lead. When Leicester lost at Sheffield Wednesday on 9th December, Notts County closed to within a point, with a 2-1 success at lowly Bradford City. This seemed to deflate the leaders, who lost their next 3 matches. Notts needed no further encouragement and eased into first place on December 16th with the first of 3 single goal successes, which lifted the club's points haul to 31 on Christmas Day. Bury, Leeds United and Blackpool, on goal average, all passed luckless Leicester.

The leaders returned to action on Boxing Day, strangely out of sorts. The defeat at Fulham proved to be the first of 5 in nine matches, which produced only 1 victory. On February 10th, County were destroyed at home by Manchester United and the club would have reached the end of the month in a far worse position had it not been for the collective failure of other leading clubs to string together a worthwhile set of results. As it turned out, County were still in a position to push back to the top if they could rediscover their form. The Notts recovery began on March 10th, with Jack Cook and Donald Cock on target in the 2-0 win over Rotherham County in front of a paltry crowd totalling around 2,000. Three wins in the next four games saw Notts County regain the Division 2 lead, on March 30th, after Leicester lost at Fulham.

By beating Stockport County 2-0 on Easter Saturday, March 31st, the Football League's oldest club retained their hold on top spot going into April. Leicester were a point behind, with Blackpool, in third, 3 points adrift. Despite further problems, County reached mid-April 2 points up on next opponents West Ham United, Manchester United and wobbling Leicester City. The Hammers were beaten 2-0 on April 18th, but defeat at Leeds United 3 days later and other results meant that May 5th, the season's final day, arrived with Notts third, on goal average, behind West Ham, who County had to visit, and Leicester. Harold Hill's goal gave County a 1-0 win. With Leicester City losing at Bury though, it also won Notts the 2nd Division title!

Notts County's '1st half' record

August	26	Coventry City	2-1
	28	SOUTH SHIELDS	2-0
September	02	COVENTRY CITY	2-0
	04	South Shields	0-1
	09	HULL CITY	0-1
	16	Hull City	2-0
	23	Sheffield Wednesday	1-0
	30	SHEFFIELD WEDNESDAY	1-0
October	07	Barnsley	0-1
	14	BARNSLEY	1-0
	21	Port Vale	0-0
	28	PORT VALE	1-0
November	04	BLACKPOOL	2-0
	11	Blackpool	1-1
	18	WOLVES	4-1
	25	Wolves	0-1
December	02	BRADFORD CITY	0-0
	09	Bradford City	2-1
	16	SOUTHAMPTON	1-0
	23	Southampton	1-0
	25	FULHAM	1-0

Notts County's '2nd half' record

December	26	Fulham	1-2
	30	Derby County	0-0
January	06	DERBY COUNTY	1-2
	20	Leicester City	1-2
	27	LEICESTER CITY	1-0
February	10	MANCHESTER UNITED	1-6
	17	Bury	2-2
	21	Manchester United	1-1
March	03	Rotherham County	0-1
	10	ROTHERHAM COUNTY	2-0
	17	CLAPTON ORIENT	3-1
	21	BURY	1-0
	24	Clapton Orient	1-2
	30	Crystal Palace	1-0
	31	STOCKPORT COUNTY	2-0
April	02	CRYSTAL PALACE	0-4
	07	Stockport County	0-0
	14	LEEDS UNITED	1-0
	18	WEST HAM UNITED	2-0
	21	Leeds United	0-3
May	05	West Ham United	1-0

Table at December 25th, 1922

1	NOTTS COUNTY	21	24	8	31
2	Bury	21	31	18	29
3	Leeds United	21	21	13	27
4	Blackpool	21	29	16	26
5	Leicester City	21	32	20	26
6	Derby County	21	27	20	23
7	West Ham United	21	26	21	23
8	Barnsley	21	30	25	23
9	Sheffield Wednesday	21	27	23	23
10	Port Vale	20	20	17	22
11	Manchester United	21	21	19	22
12	Fulham	21	15	14	20
13	Coventry City	21	26	30	20
14	South Shields	21	17	17	19
15	Southampton	21	19	21	19
16	Hull City	21	17	20	19
17	Rotherham County	22	25	33	18
18	Stockport County	20	23	30	17
19	Bradford City	21	14	22	17
20	Crystal Palace	22	20	39	14
21	Clapton Orient	21	14	29	13
22	Wolves	21	15	38	11
		462	493	493	462

Final League Division 2 Table 1923

1	NOTTS COUNTY	42	46	34	53
2	West Ham United	42	63	38	51
3	Leicester City	42	65	44	51
4	Manchester United	42	51	36	48
5	Blackpool	42	60	43	47
6	Bury	42	55	46	47
7	Leeds United	42	43	36	47
8	Sheffield Wednesday	42	54	47	46
9	Barnsley	42	62	51	45
10	Fulham	42	43	32	44
11	Southampton	42	40	40	42
12	Hull City	42	43	45	42
13	South Shields	42	35	44	40
14	Derby County	42	46	50	39
15	Bradford City	42	41	45	37
16	Crystal Palace	42	54	62	37
17	Port Vale	42	39	51	37
18	Coventry City	42	46	63	37
19	Clapton Orient	42	40	50	36
20	Stockport County	42	43	58	36
21	Rotherham County	42	44	63	35
22	Wolves	42	42	77	27
		924	1055	1055	924

Notts County and West Ham United were promoted. Wolves and Rotherham County were relegated to Division 3 North.

1922-1923 – DIVISION 3 (North) NELSON

Despite a crushing defeat in their first game of the season, Nelson won 5 of their next 6 matches to establish themselves as leaders of the division by the close of September. The club held a 2 points lead over Grimsby Town, Wigan Borough and Rochdale, all of whom had taken 8 points from 6 games. Bradford Park Avenue, Nelson's tormentors on August 26th, had not won another match, but were expected to emerge as championship contenders. Three wins in four October outings helped Nelson increase their lead at the top to three points. Although Grimsby Town and Wigan Borough only lost once each during the month, neither club managed to match the leaders' level of success. Rochdale, meanwhile, failed to win and slipped off the pace, having added only 3 points to their total. However, they then completed a double over Hartlepools United to reach mid-November in third, marginally behind Wigan, on goal average. Grimsby Town lost twice to fall out of the top four.

Despite home defeat on November 25th by Rochdale, Nelson continued to set the pace up to the end of December, even though their lead was down to one point as the New Year opened. Rochdale had moved into second slot by this time, heading Bradford Park Avenue on goal average. The former top flight club had begun to mount their expected challenge for promotion and had won 8 out of their last 12. Avenue, in fact, were one of a posse of three clubs to push past Nelson on January 6th after the leaders lost heavily at Hartlepools United.

Nelson's '1st half' record

August	26	Bradford Park Avenue	2-6
September	02	BRADFORD PARK AVENUE	1-0
	09	STALYBRIDGE CELTIC	1-0
	12	HALIFAX TOWN	2-0
	16	Stalybridge Celtic	0-2
	23	SOUTHPORT	2-0
	30	Southport	1-0
October	07	ASHINGTON	1-3
	14	Ashington	2-0
	21	Tranmere Rovers	2-0
	28	TRANMERE ROVERS	1-0
November	04	Barrow	0-1
	11	BARROW	2-1
	25	ROCHDALE	1-2
December	09	Darlington	3-2
	23	DARLINGTON	3-0
	25	Halifax Town	2-2
	30	HARTLEPOOLS UNITED	4-1
January	06	Hartlepools United	1-5

Table at January 6th, 1923

1	Bradford Park Avenue	21	34	20	26
2	Chesterfield	20	43	26	25
3	Rochdale	20	28	19	25
4	Wigan Borough	20	26	18	25
5	NELSON	19	31	25	25
6	Stalybridge Celtic	19	26	14	24
7	Walsall	20	28	26	24
8	Halifax Town	19	28	23	21
9	Darlington	20	32	29	20
10	Southport	21	16	17	20
11	Lincoln City	20	20	23	20
12	Accrington Stanley	20	29	37	20
13	Hartlepools United	22	28	37	20
14	Crewe Alexandra	21	22	22	19
15	Ashington	21	26	41	16
16	Wrexham	20	17	29	16
17	Grimsby Town	19	27	25	15
18	Barrow	20	24	26	15
19	Durham City	19	20	27	15
20	Tranmere Rovers	21	17	38	11
		402	522	522	402

Nelson returned to the top a week later, however, with a 3-0 win at Rochdale. They then slipped back on January 20th by losing at Lincoln City, only to resume the mantle of leaders once again on the last Saturday of the month when taking both points from a 2-1 success over the Red Imps, thanks to a brace from centre forward, Joe Eddleston. A double over strugglers Durham City left the Seedhillites 2 points clear of Chesterfield at mid-February.

The Spireites' two wins over Stalybridge Celtic resulted in the Derbyshire club ending the month in pole position, however, as Nelson lost at Wigan Borough on February 17th. The two leaders met head on at the beginning of March for a double date, which attracted crowds of 12,000 to both games. The Seedhillites handled the pressure much better and took all four points. Instead of pressing home their new advantage though, Nelson failed to win any of their subsequent four matches.

Only superior goal average kept the Park Ground men at the top of the table after the April 2nd fixtures and, with Bradford Park Avenue and Walsall only a point behind, the leaders came under severe pressure. Successive wins by mid-April re-established a three-point lead, however. With a game in hand on the others, Nelson could control their own destiny. Victory at Accrington on April 21st took the club to within 2 points of the title. With goals from Michael McCulloch and Richard Crawshaw, Nelson beat Wrexham 2-0 on April 24th to become champions.

Nelson's '2nd half' record

January	13	Rochdale	3-0
	20	Lincoln City	0-1
	27	LINCOLN CITY	2-1
February	03	Durham City	1-0
	10	DURHAM CITY	4-0
	17	Wigan Borough	1-3
	24	WIGAN BOROUGH	1-0
March	03	Chesterfield	2-1
	10	CHESTERFIELD	4-0
	17	CREWE ALEXANDRA	0-0
	24	Crewe Alexandra	0-1
	31	GRIMSBY TOWN	1-1
April	02	Wrexham	1-2
	07	Grimsby Town	2-0
	14	ACCRINGTON STANLEY	2-1
	21	Accrington Stanley	1-0
	24	WREXHAM	2-0
	28	WALSALL	3-0
May	05	Walsall	0-5

Final League Division 3 (North) Table 1923

1	NELSON	38	61	41	51
2	Bradford Park Avenue	38	67	38	47
3	Walsall	38	51	44	46
4	Chesterfield	38	68	52	45
5	Wigan Borough	38	64	39	44
6	Crewe Alexandra	38	48	38	43
7	Halifax Town	38	53	46	41
8	Accrington Stanley	38	59	65	41
9	Darlington	38	59	46	40
10	Wrexham	38	38	48	38
11	Stalybridge Celtic	38	42	47	36
12	Rochdale	38	42	53	36
13	Lincoln City	38	39	55	36
14	Grimsby Town	38	55	52	33
15	Hartlepools United	38	48	54	32
16	Tranmere Rovers	38	49	59	32
17	Southport	38	32	46	31
18	Barrow	38	50	60	30
19	Ashington	38	51	77	30
20	Durham City	38	43	59	28
		760	1019	1019	760

Nelson were promoted to Division 2. Ashington and Durham City (45 votes each) were re-elected. Stalybridge Celtic resigned, but the size of the division was increased to 22 clubs by the election of Doncaster Rovers and New Brighton (45 each). Nuneaton Town and Wallasey stood for election, but neither received any support.

1922-1923 – DIVISION 3 (South)   BRISTOL CITY

Portsmouth got off to the best start in the division, picking up 14 points from eight unbeaten games, and reaching the end of September in top place, with 11 goals for and none against. Plymouth Argyle, having apparently recovered from the disappointment of missing out on promotion on the last day of the previous campaign, lay second, a point worse off. Queen's Park Rangers and Bristol City occupied the next two places.

Plymouth beat Portsmouth twice at the start of October and, when Bristol City overturned Pompey home and away in early November, the Fratton Park outfit slid out of the top four. At mid-November, Argyle lay two points ahead of Bristol City, who had a game in hand. City had moved into second position on November 11th, overtaking Watford after the Brewers' 10-game unbeaten run was ended on that day by Reading.

Watford, however, came back from this reverse to join the leaders on 24 points by beating Luton Town on November 25th, while Plymouth were being held by Southend United. Bristol City moved up to the same mark a week later by drawing at Luton. With their rivals due to face each other on December 16th and 23rd, City sensed an opportunity to push their own title claims forward. With four wins in a row, the Ashton Gate club eased into the divisional lead as Argyle and Watford shared the points equally. Boxing Day closed with Bristol City two points clear.

Getting to the top was one thing – staying there was the new test to be faced as 1922 ended and 1923 began. City were helped, however, by Plymouth Argyle's relative league inactivity during the next phase of the season. The Devon club only played 4 games by mid-February, compared with City's seven, 5 of which were won to help build a 10-point gap between Bristol and Plymouth. Swansea Town, lying in second place, trailed City by four points. There was always the fear that Plymouth would come again and cause problems, even though Argyle's 3 matches in hand could not be used to make up the points deficit. Despite taking a break-even return of 8 points from eight matches up to the end of March, City still held a 9-point advantage over Plymouth and a 4-point lead over Swansea, who remained second. It began to dawn on the Ashton Gate club that the 'Plymouth problem' was not going to materialise.

A further 3 games were played by Bristol City by mid-April. The 3rd Division (South) table showed that the leaders' points advantages over both Swansea and the Argyle were unchanged. City now needed only 3 points from their remaining 3 games to become champions and return to Division 2 after only one season's absence. On April 21st, the first of these games was won 3-1 against Watford, with Billy Walker scoring twice and Jack Smith also netting. With Swansea and Plymouth kindly drawing 1-1, the 'race' was all over. Bristol City had won the title.

Bristol City's '1st half' record

August	26	READING	2-1
	28	Plymouth Argyle	1-5
September	02	Reading	0-0
	04	PLYMOUTH ARGYLE	2-0
	09	NEWPORT COUNTY	2-0
	16	Newport County	1-0
	23	BRISTOL ROVERS	0-1
	30	Bristol Rovers	2-1
October	07	Swansea Town	1-4
	14	SWANSEA TOWN	1-0
	21	SOUTHEND UNITED	5-0
	28	Southend United	3-0
November	04	PORTSMOUTH	2-1
	11	Portsmouth	2-1
	18	MILLWALL	1-1
	25	Millwall	1-1
December	02	Luton Town	1-1
	09	LUTON TOWN	1-0
	16	Queen's Park Rangers	2-1
	23	QUEEN'S PARK RANGERS	3-2
	26	SWINDON TOWN	3-1

Bristol City's '2nd half' record

December	27	Swindon Town	1-0
	30	Gillingham	1-1
January	06	GILLINGHAM	2-1
	20	Brighton & Hove Albion	1-2
	27	BRIGHTON & HOVE ALBION	3-1
February	10	Merthyr Town	1-0
	14	MERTHYR TOWN	3-0
	17	EXETER CITY	1-1
	24	Exeter City	0-0
March	03	NORTHAMPTON TOWN	1-0
	10	Northampton Town	1-2
	17	Norwich City	2-2
	24	NORWICH CITY	4-0
	30	ABERDARE ATHLETIC	0-0
	31	Brentford	0-4
April	02	Aberdare Athletic	1-0
	07	BRENTFORD	1-1
	14	Watford	1-1
	21	WATFORD	3-1
	28	Charlton Athletic	0-1
May	05	CHARLTON ATHLETIC	3-1

Table at December 26th, 1922

1	BRISTOL CITY	21	36	21	32
2	Plymouth Argyle	21	31	10	30
3	Watford	22	33	24	28
4	Swansea Town	21	43	21	27
5	Northampton Town	20	31	16	24
6	Millwall Athletic	21	18	14	24
7	Brighton & Hove Albion	21	29	20	23
8	Swindon Town	20	29	24	23
9	Luton Town	22	31	31	22
10	Portsmouth	21	23	24	21
11	Queen's Park Rangers	22	28	23	20
12	Norwich City	20	25	26	20
13	Bristol Rovers	21	17	20	20
14	Charlton Athletic	21	18	24	20
15	Exeter City	20	16	38	18
16	Southend United	20	28	29	17
17	Brentford	21	23	31	17
18	Merthyr Town	20	18	25	17
19	Reading	21	19	29	16
20	Gillingham	20	21	32	13
21	Newport County	20	14	29	13
22	Aberdare Athletic	20	18	38	11
		456	549	549	456

Final League Division 3 (South) Table 1923

1	BRISTOL CITY	42	66	40	59
2	Plymouth Argyle	42	61	29	53
3	Swansea Town	42	78	45	53
4	Brighton & Hove Albion	42	52	34	51
5	Luton Town	42	68	49	49
6	Millwall Athletic	42	45	40	46
7	Portsmouth	42	58	52	46
8	Northampton Town	42	54	44	45
9	Swindon Town	42	62	56	45
10	Watford	42	57	54	44
11	Queen's Park Rangers	42	54	49	42
12	Charlton Athletic	42	55	51	42
13	Bristol Rovers	42	35	36	42
14	Brentford	42	41	51	38
15	Southend United	42	49	54	37
16	Gillingham	42	51	59	37
17	Merthyr Town	42	39	48	36
18	Norwich City	42	51	71	36
19	Reading	42	36	55	34
20	Exeter City	42	47	84	33
21	Aberdare Athletic	42	42	70	29
22	Newport County	42	40	70	27
		924	1141	1141	924

Bristol City were promoted to Division 2. Aberdare Athletic and Newport County (45 votes each) were both re-elected. Bournemouth & Boscombe Athletic (28) were elected also, beating Llanelli (9), Pontypridd (8) and Torquay United (0) in the poll.

1923-1924 – LEAGUE DIVISION 1   HUDDERSFIELD TOWN

Eight matches unbeaten gave Cardiff City an excellent start to the campaign and the Welshmen led the 1st Division by 2 points when October began. Closest to them were Aston Villa and Bolton Wanderers, who had each played 2 games more. Both had drawn 5 out of 10 matches crammed into the opening 5 weeks of the season and had collected 11 points. Huddersfield Town were in fourth at this stage, with 10 points from 8 games and the best defensive record. The top four all took 3 points from their next 2 games, but, whereas the leading trio all lost one of their next fixture pair, Huddersfield completed a 1-0 double over Birmingham.

By October's end, therefore, Town, now unbeaten in 7 games, headed the table, from Cardiff, on goal average. The Ninian Park men soon reasserted themselves, however, a 3-0 win at West Bromwich carrying them a point clear after the Terriers were held 1-1 at Anfield. The status quo was maintained when the top two both won, a week later, on November 10th. Huddersfield lost both their next 2 away games and Cardiff pulled 2 points clear at the top, with Aston Villa taking over 2nd spot. While the leaders pushed on, with wins over Forest and Liverpool, Villa lost, at Sheffield United on December 15th and were passed, on goal average, by Bolton, who thumped Notts County 7-1, and Huddersfield, who won at Arsenal to go second again. By the end of Christmas Day, things had changed once more, with Wanderers having gone second, after Town lost at Spurs. Cardiff now led by four points.

Villa did themselves and all the other hopefuls a great favour by beating the leaders twice in the next 12 days. City's lead was halved, but it was Bolton, Huddersfield and Sunderland who benefited, as Villa lost once to the Burnden Park men and twice to the Roker club to slip out of contention. With 10 games unbeaten by February 13th, Sunderland moved into second, 3 points behind Cardiff, but 3 ahead of both Bolton Wanderers and Huddersfield Town.

What happened next was one of those mysteries which were once part of English football. Cardiff City, clear at the top of the league, failed to win any of their next 6 games. By the end of March, Sunderland, Bolton and Huddersfield had all passed the ailing Bluebirds, who managed only 2 goals in this period. Both Cardiff and Huddersfield had games in hand on the others, but the Leeds Road club, who hadn't lost in 8 outings, looked far better-placed to make good use of these. Bolton's form now deserted them and Sunderland sparkled only to fade dramatically in their last two games. This left Cardiff City and Huddersfield Town going into the final day of the season, May 3rd, to decide the outcome. City held a one point lead and had a slightly better goal average. The Welsh team seem to have thought a draw would be enough and settled for 0-0 at Birmingham. However, Huddersfield's 3-0 win over Nottingham Forest gave them equal points, a 0·024 of a goal superiority … and the League title.

Huddersfield Town's '1st half' record

August	25	MIDDLESBROUGH	1-0
	27	Preston North End	3-1
September	01	Middlesbrough	0-2
	04	PRESTON NORTH END	4-0
	08	Notts County	0-1
	15	NOTTS COUNTY	0-0
	22	Everton	1-1
	29	EVERTON	2-0
October	06	West Bromwich Albion	4-2
	13	WEST BROMWICH ALBION	0-0
	20	Birmingham	1-0
	27	BIRMINGHAM	1-0
November	03	Liverpool	1-1
	10	LIVERPOOL	3-1
	17	Bolton Wanderers	1-3
	24	BOLTON WANDERERS	1-0
December	01	Sunderland	1-2
	08	SUNDERLAND	3-2
	15	The Arsenal	3-1
	22	THE ARSENAL	6-1
	25	Tottenham Hotspur	0-1

Table at December 25th, 1923

1	Cardiff City	21	37	18	32
2	Bolton Wanderers	23	38	19	28
3	HUDDERSFIELD TOWN	21	36	19	28
4	Aston Villa	23	27	18	27
5	Sheffield United	21	34	24	26
6	Sunderland	21	37	28	26
7	Everton	22	32	27	26
8	Tottenham Hotspur	21	23	18	25
9	Newcastle United	22	33	26	24
10	Blackburn Rovers	21	35	28	23
11	Notts County	20	19	22	22
12	Manchester City	20	25	33	21
13	West Ham United	21	18	22	20
14	West Bromwich Albion	21	27	31	19
15	Burnley	21	30	29	18
16	Liverpool	21	23	28	16
17	Nottingham Forest	21	26	35	16
18	The Arsenal	20	18	33	15
19	Chelsea	22	13	28	15
20	Birmingham	21	14	30	14
21	Preston North End	21	25	43	13
22	Middlesbrough	21	19	30	12
		466	589	589	466

Huddersfield Town's '2nd half' record

December	26	TOTTENHAM HOTSPUR	2-1
	29	Blackburn Rovers	0-1
January	05	BLACKBURN ROVERS	1-0
	19	CHELSEA	0-1
	26	Chelsea	1-0
February	09	Newcastle United	1-0
	16	WEST HAM UNITED	1-1
	27	NEWCASTLE UNITED	1-1
March	01	CARDIFF CITY	2-0
	15	Sheffield United	1-0
	22	SHEFFIELD UNITED	1-0
	27	West Ham United	3-2
April	05	ASTON VILLA	1-0
	12	MANCHESTER CITY	1-1
	14	Cardiff City	0-0
	18	Burnley	1-1
	19	Manchester City	1-1
	22	BURNLEY	1-0
	26	Nottingham Forest	1-1
	30	Aston Villa	1-3
May	03	NOTTINGHAM FOREST	3-0

Final League Division 1 Table 1924

1	HUDDERSFIELD TOWN	42	60	33	57
2	Cardiff City	42	61	34	57
3	Sunderland	42	71	54	53
4	Bolton Wanderers	42	68	34	50
5	Sheffield United	42	69	49	50
6	Aston Villa	42	52	37	49
7	Everton	42	62	53	49
8	Blackburn Rovers	42	54	50	45
9	Newcastle United	42	60	54	44
10	Notts County	42	44	49	42
11	Manchester City	42	54	71	42
12	Liverpool	42	49	48	41
13	West Ham United	42	40	43	41
14	Birmingham	42	41	49	39
15	Tottenham Hotspur	42	50	56	38
16	West Bromwich Albion	42	51	62	38
17	Burnley	42	55	60	36
18	Preston North End	42	52	67	34
19	The Arsenal	42	40	63	33
20	Nottingham Forest	42	42	64	32
21	Chelsea	42	31	53	32
22	Middlesbrough	42	37	60	22
		924	1143	1143	924

Chelsea and Middlesbrough were relegated.

1923-1924 – LEAGUE DIVISION 2

LEEDS UNITED

After the opening exchanges of the season, the top of the 2nd Division showed South Shields in top spot, with 12 points from eight games. Bury and Barnsley were a point behind the leaders, with Leicester City, having started reasonably well again, in fourth, with 10 points from eight games. Of the 'bigger clubs', in terms of crowd-pulling potential, Fulham and Sheffield Wednesday were both in the bottom four as September ended, while Manchester United had followed a 3-win opening with 5 matches without a victory. By mid-November, the situation at the head of the division had changed considerably. Having beaten Bury twice, South Shields were blown off course by losses at both Clapton and Oldham. Leeds United, with 5 wins and a draw, without a goal against, took over as leaders. Stoke and Derby County both took 9 points from 6 games in this period to take over 3rd and 4th spots, as Barnsley, Bury and Leicester managed just one victory apiece and fell back into mid-table. Also starting to go well were Blackpool and Manchester United.

It was, in fact, the Red Devils who put the brakes on Leeds' charge at the top, with a 3-1 success over the top-dogs at Old Trafford. The leaders then lost twice to reviving Bury and could only draw with Oldham Athletic on Christmas Day. Despite this, however, United managed to end the first half of their 1923-24 league programme at the Second Division summit. This, it has to be said, was as much down to a 1-2 defeat for Derby County at lowly Nelson as to United's own faltering efforts. A wake-up call had been clearly sounded.

The New Year started with Derby, Leeds and Stoke all on 28 points, United having played fewer games than their rivals. The Rams lost 3 of their next four games, while Leeds United dropped 3 points in two games, before winning successive matches to get back on track. This combination of results allowed Stoke to go top and to reach mid-February 2 points ahead of Leeds. Blackpool and the recovering South Shields now occupied the two positions immediately below the Elland Road club.

The shifting patterns at the top of the 2nd Division continued into March. Stoke hit a barren patch around this time, went 7 games without winning and tumbled out of contention at the top. Bury, with a 9-game unbeaten run, which included seven wins and eight 'clean sheets', pushed themselves back into the leading group. While other clubs generally failed to come anywhere near the Shakers' standards, Leeds United took up the mantle of league leaders with a creditable 6 wins in 9 games.

With a 2-point lead over Bury and a 6-point gap separating them from third place, Leeds United looked like very good promotion prospects at the start of April. Four games later, the Yorkshire club still led the table, though the advantages of a few days before had been halved. On Easter Monday, both Bury and Blackpool lost, however, while United thumped Stockport County 4-0 to secure promotion. Five days later, on April 26th, Walter Coates' goal was enough to beat Nelson and bring the title to Elland Road.

Leeds United's '1st half' record

August	25	Stoke	1-1
	27	CRYSTAL PALACE	3-0
September	01	STOKE	0-0
	05	Crystal Palace	1-1
	08	Leicester City	0-2
	15	LEICESTER CITY	1-2
	22	Hull City	2-1
	29	HULL CITY	5-2
October	06	Clapton Orient	1-0
	13	CLAPTON ORIENT	1-0
	20	Port Vale	1-0
	27	PORT VALE	3-0
November	03	BRADFORD CITY	1-0
	10	Bradford City	0-0
	17	BARNSLEY	3-1
	24	Barnsley	3-1
December	01	MANCHESTER UNITED	0-0
	08	Manchester United	1-3
	15	BURY	1-2
	22	Bury	0-3
	25	Oldham Athletic	2-2

Table at December 25th, 1923

1	LEEDS UNITED	21	30	21	26
2	Derby County	21	39	24	25
3	Stoke	22	26	30	25
4	Manchester United	20	31	19	23
5	Blackpool	21	37	26	23
6	Leicester City	20	31	21	22
7	Southampton	22	22	18	22
8	Bury	20	28	23	22
9	South Shields	20	23	22	22
10	Sheffield Wednesday	21	29	30	21
11	Oldham Athletic	20	24	25	21
12	Bradford City	20	22	21	20
13	Barnsley	20	27	29	20
14	Stockport County	19	22	27	20
15	Coventry City	20	31	29	19
16	Hull City	21	27	27	19
17	Crystal Palace	21	28	35	19
18	Clapton Orient	19	20	15	18
19	Nelson	21	21	35	18
20	Fulham	21	26	33	17
21	Bristol City	21	20	42	15
22	Port Vale	19	20	32	13
		450	584	584	450

Leeds United's '2nd half' record

December	26	OLDHAM ATHLETIC	5-0
January	05	South Shields	0-2
	19	Sheffield Wednesday	0-0
	26	SHEFFIELD WEDNESDAY	1-0
February	09	COVENTRY CITY	3-1
	16	Bristol City	1-0
	27	SOUTH SHIELDS	2-1
March	01	Southampton	1-0
	08	SOUTHAMPTON	3-0
	10	Coventry City	1-2
	15	FULHAM	3-0
	19	BRISTOL CITY	0-0
	22	Fulham	2-0
	29	BLACKPOOL	0-0
April	05	Blackpool	1-1
	12	DERBY COUNTY	1-1
	18	Stockport County	1-1
	19	Derby County	0-2
	21	STOCKPORT COUNTY	4-0
	26	NELSON	1-0
May	03	Nelson	1-3

Final League Division 2 Table 1924

1	LEEDS UNITED	42	61	35	54
2	Bury	42	63	35	51
3	Derby County	42	75	42	51
4	Blackpool	42	72	47	49
5	Southampton	42	52	31	48
6	Stoke	42	44	42	46
7	Oldham Athletic	42	45	52	45
8	Sheffield Wednesday	42	54	51	44
9	South Shields	42	49	50	44
10	Clapton Orient	42	40	36	43
11	Barnsley	42	57	61	43
12	Leicester City	42	64	54	42
13	Stockport County	42	44	52	42
14	Manchester United	42	52	44	40
15	Crystal Palace	42	53	65	39
16	Port Vale	42	50	66	38
17	Hull City	42	46	51	37
18	Bradford City	42	35	48	37
19	Coventry City	42	52	68	35
20	Fulham	42	45	56	34
21	Nelson	42	40	74	33
22	Bristol City	42	32	65	29
		924	1125	1125	924

Leeds United and Bury were promoted. Nelson (North) and Bristol City (South) were relegated to Division 3.

1923-1924 – DIVISION 3 (North)

Three clubs went 6 games unbeaten at the start of the season – Southport, Tranmere Rovers and the promotion favourites, Wolves. Southport, for whom Peter Mee had scored all 6 goals, and Wolves both lost away games on September 22nd, which allowed Rovers to go top by beating Barrow 3-0. A week later, however, the Prenton Park men drew and surrendered pole position to Wolves, whose 5-1 drubbing of Accrington Stanley gave them the best goal average of the 4 clubs on 11 points at September 30th. Wolves were 3 points clear by the start of November.

The top team's 7-point haul in October was not matched by any other club. Southport, who lost top scorer Mee to a career-ending injury on November 3rd, and Tranmere continued to find points hard to come by. The chasing pack, including Wigan Borough and Rochdale, was headed by Darlington by November 10th, when Wolves slipped up at Grimsby Town. This kept the front-runner's lead down to 2 points, with the 3 main pursuers divided only by goal average. Wolves pressed on, winning their next 3 games and reaching December 22nd still 2 points ahead. Rochdale had managed to stay in touch, with Wigan a point further back. 'Dale then pulled level on points with Wolves on Christmas Day with a 2-0 win over Lincoln City, but the Spotland men's hopes of dislodging the leaders were disappointed over the next few days. Despite winning twice, Rochdale were left 2 points behind as Wolves completed a hat-trick of victories when beating Durham City 3-2 on New Year's Day.

Wolves' '1st half' record

August	25	Chesterfield	0-0	
	27	ROTHERHAM COUNTY	3-0	
September	01	CHESTERFIELD	2-1	
	03	Rotherham County	1-1	
	08	Crewe Alexandra	0-0	
	15	CREWE ALEXANDRA	1-0	
	22	Accrington Stanley	0-1	
	29	ACCRINGTON STANLEY	5-1	
October	06	Halifax Town	2-2	
	13	HALIFAX TOWN	4-0	
	20	Bradford Park Avenue	1-0	
	27	BRADFORD PARK AVENUE	2-0	
November	03	GRIMSBY TOWN	4-1	
	10	Grimsby Town	0-2	
	24	NEW BRIGHTON	5-1	
December	01	New Brighton	1-0	
	08	Hartlepools United	1-0	
	22	WALSALL	0-0	
	26	DURHAM CITY	2-1	
	29	ASHINGTON	1-0	
January	01	Durham City	3-2	

Table at January 1st, 1924

1	WOLVES	21	38	13	33
2	Rochdale	21	28	13	31
3	Darlington	22	40	20	29
4	Chesterfield	22	37	19	28
5	Wigan Borough	22	31	23	26
6	Ashington	20	37	23	25
7	Halifax Town	22	29	30	24
8	New Brighton	23	21	23	24
9	Southport	21	19	21	24
10	Bradford Park Avenue	21	32	28	23
11	Rotherham County	21	20	21	21
12	Grimsby Town	22	21	24	21
13	Walsall	22	22	25	20
14	Durham City	21	25	23	19
15	Wrexham	21	22	21	19
16	Doncaster Rovers	22	22	32	18
17	Accrington Stanley	21	19	31	18
18	Tranmere Rovers	20	21	32	16
19	Lincoln City	20	29	32	15
20	Hartlepools United	19	12	25	14
21	Barrow	22	17	41	11
22	Crewe Alexandra	22	12	34	9
		468	554	554	468

WOLVERHAMPTON WANDERERS

Wolves opened the second half of their 3rd Division (North) campaign with a stunning 7-1 win at sixth-placed Ashington, on January 15th. Rochdale refused to buckle under the pressure, however, and, by the time the Molineux men played again, on January 19th, the Lancashire club were top, following single goal successes over Hartlepools United and luckless Ashington. The league leadership was exchanged 3 times over the next 3 weeks, with Wolves reaching mid-February with the advantage … on goal average. The top two were well clear of other clubs by this time, with third-placed Chesterfield 7 points adrift. Clashes at both Spotland and Molineux failed to separate the pace-setters, but Wolves took advantage of 'Dale's 0-1 loss at Grimsby on March 15th to go clear.

The campaign came to the end of March with the title favourites a point ahead of their rivals. Crucially, Wolves had the psychological advantage of two games in hand as April began. How important this might prove remained to be seen. 3 away games in early April produced only 2 points for Wolves, who needed a 3-0 Easter Saturday win over Lincoln City to reclaim lead of the division from Rochdale, on goal average. The positions remained the same by the end of April 26th, with both clubs on 60 points from 40 games. On Monday 28th, Rochdale lost 1-2 at Tranmere. 3 days later, Wolves won at Doncaster Rovers 2-0, Tom Phillipson grabbing both goals. On May 3rd, Wolves secured a 0-0 draw at Tranmere, the point won being enough to win the title.

Wolves' '2nd half' record

January	05	Ashington	7-1	
	19	Wrexham	2-2	
	26	WREXHAM	3-0	
February	09	DONCASTER ROVERS	1-0	
	11	HARTLEPOOLS UNITED	2-1	
	16	Rochdale	0-0	
March	01	Southport	0-0	
	08	SOUTHPORT	2-1	
	15	DARLINGTON	2-0	
	22	Darlington	1-1	
	26	ROCHDALE	0-0	
	29	BARROW	3-0	
April	05	Barrow	2-2	
	07	Walsall	1-2	
	12	Lincoln City	0-0	
	19	LINCOLN CITY	3-0	
	21	WIGAN BOROUGH	3-3	
	22	Wigan Borough	1-1	
	26	TRANMERE ROVERS	3-0	
May	01	Doncaster Rovers	2-0	
	03	Tranmere Rovers	0-0	

Final League Division 3 (North) Table 1924

1	WOLVES	42	76	27	63
2	Rochdale	42	60	26	62
3	Chesterfield	42	70	39	54
4	Rotherham County	42	70	43	52
5	Bradford Park Avenue	42	69	43	52
6	Darlington	42	70	53	48
7	Southport	42	44	42	46
8	Ashington	42	59	61	44
9	Doncaster Rovers	42	59	53	42
10	Wigan Borough	42	55	53	42
11	Grimsby Town	42	49	47	41
12	Tranmere Rovers	42	51	60	41
13	Accrington Stanley	42	48	61	40
14	Halifax Town	42	42	59	40
15	Durham City	42	59	60	39
16	Wrexham	42	37	44	38
17	Walsall	42	44	59	36
18	New Brighton	42	40	53	35
19	Lincoln City	42	48	59	32
20	Crewe Alexandra	42	32	58	27
21	Hartlepools United	42	33	70	25
22	Barrow	42	35	80	25
		924	1150	1150	924

Wolverhampton Wanderers were promoted to Division 2. Hartlepools United and Barrow were re-elected. No vote was needed as no other clubs applied.

1923-1924 – DIVISION 3 (South)   PORTSMOUTH

A superb start to the campaign carried Swansea Town clear at the top by September 8th. Going 100% in their opening 5 fixtures, the Welshmen hit 14 goals and were playing fluent, irresistible football. This progress was interrupted, however, by defeat at Northampton a week later, with top spot lost too on September 19th, when Portsmouth won at Southend United. A double over Gillingham in their next 2 games gave Swansea joint leadership of the division at month's end, following Pompey's 1-4 crash away to Luton Town.

Both the leaders took 8 points from their next 6 games to reach mid-November equal on points, but Portsmouth now held a fractional advantage on goal average to head the table. There was a 4-point gap between the leading duo and third-placed Northampton Town, whose form had been the best of the chasing group of clubs and had included taking 3 points off the well-fancied Plymouth Argyle side. The Devon club were still expected to figure in the title race.

Swansea moved to the top with a 1-0 win over fourth-placed Brighton & Hove Albion on November 17th, when Portsmouth had no game. Pompey reclaimed the lead a week later, but the Swans made up their other game in hand on December 1st and went 2 points clear by beating Charlton Athletic 1-0 at the Vetch Field. This was how things stayed right up until Christmas, when Portsmouth lost at Millwall, while Swansea beat Watford to double their lead. A day later, Pompey fell 5 points behind, having lost again to the Lions, while Swansea drew.

With Plymouth Argyle having caught them up on points, John McCartney's charges needed a quick, positive response to a situation in which their title hopes seemed suddenly to be drifting away. Quite what the Pompey boss said to his squad can only be imagined, but Q.P.R. suffered as a result, with Portsmouth reasserting their title credentials in style. Swansea, in contrast, lost their way rather, and, by mid-February, Pompey trailed the leaders by one point only.

Defeat at Norwich City on February 16th ended the Fratton mini-surge, but 9 points from the next 6 games took the Portsmouth club top, ousting brief leaders Millwall Athletic from pole position. Swansea, beaten 3 times in the same period, were rocking badly and Portsmouth beat the former leaders 3-0 on March 29th, watched by 20,000 fans. Millwall beat Plymouth on the same day and went top on 12th April for a week. Portsmouth returned to the top on the 19th. With Millwall, Swansea and Brighton all losing on April 21st, Easter Monday, Pompey's 0-0 draw at Bournemouth was as good as a win psychologically, with the club moving a point clear at the top.

With only 3 games left, the title beckoned more than ever. Portsmouth went into their Wednesday, 30th April home game with Swindon Town needing 2 points to be certain of the title. A crowd of 18,000 watched the 4-1 win, which took Pompey to a title-clinching 57 points. Centre half Harry Foxall (2), David Watson and Jimmy Martin scored the goals which made John McCartney's team champions.

Portsmouth's '1st half' record

August	25	Plymouth Argyle	2-1
	29	NEWPORT COUNTY	5-0
September	01	PLYMOUTH ARGYLE	2-1
	06	Newport County	1-2
	08	READING	1-1
	12	Exeter City	0-0
	15	Reading	4-1
	19	Southend United	1-0
	22	LUTON TOWN	3-0
	29	Luton Town	1-4
October	06	BRIGHTON & HOVE ALBION	1-3
	13	Brighton & Hove Albion	4-0
	20	BRISTOL ROVERS	1-1
	27	Bristol Rovers	1-0
November	03	BRENTFORD	3-0
	10	Brentford	1-1
	24	SOUTHEND UNITED	3-0
December	08	EXETER CITY	4-0
	22	ABERDARE ATHLETIC	4-0
	25	Millwall	0-2
	26	MILLWALL	0-1

Table at December 26th, 1923

1	Swansea Town	21	38	21	33
2	PORTSMOUTH	21	42	18	28
3	Plymouth Argyle	22	36	18	28
4	Brighton & Hove Albion	22	37	23	27
5	Luton Town	22	28	23	26
6	Millwall Athletic	22	20	19	25
7	Northampton Town	20	23	13	23
8	Bristol Rovers	21	27	19	23
9	Swindon Town	21	24	20	22
10	Norwich City	21	26	22	21
11	Charlton Athletic	21	26	23	21
12	Queen's Park Rangers	21	22	29	20
13	Watford	22	15	16	19
14	Newport County	21	32	38	18
15	Southend United	20	23	34	18
16	Aberdare Athletic	20	21	32	18
17	Brentford	20	25	32	17
18	Gillingham	20	19	25	17
19	Merthyr Town	21	25	41	16
20	Bournemouth & B.A.	22	21	36	16
21	Reading	21	19	32	13
22	Exeter City	20	14	29	13
		462	563	563	462

Portsmouth's '2nd half' record

December	29	Queen's Park Rangers	2-0
January	05	QUEEN'S PARK RANGERS	7-0
	19	Merthyr Town	2-2
	26	MERTHYR TOWN	1-0
February	09	CHARLTON ATHLETIC	0-0
	16	Norwich City	1-3
	23	NORWICH CITY	4-0
March	01	Swindon Town	0-0
	10	Charlton Athletic	1-1
	15	WATFORD	4-0
	17	Aberdare Athletic	0-0
	22	Watford	3-2
	29	SWANSEA TOWN	3-0
April	05	Swansea Town	0-0
	12	Northampton Town	1-3
	18	BOURNEMOUTH & B.A.	3-0
	19	NORTHAMPTON TOWN	4-0
	21	Bournemouth & B.A.	0-0
	26	GILLINGHAM	3-0
	30	SWINDON TOWN	4-1
May	03	Gillingham	2-0

Final League Division 3 (South) Table 1924

1	PORTSMOUTH	42	87	30	59
2	Plymouth Argyle	42	70	34	55
3	Millwall Athletic	42	64	38	54
4	Swansea Town	42	60	48	52
5	Brighton & Hove Albion	42	68	37	51
6	Swindon Town	42	58	44	47
7	Luton Town	42	50	44	46
8	Northampton Town	42	64	47	45
9	Bristol Rovers	42	52	46	43
10	Newport County	42	56	64	43
11	Norwich City	42	60	59	40
12	Aberdare Athletic	42	45	58	38
13	Merthyr Town	42	45	65	38
14	Charlton Athletic	42	38	45	37
15	Gillingham	42	43	58	37
16	Exeter City	42	37	52	37
17	Brentford	42	54	71	36
18	Reading	42	51	57	35
19	Southend United	42	53	84	34
20	Watford	42	45	54	33
21	Bournemouth & B.A.	42	40	65	33
22	Queen's Park Rangers	42	37	77	31
		924	1177	1177	924

Portsmouth were promoted to Division 2. Bournemouth & Boscombe Athletic and Queen's Park Rangers were both re-elected. No vote was needed as no other clubs applied.

1924-1925 – LEAGUE DIVISION 1 HUDDERSFIELD TOWN

Champions, Huddersfield Town, started the season with 4 wins to take an early lead, but then drew 3 games in a row, scoring only once. This enabled Sunderland to pull level with Herbert Chapman's team on September 29th by defeating Burnley 2-1 at Turf Moor. Huddersfield remained top until the final Saturday of October. All the top 4 lost, allowing Birmingham to leapfrog into pole position by winning 1-0 at Leeds Road. The Blues held top spot for just a week, being passed on November 1st by Notts County and West Bromwich Albion.

County led the 1st Division at mid-November with 20 points from 15 games – the same as Birmingham. West Bromwich were in third and Sunderland fourth. Huddersfield lay 5th after a bad run of 4 losses in six outings. None of the top five managed to score on November 22nd and County's problems finding the net were to continue until December 13th. By this stage, Huddersfield had steadied things and, after 4 games without losing, were only a point behind the leading trio of West Bromwich Albion, Notts County and Sunderland.

With the latter two each losing their next games, Albion pulled ahead, winning at Bury and Manchester City. Also winning twice, including a 5-1 thumping of Burnley in which Chris Wilson hit 4, Huddersfield stayed in touch. Birmingham went third by beating Arsenal and Bolton scored a 1-0 win over struggling Forest to go fourth. With 5 of their next 7 matches at home, Huddersfield seemed well-placed to put pressure on the leaders over the next few weeks.

West Bromwich had their own ideas about the destination of the title, however, ending 1924 2 points clear after wins over Notts County and Manchester City. By January 17th, when both the top two lost, the gap was up to 3 points, but things continued to change and, when Albion crashed 1-4 at home to Arsenal on February 7th, Huddersfield went top by beating Aston Villa 4-1. Despite thumping Arsenal 5-0 at Highbury a week later, however, the Leeds Road men reached mid-February in second, following 2 away wins in a week by their main rivals.

Huddersfield reclaimed the leadership on goal average with a draw against Manchester City on February 21st while Albion were on F.A. Cup duty at Aston Villa. When the leaders met in West Yorkshire on March 11th, the hard-fought 1-1 draw kept the reigning champions' noses in front at the head of the table. Both clubs were, however, becoming aware of the progress of Bury and Newcastle United. Both these pursuers had enjoyed good runs since well before Christmas. The pair ended March breathing down the pace-setters' necks.

However, West Brom's 1-0 defeat of Newcastle and a double for Town over Bury at Easter opened up a key gap. Albion lost at Arsenal on April 14th, so Huddersfield moved one point clear. Four days later, both leaders had 54 points after Cardiff City drew at Leeds Road. With 3 points from the next 2 games, however, the Terriers began the last game needing only a draw to retain the title. Cawthorne's only goal of the season earned a 1-1 – and the Football League crown.

Huddersfield Town's '1st half' record

August	30	Newcastle United	3-1
September	02	NOTTINGHAM FOREST	3-0
	06	SHEFFIELD UNITED	2-1
	08	Nottingham Forest	1-0
	13	West Ham United	0-0
	20	BLACKBURN ROVERS	0-0
	27	Leeds United	1-1
October	04	Aston Villa	1-1
	11	THE ARSENAL	4-0
	18	Manchester City	1-1
	25	BIRMINGHAM	0-1
November	01	West Bromwich Albion	0-1
	08	TOTTENHAM HOTSPUR	1-2
	12	Liverpool	3-2
	15	Bolton Wanderers	0-1
	22	NOTTS COUNTY	0-0
	29	Everton	2-0
December	06	SUNDERLAND	4-0
	13	Cardiff City	2-2
	20	PRESTON NORTH END	1-0
	25	Burnley	5-1

Huddersfield Town's '2nd half' record

December	26	BURNLEY	2-0
	27	NEWCASTLE UNITED	0-0
January	03	Sheffield United	1-1
	17	WEST HAM UNITED	1-2
	24	Blackburn Rovers	3-2
	31	LEEDS UNITED	2-0
February	07	ASTON VILLA	4-1
	14	The Arsenal	5-0
	21	MANCHESTER CITY	1-1
	28	Birmingham	1-0
March	11	WEST BROMWICH ALBION	1-1
	14	Tottenham Hotspur	2-1
	21	BOLTON WANDERERS	0-0
April	04	EVERTON	2-0
	10	Bury	1-0
	11	Sunderland	1-1
	14	BURY	2-0
	18	CARDIFF CITY	0-0
	25	Preston North End	4-1
	29	Notts County	1-1
May	02	LIVERPOOL	1-1

Table at December 25th, 1924

1	West Bromwich Albion	21	31	16	28
2	HUDDERSFIELD TOWN	21	34	15	27
3	Birmingham	21	24	24	26
4	Bolton Wanderers	20	36	23	25
5	Notts County	21	19	13	24
6	Newcastle United	22	32	23	24
7	Liverpool	21	35	29	24
8	Sunderland	21	32	28	24
9	Manchester City	22	46	38	23
10	Bury	21	26	30	23
11	The Arsenal	21	28	23	22
12	Aston Villa	21	34	32	22
13	Tottenham Hotspur	22	28	22	21
14	Blackburn Rovers	22	27	30	21
15	West Ham United	21	24	29	20
16	Leeds United	21	26	29	19
17	Cardiff City	21	30	32	18
18	Sheffield United	21	23	33	17
19	Burnley	20	20	29	16
20	Everton	21	18	30	15
21	Nottingham Forest	21	17	34	15
22	Preston North End	21	16	44	10
		464	606	606	464

Final League Division 1 Table 1925

1	HUDDERSFIELD TOWN	42	69	28	58
2	West Bromwich Albion	42	58	34	56
3	Bolton Wanderers	42	76	34	55
4	Liverpool	42	63	55	50
5	Bury	42	54	51	49
6	Newcastle United	42	61	42	48
7	Sunderland	42	64	51	48
8	Birmingham	42	49	53	46
9	Notts County	42	42	31	45
10	Manchester City	42	76	68	43
11	Cardiff City	42	56	51	43
12	Tottenham Hotspur	42	52	43	42
13	West Ham United	42	62	60	42
14	Sheffield United	42	55	63	39
15	Aston Villa	42	58	71	39
16	Blackburn Rovers	42	53	66	35
17	Everton	42	40	60	35
18	Leeds United	42	46	59	34
19	Burnley	42	46	75	34
20	The Arsenal	42	46	58	33
21	Preston North End	42	37	74	26
22	Nottingham Forest	42	29	65	24
		924	1192	1192	924

Preston North End and Nottingham Forest were relegated.

1924-1925 – LEAGUE DIVISION 2   LEICESTER CITY

Pre-season title favourites, Chelsea, won 3 of their first 4 games and seemed to justify their short odds. However, the Blues failed to score in 5 of their next 6 matches or to win any of these or the following two. Derby County, with 5 wins and 2 draws in 8 games, headed the table by the end of September. The Rams were a point ahead of Manchester United, who had kept 5 clean sheets in 7 outings and had racked up 4 straight wins since held at Stoke on September 6th. Blackpool held 3rd place, with Portsmouth 4th.

The two leading clubs maintained their momentum through October, but United moved ahead of Derby on November 1st when the Rams lost 0-2 at improving Crystal Palace, while the Manchester men defeated Fulham 2-0 at Old Trafford. With Portsmouth winning only 2 in 8 and Blackpool losing 4 in a row, Leicester City emerged from the pack, with Palace, to take up the role of pursuers-in-chief. 12 points from 7 games carried the Foxes into third place by mid-November, a creditable record which left City 4 points off second spot.

Little had been seen of Chelsea since mid-September when the goals dried up, but the Blues had got back to winning ways on November 1st after 7 consecutive draws. When Wolves were beaten 1-0 on Christmas Day, Chelsea's run stretched to 14 games unbeaten and they had moved up to third, just ahead of Leicester, whose late November wobble had pegged the Foxes back. The leading pair were still clear, but Leicester's 3-0 success at Derby on December 6th and United's 5 dropped points in 6 matches from November 22nd were taken as indications that the leaders could be caught.

By New Year, both Chelsea and Leicester had moved nearer to the top, City's 3-0 defeat of Manchester United being the key result in this. Despite beating Chelsea on January 1st, United hit a bad patch at mid-month, exiting the F.A. Cup and losing 3 of 4 in the league. With Chelsea and Derby both losing twice, Leicester's 4 wins in 5, with 18 goals scored against 4, saw the Filbert Street club reach the middle of February placed second in the 2nd Division, just two points off the lead.

With 6 wins in their next 7 games, Leicester drew level with Derby on March 17th and again on March 28th, pulling clear at the top by winning at Wolves 1-0, thanks to Arthur Chandler's goal, on the 30th. Manchester United, back in 3rd, now trailed the Foxes by 5 points, with Chelsea, having lost 4 times in 5 outings, a massive 11 points adrift in fourth. Leicester had scored 40 goals in 14 games since Christmas Day, Chandler hitting 17 of these and John Duncan 10. Promotion and the title beckoned.

Typically, City's progress now faltered, with only 1 scored and 2 points taken in the next 4 matches. Derby (4 points from 4 games) and Manchester United (5 from 4) did little better, however. By mid-April, City, with 54, led Derby by one point, with United on 51. Leicester's April 25th win over Bradford City guaranteed promotion, but 2 more points were still needed from the final game of the season to make sure of the title. On May 2nd, Stockport were beaten 4-0 in front of a 25,000 Filbert Street crowd. This made Manchester United's result at Barnsley irrelevant – Leicester were champions.

Leicester City's '1st half' record

August	30	Manchester United	0-1
September	01	CHELSEA	4-0
	06	MIDDLESBROUGH	0-0
	08	Chelsea	0-4
	13	STOKE	0-1
	15	Stockport County	2-0
	20	Coventry City	2-4
	27	OLDHAM ATHLETIC	3-0
October	04	Sheffield Wednesday	4-1
	11	CLAPTON ORIENT	4-2
	18	Crystal Palace	2-0
	25	Barnsley	1-1
November	01	WOLVES	2-0
	08	Fulham	2-2
	15	PORTSMOUTH	4-0
	22	Hull City	1-2
	29	BLACKPOOL	0-2
December	06	Derby County	3-0
	13	SOUTH SHIELDS	1-1
	20	Bradford City	1-1
	25	PORT VALE	7-0

Leicester City's '2nd half' record

December	26	Port Vale	2-1
	27	MANCHESTER UNITED	3-0
January	03	Middlesbrough	5-1
	17	Stoke	1-1
	24	COVENTRY CITY	5-1
February	07	SHEFFIELD WEDNESDAY	6-1
	14	Clapton Orient	1-0
	28	BARNSLEY	6-0
March	12	CRYSTAL PALACE	3-1
	14	FULHAM	4-0
	17	Oldham Athletic	1-0
	21	Portsmouth	1-1
	28	HULL CITY	1-0
	30	Wolves	1-0
April	04	Blackpool	1-2
	11	DERBY COUNTY	0-0
	13	Southampton	0-0
	14	SOUTHAMPTON	0-0
	18	South Shields	1-1
	25	BRADFORD CITY	1-0
May	02	STOCKPORT COUNTY	4-0

Table at December 25th, 1924

1	Derby County	21	46	20	31
2	Manchester United	20	31	10	30
3	Chelsea	21	28	15	27
4	LEICESTER CITY	21	43	22	25
5	Crystal Palace	21	28	25	23
6	Clapton Orient	21	24	19	22
7	Wolves	20	30	27	22
8	Portsmouth	20	22	23	21
9	Blackpool	20	38	26	20
10	Middlesbrough	20	17	18	20
11	Sheffield Wednesday	21	29	31	20
12	Fulham	19	18	22	20
13	Stoke City	20	17	21	19
14	Southampton	21	18	23	19
15	Oldham Athletic	21	17	33	19
16	Hull City	20	26	27	18
17	Port Vale	19	23	30	18
18	Bradford City	20	19	27	16
19	South Shields	20	16	24	15
20	Barnsley	20	23	33	14
21	Stockport County	19	14	29	14
22	Coventry City	19	24	46	11
		444	551	551	444

Final League Division 2 Table 1925

1	LEICESTER CITY	42	90	32	59
2	Manchester United	42	57	23	57
3	Derby County	42	71	36	55
4	Portsmouth	42	58	50	48
5	Chelsea	42	51	37	47
6	Wolves	42	55	51	46
7	Southampton	42	40	36	44
8	Port Vale	42	48	56	42
9	South Shields	42	42	38	41
10	Hull City	42	50	49	41
11	Clapton Orient	42	42	42	40
12	Fulham	42	41	56	40
13	Middlesbrough	42	36	44	39
14	Sheffield Wednesday	42	50	56	38
15	Barnsley	42	46	59	38
16	Bradford City	42	37	50	38
17	Blackpool	42	65	61	37
18	Oldham Athletic	42	35	51	37
19	Stockport County	42	37	57	37
20	Stoke City	42	34	46	35
21	Crystal Palace	42	38	54	34
22	Coventry City	42	45	84	31
		924	1068	1068	924

Leicester City and Manchester United were promoted, Crystal Palace (South) and Coventry City (North) relegated.

1924-1925 – DIVISION 3 (North)   DARLINGTON

There was an unusual opening to the season in Division 3 (North). Accrington Stanley played 10 games by the end of September compared with Darlington's six. The Quakers were, however, a point ahead of their Lancashire rivals at this stage, the clubs occupying third and fourth spots, with Southport just ahead of both of them, on 10 points from 7 games. In pole position were the previous season's wooden spoonists, Barrow – already somewhat a surprise package.

It was not unexpected, however, when the Bluebirds failed to win any of their next 6 games and slipped rapidly down the table. Darlington, dropping only one point in 7 matches, moved to the top, on goal average, after beating Wrexham 2-0 on October 4th and went clear of Southport a fortnight later after David Brown's goal proved enough to beat hosts Chesterfield. By mid-November, the Feethams men led the division by 3 points from Rochdale.

With three wins in their next 4 games, Darlington looked well capable of building a huge lead by New Year's Eve, but, after beating Doncaster Rovers on December 20th, the 'top dogs' went 3 games without scoring and dropped 4 points. None of the other clubs could put together a decent run, however, and, having beaten Halifax Town 3-0 on January 2nd, the Quakers sat 7 points clear at the top. The form team at this time was Nelson, who were sixth, a distant 9 points adrift of the front-runners.

Over the next month, Darlington's form was good, with four games producing 3 victories and a draw. A surprise home loss against Lincoln City and a disappointing 1-1 draw at Rotherham County meant that the 7-point lead had not been extended by mid-February, as had been hoped. There was only one real niggle of concern though – Nelson, now eleven games unbeaten were up to third, with 2 games in hand on Darlington. The threat remained distant, however. By March 7th, the niggle had developed into a genuine cause for concern. Despite crushing Wigan Borough by 5-0 on 28th February, the Quakers had dropped 4 points in three other games. Nelson, 5-0 conquerors of New Brighton, were now 5 points behind, with 3 games in hand. There was huge relief at The Feethams a week later when news arrived of Nelson's loss at Grimsby. By March 29th, the Seedhill men still trailed by 5 points – with only one game in hand.

On April 4th, Darlington drew at Nelson, following this with wins over Accrington Stanley and Ashington by April 11th. In the meantime, Nelson lost at Crewe, then drew at Bradford Park Avenue. Despite their 1-2 reverse at Durham City and Nelson's 7-0 romp against Crewe on Bank Holiday Monday, the Quakers finished Easter 6 points clear. Defeat on April 18th at Southport caused a few flutters, but, when the news arrived that Nelson had crashed 2-4 at home to Wrexham, Darlington were able to celebrate the title and promotion.

Darlington's '1st half' record

August	30	Grimsby Town	2-0
September	03	NEW BRIGHTON	3-1
	06	HARTLEPOOLS UNITED	2-0
	13	Rochdale	1-2
	20	CREWE ALEXANDRA	5-1
	27	BRADFORD PARK AVENUE	2-1
October	04	Wrexham	2-0
	11	ROTHERHAM COUNTY	4-0
	18	Chesterfield	1-0
	25	Wigan Borough	1-1
November	01	WALSALL	3-0
	08	Tranmere Rovers	1-0
	15	NELSON	3-1
	22	Barrow	4-0
December	06	Ashington	2-4
	17	SOUTHPORT	2-1
	20	Doncaster Rovers	2-0
	25	DURHAM CITY	0-0
	27	GRIMSBY TOWN	0-0
January	01	Accrington Stanley	0-2
	02	HALIFAX TOWN	3-0

Darlington's '2nd half' record

January	03	Hartlepools United	1-1
	17	ROCHDALE	2-0
	24	Crewe Alexandra	5-0
February	07	WREXHAM	3-1
	11	LINCOLN CITY	0-1
	14	Rotherham County	1-1
	21	CHESTERFIELD	3-3
	24	Bradford Park Avenue	0-0
	28	WIGAN BOROUGH	5-0
March	07	Walsall	1-2
	14	TRANMERE ROVERS	2-1
	21	Lincoln City	1-0
	28	BARROW	3-0
April	04	Nelson	1-1
	10	ACCRINGTON STANLEY	2-1
	11	ASHINGTON	2-1
	13	Durham City	1-2
	14	Halifax Town	1-1
	18	Southport	0-1
	25	DONCASTER ROVERS	1-1
May	02	New Brighton	0-1

Table at January 2nd, 1925

1	DARLINGTON	21	43	14	33
2	New Brighton	21	43	23	26
3	Bradford Park Avenue	22	46	25	26
4	Southport	20	30	17	26
5	Rochdale	20	36	28	25
6	Nelson	19	31	23	24
7	Lincoln City	22	29	33	23
8	Barrow	21	29	27	22
9	Crewe Alexandra	21	27	33	22
10	Ashington	23	34	47	22
11	Walsall	22	22	22	21
	Wigan Borough	22	31	31	21
13	Chesterfield	20	24	18	20
14	Doncaster Rovers	21	30	32	20
15	Durham City	21	27	34	19
16	Halifax Town	20	19	24	18
17	Accrington Stanley	22	29	40	18
18	Tranmere Rovers	19	27	25	17
19	Grimsby Town	22	19	32	17
20	Wrexham	23	19	36	17
21	Hartlepools United	21	25	33	16
22	Rotherham County	21	21	44	11
		464	641	641	464

Final League Division 3 (North) Table 1925

1	DARLINGTON	42	78	33	58
2	Nelson	42	79	50	53
3	New Brighton	42	75	50	53
4	Southport	42	59	37	51
5	Bradford Park Avenue	42	84	42	50
6	Rochdale	42	75	53	49
7	Chesterfield	42	60	44	45
8	Lincoln City	42	53	58	44
9	Halifax Town	42	56	52	43
10	Ashington	42	68	76	42
11	Wigan Borough	42	62	65	41
12	Grimsby Town	42	60	60	39
13	Durham City	42	50	68	39
14	Barrow	42	51	74	39
15	Crewe Alexandra	42	53	78	39
16	Wrexham	42	53	61	38
17	Accrington Stanley	42	60	72	38
18	Doncaster Rovers	42	54	65	38
19	Walsall	42	44	53	37
20	Hartlepools United	42	45	63	35
21	Tranmere Rovers	42	59	78	32
22	Rotherham County	42	42	88	21
		924	1320	1320	924

Darlington were promoted to Division 2. Rotherham County amalgamated with former League club Rotherham Town and were re-elected as 'Rotherham United' (44 votes). Also re-elected were Tranmere Rovers (32), but Mansfield Town (13) and Blyth Spartans (3) were unsuccessful.

1924-1925 – DIVISION 3 (South)   SWANSEA TOWN

Bristol Rovers made an excellent start to the season, taking 9 points from their opening 5 fixtures. It came as no surprise, however, to see Plymouth Argyle, runners-up for the past 3 seasons, recover from a slow start to head the division by 24th September, after beating Queen's Park Rangers 1-0 at Home Park. The Pilgrims maintained their position at the head of things with a 3-0 win at Gillingham three days later. After 10 games unbeaten, Plymouth lost 1-3 at Aberdare Athletic, following this with a 0-1 reverse at Watford. This enabled Northampton Town to ease into first place, after a 1-0 victory over Brighton & Hove Albion. Argyle reclaimed top spot a week later, however, beating the Cobblers 2-1. Joining Northampton, a point behind Plymouth at the mid-November point, were Swindon Town and Bristol City, both of whom had been listed among the title favourites before the season.

Northampton slipped dramatically out of contention, losing 5 games in a row. Leaders Plymouth lost 3 out of 6 and were replaced at the top by Bristol City after losing at Swansea on December 20th. Defeat at Exeter City on Boxing Day saw the Argyle down to 4th, with Swindon Town and Swansea Town both moving above the former front-runner. The Vetch Field club looked particularly good value for money, having gone 8 games unbeaten and having conceded only 3 goals in these.

By New Year the Swans were top, following a 2-0 December 27th success at Swindon. John Fowler's brace lifted his total for the season to 20 goals in 22 games. Plymouth also won to go second. By mid-February, both the leading pair had added 8 points to their tallies. The key difference was that Plymouth's points had come from 6 games, while Swansea's were taken from just four. By the end of March, Swansea Town still led the 3rd Division (South) table, on goal average. Plymouth lay a point behind by this stage and it was Bristol City, having largely recovered from a barren period around New Year, who occupied the 2nd slot. The Ashton Gate men had played 2 games more than their Welsh rivals, who also had a game in hand on Argyle. Perhaps points in the bag *are* better – Swansea lost 1-3 at Aberdare on April 2nd. The title race was going to go to the wire, it seemed.

After the Easter games, the Welshmen clung to their goal average lead, by 0·07 of a goal. Plymouth lay second, with Bristol City now third. Argyle took 3 points off Reading, April 18th-20th, kept their new 1-point lead on April 25th by drawing at Swansea, and reached 56 points on April 29th by crushing Southend 6-0. The Swans beat Reading 1-0 a day later and met Exeter City on May 2nd, needing victory to lift the title. A 25,000 crowd saw Town win 2-1 to become champions.

Swansea Town's '1st half' record

August	30	SWINDON TOWN	2-0
September	01	BRISTOL ROVERS	2-2
	06	Reading	0-2
	08	Bristol Rovers	0-3
	13	MERTHYR TOWN	2-0
	20	Queen's Park Rangers	0-0
	24	Exeter City	0-2
	27	CHARLTON ATHLETIC	6-1
October	04	Northampton Town	3-1
	11	WATFORD	3-1
	18	Southend United	0-1
	25	ABERDARE ATHLETIC	2-2
November	01	Norwich City	0-2
	08	BRENTFORD	7-0
	15	Millwall	2-1
	22	LUTON TOWN	4-1
December	06	BOURNEMOUTH & B.A.	1-0
	13	Brighton & Hove Albion	0-0
	20	PLYMOUTH ARGYLE	2-0
	25	BRISTOL CITY	1-1
	26	Bristol City	0-0

Table at December 26th, 1924

1	Bristol City	22	26	19	28
2	Swindon Town	22	41	23	27
3	SWANSEA TOWN	21	37	20	26
4	Plymouth Argyle	21	35	21	26
5	Watford	22	23	20	26
6	Southend United	20	28	23	25
7	Newport County	21	27	19	24
8	Millwall Athletic	22	28	23	24
9	Exeter City	21	25	22	23
10	Charlton Athletic	21	26	26	23
11	Norwich City	20	33	23	22
12	Brighton & Hove Albion	21	29	26	22
13	Bristol Rovers	20	24	22	21
14	Northampton Town	22	24	26	20
15	Gillingham	20	18	25	18
16	Luton Town	23	24	35	18
17	Aberdare Athletic	20	26	32	17
18	Reading	19	16	17	16
19	Queen's Park Rangers	21	21	28	16
20	Merthyr Town	22	21	31	15
21	Brentford	22	17	51	14
22	Bournemouth & B.A.	19	15	32	11
		462	564	564	462

Swansea Town's '2nd half' record

December	27	Swindon Town	2-0
January	17	Merthyr Town	2-0
	24	QUEEN'S PARK RANGERS	2-0
February	07	NORTHAMPTON TOWN	2-1
	14	Watford	3-1
	16	Charlton Athletic	0-0
	21	SOUTHEND UNITED	4-0
March	07	NORWICH CITY	2-0
	14	Brentford	1-3
	18	Gillingham	0-0
	21	MILLWALL	2-2
	28	Luton Town	0-0
April	02	Aberdare Athletic	1-3
	04	GILLINGHAM	2-0
	10	Newport County	0-3
	11	Bournemouth & B.A.	2-0
	13	NEWPORT COUNTY	1-0
	18	BRIGHTON & HOVE ALBION	1-0
	25	Plymouth Argyle	1-1
	30	READING	1-0
May	02	EXETER CITY	2-1

Final League Division 3 (South) Table 1925

1	SWANSEA TOWN	42	68	35	57
2	Plymouth Argyle	42	77	38	56
3	Bristol City	42	60	41	53
4	Swindon Town	42	66	38	51
5	Millwall Athletic	42	58	38	49
6	Newport County	42	62	42	49
7	Exeter City	42	59	48	47
8	Brighton & Hove Albion	42	59	45	46
9	Northampton Town	42	51	44	46
10	Southend United	42	51	61	43
11	Watford	42	38	47	43
12	Norwich City	42	53	51	41
13	Gillingham	42	35	44	40
14	Reading	42	37	38	38
15	Charlton Athletic	42	46	48	38
16	Luton Town	42	49	57	37
17	Bristol Rovers	42	42	49	37
18	Aberdare Athletic	42	54	67	37
19	Queen's Park Rangers	42	42	63	36
20	Bournemouth & B.A.	42	40	58	34
21	Brentford	42	38	91	25
22	Merthyr Town	42	35	77	21
		924	1120	1120	924

Swansea Town were promoted to Division 2. Brentford and Merthyr Town (44 votes each) were re-elected. Mid-Rhondda received no support. In view of the crisis about to hit the coal industry, this is perhaps not such a bad thing.

SHIRT COLOURS OF ... ... LEAGUE CLUBS 1919 - 1929

Club	Colours
ABERDARE ATHLETIC	Claret, with Light Blue sleeves 1921-22; Blue and Yellow stripes from 1922
ACCRINGTON STANLEY	Red
ARSENAL	Red
ASHINGTON	Black and White stripes
ASTON VILLA	Claret and Blue
BARNSLEY	Red
BARROW	Blue – White sleeves
BIRMINGHAM	Blue – White 'V' to 1927
BLACKBURN ROVERS	Blue and White halves
BLACKPOOL	Red to 1922-23; Orange from 1923
BOLTON WANDERERS	White
BOURNEMOUTH & B.A.	Red and White stripes to 1925-26; Red from 1926
BRADFORD CITY	Claret and Yellow stripes 1919-20 and 1928-29; Claret with Yellow shoulders 1920-28
BRADFORD PARK AVENUE	Green and White hoops to 1923; Red, Yellow and Black hoops 1923-25 and 1926-29; White, with a 3 colour band 1925-26
BRENTFORD	White to 1924-25; Red and White stripes from 1925
BRIGHTON & H.A.	Blue and White stripes
BRISTOL CITY	Red
BRISTOL ROVERS	White
BURNLEY	Claret and Blue
BURY	Red and White hoops 1919-21; White from 1921
CARDIFF CITY	Light Blue
CARLISLE UNITED	Blue
CHARLTON ATHLETIC	Red, apart from 1923-24 when Light and Navy Blue stripes
CHELSEA	Blue
CHESTERFIELD	Blue, until 1928 when Blue and White stripes
CLAPTON ORIENT	White, with a Red 'V'
COVENTRY CITY	Light Blue and White stripes to 1922; Red and Green halves 1922-24; Blue and White stripes from 1924
CREWE ALEXANDRA	Scarlet
CRYSTAL PALACE	Claret and Blue
DARLINGTON	Black and White hoops
DERBY COUNTY	White, apart from 1922-23 when Black and White stripes
DONCASTER ROVERS	Red until 1926, when Red and White stripes
DURHAM CITY	Blue with a Yellow 'V' or Blue and Yellow stripes
EVERTON	Blue
EXETER CITY	Red and White stripes
FULHAM	White
GILLINGHAM	Black and White stripes to 1925; Light Blue from 1925-26
GRIMSBY TOWN	Black and White stripes
HALIFAX TOWN	Blue and White stripes to 1926; Blue from 1926-27
HARTLEPOOLS UNITED	Blue, with a White 'V'
HUDDERSFIELD TOWN	Light Blue and White stripes
HULL CITY	Black and Yellow stripes
LEEDS CITY	Blue, with a Yellow 'V'
LEEDS UNITED	Blue and White stripes
LEICESTER CITY	Blue
LINCOLN CITY	Red and White stripes
LIVERPOOL	Red
LUTON TOWN	White
MANCHESTER CITY	Sky Blue
MANCHESTER UNITED	Red, apart from 1922-26 when White with a Red
MERTHYR TOWN	Red to 1925; Red and Green stripes 1925
MIDDLESBROUGH	Red, with White
MILLWALL (ATHLETIC)	Dark Blue
NELSON	Blue
NEW BRIGHTON	White
NEWCASTLE UNITED	Black and White stripes
NEWPORT COUNTY	Yellow and Black stripes
NORTHAMPTON TOWN	Purple
NORWICH CITY	Green and Yellow stripes to 1923; White 1923-25; White with a Green and Yellow 'V' 1925-27; Green and Yellow halves from 1927
NOTTINGHAM FOREST	Red
NOTTS COUNTY	Black and White stripes, apart from 1923-26 when White, with Black 'V'
OLDHAM ATHLETIC	Broad Blue and White
PLYMOUTH ARGYLE	Green
PORT VALE	White to 1923; Red from 1923-24
PORTSMOUTH	Blue
PRESTON NORTH END	White
QUEEN'S PARK RANGERS	Green and White hoops to 1926-1927; Blue and White hoops from 1927
READING	Dark Blue and White
ROCHDALE	Black and White stripes
ROTHERHAM COUNTY/ UNITED	White to 1923-24; Black and White stripes 1924-25; Yellow, with a Black 'V' 1925-28; Red 1928-29
SHEFFIELD UNITED	Red and White stripes
SHEFFIELD WEDNESDAY	Blue and White stripes
SOUTH SHIELDS	Red and Green stripes 1919-21; Red, with Green shoulders 1921-22; Blue from 1922
SOUTHAMPTON	Red and White stripes
SOUTHEND UNITED	Blue
SOUTHPORT	Red to 1924; Red with White sleeves 1924-25; Black and White stripes from 1927
STALYBRIDGE CELTIC	Blue with White sleeves
STOCKPORT COUNTY	Blue and White hoops 1919-21; Broad Blue and White stripes 1921-24; Blue from 1924
STOKE (CITY)	Red and White stripes
SUNDERLAND	Red and White stripes
SWANSEA TOWN	White
SWINDON TOWN	Red
TORQUAY UNITED	Gold with Blue sleeves
TOTTENHAM HOTSPUR	White
TRANMERE ROVERS	Blue
WALSALL	Claret and Blue
WATFORD	Black and White stripes 1920-27; Blue from 1927
WEST BROMWICH ALBION	Dark Blue and White stripes
WEST HAM UNITED	Claret and Blue
WIGAN BOROUGH	Yellow and Black halves 1921-23 ; Red and White halves 1923-24; Yellow 1925-26, then back to halved shirts
WOLVERHAMPTON WANDERERS	Old Gold and Black stripes 1919-23; old Gold with a Black 'V' from 1923
WREXHAM	Red to 1924; Blue, with a White chest band

OTHER INFORMATION   1921-1925

Attendances 1921-1925

1st Division
(Total for year is followed by average per game)

1921-22	12,480,930	27,015
1922-23	10,646,160	23,044
1923-24	10,337,775	22,376
1924-25	10,253,760	22,194

There were 462 games played in each season.

2nd Division
(Total for year is followed by average per game)

1921-22	6,123,495	13,254
1922-23	6,262,725	13,556
1923-24	5,927,040	12,829
1924-25	6,715,065	14,535

There were 462 games played in each season.

3rd Division (North)
(Total for year is followed by average per game)

1921-22	2,431,430	6,399
1922-23	2,323,890	6,116
1923-24	2,900,940	6,279
1924-25	2,576,490	5,577

There were 380 games played in the first two seasons and 462 games played in the next two.

3rd Division (South)
(Total for year is followed by average per game)

1921-22	4,454,730	9,642
1922-23	4,268,565	9,239
1923-24	3,837,645	8,307
1924-25	3,812,655	8,253

There were 462 games played in each season.

Football League

(The total for season is followed by the average per game, with the last column showing the number of league games played altogether)

1921-22	25,490,585	14,434	1,766
1922-23	23,501,340	13,308	1,766
1923-24	23,003,400	12,448	1,848
1924-25	23,357,490	12,640	1,848

Some questions of Money

1921
An Act of Parliament banned all cash betting on soccer matches, though credit betting was still allowed.

The 'international match fee' was upped from £4 to £6 by the F.A..

1922
The maximum wage was cut from £9 to £8. A threatened players' strike never materialised.

West Ham United paid £5,000 to Falkirk for Syd Puddefoot – a new transfer record which led to a storm of protest. Arsenal proposed a limit on transfer fees at £1,650, but this was rejected and no further discussion held.

F.A. Cup 1921-1925

The 1922 F.A. Cup Final was played at Stamford Bridge, home of Chelsea. The crowd was again a good one, but was lower than had been common at Crystal Palace before 1914. The F.A. took the decision to build a new stadium at Wembley, partly in order to attract bigger crowds to English soccer's 'showpiece' game. The first Wembley Final was played in 1923.

Details of F.A. Cup Finals 1922-1925

29th April, 1922

Huddersfield Town took the trophy with a 1-0 win over Preston North End. The deciding goal was scored from the spot by Billy Smith, after Mr. J.W.D. Fowler had awarded a penalty for a foul, which most onlookers believed to have been committed outside the box. Town then held out for 23 minutes and Herbert Chapman had won his first major trophy.

28th April, 1923

The official attendance for the first-ever Cup Final played at Wembley was 126,047. There may have been as many as 240,000 crammed inside the stadium and the kick-off had to be delayed by over 40 minutes while mounted police tried to clear the pitch. The Press nicknamed the match 'The White Horse Final' after 'Billy', a police mount ridden by P.C. Scorey, was seen to play a prominent part in making play possible.

Two minutes after Mr. D.H. Asson had got the game started the ball went out of play. A West Ham defender went into to the crowd to retrieve it and returned to the pitch to find David Jack had given Bolton Wanderers the lead. There was no dispute at all about Jack Smith's 53rd minute goal for Wanderers, however, and Bolton took the game 2-0.

26th April, 1924

Scoring twice in the last 10 minutes, Newcastle United beat Aston Villa 2-0. The goals came from Neil Harris and Stan Seymour. The game was watched by an all-ticket crowd of 91,695, with W.E. Russell in charge. Newcastle's Walter Hampson was aged 41 years and 8 months – the oldest-known F.A. Cup finalist to date.

25th April, 1925

G.N. Watson took charge of the match, which was watched by 91,763. The game was settled by a first half goal from Sheffield United's Fred Tunstall, who hit the winner on the 30 minutes mark against Cardiff City.

Death of Lord Kinniard

On January 30th, 1923, Lord Kinniard, one of the greatest names in English football, died at the age of 75.

He had served as F.A. President for 33 years, after a successful amateur career. Nine times an F.A. Cup finalist and five times a competition winner, Kinniard had also been a full international for Scotland.

Towards the end of his life, Lord Kinniard reflected on the game he loved, saying :
> I believe that all right-minded people have
> good reason to thank God for the great
> progress of this popular national game.

Down the years many people have at least felt something similar.

- 96 -

OTHER INFORMATION

1921-1925 (continued)

Major changes in the Laws of the Game

In 1924 two major changes were made to the Laws of Football. One was to take immediate effect after the June 15th meeting, while the other was to come into operation for the 1925-1926 season to give clubs time to prepare.

The change made in the rules relating to corner kicks was felt necessary in order to get rid of what was thought to be unclear wording. The new statement spelled out that the player who took the corner was allowed one touch, after which he could not play the ball again until it had been played by another player.

The second change was a much bigger one, in spite of the fact that, in the end, it involved only a one word alteration in the existing statement. The subject of the change was the off-side law, which had been the cause of argument and discussion for at least 15 years.

It was decided that, from the start of the 1925-26 season, *instead of* there having to be *three defenders* between an attacker and the goal when the ball was played (for the attacker to be onside), *only two* would be *necessary*.

The aims of the change were to cut the number of off-side decisions, which averaged over 30 per game, according to some sources, and to try and prevent sterile defensive play. Both these 'evils' were felt to be turning spectators away from the game.

The change to the off-side law was made after an Amateurs v. Professionals trial match played at Highbury in 1924. The first half of the game was played using the 'new' version of the law. The second 45 minutes was then played using the 'old' version, on a pitch marked out in a way which increased the size of the 'onside area'.

While 90 minutes seems to be a ridiculously short amount of 'investigation time' on the face of it, the arguments were long-standing and could have dragged on forever. Whether the full effects that the change would have were realised at the time is highly uncertain. In terms of goal-scoring, the introduction of the new off-side law was to make a difference of over 35%.

A Fuss over Fixtures

The ban on cash betting on soccer in 1921 was not really effective and there was a rapid increase in the number of 'pools companies'. With the Law seemingly unable to stop betting companies from using Football League fixtures without any payment, it was left to the League to try and sort things out.

The exact details of what happened are not totally clear, but the principles of what was involved are as follows. The 'pools companies' found it easy to get hold of Football League fixtures because (a) these were published well in advance, (b) the pattern was fairly predictable anyway. The pattern of the first 10 games for South Shields in Division 2 1923-24, shown below, was typical – the back-to-back home and away approach in operation.

SOUTH SHIELDS 1923-24 – opening 10 games

August	25	Fulham
	27	BLACKPOOL
September	01	FULHAM
	03	Blackpool
	08	BARNSLEY
	15	Barnsley
	22	MANCHESTER UNITED
	29	Manchester United
October	06	Bury
	13	BURY

Now look at the Laides' opening to the next (1924-25) season, with only Blackpool played home and away in the first 10 matches. This took the 'predictability' out of the League's fixtures, thus overcoming that side to the problem.

SOUTH SHIELDS 1924-25 – opening 10 games

August	30	PORTSMOUTH
September	01	BLACKPOOL
	06	Fulham
	08	Blackpool
	13	WOLVES
	20	Barnsley
	27	MIDDLESBROUGH
October	04	Port Vale
	11	BRADFORD CITY
	18	Oldham Athletic

Solving the other element was more difficult. Rather than any give 'advance warning' about fixtures, the League kept them secret from everybody in the first phase of the campaign. Not even the clubs were told who they would be playing until shortly before a game – though how much notice was given is not known exactly.

Clearly, this caused problems – mainly for the clubs and a storm of protest erupted. The League had to stand firm on the issue, however, and, fortunately, the 'pools companies' caved in and agreed to pay for the use of Football League fixtures on their coupons.

The episode ended satisfactorily for everyone really. It was well-known by this time that the majority of players, managers, backroom staff and supporters did not particularly like the 'back-to-back' system. The change to the new fixtures system proved to be a very popular alteration. Only midweek matches early in the season games and 'holiday time' (Christmas/New Year and Easter) games retained a 'home then away' basis.

More ... OTHER INFORMATION   1921-1925

Goal scoring 1921-1925

The leading marksmen for each season were :

Division 1

1921-22   32 – Andy Wilson (Middlesbrough)
1922-23   30 – Charlie Buchan (Sunderland)
1923-24   28 – Wilf Chadwick (Everton)
1924-25   31 – Fred Roberts (Manchester City)

Division 2

1921-22   25 – Jimmy Broad (Stoke)
1922-23   32 – Harry Bedford (Blackpool)
1923-24   32 – Harry Bedford (Blackpool)
1924-25   32 – Arthur Chandler (Leicester City)

Division 3 (North)

1921-22   37 – Jim Carmichael (Grimsby Town)
1922-23   23 – George Beel (Chesterfield)
          Jim Carmichael (Grimsby Town)
1923-24   27 – David Brown (Darlington)
1924-25   39 – David Brown (Darlington)

Division 3 (South)

1921-22   31 – Frank Richardson (Plymouth)
1922-23   30 – Fred Pagnam (Watford)
1923-24   28 – Billy Haines (Portsmouth)
1924-25   28 – Jack Fowler (Swansea Town)

The number of goals scored in Football League matches continued to fall 1921-1924, but for the final season before the new rules on offside came into force, there was at last a slight rise of 1/18th of a goal per game across the Football League as a whole, with more goals being scored in Divisions 1 and 3 North.

1st Division
(Total for year is followed by average per game)

1921-22   1,244   2·69
1922-23   1,215   2·63
1923-24   1,143   2·47
1924-25   1,192   2·58

There were 462 games played in each season.

2nd Division
(Total for year is followed by average per game)

1921-22   1,061   2·30
1922-23   1,055   2·28
1923-24   1,125   2·44
1924-25   1,068   2·31

There were 462 games played in each season.

3rd Division (North)
(Total for year is followed by average per game)

1921-22   1,150   3·03
1922-23   1,018   2·68
1923-24   1,150   2·49
1924-25   1,320   2·86

There were 380 matches played 1921-22 and 1922-23 and 462 games played in the 1923-24 season.

3rd Division (South)
(Total for year is followed by average per game)

1921-22   1,118   2·42
1922-23   1,141   2·47
1923-24   1,177   2·55
1924-25   1,120   2·42

There were 462 games played in each season.

There continued to be some **high-scoring games** in the Football League in the years 1921-1925.

Division 1

Aston Villa produced the top feat of scoring of the 1921-22 season, smashing Bradford City 7-1 on November 12th. Just short of a year later Burnley top-scored with an 8-2 mauling of Nottingham Forest on November 4th and in the next campaign Bolton Wanderers handed out a December 15th, 7-1 beating to Notts County at Burnden Park. On April 2nd, 1925 Blackburn Rovers beat Birmingham 7-0.

Division 2

Hull City took Stoke apart on November 12th, 1921, running out 7-1 victors, while in the 1922-23 season three clubs won games in which they scored six goals – Barnsley, Derby County and Manchester United (at champions-to-be Notts County). Derby County were among the goals again early in the next campaign, with a stunning 8-0 win at Bristol City on September 29th and in 1924 Leicester City provided their supporters with a 7-0 treat on Christmas Day, thrashing visitors Port Vale.

Division 3 (North)

During the 1921-22 season, seven clubs won matches in which they scored 7 times, with Darlington managing this twice. Other high-scorers were Ashington, Crewe Alexandra, Hartlepools United, Rochdale, Southport and Tranmere Rovers. On March 3rd, 1923, Wigan Borough set a new record for the division when they demolished Lincoln City 9-1. In the 1923-24 season Chesterfield crushed Walsall 7-0 on November 10th, with Wolves hammering Ashington at Portland Park on January 5th. Ashington conceded 7 at Doncaster Rovers (3-7) on September 8th, 1924, and Bradford Park Avenue (1-7) on 17th December. Nelson beat Crewe Alexandra 7-0 on April 13th, 1925

Division 3 (South)

Southampton presented their supporters with an early Christmas present in the shape of an 8-0 trouncing of Northampton Town on Christmas Eve, 1921, while Christmas cheer was on the menu for followers of Brighton & Hove Albion as Portsmouth were sent packing with a 7-1 victory for the Dolphins on Christmas Day, 1922. In the 1923-24 season, Watford smashed Newport County 8-2 on January 5th and Northampton matched this by burying their visitors Southend United 8-0 on March 22nd. During the 1924-25 campaign Plymouth Argyle enjoyed 7-1 wins over both Brentford (September 5th) and Bristol City (April 10th). Brentford took another heavy beating on November 8th – 0-7 at Swansea Town.

Goal drought

The % of Football League matches in which more than 1 goal was scored fell in the period 1921-1924. The figures for each season were :

1921-22   70·73%
1922-23   69·77%
1923-24   68·45%
1924-25   70·29%

FURTHER INFORMATION 1921-25

Attendances 1919-1925

A small number of clubs dominated the top of the 'attendance charts' throughout. Chelsea were always prominent, along with their London rivals Arsenal and Tottenham Hotspur, Newcastle United, Aston Villa, Manchester United and the Merseyside giants, Everton and Liverpool. The success, or lack of it, of these clubs affected average attendance figures for the League.

In the 2nd Division, two more London clubs, Fulham and West Ham United, were among the well-followed outfits, with Leicester City attracting good attendances from 1922. Manchester United's crowds led the way in the second tier following their demotion from the top flight. Tottenham, Birmingham and Cardiff City were also well-supported in their promotion seasons. In the 3rd Division, clubs in the Southern section drew bigger crowds, on average, with Millwall, Plymouth Argyle, Portsmouth and Swansea Town leading the way. Bradford and Wigan Borough attracted the best attendances in the Northern section, though Wolves outshone all others during their one campaign at that level, averaging 14,670 at home games.

Having risen to an average approaching 30,000, 1st Division gates fell during 1921. This pattern was echoed in Division 2, somewhat of a distortion being caused by Manchester United's presence 1922-23. The same trends can be found in the 3rd Divisions, attendances in the Northern section being distorted for one season by crowds at Wolves' home games. The overall trend was downwards after 1921. In seeking to explain this, many have noted the fall in the number of goals being scored and greater use of the 'off-side trap'. These did, no doubt, play a part in the decline in crowd numbers, with the low-point for Division 1 being reached 1924-25 at 10.25 million. Probably more important was the economic depression which hit the country post-war, with high unemployment and increasing poverty in some areas. The hardest-hit areas were those associated with heavy industry. The connection between crowd numbers and the local economy was to become even more significant within a few years.

OTHER INFORMATION 1925-29

Attendances 1925-1929

Arsenal, Aston Villa, Chelsea, Everton, Liverpool and Manchester City were in the top 8 clubs, in terms of home support, throughout the 4-season period. It was not unusual for the 3rd Division (South) clubs drawing the largest home crowds to average higher gates than many 2nd Division clubs and Millwall, in the years before their promotion in 1928, with a mean of 15,000+ were always prominent in the attendance lists. In Division 3 (North), the top crowds were repeatedly attracted in Bradford – to Park Avenue up to 1928 and to Valley Parade to watch free-scoring City in the following season.

From the start of the 1925-26 season, clubs had to return accurate crowd figures to the League, after allegations about gate money being used to provide 'illegal incentives' to players. Before this, clubs had been able to give only 'a rough figure', which was generally a 'round number'. The numbers watching League games over the period were remarkably consistent, with top flight aggregates totalling a high of 10·57 million for both 1926-27 and 1927-28. The story was similar in all the lower levels, with the ranges being 6·41-6·89 million for the Division 2, 3·57-3·98 for the 3 South and 2·50-2·75 for the 3 North.

Variations between seasons were the result of which teams were in which division. After the promotion of Manchester United in 1925, the average 1st Division crowd for 1925-26 rose, while the average attendance at 2nd Division games fell. In 1928, Durham City were replaced by Carlisle United in the 3rd Division (North) and crowd figures for the next season went up by an average of 500.

For some sides, attendances fell because of economic factors, with 'smaller' teams from mining areas feeling the pinch from 1926 onwards. The clubs having the hardest times and lowest crowds because of this were Aberdare Athletic and Merthyr Town (South Wales) + Ashington and Durham City (North-East). It is no surprise really that this quartet provided the 3 clubs who lost their League status during this period – other clubs did not like the long journeys and poor returns from gate receipts because the locals could not afford to pay to watch football.

There were 462 games in each season in each of the 4 divisions. In all tables below, the attendance total for the season is given, followed by the average per game.

1st Division

1925-26	10,416,672	22,547
1926-27	10,571,001	22,881
1927-28	10,572,954	22,885
1928-29	10,491,999	22,710

2nd Division

1925-26	6,416,278	13,257
1926-27	6,517,896	14,108
1927-28	6,892,662	14,919
1928-29	6,697,887	14,498

3rd Division (North)

1925-26	2,630,796	5,694
1926-27	2,525,628	5,467
1927-28	2,501,373	5,414
1928-29	2,748,249	5,949

3rd Division (South)

1925-26	3,866,100	8,368
1926-27	3,755,493	8,129
1927-28	3,567,774	7,722
1928-29	3,979,878	8,614

Football League

1,848 matches were played in each season.

1925-26	23,329,846	12,624
1926-27	23,370,018	12,646
1927-28	23,534,763	12,735
1928-29	23,918,013	12,943

1925-1926 – LEAGUE DIVISION 1

The new season, with the new offside law in place, opened with a bang at Villa Park, where the home side crushed Burnley 10-0. Villa did not build on this explosive start, however, and it was Tottenham Hotspur who headed the table by September 7th, having won their opening 4 games. Spurs amassed 12 points by September 21st, but dropped to second 5 days later when beaten 0-3 at Sunderland, who ended the month in top spot, on goal average. Arsenal and West Ham were on 11 points, with Huddersfield Town, the reigning champions, unbeaten, a point worse off.

Despite 2 defeats, at Manchester City and Aston Villa, in the first 5 days of October, Sunderland reasserted themselves by beating Everton 7-3 on October 10th and pulled 2 points clear 4 days later by beating Bury 1-0. The Roker outfit were still in the driving seat at mid-November, though Arsenal were applying pressure after 3 big wins in a row, which put them second, a point off the lead. Huddersfield, 4 points behind the Gunners, had games in hand on all those above them.

Arsenal took a 1-point lead at the top by beating Sunderland 2-0 on November 28th, remaining at the 1st Division summit over the next month despite a heavy 1-4 hammering at Notts County on Boxing Day. Sunderland hung on in second, but the key movement was Huddersfield's rise to third, the 11 points won leaving the Terriers 2 points from the top, with 2 matches in hand.

HUDDERSFIELD TOWN

Sunderland's 4-1 defeat of Huddersfield on January 20th was thought to have put the Leeds Road club 'in their place', but defeats for both Arsenal and the Wearsiders three days later enabled Town to join their rivals on 33 points at the top of the 1st Division. Arsenal lost two more games in the next week, allowing Sunderland and Huddersfield to pull away a little, with wins on February 6th. When the West Yorkshire team beat Everton 3-0 a week later, it enabled them to edge ahead of Sunderland, on goal average. The 'hat-trick' of Football League titles looked to be on.

Dropping only one point in their next 7 games, the defending champions now burned off their rivals. Sunderland lost three of six games played by the end of March and, although they were unbeaten in 5 games after mid-February, Arsenal found themselves 7 points off the lead by the start of April, when the 'business end of the season' arrived. Huddersfield had 7 matches left to play and looked to have matters well under control.

A sluggish Easter start saw Town drop 3 points in 2 games, however, but Arsenal failed to profit, losing at Aston Villa on Good Friday. With the Gunners beaten at otherwise out-of-sorts Sunderland on April 10th, Huddersfield, with wins over Blackburn and West Ham, needed only one point to clinch another title. Two days later, Bolton were beaten 3-0, with goals from Billy Smith, Alex Jackson and Clem Stephenson.

Huddersfield Town's '1st half' record

August	29	WEST BROMWICH ALBION	1-1
September	05	Sheffield United	3-2
	08	BURY	2-1
	12	CARDIFF CITY	1-1
	16	Birmingham	3-1
	19	Tottenham Hotspur	5-5
	26	MANCHESTER CITY	2-2
October	03	Everton	3-2
	10	BURNLEY	2-1
	17	Leeds United	4-0
	24	NEWCASTLE UNITED	0-1
	31	Manchester United	1-1
November	14	Aston Villa	0-3
	21	LEICESTER CITY	3-0
	25	LIVERPOOL	0-0
	28	West Ham United	3-2
December	05	THE ARSENAL	2-2
	12	Bolton Wanderers	1-6
	19	NOTTS COUNTY	2-0
	26	SUNDERLAND	1-1
	28	BIRMINGHAM	4-1

Table at December 28th, 1925

1	The Arsenal	23	52	36	30
2	Sunderland	23	54	40	29
3	HUDDERSFIELD TOWN	21	43	33	28
4	Manchester United	22	39	31	26
5	Tottenham Hotspur	23	45	47	26
6	West Bromwich Albion	22	50	37	25
7	Aston Villa	22	51	40	25
8	Sheffield United	23	56	49	24
9	Bury	22	51	49	24
10	Birmingham	24	39	40	24
11	Newcastle United	22	44	43	23
12	Everton	23	48	48	23
13	Bolton Wanderers	22	43	37	22
14	Liverpool	21	33	30	20
15	Notts County	23	35	39	20
16	Cardiff City	23	33	42	20
17	West Ham United	23	33	49	20
18	Blackburn Rovers	23	46	46	19
19	Leicester City	23	42	51	18
20	Burnley	23	41	68	18
21	Manchester City	23	54	67	16
22	Leeds United	22	36	46	16
		496	968	968	496

Huddersfield Town's '2nd half' record

January	02	West Bromwich Albion	2-2
	16	SHEFFIELD UNITED	4-1
	20	Sunderland	1-4
	23	Cardiff City	2-1
February	06	Manchester City	5-1
	11	Blackburn Rovers	1-2
	13	EVERTON	3-0
	20	Burnley	1-1
	27	LEEDS UNITED	3-1
March	03	TOTTENHAM HOTSPUR	2-1
	06	Newcastle United	2-0
	13	MANCHESTER UNITED	5-0
	20	Liverpool	2-1
	27	ASTON VILLA	5-1
April	03	Leicester City	0-2
	05	Bury	0-0
	06	BLACKBURN ROVERS	3-1
	10	WEST HAM UNITED	2-1
	12	BOLTON WANDERERS	3-0
	17	The Arsenal	1-3
May	01	Notts County	2-4

Final League Division 1 Table 1926

1	HUDDERSFIELD TOWN	42	92	60	57
2	The Arsenal	42	87	63	52
3	Sunderland	42	96	80	48
4	Bury	42	85	77	47
5	Sheffield United	42	102	82	46
6	Aston Villa	42	86	76	44
7	Liverpool	42	70	63	44
8	Bolton Wanderers	42	75	76	44
9	Manchester United	42	66	73	44
10	Newcastle United	42	84	75	42
11	Everton	42	72	70	42
12	Blackburn Rovers	42	91	80	41
13	West Bromwich Albion	42	79	78	40
14	Birmingham	42	66	81	40
15	Tottenham Hotspur	42	66	79	39
16	Cardiff City	42	61	76	39
17	Leicester City	42	70	80	38
18	West Ham United	42	63	76	37
19	Leeds United	42	64	76	36
20	Burnley	42	85	108	36
21	Manchester City	42	89	100	35
22	Notts County	42	54	74	33
		924	1703	1703	924

Manchester City and Notts County were relegated.

1925-1926 – LEAGUE DIVISION 2

Chelsea dropped only one point in their opening 7 games and finished September a point clear of Middlesbrough and Sheffield Wednesday, both of whom had played more times than the Stamford Bridge men. Bobby Turnbull had scored ten of the leaders' 22 goals in their forceful start to the campaign. Although Middlesbrough had outscored Chelsea, the 16 goals Boro conceded in the process was four times what the Blues had let in.

By mid-November, Chelsea were still unbeaten, in fourteen games, but the 2nd Division had new leaders, in the shape of Middlesbrough, whose 6 wins in 7 outings put the Ayresome Park club a point ahead. Chelsea's 4 draws in 7 games had proved costly. Wednesday had lost 3 times, slipping to 4th, with Derby, 4-1 victors at Hillsborough on October 17th, now third, after an 11-match unbeaten sequence, which produced 18 points. After near misses in the previous 2 seasons, the Rams looked sure to sustain a promotion challenge this time.

There were some major developments in the next few weeks at the top of the table. Successive defeats for Chelsea and Middlesbrough, coupled with Derby's slip-up against Preston, allowed Sheffield's Owls to go top, after beating Hull City and Chelsea (4-1). As Boro continued their decline with 4 further losses by December 25th, Chelsea dropped a further 3 points by drawing games. This left Sheffield Wednesday and Derby County in a head-to-head scrap for the league leadership, which the Rams shaded, on goal average, after the fixtures played on Christmas Day.

Sheffield Wednesday's '1st half' record

August	29	FULHAM	3-0	
	31	Stockport County	2-0	
September	05	South Shields	1-1	
	07	Oldham Athletic	1-1	
	12	PRESTON NORTH END	5-1	
	19	Middlesbrough	0-3	
	21	STOCKPORT COUNTY	6-2	
	26	PORTSMOUTH	4-2	
October	03	Wolves	2-1	
	10	SWANSEA CITY	3-1	
	17	DERBY COUNTY	1-4	
	24	Nottingham Forest	0-2	
	31	BARNSLEY	3-0	
November	07	Port Vale	3-4	
	14	DARLINGTON	4-0	
	21	Hull City	1-0	
	28	CHELSEA	4-1	
December	05	Clapton Orient	0-0	
	12	SOUTHAMPTON	2-1	
	19	Blackpool	0-1	
	25	Bradford City	4-1	

Table at December 25th, 1925

1	Derby County	20	41	18	29
2	SHEFFIELD WEDNESDAY	21	49	26	29
3	Chelsea	20	41	17	28
4	Oldham Athletic	19	36	23	25
5	Middlesbrough	22	42	40	24
6	Portsmouth	22	44	50	24
7	Port Vale	21	42	34	23
8	South Shields	21	37	34	23
9	Blackpool	22	38	31	22
10	Hull City	21	30	28	22
11	Bradford City	20	24	22	20
12	Wolves	20	31	31	20
13	Preston North End	22	40	51	20
14	Swansea Town	18	35	29	19
15	Stoke City	21	29	38	19
16	Darlington	21	35	43	18
17	Nottingham Forest	21	26	35	18
18	Barnsley	20	26	37	18
19	Southampton	22	30	37	15
20	Clapton Orient	20	22	32	14
21	Fulham	21	23	44	14
22	Stockport County	21	27	48	12
		456	748	748	456

SHEFFIELD WEDNESDAY

By New Year, the two leaders had a 5-point advantage over Chelsea, who lost twice in late December. Derby County and Sheffield Wednesday continued to slug it out at the top all through January, ending the month much as they began it. Both won their games on February 6th to maintain the status quo, but then County lost twice in a week and Wednesday went two points clear by beating their visitors, Wolves, on February 13th.

The lead changed hands twice during the second week of March, but the end of the month saw Sheffield Wednesday holding first place, a point ahead of Derby County, who had a game in hand. Neither side had been able to produce consistent form in this period. Chelsea, still in third, proved unable to take advantage of the stumblings of the sides above them and drew 3 times to remain a crucial 3 points behind Derby. With games running out, a tight finish looked likely, unless one team could put together a good run.

In fact, the top two teams hit form in the first half of April. Both Wednesday and County took 7 points from 4 games, without conceding a goal. Chelsea went unbeaten in 4, but drew 3 of these to fall further back. Defeat by Middlesbrough on April 24th ended the Blues' paper-thin promotion hopes. Two days later, however, Chelsea beat Derby 2-1 at Stamford Bridge, which passed the initiative in the title race back to Sheffield Wednesday, who duly accepted this by beating Blackpool on May 1st with goals from Arthur Lowdell and Jimmy Trotter, in front of a crowd of 20,575.

Sheffield Wednesday's '2nd half' record

December	26	BRADFORD CITY	5-1	
	28	OLDHAM ATHLETIC	5-1	
January	02	Fulham	0-3	
	16	SOUTH SHIELDS	1-0	
	23	Preston North End	3-0	
February	06	Portsmouth	2-1	
	13	WOLVES	2-1	
	22	MIDDLESBROUGH	2-0	
	27	Derby County	1-4	
March	11	Swansea Town	2-2	
	13	Barnsley	1-1	
	20	PORT VALE	0-2	
	22	NOTTINGHAM FOREST	2-0	
	27	Darlington	1-5	
April	03	HULL CITY	2-0	
	05	Stoke City	1-0	
	06	STOKE CITY	2-0	
	10	Chelsea	0-0	
	17	CLAPTON ORIENT	3-0	
	24	Southampton	2-1	
May	01	BLACKPOOL	2-0	

Final League Division 2 Table 1926

1	SHEFFIELD WEDNESDAY	42	88	48	60
2	Derby County	42	77	42	57
3	Chelsea	42	76	49	52
4	Wolves	42	84	60	49
5	Swansea Town	42	77	57	49
6	Blackpool	42	76	69	45
7	Oldham Athletic	42	74	62	44
8	Port Vale	42	79	69	44
9	Middlesbrough	42	77	68	44
10	South Shields	42	74	65	44
11	Portsmouth	42	79	74	44
12	Preston North End	42	71	84	43
13	Hull City	42	63	61	41
14	Southampton	42	63	63	38
15	Darlington	42	72	77	38
16	Bradford City	42	47	66	36
17	Nottingham Forest	42	51	73	36
18	Barnsley	42	58	84	36
19	Fulham	42	46	77	34
20	Clapton Orient	42	50	65	33
21	Stoke City	42	54	77	32
22	Stockport County	42	51	97	25
		924	1487	1487	924

Sheffield Wednesday and Derby County were promoted. Stoke City and Stockport County were relegated to Division 3 (North).

- 101 -

1925-26 – DIVISION 3 (NORTH)

GRIMSBY TOWN

The early exchanges in the division produced some high scores, with Bradford and Rochdale both hitting six on the first day. Park Avenue went two better than this on 14th September by thrashing Walsall 8-0, a score matched by Grimsby Town, at home to Tranmere Rovers, on the same afternoon. The trio of high scorers ended September in the top three slots in the table, with the Mariners 2 points behind their two rivals, each of whom had 13 points.

Rochdale went clear by beating Avenue 2-0 on October 3rd, but were then beaten by both Grimsby and Ashington. This allowed Bradford to move ahead and 11 points from 6 games enabled the West Yorkshire club to reach mid-November 3 points up on 'Dale, who lost twice more in the first half of the month. A couple of heavy away defeats prevented Grimsby from staying close to the leaders, while Nelson passed the fading Ashington to go fourth.

The front-runners took 7 points from the next four games to open up a seven-point lead over Rochdale by December 19th. There seemed to be a genuine danger, for the others, that Bradford might break away and turn the title race into more of a procession. Holiday opponents Grimsby Town had other ideas and a Christmas Day-Boxing Day double over the table-toppers took the Blundell Park men second, with Rochdale and Nelson also making ground on Bradford.

Park Avenue's response to this was positive, however, and 5 games played in January yielded 9 points. Hartlepools and Rochdale were beaten in early February, leaving Bradford 7 points clear. Grimsby, having stretched to nine games their unbeaten league run, trailed the leaders by eight points, but felt that their three games in hand could be used to put pressure on their rivals. Now out of the F.A. Cup, the Mariners could focus on league matters.

When Grimsby crashed 2-5 at Rochdale on February 20th, the views changed rather – at least until the news came in that Avenue had also lost, at Tranmere. With the leaders winning only two of their next 5 games, Grimsby and Rochdale were able to close the gap at the top by the end of March. With 50 points, Bradford led. Grimsby lay 2 points behind, with a game in hand. Rochdale were a point further back. Things were 'interesting' at the top.

'Dale then produced a stunning burst of 4 consecutive wins to reach mid-April level with Avenue on 55 points. Grimsby, on 54, still had a game in hand. Rochdale lost at Lincoln on April 17th, but the crucial result was Grimsby's 4-1 victory, at Doncaster Rovers, 5 days later. This took the Mariners top, with 2 to play. Town faced their last game, at home to New Brighton, needing a win to become champions. 14,548 saw Jimmy Carmichael hit the only, title-clinching goal

Grimsby Town's '1st half' record

August	29	DONCASTER ROVERS	3-0
	31	WALSALL	5-1
September	05	Rotherham United	1-2
	07	Walsall	2-2
	12	HALIFAX TOWN	1-0
	14	TRANMERE ROVERS	8-0
	19	Accrington Stanley	0-1
	26	DURHAM CITY	3-1
October	01	Tranmere Rovers	0-0
	03	Hartlepools United	1-1
	10	ROCHDALE	3-0
	17	SOUTHPORT	3-2
	24	Lincoln City	1-4
	31	COVENTRY CITY	2-0
November	07	Wrexham	1-4
	14	WIGAN BOROUGH	1-1
	21	Ashington	2-4
December	05	Nelson	1-1
	19	New Brighton	4-1
	25	BRADFORD PARK AVENUE	3-0
	26	Bradford Park Avenue	1-0

Table at December 26th, 1925

1	Bradford Park Avenue	22	48	20	31
2	GRIMSBY TOWN	21	46	25	27
3	Rochdale	20	46	26	27
4	Nelson	21	47	25	26
5	Chesterfield	19	37	19	24
6	Halifax Town	20	32	23	24
7	Hartlepools United	21	38	37	24
8	Coventry City	21	43	33	23
9	Doncaster Rovers	20	38	32	23
10	Accrington Stanley	21	38	47	22
11	Durham City	21	37	37	21
12	Crewe Alexandra	19	35	32	20
13	Lincoln City	20	35	34	20
14	Wrexham	20	35	37	19
15	Ashington	21	30	30	18
16	Rotherham United	20	24	49	18
17	Wigan Borough	20	33	38	17
18	New Brighton	20	26	39	15
19	Tranmere Rovers	20	30	49	15
20	Southport	19	31	42	14
21	Barrow	21	29	47	10
22	Walsall	21	24	61	10
		448	782	782	448

Grimsby Town's '2nd half' record

January	16	ROTHERHAM UNITED	3-0
	23	Halifax Town	2-0
	30	ACCRINGTON STANLEY	5-2
February	06	Durham City	0-0
	13	HARTLEPOOLS UNITED	2-0
	20	Rochdale	2-5
	25	BARROW	4-0
	27	Southport	1-0
March	06	LINCOLN CITY	4-0
	13	Coventry City	1-1
	20	WREXHAM	1-0
	25	CREWE ALEXANDRA	2-0
	27	Wigan Borough	2-2
April	02	CHESTERFIELD	1-0
	03	ASHINGTON	3-1
	05	Chesterfield	0-2
	10	Barrow	3-0
	17	NELSON	3-0
	22	Doncaster Rovers	4-1
	24	Crewe Alexandra	1-1
May	01	NEW BRIGHTON	1-0

Final League Division 3 (North) Table 1926

1	GRIMSBY TOWN	42	91	40	61
2	Bradford Park Avenue	42	101	43	60
3	Rochdale	42	104	58	59
4	Chesterfield	42	100	54	55
5	Halifax Town	42	53	50	45
6	Hartlepools United	42	82	73	44
7	Tranmere Rovers	42	73	83	44
8	Nelson	42	89	71	43
9	Ashington	42	70	62	43
10	Doncaster Rovers	42	80	72	43
11	Crewe Alexandra	42	63	61	43
12	New Brighton	42	69	67	42
13	Durham City	42	63	70	42
14	Rotherham United	42	69	92	41
15	Lincoln City	42	66	82	39
16	Coventry City	42	73	82	38
17	Wigan Borough	42	68	74	37
18	Accrington Stanley	42	81	105	37
19	Wrexham	42	63	92	32
20	Southport	42	62	92	32
21	Walsall	42	58	107	26
22	Barrow	42	50	98	18
		924	1628	1628	924

Grimsby Town were promoted. Walsall (33 votes) and Barrow (25) were re-elected. Carlisle United (12), Blyth Spartans (10) and Mansfield Town (10) were unsuccessful. Coventry City transferred to Division 3 (South).

1925-26 – DIVISION 3 (SOUTH) — READING

Plymouth Argyle opened in style, with 6-2 wins over both Southend and Crystal Palace. Victories in their next two games took the Devon side to the top, but they were replaced there by Reading, after the Elm Park men won at Luton Town on September 14th. The new leaders' heavy reverse at Gillingham on the 26th, coupled with their own 7-2 destruction of Aberdare Athletic, swept promotion favourites Plymouth back ahead, but Reading won again 4 days later to regain the lead.

By the time the top two met, at Reading, on October 17th, Plymouth led the table. A 1-1 draw maintained the new status quo. Both clubs won their next two games, but then Reading lost at Norwich City, enabling Argyle to go 2 points clear after drawing with Swindon Town. Another draw for the Pilgrims seven days later saw Reading able to close the gap to one point again. Bristol City, in third, lay 3 points behind the 2nd-placed outfit.

By December 19th, the Ashton Gate club had drawn level with Reading, on 25 points. Plymouth, with 3 wins and an amazing 5-5 draw at Crystal Palace in this period, were now 5 points clear. Facing lowly Exeter in the 'Pride of Devon' derby over the Festive Season, Argyle looked capable of stretching this advantage further. To most people's utter amazement, the unfancied Grecians took 3 points off the leaders. This allowed their pursuers to gain some ground.

Plymouth's next 6 games produced only 1 win and 4 points. Reading, with a run of 3 victories, passed Argyle after a 2-1 win at Charlton Athletic on January 30th. A 2-5 reverse at Merthyr Town cost the Biscuitmen pole position on February 13th, however, as Bristol City beat Watford 1-0 to move top, on goal average. Plymouth showed signs of recovery with a 5-3 win over Brighton, but were a point off the lead. Argyle's 'renewed challenge' failed to materialise fully, however, with 3 of their next 5 games lost.

Only in late March were there clear signs that Plymouth might still be a threat and there was, by this time, a new challenger emerging in the form of Millwall. The East End side had gone 7 matches unbeaten, without conceding a goal. Reading led the table as April began, 2 points clear of Bristol City, each having 7 games left to play. Millwall won 3 times over Easter to move 2nd, while the pressure proved too much for Bristol City, who faded away.

Reading stayed top, but wins for Millwall and Argyle on 10th April cut the gap to 2 points. The Den men then fell apart, leaving Plymouth to profit from Reading's loss at Palace to grab the lead by beating Charlton. On May 1st, last day of the season, Argyle lost 0-2 at Gillingham. Reading, cheered on by 17,432 fans, crushed Brentford 7-1, with 4 goals from Frank Richardson and 3 from Hugh Davey. The 3rd Division (South) title pennant would fly at Elm Park after all.

Reading's '1st half' record

August	29	EXETER CITY	3-2
September	03	Queen's Park Rangers	2-1
	05	Southend United	2-2
	09	QUEEN'S PARK RANGERS	2-1
	12	Bournemouth & B.A.	1-1
	14	Luton Town	1-0
	19	CHARLTON ATHLETIC	1-1
	26	Gillingham	1-4
	30	LUTON TOWN	3-0
October	03	MERTHYR TOWN	1-1
	10	Newport County	1-1
	17	PLYMOUTH ARGYLE	1-1
	24	Bristol City	1-0
	31	MILLWALL	2-0
November	07	Norwich City	1-3
	14	WATFORD	4-1
	21	Brighton & Hove Albion	2-2
December	05	Northampton Town	1-0
	19	Brentford	0-1
	25	SWINDON TOWN	2-0
	26	Swindon Town	1-1

Reading's '2nd half' record

December	28	CRYSTAL PALACE	2-1
January	02	Exeter City	2-3
	16	SOUTHEND UNITED	1-0
	23	BOURNEMOUTH & B.A.	5-2
	30	Charlton Athletic	2-1
February	06	GILLINGHAM	1-0
	13	Merthyr Town	2-5
	20	NEWPORT COUNTY	2-1
	27	Plymouth Argyle	3-1
March	06	BRISTOL CITY	1-1
	13	Millwall	0-1
	20	NORWICH CITY	2-0
	24	ABERDARE ATHLETIC	2-1
	27	Watford	1-0
April	02	Bristol Rovers	2-4
	03	BRIGHTON & HOVE ALBION	0-0
	05	BRISTOL ROVERS	3-0
	10	Aberdare Athletic	2-2
	17	NORTHAMPTON TOWN	4-2
	24	Crystal Palace	0-3
May	01	BRENTFORD	7-1

Table at December 26th, 1925

1	Plymouth Argyle	20	61	30	31
2	READING	21	33	23	28
3	Bristol City	21	39	26	27
4	Brighton & Hove Albion	21	49	39	26
5	Northampton Town	20	39	37	24
6	Millwall	20	39	21	23
7	Southend United	21	46	36	23
8	Watford	21	36	37	23
9	Merthyr Town	21	35	34	21
10	Swindon Town	21	31	32	21
11	Norwich City	22	29	35	21
12	Gillingham	20	27	23	20
13	Bristol Rovers	21	35	29	19
14	Charlton Athletic	20	19	22	19
15	Bournemouth & B.A.	21	29	45	19
16	Luton Town	21	34	46	17
17	Crystal Palace	20	37	42	16
18	Exeter City	21	28	36	16
19	Aberdare Athletic	21	35	44	16
20	Brentford	20	29	42	16
21	Newport County	20	25	37	16
22	Queen's Park Rangers	20	18	37	12
		454	753	753	454

Final League Division 3 (South) Table 1926

1	READING	42	77	52	57
2	Plymouth Argyle	42	107	67	56
3	Millwall	42	73	39	53
4	Bristol City	42	72	51	51
5	Brighton & Hove Albion	42	84	73	47
6	Swindon Town	42	69	64	46
7	Luton Town	42	80	75	43
8	Bournemouth & B.A.	42	75	91	43
9	Aberdare Athletic	42	74	66	42
10	Gillingham	42	53	49	42
11	Southend united	42	78	73	42
12	Northampton Town	42	82	80	41
13	Crystal Palace	42	75	79	41
14	Merthyr Town	42	69	75	39
15	Watford	42	73	89	39
16	Norwich City	42	58	73	39
17	Newport County	42	64	74	38
18	Brentford	42	69	94	38
19	Bristol Rovers	42	66	69	36
20	Exeter City	42	72	70	35
21	Charlton Athletic	42	48	68	35
22	Queen's Park Rangers	42	37	84	21
		924	1555	1555	924

Reading were promoted. Charlton Athletic and Queen's Park Rangers were re-elected without a vote as there were no other applicants.

1926-1927 – LEAGUE DIVISION 1

NEWCASTLE UNITED

With 3 wins and 2 draws, Burnley were early leaders of the 1st Division, at September 11th. Defeat at Manchester United a week later saw the Turf Moor men slip to third, with both Leicester City and Birmingham winning to go past them. A 1-0 win over Everton took the Blues top 2 days later, but City claimed a goal average advantage by sinking Blackburn 4-0 on September 25th, while Birmingham were held by Bury at St. Andrew's. After indifferent starts, Sunderland and arch-rivals Newcastle United were beginning to make progress.

Both leaders lost 4 of their next 7 and were overhauled by several other clubs, including Burnley and Sunderland. The form teams, however, were Huddersfield Town and Spurs as the season moved into November. Town went unbeaten in 7 to go third, on 19 points, by November 13th. With 5 wins in 7 outings, Tottenham headed the table, on 20 points, after a 4-1 win over Cardiff City.

A week later, Burnley crushed Spurs and the London club slipped off the pace over the next 3 weeks. Sunderland took over at the top and stayed there, apart from the first full week of December, when Newcastle replaced them briefly, until Christmas Day. A 4-5 defeat for the Roker men away at Everton let in Burnley, whose 4-0 mauling of Liverpool took them two points clear. The standings showed, however, that there were still several clubs in contention.

Burnley drew at Anfield on Boxing Day and went into the New Year as leaders of the top flight. The Clarets then lost at Everton on New Year's Day and Newcastle, with a 1-0 win over Leeds United, went top, hoping this time to stay there a little longer than they had in December. Three further wins did the trick in this respect and by February 5th the Geordies held a 2-point lead over Burnley and Sunderland. Successive away defeats in the next seven days left United vulnerable, however.

Sunderland drew level by beating Birmingham on February 16th. Three days later, both North-East clubs were passed by champions Huddersfield, who won 4-2 at Leicester. With the Terriers then held 0-0 by Everton on the 26th, Newcastle regained pole position by winning at Anfield, moving clear a week later after beating Everton 7-3. By the end of March, United led the table from Huddersfield by one point.

The top two reached Easter, when they would clash twice, with 3 points separating them. Each won the home match of their head-to-head 1-0, but in the third holiday fixture Town only drew whereas the Magpies won to lead by 4 points with 3 to play. Both drew their next game, leaving Newcastle in need of 1 point from 2 matches to become champions. On April 30th, Sheffield Wednesday were beaten 2-1 at St. James Park and the title returned to Tyneside after 18 years.

Newcastle United's '1st half' record

August	28	ASTON VILLA	4-0
September	01	BURNLEY	1-5
	04	Bolton Wanderers	1-2
	06	Burnley	3-3
	11	MANCHESTER UNITED	4-2
	18	Derby County	1-1
	20	Cardiff City	1-1
	25	SHEFFIELD UNITED	2-0
October	02	The Arsenal	2-2
	09	LIVERPOOL	1-0
	16	Everton	3-1
	23	BLACKBURN ROVERS	6-1
	30	Sunderland	0-2
November	06	WEST BROMWICH ALBION	5-2
	13	Bury	2-3
	20	BIRMINGHAM	5-1
	27	Tottenham Hotspur	3-1
December	04	WEST HAM UNITED	2-0
	11	Sheffield Wednesday	2-3
	18	LEICESTER CITY	1-1
	25	CARDIFF CITY	5-0

Newcastle United's '2nd half' record

December	27	Leeds United	2-1
January	01	LEEDS UNITED	1-0
	15	Aston Villa	2-1
	22	BOLTON WANDERERS	1-0
February	05	DERBY COUNTY	3-0
	09	Manchester United	1-3
	12	Sheffield United	1-2
	26	Liverpool	2-1
March	05	EVERTON	7-3
	12	Blackburn Rovers	2-1
	19	SUNDERLAND	1-0
	26	West Bromwich Albion	2-4
April	02	BURY	3-1
	06	THE ARSENAL	6-1
	09	Birmingham	0-2
	15	HUDDERSFIELD TOWN	1-0
	16	TOTTENHAM HOTSPUR	3-2
	19	Huddersfield Town	0-1
	23	West Ham United	1-1
	30	SHEFFIELD WEDNESDAY	2-1
May	07	Leicester City	1-2

Table at December 25th, 1926

1	Burnley	22	56	35	29
2	NEWCASTLE UNITED	21	54	31	27
3	Sunderland	23	52	37	27
4	Bolton Wanderers	20	43	26	25
5	Huddersfield Town	21	40	34	25
6	Leicester City	21	52	42	24
7	Tottenham Hotspur	21	47	38	24
8	West Ham United	20	35	28	22
9	Sheffield Wednesday	22	38	45	22
10	Birmingham	21	26	31	21
11	Leeds United	20	42	38	20
12	Aston Villa	21	40	42	20
13	The Arsenal	20	37	40	20
14	Bury	22	38	43	20
15	Sheffield United	21	37	48	20
16	Manchester United	20	28	37	20
17	Blackburn Rovers	21	39	53	20
18	Liverpool	20	30	32	18
19	Everton	23	38	55	16
20	Cardiff City	21	26	38	16
21	Derby County	20	37	38	15
22	West Bromwich Albion	21	29	53	11
		462	864	864	462

Final League Division 1 Table 1927

1	NEWCASTLE UNITED	42	96	58	56
2	Huddersfield Town	42	76	60	51
3	Sunderland	42	98	70	49
4	Bolton Wanderers	42	84	62	48
5	Burnley	42	91	80	47
6	West Ham United	42	86	70	46
7	Leicester City	42	85	70	46
8	Sheffield United	42	74	86	44
9	Liverpool	42	69	61	43
10	Aston Villa	42	81	83	43
11	The Arsenal	42	77	86	43
12	Derby County	42	86	73	41
13	Tottenham Hotspur	42	76	78	41
14	Cardiff City	42	55	65	41
15	Manchester United	42	52	64	40
16	Sheffield Wednesday	42	75	92	39
17	Birmingham	42	64	73	38
18	Blackburn Rovers	42	77	96	38
19	Bury	42	68	77	36
20	Everton	42	64	90	34
21	Leeds United	42	69	88	30
22	West Bromwich Albion	42	65	86	30
		924	1668	1668	924

Leeds United and West Bromwich Albion were relegated.

1926-1927 – LEAGUE DIVISION 2

Manchester City and Preston North End enjoyed the best starts to the campaign, reaching the end of September with 13 points each from 8 games. In third place, a point behind, were Port Vale, whose 7-match unbeaten run, since the 3-4 August loss at Darlington, made the Burslem club the surprise package among the early pace-setters. The other team in the top four was Swansea Town, who shared the points lead until a 1-3 loss at Maine Road on September's final Saturday.

Five wins in the next 7 matches lifted the Vetch Field men to the top by mid-November. Two defeats for Manchester City and Preston in this phase of the season left those clubs a point behind the Welsh outfit. Hull City lay in fourth, after taking 10 points from 7 matches, but all the leading clubs were watching Middlesbrough's progress with some concern. Boro, beaten in their opening 3 games, had introduced a new centre-forward, George Camsell. In 11 games he had scored 15 times. The ex-Durham City player hit 18 goals in Boro's next 6 matches, from which his team took 11 points.

Middlesbrough's charge between mid-November and December 27th swept them to the top of the table on the latter date, after the completion of 'a double' over out-of-sorts Manchester City. The Ayresome Park men replaced Hull City, who lost at home to Chelsea, whose mid-table standing continued to surprise football followers. With a cluster of clubs at the top, could Boro stay there?

MIDDLESBROUGH

The Teessiders followed a 5-2 hammering of Port Vale on New Year's Day with 3 draws. None of the rest of the top six proved able to take advantage of Middlesbrough's dropped points, however. With wins over both Grimsby Town and Wolves, the leaders reached the mid-point in February two points ahead of Nottingham Forest, who were themselves two clear of resurgent Manchester City and Portsmouth, who had shown the division's best form during January.

Boro gathered 12 points in the next 7 matches, extending their run without losing to 19 games by beating Portsmouth 1-0 on March 26th. Camsell, who hit the winner, had now hit 51 goals in 29 2nd Division games. Middlesbrough had an 8-point lead with 8 games to go – only a disaster could stop a return to Division 1. Wins over Oldham Athletic, the last side to beat Boro in the league, and Fulham brought promotion and the title ever closer. Despite losing at Port Vale on Good Friday, Middlesbrough moved closer to the top flight with a 3-0 win over Grimsby Town the next day.

Promotion came on Easter Monday, when Preston lost at Hull. Boro only needed 1 point to become champions, but lost at Reading on April 20th to drag things out more. Still short of the mark, the leaders travelled to Blackpool on April 23rd hoping to settle matters. George Camsell hit his 55th of the campaign, the match ended 2-2 and Middlesbrough were 2nd Division champions, at last.

Middlesbrough's '1st half' record

August	28	Chelsea	0-3
	30	Southampton	1-2
September	04	PRESTON NORTH END	0-2
	11	South Shields	0-0
	18	HULL CITY	2-0
	22	BRADFORD CITY	4-3
	25	Wolves	2-1
	29	Bradford City	1-0
October	02	NOTTS COUNTY	4-2
	09	Clapton Orient	3-2
	16	Nottingham Forest	3-4
	23	BARNSLEY	5-1
	30	Darlington	4-1
November	06	PORTSMOUTH	7-3
	13	Oldham Athletic	1-2
	20	FULHAM	6-1
	27	SOUTHAMPTON	3-1
December	04	BLACKPOOL	4-4
	18	SWANSEA TOWN	7-1
	25	Manchester City	5-3
	27	MANCHESTER CITY	2-1

Table at December 27th, 1926

1	MIDDLESBROUGH	21	64	37	30
2	Hull City	22	32	15	29
3	Nottingham Forest	22	41	30	29
4	Swansea Town	22	42	32	29
5	Preston North End	21	43	32	28
6	Southampton	22	41	33	28
7	Portsmouth	22	38	27	27
8	Chelsea	22	33	32	26
9	Manchester City	22	52	37	25
10	Port Vale	23	44	42	24
11	Oldham Athletic	22	34	33	24
12	Blackpool	22	47	42	20
13	Reading	21	33	35	19
14	Fulham	22	31	43	19
15	South Shields	20	38	33	18
16	Wolves	22	39	40	16
17	Darlington	23	41	50	16
18	Grimsby Town	20	30	40	16
19	Notts County	21	35	51	15
20	Clapton Orient	21	29	50	14
21	Barnsley	20	29	58	14
22	Bradford City	23	24	48	10
		476	840	840	476

Middlesbrough's '2nd half' record

January	01	PORT VALE	5-2
	15	CHELSEA	0-0
	22	Preston North End	2-2
February	05	Hull City	3-3
	08	Grimsby Town	7-4
	12	WOLVES	2-0
	23	Notts County	2-2
	26	CLAPTON ORIENT	6-0
March	05	NOTTINGHAM FOREST	1-0
	12	Barnsley	1-1
	16	SOUTH SHIELDS	5-0
	19	DARLINGTON	4-1
	26	Portsmouth	1-0
April	02	OLDHAM ATHLETIC	3-1
	09	Fulham	3-0
	15	Port Vale	1-3
	16	GRIMSBY TOWN	3-0
	20	Reading	1-2
	23	Blackpool	2-2
	30	READING	5-0
May	07	Swansea Town	1-0

Final League Division 2 Table 1927

1	MIDDLESBROUGH	42	122	60	62
2	Portsmouth	42	87	49	54
3	Manchester City	42	108	61	54
4	Chelsea	42	62	52	52
5	Nottingham Forest	42	80	55	50
6	Preston North End	42	74	72	49
7	Hull City	42	63	52	47
8	Port Vale	42	88	78	45
9	Blackpool	42	95	80	44
10	Oldham Athletic	42	74	84	44
11	Barnsley	42	88	87	43
12	Swansea Town	42	68	72	43
13	Southampton	42	60	62	42
14	Reading	42	64	72	40
15	Wolves	42	73	75	35
16	Notts County	42	70	96	35
17	Grimsby Town	42	74	91	34
18	Fulham	42	58	92	34
19	South Shields	42	71	96	33
20	Clapton Orient	42	60	96	31
21	Darlington	42	79	98	30
22	Bradford City	42	50	88	23
		924	1668	1668	924

Middlesbrough and Portsmouth were promoted. Bradford City and Darlington were relegated to Division 3 (North). This led to Walsall being transferred to Division 3 (South).

1926-27 – DIVISION 3 (NORTH)   STOKE CITY

It was unusual in these times for one team to dominate a title race from almost start to finish, but Stoke City, relegated from Division 2 the previous season, achieved this in the 3rd Division (North) in the 1926-27 campaign. Held at home by Bradford Park Avenue on the opening day of the season, the Potters reeled off 5 wins in a row before dropping their next point. Two further wins, including a 7-0 destruction of the decent Ashington side, put City four points clear by the end of September. A 0-5 collapse at New Brighton on October 2nd was only a blip for Stoke, who resumed their onward and upward march with 3 more wins to reassert their superiority. Beaten again on October 30th, the Potteries club followed this irritation with further wins, over Southport and Rochdale, to reach mid-November 4 points ahead of 2nd-placed Chesterfield, with 26 points from 16 games.

With a settled nucleus to the side, Stoke eased through the next 5 league matches unbeaten, overcoming the shock of elimination from the F.A. Cup by non-league Rhyl Athletic, to remain top of the table at December 27th. Their lead was by now down to 3 points, with Rochdale, for whom ex-Stoke man, Bert Whitehurst, scored 12 goals in five December games, threatening to make a contest of things after all. City, for whom Charlie Wilson had hit 22 goals in 21 games, were not to be distracted, however.

Rochdale lost twice in early January, which allowed Stoke to move away again, but by mid-February the leaders had been beaten on 2 occasions themselves. These included a 0-1 loss at Nelson, whose 6 wins in seven games carried them to third, with games in hand on City. Also going very well at this stage were unfashionable Halifax Town, with 7 wins and 15 points from 8 matches. Stoke still led the table by four points, however, and continued to set the standards for the others to try and match. Part of the reason for the Potters' success was their ability to recover from setbacks. Also, the team had proved it could grind out results consistently since the league began back in August. Nine more points were added in the 6 games played up to the end of March. Other clubs could not match this continuing high level of performance and April began with Stoke 6 points ahead of Nelson.

Even after losing twice in the next 4 matches, City were 5 points clear at April 16th, with the title in sight. The crucial day proved to be Saturday, April 23rd. Nelson lost at home to Southport, 1-2, and Rochdale fell, 1-4, at Walsall. With a 1-0 win over Accrington Stanley, courtesy of Jack Eyres' goal, Stoke City moved out of reach of the other leading clubs in the northern section and completed a quick return to Division 2. All those linked with the club believed that the Potters were due for even better things.

Stoke City's '1st half' record

August	28	BRADFORD PARK AVENUE	0-0
	30	WIGAN BOROUGH	2-0
September	04	Walsall	1-0
	06	Wigan Borough	3-0
	11	NELSON	4-1
	13	HARTLEPOOLS UNITED	3-1
	18	Chesterfield	1-1
	22	Hartlepools United	3-1
	25	ASHINGTON	7-0
October	02	New Brighton	0-5
	09	WREXHAM	2-0
	16	BARROW	4-0
	23	Crewe Alexandra	2-0
	30	STOCKPORT COUNTY	0-1
November	06	Southport	3-0
	13	ROCHDALE	3-1
	20	Tranmere Rovers	1-1
December	04	Accrington Stanley	1-0
	18	Halifax Town	2-2
	25	ROTHERHAM UNITED	4-1
	27	Rotherham United	2-2

Stoke City's '2nd half' record

January	01	LINCOLN CITY	2-0
	08	DURHAM CITY	4-0
	15	Bradford Park Avenue	0-3
	22	WALSALL	4-1
	29	Nelson	0-1
February	05	CHESTERFIELD	3-2
	12	Ashington	2-0
	19	NEW BRIGHTON	1-1
	26	Wrexham	6-2
March	05	Barrow	0-0
	12	CREWE ALEXANDRA	2-1
	19	Stockport County	2-2
	26	SOUTHPORT	4-0
April	02	Rochdale	0-4
	09	TRANMERE ROVERS	2-0
	15	Doncaster Rovers	1-3
	16	Durham City	2-1
	18	DONCASTER ROVERS	0-0
	23	ACCRINGTON STANLEY	1-0
	30	Lincoln City	3-1
May	07	HALIFAX TOWN	5-1

Table at December 27th, 1926

1	STOKE CITY	21	48	17	33
2	Rochdale	21	55	34	30
3	Stockport County	19	45	22	27
4	Nelson	18	52	27	26
5	Bradford Park Avenue	21	44	31	26
6	Chesterfield	20	49	34	25
7	New Brighton	21	41	29	25
8	Halifax Town	19	30	22	24
9	Tranmere Rovers	20	34	30	21
10	Rotherham United	21	38	44	20
11	Walsall	20	32	35	19
12	Durham City	21	25	35	19
13	Southport	20	34	39	18
14	Ashington	20	29	46	18
15	Wrexham	20	29	32	17
16	Hartlepools United	21	31	37	17
17	Doncaster Rovers	19	31	41	17
18	Lincoln City	21	39	45	15
19	Wigan Borough	22	39	49	15
20	Crewe Alexandra	20	30	38	15
21	Accrington Stanley	21	28	50	11
22	Barrow	20	15	61	8
		446	798	798	446

Final League Division 3 (North) Table 1927

1	STOKE CITY	42	92	40	63
2	Rochdale	42	105	65	58
3	Bradford Park Avenue	42	101	59	55
4	Halifax Town	42	70	53	53
5	Nelson	42	104	75	51
6	Stockport County*	42	93	69	49
7	Chesterfield	42	92	68	47
8	Doncaster Rovers	42	81	65	47
9	Tranmere Rovers	42	85	67	46
10	New Brighton	42	79	67	46
11	Lincoln City	42	90	78	42
12	Southport	42	80	85	39
13	Wrexham	42	65	73	38
14	Walsall	42	68	81	38
15	Crewe Alexandra	42	71	81	37
16	Ashington	42	60	90	36
17	Hartlepools United	42	66	81	34
18	Wigan Borough	42	66	83	32
19	Rotherham United	42	70	92	32
20	Durham City	42	58	105	30
21	Accrington Stanley	42	62	98	27
22	Barrow	42	34	117	22
		924	1692	1692	922

*Stockport County deducted 2 points for fielding ineligible player (Joe Smith) against Stoke City on March 19th, 1927 Stoke City were promoted. Accrington Stanley (36 votes) and Barrow (30) were re-elected. Mansfield Town (8), York City (6), Carlisle United (5) and Blyth Spartans (3) were unsuccessful.

1926-27 – DIVISION 3 (SOUTH) — BRISTOL CITY

By the end of September, Swindon Town led the table, with 13 points from 8 games. This put the Robins 1 point up on Bristol City, Millwall and Newport County. Town's one loss had been suffered at Brighton & Hove Albion on September 18th – by an amazing 3-9. The Goldstone Ground men, who had also beaten 3rd-placed Millwall by this stage, had collected only 7 points to date – from 6 games. Clearly, however, the Dolphins could turn on the style at times.

This promise became reality during October, when Albion won 7 matches to join Bristol City at the head of the table on 21 points. The Ashton Gate side were themselves unbeaten in the month, unlike Swindon, Millwall and Newport. Victory over Queen's Park Rangers carried Brighton clear on November 6th, but Bristol City got back on terms a week later by defeating Northampton 4-3. Swindon and Newport were 3 points behind the leaders.

Brighton beat Bristol City 3-0 on November 20th to pull clear again. The Sussex club stayed top until December 11th when Swindon took advantage of Albion's F.A. Cup duty to ease into first place by winning 4-1 at Aberdare Athletic. By winning their next 4 games, the Wiltshire club took a firm grip on top spot, ending the year 4 points ahead of Brighton. By January 15th, Swindon led by 3 points from Millwall, with Albion and Bristol City, each with a clutch of games in hand, 2 points behind the Lions.

Swindon dropped 5 points in their next 4 matches, allowing Brighton and Millwall to close in on them. However, with 9 points from 5 games played up to mid-February, Bristol City caught and passed the New Year top-dogs. With 31 goals in 7 games, Christmas Day to February 12th, City had struck a rich vein of form which threatened to blow away all the other challengers. Leading the way in the Ashton Gate club's goal-fest were Tommy Walsh and Albert Keating.

By taking 13 points from their next seven fixtures, Bristol City opened up a yawning 8-point gap by March's end. 1-0 wins over both Millwall and Swindon Town helped in this. As Swindon wilted and slid out of the top 4, Plymouth, unbeaten in 10 games after January 1st, tried to mount a late challenge. Encouragingly for the Devon side, by the end of the Easter games, Bristol City had lost 3 times in 5 matches, but still led the table by 4 points, from Millwall.

Plymouth were 6 points off the lead with a game in hand. The Pilgrims' storming end-of-season run had, however, come just too late. Although Argyle beat Bristol City 4-2 at Home Park on May 4th, the Ashton Gate club, with a vastly better goal average of 1·87 to their rivals' 1·54, held a 2-point lead with 1 match left to play. Plymouth had run out of games and it was effectively all over. Bristol City's title triumph was confirmed on May 7th when they won their final fixture against Merthyr Town 3-0.

Bristol City's '1st half' record

August	28	Gillingham	1-1
September	01	NEWPORT COUNTY	4-1
	04	WATFORD	5-0
	09	Newport County	0-0
	11	Crystal Palace	2-4
	18	COVENTRY CITY	3-0
	22	PLYMOUTH ARGYLE	4-2
	25	Queen's Park Rangers	2-1
October	02	CHARLTON ATHLETIC	4-1
	09	Bristol Rovers	5-0
	16	EXETER CITY	3-2
	23	Swindon Town	2-2
	30	MILLWALL	4-1
November	06	Brentford	0-3
	13	NORTHAMPTON TOWN	4-3
	20	Brighton & Hove Albion	0-3
December	04	Luton Town	0-0
	18	Merthyr Town	1-1
	25	Aberdare Athletic	7-3
	27	ABERDARE ATHLETIC	2-1
January	15	GILLINGHAM	9-4

Bristol City's '2nd half' record

January	22	Watford	1-0
	29	CRYSTAL PALACE	5-4
February	05	Coventry City	5-2
	09	NORWICH CITY	1-1
	12	QUEEN'S PARK RANGERS	1-0
	19	Charlton Athletic	1-0
	23	SOUTHEND UNITED	5-1
	26	BRISTOL ROVERS	3-1
March	05	Exeter City	1-1
	12	SWINDON TOWN	2-0
	19	Millwall	1-0
	26	BRENTFORD	1-0
April	02	Northampton Town	0-2
	09	BRIGHTON & HOVE ALBION	0-2
	15	BOURNEMOUTH & B.A.	2-0
	16	Norwich City	1-1
	18	Bournemouth & B.A.	0-2
	23	LUTON TOWN	6-0
	30	Southend United	1-0
May	04	Plymouth Argyle	2-4
	07	MERTHYR TOWN	3-0

Table at January 15th, 1927

1	Swindon Town	24	66	42	36
2	Millwall	25	55	34	33
3	Brighton & Hove Albion	21	46	22	31
4	BRISTOL CITY	21	62	33	31
5	Newport County	24	29	35	29
6	Plymouth Argyle	23	46	37	28
7	Luton Town	22	39	37	25
8	Brentford	21	47	33	24
9	Exeter City	22	46	36	23
10	Crystal Palace	21	38	32	23
11	Southend United	23	45	42	23
12	Bournemouth & B.A.	21	41	38	21
13	Watford	24	35	46	20
14	Norwich City	22	36	48	19
15	Coventry City	24	41	56	19
16	Queen's Park Rangers	24	40	55	18
17	Bristol Rovers	22	31	37	18
18	Merthyr Town	22	34	41	18
19	Charlton Athletic	20	25	31	17
20	Northampton Town	25	33	55	16
21	Gillingham	23	30	46	15
22	Aberdare Athletic	24	31	60	11
		498	896	896	498

Final League Division 3 (South) Table 1927

1	BRISTOL CITY	42	104	54	62
2	Plymouth Argyle	42	95	61	60
3	Millwall	42	89	51	56
4	Brighton & Hove Albion	42	79	50	53
5	Swindon Town	42	100	85	51
6	Crystal Palace	42	84	81	45
7	Bournemouth & B.A.	42	78	66	44
8	Luton Town	42	68	66	44
9	Newport County	42	57	71	44
10	Bristol Rovers	42	78	80	41
11	Brentford	42	70	61	40
12	Exeter City	42	76	73	40
13	Charlton Athletic	42	60	61	40
14	Queen's Park Rangers	42	65	71	39
15	Coventry City	42	71	86	37
16	Norwich City	42	59	71	35
17	Merthyr Town	42	63	80	35
18	Northampton Town	42	59	87	35
19	Southend United	42	64	77	34
20	Gillingham	42	54	72	32
21	Watford	42	57	87	32
22	Aberdare Athletic	42	62	101	25
		924	1592	1592	924

Bristol City were promoted to Division 2. Watford (44 votes) were re-elected, but Aberdare Athletic tied with Torquay United in second place, with both clubs receiving 21 votes. Kettering Town (1), Yeovil & Petters United (1) and Ebbw Vale (0) were eliminated from the ballot and a second vote was held. Torquay United won this by 26-19 and replaced Aberdare as a Football League club.

1927-1928 – LEAGUE DIVISION 1 — EVERTON

Defending champions, Newcastle United, began the season well, winning 4 and drawing two of their opening 6 games, to head the table by September 17th. Joined by Bury, two days later, after the Shakers beat Liverpool 5-2, the Geordies lost for the first time, on September 24th, to Cardiff City. As Bury also lost, this led to four teams ending September with a share of the points lead, on 10. Joining the champions and Bury on this mark were Cardiff and West Ham United.

Of the top four, Cardiff City had the worst result on October 1st, crashing 2-8 at Huddersfield, but only Bury won. The Gigg Lane men had a lean time afterwards, however, taking just 3 points from their next 6 games, which included a 1-4 home loss to Newcastle, on November 12th. This win left the Tynesiders second in the table, 3 points ahead of Blackburn Rovers, but one behind Everton, who had stormed to the top by the end of October and reached mid-November unbeaten in 12.

With Newcastle failing to produce a win in their next seven games, Everton were able to overcome the setback of home defeat by Sunderland on November 19th to open up a clear lead at the top. Clubs trying to stay in touch were headed by Leicester and Blackburn, though it was most probably Huddersfield Town, in fourth after the Boxing Day matches, that Everton were most wary of as New Year approached. In 33-goal 'Dixie' Dean, however, the Goodison Park team had a real trump card in their hand.

Huddersfield had moved up to second by New Year and outpointed the leaders during January to make their meeting at Leeds Road on February 4th of key importance. Town won 4-1 to move to within a point of Everton, whose wobble was to continue a week later when they crumbled at home, 2-5, against Spurs. Huddersfield, however, crashed 0-4 away at Cardiff City, leaving Everton still clinging to their top of the league spot at mid-February, but nervous.

Having failed to win in 3, the Merseysiders really seemed to have lost their way in this phase of the campaign, playing 6 more times without victory. This appalling run ended on March 31st, when Sunderland were beaten 2-0. Huddersfield, despite the distraction of 4 F.A. Cup ties had gone top and led by 3 points as April arrived. In addition to this, Town also had two games in hand on Everton. Things looked to be going very much the Terriers' way – but, it's never over 'until the final whistle'.

As come-backs go, Everton's revival over the next few weeks was as remarkable as Huddersfield Town's throwing away of their title chance. 5 points in 3 games left the Toffees one point off the lead by mid-April. Wins over Newcastle, Villa and Burnley lifted Everton back to the top, with a three-point lead by April 28th. Huddersfield, beaten in the F.A. Cup Final a week before, had 2 games in hand, however. When Town lost the second of these, on May 2nd, Everton became Football League champions.

Everton's '1st half' record

August	27	SHEFFIELD WEDNESDAY	4-0
September	03	Middlesbrough	2-4
	05	Bolton Wanderers	1-1
	10	BIRMINGHAM	5-2
	14	BOLTON WANDERERS	2-2
	17	Newcastle United	2-2
	24	HUDDERSFIELD TOWN	2-2
October	01	Tottenham Hotspur	3-1
	08	MANCHESTER UNITED	5-2
	15	LIVERPOOL	1-1
	22	WEST HAM UNITED	7-0
	29	Portsmouth	3-1
November	05	LEICESTER CITY	7-1
	12	Derby County	3-0
	19	SUNDERLAND	0-1
	26	Bury	3-2
December	03	SHEFFIELD UNITED	0-0
	10	Aston Villa	3-2
	17	BURNLEY	4-1
	24	Arsenal	2-3
	26	CARDIFF CITY	2-1

Everton's '2nd half' record

December	27	Cardiff City	0-2
	31	Sheffield Wednesday	2-1
January	02	Blackburn Rovers	2-4
	07	MIDDLESBROUGH	3-1
	21	Birmingham	2-2
February	04	Huddersfield Town	1-4
	11	TOTTENHAM HOTSPUR	2-5
	25	Liverpool	3-3
March	03	West Ham United	0-0
	10	PORTSMOUTH	0-0
	14	Manchester United	0-1
	17	Leicester City	0-1
	24	DERBY COUNTY	2-2
	31	Sunderland	2-0
April	06	BLACKBURN ROVERS	4-1
	07	BURY	1-1
	14	Sheffield United	3-1
	18	NEWCASTLE UNITED	3-0
	21	ASTON VILLA	3-2
	28	Burnley	5-3
May	05	ARSENAL	3-3

Table at December 26th, 1927

1	EVERTON	21	61	29	30
2	Leicester City	22	49	35	26
3	Blackburn Rovers	22	31	32	25
4	Huddersfield Town	20	45	33	24
5	Newcastle United	21	43	40	23
6	Cardiff City	21	38	40	23
7	Tottenham Hotspur	21	39	44	22
8	Liverpool	20	47	35	21
9	Middlesbrough	21	46	43	21
10	Arsenal	19	40	39	21
11	West Ham United	20	45	49	21
12	Bury	21	41	45	21
13	Aston Villa	21	43	43	20
	Sunderland	21	37	37	20
15	Manchester United	22	37	40	20
16	Bolton Wanderers	20	36	31	19
17	Sheffield United	21	33	43	19
18	Burnley	21	37	52	19
19	Derby County	20	51	48	17
20	Birmingham	21	33	45	16
21	Sheffield Wednesday	21	38	45	15
22	Portsmouth	21	34	56	15
		458	904	904	458

Final League Division 1 Table 1928

1	EVERTON	42	102	66	53
2	Huddersfield Town	42	91	68	51
3	Leicester City	42	96	72	48
4	Derby County	42	96	83	44
5	Bury	42	80	80	44
6	Cardiff City	42	70	80	44
7	Bolton Wanderers	42	81	66	43
8	Aston Villa	42	78	73	43
9	Newcastle United	42	79	81	43
10	Arsenal	42	82	86	41
11	Birmingham	42	70	75	41
12	Blackburn Rovers	42	66	78	41
13	Sheffield United	42	79	86	40
14	Sheffield Wednesday	42	81	78	39
15	Sunderland	42	74	76	39
16	Liverpool	42	84	87	39
17	West Ham United	42	81	88	39
18	Manchester United	42	72	80	39
19	Burnley	42	82	98	39
20	Portsmouth	42	66	90	39
21	Tottenham Hotspur	42	74	86	38
22	Middlesbrough	42	81	88	37
		924	1765	1765	924

Tottenham Hotspur and Middlesbrough were relegated.

1927-1928 – LEAGUE DIVISION 2

MANCHESTER CITY

Clapton Orient had the best start to the season, dropping only one point in their first 6 games to lead Division Two at September 17th. A 2-4 reverse at Barnsley brought the O's' unbeaten opening to an end a week later, however, and they were joined on 11 points by Manchester City, whose 5-4 win at Nottingham Forest put the Citizens second, with a highly interesting goals aggregate of 21-16. Preston North End and Bristol City were a point behind the leaders.

Three defeats for Orient in October saw the Millfields Road outfit begin a long slide down the table, which eventually almost resulted in relegation. City fared rather better, but two defeats at the start of November resulted in the Maine Road side slipping to fourth, with 18 points from 14 games. Stoke City and Bristol City, the two promoted sides, sat just above the Mancunians, on goal average. Five points ahead at the top were Chelsea, following 7 consecutive victories.

The leaders could not maintain this invincible form, dropping 6 points in 4 away games by Boxing Day. Manchester City, with 5 wins and a draw after mid-November clawed their way back into contention. The 3-0 win achieved at Barnsley on December 26th took the Maine Road men to within two points of Chelsea. Also producing five wins in this period, Preston North End and Leeds United threw their hats into the championship ring. Signs of something of a dog-fight were beginning to develop.

Results before New Year tightened things even more, with two wins for Preston and Leeds, one win for Manchester City and a 0-0 draw for Chelsea, at home to Reading. By the middle of February, the Londoners, having managed four wins, were clear again, 2 points ahead of City and Preston North End, with Leeds United a further two points back. It was still very much a case of 'anything could happen' and, sure enough, things were about to change once again.

Chelsea lost their next two games, Leeds United went seven matches unbeaten and Preston took ten points from their 7 fixtures up to the end of March. Manchester City played six without losing in this period, including a 1-0, March 24th win at Stamford Bridge, which was Chelsea's only defeat during the month. All four leaders had 48 points at the beginning of April, with Leeds United holding a goal average advantage over the others.

By the middle of the month, North End had lost three times and Chelsea twice. Leeds United, with 55 points, headed the table, two up on Manchester City, who had 2 games in hand. On April 25th, Tommy Tait's goal enabled the Citizens to grab a 1-0 win at Elland Road, securing promotion for the visitors in the process. City then thrashed Southampton 6-1 to go clear of Leeds. Now needing 1 point at Notts County on May 5th to take the title, the Maine Road side lost 1-2, but Leeds crashed 1-5 at Stoke and City became champions.

Manchester City's '1st half' record

August	27	Wolves	2-2
	29	SWANSEA TOWN	7-4
September	03	PORT VALE	1-0
	05	Swansea Town	3-5
	10	South Shields	1-0
	17	LEEDS UNITED	2-1
	24	Nottingham Forest	5-4
October	01	OLDHAM ATHLETIC	3-1
	08	HULL CITY	2-1
	15	Preston North End	0-1
	22	Blackpool	2-2
	29	READING	4-1
November	05	Grimsby Town	1-4
	12	CHELSEA	0-1
	19	Clapton Orient	2-0
	26	STOKE CITY	4-0
December	03	Bristol City	0-2
	10	WEST BROMWICH ALBION	3-1
	17	Southampton	1-1
	24	NOTTS COUNTY	3-1
	26	Barnsley	3-0

Table at December 26th, 1927

1	Chelsea	21	43	19	31
2	MANCHESTER CITY	21	49	32	29
3	Preston North End	21	45	28	28
4	Leeds United	21	53	27	27
5	Bristol City	21	45	33	26
6	Oldham Athletic	20	39	25	25
7	Nottingham Forest	21	53	40	25
8	Port Vale	21	40	31	24
9	West Bromwich Albion	21	46	42	22
10	Stoke City	20	33	31	21
11	Swansea Town	21	45	45	21
12	Grimsby Town	21	37	39	21
13	Clapton Orient	20	36	41	20
14	Barnsley	21	30	40	19
15	Hull City	20	22	28	18
16	Notts County	21	35	40	17
17	Fulham	20	33	47	15
18	Blackpool	21	36	54	15
19	Reading	21	30	47	15
20	Southampton	21	28	42	14
21	Wolves	21	34	51	14
22	South Shields	20	29	59	9
		456	841	841	456

Manchester City's '2nd half' record

December	31	WOLVES	3-0
January	02	BARNSLEY	7-3
	07	Port Vale	2-1
	21	SOUTH SHIELDS	3-0
February	04	NOTTINGHAM FOREST	3-3
	11	Oldham Athletic	2-3
	25	PRESTON NORTH END	2-2
March	03	BLACKPOOL	4-1
	10	Reading	1-1
	17	GRIMSBY TOWN	2-0
	24	Chelsea	1-0
	31	CLAPTON ORIENT	5-3
April	06	FULHAM	2-1
	07	Stoke City	0-2
	09	Fulham	1-1
	14	BRISTOL CITY	4-2
	16	Hull City	0-0
	21	West Bromwich Albion	1-1
	25	Leeds United	1-0
	28	SOUTHAMPTON	6-1
May	05	Notts County	1-2

Final League Division 2 Table 1928

1	MANCHESTER CITY	42	100	59	59
2	Leeds United	42	98	49	57
3	Chelsea	42	75	45	54
4	Preston North End	42	100	66	53
5	Stoke City	42	78	59	52
6	Swansea Town	42	75	63	48
7	Oldham Athletic	42	75	51	46
8	West Bromwich Albion	42	90	70	46
9	Port Vale	42	68	57	44
10	Nottingham Forest	42	83	84	40
11	Grimsby Town	42	69	83	40
12	Bristol City	42	76	79	39
13	Barnsley	42	65	85	39
14	Hull City	42	41	54	39
15	Notts County	42	68	74	38
16	Wolves	42	63	91	36
17	Southampton	42	68	77	35
18	Reading	42	53	75	35
19	Blackpool	42	83	101	34
20	Clapton Orient	42	55	85	34
21	Fulham	42	68	89	33
22	South Shields	42	56	111	23
		924	1607	1607	924

Manchester City and Leeds United were promoted. Fulham (South) and South Shields (North) were relegated to Division 3.

- 109 -

1927-28 – DIVISION 3 (NORTH)

In an uneven start to the season, Halifax Town played 9 times by the end of September and, with 12 points, topped the table. Wrexham, with 11 from eight, lay second and Rochdale, having won 5 of their six games to date, were third, ahead of Bradford Park Avenue, who had played 7 games, on goal average. These standings looked likely to change as the games played evened up.

Halifax's tenure in top place lasted rather longer than many expected, however, and it was not until October 29th that the Shaymen were caught and passed, on goal average. The new leaders were Bradford, who were thus rewarded for a 10-match unbeaten sequence, which had produced 17 points since the start of September. Wins over both Halifax Town and Darlington kept Avenue top at mid-November.

On the 19th of the month, however, Bradford lost at home to Doncaster Rovers, 0-2, and were replaced at the head of the table by their conquerors. Despite going 4 games unbeaten, Avenue remained second until after Christmas. However, New Year's Eve saw Rovers dip 0-2 at third-placed Lincoln City, while Bradford won 1-0 at Durham City to reclaim the league leadership. Avenue's 4-0 win at Rochdale, on 3rd January, set up a 3-point buffer.

Bradford Park Avenue's '1st half' record

August	27	DURHAM CITY	4-0
	30	Southport	1-2
September	03	Wrexham	1-1
	05	SOUTHPORT	5-3
	10	CHESTERFIELD	1-0
	17	Bradford City	3-2
	24	Tranmere Rovers	2-2
October	01	STOCKPORT COUNTY	2-0
	08	Barrow	0-0
	15	NELSON	3-2
	22	ASHINGTON	5-0
	29	Crewe Alexandra	3-1
November	05	HALIFAX TOWN	3-2
	12	Darlington	3-1
	19	DONCASTER ROVERS	0-2
December	03	ACRRINGTON STANLEY	3-3
	17	LINCOLN CITY	3-0
	24	New Brighton	2-1
	27	ROCHDALE	4-1
	31	Durham City	1-0
January	03	Rochdale	4-0

Table at January 3rd, 1928

1	BRADFORD PARK AVENUE	21	53	23	34
2	Doncaster Rovers	21	46	17	31
3	Lincoln City	23	45	38	28
4	Tranmere Rovers	20	38	25	26
5	Accrington Stanley	21	44	30	26
6	Stockport County	21	36	26	25
7	Halifax Town	22	43	32	25
8	Wrexham	22	37	33	25
9	Rochdale	20	43	38	23
10	Hartlepools United	23	41	44	23
11	Bradford City	21	48	34	22
12	Southport	21	42	36	20
13	Darlington	21	37	35	20
14	New Brighton	20	34	31	19
15	Chesterfield	22	34	43	18
16	Rotherham United	21	34	36	17
17	Crewe Alexandra	22	40	47	17
18	Durham City	22	31	43	17
19	Nelson	21	37	62	15
20	Wigan Borough	21	26	50	13
21	Barrow	22	29	62	13
22	Ashington	22	28	61	13
		470	846	846	470

BRADFORD PARK AVENUE

Rovers, of course, came again, following a 1-1 draw, against Hartlepools United, with three wins by the end of January to apply pressure on the leaders. Avenue's nerve held though, with 6 points taken from 4 games, the last of which involved a 5-0 humbling of neighbours Bradford City. Doncaster then lost twice and Bradford reached the mid-February stage with a 7-point advantage.

An excellent record of four wins and two draws over the next six weeks stretched this lead to a massive 12 points because Avenue's closest rivals lost three further times by March 24th. When they travelled to Doncaster Rovers on the final day of the month, Bradford Park Avenue were looking to kill off the Belle Vue side's challenge. A 0-2 reverse meant that only a 10-point lead was taken into April.

Despite losing twice in their next four games, Avenue were boosted by the fact that Doncaster had shot their bolt and dropped 5 points in the same spell up to mid-April. With three games still to play, Bradford needed only 1 point to ensure that they became champions and returned to the Division 2. On April 21st, a crowd of 11,236 watched the comprehensive 5-1 home win over Wigan Borough which brought the title to Park Avenue.

Bradford Park Avenue's '2nd half' record

January	07	WREXHAM	2-0
	14	Hartlepools United	1-1
	21	Chesterfield	0-0
	28	BRADFORD CITY	5-0
February	01	Wigan Borough	3-1
	04	TRANMERE ROVERS	6-2
	11	Stockport County	2-2
	18	BARROW	1-1
	25	Nelson	2-1
March	03	Ashington	3-0
	10	CREWE ALEXANDRA	2-0
	17	Halifax Town	1-1
	24	DARLINGTON	6-3
	31	Doncaster Rovers	0-2
April	07	HARTLEPOOLS UNITED	3-0
	09	Rotherham United	0-1
	10	ROTHERHAM UNITED	3-1
	14	Accrington Stanley	1-2
	21	WIGAN BOROUGH	5-1
	28	Lincoln City	0-2
May	05	NEW BRIGHTON	2-1

Final League Division 3 (North) Table 1928

1	BRADFORD PARK AVENUE	42	101	45	63
2	Lincoln City	42	91	64	55
3	Stockport County	42	89	51	54
4	Doncaster Rovers	42	80	44	53
5	Tranmere Rovers	42	105	72	53
6	Bradford City	42	85	60	48
7	Darlington	42	89	74	47
8	Southport	42	79	70	45
9	Accrington Stanley	42	76	67	44
10	New Brighton	42	72	62	42
11	Wrexham	42	64	67	42
12	Halifax Town	42	73	71	41
13	Rochdale	42	74	77	41
14	Rotherham United	42	65	69	39
15	Hartlepools United	42	69	81	38
16	Chesterfield	42	71	78	36
17	Crewe Alexandra	42	77	86	34
18	Ashington	42	77	103	33
19	Barrow	42	54	102	31
20	Wigan Borough	42	56	97	30
21	Durham City	42	53	100	29
22	Nelson	42	76	136	26
		924	1676	1676	924

Bradford Park Avenue were promoted. Nelson (37 votes) were re-elected but Durham City (11) were replaced by Carlisle United (33). York City (7) and Chester (2) were unsuccessful.

1927-28 – DIVISION 3 (SOUTH) — MILLWALL

Queen's Park Rangers made a good start to the campaign, dropping only 3 points in their opening 7 games to lead the table by a point from Norwich City by September 21st. Away defeats for the top two on the 24th had no immediate effect on their positions, but it did result in Northampton Town and Southend United matching the Canaries' 10 points total. A run of four consecutive wins made Northampton look the major threat to those above them.

Despite losing 0-2 at Southend on October 8th, the Cobblers proved to be among the strongest outfits in the division by winning four other games in the month, then handing out a 10-0 thrashing to Walsall on November 5th. Also going well by this stage were Millwall, whose 3-1 win away at Newport on November 12th pulled the Lions level with Northampton, who drew 2-2 at Bristol Rovers, at the top. Q.P.R., Norwich and Southend had all faltered by this time.

Millwall's next two games produced stunning wins – 9-1 over Coventry City and 7-1 over Walsall. Despite losing away to Plymouth Argyle on December 10th, the Lions added 3 more victories by December 27th to establish a 2-point advantage over Northampton at the top. Town had 2 games in hand, but were looking a little unstable in defence, as their 4-2 win at Coventry and 6-5 Boxing Day success against Luton Town show.

The top two met at The Den on December 31st. Millwall won 3-0 in front of 26,334 and now led the division by 4 points. Exeter City joined Northampton on 29 points by hammering Torquay United 5-0. Having beaten Plymouth twice over the holiday, the Grecians were looking a possible threat. By mid-February though, City had fallen back and Millwall's 4-point lead over Northampton was intact, in spite of a 0-5 slump at Bournemouth.

During the past few seasons, Plymouth had been involved in the promotion battle repeatedly and 12 months earlier Argyle had mounted a superb late challenge which had materialised during March. This time round, the Devonshire men, though third, remained well off the pace, going into April trailing the leaders, Millwall by a distant 10 points. With 5 wins in the 7 matches played after February 11th, the Lions now lay 6 six points clear of Northampton at the top.

By mid-April, after 4 more victories, Millwall needed 3 points from four games to win the 3rd Division (South) title. On 18th April, this was reduced to a '1 point required', as a result of Northampton's 0-2 defeat at Watford. Watched by a crowd of 20,744, Millwall crushed visitors Gillingham 6-0 on April 21st to become champions and secure promotion to the 2nd Division for the first time. Jack Cock led the way in the title-winning show by hitting a hat-trick.

Millwall's '1st half' record

August	27	Northampton Town	2-5
	29	TORQUAY UNITED	9-1
September	03	SOUTHEND UNITED	5-1
	07	Torquay United	1-0
	10	Brighton & Hove Albion	1-3
	17	BOURNEMOUTH & B.A.	2-0
	24	Brentford	1-6
October	01	LUTON TOWN	3-2
	03	Merthyr Town	0-0
	08	Charlton Athletic	1-1
	15	Crystal Palace	4-0
	22	SWINDON TOWN	3-3
	29	Queen's Park Rangers	1-0
November	05	WATFORD	4-2
	12	Newport County	3-1
	19	COVENTRY CITY	9-1
December	03	WALSALL	7-1
	10	Plymouth Argyle	2-3
	17	PLYMOUTH ARGYLE	2-0
	24	Bristol Rovers	6-1
	27	NORWICH CITY	2-1

Millwall's '2nd half' record

December	31	NORTHAMPTON TOWN	3-0
January	07	Southend United	1-0
	21	BRIGHTON & HOVE ALBION	6-0
	28	Bournemouth & B.A.	0-5
February	04	BRENTFORD	3-0
	11	Luton Town	1-1
	18	CHARLTON ATHLETIC	5-0
	25	CRYSTAL PALACE	1-1
March	03	Swindon Town	0-3
	10	QUEEN'S PARK RANGERS	6-1
	17	Watford	3-0
	24	NEWPORT COUNTY	5-1
	31	Coventry City	3-0
April	06	EXETER CITY	2-0
	07	MERTHYR TOWN	3-0
	09	Exeter City	4-2
	14	Walsall	5-2
	21	GILLINGHAM	6-0
	25	Gillingham	1-0
	30	Norwich City	0-2
May	05	BRISTOL ROVERS	1-0

Table at December 27th, 1927

1	MILLWALL	21	68	32	31
2	Northampton Town	19	57	28	29
3	Exeter City	20	36	24	27
4	Plymouth Argyle	21	45	32	25
5	Charlton Athletic	19	28	27	24
6	Swindon Town	18	50	37	23
7	Queen's Park Rangers	20	28	23	22
8	Southend United	18	37	31	22
9	Newport County	20	35	33	21
10	Brighton & Hove Albion	20	38	36	20
11	Brentford	21	41	43	19
12	Bournemouth & B.A.	21	35	39	19
13	Norwich City	19	39	34	18
14	Coventry City	20	36	47	18
15	Crystal Palace	19	30	40	18
16	Merthyr Town	22	31	45	16
17	Watford	20	32	38	15
18	Bristol Rovers	20	39	52	14
19	Gillingham	19	28	41	14
20	Walsall	19	27	53	14
21	Torquay United	19	18	43	13
22	Luton Town	19	46	46	12
		434	824	824	434

Final League Division 3 (South) Table 1928

1	MILLWALL	42	127	50	65
2	Northampton Town	42	102	64	55
3	Plymouth Argyle	42	85	54	53
4	Brighton & Hove Albion	42	81	69	48
5	Crystal Palace	42	79	72	48
6	Swindon Town	42	90	69	47
7	Southend United	42	80	64	46
8	Exeter City	42	70	60	46
9	Newport County	42	81	84	45
10	Queen's Park Rangers	42	72	71	43
11	Charlton Athletic	42	60	70	43
12	Brentford	42	76	74	40
13	Luton Town	42	94	87	39
14	Bournemouth & B.A.	42	72	79	38
15	Watford	42	68	78	38
16	Gillingham	42	62	81	37
17	Norwich City	42	66	70	36
18	Walsall	42	75	101	33
19	Bristol Rovers	42	67	93	32
20	Coventry City	42	67	96	31
21	Merthyr Town	42	53	91	31
22	Torquay United	42	53	103	30
		924	1680	1680	924

Millwall were promoted to Division 2. Torquay United (42 votes) and Merthyr Town (27) were both re-elected. An amateur team named 'The Argonauts', who planned to play home games at Wembley, came third in the poll with 11 votes. Other unsuccessful teams were Kettering Town (3) and Peterborough & Fletton United (2). There had been an application planned from Aberdare & Aberaman, but this was withdrawn before the ballot was held.

1928-1929 – LEAGUE DIVISION 1

SHEFFIELD WEDNESDAY

In the Final Table for the previous season, Derby County, in fourth, finished only 7 points ahead of Middlesbrough, who ended the campaign in 22nd place. The remarkably even nature of top flight football around this time, though belied by some of the scores, can be further seen in the start of the 1928-29 season. By September 29th, Burnley led the table with 12 points from 9 games – hardly barn-storming stuff. Derby County lay second (11 from 8), Blackburn Rovers third (10 from 9) and Birmingham fourth (10 from 8).

Derby and Blackburn both showed better form over the next 6 weeks, each taking 9 points from 6 games to reach mid-November occupying the top 2 places. Staying with these two during this phase were two Yorkshire clubs, Sheffield Wednesday and Leeds United, the latter blowing the chance of sharing the league leadership by crashing 1-4 at Bolton Wanderers on November 10th. It remained difficult to see where the season's champions might emerge from.

After a further 6 weeks' action, which took the campaign as far as December 25th, the top 4 were exactly the same. There was, however, a key change. Sheffield Wednesday achieved 6 wins in 7 league matches. They had moved to the top on November 24th, after beating Liverpool, while Derby lost to Leeds, and, after sinking Manchester City 4-0 on Christmas Day, the Owls had opened a 4-point lead. 12 months earlier, Wednesday had lain 21st in the table. This was some transformation!

Successive 2-2 draws before New Year could have seen the Sheffield club's lead reduced, but, with Derby and Leeds both beaten twice, the Owls stayed 4 points clear. With only five points from their next 5 games though, Wednesday reached mid-February with their advantage cut down to three points. Blackburn Rovers were now in second place, with Sunderland and Aston Villa having moved into the top four, two points behind the Ewood Park club. The battle for Football League honours looked likely to go all the way.

In the next, often crucial, stage of the season, up to the end of March, Wednesday lost 3 times, all away, but took all ten points from 5 home matches. None of the pursuing sides bettered this, with only Sunderland and improving Leicester City matching it. At the start of April, therefore, the Owls led the table by 5 points from Sunderland. Leicester, with two games in hand, were 7 points off the lead. Wednesday had not been great, but they had been allowed to get away.

A 6-0 thrashing of West Ham United on April 13th made up for 3 points dropped in the Owls' previous 2 games. With 3 fixtures left, Wednesday still led by 5 points, but the title still remained to be won and Leicester and Villa could still catch the leaders. Despite losing 1-2 at Newcastle on April 20th, the Yorkshire club had only a week to wait to be crowned champions. A draw at Burnley on April 27th took the Owls to 52 points – clear of Leicester, who had drawn at Huddersfield, and Villa, who lost at Manchester City.

Sheffield Wednesday's '1st half' record

August	25	ARSENAL	3-2
	29	Everton	0-0
September	01	Blackburn Rovers	1-4
	03	EVERTON	1-0
	08	SUNDERLAND	2-1
	15	Derby County	0-6
	22	SHEFFIELD UNITED	5-2
	29	BOLTON WANDERERS	0-0
October	06	Portsmouth	2-3
	13	BIRMINGHAM	3-0
	20	Bury	4-0
	27	CARDIFF CITY	1-0
November	03	Leicester City	1-1
	10	MANCHESTER UNITED	2-1
	17	Leeds United	2-0
	24	LIVERPOOL	3-2
December	01	West Ham United	2-3
	08	NEWCASTLE UNITED	3-1
	15	Burnley	2-0
	22	ASTON VILLA	4-1
	25	MANCHESTER CITY	4-0

Table at December 25th, 1928

1	SHEFFIELD WEDNESDAY	21	45	27	31
2	Derby County	21	49	29	27
3	Blackburn Rovers	22	43	29	27
4	Leeds United	20	43	41	25
5	Sunderland	21	50	38	23
6	Everton	21	35	30	23
7	Burnley	22	51	54	23
8	Leicester City	21	49	41	22
9	Aston Villa	20	47	41	22
10	Liverpool	21	43	35	21
11	West Ham United	22	40	49	21
12	Huddersfield Town	21	44	32	20
13	Bolton Wanderers	21	37	36	20
14	Newcastle United	22	38	50	20
15	Birmingham	20	38	40	18
16	Arsenal	21	34	39	18
17	Manchester City	20	41	49	18
18	Portsmouth	21	28	43	18
19	Sheffield United	21	33	51	17
20	Manchester United	20	28	37	16
21	Cardiff City	21	24	28	15
22	Bury	18	20	41	13
		458	860	860	458

Sheffield Wednesday's '2nd half' record

December	26	Manchester City	2-2
	29	Arsenal	2-2
January	01	HUDDERSFIELD TOWN	1-1
	05	BLACKBURN ROVERS	1-0
	19	Sunderland	3-4
February	02	Sheffield United	1-1
	09	Bolton Wanderers	2-2
	18	DERBY COUNTY	5-0
	23	Birmingham	1-4
March	02	BURY	3-1
	04	PORTSMOUTH	2-1
	09	Cardiff City	1-3
	16	LEICESTER CITY	1-0
	23	Manchester United	1-2
	30	LEEDS UNITED	4-2
April	02	Huddersfield Town	0-0
	06	Liverpool	2-3
	13	WEST HAM UNITED	6-0
	20	Newcastle United	1-2
	27	BURNLEY	1-1
May	04	Aston Villa	1-4

Final League Division 1 Table 1929

1	SHEFFIELD WEDNESDAY	42	86	62	52
2	Leicester City	42	96	67	51
3	Aston Villa	42	98	81	50
4	Sunderland	42	93	75	47
5	Liverpool	42	90	64	46
6	Derby County	42	86	71	46
7	Blackburn Rovers	42	72	63	45
8	Manchester City	42	95	86	45
9	Arsenal	42	77	72	45
10	Newcastle United	42	70	72	44
11	Sheffield United	42	86	85	41
12	Manchester United	42	66	76	41
13	Leeds United	42	71	84	41
14	Bolton Wanderers	42	73	80	40
15	Birmingham	42	68	77	40
16	Huddersfield Town	42	70	61	39
17	West Ham United	42	86	96	39
18	Everton	42	63	75	38
19	Burnley	42	81	103	38
20	Portsmouth	42	56	80	36
21	Bury	42	62	99	31
22	Cardiff City	42	43	59	29
		924	1688	1688	924

Bury and Cardiff City were relegated.

1928-1929 – LEAGUE DIVISION 2 — MIDDLESBROUGH

For several years, Chelsea had been named among the promotion favourites. Just as they had done three years earlier, the Blues made a cracking start to the campaign, taking 15 points from 8 games. In second spot at the start of October, a point behind, were Hull City, who were still unbeaten in 9 games. Also having started well, Notts County and Preston North End were tucked in behind the Tigers, both on 13 points from 8 matches.

Chelsea suffered the all-too-familiar loss of form during October and failed to win again until Preston were beaten 2-1 at Stamford Bridge on November 10th. Surprisingly, this left the Blues second, only one point behind leaders Notts County, whose 6 points from 6 games since September was form which was hardly sparkling. Southampton had moved into the top four, behind Hull, both sides having 'broken even' with 6 points from 6 games in the last 6 weeks.

The two clubs relegated at the end of the previous season, Middlesbrough and Tottenham Hotspur, had not made much impact over the first third of the season. While the White Hart Lane men's form continued to fluctuate between cool and tepid, Boro finally shook off their lethargy and stupor in December to go five unbeaten. This lifted the Teesside club up to third place, after a Christmas Day roasting of Port Vale, 5-1. Chelsea headed Boro on goal average, while Notts County maintained their lead of the 2nd Division, having lost only once in 7 outings.

With the front-runners beaten in each of their next 3 games, however, Chelsea and Middlesbrough were able to go past them, Boro holding top spot after beating Tottenham 3-0 on New Year's Day. The leading pair then clashed head on at Stamford Bridge, on January 19th, with Chelsea shading an enthralling encounter 5-4. At mid-February, the Blues had a 1-point lead over Boro, with Notts County 2 points further back and Grimsby up to fourth after 6 successive wins.

The Cleethorpes-based club continued its amazing run into March, by the end of which 7 more wins had been racked up. Town led the 2nd Division by 2 points from Boro and had a game in hand. Notts County, in third, trailed the leaders by 5 points, with Chelsea, beaten seven times in 8 games, completely out of the reckoning. As often happened with leaders at this point, however, Grimsby stumbled, losing twice in 6 days at the start of April.

Boro seized their chance and went top again on April 6th, staying ahead as the month's mid-point arrived. Both clubs won promotion with wins on April 20th, but Grimsby still held the advantage, it seemed, in the title race. A defeat for Town at Bradford on the 22nd swung things in Boro's favour, making the May 4th 'last day showdown' at Ayresome Park, all the more interesting. Two goals from George Camsell delighted home fans in the 36,503 crowd and helped Boro win the game 3-0. For the second time in three years, Middlesbrough were 2nd Division champions.

Middlesbrough's '1st half' record

August	25	Reading	3-2
	27	Tottenham Hotspur	5-2
September	01	PRESTON NORTH END	2-3
	08	Chelsea	0-2
	12	HULL CITY	1-1
	15	Oldham Athletic	3-1
	22	SOUTHAMPTON	1-2
	29	Wolves	3-3
October	06	NOTTS COUNTY	3-1
	13	Millwall	3-2
	20	BLACKPOOL	4-1
	27	Swansea Town	0-2
November	03	BRADFORD PARK AVENUE	5-3
	10	Barnsley	2-2
	17	STOKE CITY	1-0
	24	Clapton Orient	0-3
December	01	WEST BROMWICH ALBION	1-1
	08	Nottingham Forest	1-1
	15	BRISTOL CITY	3-1
	22	Grimsby Town	4-1
	25	PORT VALE	5-1

Table at December 25th, 1928

1	Notts County	21	40	21	29
2	Chelsea	21	34	23	27
3	MIDDLESBROUGH	21	50	35	27
4	Hull City	22	42	31	27
5	Bradford Park Avenue	21	55	38	26
6	Southampton	21	35	24	24
7	Preston North End	21	50	43	24
8	Stoke City	21	33	21	22
9	Blackpool	21	46	40	22
10	Millwall	21	39	38	22
11	West Bromwich Albion	21	35	38	21
12	Grimsby Town	20	41	38	20
13	Wolves	21	42	40	20
14	Nottingham Forest	20	38	42	19
15	Tottenham Hotspur	20	33	38	19
16	Swansea Town	21	31	43	18
17	Port Vale	21	34	42	17
18	Clapton Orient	21	27	41	17
19	Reading	21	30	51	17
20	Barnsley	20	32	38	16
21	Bristol City	21	30	43	15
22	Oldham Athletic	20	16	45	9
		458	813	813	458

Middlesbrough's '2nd half' record

December	26	Port Vale	3-2
	29	READING	0-0
January	01	TOTTENHAM HOTSPUR	3-0
	05	Preston North End	0-0
	19	CHELSEA	4-5
February	02	Southampton	1-1
	09	WOLVES	8-3
	16	Notts County	3-0
	20	OLDHAM ATHLETIC	1-0
	23	MILLWALL	3-0
March	02	Blackpool	0-3
	09	SWANSEA TOWN	0-0
	16	Bradford Park Avenue	2-3
	23	BARNSLEY	1-0
	30	Stoke City	2-3
April	01	Hull City	1-1
	06	CLAPTON ORIENT	4-0
	13	West Bromwich Albion	1-1
	20	NOTTINGHAM FOREST	1-0
	27	Bristol City	1-0
May	04	GRIMSBY TOWN	3-0

Final League Division 2 Table 1929

1	MIDDLESBROUGH	42	92	57	55
2	Grimsby Town	42	82	61	53
3	Bradford Park Avenue	42	88	70	48
4	Southampton	42	74	60	48
5	Notts County	42	78	65	47
6	Stoke City	42	74	51	46
7	West Bromwich Albion	42	80	79	46
8	Blackpool	42	92	76	45
9	Chelsea	42	64	65	44
10	Tottenham Hotspur	42	75	81	43
11	Nottingham Forest	42	71	70	42
12	Hull City	42	58	63	40
13	Preston North End	42	78	79	39
14	Millwall	42	71	86	39
15	Reading	42	63	86	39
16	Barnsley	42	69	66	38
17	Wolves	42	77	81	37
18	Oldham Athletic	42	54	75	37
19	Swansea Town	42	62	75	36
20	Bristol City	42	58	72	36
21	Port Vale	42	71	86	34
22	Clapton Orient	42	45	72	32
		924	1576	1576	924

Middlesbrough and Grimsby Town were promoted. Port Vale (North) and Clapton Orient (South) were relegated to Division 3.

1928-29 – DIVISION 3 (NORTH) — BRADFORD CITY

Wrexham produced their best-ever start to date, taking 13 points from 8 unbeaten games by the end of September. The 3 clubs which completed the top quartet by this stage, Stockport County, newly-elected Carlisle United and Bradford City, all lost twice in the opening phase, but were the 'best of the rest' gathered behind the Welsh leaders of the division.

There was little change at the top, in relative terms, during the next few weeks. Wrexham crashed 2-6 at Stockport on October 26th, but took 8 points from their other 5 matches. The Red Dragons kept a firm grip on top spot by beating high-scoring Bradford City 2-1 at the Racecourse Ground on November 10th. Wrexham ended the day three points ahead of their victims, whose 18 points total was matched by both Stockport and Carlisle as the one-third stage in the season was reached.

Big wins for Bradford City and Stockport County enabled the two to catch Wrexham on December 1st, but their F.A. Cup commitments a week later allowed the Welshmen to go clear again. The leaders struggled in the next fortnight and on December 22nd County passed them after winning at Barrow 4-2. Stockport soon had problems of their own though, with defeat at Tranmere Rovers 2 days before New Year limiting their lead over Bradford City to just one point as 1928 drew to a close.

Four wins in January and a 2-1 victory over Bradford City on February 2nd boosted the Hatters, however, and, by the two-thirds point in the campaign, County led the table by 3 points from Wrexham, with City a point further away, but with a game in hand. Carlisle United, having gone 4 without losing were back in fourth, but had clocked up more games.

The former front-runners put in a good spell from mid-February to late March. In other seasons, an 11-point haul from 8 games might have seen the club advance, but Stockport did even better, winning 6 and drawing 1 of their matches. Bradford City, though, outdid the leaders, collecting 15 points from 8 games and moving to within two points of County, with a game in hand still. Stockport felt the pressure and flopped at Wigan Borough on April 1st, but then dug in to battle out the final stages.

The leaders reached the middle of April with a 1-point lead and, after the matches played on April 27th, the situation at the top of Division 3 (North) remained exactly the same – County led the table by a point, but City had a game in hand. This was played three days later, with the Bradford men 3-1 winners at Rochdale and going to the top of the table. The Valley Parade team completed their season in front of 28,850 spectators on May 4th, when a 3-1 victory over South Shields sealed the club's title triumph.

Bradford City's '1st half' record

August	25	ROTHERHAM UNITED	11-1
	30	Carlisle United	2-2
September	01	Wigan Borough	0-2
	03	CARLISLE UNITED	4-2
	08	CREWE ALEXANDRA	4-1
	15	Tranmere Rovers	0-1
	22	STOCKPORT COUNTY	2-1
	29	Halifax Town	1-1
October	06	LINCOLN CITY	2-3
	13	Ashington	8-2
	20	DONCASTER ROVERS	3-0
	27	Barrow	3-1
November	03	CHESTERFIELD	6-1
	10	Wrexham	1-2
	17	NEW BRIGHTON	5-2
December	01	SOUTHPORT	5-0
	15	NELSON	0-2
	22	South Shields	1-1
	25	Accrington Stanley	1-0
	26	ACCRINGTON STANLEY	4-1
	29	Rotherham United	2-2

Bradford City's '2nd half' record

January	01	Hartlepools United	3-1
	02	Darlington	3-3
	05	WIGAN BOROUGH	1-0
	19	Crewe Alexandra	0-0
February	02	Stockport County	1-2
	09	HALIFAX TOWN	2-2
	16	Lincoln City	4-3
	23	ASHINGTON	2-0
March	02	Doncaster Rovers	1-1
	06	TRANMERE ROVERS	8-0
	09	BARROW	8-0
	16	Chesterfield	5-0
	23	WREXHAM	5-0
	30	New Brighton	3-0
April	02	HARTLEPOOLS UNITED	4-1
	06	ROCHDALE	0-0
	13	Southport	3-0
	20	DARLINGTON	3-0
	27	Nelson	1-0
	30	Rochdale	3-1
May	04	SOUTH SHIELDS	3-1

Table at December 29th, 1928

1	Stockport County	21	67	33	29
2	BRADFORD CITY	21	65	28	28
3	Wrexham	22	50	41	28
4	Lincoln City	22	51	39	26
5	Carlisle United	23	54	46	26
6	Wigan Borough	20	32	18	25
7	Doncaster Rovers	21	40	32	25
8	South Shields	21	42	33	24
9	Crewe Alexandra	21	40	38	24
10	Tranmere Rovers	20	39	37	23
11	Nelson	22	42	45	22
12	Chesterfield	20	45	41	21
13	Halifax Town	22	30	31	21
14	Rochdale	22	47	50	19
15	New Brighton	21	40	43	19
16	Rotherham United	22	31	42	19
17	Darlington	21	35	44	16
18	Southport	21	36	55	16
19	Accrington Stanley	20	31	44	15
20	Hartlepools United	22	32	61	15
21	Barrow	20	28	43	14
22	Ashington	23	27	60	13
		468	904	904	468

Final League Division 3 (North) Table 1929

1	BRADFORD CITY	42	128	43	63
2	Stockport County	42	111	58	62
3	Wrexham	42	91	69	52
4	Wigan Borough	42	82	49	51
5	Doncaster Rovers	42	76	66	50
6	Lincoln City	42	91	67	48
7	Tranmere Rovers	42	79	77	47
8	Carlisle United	42	86	77	46
9	Crewe Alexandra	42	80	68	44
10	South Shields	42	83	74	44
11	Chesterfield	42	71	77	41
12	Southport	42	75	85	40
13	Halifax Town	42	63	62	39
14	New Brighton	42	64	71	39
15	Nelson	42	77	90	39
16	Rotherham United	42	60	77	39
17	Rochdale	42	79	96	36
18	Accrington Stanley	42	68	82	34
19	Darlington	42	64	88	33
20	Barrow	42	64	93	28
21	Hartlepools United	42	59	112	26
22	Ashington	42	45	115	23
		924	1696	1696	924

Bradford City were promoted to Division 2. Hartlepools United (33 votes) were re-elected, but Ashington (14) were replaced by York City (24). Mansfield Town (16) finished third in the poll, but were unsuccessful, along with Manchester Central (2), Prescot Cables (1), Chester (0), Rhyl (0), and Workington (0).

1928-29 – DIVISION 3 (SOUTH)   CHARLTON ATHLETIC

The scramble for the early leadership of the southern section of the 3rd Division saw Luton Town emerge from the pack to establish a 2-point advantage by the end of September. Six wins in a row gave the Hatters 14 points from eight games to lead the table from London-based trio Q.P.R., Brentford and Crystal Palace. Below these teams, a number of others were showing touches of form only, though Charlton Athletic had won 4 in a row.

Luton continued to go well and, despite losing 2-3 at Watford on October 20th, still led by 2 points at mid-November. Up to second by this time were Plymouth Argyle, who had taken up their familiarly prominent position after producing 6 wins in 8 games, the other two having ended all square. Queen's Park Rangers remained in touch in third place, with Coventry City, unbeaten in six, moving up to fourth after a 4-1 win over Swindon Town.

In the run-up to New Year there was a tightening up at the top of the table. As Luton Town slipped to three successive defeats, Fulham won 6 out of seven to end 1928 at the head of things. The Craven Cottage men held a goal average lead over Plymouth and Q.P.R., with Northampton Town 2 points behind. The Cobblers reached the 29-point mark with a 2-0 win over Norwich City on January 5th, but the key result was Argyle's 4-2 beating of Fulham. This took the Devon club to the top.

Plymouth failed to win in their next 3 games. With things so close at the top, the Home Park men were dropped from the top four by mid-February. By this time, Northampton Town had gone ahead, closely pursued by Fulham and Luton. The biggest movement, however, came from Charlton Athletic, whose 4 consecutive wins lifted the club from mid-table on January 5th to fourth. The Haddicks were only three points behind the leaders.

By the time the end of March was reached, a 'battle royal' was developing for the single promotion place. The top 4 clubs all had 44 points. While Northampton Town had the much better goal average, only 0·2 of a goal separated the other 3 – Charlton, Q.P.R. and Crystal Palace. By 13th April, the Cobblers had 49 points from 39 games, Q.P.R. and Luton Town were on 48 from 38, Charlton stood at 47 from 37, and Crystal Palace's record was 46 from 37.

Q.P.R. beat Northampton 4-1 on April 20th to go top. With Charlton and Luton both losing, this looked a possibly decisive result. However, 2 days later, the 'Rs' lost away at Norwich, while Charlton beat Brentford to take a 1 goal lead at the top, turning this into a 1-point advantage by beating Watford on April 27th. On May 1st, in another twist in the tale, Crystal Palace beat Gillingham 3-0 and pulled level with the leaders. Charlton had to win their last game to take the title. A 2-0 success at Walsall on May 4th did the trick!

Charlton Athletic's '1st half' record

August	25	Northampton Town	1-4
September	01	NEWPORT COUNTY	2-2
	03	Brentford	0-1
	08	NORWICH CITY	1-0
	15	Brighton & Hove Albion	3-2
	22	EXETER CITY	3-1
	29	Southend United	3-1
October	06	MERTHYR TOWN	2-2
	13	Bournemouth & B.A.	2-4
	20	Crystal Palace	2-0
	27	SWINDON TOWN	4-1
November	03	Torquay United	1-3
	10	GILLINGHAM	1-1
	17	Plymouth Argyle	2-2
December	01	Queen's Park Rangers	2-2
	15	Watford	1-3
	22	WALSALL	5-0
	25	Coventry City	1-0
	26	COVENTRY CITY	3-1
	29	NORTHAMPTON TOWN	3-1
January	05	Newport County	0-2

Table at January 5th, 1929

1	Plymouth Argyle	23	49	28	31
2	Queen's Park Rangers	23	43	32	30
3	Fulham	22	55	33	29
4	Northampton Town	24	58	36	29
5	Luton Town	22	49	36	29
6	Coventry City	23	38	25	27
7	Bournemouth & B.A.	22	48	37	26
8	Swindon Town	23	48	41	26
9	CHARLTON ATHLETIC	21	42	33	25
10	Crystal Palace	22	39	40	25
11	Watford	22	36	41	24
12	Walsall	22	43	48	23
13	Southend United	22	38	38	21
14	Torquay United	22	39	45	18
15	Brentford	22	28	35	18
16	Bristol Rovers	22	30	41	17
17	Brighton & Hove Albion	22	29	44	17
18	Gillingham	23	26	40	17
19	Norwich City	22	32	40	16
20	Exeter City	22	32	46	14
21	Newport County	22	29	43	14
22	Merthyr Town	22	27	56	14
		490	858	858	490

Charlton Athletic's '2nd half' record

January	19	Norwich City	1-0
	26	BRIGHTON & HOVE ALBION	3-0
February	02	Exeter City	5-2
	09	SOUTHEND UNITED	3-2
	16	Merthyr Town	3-2
	23	BOURNEMOUTH & B.A.	6-2
March	02	CRYSTAL PALACE	1-3
	09	Swindon Town	1-1
	14	BRISTOL ROVERS	1-2
	16	TORQUAY UNITED	2-0
	23	Gillingham	0-1
	29	LUTON TOWN	4-1
	30	PLYMOUTH ARGYLE	2-1
April	01	Luton Town	0-3
	06	Fulham	5-2
	13	QUEEN'S PARK RANGERS	2-2
	17	FULHAM	0-0
	20	Bristol Rovers	0-3
	22	BRENTFORD	1-0
	27	WATFORD	2-0
May	04	Walsall	2-0

Final League Division 3 (South) Table 1929

1	CHARLTON ATHLETIC	42	86	60	54
2	Crystal Palace	42	81	67	54
3	Northampton Town	42	96	57	52
4	Plymouth Argyle	42	83	51	52
5	Fulham	42	101	71	52
6	Queen's Park Rangers	42	82	61	52
7	Luton Town	42	89	73	49
8	Watford	42	79	74	48
9	Bournemouth & B.A.	42	84	77	47
10	Swindon Town	42	75	72	43
11	Coventry City	42	62	57	42
12	Southend United	42	80	75	41
13	Brentford	42	56	60	38
14	Walsall	42	73	79	38
15	Brighton & Hove Albion	42	58	76	38
16	Newport County	42	69	86	35
17	Norwich City	42	69	81	34
18	Torquay United	42	66	84	34
19	Bristol Rovers	42	60	79	33
20	Merthyr Town	42	55	103	30
21	Exeter City	42	67	88	29
22	Gillingham	42	43	83	29
		924	1614	1614	924

Charlton Athletic were promoted to Division 2. Exeter City (42 votes) and Gillingham (35) were both re-elected. Unsuccessful clubs on this occasion were The Argonauts (6), Aldershot (5), Kettering Town (1), Thames Association (1) and Llanelli (0). Mansfield Town also applied to join the 3rd Division (South) but withdrew before the ballot was held.

MORE INFORMATION   1925-1929

Goal scoring 1925-1929

The leading marksmen for each season were :

Division 1

1925-26 43 – Ted Harper (Blackburn Rovers)
1926-27 37 – Jimmy Trotter (Sheffield Wednesday)
1927-28 60 – 'Dixie' Dean (Everton)
1928-29 43 – Dave Halliday (Sunderland)

Division 2

1925-26 29 – Bob Turnbull (Chelsea)
1926-27 59 – George Camsell (Middlesbrough)
1927-28 38 – Jimmy Cookson (West Bromwich Albion)
1928-29 40 – Jimmy Hampson (Blackpool)

Division 3 (North)

1925-26 44 – Jimmy Cookson (Chesterfield)
1926-27 44 – Albert Whitehurst (Rochdale)
1927-28 38 – Joe Smith (Stockport County)
1928-29 42 – Jimmy McConnell (Carlisle United)

Division 3 (South)

1925-26 31 – Jack Cock (Plymouth Argyle)
1926-27 47 – Harry Morris (Swindon Town)
1927-28 38 – Harry Morris (Swindon Town)
1928-29 43 – Andrew Rennie (Luton Town)

The change in the offside law had a dramatic effect on the number of high-scoring games in all four divisions of the Football League in these years. In the final season under the 'old law', 1924-25, there were eight games in which the winning side scored seven goals. During the following four campaigns, there were 144 cases of the victors hitting 7, or more, in Football League matches – an average of 36 a season.

DIVISIONAL HIGH SCORES 1929-1932

Division 1

1925-26
29/08 Aston Villa   10-0 Burnley
01/01 Sheffield United   11-2 Cardiff City

Nine other games involved the winners scoring at least 7 goals and Bury, Manchester City and Sheffield United all hit eight goals in one game.

1926-27
19/03 Derby County   8-0 Sheffield Wednesday

Five teams hit seven goals in a game, with three of the winning results being 7-3.

1927-28
01/10 Huddersfield Town   8-2 Cardiff City
01/10 Liverpool   8-2 Portsmouth

There were 7 goals for the victors 8 times, with Newcastle United's 7-5 March 10th win over Aston Villa, the highest aggregate.

1928-29
20/10 Leicester City   10-0 Portsmouth
19/01 Sheffield United   10-0 Burnley

Liverpool and West Ham United both won matches in which they scored eight goals and there were five cases of 7 being scored by winners of matches.

Division 2

1925-26
01/05 Oldham Athletic   8-3 Nottingham Forest

The Latics were also one of 4 sides to hit seven in a game.

1926-27
06/11 Wolves   9-1 Barnsley
09/04 Portsmouth   9-1 Notts County

Manchester City and Darlington both scored 8 in a game, while there were seven 7s, including Middlesbrough's 7-4 triumph at Grimsby Town.

Division 2 high scores (continued)

1927-28
19/11 Notts County   9-0 Barnsley

The Colliers, however, beat Fulham 8-4 on January 28th. There were 6 scores of 7 goals in a game, with Manchester City and Nottingham Forest managing the feat twice each.

1928-29
03/11 Southampton   8-2 Blackpool
09/03 Port Vale   8-1 West Bromwich Albion

4 'sevens' were scored, Preston North End being involved in 3 of the games – twice winning (v. Port Vale 23/02 and Reading 27/08), once losing – at Bradford 27/10.

Division 3 (North)

1925-26
23/01 Hartlepools United   9-3 Walsall

In 3 matches, the winners scored 8 and five scores of 7 were recorded.

1926-27

The highest number of games in which a team scored 7+ goals in this time was 17 - in Division 3 (North), 1926-27. There were 4 cases of 8 goals being scored – Chesterfield-Barrow (8-1), Rochdale-Chesterfield (8-1), Tranmere Rovers-Durham City (8-3) and Wigan Borough-Barrow (8-0). Nelson, Rochdale and Stockport County each hit 7 goals twice, while Barrow shipped 7 on three occasions.

1927-28
07/01 Tranmere Rovers   11-1 Durham City

Bradford City and Darlington both netted 9 times in games and there were 3 scores of seven by winning teams.

1928-29
25/08 Bradford City   11-1 Rotherham United
16/03 South Shields   10-1 Rotherham United

Bradford City managed 8 goals on 3 other occasions, a total only achieved by one other club – Carlisle United.

Division 3 (South)

1925-26
19/09 Millwall   8-1 Southend United
02/01 Aberdare Athletic   8-1 Watford
02/01 Swindon Town   8-2 Bournemouth & B.A.

1926-27
18/09 Brighton & H.A.   9-3 Swindon Town
15/01 Bristol City   9-4 Gillingham

The 8 scores of seven in the division were surpassed by Exeter City, who hammered Coventry City 8-1 (04/12).

1927-28

On November 5th, there were fireworks at Northampton, where Town blew away Walsall 10-0. Millwall won 9-1 twice, Merthyr Town had an 8-2 success over Swindon Town and there were five scores of seven by winners.

1928-29

Three teams hit 8 goals in games they won – Luton Town v. Gillingham (8-0, April 13th), Northampton Town v. Crystal Palace (8-1, October 27th) and Q.P.R. v. Merthyr Town (8-0, March 9th). Two cases of seven goals being hit completed the high-scoring for the division.

The number of goals scored in Football League matches shot up from 4,700 in the 1924-25 season to 6,373, 1925-26 – an increase by 35·6%. There was another rise 1926-27, by 247 goals and a further increase 1927-28 when a total of 6,728 were scored. This represented a 43·1% rise from the last season before the change in the offside law. The total for 1928-29 was, however, down, by 154 goals scored, to 6,574. Looking at figures which are a bit easier to take in, however, we can see that for the 1924-25 season, a mean of 2·54 goals were scored in Football League matches, compared with an average of 3·56 in the 1928-29 campaign, when the total was slightly down. This means, on average, crowds were seeing a goal a game more – roughly.

... AND

Goal-scoring (continued)

There were 462 games played in each season in each division. The total for the campaign is followed by the average number of goals per game.

1st Division

1925-26	1,703	3·69 (+42·9%)
1926-27	1,668	3·61
1927-28	1,765	3·82 (+48·1% on 1923-24)
1928-29	1,688	3·65

2nd Division

1925-26	1,487	3·22 (+39·2%)
1926-27	1,668	3·61
1927-28	1,607	3·48 (+50·7% on 1923-24)
1928-29	1,688	3·41

3rd Division (North)

1925-26	1,628	3·52 (+23·3%)
1926-27	1,692	3·66
1927-28	1,676	3·63 (+27% on 1923-24)
1928-29	1,696	3·67

3rd Division (South)

1925-26	1,555	3·37 (+38·9%)
1926-27	1,592	3·45
1927-28	1,680	3·64 (+50% on 1923-24)
1928-29	1,614	3·49

Goal drought turns to goal glut

The % of Football League matches in which more than 1 goal was scored rose in every season during the period 1925-1929. The figures for each season were :

1925-26	83·83%
1926-27	84·25%
1927-28	85·01%
1928-29	85·07%

F.A. Cup 1925-1929

All four F.A.Cup Finals 1925-29 took place at Wembley Stadium. All these games were all-ticket, with the attendance set at around 92,000. As had been the case in the past, the games were played in April, before the end of the league season.

24th April, 1926

Another 1-0 final score was recorded, with David Jack's second-half winner for Bolton Wanderers defeating Manchester City, a club about to suffer relegation from Division 1. A crowd of 91,447 saw the match, which was refereed by I. Baker.

23rd April, 1927

For the only time in the history of the competition, the F.A. Cup left England after Cardiff City beat Arsenal in the Final, 1-0. City's goal came after 75 minutes and was scored by Hughie Ferguson. W.F. Bunnell was the referee and the attendance was 91,206.

21st April, 1928

A crowd of 92,041 watched the first 4-goal Final for 20 years. T.G. Bryan was the official of this game, which was won 3-1 by Blackburn Rovers, for whom Jack Roscamp scored twice and Tommy McLean once. Huddersfield Town, the losers, whose consolation goal came from Alex Jackson, had a terrible week after the Wembley disappointment, losing two games and their chance of the 1st Division title.

27th April, 1929

The 1929 Final was attended by 92,576 people - the biggest crowd since 1923. Once again the winners were Bolton Wanderers, who beat Portsmouth 2-0. The match, with A. Josephs in charge, was a generally tame affair, but burst into life after 79 minutes when Bill Butler scored for the Trotters. The game was made safe ten minutes later when Harold Blackmore hit the Lancashire club's second.

MORE ...

Live commentary

On January 22nd, 1927, the first live radio broadcast of a Football League match took place, with the B.B.C. providing commentary of the Arsenal v. Sheffield United game. Listeners could follow play by listening to the commentary and using a pitch-shaped chart divided into numbered areas. A 'second B.B.C. man' could be heard in the background shouting out the numbers of the squares on the chart to help the audience keep up with play. The expression 'back to square 1' is said to have entered the English language through this development.

'Ins and Outs'

As stated above, 3 clubs left the Football League 1927-29, the unfortunate trio being Aberdare Athletic, Durham City and Ashington. These clubs had 3 things in common. They finished in the re-election places in the table for a 2nd time in the season at the end of which they were voted out. Also, they were bottom of their division in the 'average home crowds league' table. Thirdly, they were all based in mining areas and the coal industry was hit by strikes, short-time and unemployment in the second part of the 1920s.

Aberdare were first to go, losing their place to the 1927 Southern League (Western Section) champions, Torquay United, after a 2nd ballot. During the 1924-25 season, the Welsh team's home gates averaged 5,590, but this had fallen to 4,815 the next year and the figure was down to 2,500 for 1926-27. With high unemployment preventing fans from being able to attend, Aberdare was 'unpopular' with the other clubs in the division. With money probably the key factor, because there was so little to show from a visit to the Ynys Stadium, many clubs voted against the Darians and this cost the club its League place.

By the bringing of Torquay United into the League in 1927, a potentially well-supported club was added to the ranks. The Gulls average 4,175 for home games in their first campaign and had no trouble at all being re-elected in 1928, having finished bottom. Clubs overlooked for election to the Third Division (South) included Kettering Town (1927-29) and Aldershot Town (1929) despite their impressive and consistent efforts in the Southern League.

Durham City's crowds were the lowest in Division 3 (North) 1924-28 and they paid the price for this by being replaced by Carlisle United, despite not having finished bottom. Ashington, with crowds down to an average 1,666, because, like Durham, of 'Aberdare-like problems' followed in 1929, being replaced by York City. The Cumbrians, drawing crowds of almost 8,000, and City, with a following of over 5,000 for home games, were far more welcome among other clubs.

Some good northern sides failed to gain entry into the Football League. Mansfield Town had 4 unsuccessful applications in the period, despite an excellent playing record. Fellow Midland Leaguers, Scunthorpe United, Gainsborough Trinity and Scarborough could probably have at least held their own in 3 North at the time, but, with limits to their support, never bothered to make an application.

Some questions of Money

1925
There were 2 major transfers. Charles Buchan moved from Sunderland to Arsenal for £2,000 + £100 per goal he scored. A new record was set in December, when Hughie Gallacher joined Newcastle from Airdrieonians for £5,500.

1928
Arsenal, who a few years earlier had campaigned for a 'maximum transfer fee', broke the existing record paid for a player by paying £10,890 to Bolton Wanderers for David Jack. Managed by Herbert Chapman, who, with Charles Buchan, was trying to build a side which could get the best out of the 'W formation', Arsenal spent a further £9,000 in June 1929 to bring Preston North End's Alex James to Highbury. While Chairmen at other clubs scoffed at this inflation in transfer fees, Arsenal trusted in their manager's judgement and 'spent to accumulate'.

1929-30 – LEAGUE DIVISION 1

1st Division Table (top 6) at 28/12/29

1	SHEFFIELD WEDNESDAY	21	53-24	30
2	Manchester City	22	54-37	30
3	Aston Villa	23	49-41	28
4	Derby County	23	45-40	28
5	Leeds United	23	43-33	26
6	Liverpool	23	39-43	26

FINAL PHASE ... AT THE TOP

By April 14th, Sheffield Wednesday looked to have a firm grip on the title race, being 3 points ahead of Derby County and having two games in hand on all the teams in the 5 places below them.

Top 3 at 14/04/30

1	SHEFFIELD WEDNESDAY	35	86-46	49	1.81
2	Derby County	37	77-66	46	1.17
3	Manchester City	37	82-68	44	1.21

(Figure in the right-hand column is goal average)

On April 19th, Wednesday won 1-0 at Blackburn, while Derby (1-2 at Grimsby) and Manchester City (1-3 at Leicester) both lost. Just as it looked all over, the Owls then crashed 1-4 at Derby, two days later, to revive the Rams' hopes. The reigning champions were having none of that, however, and, 24 hours later, on April 22nd, crushed County at Hillsborough 6-3 and this ensured that they secured the Division 1 title again.

1st Division Table (bottom 6) at 28/12/29

17	Birmingham	23	38-36	20
18	Portsmouth	23	35-39	20
19	Sunderland	22	33-44	18
20	Newcastle United	23	43-60	18
21	Everton	24	39-53	17
22	Grimsby Town	22	37-53	16

FINAL PHASE ... AT THE BOTTOM

Things were looking grim for Everton by mid-April. Four points behind Newcastle United, who held 20th place, the Toffees had just 5 games in which to try and save themselves. Better off, but still in danger, were Grimsby Town and time was starting to run out.

Bottom 7 at 14/04/30

16	Burnley	39	72-89	34	0.81
17	Manchester United	37	59-75	34	0.79
18	Middlesbrough	38	73-77	33	0.95
19	Sheffield United	38	81-88	33	0.92
20	Newcastle United	37	64-87	30	0.74
21	Grimsby Town	37	66-86	29	0.77
22	Everton	37	65-85	26	0.76

(Figure in the right-hand column is goal average)

By the time the Easter programme closed on April 22nd, there had been some dramatic changes to the picture. Grimsby Town won 3 games in a row and all the other sides in the bottom six, apart from Sheffield United, had won at least once. For Burnley, who lost twice, this was disastrous and they slipped to 21st place, below even the winless Blades, whose draw with Villa took them above the Turf Moor men on goal average. Manchester United were the only lowly club to reach safety.

Everton added two more wins to their 3 Easter points and, with none of the other struggglers winning their next game, it all went to the final day of the season, May 3rd – two to go down from six. Anybody betting on all 6 threatened teams winning would have got very long odds, but this is what now happened. Burnley top-scored with a 6-3 win over Derby County, but it was not enough. Sheffield United won 5-1 at Manchester United to stay in the top flight. Going down with Burnley were Everton, despite beating Sunderland 4-1.

- 118 -

SHEFFIELD WEDNESDAY

August	31	Portsmouth	4-0
September	02	BOLTON WANDERERS	1-0
	07	ARSENAL	0-2
	14	Aston Villa	3-1
	21	LEEDS UNITED	1-2
	25	Bolton Wanderers	3-1
	28	Sheffield United	2-2
October	05	Burnley	4-2
	12	SUNDERLAND	1-1
	19	HUDDERSFIELD TOWN	3-1
	26	Birmingham	0-1
November	02	LEICESTER CITY	4-0
	09	Newcastle United	3-1
	16	MANCHESTER UNITED	7-2
	23	West Ham United	1-1
	30	LIVERPOOL	2-1
December	07	Middlesbrough	1-4
	14	BLACKBURN ROVERS	4-0
	25	Everton	4-1
	26	EVERTON	4-0
	28	PORTSMOUTH	1-1
January	01	Manchester City	3-3
	04	Arsenal	3-2
	18	ASTON VILLA	3-0
February	01	SHEFFIELD UNITED	1-1
	05	Grimsby Town	5-0
	08	BURNLEY	4-1
	22	Huddersfield Town	1-4
March	08	Leicester City	1-2
	15	NEWCASTLE UNITED	4-2
	29	WEST HAM UNITED	2-1
April	05	Liverpool	3-1
	09	Leeds United	0-3
	12	MIDDLESBROUGH	1-0
	14	Manchester United	2-2
	19	Blackburn Rovers	1-0
	21	Derby County	1-4
	22	DERBY COUNTY	6-3
	26	GRIMSBY TOWN	1-0
	28	BIRMINGHAM	1-1
	30	Sunderland	4-2
May	03	MANCHESTER CITY	5-1

1st Division Final Table 1929-30

1	SHEFFIELD WEDNESDAY	42	105	57	60
2	Derby County	42	90	82	50
3	Manchester City	42	91	81	47
4	Aston Villa	42	92	83	47
5	Leeds United	42	79	63	46
6	Blackburn Rovers	42	99	93	45
7	West Ham United	42	86	79	43
8	Leicester City	42	86	90	43
9	Sunderland	42	76	80	43
10	Huddersfield Town	42	63	69	43
11	Birmingham	42	67	62	41
12	Liverpool	42	63	79	41
13	Portsmouth	42	66	62	40
14	Arsenal	42	78	66	39
15	Bolton Wanderers	42	74	74	39
16	Middlesbrough	42	82	84	38
17	Manchester United	42	67	88	38
18	Grimsby Town	42	73	89	37
19	Newcastle United	42	71	92	37
20	Sheffield United	42	91	96	36
21	Burnley	42	79	97	36
22	Everton	42	80	92	35
		924	1758	1758	924

Burnley and Everton were relegated to Division 2.

1929-30 – LEAGUE DIVISION 2

BLACKPOOL

Division 2 (top 6) at 26/12/29

1	BLACKPOOL	21	58-36	32
2	Oldham Athletic	21	51-26	31
3	Chelsea	21	41-22	27
4	Bury	21	44-37	25
5	Wolves	22	41-37	25
6	Bradford Park Avenue	22	42-41	25

FINAL PHASE … AT THE TOP

Three clubs were left in contention for the 2 promotion places by mid-April. Oldham Athletic, with a 2.07 goal average, led Blackpool, with both clubs on 51 points with 5 games to play. Chelsea, with same number of matches completed, lay 2 points behind.

Top 3 at 14/04/30

1	Oldham Athletic	37	85-41	51	2.07
2	BLACKPOOL	37	90-63	51	1.43
3	Chelsea	37	68-41	49	1.66

(Figure in the right-hand column is goal average)

As luck would have it the top two met twice over the Easter weekend. Blackpool took the honours on Good Friday, with a 3-0 win at Bloomfield Road, then completed a 'double' by winning 2-1 at Oldham on Easter Monday. In between, on Saturday 19th, the Seasiders had beaten Bradford City, while the Latics drew 2-2 with Bristol City. Chelsea, with two wins over the holiday were now second. Oldham had lost the plot, drew at Notts County on the 26th, then lost at Barnsley on May 3rd. Blackpool, already promoted, lifted the Division 2 crown by drawing at Nottingham Forest on the latter date.

Division 2 (bottom 6) at 26/12/29

17	Notts County	23	31-40	18
18	Preston North End	22	34-45	18
19	Bristol City	22	36-52	18
20	Millwall	22	34-48	17
21	Barnsley	21	27-38	15
22	Swansea Town	22	29-41	13

FINAL PHASE … AT THE BOTTOM

As the end of the season approached, nine clubs were still in danger, though it seemed as if bottom-of-the-pile Bristol City, 3 points adrift of the rest, would almost certainly fill one of the relegation places. Hull City, in 21st spot, had games in hand on everyone else and victory in one of these could lift the Tigers 5 places in the table.

Bottom 9 at 14/04/30

14	Reading	38	48-60	33	0.80
15	Notts County	38	52-61	32	0.85
16	Swansea Town	38	50-60	31	0.83
17	Bradford City	37	55-71	31	0.78
18	Millwall	37	50-65	31	0.77
19	Barnsley	37	48-65	30	0.74
20	Preston North End	37	52-73	30	0.71
21	Hull City	35	44-66	30	0.67
22	Bristol City	36	49-75	27	0.65

(Figure in the right-hand column is goal average)

By April 23rd, Hull had added only 1 point to their total – from 4 games. Millwall had moved to safety by this stage, but Notts County had lost 3 times and were looking like a team destined for the drop. Bristol City, on the other hand, were making a fight of it, taking 3 points from 3 Easter matches against promotion contenders, Chelsea and Oldham. On April 26th, Hull and Bristol City both won, Swansea Town pulled to safety and Notts County only drew, which guaranteed them a return to Division 3. In the crunch match on May 1st, Bristol City won 1-0 at Hull. Despite beating Wolves on May 3rd, the Tigers went down, on goal average, after Bristol's draw with Preston.

August	31	MILLWALL	4-3
September	02	BURY	2-1
	07	Southampton	2-4
	09	NOTTINGHAM FOREST	5-1
	14	TOTTENHAM HOTSPUR	3-2
	21	West Bromwich Albion	1-5
	28	BRADFORD PARK AVENUE	1-0
October	05	Barnsley	4-2
	12	CARDIFF CITY	3-0
	19	Preston North End	6-4
	26	BRISTOL CITY	7-1
November	02	Notts County	2-0
	09	READING	4-2
	16	Charlton Athletic	4-1
	23	HULL CITY	1-2
	30	Stoke City	1-0
December	07	WOLVES	3-2
	14	Bradford City	1-1
	21	SWANSEA TOWN	3-0
	25	CHELSEA	1-1
	26	Chelsea	0-4
	28	Millwall	1-3
January	01	Bury	1-0
	04	SOUTHAMPTON	5-1
	18	Tottenham Hotspur	1-6
February	01	Bradford Park Avenue	0-5
	08	BARNSLEY	2-1
	15	Cardiff City	2-4
	22	PRESTON NORTH END	5-1
March	01	Bristol City	1-0
	05	WEST BROMWICH ALBION	1-0
	08	NOTTS COUNTY	1-2
	15	Reading	1-1
	22	CHARLTON ATHLETIC	6-0
	29	Hull City	3-0
April	05	STOKE CITY	0-2
	12	Wolves	2-1
	18	OLDHAM ATHLETIC	3-0
	19	BRADFORD CITY	3-0
	21	Oldham Athletic	2-1
	26	Swansea Town	0-3
May	03	Nottingham Forest	0-0

2nd Division Final Table 1929-30

1	BLACKPOOL	42	98	67	58
2	Chelsea	42	74	46	55
3	Oldham Athletic	42	90	51	53
4	Bradford Park Avenue	42	91	70	50
5	Bury	42	78	67	49
6	West Bromwich Albion	42	105	73	47
7	Southampton	42	77	76	45
8	Cardiff City	42	61	59	44
9	Wolves	42	77	79	41
10	Nottingham Forest	42	55	69	41
11	Stoke City	42	74	72	40
12	Tottenham Hotspur	42	59	61	39
13	Charlton Athletic	42	59	63	39
14	Millwall	42	57	73	39
15	Swansea Town	42	57	61	37
16	Preston North End	42	65	80	37
17	Barnsley	42	56	71	36
18	Bradford City	42	60	77	36
19	Reading	42	54	67	35
20	Bristol City	42	61	83	35
21	Hull City	42	51	78	35
22	Notts County	42	54	70	33
		924	1513	1513	924

Blackpool and Chelsea were promoted to Division 1. Hull City (North) and Notts County (South) were relegated to Division 3.

1929-30 – DIVISION 3 (NORTH) PORT VALE

Division 3 (North) (top 6) at 26/12/29

1	PORT VALE	21	53-23	33
2	Stockport County	18	51-21	29
3	Crewe Alexandra	19	44-27	24
4	Accrington Stanley	20	44-31	24
5	Darlington	21	48-38	24
6	Carlisle United	19	50-43	22

FINAL PHASE ... AT THE TOP

The battle for promotion was a two-horse race as the season moved towards mid-April. Stockport County led by a point, but Port Vale, with a better goal average, had a game in hand.

Top 2 at 12/04/30

1	Stockport County	37	96-39	57	2.46
2	PORT VALE	36	86-33	56	2.61

(Figure in the right-hand column is goal average)

Despite dropping a home point on Good Friday against York City, Vale went top on goal average because Stockport lost 2-3 at New Brighton. Both leaders won their games on April 19th, but the next matches made an important difference. On Easter Monday Port Vale won at York City, while on Wednesday, April 23rd, County lost 0-1 at Lincoln City. This left Port Vale 3 points short of the title, which reduced to 1 point after their crushing win at Tranmere on April 26th. The key blow was struck on May 1st when the Valiants won at Doncaster 1-0.

Division 3 (North) (bottom 6) at 26/12/29

17	Doncaster Rovers	21	30-39	17
18	Halifax Town	22	27-34	16
19	Wrexham	21	29-40	16
20	Rotherham United	19	24-43	13
21	New Brighton	20	23-53	13
22	Barrow	19	19-47	10

FINAL PHASE ... AT THE BOTTOM

Barrow still harboured hopes of escaping the re-election zone at April 12th, but, with the safety mark 4 points away and only 4 games left to play, the Holker Street men's chances looked slim to say the least. Halifax Town were in 21st place, a point behind Rotherham United, but with two matches more completed.

Bottom 5 at 12/04/30

18	Wrexham	37	53-78	28	0.68
19	Wigan Borough	38	54-81	28	0.67
20	Rotherham United	37	64-103	27	0.62
21	Halifax Town	39	40-73	26	0.55
22	Barrow	38	39-95	23	0.41

(Figure in the right-hand column is goal average)

Wrexham and Wigan Borough both ended April 19th clear of the re-election threat after the Welshmen beat Halifax Town 2-1 and the Springfield Park club followed victory at Nelson on Good Friday by drawing with Rotherham. The Millers did not have long to wait to reach safety, achieving this after beating Doncaster Rovers 1-0 on Easter Monday, April 21st. Halifax, after losing two Easter games managed a Monday success, 3-2 against Chesterfield. Barrow, having drawn their opening 2 holiday fixtures defeated Crewe 1-0 on the same day. For both clubs, these wins came too late to stave off a re-election application.

August	31	Halifax Town	2-1
September	02	New Brighton	1-0
	07	BARROW	5-0
	09	NEW BRIGHTON	5-1
	14	Wrexham	2-0
	16	Lincoln City	2-3
	21	WIGAN BOROUGH	4-0
	23	CREWE ALEXANDRA	2-0
	28	Carlisle United	4-1
October	05	NELSON	3-1
	12	Southport	2-1
	19	Rotherham United	2-2
	26	ROCHDALE	3-3
November	02	South Shields	0-0
	09	ACCRINGTON STANLEY	5-2
	16	Darlington	1-0
	23	HARTLEPOOLS UNITED	2-1
December	07	CHESTERFIELD	4-1
	21	TRANMERE ROVERS	1-0
	25	STOCKPORT COUNTY	1-2
	26	Stockport County	2-4
	28	HALIFAX TOWN	3-0
January	04	Barrow	1-1
	18	WREXHAM	3-0
	25	Wigan Borough	3-0
February	01	CARLISLE UNITED	4-0
	08	Nelson	3-2
	15	SOUTHPORT	1-0
	22	ROTHERHAM UNITED	7-1
March	01	Rochdale	0-0
	08	SOUTH SHIELDS	3-0
	15	Accrington Stanley	2-0
	22	DARLINGTON	0-2
	29	Hartlepools United	0-2
April	05	DONCASTER ROVERS	2-1
	12	Chesterfield	1-1
	18	YORK CITY	1-1
	19	LINCOLN CITY	5-2
	21	York City	2-0
	26	Tranmere Rovers	5-1
May	01	Doncaster Rovers	2-0
	03	Crewe Alexandra	2-0

3rd Division (North) Final Table 1929-30

1	PORT VALE	42	103	37	67
2	Stockport County	42	106	44	63
3	Darlington	42	108	73	50
4	Chesterfield	42	76	56	50
5	Lincoln City	42	83	61	48
6	York City	42	77	64	46
7	South Shields	42	77	74	46
8	Hartlepools United	42	81	74	45
9	Southport	42	81	74	43
10	Rochdale	42	89	91	43
11	Crewe Alexandra	42	82	71	42
12	Tranmere Rovers	42	83	86	41
13	New Brighton	42	69	79	40
14	Doncaster Rovers	42	62	69	39
15	Carlisle United	42	90	101	39
16	Accrington Stanley	42	84	81	37
17	Wrexham	42	67	88	34
18	Wigan Borough	42	60	88	33
19	Nelson	42	51	80	33
20	Rotherham United	42	67	113	30
21	Halifax Town	42	44	79	28
22	Barrow	42	41	98	27
		924	1681	1681	924

Port Vale were promoted to Division 2. *Halifax Town* (40 votes) and *Barrow* (22) were re-elected. Unsuccessful applicants were Mansfield Town (15), Manchester Central (13) and Prescot Cables (0).

1929-30 – DIVISION 3 (SOUTH)

Division 3 (South) (top 6) at 28/12/29

1	PLYMOUTH ARGYLE	21	54-18	34
2	Brentford	21	47-22	31
3	Brighton & Hove Albion	21	48-27	30
4	Northampton Town	20	33-19	27
5	Bournemouth & B.A.	19	40-22	25
6	Crystal Palace	24	44-49	24

FINAL PHASE ... AT THE TOP

Only Brentford stood between Plymouth Argyle and a long-awaited promotion to Division Two by April 14th. The Devon club held a 3-point lead over the Bees, who had played one game more. Surely this time the Home Park club would make it.

Top 4 at 14/04/30

1	PLYMOUTH ARGYLE	36	85-31	58	2.74
2	Brentford	37	86-37	55	2.32
3	Brighton & Hove Albion	37	80-50	47	1.60
4	Northampton Town	37	68-45	46	1.51

(Figure in the right-hand column is goal average)

Plymouth moved closer to promotion on Good Friday, April 18th. A 3-1 win over Newport County carried Argyle 5 points clear because Brentford lost 1-2 at Queen's Park Rangers. Plymouth defeated Norwich City on the 19th, but Brentford forced the promotion celebration to be put on hold by beating Bournemouth 1-0 at Griffin Park. This only served to delay the inevitable, however, and on April 21st Plymouth became champions by defeating Newport County 2-0 in South Wales.

Division 3 (South) (bottom 6) at 28/12/29

17	Clapton Orient	21	16-29	16
18	Watford	21	24-36	15
19	Newport County	20	35-41	14
20	Bristol Rovers	20	38-45	14
21	Gillingham	22	20-45	14
22	Merthyr Town	19	20-54	10

FINAL PHASE ... AT THE BOTTOM

Despite an awful season, Merthyr Town still reached mid-April with a mathematical chance of escaping re-election trauma, though there were very long odds against this, with their 15 points leaving them 9 points behind 20th place with only five games left. Gillingham, in 21st place, were just 2 points from safety, but were looking in real trouble too.

Bottom 4 at 14/04/30

19	Torquay United	37	55-87	25	0.63
20	Bristol Rovers	36	59-86	24	0.69
21	Gillingham	37	41-79	22	0.52
22	Merthyr Town	37	47-122	15	0.39

(Figure in the right-hand column is goal average)

On Easter Saturday, April 19th, the Merthyr team produced one of their best performances of the season to thrash Crystal Palace 5-2. Ironically, both Bristol Rovers and Gillingham took their Easter points hauls to three on the same afternoon, leaving the Martyrs doomed to seek re-election. The fight to avoid the other 'begging' slot went right down to the wire and was not settled until May 3rd, the final Saturday of the season. Torquay managed to avoid dropping to 21st place over the closing stages, but still had to beat Exeter City at Plainmoor to guarantee safety. Gillingham's 6-0 hammering of Merthyr on April 26th lifted the Kent club briefly above Bristol Rovers, but the Pirates edged ahead four days later, on goal average, by drawing 0-0 at Walsall. Gillingham beat Luton Town on May 3rd, but Rovers sank Brentford 4-1 at Eastville and escaped by the skin of their teeth.

PLYMOUTH ARGYLE

August	31	Clapton Orient	2-0
September	04	Torquay United	4-3
	07	BRENTFORD	1-1
	11	TORQUAY UNITED	5-0
	14	Bristol Rovers	3-2
	21	BRIGHTON & HOVE ALBION	1-1
	25	Watford	2-0
	28	Swindon Town	2-1
October	05	GILLINGHAM	3-0
	12	MERTHYR TOWN	2-1
	19	Northampton Town	1-1
	26	EXETER CITY	4-1
November	02	Southend United	1-1
	09	LUTON TOWN	6-1
	16	Bournemouth & B.A.	1-1
	23	WALSALL	1-1
December	07	FULHAM	3-1
	21	CRYSTAL PALACE	6-1
	25	Coventry City	0-1
	26	COVENTRY CITY	3-0
	28	CLAPTON ORIENT	3-0
January	04	Brentford	0-3
	18	BRISTOL ROVERS	3-0
February	08	Gillingham	0-0
	15	Merthyr Town	3-0
	22	NORTHAMPTON TOWN	1-0
March	01	Exeter City	1-1
	08	SOUTHEND UNITED	1-0
	13	Queen's Park Rangers	2-1
	15	Luton Town	2-5
	22	BOURNEMOUTH & B.A.	2-1
	26	SWINDON TOWN	5-0
	29	Walsall	3-1
April	02	Brighton & Hove Albion	1-0
	05	QUEEN'S PARK RANGERS	4-0
	12	Fulham	3-1
	18	NEWPORT COUNTY	3-1
	19	NORWICH CITY	4-1
	21	Newport County	2-0
	26	Crystal Palace	0-3
	28	Norwich City	2-1
May	03	WATFORD	2-1

3rd Division (South) Final Table 1929-30

1	PLYMOUTH ARGYLE	42	98	38	68
2	Brentford	42	94	44	61
3	Queen's Park Rangers	42	80	68	51
4	Northampton Town	42	82	58	50
5	Brighton & Hove Albion	42	87	63	50
6	Coventry City	42	88	73	47
7	Fulham	42	87	83	47
8	Norwich City	42	88	77	46
9	Crystal Palace	42	81	74	46
10	Bournemouth & B.A.	42	72	61	43
11	Southend United	42	69	59	43
12	Clapton Orient	42	55	62	41
13	Luton Town	42	64	78	40
14	Swindon Town	42	73	83	38
15	Watford	42	60	73	38
16	Exeter City	42	67	73	35
17	Walsall	42	71	78	34
18	Newport County	42	74	85	34
19	Torquay United	42	64	94	31
20	Bristol Rovers	42	67	93	30
21	Gillingham	42	51	80	30
22	Merthyr Town	42	60	135	21
		924	1632	1632	924

Plymouth Argyle were promoted to Division 2. *Gillingham* (33 votes) were re-elected, but *Merthyr Town* (14) were replaced by *Thames Association* (20). Aldershot (19), Llanelli (4) and Argonauts (0) were unsuccessful.

1930-31 – LEAGUE DIVISION 1

ARSENAL

Division 1 (top 6) at 26/12/30

1	ARSENAL	21	61-31	33
2	Sheffield Wednesday	21	58-33	29
3	Aston Villa	22	60-47	28
4	Derby County	22	52-36	27
5	Portsmouth	22	52-39	27
6	West Ham United	22	51-44	27

FINAL PHASE … AT THE TOP

With 5 games left, Arsenal needed 5 points to win the title. Only Aston Villa were left with any hope of stopping the Gunners.

Top 4 at 04/04/31

1	ARSENAL	37	114-56	57	2.04
2	Aston Villa	37	114-70	51	1.63
3	Sheffield Wednesday	36	92-65	46	1.42
4	Portsmouth	37	77-62	43	1.24

(Figure in the right-hand column is goal average)

There was a slight pause in Arsenal's march to the title when Portsmouth drew at Highbury on April 6th. Aston Villa won 4-3 against Newcastle United the next day to move a point closer to the Gunners, but when the leaders won at Grimsby Town the following Saturday, Villa knew it was just about all over, despite their 4-0 victory over Sheffield United. Sure enough, on April 18th, Arsenal beat Liverpool 3-1 and moved out of Aston Villa's reach to become champions.

Division 1 (bottom 6) at 26/12/30

17	Sunderland	22	48-58	19
18	Leeds United	22	48-47	18
19	Bolton Wanderers	21	31-40	18
20	Grimsby Town	21	34-34	17
21	Blackpool	22	38-69	17
22	Manchester United	22	27-72	7

FINAL PHASE … AT THE BOTTOM

Manchester United's slim hopes of avoiding the drop had run out by the end of March, with Leeds United looking favourites to join the Red Devils en route for Division 2. The Elland Road side were 3 points behind Birmingham and 4 down on 19th-placed Blackpool, despite the Seasiders' tendency to ship goals all too often. All three clubs had 5 games left.

Bottom 4 at 04/04/31

19	Blackpool	37	62-110	30	0.56
20	Birmingham	37	50-68	29	0.73
21	Leeds United	37	60-75	26	0.80
22	Manchester United	38	44-103	19	0.43

(Figure in the right-hand column is goal average)

Birmingham struck a major blow in their survival bid with a 1-0 win over Sunderland on April 6th. Blackpool lost at Derby and Leeds United drew at Sheffield United. A day later, Leeds thrashed the Blades 4-0, which livened the relegation battle up even more. All three clubs seeking to avoid joining bottom club Manchester United on the demotion train lost their games on Saturday 11th April, but, one week on, Birmingham moved to safety by adding a 2-0 win over Sheffield Wednesday to their midweek draw at Liverpool.

Blackpool drew at home to Huddersfield Town, but Leeds lost to Villa. United now trailed their rivals by 2 points, on top of which the Seasiders had a game in hand. On the 25th, a 2-6 defeat for Blackpool at Grimsby meant the issue went to the final day of the campaign – May 2nd. Leeds United defeated Derby County 3-1 at Elland Road, but were relegated because Blackpool fought out a 2-2 draw with Manchester City.

Month	Date	Opponent	Score
August	30	Blackpool	4-1
September	01	Bolton Wanderers	4-1
	06	LEEDS UNITED	3-1
	10	BLACKBURN ROVERS	3-2
	13	Sunderland	4-1
	15	Blackburn Rovers	2-2
	20	LEICESTER CITY	4-1
	27	Birmingham	4-2
October	04	SHEFFIELD UNITED	1-1
	11	Derby County	2-4
	18	Manchester United	2-1
	25	WEST HAM UNITED	1-1
November	01	Huddersfield Town	1-1
	08	ASTON VILLA	5-2
	15	Sheffield Wednesday	2-1
	22	MIDDLESBROUGH	5-3
	29	Chelsea	5-1
December	13	Liverpool	1-1
	20	NEWCASTLE UNITED	1-2
	25	Manchester City	4-1
	26	MANCHESTER CITY	3-1
	27	BLACKPOOL	7-1
January	17	SUNDERLAND	1-3
	28	GRIMSBY TOWN	9-1
	31	BIRMINGHAM	1-1
February	05	Leicester City	7-2
	07	Sheffield United	1-1
	14	DERBY COUNTY	6-3
	21	MANCHESTER UNITED	4-1
	28	West Ham United	4-2
March	07	HUDDERSFIELD TOWN	0-0
	11	Leeds United	2-1
	14	Aston Villa	1-5
	21	SHEFFIELD WEDNESDAY	2-0
	28	Middlesbrough	5-2
April	03	Portsmouth	1-1
	04	CHELSEA	2-1
	06	PORTSMOUTH	1-1
	11	Grimsby Town	1-0
	18	LIVERPOOL	3-1
	25	Newcastle United	3-1
May	02	BOLTON WANDERERS	5-0

1st Division Final Table 1930-31

1	ARSENAL	42	127	59	66
2	Aston Villa	42	128	78	59
3	Sheffield Wednesday	42	102	75	52
4	Portsmouth	42	84	67	49
5	Huddersfield Town	42	81	65	48
6	Derby County	42	94	79	46
7	Middlesbrough	42	98	90	46
8	Manchester City	42	75	70	46
9	Liverpool	42	86	85	42
10	Blackburn Rovers	42	83	84	42
11	Sunderland	42	89	85	41
12	Chelsea	42	64	67	40
13	Grimsby Town	42	82	87	39
14	Bolton Wanderers	42	68	81	39
15	Sheffield United	42	78	84	38
16	Leicester City	42	80	95	38
17	Newcastle United	42	78	87	36
18	West Ham United	42	79	94	36
19	Birmingham	42	55	70	36
20	Blackpool	42	71	125	32
21	Leeds United	42	68	81	31
22	Manchester United	42	53	115	22
		924	1823	1823	924

Leeds United and Manchester United were relegated.

1930-31 – LEAGUE DIVISION 2   EVERTON

Division 2 (top 6) at 25/12/30

1	EVERTON	21	61-33	32
2	West Bromwich Albion	21	44-24	28
3	Burnley	21	48-41	27
4	Tottenham Hotspur	21	53-28	26
5	Preston North End	21	53-32	26
6	Wolves	21	50-33	26

FINAL PHASE … AT THE TOP

As the end of March drew close, Everton lay well clear of Spurs at the head of the table. West Bromwich Albion, in third, still hoped to catch Tottenham, who were 3 points ahead of the Baggies, having played one game more.

Top 3 at 28/03/31

1	EVERTON	35	107-52	54	2.06
2	Tottenham Hotspur	35	80-44	46	1.82
3	West Bromwich Albion	34	68-41	43	1.66

(Figure in the right-hand column is goal average)

A 1-0 win at Bristol City on Good Friday eased Everton closer to the title because Tottenham were held at home by Cardiff City and West Bromwich Albion lost at Port Vale. On April 4th, Spurs lost at Port Vale, 0-3, and Everton, who beat Bradford Park Avenue 4-2 at Goodison became champions. In the battle for second place, Tottenham found the pressure just too great and managed only one win in their last 7 matches. Albion closed the gap, then secured promotion on the last day of the season by beating Charlton Athletic 3-2 while Spurs lost 0-1 at Burnley.

Division 2 (bottom 6) at 25/12/30

17	Barnsley	20	19-33	16
18	Bristol City	21	26-49	16
19	Millwall	21	40-50	15
20	Plymouth Argyle	20	28-39	15
21	Cardiff City	21	33-48	14
22	Reading	21	25-59	11

FINAL PHASE … AT THE BOTTOM

Cardiff City looked doomed as April approached. Six points behind Plymouth Argyle and Reading, the Bluebirds had won only 8 times all season and had a mountain to climb in their last 7 games if they were to escape the drop. Nottingham Forest, Swansea Town and Barnsley were 2 points clear of the pair closest to struggling Cardiff.

Bottom 6 at 28/03/31

17	Nottingham Forest	35	63-70	29	0.90
18	Swansea Town	35	47-63	29	0.75
19	Barnsley	35	48-67	29	0.72
20	Plymouth Argyle	35	55-71	27	0.78
21	Reading	35	60-80	27	0.75
22	Cardiff City	35	44-78	21	0.56

(Figure in the right-hand column is goal average)

After drawing at Spurs on Good Friday, Cardiff City stopped scoring and were relegated on April 11th after a 0-0 draw with Millwall meant the Bluebirds could no longer catch Swansea in 20th place. Reading's 1-3 defeat at Plymouth Argyle on the 18th pushed the Elm Park club to the edge, while guaranteeing safety for Argyle, Barnsley and Nottingham Forest. Defeat by Bury by 3-4 on April 25th sent Reading down, leaving Swansea in the clear despite a 1-5 roasting at Bradford Park Avenue.

August	30	Plymouth Argyle	3-2
September	03	PRESTON NORTH END	2-1
	06	SWANSEA TOWN	5-1
	08	Cardiff City	2-1
	13	West Bromwich Albion	2-1
	17	CARDIFF CITY	1-1
	20	PORT VALE	2-3
	27	Bradford City	3-0
October	04	CHARLTON ATHLETIC	7-1
	11	Barnsley	1-1
	18	Nottingham Forest	2-2
	25	TOTTENHAM HOTSPUR	4-2
November	01	Reading	2-0
	08	WOLVES	4-0
	15	Millwall	3-1
	22	STOKE CITY	5-0
	29	Bradford Park Avenue	1-4
December	06	OLDHAM ATHLETIC	6-4
	13	Burnley	2-5
	20	SOUTHAMPTON	2-1
	25	Bury	2-2
	27	PLYMOUTH ARGYLE	9-1
January	01	BURY	3-2
	03	Swansea Town	5-2
	17	WEST BROMWICH ALBION	2-1
	26	Port Vale	3-1
	31	BRADFORD CITY	4-2
February	07	Charlton Athletic	7-0
	18	BARNSLEY	5-2
	21	NOTTINGHAM FOREST	2-0
March	07	READING	3-2
	16	Tottenham Hotspur	0-1
	21	MILLWALL	2-0
	25	Wolves	1-3
	28	Stoke City	0-2
April	03	Bristol City	1-0
	04	BRADFORD PARK AVENUE	4-2
	06	BRISTOL CITY	1-3
	11	Oldham Athletic	3-3
	18	BURNLEY	3-2
	25	Southampton	1-2
May	02	Preston North End	1-2

2nd Division Final Table 1930-31

1	EVERTON	42	121	66	61
2	West Bromwich Albion	42	83	49	54
3	Tottenham Hotspur	42	88	55	51
4	Wolves	42	84	67	47
5	Port Vale	42	67	61	47
6	Bradford Park Avenue	42	97	66	46
7	Preston North End	42	83	64	45
8	Burnley	42	81	77	45
9	Southampton	42	74	62	44
10	Bradford City	42	61	63	44
11	Stoke City	42	64	71	44
12	Oldham Athletic	42	61	72	42
13	Bury	42	75	82	41
14	Millwall	42	71	80	39
15	Charlton Athletic	42	59	86	39
16	Bristol City	42	54	82	38
17	Nottingham Forest	42	80	85	37
18	Plymouth Argyle	42	76	84	36
19	Barnsley	42	59	79	35
20	Swansea Town	42	51	74	34
21	Reading	42	72	96	30
22	Cardiff City	42	47	87	25
		924	1608	1608	924

Everton and West Bromwich Albion were promoted. Reading and Cardiff City were relegated to Division 3 (South).

1930-31 – DIVISION 3 (NORTH)

Division 3 (North) (top 6) at 26/12/30

1	Lincoln City	20	47-22	31
2	Tranmere Rovers	21	64-44	30
3	CHESTERFIELD	21	50-30	28
4	Stockport County	20	46-29	28
5	Hull City	21	53-31	27
6	Wrexham	21	49-34	26

FINAL PHASE ... AT THE TOP

Lincoln City, a point clear with one match fewer played, held the advantage over Tranmere Rovers at April 11th. Back in third, Chesterfield were 3 points down on the leaders and had played one game more.

Top 4 at 11/04/31

1	Lincoln City	38	95-48	55	1.98
2	Tranmere Rovers	39	110-66	54	1.67
3	CHESTERFIELD	39	88-53	52	1.66
4	Wrexham	39	86-59	49	1.46

(Figure in the right-hand column is goal average)

On April 18th, Lincoln City suffered a surprise 1-3 home defeat by Rotherham United and Tranmere Rovers slumped 0-3 away at Gateshead. Chesterfield, 3-1 winners at Hartlepools United, were right back in contention and the Spireites' 3-2 win over Lincoln on April 22nd took them top. Three days later, on 25th April, the quite amazing turnaround was completed, with City losing 3-5 at Accrington, Rovers beaten at home by Darlington and Chesterfield taking the title by sinking Gateshead 8-1 at Saltergate.

Division 3 (North) (bottom 6) at 26/12/30

17	Hartlepools United	20	40-41	16
18	New Brighton	21	25-42	16
19	Rochdale	20	38-58	14
20	Crewe Alexandra	20	34-54	14
21	Barrow	21	26-50	14
22	Nelson	20	23-46	10

FINAL PHASE ... AT THE BOTTOM

Nelson were already sentenced to a re-election application as the campaign entered its final stages. With 28 points from 38 games, Hartlepools United lay 21st, but, with a game in hand on Rochdale (30 points) and two in hand on New Brighton (31), all was not yet lost.

Bottom 6 at 11/04/31

17	Halifax Town	39	51-80	33	0.64
18	Crewe Alexandra	39	62-87	31	0.71
19	New Brighton	40	45-72	31	0.63
20	Rochdale	39	60-102	30	0.59
21	Hartlepools United	38	64-75	28	0.85
22	Nelson	39	41-100	19	0.41

(Figure in the right-hand column is goal average)

When Hartlepools lost 0-5 at Hull City on April 20th, it meant that New Brighton were safe, while United were in even more trouble, having only two games left. Rochdale's home defeat by Darlington a day later offered 'Pools some hope though and their visit to Spotland on April 25th effectively became the 're-election decider'. The result, a 2-1 win for Hartlepools, meant Rochdale would accompany Nelson in seeking another chance – unless United crashed by 30+ goals at Southport on May 2nd. They didn't.

CHESTERFIELD

August	30	CARLISLE UNITED	2-1
September	01	Rochdale	3-2
	06	York City	2-2
	08	CREWE ALEXANDRA	2-0
	13	ROTHERHAM UNITED	2-1
	17	Crewe Alexandra	1-2
	20	Hull City	1-3
	27	Barrow	3-0
October	04	SOUTHPORT	2-1
	11	Accrington Stanley	3-1
	18	DONCASTER ROVERS	2-1
	25	Lincoln City	1-1
November	01	STOCKPORT COUNTY	1-1
	08	New Brighton	1-3
	15	HALIFAX TOWN	7-0
	22	Darlington	1-5
December	06	Wigan Borough	5-1
	13	HARTLEPOOLS UNITED	3-0
	20	Gateshead	3-3
	25	WREXHAM	4-0
	26	Wrexham	1-2
	27	Carlisle United	0-0
January	01	TRANMERE ROVERS	5-1
	03	YORK CITY	3-1
	10	NELSON	2-1
	17	Rotherham United	1-0
	24	HULL CITY	0-4
	31	BARROW	3-1
February	07	Southport	0-3
	14	ACCRINGTON STANLEY	7-3
	21	Doncaster Rovers	0-1
March	07	Stockport County	1-2
	14	NEW BRIGHTON	1-0
	21	Halifax Town	1-1
	28	DARLINGTON	2-1
April	03	Tranmere Rovers	0-2
	04	Nelson	5-0
	06	ROCHDALE	4-1
	11	WIGAN BOROUGH	3-1
	18	Hartlepools United	3-1
	22	LINCOLN CITY	3-2
	25	GATESHEAD	8-1

3rd Division (North) Final Table 1930-31

1	CHESTERFIELD	42	102	57	58
2	Lincoln City	42	102	59	57
3	Wrexham	42	94	62	54
4	Tranmere Rovers	42	111	74	54
5	Southport	42	88	56	53
6	Hull City	42	99	55	50
7	Stockport County	42	77	61	49
8	Carlisle United	42	98	81	45
9	Gateshead	42	71	73	45
10	Wigan Borough	42	76	86	43
11	Darlington	42	71	59	42
12	York City	42	85	82	42
13	Accrington Stanley	42	84	108	39
14	Rotherham United	42	81	83	38
15	Doncaster Rovers	42	65	65	37
16	Barrow	42	68	89	37
17	Halifax Town	42	55	89	35
18	Crewe Alexandra	42	66	93	34
19	New Brighton	42	49	76	33
20	Hartlepools United	42	67	86	30
21	Rochdale	42	62	107	30
22	Nelson	42	43	113	19
		924	1714	1714	924

Chesterfield were promoted. *Rochdale* (40 votes) were re-elected, but *Nelson* (27) were replaced by *Chester* (27) after a second ballot, which the newcomers won 28-20. Manchester Central (4) and Merthyr Town (0) were unsuccessful.

1930-31 – DIVISION 3 (SOUTH)

Division 3 (South) (top 6) at 25/12/30

1	NOTTS COUNTY	21	54-26	32
2	Southend United	21	46-30	28
3	Northampton Town	20	34-17	27
4	Crystal Palace	20	58-42	25
5	Brentford	21	51-37	24
6	Swindon Town	21	45-39	24

FINAL PHASE ... AT THE TOP

Notts County held an 8-point lead from Southend United as March came to an end. County had dominated matters for some time and, with seven matches left, looked very firm favourites to be crowned champions.

Top 5 at 28/03/31

1	NOTTS COUNTY	35	87-38	52	2.29
2	Southend United	35	71-50	44	1.42
3	Northampton Town	35	67-43	42	1.56
4	Brentford	35	77-57	40	1.35
5	Crystal Palace	34	86-61	39	1.41

(Figure in the right-hand column is goal average)

Notts County homed in on the Division 3 (South) crown by defeating Walsall 6-1 on April 3rd, Good Friday, and then following this, a day afterwards, with a 1-0 success over Brentford. On April 6th, the leaders lost 1-2 in the return fixture against Walsall, but could still celebrate becoming champions because Northampton Town, the only side left able to catch County before kick-off, crashed 0-4 at Luton Town.

Division 3 (South) (bottom 6) at 25/12/30

17	Luton Town	20	27-34	17
18	Exeter City	20	34-47	17
19	Norwich City	20	25-37	14
20	Walsall	19	36-49	13
21	Newport County	20	40-61	12
22	Thames Association	20	22-51	12

FINAL PHASE ... AT THE BOTTOM

The three-point gap between Thames Association, in 20th place, and Newport County, one spot below them, did not look at all unbridgeable with 7 matches still to play, but March came to an end with the Londoners having that all-important psychological advantage. One point behind County, Norwich City had it that bit harder by this time.

Bottom 4 at 28/03/31

19	Walsall	35	67-80	29	0.84
20	Thames Association	35	47-82	27	0.57
21	Newport County	35	62-96	24	0.65
22	Norwich City	35	41-67	23	0.61

(Figure in the right-hand column is goal average)

Thames Association and Walsall both had good results over the Easter weekend, winning two games apiece. Newport and Norwich City won one game each, the Canaries also earning a draw. This all left the bottom two 6 points adrift of Thames, with 4 games left. With all four clubs at the foot of the table losing on April 11th, issues were all but resolved, and the first side condemned to seek re-election were Newport County after a 1-4 defeat at Norwich on April 18th. With Thames beaten at home by Bristol Rovers, City still had a slight hope of escaping, but this disappeared on April 25th when the East Anglian side lost at Gillingham 1-2, while Thames drew with Newport.

NOTTS COUNTY

August	30	Coventry City	2-1
September	03	THAMES ASSOCIATION	4-0
	06	FULHAM	6-1
	08	Norwich City	2-2
	13	Swindon Town	2-1
	20	BOURNEMOUTH & B.A.	2-0
	24	Brentford	2-2
	27	Watford	1-0
October	02	NORWICH CITY	4-0
	04	BRISTOL ROVERS	3-0
	11	CLAPTON ORIENT	5-0
	18	Newport County	3-2
	25	GILLINGHAM	2-2
November	01	Exeter City	3-3
	08	BRIGHTON & HOVE ALBION	2-2
	15	Torquay United	4-1
	22	NORTHAMPTON TOWN	2-2
December	06	CRYSTAL PALACE	2-2
	17	Southend United	1-2
	20	LUTON TOWN	1-0
	25	Queen's Park Rangers	1-4
	26	QUEEN'S PARK RANGERS	2-0
	27	COVENTRY CITY	4-1
January	03	Fulham	1-3
	17	SWINDON TOWN	2-0
	28	Bournemouth & B.A.	1-2
	31	WATFORD	1-0
February	07	Bristol Rovers	2-2
	14	Clapton Orient	4-1
	21	NEWPORT COUNTY	5-0
	28	Gillingham	5-0
March	07	EXETER CITY	1-2
	14	Brighton & Hove Albion	3-1
	21	TORQUAY UNITED	2-0
	28	Northampton Town	0-0
April	03	WALSALL	6-1
	04	BRENTFORD	1-0
	06	Walsall	1-2
	11	Crystal Palace	1-1
	18	SOUTHEND UNITED	1-1
	25	Luton Town	0-3
May	02	Thames Association	0-0

3rd Division (South) Final Table 1930-31

1	NOTTS COUNTY	42	97	46	59
2	Crystal Palace	42	107	71	51
3	Brentford	42	90	64	50
4	Brighton & Hove Albion	42	68	53	49
5	Southend United	42	76	60	49
6	Northampton Town	42	77	59	48
7	Luton Town	42	76	51	46
8	Queen's Park Rangers	42	82	75	43
9	Fulham	42	77	75	43
10	Bournemouth & B.A.	42	72	73	43
11	Torquay United	42	80	84	43
12	Swindon Town	42	89	94	42
13	Exeter City	42	84	90	42
14	Coventry City	42	75	65	41
15	Bristol Rovers	42	75	92	40
16	Gillingham	42	61	76	38
17	Walsall	42	78	95	37
18	Watford	42	72	75	35
19	Clapton Orient	42	63	91	35
20	Thames Association	42	54	93	34
21	Newport County	42	69	111	28
22	Norwich City	42	47	76	28
		924	1669	1669	924

Notts County were promoted. *Norwich City* (38 votes) were re-elected, but *Newport County* (19) were replaced by Mansfield Town (25). Aldershot (14), Merthyr Town (2) and Llanelli (0) were unsuccessful. Walsall were transferred to Division 3 (North).

1931-32 – LEAGUE DIVISION 1   EVERTON

Division 1 (top 6) at 25/12/31

1	EVERTON	21	73-39	29
2	West Bromwich Albion	22	43-23	27
3	Arsenal	21	50-31	26
4	Liverpool	21	45-41	25
5	Huddersfield Town	21	39-29	24
6	Sheffield United	21	51-38	24

FINAL PHASE ... AT THE TOP

Everton were tantalisingly close to the title by April 9th. Having played 37 league matches, the Goodison Park club held a 5-point advantage over Yorkshire pair Huddersfield Town and Sheffield Wednesday, both of whom had played a game more. Arsenal, who also had 5 fixtures to complete, were a point further back.

Top 4 at 09/04/32

1	Everton	37	109-61	51	1.79
2	Huddersfield Town	38	76-54	46	1.41
3	Sheffield Wednesday	38	89-73	46	1.22
4	Arsenal	37	75-45	45	1.67

(Figure in the right-hand column is goal average)

Everton's pursuit of the League title continued with a 6-1 win over West Ham United on April 16th. Huddersfield Town and Arsenal both won to keep their hopes alive, but defeat by the Gunners ended Sheffield Wednesday's chances. Defeat at Middlesbrough on April 23rd left Everton still short of the mark needed to become champions, but Arsenal dropped a point at Villa two days later and then ended Huddersfield's bid with a 2-1 victory at Leeds Road. On April 30th, Everton took the 2 points they required by beating Bolton Wanderers 1-0.

Division 1 (bottom 6) at 25/12/31

17	Chelsea	21	34-48	17
18	Portsmouth	19	20-29	17
19	West Ham United	21	32-54	17
20	Derby County	21	34-46	16
21	Blackpool	21	32-56	15
22	Grimsby Town	21	32-51	13

FINAL PHASE ... AT THE BOTTOM

Each of the bottom five had 4 games left after April 9th. On 33 points, Bolton Wanderers were almost safe, while Leicester City and Grimsby Town occupied the relegation berths.

Bottom 4 at 09/04/32

19	West Ham United	38	57-92	31	0.62
20	Leicester City	38	69-92	30	0.75
21	Blackpool	38	58-96	28	0.60
22	Grimsby Town	38	56-89	26	0.63

(Figure in the right-hand column is goal average)

Of the bottom four, only Leicester City won on April 16th. A week later, City won again to move the verge of safety, while Grimsby began a late bid to escape the drop with victory over Derby County. West Ham lost at home to Birmingham and started to look extremely vulnerable. Hammers' chances of survival suffered further setbacks over the next few days. Blackpool drew at Newcastle on the 27th, then moved to 31 points by defeating Huddersfield on April 30th. With Leicester and Grimsby winning again, West Ham's fourth successive defeat, 0-2 at Sunderland meant the storm clouds gathered round the Boleyn Ground. On May 7th, Hammers lost 2-3 at Chelsea and went down because Blackpool (3-1 v. Sheffield United) and Grimsby Town (3-1 v. Sheffield Wednesday) both won. Grimsby were also relegated.

August	29	BIRMINGHAM	3-2
September	02	Portsmouth	3-0
	05	Sunderland	3-2
	12	MANCHESTER CITY	0-1
	16	Derby County	0-3
	19	Liverpool	3-1
	23	DERBY COUNTY	2-1
	26	Arsenal	2-3
October	03	BLACKPOOL	3-2
	10	Sheffield United	5-1
	17	SHEFFIELD WEDNESDAY	9-3
	24	Aston Villa	3-2
	31	NEWCASTLE UNITED	8-1
November	07	Huddersfield Town	0-0
	14	CHELSEA	7-2
	21	Grimsby Town	2-1
	28	LEICESTER CITY	9-2
December	05	West Ham United	2-4
	12	MIDDLESBROUGH	5-1
	19	Bolton Wanderers	1-2
	25	Blackburn Rovers	3-5
	26	BLACKBURN ROVERS	5-0
January	02	Birmingham	0-4
	16	SUNDERLAND	4-2
	27	Manchester City	0-1
	30	LIVERPOOL	2-1
February	06	ARSENAL	1-3
	13	Blackpool	0-2
	20	SHEFFIELD UNITED	5-1
	27	Sheffield Wednesday	3-1
March	05	ASTON VILLA	4-2
	19	HUDDERSFIELD TOWN	4-1
	25	WEST BROMWICH ALBION	2-1
	26	Chelsea	0-0
	28	West Bromwich Albion	1-1
April	02	GRIMSBY TOWN	4-2
	09	Leicester City	1-0
	16	WEST HAM UNITED	6-1
	23	Middlesbrough	0-1
	30	BOLTON WANDERERS	1-0
May	04	Newcastle United	0-0
	07	PORTSMOUTH	0-1

1st Division Final Table 1931-32

1	EVERTON	42	116	64	56
2	Arsenal	42	90	48	54
3	Sheffield Wednesday	42	96	82	50
4	Huddersfield Town	42	80	63	48
5	Aston Villa	42	104	72	46
6	West Bromwich Albion	42	77	55	46
7	Sheffield United	42	80	75	46
8	Portsmouth	42	62	62	45
9	Birmingham	42	78	67	44
10	Liverpool	42	81	93	44
11	Newcastle United	42	80	87	42
12	Chelsea	42	69	73	40
13	Sunderland	42	67	73	40
14	Manchester City	42	83	73	38
15	Derby County	42	71	75	38
16	Blackburn Rovers	42	89	95	38
17	Bolton Wanderers	42	72	80	38
18	Middlesbrough	42	64	89	38
19	Leicester City	42	74	94	37
20	Blackpool	42	65	102	33
21	Grimsby Town	42	67	98	32
22	West Ham United	42	62	107	31
		924	1727	1727	924

Grimsby Town and West Ham United were relegated.

1931-32 – LEAGUE DIVISION 2

Division 2 (top 6) at 26/12/31

1	Leeds United	22	49-24	32
2	WOLVES	21	65-23	30
3	Plymouth Argyle	21	47-28	28
4	Bradford Park Avenue	22	43-26	28
5	Stoke City	22	38-23	28
6	Bury	21	47-34	27

FINAL PHASE ... AT THE TOP

By April 9th, Wolves required only 2 points from 4 games to guarantee promotion. For second-placed Leeds United, three points behind the leaders, but 4 ahead of Stoke City and West Yorkshire rivals Bradford Park Avenue, hopes of a late steal of the title lingered on, but the concentration had to be on trying to hold on to the promotion slot.

Top 4 at 09/04/32

1	WOLVES	38	110-42	54	2.62
2	Leeds United	38	75-48	51	1.56
3	Stoke City	38	66-46	47	1.44
4	Bradford Park Avenue	38	67-55	47	1.22

(Figure in the right-hand column is goal average)

Despite losing at Bury on April 16th, Wolves secured a return to the top flight a week later with a 2-0 win over Port Vale. Their vastly superior goal average meant the Molineux club needed only to avoid dramatic defeats in their last two games to become champions because second-placed Leeds had taken only one point from two matches. Wolves lost their closing fixtures, but were confirmed as Division 2 winners on May 7th after Leeds failed to produce a 'last day miracle'.

Division 2 (bottom 6) at 26/12/31

17	Oldham Athletic	22	32-44	18
18	Preston North End	22	34-50	18
19	Chesterfield	21	32-48	18
20	Port Vale	22	35-55	18
21	Charlton Athletic	20	26-44	14
22	Bristol City	22	23-41	12

FINAL PHASE ... AT THE BOTTOM

With Bristol City already down, only one relegation place had still to be filled as the middle of April drew closer. From 16th-placed Preston North End on 34 points, the candidates queued neatly, a point separating them, down to Port Vale with 29 points in 21st spot.

Bottom 6 at 09/04/32

17	Notts County	38	67-69	33	0.97
18	Oldham Athletic	38	57-79	32	0.72
19	Barnsley	38	50-82	31	0.61
20	Burnley	38	56-84	30	0.67
21	Port Vale	38	53-83	29	0.64
22	Bristol City	38	36-73	19	0.49

(Figure in the right-hand column is goal average)

On April 16th, Burnley beat Barnsley 1-0, increasing the losers' worries while improving their own chances of survival. There was also a win for Oldham, but defeat for Port Vale as the season reached its climax. Vale lost a week later, while the three clubs above them all drew to leave the Staffordshire side 3 points adrift of Barnsley with only 2 games to play. On April 30th, however, Barnsley crashed 1-4 at home to Charlton Athletic, offering Port Vale, who beat Chesterfield 2-1, a life-line. Decision day arrived on May 7th, with Barnsley's hopes pinned on at least matching Vale's result. The Oakwell men drew 2-2 at Oldham, but this was not enough, as Port Vale won 2-0 at Leeds United and achieved safety on goal average.

WOLVERHAMPTON WANDERERS

August	29	TOTTENHAM HOTSPUR	4-0
September	05	Nottingham Forest	0-2
	07	Bradford City	2-2
	12	CHESTERFIELD	6-0
	14	BRADFORD CITY	3-1
	19	Burnley	3-1
	26	PRESTON NORTH END	3-2
October	03	Southampton	3-1
	10	STOKE CITY	0-1
	17	Leeds United	1-2
	24	SWANSEA TOWN	2-0
	31	Barnsley	2-2
November	07	MILLWALL	5-0
	14	Plymouth Argyle	3-3
	21	BRISTOL CITY	4-2
	28	Oldham Athletic	2-0
December	05	BURY	6-0
	12	Port Vale	7-1
	19	NOTTS COUNTY	0-0
	25	Manchester United	2-3
	26	MANCHESTER UNITED	7-0
	28	CHARLTON ATHLETIC	3-1
January	02	Tottenham Hotspur	3-3
	16	NOTTINGHAM FOREST	0-0
	27	Chesterfield	2-1
	30	BURNLEY	3-1
February	06	Preston North End	2-4
	13	SOUTHAMPTON	5-1
	20	Stoke City	1-2
	27	LEEDS UNITED	1-1
March	05	Swansea Town	1-1
	12	BARNSLEY	2-0
	19	Millwall	2-1
	26	PLYMOUTH ARGYLE	2-0
	28	BRADFORD PARK AVENUE	6-0
	29	Bradford Park Avenue	1-2
April	02	Bristol City	4-0
	09	OLDHAM ATHLETIC	7-1
	16	Bury	0-1
	23	PORT VALE	2-0
	30	Notts County	1-3
May	07	Charlton Athletic	2-3

2nd Division Final Table 1931-32

1	WOLVES	42	115	49	56
2	Leeds United	42	78	54	54
3	Stoke City	42	69	48	52
4	Plymouth Argyle	42	100	66	49
5	Bury	42	70	58	49
6	Bradford Park Avenue	42	72	63	49
7	Bradford City	42	80	61	45
8	Tottenham Hotspur	42	87	78	43
9	Millwall	42	61	61	43
10	Charlton Athletic	42	61	66	43
11	Nottingham Forest	42	77	72	42
12	Manchester United	42	71	72	42
13	Preston North End	42	75	77	42
14	Southampton	42	66	77	41
15	Swansea Town	42	73	75	39
16	Notts County	42	75	75	38
17	Chesterfield	42	64	86	37
18	Oldham Athletic	42	62	84	36
19	Burnley	42	59	87	35
20	Port Vale	42	58	89	33
21	Barnsley	42	55	91	33
22	Bristol City	42	39	78	23
		924	1567	1567	924

Wolverhampton Wanderers and Leeds United were promoted. Barnsley (North) and Bristol City (South) were relegated to Division 3.

1931-32 – DIVISION 3 (NORTH)   LINCOLN CITY

Division 3 (North) (top 6) 02/01/32

1	Gateshead	21	56-25	31
2	LINCOLN CITY	20	54-23	30
3	Crewe Alexandra	21	54-30	27
4	Southport	22	34-30	27
5	York City	23	37-37	27
6	Tranmere Rovers	21	67-33	26

FINAL PHASE ... AT THE TOP

Gateshead held a 1-point lead over Lincoln City after the opening matches of April, but the Red Imps had a match in hand on the Laides. The top two were well clear of the pack, with 3rd-placed Barrow 6 points off the lead, with 4 to play.

Top 4 at 02/04/32

1	Gateshead	36	87-44	51	1.98
2	LINCOLN CITY	35	90-39	50	2.31
3	Barrow	36	80-52	45	1.54
4	Crewe Alexandra	36	89-57	44	1.56

(Figure in the right-hand column is goal average)

Both Gateshead and Lincoln City won their games on April 9th and 16th, the Laides achieving odd goal successes while the Imps blasted 10 goals against 4. The key change came on April 23rd, with Gateshead going down 1-2 at Rotherham while Lincoln picked up a 3-0 win at Carlisle United. It could all have been over a week later, but a strangely subdued Lincoln City were held 0-0 at Sincil Bank by Wrexham. The Imps' much better goal average required remarkable results on the last day, May 7th, to change things. Although City lost 3-4 at Hartlepools and Gateshead beat Walsall 2-0, Lincoln became champions.

Division 3 (North) (bottom 6) 02/01/32

16	Halifax Town	20	29-36	17
17	Walsall	21	24-44	16
18	Doncaster Rovers	21	27-44	15
19	Rotherham United	21	30-45	13
20	Rochdale	21	27-66	10
21	New Brighton	22	12-44	8

FINAL PHASE ... AT THE BOTTOM

Rochdale's chances of avoiding the season's one re-election place, because of Wigan Borough's October resignation, were so thin by April 2nd as to be transparent. 'Dale had 4 games left, but lay 7 points behind New Brighton. The Spotland club had won only 4 matches all term, so nobody gave them even the slightest chance of pulling up to 20th place.

Bottom 4 at 02/04/32

18	Hartlepools United	36	64-95	29	0.67
19	Rotherham United	35	51-64	26	0.80
20	New Brighton	35	29-69	18	0.42
21	Rochdale	36	41-116	11	0.35

(Figure in the right-hand column is goal average)

The pundits were, of course, right. Rochdale had to beat 2nd-placed Lincoln City on April 9th to keep any lingering hopes of avoiding a re-election application alive. They lost 3-5, which relieved New Brighton of any further worries. The Rakers went on to celebrate with 3 wins in their last four fixtures. For 'Dale there followed three more defeats.

Month	Day	Opponent	Score
August	29	DARLINGTON	2-0
	31	HARTLEPOOLS UNITED	6-0
September	05	Halifax Town	0-3
	12	WALSALL	3-0
	19	Gateshead	3-2
	26	NEW BRIGHTON	3-0
October	03	Barrow	2-0
	10	HULL CITY	1-0
	17	STOCKPORT COUNTY	1-2
	24	Rotherham United	1-0
	31	TRANMERE ROVERS	4-2
November	07	York City	1-1
	14	SOUTHPORT	7-0
	21	Doncaster Rovers	3-0
December	05	Crewe Alexandra	1-8
	19	Wrexham	1-3
	25	Chester	1-2
	26	CHESTER	4-0
January	01	Accrington Stanley	2-2
	02	Darlington	6-0
	09	ROCHDALE	3-0
	16	HALIFAX TOWN	9-1
	23	Walsall	3-0
	30	GATESHEAD	1-0
February	06	New Brighton	1-2
	13	BARROW	3-1
	20	Hull City	1-4
	24	CARLISLE UNITED	3-1
	27	Stockport County	1-0
March	05	ROTHERHAM UNITED	3-1
	12	Tranmere Rovers	0-1
	19	YORK CITY	1-1
	25	ACCRINGTON STANLEY	5-1
	26	Southport	1-1
April	02	DONCASTER ROVERS	1-2
	09	Rochdale	5-3
	16	CREWE ALEXANDRA	5-1
	23	Carlisle United	3-0
	30	WREXHAM	0-0
May	07	Hartlepools United	3-4

3rd Division (North) Final Table 1931-32

1	LINCOLN CITY	40	106	47	57
2	Gateshead	40	94	48	57
3	Chester	40	78	60	50
4	Tranmere Rovers	40	107	58	49
5	Barrow	40	86	59	49
6	Crewe Alexandra	40	95	66	48
7	Southport	40	58	53	46
8	Hull City	40	82	53	45
9	York City	40	76	81	43
10	Wrexham	40	64	69	43
11	Darlington	40	66	69	38
12	Stockport County	40	55	53	37
13	Hartlepools United	40	78	100	37
14	Accrington Stanley	40	75	80	36
15	Doncaster Rovers	40	59	80	36
16	Walsall	40	57	85	35
17	Halifax Town	40	61	87	34
18	Carlisle United	40	64	79	33
19	Rotherham United	40	63	72	32
20	New Brighton	40	38	76	24
21	Rochdale	40	48	135	11
		840	1510	1510	840

Lincoln City were promoted. *Rochdale* (47 votes) were re-elected and the division was made up to 22 clubs by the transfer of *Mansfield Town* from Division 3 (South). Rhyl (2 votes) and Wigan Athletic were unsuccessful.

1931-32 – DIVISION 3 (SOUTH)   FULHAM

Division 3 (South) (top 6) at 28/12/31

1	Brentford	20	40-21	29
2	FULHAM	21	57-34	28
3	Crystal Palace	20	41-27	26
4	Exeter City	22	44-37	26
5	Brighton & Hove Albion	21	37-29	25
6	Watford	21	47-40	25

FINAL PHASE … AT THE TOP

Four points ahead with 4 games to play, Fulham looked to be on course for the 2nd Division at April 9th. Southend United and Reading still entertained other ideas, of course, but time was running out for the leaders' nearest rivals.

Top 4 at 09/04/32

1	FULHAM	38	101-56	51	1.80
2	Southend United	38	69-51	47	1.35
3	Reading	38	83-66	47	1.26
4	Exeter City	38	73-57	45	1.28

(Figure in the right-hand column is goal average)

Fulham beat Bournemouth on April 16th, but lost at Queen's Park Rangers on the 23rd. With Southend United drawing on both dates, Reading came through as the leaders' main rivals, with victories over Bristol Rovers and at Torquay United. A narrow win over Bristol Rovers on April 30th lifted Fulham to 55 points, two points ahead of Reading and with a vastly better goal average. The leaders had no need to do sums, however, winning their final game, against Exeter City, 3-1 on May 7th to take the title.

Division 3 (South) (bottom 6) at 28/12/31

17	Cardiff City	20	31-37	16
18	Torquay United	21	36-57	16
19	Clapton Orient	20	30-41	15
20	Northampton Town	22	24-38	14
21	Thames Association	21	21-43	13
22	Gillingham	20	17-39	12

FINAL PHASE … AT THE BOTTOM

Thames were virtually doomed to finish in the bottom two after April 9th, being 8 points adrift of 20th-placed Mansfield Town and having only 4 matches left to play. Five points behind the Stags, though at least having the consolation of a game in hand, Gillingham faced another end-of-season battle to escape from the re-election zone.

Bottom 4 at 09/04/32

19	Clapton Orient	37	71-74	32	0.96
20	Mansfield Town	38	67-98	29	0.68
21	Gillingham	37	35-70	24	0.50
22	Thames Association	38	47-99	21	0.48

(Figure in the right-hand column is goal average)

A 1-3 defeat by Crystal Palace on April 16th meant Thames would finish in the bottom two and it was around this time that the decision to resign from the Football League at the end of the season was taken. Gillingham, having drawn on both the previous Saturdays, crashed 0-7 at Brighton on April 23rd, leaving the Kent club 4 points behind Mansfield with two to play. One of these was against the Stags and was won 2-0, meaning the final day of the campaign, May 7th, became all-important. Gillingham lost at Reading, however, while Mansfield Town beat Northampton 5-2. The Gills would have to seek re-election.

August	29	COVENTRY CITY	5-3
September	02	Exeter City	3-0
	05	Gillingham	1-2
	07	TORQUAY UNITED	10-2
	12	LUTON TOWN	3-2
	16	Torquay United	3-2
	19	Cardiff City	3-0
	26	NORTHAMPTON TOWN	1-3
October	03	Reading	2-4
	10	SOUTHEND UNITED	1-1
	17	CLAPTON ORIENT	5-1
	24	Swindon Town	2-2
	31	NORWICH CITY	4-0
November	07	Brighton & Hove Albion	3-2
	14	MANSFIELD TOWN	2-1
	21	Watford	1-3
December	05	Bournemouth & B.A.	3-0
	19	Bristol Rovers	2-2
	25	Brentford	0-0
	26	BRENTFORD	2-1
	28	QUEEN'S PARK RANGERS	1-3
January	02	Coventry City	5-5
	16	GILLINGHAM	0-2
	18	CRYSTAL PALACE	4-0
	23	Luton Town	3-1
	30	CARDIFF CITY	4-0
February	06	Northampton Town	1-0
	13	READING	3-3
	20	Southend United	1-4
	27	Clapton Orient	1-0
March	05	SWINDON TOWN	2-2
	12	Norwich City	2-2
	19	BRIGHTON & HOVE ALBION	3-0
	25	Thames Association	0-0
	26	Mansfield Town	2-1
	28	THAMES ASSOCIATION	8-0
April	02	WATFORD	5-0
	09	Crystal Palace	0-2
	16	BOURNEMOUTH & B.A.	3-0
	23	Queen's Park Rangers	1-3
	30	BRISTOL ROVERS	3-2
May	07	EXETER CITY	3-1

3rd Division (South) Final Table 1931-32

1	FULHAM	42	111	62	57
2	Reading	42	97	67	55
3	Southend United	42	77	53	53
4	Crystal Palace	42	74	63	51
5	Brentford	42	68	52	48
6	Luton Town	42	95	70	47
7	Exeter City	42	77	62	47
8	Brighton & Hove Albion	42	73	58	46
9	Cardiff City	42	87	73	46
10	Norwich City	42	76	67	46
11	Watford	42	81	79	46
12	Coventry City	42	108	97	44
13	Queen's Park Rangers	42	79	73	42
14	Northampton Town	42	69	69	39
15	Bournemouth & B.A.	42	70	78	38
16	Clapton Orient	42	77	90	35
17	Swindon Town	42	70	84	34
18	Bristol Rovers	42	65	92	34
19	Torquay United	42	72	106	33
20	Mansfield Town	42	75	108	32
21	Gillingham	42	40	82	26
22	Thames Association	42	53	109	23
		924	1694	1694	922

Fulham were promoted. *Mansfield Town* transferred to Division 3 (North) and *Thames Association* resigned. *Gillingham* (41 votes) were re-elected and *Newport County* (36) and *Aldershot* (35) elected. Llanelli (25), Guildford City (8) and Merthyr Town (2) were unsuccessful.

OTHER INFORMATION   1929-1932

GOALSCORING 1929-1932

GOALS PER GAME

FOOTBALL LEAGUE

1929-30 – 6,584 in 1,848 - 3.56 goals per game
1930-31 – 6,814 in 1,848 - 3.69 goals per game
1931-32 – 6,498 in 1,806 - 3.60 goals per game

DIVISION 1

1929-30 – 1,758 in 462 - 3.81
1930-31 – 1,823 in 462 - 3.95
1931-32 – 1,727 in 462 - 3.74

DIVISION 2

1929-30 – 1,513 in 462 - 3.28
1930-31 – 1,608 in 462 - 3.48
1931-32 – 1,567 in 462 - 3.39

DIVISION 3 NORTH

1929-30 – 1,681 in 462 - 3.64
1930-31 – 1,714 in 462 - 3.71
1931-32 – 1,510 in 420 - 3.60

DIVISION 3 SOUTH

1929-30 – 1,632 in 462 - 3.53
1930-31 – 1,669 in 462 - 3.61
1931-32 – 1,694 in 462 - 3.67

LOW SCORES ANALYSIS

Number of games in which fewer than 2 goals were scored in Football League matches and percentage of total games.

1929-30 – 260 out of 1,848 – 14.07%
1930-31 – 264 out of 1,848 – 14.29%
1931-32 – 248 out of 1,806 – 13.74%

DIVISIONAL HIGH SCORES 1929-1932

1929-30

Division 1
09/11	Blackburn Rovers	8-3	Burnley
12/04	Arsenal	8-0	Sheffield United

Division 2
26/10	Blackpool	7-1	Bristol City
19/04	West Bromwich A.	7-1	Hull City
28/12	West Bromwich A.	7-3	Wolves

Division 3 North
15/02	Darlington	8-1	Rotherham United
01/01	Darlington	8-3	South Shields
21/04	Hartlepools United	2-8	Rochdale
25/09	Wigan Borough	8-0	Carlisle United
28/09	Wrexham	8-0	Rochdale

Division 3 South
10/04	Newport County	10-0	Merthyr Town
15/03	Norwich City	10-2	Coventry City

1930-31

Division 1
13/12	Huddersfield Town	10-1	Blackpool

Division 2
27/12	Everton	9-1	Plymouth Argyle

Division 3 North
26/12	Hull City	10-0	Halifax Town

Division 3 South
25/12	Brentford	8-2	Crystal Palace
11/04	Luton Town	8-0	Thames Association

1931-32

Division 1
17/10	Everton	9-3	Sheffield Wednes.
28/11	Everton	9-2	Leicester City

Division 2
21/11	Tottenham Hotspur	9-3	Port Vale
02/01	Bradford City	9-1	Barnsley

Division 3 North
25/12	Tranmere Rovers	9-1	Rochdale

Division 3 South
07/09	Fulham	10-2	Torquay United

LEADING GOAL SCORERS 1929-1932

Division 1
1929-30	Vic Watson (West Ham United)	45
1930-31	Pongo Waring (Aston Villa)	49
1931-32	Dixie Dean (Everton)	45

Division 2
1929-30	Jimmy Hampson (Blackpool)	45
1930-31	Dixie Dean (Everton)	39
1931-32	Cyril Pearce (Swansea Town)	35

Division 3 North
1929-30	Frank Newton (Stockport County)	36
1930-31	Jimmy McConnell (Carlisle United)	37
1931-32	Alan Hall (Lincoln City)	42

Division 3 South
1929-30	George Goddard (QPR)	37
1930-31	Peter Simpson (Crystal Palace)	46
1931-32	Clarrie Bourton (Coventry City)	49

ATTENDANCES 1929-1932

FOOTBALL LEAGUE

There were 1,848 matches played in each of the three seasons covered. In the figures below, the total for each season is followed by the average per game. There was a significant fall in numbers watching Football League games between the 1929-30 and 1930-31 seasons because of the effects of the Great Depression, which began with the Wall Street Crash in October 1929 and developed into the World Economic Crisis over the next few months.

1929-30	22,947,793	12,418 per game
1930-31	21,083,479	11,409 per game
1931-32	21,645,318	11,985 per game

462 matches were played in each division in each of the 3 seasons – apart from the 1931-32 campaign for Division 3 North. Due at least partly to the economic problems of the time, Wigan Borough resigned from the League in October 1931, so only 420 fixtures were officially completed in that section for that season.

Arsenal drew the biggest crowds in all 3 seasons. The loss of first Chelsea, then Everton from Division 1 affected 2nd Division attendances adversely, despite large attendances in all three campaigns at Tottenham Hotspur. In the 3rd Division North, average crowds fell once Port Vale had left, but the close race between Lincoln City and Gateshead 1931-32 boosted crowds at both clubs' games. In Division 3 South, Plymouth Argyle's promotion in 1930 helped cut the mean attendance, but a successful season for Fulham 1931-32 had the opposite effect.

DIVISION 1

1929-30	10,462,717	22,647 per game
1930-31	9,453,375	20,462 per game
1931-32	9,946,506	21,529 per game

DIVISION 2

1929-30	6,306,594	13,651 per game
1930-31	6,149,721	13,311 per game
1931-32	5,642,309	12,213 per game

DIVISION 3 NORTH

1929-30	2,253,810	4,878 per game
1930-31	2,270,637	4,915 per game
1931-32	2,132,851	5,078 per game

DIVISION 3 SOUTH

1929-30	3,924,672	8,495 per game
1930-31	3,209,746	6,948 per game
1931-32	3,923,652	8,493 per game

F.A. CUP FINALS

F.A. CUP FINALS 1930-1932

April 26th, 1930 - Wembley

Arsenal   2-0   Huddersfield Town (1-0)
James, Lambert
Crowd – 92,488   Referee – T. Crew

April 25th, 1931 - Wembley

Birmingham   1-2   **West Bromwich Albion** (0-1)
Bradford   *W.G. Richardson (2)*
Crowd – 92,406   Referee – A.H. Kingscott

April 23rd, 1932 - Wembley

Arsenal   1-2   **Newcastle United** (1-1)
John   *Allen (2)*
Crowd – 92,298   Referee – W.P. Harper

... AND ALSO 1929-1932

CLUBS

Five days before the 1930 F.A. Cup Final, **Arsenal** drew 6-6 at Leicester City – the highest-scoring draw in British senior football.

All 5 **Everton** forwards scored in the club's 7-0 Division 2 victory over Charlton Athletic on February 7th, 1931

Southport, from Division 3 (North), battled through to the last eight in the F.A. Cup in the 1930-1931 competition – then crashed 1-9 to Everton.

Arsenal set a new Division 1 points total record of 66 in the 1930-31 season. The Gunners' 60 away goals and 33 away points were also new records.

Aston Villa equalled Bradford City's scoring record for a season by netting 128 times in Division 1, 1930-31. With 78 conceded, Villa's goals aggregate was 206 – almost 5 goals per game.

In 1931 **West Bromwich Albion** became the first team to win promotion and the F.A Cup in the same season.

When **Wigan Borough** resigned from the League in October 1931, they became the first club to do so during a season.

After beating New Brighton 2-1 on November 7th, 1931, **Rochdale** lost a record 17 league games in a row.

On December 5th, 1931, **Newcastle United** and **Portsmouth** drew 0-0 in the only Football League game believed to have been played without a corner being awarded to either side.

Rochdale's 135 goals against in the 1931-32 season equalled **Merthyr Town**'s conceded total 1929-30, but was one fewer than the number let in by **Nelson** 1927-28. 'Dale played only 40 matches, however, compared with 42 by the others.

INDIVIDUALS

When he played for Bradford Park Avenue against Millwall on September 16th, 1929, **Albert Geldard** became the youngest player ever to appear in a Football League match. His age was 15 years and 158 days.

On March 19th, 1932, **Stanley Matthews** played his first League game, appearing for Stoke City in a 1-0 win at Bury. He went on to make 318 appearances for Stoke City and played 380 times for Blackpool. Matthews won 54 full England cap, played in 29 wartime internationals and made 14 appearances for the Football League side. He went on to become the oldest man ever to play in English first-class football and was regarded as a footballing genius.

WORLD CUP

Uruguay won the first World Cup Final, beating Argentina 4-2 in Montevideo.

NUMBERS

Numbered shirts, worn for the first time in League games, by Arsenal and Chelsea, in August 1928, were adopted by more clubs 1929-1932 – but the practice was not compulsory.

INCIDENT

The crowd at the 1930 F.A. Cup Final had more than the match to watch. About 20 minutes after the game started the huge German airship, the *Graf Zeppelin*, appeared in the sky over Wembley Stadium, hovering there for some time. There is considerable disagreement as to exactly what happened in the minutes the airship was there.

POWER GAMES

During the 1929-1930 season, the Football League acquired a greater say in the running of the game in England after eight seats were won on the F.A. Council.

1932-33 – LEAGUE DIVISION 1 ARSENAL

Division 1 (top 6) at 26/12/32

1	ARSENAL	21	69-33	34
2	Aston Villa	21	51-33	28
3	Sheffield Wednesday	21	47-31	28
4	Leeds United	21	31-23	28
5	Derby County	21	46-33	27
6	Newcastle United	20	38-25	25

FINAL PHASE … AT THE TOP

By April 8th, Arsenal held a 3-point lead at the head of the 1st Division from Sheffield Wednesday. Back in third, a further 3 points from the top, were Aston Villa, who might yet manage to put pressure on the Gunners.

Top 4 at 08/04/33

1	ARSENAL	37	106-53	51	2.00
2	Sheffield Wednesday	37	74-57	48	1.30
3	Aston Villa	35	79-63	45	1.25
4	Newcastle United	36	62-47	45	1.32

(Figure in the right-hand column is goal average)

On April 14th, the top two clashed at Highbury, with Arsenal winning 4-2. Wednesday lost at home to Villa the following day, while Arsenal defeated Portsmouth 2-0 to end April 15th seven points clear at the head of the table. Aston Villa and Newcastle United then met twice at the end of the Easter fixtures, both winning the home game. This left the London side in need of one point from 3 matches. The 3-1 win at Chelsea on April 22nd meant Arsenal became champions.

Division 1 (bottom 6) at 26/12/32

17	Birmingham	21	30-32	17
18	Blackpool	21	33-46	17
19	Chelsea	21	30-44	16
20	Wolves	21	37-60	11
21	Middlesbrough	19	29-45	10
22	Leicester City	21	27-51	10

FINAL PHASE … AT THE BOTTOM

With only 3 points covering the bottom six clubs, there was the prospect of a nervy end to the campaign. Any club able to string 2-3 wins together over the final 5-6 matches had a decent chance of escaping the drop. There was precious little difference in the goal averages of the sides at the foot of the table.

Bottom 6 at 08/04/33

17	Bolton Wanderers	37	68-83	30	0.82
18	Chelsea	36	50-63	29	0.79
19	Middlesbrough	36	54-69	28	0.78
20	Wolves	36	68-88	28	0.77
21	Leicester City	36	58-76	28	0.76
22	Blackpool	37	61-80	27	0.76

(Figure in the right-hand column is goal average)

By the time the Easter fixtures were over on April 18th, both Chelsea and Middlesbrough had won twice, Bolton Wanderers and Leicester had lost twice, and Blackpool and Wolves were up to 30 points. Middlesbrough became the first to reach safety when winning 1-0 at Leeds on April 29th, Chelsea's 4-1 win at Manchester City on May 3rd securing their Division 1 status soon afterwards.

This left 4 strugglers going into the last day with the spectre of relegation hanging over them, with Wolves' draw at Blackpool on April 29th a key score as the end approached. Leicester and Wolves began the day on 33 points, with Bolton and Blackpool on 31. All four clubs won their May 6th matches, Bolton thrashing Leeds United 5-0 and Leicester adding West Bromwich Albion to their list of 'end-of-season victims' by 6-2. Bolton Wanderers and Blackpool were now relegated.

August	27	Birmingham	1-0
	31	WEST BROMWICH ALBION	1-2
September	03	SUNDERLAND	6-1
	10	Manchester City	3-2
	14	West Bromwich Albion	1-1
	17	BOLTON WANDERERS	3-2
	24	EVERTON	2-1
October	01	Blackpool	2-1
	08	DERBY COUNTY	3-3
	15	Blackburn Rovers	3-2
	22	Liverpool	3-2
	29	LEICESTER CITY	8-2
November	05	Wolves	7-1
	12	NEWCASTLE UNITED	1-0
	19	Aston Villa	3-5
	26	MIDDLESBROUGH	4-1
December	03	Portsmouth	3-1
	10	CHELSEA	4-1
	17	Huddersfield Town	1-0
	24	SHEFFIELD UNITED	9-2
	26	LEEDS UNITED	1-2
	27	Leeds United	0-0
	31	BIRMINGHAM	3-0
January	02	Sheffield Wednesday	2-3
	07	Sunderland	2-3
	21	MANCHESTER CITY	2-1
February	01	Bolton Wanderers	4-0
	04	Everton	1-1
	11	BLACKPOOL	1-1
	22	Derby County	2-2
	25	BLACKBURN ROVERS	8-0
March	04	LIVERPOOL	0-1
	11	Leicester City	1-1
	18	WOLVES	1-2
	25	Newcastle United	1-2
April	01	ASTON VILLA	5-0
	08	Middlesbrough	4-3
	14	SHEFFIELD WEDNESDAY	4-2
	15	PORTSMOUTH	2-0
	22	Chelsea	3-1
	29	HUDDERSFIELD TOWN	2-2
May	06	Sheffield United	1-3

1st Division Final Table 1932-33

1	ARSENAL	42	118	61	58
2	Aston Villa	42	92	67	54
3	Sheffield Wednesday	42	80	68	51
4	West Bromwich Albion	42	83	70	49
5	Newcastle United	42	71	63	49
6	Huddersfield Town	42	66	53	47
7	Derby County	42	76	69	44
8	Leeds United	42	59	62	44
9	Portsmouth	42	74	76	43
10	Sheffield United	42	74	80	43
11	Everton	42	81	74	41
12	Sunderland	42	63	80	40
13	Birmingham	42	57	57	39
14	Liverpool	42	79	84	39
15	Blackburn Rovers	42	76	102	38
16	Manchester City	42	68	71	37
17	Chelsea	42	63	73	37
18	Middlesbrough	42	63	73	35
19	Leicester City	42	75	89	35
20	Wolves	42	80	96	35
21	Bolton Wanderers	42	78	92	33
22	Blackpool	42	69	85	33
		924	1645	1645	924

Bolton Wanderers and Blackpool were relegated.

1932-33 – LEAGUE DIVISION 2

STOKE CITY

Division 2 (top 6) at 26/12/32

1	STOKE CITY	21	38-18	30
2	Bradford City	21	42-20	29
3	Bury	21	40-28	28
4	Swansea Town	21	30-26	27
5	Tottenham Hotspur	21	58-29	26
6	Fulham	20	41-35	23

As Easter approached, Stoke City and Tottenham Hotspur seemed to be on course for Division 1 and likely to contest the title battle rather than worry about missing out on promotion. Bury and Fulham might be able to apply pressure, but there was an important gap between second and third.

Top 4 at 08/04/33

1	STOKE CITY	36	63-31	48	2.03
2	Tottenham Hotspur	35	88-46	47	1.91
3	Bury	37	77-53	44	1.45
4	Fulham	36	72-61	43	1.18

(Figure in the right-hand column is goal average)

Good Friday results changed the picture slightly. Stoke lost at lowly Charlton, Spurs were held at home by Plymouth Argyle and Fulham beat Preston North End 1-0. All the top 3 won their matches the next day and both Stoke and Fulham won again on Easter Monday, April 17th. Spurs drew again with Plymouth and began to cast nervous backward glances as Fulham were now just 2 points behind and next up at White Hart Lane. The pair drew 0-0 on April 22nd maintaining the status quo between them, which favoured Stoke, whose 5-2 win over Lincoln City left them needing 1 point for promotion.

Spurs drew 1-1 at Burnley on April 24th to create a 3-point lead over Fulham and keep their title ambitions afloat with 2 games left. When Fulham lost to Grimsby Town on April 29th, the top two were promoted, despite both losing and the title was decided on May 6th when Stoke defeated Bradford City 4-1 to finish a point clear of Tottenham.

Division 2 (bottom 6) at 26/12/32

17	Grimsby Town	21	31-44	18
18	West Ham United	21	43-55	16
19	Burnley	21	35-46	15
20	Preston North End	21	36-49	15
21	Chesterfield	20	27-41	14
22	Charlton Athletic	20	26-52	11

FINAL PHASE ... AT THE BOTTOM

Four clubs were still in trouble on the eve of Easter 1933, with West Ham United and Chesterfield due to play each other twice over the holiday period and Charlton Athletic to play the Derbyshire men on the last day of the season.

Bottom 4 at 08/04/33

19	Burnley	35	59-69	29	0.86
20	West Ham United	36	59-69	27	0.86
21	Charlton Athletic	35	64-83	27	0.77
22	Chesterfield	36	53-74	27	0.72

(Figure in the right-hand column is goal average)

Burnley drew with Oldham on Good Friday, Charlton beat Stoke and Chesterfield moved off the bottom by winning 1-0 against West Ham, who sank to 22nd place. This seemed to wake the Hammers up - they won their next 2 games, leaving twice-beaten Charlton and Chesterfield in the relegation slots after the April 17th fixtures were over. A further West Ham win (2-1 v. Manchester United), on April 22nd, when Burnley also won, piled the pressure on the bottom 2, Charlton having a 3rd loss in a row and Chesterfield drawing at Grimsby Town. Charlton earned a much-needed victory over Port Vale 4 days later, but lost again on April 29th and were relegated as West Ham beat Tottenham, from whom Burnley had also taken a point earlier in the week. Hammers were safe, but Burnley needed 1 more point from their final game, at home to Bury on May 6th. A 1-0 win took the Turf Moor club out of reach of Chesterfield, who went down despite a 5-2 win at Charlton.

August	27	Manchester United	2-0
	29	MILLWALL	1-2
September	03	TOTTENHAM HOTSPUR	2-0
	05	Millwall	0-0
	10	Grimsby Town	1-0
	17	OLDHAM ATHLETIC	4-0
	24	Preston North End	3-1
October	01	BURNLEY	3-0
	08	Bradford Park Avenue	2-2
	15	PLYMOUTH ARGYLE	2-0
	22	PORT VALE	1-0
	29	Notts County	4-3
November	05	SWANSEA TOWN	2-0
	12	Southampton	0-1
	19	WEST HAM UNITED	0-0
	26	Fulham	3-1
December	03	CHESTERFIELD	2-1
	10	Lincoln City	3-2
	17	BURY	2-3
	24	Bradford City	1-1
	26	NOTTINGHAM FOREST	0-1
	27	Nottingham Forest	0-1
	31	MANCHESTER UNITED	0-0
January	07	Tottenham Hotspur	2-3
	21	GRIMSBY TOWN	2-0
	31	Oldham Athletic	4-0
February	04	PRESTON NORTH END	1-1
	11	Burnley	2-1
	18	BRADFORD PARK AVENUE	4-0
	25	Plymouth Argyle	0-1
March	04	Port Vale	3-1
	11	NOTTS COUNTY	0-2
	18	Swansea Town	2-0
	25	SOUTHAMPTON	3-1
April	01	West Ham United	2-1
	08	FULHAM	0-1
	14	Charlton Athletic	0-1
	15	Chesterfield	2-1
	17	CHARLTON ATHLETIC	2-0
	22	LINCOLN CITY	5-2
	29	Bury	2-3
May	06	BRADFORD CITY	4-1

2nd Division Final Table 1932-33

1	STOKE CITY	42	78	39	56
2	Tottenham Hotspur	42	96	51	55
3	Fulham	42	78	65	50
4	Bury	42	84	59	49
5	Nottingham Forest	42	67	59	49
6	Manchester United	42	71	68	43
7	Millwall	42	59	57	43
8	Bradford Park Avenue	42	77	71	42
9	Preston North End	42	74	70	42
10	Swansea Town	42	50	54	42
11	Bradford City	42	65	61	41
12	Southampton	42	66	66	41
13	Grimsby Town	42	79	84	41
14	Plymouth Argyle	42	63	67	41
15	Notts County	42	67	78	40
16	Oldham Athletic	42	67	80	38
17	Port Vale	42	66	79	38
18	Lincoln City	42	72	87	37
19	Burnley	42	67	79	36
20	West Ham United	42	75	93	35
21	Chesterfield	42	61	84	34
22	Charlton Athletic	42	60	91	31
		924	1542	1542	924

Stoke City and Tottenham Hotspur were promoted. Chesterfield (North) and Charlton Athletic (South) were relegated to Division 3.

1932-33 DIVISION 3 (NORTH)   HULL CITY

Division 3 (North) (top 6) at 31/12/32

1	Chester	23	51-28	32
2	HULL CITY	21	47-23	29
3	Barnsley	23	56-49	26
4	Barrow	20	32-23	25
5	Gateshead	21	43-31	25
6	Wrexham	20	52-35	24

FINAL PHASE ... AT THE TOP

By mid-April, it was a case of 'all to play for' at the top of Division 3 (North). Hull City led the way, with Chester for company, on 51 points, though Wrexham still looked as if they might stage a late title push.

Top 4 at 15/04/33

1	HULL CITY	37	88-40	51	2.20
2	Chester	38	86-50	51	1.72
3	Wrexham	36	98-50	48	1.96
4	Stockport County	38	82-49	46	1.67

(Figure in the right-hand column is goal average)

Hull City went clear at the top on April 17th after a 3-0 victory over Tranmere Rovers while Chester were losing 0-2 at Rochdale. Wrexham also won 3-0 to remain a threat. Hull won again on the 22nd, 2-1 at York, and Wrexham moved 2nd after a 2-0 success at Rotherham. Two days later, the North Wales club drew with Tranmere and so failed to exert strong pressure on the leaders. Both the top two won their games on the 29th, leaving 2 matches each to play and their rivals now out of the running. Stockport still had a crucial role to play, however, beating Wrexham 1-0 on May 1st. Hull City beat York 2-1 on the same day and became champions.

Division 3 (North) (bottom 6) at 31/12/32

17	Halifax Town	22	34-40	17
18	York City	20	36-44	17
19	Carlisle United	21	19-27	17
20	Hartlepools United	21	44-68	14
21	New Brighton	22	29-56	14
22	Darlington	19	29-43	13

FINAL PHASE ... AT THE BOTTOM

Rochdale propped up the section again as the final stages were reached. This time, however, things were much tighter at the foot of Division 3 (North) with none of the bottom six clear from the possibility of having to seek re-election.

Bottom 6 at 15/04/33

17	York City	36	62-82	30	0.76
18	Carlisle United	37	43-64	29	0.67
19	Rotherham United	37	50-78	29	0.64
20	New Brighton	38	60-84	28	0.71
21	Darlington	37	60-90	26	0.67
22	Rochdale	37	43-73	25	0.59

(Figure in the right-hand column is goal average)

By April 22nd, things had changed significantly. Rochdale had won twice, York and Darlington had lost twice, and all the other three strugglers had gained at least two points. York and Darlington lost again over the next 5 days, while Carlisle moved up to 33 points by beating the Quakers. Defeats for Rochdale and York on April 29th left both sides in trouble, while Darlington thumped Carlisle 5-2 to keep their hopes alive. Rotherham and New Brighton failed to pull clear, but, despite losing, Carlisle could at last breathe easily. York suffered another reverse on May 1st, slipping to 21st place a day later, May 2nd, when Rochdale won 3-0 at Accrington and ended Darlington's hopes of avoiding re-election. This meant that one re-election spot remained to be filled when the final day of the season, May 6th, arrived. Rotherham United and York City both won their closing matches 6-1, while Rochdale defeated Hull City 3-2. New Brighton, who lost 0-2 at Wrexham, slipped two places to 21st and faced re-election.

- 134 -

August	27	Walsall	0-1
	29	WREXHAM	4-1
September	03	GATESHEAD	1-1
	07	Wrexham	1-3
	10	Stockport County	5-3
	17	DARLINGTON	3-1
	24	Doncaster Rovers	1-1
October	01	SOUTHPORT	4-0
	08	BARNSLEY	5-1
	15	Hartlepools United	1-0
	22	Mansfield Town	1-2
	29	ROTHERHAM UNITED	4-2
November	05	Accrington Stanley	2-1
	12	NEW BRIGHTON	5-0
	19	Chester	1-1
December	03	Carlisle United	1-1
	17	Crewe Alexandra	1-1
	24	ROCHDALE	1-1
	26	HALIFAX TOWN	3-1
	27	Halifax Town	3-1
	31	WALSALL	0-0
January	07	Gateshead	3-2
	19	BARROW	3-0
	21	STOCKPORT COUNTY	3-0
February	01	Darlington	2-3
	04	DONCASTER ROVERS	6-1
	11	Southport	1-0
	18	Barnsley	0-1
	25	HARTLEPOOLS UNITED	3-0
March	04	MANSFIELD TOWN	4-1
	11	Rotherham United	2-3
	18	ACCRINGTON STANLEY	4-2
	25	New Brighton	0-1
April	01	CHESTER	2-0
	08	Barrow	2-0
	14	Tranmere Rovers	0-2
	15	CARLISLE UNITED	6-1
	17	TRANMERE ROVERS	3-0
	22	York City	2-1
	29	CREWE ALEXANDRA	3-0
May	01	YORK CITY	2-1
	06	Rochdale	2-3

3rd Division (North) Final Table 1932-33

1	HULL CITY	42	100	45	59
2	Wrexham	42	106	51	57
3	Stockport County	42	99	58	54
4	Chester	42	94	66	52
5	Walsall	42	75	58	48
6	Doncaster Rovers	42	77	79	48
7	Gateshead	42	78	67	47
8	Barnsley	42	92	80	46
9	Barrow	42	60	60	43
10	Crewe Alexandra	42	80	84	43
11	Tranmere Rovers	42	70	66	42
12	Southport	42	70	67	41
13	Accrington Stanley	42	78	76	40
14	Hartlepools United	42	87	116	39
15	Halifax Town	42	71	90	38
16	Mansfield Town	42	84	100	35
17	Rotherham United	42	60	84	34
18	Rochdale	42	58	80	33
19	Carlisle United	42	51	75	33
20	York City	42	72	92	32
21	New Brighton	42	63	88	32
22	Darlington	42	66	109	28
		924	1691	1691	924

Hull City were promoted to Division 2. *Darlington* and *New Brighton* (47 votes each) were both re-elected, leaving the only other applicant, Scarborough (4), unsuccessful.

1932-33 – DIVISION 3 (SOUTH)

Division 3 (South) (top 6) at 31/12/32

1	BRENTFORD	21	43-21	34
2	Reading	21	54-30	29
3	Exeter City	21	46-27	28
4	Norwich City	21	39-23	28
5	Crystal Palace	22	41-32	26
6	Southend United	22	37-41	23

FINAL PHASE ... AT THE TOP

Three teams were still slugging it out at the head of the section by the end of April 8th. Brentford, with a 1-point lead and fewer games played were in a strong position, but neither Norwich nor Exeter were ready to concede.

Top 3 at 08/04/33

1	BRENTFORD	34	78-41	50	1.90
2	Norwich City	36	78-47	49	1.66
3	Exeter City	35	77-41	48	1.88

(Figure in the right-hand column is goal average)

Brentford's hopes of finishing on top of the pile were improved by results on April 14th. The Bees overcame Bristol City at Griffin Park, while Norwich crashed 0-4 at Crystal Palace and Exeter drew 2-2 at Clapton Orient. A day later, the leaders' match with Norwich ended 2-2, leaving a 3-point gap between the two, and although Exeter won 1-0 against Bristol Rovers, Brentford were 2 points ahead of the Grecians with a game in hand.

All the top three won their Easter Monday matches and there were 2-1 victories for both Brentford and Norwich City on April 22nd. Exeter, on the other hand, fell 1-4 at Aldershot, leaving Brentford needing just three points from 4 games to become champions. Only one of these matches was needed. On April 26th, Brentford defeated Brighton & Hove Albion 2-1 to move onto 59 points. Exeter City drew 0-0 with Aldershot and could now only reach 58 – Brentford were champions.

Division 3 (South) (bottom 6) at 31/12/32

17	Queen's Park Rangers	21	39-45	18
18	Bristol City	21	37-42	17
19	Clapton Orient	22	29-50	17
20	Swindon Town	21	40-54	16
21	Cardiff City	21	37-51	16
22	Newport County	22	27-59	12

FINAL PHASE ... AT THE BOTTOM

There was little to choose between the bottom four as the final phase began. Cardiff City held a point advantage over their rivals, the most troubled of whom was Newport County, who had played more matches than any of the others.

Bottom 4 at 08/04/33

19	Cardiff City	35	57-88	26	0.65
20	Clapton Orient	36	51-82	25	0.62
21	Swindon Town	35	53-89	25	0.60
22	Newport County	38	53-98	25	0.54

(Figure in the right-hand column is goal average)

Newport County had the best Easter of the bottom 4, winning both their games to end the holiday period on 29 points from 40 games. By beating Northampton Town 6-0 on April 22nd, Cardiff City got to the same situation, following an awful run of three losses and a draw. The Welsh pair headed Swindon Town (28 from 39) and Clapton Orient (27 from 40) by this stage, after poor returns from their Easter fixtures. Swindon added a point to their total by drawing with Gillingham 1-1 on the 26th, but the real difference was made on April 29th. In a key clash, Orient beat Cardiff 3-0, while defeats for the other two left all four strugglers on 29 points with only the May 6th games left. Cardiff City beat Swindon Town 3-0 and pulled clear. Both Clapton and Newport lost. Goal average was used to separate the last three, with Orient escaping re-election.

BRENTFORD

August	27	Queen's Park Rangers	3-2
	29	Coventry City	3-2
September	03	TORQUAY UNITED	3-1
	08	COVENTRY CITY	2-1
	10	Exeter City	2-1
	17	LUTON TOWN	1-0
	24	Newport County	6-1
October	01	BOURNEMOUTH & B.A.	1-1
	08	Swindon Town	0-0
	15	CLAPTON ORIENT	4-2
	22	Southend United	1-0
	29	CRYSTAL PALACE	2-0
November	05	Gillingham	3-1
	12	WATFORD	2-1
	19	Cardiff City	1-2
December	03	Norwich City	0-3
	17	Bristol Rovers	4-2
	24	ALDERSHOT	2-0
	26	Northampton Town	0-1
	27	NORTHAMPTON TOWN	1-0
	31	QUEEN'S PARK RANGERS	2-0
January	07	Torquay United	1-1
	21	EXETER CITY	0-2
February	01	Luton Town	5-5
	04	NEWPORT COUNTY	6-0
	11	Bournemouth & B.A.	1-1
	18	SWINDON TOWN	1-0
	25	Clapton Orient	5-1
March	04	SOUTHEND UNITED	3-1
	11	Crystal Palace	1-2
	18	GILLINGHAM	1-2
	25	Watford	1-1
April	01	CARDIFF CITY	7-3
	08	Reading	3-1
	14	Bristol City	2-1
	15	NORWICH CITY	2-2
	17	BRISTOL CITY	2-1
	22	Brighton & Hove Albion	2-1
	26	BRIGHTON & HOVE ALBION	2-1
	29	BRISTOL ROVERS	0-0
May	03	READING	1-1
	06	Aldershot	1-1

3rd Division (South) Final Table 1932-33

1	BRENTFORD	42	90	49	62
2	Exeter City	42	88	48	58
3	Norwich City	42	88	55	57
4	Reading	42	103	71	51
5	Crystal Palace	42	78	64	46
6	Coventry City	42	106	77	44
7	Gillingham	42	72	61	44
8	Northampton Town	42	76	66	44
9	Bristol Rovers	42	61	56	44
10	Torquay United	42	72	67	44
11	Watford	42	66	63	44
12	Brighton & Hove Albion	42	66	65	42
13	Southend United	42	65	82	41
14	Luton Town	42	78	78	39
15	Bristol City	42	83	90	37
16	Queen's Park Rangers	42	72	87	37
17	Aldershot	42	61	72	36
18	Bournemouth & B.A.	42	60	81	36
19	Cardiff City	42	69	99	31
20	Clapton Orient	42	59	93	29
21	Newport County	42	61	105	29
22	Swindon Town	42	60	105	29
		924	1634	1634	924

Brentford were promoted to Division 2. *Swindon Town* (45 votes) and *Newport County* (26) were re-elected, having finished ahead of Llanelli (20), Folkestone (5), Merthyr Town (1) and Nuneaton (1) in the voting.

1933-34 – LEAGUE DIVISION 1   ARSENAL

Division 1 (top 6) at 25/12/33

1	ARSENAL	21	39-20	31
2	Derby County	20	41-21	28
3	Huddersfield Town	21	49-34	27
4	Tottenham Hotspur	21	38-23	26
5	Manchester City	21	29-32	24
6	West Bromwich Albion	20	33-26	23

FINAL PHASE … AT THE TOP

Mid-April arrived with reigning champions once again in pole position with four games to go. 4 points behind the leaders lay Huddersfield Town, the only team left who could scupper the Gunners' chances of another success.

Top 2 at 14/04/34

1	ARSENAL	38	69-43	54	1.60
2	Huddersfield Town	38	81-54	50	1.50

(Figure in the right-hand column is goal average)

Huddersfield's hopes received a boost on April 18th when their rivals lost 0-1 at Portsmouth. Any further slip by Arsenal and Town needed to be ready to pounce. As it turned out though, it was Huddersfield who faltered, losing 0-3 at Middlesbrough on April 21st, while Arsenal defeated Sunderland 2-1. Town beat Everton 1-0 on the 25th to keep their much-faded hopes just about alive, but the race ended on April 28th when the point Arsenal needed to retain their title was gathered in a 2-2 draw at Chelsea. 5-3 winners against Blackburn Rovers at Leeds Road, Huddersfield had to settle for second place.

Division 1 (bottom 6) at 25/12/33

17	Newcastle United	21	31-40	18
18	Birmingham	20	21-20	17
19	Stoke City	21	22-40	17
20	Leicester City	20	28-33	15
21	Sheffield United	21	26-54	15
22	Chelsea	20	24-47	9

FINAL PHASE … AT THE BOTTOM

Sheffield United's fate was virtually sealed by the middle of April, with the struggling Blades 4 points behind 20th-placed Birmingham, who headed Newcastle United by 0.04 of a goal, with both sides a point down on Chelsea. The Londoners had, however, played two games fewer than the Geordies and one less than Birmingham.

Bottom 4 at 14/04/34

19	Chelsea	38	60-60	33	1.00
20	Birmingham	39	44-50	32	0.88
21	Newcastle United	40	62-74	32	0.84
22	Sheffield United	39	55-98	28	0.56

(Figure in the right-hand column is goal average)

The first relegation issue was settled on April 21st when Sheffield United's expected demotion was confirmed. The Blades drew at Leeds United, but home wins for both Birmingham and Newcastle meant these clubs pulled out of reach. Chelsea, 2-4 losers at Manchester City slipped to 21st in the table. Two days later, however, the Stamford Bridge side clambered back up to 19th place by beating Leicester City 2-0.

The second relegation place was sorted out on April 28th. Chelsea, with a vastly superior goal average to their rivals, needed a draw against Arsenal, who needed only a point to become champions. Both teams got what they wanted from a match ending 2-2. Birmingham and Newcastle both needed to win. The Blues did – 7-3 at Leicester. The Tyneside club did not, losing 1-2 at Stoke City and dropping out of Division 1 as a result.

August	26	BIRMINGHAM	1-1
September	02	Sheffield Wednesday	2-1
	06	WEST BROMWICH ALBION	3-1
	09	MANCHESTER CITY	1-1
	13	West Bromwich Albion	0-1
	16	Tottenham Hotspur	1-1
	23	Everton	1-3
	30	MIDDLESBROUGH	6-0
October	07	Blackburn Rovers	2-2
	14	NEWCASTLE UNITED	3-0
	21	LEICESTER CITY	2-0
	28	Aston Villa	3-2
November	04	PORTSMOUTH	1-1
	11	Wolves	1-0
	18	STOKE CITY	3-0
	25	Huddersfield Town	1-0
December	02	LIVERPOOL	2-1
	09	Sunderland	0-3
	16	CHELSEA	2-1
	23	Sheffield United	3-1
	25	Leeds United	1-0
	26	LEEDS UNITED	2-0
	30	Birmingham	0-0
January	06	SHEFFIELD WEDNESDAY	1-1
	20	Manchester City	1-2
	31	TOTTENHAM HOTSPUR	1-3
February	03	EVERTON	1-2
	10	Middlesbrough	2-0
	21	BLACKBURN ROVERS	2-1
	24	Newcastle United	1-0
March	08	Leicester City	1-4
	10	ASTON VILLA	3-2
	24	WOLVES	3-2
	30	DERBY COUNTY	1-0
	31	Stoke City	1-1
April	02	Derby County	4-2
	07	HUDDERSFIELD TOWN	3-1
	14	Liverpool	3-2
	18	Portsmouth	0-1
	21	SUNDERLAND	2-1
	28	Chelsea	2-2
May	05	SHEFFIELD UNITED	2-0

1st Division Final Table 1933-34

1	ARSENAL	42	75	47	59
2	Huddersfield Town	42	90	61	56
3	Tottenham Hotspur	42	79	56	49
4	Derby County	42	68	54	45
5	Manchester City	42	65	72	45
6	Sunderland	42	81	56	44
7	West Bromwich Albion	42	78	70	44
8	Blackburn Rovers	42	74	81	43
9	Leeds United	42	75	66	42
10	Portsmouth	42	52	55	42
11	Sheffield Wednesday	42	62	67	41
12	Stoke City	42	58	71	41
13	Aston Villa	42	78	75	40
14	Everton	42	62	63	40
15	Wolves	42	74	86	40
16	Middlesbrough	42	68	80	39
17	Leicester City	42	59	74	39
18	Liverpool	42	79	87	38
19	Chelsea	42	67	69	36
20	Birmingham	42	54	56	36
21	Newcastle United	42	68	77	34
22	Sheffield United	42	58	101	31
		924	1524	1524	924

Newcastle United and Sheffield United were relegated.

1933-34 – LEAGUE DIVISION 2 GRIMSBY TOWN

Division 2 (top 6) at 25/12/33

1	GRIMSBY TOWN	21	52-27	30
2	Blackpool	21	35-23	26
3	Brentford	21	47-35	25
4	Bolton Wanderers	21	40-32	25
5	West Ham United	21	44-34	23
6	Preston North End	21	37-29	23

FINAL PHASE … AT THE TOP

By the end of March, Grimsby Town were on the verge of promotion back to Division 1 and their 8-point lead suggested only a dramatic slump could deprive them of the title. Who else would go up was much harder to work out as the contest for second place was a much tighter affair.

Top 5 at 31/03/34

1	GRIMSBY TOWN	36	87-51	51	1.71
2	Bolton Wanderers	36	69-51	43	1.353
3	Brentford	36	73-54	43	1.352
4	Preston North End	36	65-49	42	1.37
5	Bradford Park Avenue	35	71-61	40	1.16

(Figure in the right-hand column is goal average)

Grimsby eased closer to their goals by beating Brentford 2-1 at Griffin Park on April 2nd. Bolton Wanderers and Preston moved above the Bees and Bradford suggested they might be contenders for promotion by sinking Burnley 5-0 on April 3rd. Grimsby Town took the 2nd Division crown on April 7th with a 1-0 win at Hull City, while Preston moved into 2nd spot by winning 1-0 at Lincoln.

Home defeat by Bury on April 14th cost North End their place after both Bolton and Brentford won, but results worked out in the Deepdale side's favour a week later when victory at Hull left them level with Bolton, though slightly worse off in terms of goal average. After the games played on the 28th, Bolton and Preston had 50 points, Brentford had 49 and Bradford had 48. There was one away match left for each club. The key games of May 5th resulted in Bolton drawing 2-2 at relegated Lincoln while Preston won at Southampton and went up.

Division 2 (bottom 6) at 25/12/33

17	Manchester United	21	32-42	19
18	Bury	21	31-45	19
19	Burnley	21	31-39	18
20	Swansea Town	21	28-35	16
21	Millwall	21	15-29	16
22	Lincoln City	21	16-29	15

FINAL PHASE … AT THE BOTTOM

As the season reached April, Lincoln City were in deep trouble, being 4 points adrift of three other worried clubs, all on 27 points. Importantly, Manchester United's last two games would be against Swansea Town and Millwall.

Bottom 4 at 31/03/34

19	Swansea Town	36	44-56	27	0.79
20	Manchester United	36	52-81	27	0.64
21	Millwall	35	34-58	27	0.59
22	Lincoln City	36	38-63	23	0.60

(Figure in the right-hand column is goal average)

Lincoln City were relegated on April 14th after losing 3 more times, without scoring. Above the Imps, Millwall and Swansea had both picked up 4 more points by this time, having won twice each, while Manchester United, with a win and a draw were in 21st place. United were a point behind their rivals and all three had 3 games left. The position worsened for the Old Trafford club on April 21st, despite a point being earned at Notts County, because Swansea also drew and Millwall beat Brentford. United remained next-to-bottom after the games of April 28th when they drew 1-1 with Swansea. There was some good news though – Millwall had lost 0-5 at Bolton and were only one point ahead. On May 5th, Manchester United arrived at The Den needing to win to stay up. A 2-0 victory did the job and Millwall were the ones to go down.

August	26	BURNLEY	1-0
	29	BOLTON WANDERERS	2-3
September	02	Oldham Athletic	5-1
	04	Bolton Wanderers	4-0
	09	PRESTON NORTH END	3-0
	16	Bradford Park Avenue	1-2
	23	PORT VALE	1-2
	30	NOTTINGHAM FOREST	2-1
October	07	West Ham United	1-3
	14	PLYMOUTH ARGYLE	5-1
	21	Notts County	2-1
	28	SWANSEA TOWN	3-1
November	04	Millwall	1-0
	11	LINCOLN CITY	3-0
	18	Bury	3-1
	25	HULL CITY	4-1
December	02	Fulham	0-1
	09	SOUTHAMPTON	3-1
	16	Blackpool	4-3
	23	BRADFORD CITY	1-4
	25	Manchester United	3-1
	26	MANCHESTER UNITED	7-3
	30	Burnley	0-2
January	06	OLDHAM ATHLETIC	2-1
	20	Preston North End	2-1
	30	BRADFORD PARK AVENUE	3-2
February	05	Port Vale	1-0
	10	Nottingham Forest	2-4
	17	WEST HAM UNITED	1-1
	24	Plymouth Argyle	2-0
March	03	NOTTS COUNTY	2-2
	10	Swansea Town	1-1
	17	MILLWALL	5-2
	24	Lincoln City	3-3
	30	BRENTFORD	2-2
	31	BURY	2-0
April	02	Brentford	2-1
	07	Hull City	1-0
	14	FULHAM	3-1
	21	Southampton	2-4
	28	BLACKPOOL	7-0
May	05	Bradford City	1-2

2nd Division Final Table 1933-34

1	GRIMSBY TOWN	42	103	59	59
2	Preston North End	42	71	52	52
3	Bolton Wanderers	42	79	55	51
4	Brentford	42	85	60	51
5	Bradford Park Avenue	42	86	67	49
6	Bradford City	42	73	67	46
7	West Ham United	42	78	70	45
8	Port Vale	42	60	55	45
9	Oldham Athletic	42	72	60	44
10	Plymouth Argyle	42	69	70	43
11	Blackpool	42	62	64	43
12	Bury	42	70	73	43
13	Burnley	42	60	72	42
14	Southampton	42	54	58	38
15	Hull City	42	52	68	38
16	Fulham	42	48	67	37
17	Nottingham Forest	42	73	74	35
18	Notts County	42	53	62	35
19	Swansea Town	42	51	60	35
20	Manchester United	42	59	85	34
21	Millwall	42	39	68	33
22	Lincoln City	42	44	75	26
		924	1441	1441	924

Grimsby Town and Preston North End were promoted. Millwall (South) and Lincoln City (North) were relegated to Division 3.

1933-34 – DIVISION 3 (NORTH) BARNSLEY

Division 3 (North) (top 6) at 30/12/33

1	Chesterfield	22	51-20	34
2	Stockport County	21	51-25	30
3	Walsall	21	44-24	28
4	Halifax Town	21	39-34	26
5	BARNSLEY	21	52-42	25
6	Tranmere Rovers	20	41-23	24

FINAL PHASE ... AT THE TOP

With 3 games left to play, the battle to take the 3rd Division North's single promotion place had the look of having turned into a straight fight between Chesterfield and Barnsley. In third place, Stockport County were not completely out of contention, but it would take a peculiar turn of events for the Cheshire side to emerge as champions.

Top 3 at 14/04/34

1	Chesterfield	39	82-41	58	2.00
2	BARNSLEY	39	111-58	57	1.91
3	Stockport County	38	111-49	54	2.27

(Figure in the right-hand column is goal average)

On April 21st, Chesterfield lost 0-2 at Barrow. Barnsley drew 1-1 at Halifax Town and pulled level on points at the top, though Chesterfield still led the table by virtue of their superior goal average. Stockport County beat Tranmere 2-1 to move closer, but only drew against the same opposition two days later and missed the chance to go top.

The Hatters were held again on the 28th, at Rochdale, and both the top two won their home games to reach 60 points with one fixture left. Importantly, Chesterfield had to go to Stockport on May 5th and this game ended in a 0-0 draw. At New Brighton, Barnsley faced an easier test and won 1-0 to take 2 points and the title.

Division 3 (North) (bottome 6) at 30/12/33

17	Carlisle United	21	26-38	18
18	New Brighton	21	24-37	17
19	Darlington	22	35-52	16
20	Rotherham United	20	26-39	16
21	Mansfield Town	22	29-45	15
22	Rochdale	21	27-44	15

FINAL PHASE ... AT THE BOTTOM

One re-election place was already filled by April 14th, Rochdale again facing a cap-in-hand trip to the League A.G.M.. The struggle to avoid a similar fate involved 7 other teams by this stage and the scrap for points looked likely to go down to the wire.

Bottom 8 at 14/04/34

15	Gateshead	38	72-87	33	0.83
16	Southport	40	62-85	33	0.73
17	Accrington Stanley	39	64-89	33	0.72
18	Chester	38	77-85	32	0.91
19	Crewe Alexandra	39	74-90	32	0.82
20	Mansfield Town	39	73-83	30	0.88
21	Rotherham United	39	51-82	28	0.62
22	Rochdale	39	50-95	23	0.53

(Figure in the right-hand column is goal average)

Rotherham United's 1-3 home defeat by Wrexham on April 21st meant 5 of the 7 sides worried by the re-election threat were now 'free' and could relax. A couple of them rather overdid the 'take it easy finish', Accrington losing twice without scoring and Gateshead conceding a scary 19 goals in their last 3 games, including dipping 1-12 at Barrow on May 5th. By the time the Laides were crushed at Holker Street, the second re-election spot had been sorted out. On April 28th, Mansfield Town beat New Brighton 5-2, while Rotherham lost 0-4 at Hartlepools United. This set of results left Rotherham doomed to a bottom-2 finish and seeking re-election.

August	26	WREXHAM	3-0
	28	Rotherham United	2-0
September	02	Southport	2-2
	09	DARLINGTON	4-0
	16	Gateshead	4-1
	23	ACCRINGTON STANLEY	6-0
	30	Chesterfield	0-3
October	07	ROCHDALE	4-1
	14	Tranmere Rovers	2-5
	21	Walsall	1-5
	28	YORK CITY	1-0
November	04	Chester	2-4
	11	DONCASTER ROVERS	2-2
	18	Barrow	4-3
December	02	Stockport County	1-1
	09	Rochdale	1-3
	16	Crewe Alexandra	2-4
	23	NEW BRIGHTON	2-0
	25	Hartlepools United	2-0
	26	HARTLEPOOLS UNITED	5-4
	30	Wrexham	2-4
January	01	ROTHERHAM UNITED	5-1
	06	SOUTHPORT	3-2
	13	CARLISLE UNITED	1-0
	20	Darlington	4-0
	27	GATESHEAD	0-0
February	03	Accrington Stanley	9-0
	10	CHESTERFIELD	3-2
	19	HALIFAX TOWN	1-0
	24	TRANMERE ROVERS	5-1
March	03	WALSALL	1-1
	10	York City	1-1
	17	CHESTER	2-0
	24	Doncaster Rovers	4-4
	30	Mansfield Town	5-1
	31	BARROW	3-1
April	02	MANSFIELD TOWN	6-1
	07	Carlisle United	4-1
	14	STOCKPORT COUNTY	2-0
	21	Halifax Town	1-1
	28	CREWE ALEXANDRA	5-2
May	05	New Brighton	1-0

3rd Division (North) Final Table 1933-34

1	BARNSLEY	42	118	61	62
2	Chesterfield	42	86	43	61
3	Stockport County	42	115	52	59
4	Walsall	42	97	60	53
5	Doncaster Rovers	42	83	61	53
6	Wrexham	42	102	73	51
7	Tranmere Rovers	42	84	63	47
8	Barrow	42	116	94	47
9	Halifax Town	42	80	91	44
10	Chester	42	89	86	40
11	Hartlepools United	42	89	93	39
12	York City	42	71	74	38
13	Carlisle United	42	66	81	38
14	Crewe Alexandra	42	81	97	36
15	New Brighton	42	62	87	36
16	Darlington	42	70	101	35
17	Mansfield Town	42	81	88	34
18	Southport	42	63	90	33
19	Gateshead	42	76	110	33
20	Accrington Stanley	42	65	101	33
21	Rotherham United	42	53	91	28
22	Rochdale	42	53	103	24
		924	1800	1800	924

Barnsley were promoted to Division 2. *Rotherham United* and *Rochdale* were re-elected without a vote being needed as there were no other applicants.

1933-34 – DIVISION 3 (SOUTH)

Division 3 (South) (top 6) 26/12/33

1	NORWICH CITY	21	47-27	30
2	Queen's Park Rangers	20	40-21	28
3	Coventry City	21	49-27	27
4	Reading	20	45-25	26
5	Charlton Athletic	20	49-30	26
6	Exeter City	22	41-32	24

FINAL PHASE ... AT THE TOP

By the end of March, Norwich City were seven points clear of the field. The Canaries had played one more game than their closest rivals, but there seemed enough daylight between the Carrow Road club and the others for it to be a foregone conclusion as to who would win the title.

Top 4 at 31/03/34

1	NORWICH CITY	36	80-45	53	1.78
2	Queen's Park Rangers	35	58-42	46	1.38
3	Coventry City	35	77-45	44	1.71
4	Reading	35	70-44	43	1.59

(Figure in the right-hand column is goal average)

Wins over Newport County and Watford in their first 2 games of April kept Norwich on course for promotion, but the chasing group continued their pursuit of the leaders, with Coventry City's victory over Queen's Park Rangers on April 7th being the only case of a reverse among the three contenders. When, on April 14th, Reading beat Norwich 1-0 there seemed hope that the leaders could still be caught, but this proved to be only an illusion. On the 18th, Q.P.R. lost at Bristol Rovers and Reading were held at home by Bristol City. On April 21st, Norwich City defeated Coventry City 3-1 and this sealed their title success.

Division 3 (South) (bottom 6) at 26/12/33

17	Newport County	20	19-29	17
18	Watford	21	35-35	16
19	Gillingham	20	36-48	16
20	Southend United	20	21-33	16
21	Bristol City	20	26-44	14
22	Cardiff City	20	28-50	13

FINAL PHASE ... AT THE BOTTOM

Cardiff City had the look of a doomed side as April began. Ten years after almost winning the 1st Division, the Bluebirds were 5 points from safety at the foot of Division 3 (South) with only 7 matches outstanding. None of the 5 clubs above them were safe yet, however.

Bottom 6 at 31/03/34

17	Bristol City	34	49-66	29	0.74
18	Newport County	36	41-59	29	0.69
19	Gillingham	35	64-80	27	0.80
20	Torquay United	35	41-80	26	0.51
21	Bournemouth & B.A.	34	52-79	24	0.66
22	Cardiff City	35	48-85	21	0.56

(Figure in the right-hand column is goal average)

Torquay United and Gillingham both managed two wins by April 11th, something which eluded the other four clubs near the foot of Division 3 (South). Cardiff City, who drew with Southend United before losing 3-6 at Swindon Town, were kept alive by others' failures at this time. A further defeat on the 14th meant, however, that the Bluebirds' chances were all but gone and when Newport and Torquay both won their 21st April fixtures, Cardiff were doomed to a bottom-two finish. Beaten 0-6 by Brighton on the same day, Bournemouth were also in deep trouble, being 4 points from safety with only 2 games left to play. A 1-2 home defeat by Aldershot on April 28th made sure the Dean Court side joined Cardiff in having to apply for re-election.

NORWICH CITY

August	26	CLAPTON ORIENT	3-0
	28	BRISTOL CITY	7-2
September	02	Swindon Town	0-0
	06	Bristol City	1-0
	09	BRIGHTON & HOVE ALBION	4-3
	16	Aldershot	1-2
	23	LUTON TOWN	4-0
	30	Northampton Town	2-2
October	07	TORQUAY UNITED	0-2
	14	Queen's Park Rangers	2-5
	21	GILLINGHAM	4-1
	28	Exeter City	4-3
November	04	CARDIFF CITY	2-0
	11	Bournemouth & B.A.	4-2
	18	CHARLTON ATHLETIC	3-0
December	02	READING	3-2
	14	Coventry City	0-0
	16	SOUTHEND UNITED	0-0
	23	Bristol Rovers	0-3
	25	Crystal Palace	1-0
	26	CRYSTAL PALACE	2-0
	30	Clapton Orient	2-3
January	06	SWINDON TOWN	3-2
	13	Watford	3-1
	20	Brighton & Hove Albion	1-1
	27	ALDERSHOT	2-2
February	03	Luton Town	3-2
	10	NORTHAMPTON TOWN	2-0
	17	Torquay United	2-1
	24	QUEEN'S PARK RANGERS	1-0
March	03	Gillingham	2-1
	10	EXETER CITY	1-1
	17	Cardiff City	2-0
	24	BOURNEMOUTH & B.A.	6-1
	30	Newport County	0-0
	31	Charlton Athletic	3-3
April	02	NEWPORT COUNTY	2-1
	07	WATFORD	3-1
	14	Reading	0-1
	21	COVENTRY CITY	3-1
	28	Southend United	0-0
May	05	BRISTOL ROVERS	0-0

3rd Division (South) Final Table 1933-34

1	NORWICH CITY	42	88	49	61
2	Coventry City	42	100	54	54
3	Reading	42	82	50	54
4	Queen's Park Rangers	42	70	51	54
5	Charlton Athletic	42	83	56	52
6	Luton Town	42	83	61	52
7	Bristol Rovers	42	77	47	51
8	Swindon Town	42	64	68	45
9	Exeter City	42	68	57	43
10	Brighton & Hove Albion	42	68	60	43
11	Clapton Orient	42	75	69	42
12	Crystal Palace	42	71	67	41
13	Northampton Town	42	71	78	40
14	Aldershot	42	52	71	38
15	Watford	42	71	63	37
16	Southend United	42	51	74	34
17	Gillingham	42	75	96	33
18	Newport County	42	49	70	33
19	Bristol City	42	58	85	33
20	Torquay United	42	53	93	33
21	Bournemouth & B.A.	42	60	102	27
22	Cardiff City	42	57	105	24
		924	1526	1526	924

Norwich City were promoted to Division 2. *Bournemouth & Boscombe Athletic* and *Cardiff City* (48 votes each) were re-elected. Folkestone attracted no support.

1934-35 – LEAGUE DIVISION 1 — ARSENAL

Division 1 (top 6) at 25/12/34

1	ARSENAL	21	68-29	28
2	Sunderland	21	46-30	27
3	Manchester City	21	41-33	27
4	West Bromwich Albion	21	53-43	26
5	Stoke City	21	45-33	25
6	Grimsby Town	21	42-29	24

FINAL PHASE … AT THE TOP

Arsenal, seeking a hat-trick of League titles, reached the end of April 13th with a 3-point advantage over their nearest challengers, who this time round were Sunderland. Just below the Wearsiders were Manchester City, who, like the teams above them, had 5 matches left to play.

Top 4 at 13/04/35

1	ARSENAL	37	100-42	50	2.38
2	Sunderland	37	78-44	47	1.77
3	Manchester City	37	70-53	46	1.32
4	Sheffield Wednesday	38	65-60	44	1.08

(Figure in the right-hand column is goal average)

On Good Friday, April 19th, Arsenal took another step towards their goal by destroying Middlesbrough 8-0 at Highbury. The gap to second place remained at three points, however, as Sunderland beat Preston North End 3-1. Manchester City, on the other hand, lost 2-4 at home to Portsmouth and dropped out of real contention. Arsenal won again the next day, 1-0 at home to Huddersfield. Sunderland drew at Birmingham and it was virtually all over – a 4-point gap and just 3 games left. On April 22nd, Arsenal won 1-0 at Middlesbrough to move onto 56 points. Sunderland travelled to Preston where the match finished all square at 1-1, leaving the Rokerites on 51 points with two to play. Arsenal were champions once again.

Division 1 (bottom 6) at 25/12/34

17	Preston North End	21	32-42	17
18	Blackburn Rovers	21	28-39	17
19	Chelsea	21	30-43	17
20	Birmingham	21	27-44	17
21	Middlesbrough	20	30-36	15
22	Leicester City	21	29-47	14

FINAL PHASE … AT THE BOTTOM

By April 13th, Spurs, with 4 matches left, lay 4 points behind Leicester at the foot of Division 1. The Foxes were a point behind the 2 clubs above them – Birmingham and Middlesbrough. These three all had 5 games to go in which to pull clear from the relegation zone.

Bottom 4 at 13/04/35

19	Middlesbrough	37	65-77	31	0.84
20	Birmingham	37	53-72	31	0.74
21	Leicester City	37	53-74	30	0.72
22	Tottenham Hotspur	38	44-84	26	0.52

(Figure in the right-hand column is goal average)

Easter began in disastrous style for Middlesbrough, who were overrun at Highbury and lost 0-8. Birmingham drew 1-1 at Leeds United to move above Boro, but Leicester stayed in the relegation hole after losing 1-3 at Grimsby. A day later, on April 20th, Birmingham drew again and Leicester also picked up a point against Sheffield Wednesday. Middlesbrough lost at home to Grimsby 0-2 and only stayed ahead of Leicester on goal average. Spurs beat Blackburn to keep their slender hopes alive.

Birmingham boosted their survival chances further on Easter Monday by beating Leeds 3-1, while Boro and Spurs both lost and Leicester drew to go 20th. On April 27th, Tottenham were relegated, despite crushing Liverpool 5-1. While Leicester lost 3-5 to Arsenal, Middlesbrough won 3-0 at Aston Villa and Birmingham reached safety by drawing at Huddersfield. The remaining relegation issue would be settled on the final day of the season – Saturday, May 4th. Middlesbrough, with a better goal average, had to match Leicester's result. A 2-2 home draw against Chelsea proved to be enough as City drew 1-1 at Portsmouth.

Month	Date	Opponent	Score
August	25	Portsmouth	3-3
September	01	LIVERPOOL	8-1
	05	BLACKBURN ROVERS	4-0
	08	Leeds United	1-1
	15	WEST BROMWICH ALBION	4-3
	17	Blackburn Rovers	0-2
	22	Sheffield Wednesday	0-0
	29	BIRMINGHAM	5-1
October	06	Stoke City	2-2
	13	MANCHESTER CITY	3-0
	20	TOTTENHAM HOTSPUR	5-1
	27	Sunderland	1-2
November	03	EVERTON	2-0
	10	Grimsby Town	2-2
	17	ASTON VILLA	1-2
	24	Chelsea	5-2
December	01	WOLVES	7-0
	08	Huddersfield Town	1-1
	15	LEICESTER CITY	8-0
	22	Derby County	1-3
	25	PRESTON NORTH END	5-3
	26	Preston North End	1-2
	29	PORTSMOUTH	1-1
January	05	Liverpool	2-0
	19	LEEDS UNITED	3-0
	30	West Bromwich Albion	3-0
February	02	SHEFFIELD WEDNESDAY	4-1
	09	Birmingham	0-3
	20	STOKE CITY	2-0
	23	Manchester City	1-1
March	06	Tottenham Hotspur	6-0
	09	SUNDERLAND	0-0
	16	Everton	2-0
	23	GRIMSBY TOWN	1-1
	30	Aston Villa	3-1
April	06	CHELSEA	2-2
	13	Wolves	1-1
	19	MIDDLESBROUGH	8-0
	20	HUDDERSFIELD TOWN	1-0
	22	Middlesbrough	1-0
	27	Leicester City	5-3
May	04	DERBY COUNTY	0-1

1st Division Final Table 1934-35

1	ARSENAL	42	115	46	58
2	Sunderland	42	90	51	54
3	Sheffield Wednesday	42	70	64	49
4	Manchester City	42	82	67	48
5	Grimsby Town	42	78	60	45
6	Derby County	42	81	66	45
7	Liverpool	42	85	88	45
8	Everton	42	89	88	44
9	West Bromwich Albion	42	83	83	44
10	Stoke City	42	71	70	42
11	Preston North End	42	62	67	42
12	Chelsea	42	73	82	41
13	Aston Villa	42	74	88	41
14	Portsmouth	42	71	72	40
15	Blackburn Rovers	42	66	78	39
16	Huddersfield Town	42	76	71	38
17	Wolves	42	88	94	38
18	Leeds United	42	75	92	38
19	Birmingham	42	63	81	36
20	Middlesbrough	42	70	90	34
21	Leicester City	42	61	86	33
22	Tottenham Hotspur	42	54	93	30
		924	1677	1677	924

Leicester City and Tottenham Hotspur were relegated.

1934-35 – LEAGUE DIVISION 2   BRENTFORD

Division 2 (top 6) at 25/12/34

1	BRENTFORD	21	53-26	31
2	Bolton Wanderers	21	55-29	30
3	Manchester United	21	46-28	30
4	West Ham United	21	46-33	30
5	Nottingham Forest	21	43-30	27
6	Blackpool	21	43-31	26

FINAL PHASE ... AT THE TOP

With 6 games left to play, Brentford ended April 13th two points ahead of West Ham United, who held a 2-point lead over third-placed Blackpool. Bolton Wanderers, a point behind the Seasiders, had a game in hand and a much better goal average than the two clubs just above them.

Top 4 at 13/04/35

1	BRENTFORD	36	75-40	52	1.88
2	West Ham United	37	71-55	50	1.29
3	Blackpool	37	71-49	48	1.45
4	Bolton Wanderers	36	85-43	47	1.98

(Figure in the right-hand column is goal average)

Brentford moved smoothly through their Easter programme, winning all three, including an 8-0 demolition of lowly Port Vale on April 20th. All the other three promotion chasers won twice and lost once, Blackpool and West Ham sharing the honours in their two meetings. Brentford therefore needed one more point to become champions and took this from a 3-3 draw at Barnsley on April 27th. Blackpool lost at Southampton 0-2 and, in the day's most crucial clash, Bolton beat West Ham 3-1 to move into third place. Wanderers defeated Brentford 2-0 four days later to climb into second place, with one match to go. West Ham defeated Oldham 2-0 on May 4th, but this was not enough because Bolton drew 1-1 at Blackpool and stayed in second place because of their better goal average.

Division 2 (bottom 6) at 25/12/34

17	Hull City	21	31-46	17
18	Sheffield United	20	38-35	16
19	Norwich City	21	36-39	15
20	Swansea Town	21	27-35	15
21	Oldham Athletic	21	27-52	13
22	Notts County	21	20-48	9

FINAL PHASE ... AT THE BOTTOM

With 5 matches each to play, the bottom two, Oldham and Notts County, trailed 20th-placed Bradford City by 5 points. Two points better off than City, neither Port Vale nor Southampton were in the clear at mid-April, but it would need a dramatic turn of events to alter the standings drastically.

Bottom 5 at 13/04/35

18	Port Vale	37	46-58	30	0.79
19	Southampton	38	41-69	30	0.59
20	Bradford City	37	45-60	28	0.75
21	Oldham Athletic	37	50-85	23	0.59
22	Notts County	37	37-80	23	0.46

(Figure in the right-hand column is goal average)

On April 19th, Oldham Athletic lost at Burnley 2-4 and Notts County went down 3-5 at Port Vale, who were now in the safety zone. County lost again the following day, while Oldham forced a draw at Norwich City. With Southampton and Bradford City both losing, the bottom two remained just about alive.

Notts County produced a 3-2 success over Port Vale on Easter Monday. Another defeat for Oldham meant the Latics were now bottom of the pile. Southampton went safe by beating Manchester United 1-0, but, as Bradford City lost again, both Notts and Oldham still had a chance of survival. This lingering hope ended on April 23rd. In their return game with Barnsley, Bradford City produced a 1-0 victory and sent County and Oldham down to Division 3.

August	25	NORWICH CITY	2-1
	27	Fulham	2-2
September	01	Newcastle United	5-2
	05	FULHAM	1-0
	08	WEST HAM UNITED	4-1
	15	Blackpool	2-2
	22	BURY	1-2
	29	Hull City	1-2
October	06	NOTTINGHAM FOREST	1-1
	13	Bradford City	0-3
	20	NOTTS COUNTY	4-1
	27	Southampton	0-1
November	03	BOLTON WANDERERS	1-0
	10	Oldham Athletic	3-1
	17	BURNLEY	6-1
	24	Swansea Town	4-2
December	01	MANCHESTER UNITED	3-1
	08	Port Vale	2-2
	15	BARNSLEY	8-1
	22	Sheffield United	2-1
	25	PLYMOUTH ARGYLE	0-0
	26	Plymouth Argyle	1-1
	29	Norwich City	1-2
January	05	NEWCASTLE UNITED	3-0
	19	West Ham United	0-2
	26	BLACKPOOL	2-1
February	02	Bury	1-4
	09	HULL CITY	2-1
	23	BRADFORD CITY	2-0
	28	Nottingham Forest	0-0
March	02	Notts County	1-0
	09	SOUTHAMPTON	3-2
	23	OLDHAM ATHLETIC	2-1
	30	Burnley	3-0
April	06	SWANSEA TOWN	1-0
	13	Manchester United	0-0
	19	BRADFORD PARK AVENUE	1-0
	20	PORT VALE	8-0
	22	Bradford Park Avenue	3-2
	27	Barnsley	3-3
May	01	Bolton Wanderers	0-2
	04	SHEFFIELD UNITED	3-1

2nd Division Final Table 1934-35

1	BRENTFORD	42	93	48	61
2	Bolton Wanderers	42	96	48	56
3	West Ham United	42	80	63	56
4	Blackpool	42	79	57	53
5	Manchester United	42	76	55	50
6	Newcastle United	42	89	68	48
7	Fulham	42	76	56	46
8	Plymouth Argyle	42	75	64	46
9	Nottingham Forest	42	76	70	42
10	Bury	42	62	73	42
11	Sheffield United	42	79	70	41
12	Burnley	42	63	73	41
13	Hull City	42	63	74	40
14	Norwich City	42	71	61	39
15	Bradford Park Avenue	42	55	63	38
16	Barnsley	42	60	83	38
17	Swansea Town	42	56	67	36
18	Port Vale	42	55	74	34
19	Southampton	42	46	75	34
20	Bradford City	42	50	68	32
21	Oldham Athletic	42	56	95	26
22	Notts County	42	46	97	25
		924	1502	1502	924

Brentford and Bolton Wanderers were promoted. Oldham Athletic (North) and Notts County (South) were relegated to Division 3.

- 141 -

1934-35 – DIVISION 3 (NORTH)

Division 3 (North) (top 6) at 05/01/35

1	Tranmere Rovers	23	47-19	36
2	Halifax Town	23	40-34	31
3	Chester	23	47-23	30
4	Darlington	23	48-33	29
5	Mansfield Town	23	44-31	28
6	DONCASTER ROVERS	21	36-22	27

FINAL PHASE ... AT THE TOP

As the middle of April neared, Doncaster Rovers held a goal average lead from Chester. The fact that Rovers had 2 games in hand on their rivals made them firm favourites to go up.

Top 4 at 13/04/35

1	DONCASTER ROVERS	36	77-35	51	2.20
2	Chester	38	85-51	51	1.67
3	Tranmere Rovers	38	69-45	49	1.53
4	Halifax Town	37	69-63	47	1.10

(Figure in the right-hand column is goal average)

Doncaster's 3-5 home loss against Rotherham United on April 19th might have been expected to present one of their rivals with a chance to take advantage, but Tranmere Rovers also lost, Chester drew at home to Crewe Alexandra and Halifax Town did not even play. Chester did go top, but another draw, plus a Doncaster win at Tranmere, ended this a day later and saw the Belle Vue men back in the driving seat.

Doncaster Rovers followed with a 3-1 at Rotherham United on Easter Monday, while Chester drew again with Crewe. Though Tranmere won, 4th-placed Halifax lost and their threat ended. In fact, issues were settled on Saturday, April 27th after both Chester (v. Lincoln City) and Tranmere (at Southport) lost and Doncaster Rovers defeated Wrexham 2-1.

Division 3 (North) (bottom 6) at 05/01/35

17	Hartlepools United	22	36-48	17
18	Gateshead	22	32-47	17
19	Rochdale	22	24-45	17
20	Walsall	23	34-41	16
21	Southport	22	32-48	16
22	Carlisle United	22	29-49	15

FINAL PHASE ... AT THE BOTTOM

With Carlisle United eight points adrift at the foot of the table, the question appeared to be one of who would fill the other re-election slot. Accrington Stanley and Walsall, having played more games than the clubs around them, looked to have the most testing run-ins to the campaign.

Bottom 7 at 13/04/35

16	Gateshead	37	54-82	31	0.66
17	York City	37	62-78	30	0.79
18	Accrington Stanley	39	59-88	29	0.67
19	Southport	37	48-73	29	0.66
20	Walsall	38	65-71	28	0.92
21	Rochdale	37	45-66	27	0.68
22	Carlisle United	36	44-88	19	0.50

(Figure in the right-hand column is goal average)

3 points from 2 games at the start of the Easter programme briefly raised Carlisle's hopes of a dramatic escape from the re-election zone, but defeat at Rochdale on Easter Monday, April 22nd, and other results, ended this. Above the Cumbrians, Walsall and York hit decent veins of form to reach safety on April 27th. This left last-day problems for 4 clubs, 2 of whom reacted by winning their final, May 4th fixtures – Accrington and Rochdale. Gateshead, after 3 successive losses, drew 1-1 with Mansfield Town to go clear. This left Southport, who lost 0-3 at Wrexham, in 21st place to face the re-election vote.

- 142 -

DONCASTER ROVERS

August	25	Crewe Alexandra	1-1
	28	Southport	2-1
September	01	STOCKPORT COUNTY	3-4
	03	SOUTHPORT	2-0
	08	Gateshead	0-0
	15	ACCRINGTON STANLEY	2-1
	22	Darlington	1-1
	29	YORK CITY	4-1
October	06	New Brighton	1-1
	13	CHESTER	3-0
	20	Walsall	2-0
	27	CHESTERFIELD	0-2
November	03	Mansfield Town	0-2
	10	BARROW	2-0
	17	Carlisle United	1-1
December	01	Lincoln City	2-0
	15	Wrexham	2-1
	25	Hartlepools United	1-2
	26	HARTLEPOOLS UNITED	3-1
	29	CREWE ALEXANDRA	2-0
January	05	Stockport County	2-3
	12	ROCHDALE	1-0
	19	GATESHEAD	5-0
	26	Accrington Stanley	5-1
February	02	DARLINGTON	2-0
	09	York City	2-1
	16	NEW BRIGHTON	7-1
	23	Chester	3-1
March	02	WALSALL	4-0
	09	Chesterfield	2-3
	16	MANSFIELD TOWN	2-1
	23	Barrow	1-2
	30	CARLISLE UNITED	3-0
April	06	Rochdale	1-0
	10	TRANMERE ROVERS	2-0
	13	LINCOLN CITY	1-3
	19	ROTHERHAM UNITED	3-5
	20	Tranmere Rovers	2-0
	22	Rotherham United	3-1
	27	WREXHAM	2-1
May	02	HALIFAX TOWN	0-1
	04	Halifax Town	0-1

3rd Division (North) Final Table 1934-35

1	DONCASTER ROVERS	42	87	44	57
2	Halifax Town	42	76	67	55
3	Chester	42	91	58	54
4	Lincoln City	42	87	58	51
5	Darlington	42	80	59	51
6	Tranmere Rovers	42	74	55	51
7	Stockport County	42	90	72	47
8	Mansfield Town	42	75	62	47
9	Rotherham United	42	86	73	45
10	Chesterfield	42	71	52	44
11	Wrexham	42	76	69	43
12	Hartlepools United	42	80	78	41
13	Crewe Alexandra	42	66	86	39
14	Walsall	42	81	72	36
15	York City	42	76	82	36
16	New Brighton	42	59	76	36
17	Barrow	42	58	87	35
18	Accrington Stanley	42	63	89	34
19	Gateshead	42	58	96	34
20	Rochdale	42	53	71	33
21	Southport	42	55	85	32
22	Carlisle United	42	51	102	23
		924	1593	1593	924

Doncaster Rovers were promoted to Division 2. *Carlisle United* and *Southport* (46 votes each) were re-elected. Shrewsbury Town (6) were unsuccessful.

1934-35 – DIVISION 3 (SOUTH)

Division 3 (South) (top 6) at 26/12/34

1	CHARLTON ATHLETIC	21	53-28	30
2	Reading	20	49-24	27
3	Coventry City	20	47-22	26
4	Watford	20	43-24	25
5	Luton Town	21	38-27	24
6	Crystal Palace	20	40-38	24

FINAL PHASE ... AT THE TOP

Charlton's 7-point lead after the April 13th games had the look of a winning margin. The formalities of completing the full programme remained, of course, but the other clubs faced an almost impossible task.

Top 3 at 13/04/35

1	CHARLTON ATHLETIC	37	91-47	54	1.94
2	Reading	36	77-49	47	1.57
3	Coventry City	36	80-45	45	1.78

(Figure in the right-hand column is goal average)

On April 19th, Easter got off to a bad start for the leaders as they lost 2-3 at Aldershot. The biggest consolation for the Haddicks was that Reading and Coventry City were playing each other in the first of two holiday meetings – they couldn't both win twice. In the first encounter, it was Reading who took the points, but the Elm Park side dropped a point the following day against Brighton, while Charlton won 2-0 away at Newport and followed this by defeating Aldershot 4-0 on Easter Monday, April 22nd. Reading completed the 'double' over Coventry a day later, but lost at Crystal Palace on April 26th. Charlton Athletic, who beat 2-0 on the same afternoon, were now champions.

Division 3 (South) (bottom 6) at 26/12/34

17	Exeter City	20	34-36	17
18	Queen's Park Rangers	20	26-34	17
19	Bournemouth & B.A.	20	26-39	14
20	Gillingham	21	29-46	14
21	Aldershot	20	19-32	13
22	Southend United	20	26-45	12

FINAL PHASE ... AT THE BOTTOM

Newport County and Southend United lay an awkward three points behind 20th place as mid-April approached. There was a further three-point gap to 19th-spot and things were drawing quickly to a conclusion in Division 3 (South).

Bottom 5 at 13/04/35

18	Aldershot	36	41-55	31	0.74
19	Cardiff City	37	41-55	31	0.70
20	Gillingham	36	48-68	28	0.71
21	Southend United	36	52-67	25	0.78
22	Newport County	37	48-97	25	0.49

(Figure in the right-hand column is goal average)

Aldershot and Cardiff both picked up important wins on April 19th, increasing their advantage over Gillingham, who drew with Clapton Orient. Southend also drew, but Newport lost to sink into deeper trouble. On the 20th, Gillingham defeated Cardiff 1-0, while the other three sides in the bottom five all lost, with Newport beaten again 2 days later, on April 22nd, and destined therefore for the re-election lottery. Gillingham won again, but so did Southend to stay just about alive.

April 27th saw Aldershot and Cardiff take the points needed for safety, but Gillingham lost at Charlton, while Southend United grabbed another point against Coventry to keep their flagging hopes going. A 6-1 blasting of Reading on May 1st seemed just the tonic the Roots Hall men needed, but news came in that Gillingham had drawn at Luton, so Southend finished 21st.

CHARLTON ATHLETIC

August	25	Cardiff City	1-2
	27	TORQUAY UNITED	3-2
September	01	BRIGHTON & HOVE ALBION	3-1
	05	Torquay United	2-1
	08	Luton Town	2-1
	15	SOUTHEND UNITED	3-0
	22	Bristol Rovers	0-0
	29	MILLWALL	3-1
October	06	CRYSTAL PALACE	2-2
	13	Queen's Park Rangers	3-0
	20	Coventry City	0-4
	27	CLAPTON ORIENT	2-1
November	03	Exeter City	1-3
	10	BRISTOL CITY	4-1
	17	Northampton Town	1-1
December	01	Watford	0-2
	08	NEWPORT COUNTY	6-0
	15	Gillingham	6-3
	22	READING	3-1
	25	SWINDON TOWN	6-0
	26	Swindon Town	2-2
	29	CARDIFF CITY	3-1
January	05	Brighton & Hove Albion	1-2
	12	BOURNEMOUTH & B.A.	0-1
	19	LUTON TOWN	4-2
	26	Southend United	3-0
February	02	BRISTOL ROVERS	2-0
	09	Millwall	3-1
	16	Crystal Palace	2-1
	23	QUEEN'S PARK RANGERS	3-1
March	02	COVENTRY CITY	3-3
	09	Clapton Orient	2-1
	16	EXETER CITY	1-0
	23	Bristol City	4-1
	30	NORTHAMPTON TOWN	0-1
April	06	Bournemouth & B.A.	2-2
	13	WATFORD	5-2
	19	Aldershot	2-3
	20	Newport County	2-0
	22	ALDERSHOT	4-0
	27	GILLINGHAM	2-0
May	04	Reading	2-2

3rd Division (South) Final Table 1934-35

1	CHARLTON ATHLETIC	42	103	52	61
2	Reading	42	89	65	53
3	Coventry City	42	86	50	51
4	Luton Town	42	92	60	50
5	Crystal Palace	42	86	64	48
6	Watford	42	76	49	47
7	Northampton Town	42	65	67	46
8	Bristol Rovers	42	73	77	44
9	Brighton & Hove Albion	42	69	62	43
10	Torquay United	42	81	75	42
11	Exeter City	42	70	75	41
12	Millwall	42	57	62	41
13	Queen's Park Rangers	42	63	72	41
14	Clapton Orient	42	65	65	40
15	Bristol City	42	52	68	39
16	Swindon Town	42	67	78	38
17	Bournemouth & B.A.	42	54	71	37
18	Aldershot	42	50	75	36
19	Cardiff City	42	62	82	35
20	Gillingham	42	55	75	35
21	Southend United	42	65	78	31
22	Newport County	42	54	112	25
		924	1534	1534	924

Charlton Athletic were promoted to Division 2. *Southend United* (48 votes) and *Newport County* (43) were re-elected. Bath City (1) and Folkestone (1) were unsuccessful.

1935-36 – LEAGUE DIVISION 1

Division 1 (top 6) at 26/12/35

1	SUNDERLAND	21	63-31	32
2	Huddersfield Town	21	33-28	27
3	Arsenal	21	46-20	26
4	Derby County	22	30-22	26
5	Stoke City	22	34-30	25
6	Liverpool	22	40-30	24

FINAL PHASE … AT THE TOP

As the campaign entered its final stages, Sunderland held a 7-point lead over Derby County with four matches left to play. The leaders needed only 2 points, therefore, from their closing fixtures to become champions, even if their rivals won all their games.

Top 3 at 11/04/36

1	SUNDERLAND	38	98-62	52	1.58
2	Derby County	38	55-41	45	1.34
3	Huddersfield Town	38	53-50	44	1.06

(Figure in the right-hand column is goal average)

There are times when the team which becomes the champions of a league do something special in actually winning the title. April 13th, 1936 provides us with an excellent example of such an occasion. Sunderland arrived at St. Andrew's, Birmingham knowing a win would guarantee them the Football League crown. The Roker Park club took their hosts apart, winning 7-2 and leaving the field worthy champions. Sunderland went on to finish eight points clear at the head of the Division 1 table.

Division 1 (bottom 6) at 26/12/35

17	Blackburn Rovers	21	34-50	18
18	Sheffield Wednesday	21	34-44	17
19	Grimsby Town	21	30-41	17
20	Brentford	21	34-40	16
21	Everton	21	35-49	16
22	Aston Villa	22	38-69	14

FINAL PHASE … AT THE BOTTOM

As mid-April drew near, seven sides faced the possibility of relegation, though the feeling was that it would be Blackburn and one other, as Rovers were 5 points from safety with only 4 matches left to play. The differences in the number of games played by the teams involved made for an interesting finish.

Bottom 7 at 11/04/36

16	Wolves	37	63-67	34	0.94
17	Liverpool	38	55-61	34	0.90
18	Sheffield Wednesday	36	59-67	34	0.88
19	Chelsea	36	49-64	34	0.76
20	Aston Villa	39	77-103	34	0.75
21	West Bromwich Albion	38	81-83	32	0.97
22	Blackburn Rovers	38	46-84	29	0.55

(Figure in the right-hand column is goal average)

Blackburn Rovers were quick to fold, losing 1-4 at Liverpool on April 13th and being therefore relegated for the first time in the club's history. West Bromwich Albion, just above Rovers, fared better, beating Arsenal 1-0 and climbing above Sheffield Wednesday, who crashed 0-5 at Middlesbrough. Villa, Wolves and Chelsea all drew, and Wednesday joined these teams on 35 points a day later after drawing the return game with Boro.

The Owls followed this by winning 3-0 at Stoke on the 18th. Chelsea also won. Liverpool and West Bromwich took points from their fixtures, while Wolves and Aston Villa both lost. This left Villa in 21st place, with one game left, with by far the worst goal average of the strugglers and 35 points. Wolves beat Preston 4-2 on the 20th to reach 37 points, adding to Villa's woes. Chelsea reached safety by beating Portsmouth on April 22nd, but the crucial relegation action took place on April 25th. In their final fixture Aston Villa, desperate for a win, entertained already-relegated Blackburn Rovers … and lost 2-4 This meant a first-ever relegation for the Villains … just like it was for Blackburn.

- 144 -

SUNDERLAND

August	31	Arsenal	1-3
September	04	West Bromwich Albion	3-1
	07	MANCHESTER CITY	2-0
	11	WEST BROMWICH ALBION	6-1
	14	Stoke City	2-0
	16	Aston Villa	2-2
	21	BLACKBURN ROVERS	7-2
	28	Chelsea	1-3
October	05	LIVERPOOL	2-0
	12	Grimsby Town	0-4
	19	Wolves	4-3
	26	SHEFFIELD WEDNESDAY	5-1
November	02	Portsmouth	2-2
	09	PRESTON NORTH END	4-2
	16	Brentford	5-1
	23	MIDDLESBROUGH	2-1
	30	Everton	3-0
December	07	BOLTON WANDERERS	7-2
	14	Huddersfield Town	0-1
	21	DERBY COUNTY	3-1
	26	LEEDS UNITED	2-1
	28	ARSENAL	5-4
January	01	ASTON VILLA	1-3
	04	Manchester City	1-0
	18	STOKE CITY	1-0
February	01	CHELSEA	3-3
	08	Liverpool	3-0
	15	Blackburn Rovers	1-1
	19	GRIMSBY TOWN	3-1
	22	WOLVES	3-1
	29	Preston North End	2-3
March	07	EVERTON	3-3
	14	Sheffield Wednesday	0-0
	21	BRENTFORD	1-3
	28	Middlesbrough	0-6
April	04	PORTSMOUTH	5-0
	10	BIRMINGHAM	2-1
	11	Bolton Wanderers	1-2
	13	Birmingham	7-2
	18	HUDDERSFIELD TOWN	4-3
	22	Leeds United	0-3
	25	Derby County	0-4

1st Division Final Table 1935-36

1	SUNDERLAND	42	109	74	56
2	Derby County	42	61	52	48
3	Huddersfield Town	42	59	56	48
4	Stoke City	42	57	57	47
5	Brentford	42	81	60	46
6	Arsenal	42	78	48	45
7	Preston North End	42	67	64	44
8	Chelsea	42	65	72	43
9	Manchester City	42	68	60	42
10	Portsmouth	42	54	67	42
11	Leeds United	42	66	64	41
12	Birmingham	42	61	63	41
13	Bolton Wanderers	42	67	76	41
14	Middlesbrough	42	84	70	40
15	Wolves	42	77	76	40
16	Everton	42	89	89	39
17	Grimsby Town	42	65	73	39
18	West Bromwich Albion	42	89	88	38
19	Liverpool	42	60	64	38
20	Sheffield Wednesday	42	63	77	38
21	Aston Villa	42	81	110	35
22	Blackburn Rovers	42	55	96	33
		924	1556	1556	924

Aston Villa and Blackburn Rovers were relegated.

1935-36 – LEAGUE DIVISION 2

Division 2 (top 6) at 28/12/35

1	Leicester City	22	47-29	29
2	Charlton Athletic	23	39-28	29
3	Doncaster Rovers	23	34-35	28
4	Tottenham Hotspur	23	52-34	27
5	Blackpool	23	50-36	27
6	Sheffield United	23	50-32	26

FINAL PHASE … AT THE TOP

For the second year running, West Ham United reached the business end of the 2nd Division season in a promotion slot. Second-placed Manchester United were many people's title favourites, however, because of their game in hand on the leaders and superior goal average.

Top 4 at 11/04/36

1	West Ham United	38	83-58	49	1.43
2	MANCHESTER UNITED	37	74-38	48	1.95
3	Charlton Athletic	38	76-54	48	1.41
4	Sheffield United	39	70-46	47	1.52

(Figure in the right-hand column is goal average)

Manchester United moved into top spot by beating Burnley 4-0 on April 13th, while West Ham drew at Leicester City 1-1. Also ending the day on 50 points were Charlton Athletic, who had beaten Tottenham Hotspur 3-1. On April 18th, Charlton won 3-1 at West Ham, climbing into pole position after the Manchester leaders were held 1-1 at Nottingham Forest. All the top three won their next game, on April 25th, but, in a key move, Manchester United returned to the top of the table by completing the 'double' over Bury, with a 3-2 success at Gigg Lane on the 29th. This win meant United were promoted. The leading trio had one remaining match each, with Charlton needing a point to go up or a win plus a defeat for United to become champions. In the May 2nd matches the top two both drew, making Manchester United champions and securing a second successive promotion for Charlton Athletic.

Division 2 (bottom 6) at 28/12/35

17	Bury	22	34-41	18
18	Swansea Town	23	34-51	18
19	Burnley	22	26-36	17
20	Bradford City	22	22-34	16
21	Port Vale	22	27-59	14
22	Hull City	22	25-56	13

FINAL PHASE … AT THE BOTTOM

Hull City were already down as the final stages of the season were reached. In the battle to escape from the other 'drop spot', Port Vale led Barnsley by two points, but the Yorkshire side had played one match fewer and had an advantage in terms of goal average.

Bottom 3 at 11/04/36

20	Port Vale	38	52-92	31	0.57
21	Barnsley	37	50-75	29	0.67
22	Hull City	38	41-99	18	0.41

(Figure in the right-hand column is goal average)

On April 13th, struggling Vale crashed 0-7 at Fulham. Their only consolation was that Barnsley had also been beaten, going down 0-1 at home to Bradford City. 24 hours later, however, Barnsley drew the return game at Valley Parade to narrow the gap at the bottom to a single point. Both the troubled teams lost their away games on April 18th, but on the 25th there was a significant change made. Whereas Port Vale slipped to yet another loss, 2-3 to West Ham, Barnsley won their match with Southampton 3-1. With one game to go, the Oakwell club led Port Vale by one point and were better off on goal average. As long as Barnsley avoided defeat on the last day of the campaign and Port Vale did not rack up over 20 goals at Charlton, the Yorkshiremen would stay up. In the event both teams drew their May 2nd games and Port Vale were relegated.

MANCHESTER UNITED

August	31	Plymouth Argyle	1-3
September	04	CHARLTON ATHLETIC	3-0
	07	BRADFORD CITY	3-1
	09	Charlton Athletic	0-0
	14	Newcastle United	2-0
	18	HULL CITY	2-0
	21	TOTTENHAM HOTSPUR	0-0
	28	Southampton	1-2
October	05	Port Vale	3-0
	12	FULHAM	1-0
	19	SHEFFIELD UNITED	3-1
	26	Bradford Park Avenue	0-1
November	02	LEICESTER CITY	0-1
	09	Swansea Town	1-2
	16	WEST HAM UNITED	2-3
	23	Norwich City	5-3
	30	DONCASTER ROVERS	0-0
December	07	Blackpool	1-4
	14	NOTTINGHAM FOREST	5-0
	26	BARNSLEY	1-1
	28	PLYMOUTH ARGYLE	3-2
January	01	Barnsley	3-0
	04	Bradford City	0-1
	18	NEWCASTLE UNITED	3-1
February	01	SOUTHAMPTON	4-0
	05	Tottenham Hotspur	0-0
	08	PORT VALE	7-2
	22	Sheffield United	1-1
	29	BLACKPOOL	3-2
March	07	West Ham United	2-1
	14	SWANSEA TOWN	3-0
	21	Leicester City	1-1
	28	NORWICH CITY	2-1
April	01	Fulham	2-2
	04	Doncaster Rovers	0-0
	10	Burnley	2-2
	11	BRADFORD PARK AVENUE	4-0
	13	BURNLEY	4-0
	18	Nottingham Forest	1-1
	25	BURY	2-1
	29	Bury	3-2
May	02	Hull City	1-1

2nd Division Final Table 1935-36

1	MANCHESTER UNITED	42	85	43	56
2	Charlton Athletic	42	85	58	55
3	Sheffield United	42	79	50	52
4	West Ham United	42	90	68	52
5	Tottenham Hotspur	42	91	55	49
6	Leicester City	42	79	57	48
7	Plymouth Argyle	42	71	57	48
8	Newcastle United	42	88	79	46
9	Fulham	42	76	52	44
10	Blackpool	42	93	72	43
11	Norwich City	42	72	65	43
12	Bradford City	42	55	65	43
13	Swansea Town	42	67	76	39
14	Bury	42	66	84	38
15	Burnley	42	50	59	37
16	Bradford Park Avenue	42	62	84	37
17	Southampton	42	47	65	37
18	Doncaster Rovers	42	51	71	37
19	Nottingham Forest	42	69	76	35
20	Barnsley	42	54	80	33
21	Port Vale	42	56	106	32
22	Hull City	42	47	111	20
		924	1533	1533	924

Manchester United and Charlton Athletic were promoted.
Port Vale and Hull City were relegated to Division 3 (North).

1935-36 – DIVISION 3 (NORTH)

Division 3 (North) (top 6) at 01/01/36

1	Tranmere Rovers	21	55-25	33
2	CHESTERFIELD	21	49-21	30
3	Stockport County	23	44-32	28
4	Lincoln City	21	45-26	26
5	Walsall	21	48-27	25
6	Wrexham	24	38-32	25

FINAL PHASE … AT THE TOP

Chesterfield's 5-point lead at the end of April 11th had an unassailable look about it. Tranmere had a game in hand on the leaders, but the gap was big enough for the Spireites to feel the championship was just about theirs for the taking.

Top 3 at 11/04/36

1	CHESTERFIELD	37	83-35	55	2.37
2	Tranmere Rovers	36	87-48	50	1.81
3	Chester	38	90-38	49	2.37

(Figure in the right-hand column is goal average)

Chesterfield's form deserted them in their next two outings, home defeat by Lincoln City on April 13th being followed by a further setback, 1-2, at Hartlepools United, on the 18th. Both Tranmere Rovers and Chester lost on the 13th, but victories for the chasing pair 5 days later suggested an upset was possible. However, Rovers were beaten at York City on April 22nd and although Chester won, they had only one game left to the leaders' three.

Chesterfield returned to form on April 25th with a 5-0 crushing of Carlisle. With Tranmere held at Barrow, the Spireites were back on track. The title was won on April 27th. Chesterfield defeated Hartlepools United 2-0 at Saltergate, while Rovers crashed 0-5 at Lincoln City

Division 3 (North) (bottom 6) at 01/01/36

17	Carlisle United	21	24-33	19
18	York City	20	33-49	16
19	Mansfield Town	22	36-56	16
20	Rochdale	22	32-54	15
21	Southport	22	23-51	13
22	New Brighton	22	22-62	10

FINAL PHASE … AT THE BOTTOM

Six points from safety, with four games left to play, bottom club New Brighton seemed destined to fill one re-election berth. Only one point separated 21st-placed Southport from the two clubs above them, but both these had played fewer matches than the troubled Sandgrounders.

Bottom 4 at 11/04/36

19	Mansfield Town	37	65-85	29	0.76
20	Rochdale	38	55-85	29	0.65
21	Southport	39	45-84	28	0.53
22	New Brighton	38	42-95	23	0.44

(Figure in the right-hand column is goal average)

New Brighton lost 0-1 at Rochdale on April 13th. A 1-1 draw for Mansfield Town at Accrington sentenced the Rakers to a bottom-two finish. The Stags ended their own worries by beating Gateshead on the 14th and Stockport County on the 18th, when a 0-4 defeat for Southport at Oldham Athletic left the Sandgrounders 'on the brink'. On April 25th, Southport drew with Wrexham at Haig Avenue. Rochdale also drew, at home to Darlington, to move out of Southport's reach.

CHESTERFIELD

August	31	Barrow	1-1
September	02	YORK CITY	2-2
	07	NEW BRIGHTON	3-1
	11	York City	1-1
	14	Walsall	1-1
	21	Stockport County	2-2
	28	CREWE ALEXANDRA	6-0
October	05	Accrington Stanley	1-0
	12	SOUTHPORT	5-0
	19	TRANMERE ROVERS	0-1
	26	Gateshead	3-3
November	02	DARLINGTON	5-1
	09	Halifax Town	3-2
	16	OLDHAM ATHLETIC	3-0
	23	Wrexham	1-0
December	07	Mansfield Town	1-0
	21	Carlisle United	1-2
	25	Chester	1-1
	26	CHESTER	1-0
	28	BARROW	6-1
January	01	ROCHDALE	2-2
	04	New Brighton	2-1
	11	ROTHERHAM UNITED	5-0
	18	WALSALL	3-0
February	01	Crewe Alexandra	6-5
	08	ACCRINGTON STANLEY	0-3
	15	Southport	0-1
	22	Tranmere Rovers	3-1
	29	HALIFAX TOWN	3-1
March	07	Darlington	2-1
	14	GATESHEAD	2-0
	21	Oldham Athletic	0-0
	28	WREXHAM	5-0
	30	STOCKPORT COUNTY	0-0
April	04	Rotherham United	0-0
	10	Lincoln City	1-0
	11	MANSFIELD TOWN	2-1
	13	LINCOLN CITY	0-1
	18	Hartlepools United	1-2
	25	CARLISLE UNITED	5-0
	27	HARTLEPOOLS UNITED	2-0
May	02	Rochdale	1-1

3rd Division (North) Final Table 1935-36

1	CHESTERFIELD	42	92	39	60
2	Chester	42	100	45	55
3	Tranmere Rovers	42	93	58	55
4	Lincoln City	42	91	51	53
5	Stockport County	42	65	49	48
6	Crewe Alexandra	42	80	76	47
7	Oldham Athletic	42	86	73	45
8	Hartlepools United	42	57	61	42
9	Accrington Stanley	42	63	72	42
10	Walsall	42	79	59	41
11	Rotherham United	42	69	66	41
12	Darlington	42	74	79	40
13	Carlisle United	42	56	62	40
14	Gateshead	42	56	76	40
15	Barrow	42	58	65	38
16	York City	42	62	95	38
17	Halifax Town	42	57	61	37
18	Wrexham	42	66	75	37
19	Mansfield Town	42	80	91	37
20	Rochdale	42	58	88	33
21	Southport	42	48	90	31
22	New Brighton	42	43	102	24
		924	1533	1533	924

Chesterfield were promoted to Division 2. *Southport* (47 votes) and *New Brighton* (38) were re-elected. Shrewsbury Town (7) and Wigan Athletic (6) were unsuccessful. Walsall were transferred to Division 3 (South)

1935-36 – DIVISION 3 (SOUTH)

Division 3 (South) (top 6) at 28/12/35

1	Luton Town	21	41-18	30
2	COVENTRY CITY	21	57-21	29
3	Reading	21	48-35	28
4	Queen's Park Rangers	21	46-30	25
5	Bournemouth & B.A.	21	31-22	25
6	Crystal Palace	22	49-43	25

FINAL PHASE ... AT THE TOP

After the games of April 11th, Luton Town and Reading sat at the head on 49 points. Coventry City, with a vastly better goal average than the top two, were third, with a game in hand on Luton and two in hand on Reading. A close finish beckoned.

Top 4 at 11/04/36

1	Luton Town	37	66-44	49	1.50
2	Reading	38	82-59	49	1.39
3	COVENTRY CITY	36	92-41	47	2.24
4	Queen's Park Rangers	37	77-51	46	1.51

(Figure in the right-hand column is goal average)

Luton Town defeated Bristol Rovers 12-0 on April 13th, while Reading lost to Crystal Palace. In terms of the title, these two scores seemed to have the utmost importance and certainly overshadowed Coventry City's 2-1 win at Swindon. One day later, however, Coventry beat Swindon again, moving to the top of the table, on goal average, as a result.

Both Coventry and Luton had 2-0 wins on the 18th and pulled three points clear of Reading, who drew 0-0 at Torquay United. The top two then met twice in the space of 3 days. With both games ending all square, the clubs' final fixtures of the season on May 2nd became all-important. Luton took a point from the visit to Q.P.R., but Coventry City beat Torquay 2-1 at Highfield Road to become champions.

Division 3 (South) (bottom 6) at 28/12/35

17	Southend United	21	33-31	17
18	Cardiff City	20	26-32	17
19	Bristol City	20	18-28	17
20	Bristol Rovers	21	32-48	16
21	Newport County	21	32-64	15
22	Northampton Town	23	31-62	15

FINAL PHASE ... AT THE BOTTOM

Although the bottom two, Newport County and Exeter City, were firm favourites to fill the re-election places at the end of the season, not even 13th-placed Cardiff City could consider themselves safe as the middle of April approached. The bottom two would, however, have to show much better form if either was to escape the re-election trial.

Bottom 6 at 11/04/36

17	Southend United	36	55-51	32	1.08
18	Swindon Town	36	56-64	32	0.88
19	Northampton Town	38	55-87	32	0.63
20	Bristol Rovers	37	57-77	31	0.74
21	Newport County	38	53-101	28	0.52
22	Exeter City	38	56-84	25	0.67

(Figure in the right-hand column is goal average)

Exeter's faint hopes of avoiding a bottom-two finish lessened when they could only draw with Torquay United on April 13th. Newport also drew, but were happier with their point as the side just above them, Bristol Rovers, were overrun 0-12 by Luton. County's belief that Rovers would be so traumatised that they could be caught up with was shattered a day later, April 14th, when the Pirates, perhaps surprisingly, comfortably beat Torquay 3-0 at Eastville. This result sealed Exeter's fate. On the 18th, Newport lost at home to Luton. This was good news for Cardiff, Northampton, Southend and Swindon who were all now safe. Only Bristol Rovers, beaten 1-4 away at Brighton, remained in danger of being passed by Newport. On April 25th, however, Rovers sank beleaguered Exeter City 6-1, while Newport County crashed 2-6 at Notts County and faced another re-election 'begging act'.

COVENTRY CITY

August	31	Reading	1-2
September	02	Millwall	2-2
	07	NEWPORT COUNTY	7-1
	09	MILLWALL	5-0
	14	Exeter City	3-1
	18	Torquay United	3-3
	21	BRIGHTON & HOVE ALBION	5-0
	28	Queen's Park Rangers	0-0
October	05	WATFORD	2-0
	12	Bristol City	0-0
	19	Cardiff City	0-1
	26	GILLINGHAM	4-0
November	02	Bournemouth & B.A.	1-1
	09	CRYSTAL PALACE	8-1
	16	Notts County	1-2
	23	BRISTOL ROVERS	3-1
December	07	SOUTHEND UNITED	3-0
	14	Northampton Town	4-2
	25	ALDERSHOT	0-2
	26	Aldershot	2-1
	28	READING	3-1
January	04	Newport County	1-2
	16	Clapton Orient	1-0
	18	EXETER CITY	3-0
	25	Brighton & Hove Albion	1-2
February	01	QUEEN'S PARK RANGERS	6-1
	08	Watford	0-5
	15	BRISTOL CITY	3-1
	22	CARDIFF CITY	5-1
	29	Crystal Palace	1-3
March	07	NORTHAMPTON TOWN	4-0
	14	Gillingham	1-1
	21	NOTTS COUNTY	5-1
	28	Bristol Rovers	2-3
April	04	CLAPTON ORIENT	2-0
	11	Southend United	0-0
	13	Swindon Town	2-1
	14	SWINDON TOWN	3-1
	18	BOURNEMOUTH & B.A.	2-0
	25	Luton Town	1-1
	27	LUTON TOWN	0-0
May	02	TORQUAY UNITED	2-1

3rd Division (South) Final Table 1935-36

1	COVENTRY CITY	42	102	45	57
2	Luton Town	42	81	45	56
3	Reading	42	87	62	54
4	Queen's Park Rangers	42	84	53	53
5	Watford	42	80	54	49
6	Crystal Palace	42	96	74	49
7	Brighton & Hove Albion	42	70	63	44
8	Bournemouth & B.A.	42	60	56	43
9	Notts County	42	60	57	42
10	Torquay United	42	62	62	41
11	Aldershot	42	53	61	40
12	Millwall	42	58	71	40
13	Bristol City	42	48	59	40
14	Clapton Orient	42	55	61	38
15	Northampton Town	42	62	90	38
16	Gillingham	42	66	77	37
17	Bristol Rovers	42	69	95	37
18	Southend United	42	61	62	36
19	Swindon Town	42	64	73	36
20	Cardiff City	42	60	73	36
21	Newport County	42	60	111	31
22	Exeter City	42	59	93	27
		924	1497	1497	924

Coventry City were promoted to Division 2. *Exeter City* (48 votes) and *Newport County* (40) were re-elected. Bath City (9), Dartford (10 and Folkestone (1) were all unsuccessful.

1936-37 – LEAGUE DIVISION 1

Division 1 (top 6) at 26/12/36

1	Arsenal	21	45-29	26
2	Brentford	21	42-35	26
3	Sunderland	21	45-38	26
4	Charlton Athletic	22	28-26	26
5	Portsmouth	22	31-32	25
6	Derby County	22	48-46	24

FINAL PHASE ... AT THE TOP

For the first time in some time, it seemed as if there would be a tight finish in the fight to become champions of the Football League. After the April 10th games, Manchester City headed the table, just 1 point ahead of Arsenal and Charlton Athletic. Importantly, however, City had a game in hand on both their rivals.

Top 3 at 10/04/37

1	MANCHESTER CITY	38	93-55	50	1.69
2	Arsenal	39	76-47	49	1.62
3	Charlton Athletic	39	53-46	49	1.15

(Figure in the right-hand column is goal average)

City moved closer to lifting the Division 1 crown on April 14th by winning 3-1 at Sunderland, following this with a 5-2 win at Preston North End on the 17th. Arsenal stayed on the case by beating Portsmouth 4-0 at Highbury, but Charlton dropped a point at Everton and were now 4 points behind the leaders with only 2 games left. Manchester City seemed in no mood to postpone their celebrations any longer than necessary and became champions a week later on April 24th by defeating Sheffield Wednesday 4-1 at Maine Road. This took City onto an unassailable 56 points total.

Division 1 (bottom 6) at 26/12/36

17	Liverpool	22	38-44	19
18	Preston North End	21	30-38	19
19	Sheffield Wednesday	21	33-32	18
20	Leeds United	21	33-40	17
21	West Bromwich Albion	20	34-46	15
22	Manchester United	21	29-48	13

FINAL PHASE ... AT THE BOTTOM

By the middle of April, six clubs were left in danger of the drop and, of these, Manchester United and Sheffield Wednesday looked to be in the gravest danger at the foot of the table as the games began to run out.

Bottom 6 at 10/04/37

17	Liverpool	39	58-78	33	0.74
18	West Bromwich Albion	37	66-87	32	0.76
19	Bolton Wanderers	39	43-65	32	0.66
20	Leeds United	38	54-75	30	0.72
21	Manchester United	39	52-75	29	0.69
22	Sheffield Wednesday	38	47-59	28	0.80

(Figure in the right-hand column is goal average)

On April 17th, West Bromwich, having lost at Wolves 3 days before, won 3-2 at Sheffield Wednesday. Manchester United also won, but Leeds United lost 0-3 at Wolves to drop to 21st place. Four days later Leeds lost to Wolves again and sank to the bottom of Division 1 after Sheffield Wednesday won at West Bromwich. With Manchester United drawing at Sunderland, the Elland Road side looked to be in dire straits.

On April 24th, however, there was a reversal of fortunes as Manchester United lost their final game 0-1, away at West Bromwich, and Leeds defeated Sunderland 3-0. The West Yorkshire club moved up to 20th, above their Old Trafford rivals on goal average. Bolton, Liverpool and West Bromwich Albion all moved to safety on this day.

Leeds United had one game left and an interesting situation. If they lost 0-2 they would drop below Manchester United. If they lost 0-1 they would stay ahead of United, but might be passed by Wednesday, if the Sheffield side won its last match at Huddersfield. A draw would be enough to guarantee safety on May 1st. Leeds beat Portsmouth 3-1 in their final fixture, which sent Manchester United and Sheffield Wednesday down.

MANCHESTER CITY

August	29	Middlesbrough	0-2
September	02	LEEDS UNITED	4-0
	05	WEST BROMWICH ALBION	6-2
	09	Leeds United	1-1
	12	Manchester United	2-3
	16	BIRMINGHAM	1-1
	19	Portsmouth	1-2
	26	CHELSEA	0-0
October	03	Stoke City	2-2
	10	CHARLTON ATHLETIC	1-1
	17	DERBY COUNTY	3-2
	24	Wolves	1-2
	31	SUNDERLAND	2-4
November	07	Huddersfield Town	1-1
	14	EVERTON	4-1
	21	Bolton Wanderers	2-0
December	05	Arsenal	3-1
	12	PRESTON NORTH END	4-1
	19	Sheffield Wednesday	1-5
	25	Grimsby Town	3-5
	26	MIDDLESBROUGH	2-1
	28	GRIMSBY TOWN	1-1
January	02	West Bromwich Albion	2-2
	09	MANCHESTER UNITED	1-0
	23	PORTSMOUTH	3-1
February	03	Chelsea	4-4
	06	STOKE CITY	2-1
	13	Charlton Athletic	1-1
	24	Derby County	5-0
	27	WOLVES	4-1
March	13	HUDDERSFIELD TOWN	3-0
	20	Everton	1-1
	26	Liverpool	5-0
	27	BOLTON WANDERERS	2-2
	29	LIVERPOOL	5-1
April	03	Brentford	6-2
	07	BRENTFORD	2-1
	10	ARSENAL	2-0
	14	Sunderland	3-1
	17	Preston North End	5-2
	24	SHEFFIELD WEDNESDAY	4-1
May	01	Birmingham	2-2

1st Division Final Table 1936-37

1	MANCHESTER CITY	42	107	61	57
2	Charlton Athletic	42	58	49	54
3	Arsenal	42	80	49	52
4	Derby County	42	96	90	49
5	Wolves	42	84	67	47
6	Brentford	42	82	78	46
7	Middlesbrough	42	74	71	46
8	Sunderland	42	89	87	44
9	Portsmouth	42	62	66	44
10	Stoke City	42	72	57	42
11	Birmingham	42	64	60	41
12	Grimsby Town	42	86	81	41
13	Chelsea	42	52	55	41
14	Preston North End	42	56	67	41
15	Huddersfield Town	42	62	64	39
16	West Bromwich Albion	42	77	98	38
17	Everton	42	81	78	37
18	Liverpool	42	62	84	35
19	Leeds United	42	60	80	34
20	Bolton Wanderers	42	43	66	34
21	Manchester United	42	55	78	32
22	Sheffield Wednesday	42	53	69	30
		924	1555	1555	924

Manchester United and Sheffield Wednesday were relegated.

1936-37 – LEAGUE DIVISION 2

LEICESTER CITY

Division 2 (top 6) at 25/12/36

1	Blackpool	21	52-23	31
2	Plymouth Argyle	21	44-24	29
3	Bury	21	32-24	27
4	Coventry City	21	33-21	26
5	LEICESTER CITY	21	40-26	25
6	Newcastle United	21	41-25	24

FINAL PHASE ... AT THE TOP

After the April 3rd fixtures were over, Blackpool held a three-point lead over Leicester City and Bury, who had played a game more. Two points behind third place were Plymouth Argyle, the only one of the top four never to have played in the top flight.

Top 3 at 03/04/37

1	Blackpool	38	84-50	51	1.68
2	LEICESTER CITY	38	77-53	48	1.45
3	Bury	39	68-54	48	1.26
4	Plymouth Argyle	38	68-49	46	1.39

(Figure in the right-hand column is goal average)

On April 10th, Argyle drew 1-1 at Blackpool, a result which worked in favour of both Leicester City and Bury, whose wins enabled them to close the gap on the leaders to two points. A week later, Bury lost at Nottingham Forest, which all but ended their promotion chances as the other three contenders all won, with Blackpool's victory at Coventry City guaranteeing their promotion.

The leaders completed their fixtures on April 24th with a 1-1 home draw against bottom club Doncaster Rovers. Bury beat Plymouth, while in the day's most important game Leicester defeated Nottingham Forest 2-1 to move to within a point of the top with one game left. On May 1st, Leicester City beat Tottenham Hotspur 4-1 at Filbert Street and leapfrogged into first place to become champions.

Division 2 (bottom 6) at 25/12/36

17	Chesterfield	20	33-39	17
18	Southampton	21	30-41	17
19	West Ham United	20	25-35	16
20	Bradford City	22	28-45	16
21	Bradford Park Avenue	21	28-47	16
22	Doncaster Rovers	20	11-47	9

FINAL PHASE ... AT THE BOTTOM

With the season drawing to a close, six sides were still in danger of relegation from Division 2. Doncaster's plight was by far the worst as they were 6 points adrift, but any one of the other five could face the drop if results went against them.

Bottom 6 at 03/04/37

17	Southampton	38	52-69	33	0.75
18	Norwich City	38	55-67	32	0.82
19	Bradford Park Avenue	39	49-87	29	0.56
20	Nottingham Forest	37	59-79	28	0.75
21	Bradford City	39	51-88	28	0.58
22	Doncaster Rovers	38	27-78	22	0.35

(Figure in the right-hand column is goal average)

For Doncaster relegation was not long in coming. Defeat at Sheffield United on the 10th was followed by a 1-1 draw with Tottenham on April 17th and the point dropped was enough to take the club back to the 3rd Division. In the meantime, Norwich City and Southampton had secured safety and three points from two games had improved Bradford Park Avenue's survival hopes.

After heavy defeats on April 10th, both Nottingham Forest and Bradford City had won their matches on April 17th, but City had only one game left and, when Forest beat Tottenham 3-0 on the 21st, the West Yorkshire side slipped to edge of the abyss. Their fate was decided on April 24th. Although Forest lost 1-2 at Leicester City, Bradford City were themselves on the wrong end of a 0-2 score-line at Newcastle United and were relegated as a result.

August	29	BLACKPOOL	1-2
	31	BRADFORD PARK AVENUE	5-0
September	05	Blackburn Rovers	0-0
	09	Bradford Park Avenue	2-1
	12	BURY	0-3
	14	Tottenham Hotspur	2-4
	19	Plymouth Argyle	1-2
	26	West Ham United	1-4
October	03	NORWICH CITY	2-2
	10	Newcastle United	0-1
	17	COVENTRY CITY	1-0
	24	Doncaster Rovers	0-0
	31	FULHAM	2-0
November	07	Burnley	0-0
	14	SOUTHAMPTON	2-2
	21	Swansea Town	3-1
	28	BRADFORD CITY	4-1
December	05	Aston Villa	3-1
	12	CHESTERFIELD	3-1
	19	Nottingham Forest	3-0
	25	BARNSLEY	5-1
	26	Blackpool	2-6
	28	Barnsley	2-1
January	01	Sheffield United	1-3
	02	BLACKBURN ROVERS	1-0
	09	Bury	1-0
	23	PLYMOUTH ARGYLE	3-2
February	04	WEST HAM UNITED	2-2
	06	Norwich City	2-1
	13	NEWCASTLE UNITED	3-2
	25	Coventry City	2-0
	27	DONCASTER ROVERS	7-1
March	06	Fulham	0-2
	13	BURNLEY	7-3
	20	Southampton	1-1
	27	SWANSEA TOWN	0-0
	29	SHEFFIELD UNITED	1-2
April	03	Bradford City	2-1
	10	ASTON VILLA	1-0
	17	Chesterfield	5-2
	24	NOTTINGHAM FOREST	2-1
May	01	TOTTENHAM HOTSPUR	4-1

2nd Division Final Table 1936-37

1	LEICESTER CITY	42	89	57	56
2	Blackpool	42	88	53	55
3	Bury	42	74	55	52
4	Newcastle United	42	80	56	49
5	Plymouth Argyle	42	71	53	49
6	West Ham United	42	73	55	49
7	Sheffield United	42	66	54	46
8	Coventry City	42	66	54	45
9	Aston Villa	42	82	70	44
10	Tottenham Hotspur	42	88	66	43
11	Fulham	42	71	61	43
12	Blackburn Rovers	42	70	62	42
13	Burnley	42	57	61	42
14	Barnsley	42	50	64	41
15	Chesterfield	42	84	89	40
16	Swansea Town	42	50	65	37
17	Norwich City	42	63	71	36
18	Nottingham Forest	42	68	90	34
19	Southampton	42	53	77	34
20	Bradford Park Avenue	42	52	88	33
21	Bradford City	42	54	94	30
22	Doncaster Rovers	42	30	84	24
		924	1479	1479	924

Leicester City and Blackpool were promoted. Bradford City and Doncaster Rovers were relegated to Division 3 (North).

1936-37 – DIVISION 3 (NORTH)

Division 3 (North) (top 6) at 28/12/36

1	Chester	23	50-28	30
2	STOCKPORT COUNTY	21	46-20	28
3	Hull City	20	32-22	28
4	Lincoln City	21	53-36	27
5	Port Vale	23	38-33	27
6	Oldham Athletic	21	43-31	26

FINAL PHASE ... AT THE TOP

Lincoln City sat in pole position at April 10th, with a 2-point lead over Stockport County. With 4 games to go, the leaders' fate lay in their own hands, while County could only hope for a slip-up by the Imps which would give them the chance to step in.

Top 3 at 10/04/37

1	Lincoln City	38	98-49	55	2.00
2	STOCKPORT COUNTY	38	78-37	53	2.11
3	Chester	38	77-53	48	1.45

(Figure in the right-hand column is goal average)

Lincoln lost 1-3 at Carlisle United on April 15th and, despite a 3-0 win over the same opposition two days later, were now under serious threat from Stockport because of County's goal average being much better. The Hatters beat Crewe 1-0 on April 17th and went top after completing 'the double' on the 19th. On April 24th, Lincoln lost at Hartlepools United 1-3 and this allowed Stockport to go a point clear by drawing away to Chester. In spite of all this, the fight was not yet over as the top two had to meet in the final game of the season, on May 1st, at Edgeley Park. Stockport County won the match 2-0 and took the title.

Division 3 (North) (bottom 6) at 28/12/36

17	Crewe Alexandra	21	29-43	17
18	Southport	20	34-45	16
19	Barrow	19	28-37	15
20	Rochdale	21	25-44	15
21	Darlington	20	29-43	14
22	Tranmere Rovers	21	31-54	11

FINAL PHASE ... AT THE BOTTOM

Only two points separated the bottom 5 after the fixtures of April 10th had been completed. Having played a game more than the rest, Rochdale were perhaps the most nervous of the quintet, while Gateshead, having completed a match fewer than the others, seemed to have an even chance of escaping the re-election test.

Bottom 5 at 10/04/37

18	Crewe Alexandra	38	52-75	31	0.69
19	Tranmere Rovers	38	63-80	30	0.79
20	Rochdale	39	63-84	30	0.75
21	Gateshead	37	55-81	30	0.68
22	Darlington	38	58-82	29	0.71

(Figure in the right-hand column is goal average)

Tranmere Rovers drew with Wrexham on the 12th, but lost 0-4 at Gateshead on April 17th. This meant the Laides climbed 3 places in the table as none of the other sides in the bottom five won. Crewe, Darlington and Tranmere all lost on the 19th, with Gateshead catching the 'defeat bug' on April 21st and sinking 0-6 at Chester. On the 24th, Rochdale defeated Rotherham United 1-0 and ended the day level on points with Crewe, who drew with Wrexham, and Gateshead. Tranmere and Darlington were in the re-election spots. This changed on April 26th, when Tranmere Rovers blasted Gateshead 6-1 at Prenton Park to finish on 33 points – 3 up on Darlington, one ahead of Crewe and their victims and shading Rochdale on goal average. 'Dale beat Accrington 4-1 the next day to pull clear, leaving Crewe, Darlington and Gateshead going into their last games, on May 1st, needing to win. All three lost, saving Tranmere in the process. Crewe were also safe, thanks to goal average.

- 150 -

STOCKPORT COUNTY

August	29	DARLINGTON	3-3
September	02	Gateshead	0-0
	05	Wrexham	0-0
	07	GATESHEAD	4-2
	12	ROCHDALE	3-0
	14	Lincoln City	2-0
	19	ROTHERHAM UNITED	4-2
	26	Port Vale	0-3
October	03	OLDHAM ATHLETIC	4-1
	10	Accrington Stanley	1-2
	17	Barrow	0-0
	24	YORK CITY	6-0
	31	Carlisle United	0-1
November	07	HARTLEPOOLS UNITED	1-1
	14	Southport	1-1
	21	TRANMERE ROVERS	5-0
December	05	MANSFIELD TOWN	3-1
	19	CHESTER	4-0
	25	New Brighton	1-1
	26	Darlington	1-1
	28	NEW BRIGHTON	3-1
January	02	WREXHAM	2-0
	09	Rochdale	2-2
	16	Halifax Town	1-1
	23	Rotherham United	1-1
	30	PORT VALE	1-0
February	06	Oldham Athletic	2-0
	13	ACCRINGTON STANLEY	3-2
	20	BARROW	4-1
	27	York City	1-2
March	06	CARLISLE UNITED	1-2
	13	Hartlepools United	4-2
	20	SOUTHPORT	2-1
	26	HULL CITY	3-1
	27	Tranmere Rovers	2-2
	29	Hull City	1-0
April	03	HALIFAX TOWN	0-0
	10	Mansfield Town	2-0
	17	CREWE ALEXANDRA	1-0
	19	Crewe Alexandra	2-1
	24	Chester	1-1
May	01	LINCOLN CITY	2-0

3rd Division (North) Final Table 1936-37

1	STOCKPORT COUNTY	42	84	39	60
2	Lincoln City	42	103	57	57
3	Chester	42	87	57	53
4	Oldham Athletic	42	77	59	51
5	Hull City	42	68	69	46
6	Hartlepools United	42	75	69	45
7	Halifax Town	42	68	63	45
8	Wrexham	42	71	57	44
9	Mansfield Town	42	91	76	44
10	Carlisle United	42	65	68	44
11	Port Vale	42	58	64	44
12	York City	42	79	70	43
13	Accrington Stanley	42	76	69	41
14	Southport	42	73	87	37
15	New Brighton	42	55	70	37
16	Barrow	42	70	86	36
17	Rotherham United	42	78	91	35
18	Rochdale	42	69	86	35
19	Tranmere Rovers	42	71	88	33
20	Crewe Alexandra	42	55	83	32
21	Gateshead	42	63	98	32
22	Darlington	42	66	96	30
		924	1602	1602	924

Stockport County were promoted to Division 2. *Darlington* (47 votes) and *Gateshead* (34) were both re-elected. The unsuccessful applicants were Shrewsbury Town (12), South Liverpool (4) and Wigan Athletic (1). Mansfield Town were transferred to Division 3 (South).

1936-37 – DIVISION 3 (SOUTH)

Division 3 (South) (top 6) at 28/12/36

1	Brighton & Hove Albion	22	37-20	28
2	Watford	22	42-26	27
3	LUTON TOWN	21	42-27	27
4	Bournemouth & B.A.	21	31-22	27
5	Northampton Town	21	42-27	26
6	Notts County	22	39-34	26

FINAL PHASE ... AT THE TOP

Notts County held a 2-point lead by the close of April 10th, but Luton's game in hand and better goal average made things much less than comfortable for the leaders. Brighton and Watford, lying in 3rd and 4th places, were effectively out of contention by this point.

Top 4 at 10/04/37

1	Notts County	39	71-49	54	1.45
2	LUTON TOWN	38	91-51	52	1.78
3	Brighton & Hove Albion	39	67-41	48	1.63
4	Watford	39	82-54	48	1.52

(Figure in the right-hand column is goal average)

On April 17th, Notts County won 2-0 at Watford while Luton Town lost 0-1 at Gillingham. The race for the title and the one promotion spot seemed virtually over. Nobody had yet heard the laterally challenged lady strike up a song, however, and Luton forced a rethink by beating Swindon Town 5-1 on the 21st.

It might have been this which unnerved the league leaders, but, whatever the case, Notts County were beaten at home on April 24th by Brighton. Luton Town's 5-0 romp against lowly Newport lifted the Hatters to the top of the table, on goal average, with one match left to play. Notts County were all at sea again on May 1st and went down 1-2 at Walsall. Luton Town, who clearly had 'the force' with them now, beat Torquay United 2-0 and were promoted to Division 2.

Division 3 (South) (bottom 6) at 28/12/36

17	Crystal Palace	21	31-34	17
18	Walsall	21	28-44	16
19	Bristol City	21	24-44	15
20	Exeter City	21	21-48	11
21	Aldershot	21	23-45	10
22	Newport County	21	26-59	10

FINAL PHASE ... AT THE BOTTOM

Eight points behind 20th place with 4 games to go was the sorry situation Aldershot found themselves in with mid-April still not yet reached. Only 3 points covered the sides in 17th-21st places and the struggle to pull free from joining the Shots in applying for re-election looked as if it would go on for some time before being resolved.

Bottom 6 at 10/04/37

17	Torquay United	39	56-73	31	0.78
18	Newport County	38	62-88	31	0.70
19	Walsall	38	55-81	30	0.68
20	Cardiff City	37	46-83	29	0.55
21	Exeter City	39	53-84	28	0.63
22	Aldershot	38	47-80	21	0.59

(Figure in the right-hand column is goal average)

Having lost to Millwall on the 12th, Cardiff City won the game which really mattered, at Aldershot, on April 17th, meaning the bottom side would occupy one re-election slot. Cardiff then improved their chances of not filling the other unwanted berth by defeating the Shots 4-1 on the 19th. The Bluebirds' were able to say 'mission accomplished' 5 days later after winning 2-0 against Gillingham. Also reaching safety on the same day were Walsall, after beating Southend 3-0.

Newport County's 2-1 win over Walsall on April 26th freed the Welshmen from the threat of yet another begging act, which left Devonshire pair Torquay United and Exeter City to scrap it out to escape the cut. On May 1st, Exeter City won 2-0 at Reading, but it was not enough. Torquay lost, but not by the 10+ goals needed, and survived on goal average.

LUTON TOWN

August	29	SOUTHEND UNITED	1-0
	31	Walsall	1-0
September	05	Cardiff City	0-3
	07	WALSALL	2-0
	12	CRYSTAL PALACE	5-2
	16	Torquay United	2-2
	19	Exeter City	4-2
	26	READING	4-0
October	03	Queen's Park Rangers	1-2
	10	BRISTOL CITY	4-0
	17	WATFORD	4-1
	24	Brighton & Hove Albion	1-2
	31	BOURNEMOUTH & B.A.	1-0
November	07	Northampton Town	1-3
	14	BRISTOL ROVERS	2-0
	21	Millwall	2-0
December	05	Aldershot	3-2
	19	Newport County	1-2
	25	NOTTS COUNTY	2-1
	26	Southend United	0-3
	28	Notts County	1-2
January	02	CARDIFF CITY	8-1
	09	Crystal Palace	4-0
	23	EXETER CITY	2-2
February	06	QUEEN'S PARK RANGERS	0-1
	10	Reading	2-2
	13	Bristol City	3-2
	20	Watford	3-1
	27	BRIGHTON & HOVE ALBION	2-1
March	06	Bournemouth & B.A.	1-2
	13	NORTHAMPTON TOWN	3-2
	20	Bristol Rovers	0-4
	26	Clapton Orient	2-0
	27	MILLWALL	5-0
	29	CLAPTON ORIENT	2-0
April	03	Swindon Town	2-2
	07	GILLINGHAM	5-2
	10	ALDERSHOT	5-2
	17	Gillingham	0-1
	21	SWINDON TOWN	5-1
	24	NEWPORT COUNTY	5-0
May	01	TORQUAY UNITED	2-0

3rd Division (South) Final Table 1936-37

1	LUTON TOWN	42	103	53	58
2	Notts County	42	74	52	56
3	Brighton & Hove Albion	42	74	43	53
4	Watford	42	85	60	49
5	Reading	42	76	60	49
6	Bournemouth & B.A.	42	65	59	49
7	Northampton Town	42	85	68	46
8	Millwall	42	64	54	46
9	Queen's Park Rangers	42	73	52	45
10	Southend United	42	78	67	45
11	Gillingham	42	52	66	44
12	Clapton Orient	42	52	52	43
13	Swindon Town	42	75	73	39
14	Crystal Palace	42	62	61	38
15	Bristol Rovers	42	71	80	36
16	Bristol City	42	58	70	36
17	Walsall	42	62	84	36
18	Cardiff City	42	54	87	35
19	Newport County	42	67	98	34
20	Torquay United	42	57	80	32
21	Exeter City	42	59	88	32
22	Aldershot	42	50	89	23
		924	1496	1496	924

Luton Town were promoted to Division 2. *Exeter City* (40 votes) and *Aldershot* (34) were re-elected. Ipswich Town (24) were unsuccessful.

1937-38 – LEAGUE DIVISION 1 — ARSENAL

Division 1 (top 6) at 25/12/37

1	Brentford	22	37-30	27
2	Leeds United	21	37-31	26
3	Bolton Wanderers	20	35-26	24
4	ARSENAL	21	39-25	23
5	Wolves	19	30-21	23
6	Preston North End	21	35-25	23

FINAL PHASE … AT THE TOP

As the last chapter in the 1937-38 Division 1 story opened, Arsenal led the way, 1 point up on Preston and Wolves. The Gunners were chasing their fifth title in eight years, but Wolves had a game in hand.

Top 3 at 16/04/38

1	ARSENAL	38	68-40	46	1.70
2	Preston North End	38	61-41	45	1.49
2	Wolves	37	65-45	45	1.44

(Figure in the right-hand column is goal average)

On April 18th, Arsenal finished well beaten at Brentford, only hanging on at the top thanks to goal average after their main rivals both drew. 5 days later, the leaders returned to form and won 3-1 at Preston, who were replaced in 2nd spot by Wolves, who won 3-0 at Middlesbrough. Arsenal then won 1-0 against Liverpool and moved a point clear because Chelsea drew at Molineux, but there was real drama still to come. On May 2nd, Wolves beat West Bromwich and eased into 1st place. There was 1 fixture left for each of the top 2. Arsenal blasted Bolton Wanderers 5-0 on May 7th and waited for news from Roker Park, where Sunderland were at home to Wolves. The hosts won 1-0 and this meant Arsenal were champions again.

Division 1 (bottom 6) at 25/12/37

17	West Bromwich Albion	19	34-39	18
18	Grimsby Town	21	24-35	18
19	Liverpool	20	29-36	17
20	Everton	21	33-39	16
21	Blackpool	22	25-38	16
22	Portsmouth	21	30-45	14

FINAL PHASE … AT THE BOTTOM

Nine clubs were still in danger of relegation from Division 1 after the matches of April 16th. Most of the teams involved had 4 games left, though 2 of the bottom 3 had a match in hand on the rest. It seemed a case of whose nerve would hold best.

Bottom 9 at 16/04/38

14	Stoke City	37	54-51	36	1.06
15	Everton	38	70-70	34	1.00
16	Birmingham	38	49-53	34	0.92
17	Leicester City	38	49-69	34	0.71
18	Manchester City	38	73-72	33	1.01
19	Portsmouth	38	52-63	32	0.83
20	West Bromwich Albion	37	62-78	32	0.79
21	Grimsby Town	38	46-64	32	0.72
22	Huddersfield Town	37	44-63	31	0.70

(Figure in the right-hand column is goal average)

Over the next week, Huddersfield, Portsmouth and West Bromwich all won twice, while Stoke City lost 3 times, Birmingham fell twice and Manchester City took only 1 point from 2 games. On April 30th, Everton and Leicester City reached safety after winning their games, leaving six teams below them all on 36 points and Huddersfield Town at the foot of the table on 35. On May 2nd, Huddersfield beat Stoke City 3-0 and West Bromwich lost at Wolves.

Seven teams therefore went into the last day of the campaign facing the drop and only two of these were to play each other. The 'relegation results' of May 7th produced 5 winners and 2 losers. Staying up after a last day victory were Grimsby Town, Huddersfield Town, Portsmouth, and Stoke City, who all won at home, plus Birmingham who won 4-1 at Leicester. Going down were West Bromwich Albion, after crashing 1-4 at Middlesbrough, and Manchester City, champions 12 months before, after a 0-1 defeat at Leeds Road, Huddersfield.

Month	Date	Opponent	Score
August	28	Everton	4-1
September	01	HUDDERSFIELD TOWN	3-1
	04	WOLVES	5-0
	08	Huddersfield Town	1-2
	11	Leicester City	1-1
	15	Bolton Wanderers	0-1
	18	SUNDERLAND	4-1
	25	Derby County	0-2
October	02	MANCHESTER CITY	2-1
	09	Chelsea	2-2
	16	PORTSMOUTH	2-2
	23	Stoke City	1-1
	30	MIDDLESBROUGH	1-2
November	06	Grimsby Town	1-2
	13	WEST BROMWICH ALBION	1-1
	20	Charlton Athletic	3-0
	27	LEEDS UNITED	4-1
December	04	Birmingham	2-1
	11	PRESTON NORTH END	2-0
	18	Liverpool	0-2
	25	Blackpool	1-2
	27	BLACKPOOL	2-1
January	01	EVERTON	2-1
	15	Wolves	1-3
	29	Sunderland	1-1
February	02	LEICESTER CITY	3-1
	05	DERBY COUNTY	3-0
	16	Manchester City	2-1
	19	CHELSEA	2-0
	26	Portsmouth	0-0
March	05	STOKE CITY	4-0
	12	Middlesbrough	1-2
	19	GRIMSBY TOWN	5-1
	26	West Bromwich Albion	0-0
April	02	CHARLTON ATHLETIC	2-2
	09	Leeds United	1-0
	15	BRENTFORD	0-2
	16	BIRMINGHAM	0-0
	18	Brentford	0-3
	23	Preston North End	3-1
	30	LIVERPOOL	1-0
May	07	BOLTON WANDERERS	5-0

1st Division Final Table 1937-38

1	ARSENAL	42	77	44	52
2	Wolves	42	72	49	51
3	Preston North End	42	64	44	49
4	Charlton Athletic	42	65	51	46
5	Middlesbrough	42	72	65	46
6	Brentford	42	69	59	45
7	Bolton Wanderers	42	64	60	45
8	Sunderland	42	55	57	44
9	Leeds United	42	64	69	43
10	Chelsea	42	65	65	41
11	Liverpool	42	65	71	41
12	Blackpool	42	61	66	40
13	Derby County	42	66	87	40
14	Everton	42	79	75	39
15	Huddersfield Town	42	55	68	39
16	Leicester City	42	54	75	39
17	Stoke City	42	58	59	38
18	Birmingham	42	58	62	38
19	Portsmouth	42	62	68	38
20	Grimsby Town	42	51	68	38
21	Manchester City	42	80	77	36
22	West Bromwich Albion	42	74	91	36
		924	1430	1430	924

Manchester City and West Bromwich Albion were relegated.

1937-38 – LEAGUE DIVISION 2

ASTON VILLA

Division 2 (top 6) at 27/12/37

1	Sheffield United	23	40-29	31
2	Coventry City	21	35-21	29
3	ASTON VILLA	21	36-18	28
4	Bradford Park Avenue	21	32-24	25
5	Chesterfield	21	38-31	25
6	Burnley	23	32-29	24

FINAL PHASE ... AT THE TOP

By mid-April 1938, the fight for promotion to the 1st Division was at a fascinating stage, with 4 sides in the mix and no real clarity as to which 2 would triumph. Villa led the way, but their lead over 4th-placed Manchester United was just two points. Villa and Coventry had played fewer games than their rivals.

Top 4 at 16/04/38

1	ASTON VILLA	37	61-32	49	1.91
2	Sheffield United	39	68-53	49	1.28
3	Coventry City	37	62-39	48	1.59
4	Manchester United	38	73-48	47	1.52

(Figure in the right-hand column is goal average)

When Villa lost at Swansea on April 18th, Sheffield United went 2 points clear after beating Spurs 1-0, while Coventry and Manchester United joined the former leaders on 49 points. With wins on the 19th, Villa and City moved up to 1st and 2nd places, but Coventry's defeat by Fulham on April 23rd, plus 3-1 successes for the other 3 clubs at the top, saw things change again, with the Sky Blues down to 4th. Aston Villa held their nerve and went clear at the top on the 27th by beating Bradford Park Avenue 2-0. Three days later, on April 30th, all Villa's rivals lost and they became champions without kicking a ball themselves. On May 7th, Manchester United joined the Birmingham side en route for Division 1 by beating Norwich City 2-0 and edging out Sheffield United on goal average.

Division 2 (bottom 6) at 27/12/37

17	Blackburn Rovers	22	39-45	19
18	Southampton	21	31-44	19
19	Sheffield Wednesday	22	26-33	18
20	Swansea Town	22	24-34	17
21	Fulham	21	20-35	14
22	Plymouth Argyle	22	26-45	13

FINAL PHASE ... AT THE BOTTOM

Another complex situation, at the foot of Division 2 in 1938, left 8 clubs in relegation danger at mid-April. In 22nd place Stockport County had 30 points, two fewer than Swansea and Forest, both of whom trailed 5 others by a single point.

Bottom 8 at 16/04/38

15	Newcastle United	37	46-48	33	0.96
16	Blackburn Rovers	37	65-72	33	0.91
17	Luton Town	38	74-82	33	0.90
18	Sheffield Wednesday	37	44-50	33	0.88
19	Barnsley	38	47-60	33	0.78
20	Nottingham Forest	38	42-55	32	0.76
21	Swansea Town	37	39-63	32	0.62
22	Stockport County	38	40-61	30	0.66

(Figure in the right-hand column is goal average)

None of the threatened clubs proved at all convincing as the situation moved to a head, though Luton, Blackburn, Forest and Newcastle did manage to gather 3 points each by April 30th. Stockport's loss that day meant relegation for the Cheshire side, while wins for Blackburn and Luton Town finally secured their escape from the drop. The situation, with one match left, was now quite fascinating. Newcastle United, Sheffield Wednesday and Swansea Town had 36 points, while Barnsley and Nottingham Forest had 35 points. With the last 2 due to play each other, Newcastle and Wednesday were more or less safe, unless there was a quite bizarre turn of events, because of goal average. Swansea needed a point to be sure of staying up, as did Forest, who held a 0.0017 goal average over Barnsley. The Colliers-Forest game on May 7th ended 2-2 and it was the Oakwell men who went down.

August	28	WEST HAM UNITED	2-0
September	01	Luton Town	2-3
	04	Southampton	0-0
	06	LUTON TOWN	4-1
	11	BLACKBURN ROVERS	2-1
	16	Norwich City	0-1
	18	Sheffield Wednesday	2-1
	25	FULHAM	2-0
October	02	Plymouth Argyle	3-0
	09	CHESTERFIELD	0-2
	16	NEWCASTLE UNITED	2-0
	23	Nottingham Forest	2-0
	30	COVENTRY CITY	1-1
November	06	Bury	1-1
	13	BURNLEY	0-0
	20	Manchester United	1-3
	27	SHEFFIELD UNITED	1-0
December	04	Tottenham Hotspur	1-2
	11	STOCKPORT COUNTY	7-1
	18	Barnsley	1-0
	27	Bradford Park Avenue	2-1
	28	BARNSLEY	3-0
January	01	West Ham United	1-1
	15	SOUTHAMPTON	3-0
	27	Blackburn Rovers	0-1
	29	SHEFFIELD WEDNESDAY	4-3
February	05	Fulham	1-1
	19	Chesterfield	1-0
	23	PLYMOUTH ARGYLE	3-0
	26	Newcastle United	0-2
March	09	NOTTINGHAM FOREST	1-2
	12	Coventry City	1-0
	19	BURY	2-1
April	02	MANCHESTER UNITED	3-0
	05	Burnley	0-3
	09	Sheffield United	0-0
	16	TOTTENHAM HOTSPUR	2-0
	18	Swansea Town	1-2
	19	SWANSEA TOWN	4-0
	23	Stockport County	3-1
	27	BRADFORD PARK AVENUE	2-0
May	07	NORWICH CITY	2-0

2nd Division Final Table 1937-38

1	ASTON VILLA	42	73	35	57
2	Manchester United	42	82	50	53
3	Sheffield United	42	73	56	53
4	Coventry City	42	66	45	52
5	Tottenham Hotspur	42	76	54	44
6	Burnley	42	54	54	44
7	Bradford Park Avenue	42	69	56	43
8	Fulham	42	61	57	43
9	West Ham United	42	53	52	42
10	Bury	42	63	60	41
11	Chesterfield	42	63	63	41
12	Luton Town	42	89	86	40
13	Plymouth Argyle	42	57	65	40
14	Norwich City	42	56	75	39
15	Southampton	42	55	77	39
16	Blackburn Rovers	42	71	80	38
17	Sheffield Wednesday	42	49	56	38
18	Swansea Town	42	45	73	38
19	Newcastle United	42	51	58	36
20	Nottingham Forest	42	47	60	36
21	Barnsley	42	50	64	36
22	Stockport County	42	43	70	31
		924	1346	1346	924

Aston Villa and Manchester United were promoted. Barnsley and Stockport County were relegated to Division 3 (North).

1937-38 – DIVISION 3 (NORTH)

Division 3 (North) (top 6) at 01/01/38

1	Rotherham United	21	43-31	29
2	Hull City	21	39-22	28
3	TRANMERE ROVERS	21	39-19	27
4	Oldham Athletic	20	35-20	27
5	Gateshead	20	40-29	27
6	Lincoln City	20	39-18	25

FINAL PHASE ... AT THE TOP

After the completion of the April 16th programme there was a tight situation at the top of Division 3 (North). Hull City and Tranmere Rovers both had 47 points, with 2 others only a point behind and fifth-placed Rotherham United on 45 points. Whose nerve would hold the best?

Top 5 at 16/04/38

1	Hull City	37	75-40	47	1.88
2	TRANMERE ROVERS	37	69-38	47	1.82
3	Oldham Athletic	36	62-41	46	1.51
4	Doncaster Rovers	37	68-46	46	1.48
5	Rotherham United	38	62-50	45	1.24

(Figure in the right-hand column is goal average)

Tranmere Rovers moved to the front of the pack with a 7-2 demolition of Southport on April 18th. Hull were held 0-0 at home by Port Vale, and only Doncaster Rovers were winners out of the other 3. The top 3 all won their games on April 23rd, Doncaster beating Oldham Athletic. Hull City then clambered back into pole position on the 25th by beating York 3-1.

This set up a crucial game between Tranmere and the Tigers on April 30th, which Rovers won 1-0. Doncaster were held 1-1 at Darlington and with Oldham, who beat Southport 2-0, were two points off the lead as the day ended. While things were still close, the pendulum had swung in Tranmere's favour and a 1-0 win at Lincoln on May 2nd kept the Prenton Park momentum going. Doncaster also won, 2-1 against York, to add a little spice to their last day meeting with the leaders. If Tranmere had lost by a League record score on May 7th, Doncaster would have gone up in their place, but the game ended 1-1.

Division 3 (North) (bottom 6) at 01/01/38

17	New Brighton	19	28-32	17
18	Crewe Alexandra	21	23-29	17
19	Accrington Stanley	20	19-33	14
20	Darlington	22	27-47	13
21	Hartlepools United	21	29-55	10
22	Barrow	21	14-41	8

FINAL PHASE ... AT THE BOTTOM

Five matches remained for each of the bottom four at mid-April. Barrow, with a 3-point cushion between themselves and Accrington in 21st place, were least threatened, but nothing was certain as the final phase began.

Bottom 4 at 16/04/38

19	Barrow	37	37-66	28	0.56
20	Darlington	37	47-71	26	0.66
21	Accrington Stanley	37	41-69	25	0.59
22	Hartlepools United	37	45-79	24	0.57

(Figure in the right-hand column is goal average)

Darlington and Hartlepools United produced good sequences over their next 4 matches, each winning two and drawing twice. Accrington only lost one of their four fixtures, but won just once. Barrow failed to score in any of their quartet of games and took a mere two points. This meant that Barrow dropped to 21st place and Accrington Stanley were at the foot of the table as the final day arrived. Accrington lost 1-3 at Chester to take the wooden spoon. Barrow snapped out of their stupor to hammer Lincoln City 4-1 at Holker Street, but this was not enough, because Hartlepools' May 7th win over Wrexham and the fact that Darlington did not lose by a cricket score at Gateshead meant Barrow finished 21st in the table.

- 154 -

TRANMERE ROVERS

August	28	Rotherham United	1-2
	30	ROCHDALE	3-2
September	04	CHESTER	0-0
	07	Rochdale	0-0
	11	Accrington Stanley	1-0
	13	DONCASTER ROVERS	2-0
	18	CARLISLE UNITED	5-0
	25	Halifax Town	0-1
October	02	NEW BRIGHTON	5-2
	09	YORK CITY	1-2
	16	Gateshead	1-2
	23	OLDHAM ATHLETIC	1-1
	30	Darlington	2-0
November	06	PORT VALE	2-1
	13	Crewe Alexandra	0-1
	20	BARROW	3-0
December	04	HARTLEPOOLS UNITED	4-0
	18	HULL CITY	3-1
	25	Bradford City	3-1
	27	BRADFORD CITY	2-1
January	01	ROTHERHAM UNITED	0-2
	12	Wrexham	3-1
	15	Chester	1-1
	22	ACCRINGTON STANLEY	5-0
	29	Carlisle United	0-0
February	05	HALIFAX TOWN	2-0
	12	New Brighton	1-0
	19	York City	0-2
	26	GATESHEAD	4-1
March	05	Oldham Athletic	1-2
	12	DARLINGTON	1-1
	19	Port Vale	0-1
	26	CREWE ALEXANDRA	2-2
April	02	Barrow	2-2
	09	WREXHAM	3-2
	15	Southport	3-1
	16	Hartlepools United	2-2
	18	SOUTHPORT	7-2
	23	LINCOLN CITY	2-0
	30	Hull City	1-0
May	02	Lincoln City	1-0
	07	Doncaster Rovers	1-1

3rd Division (North) Final Table 1937-38

1	TRANMERE ROVERS	42	81	41	56
2	Doncaster Rovers	42	74	49	54
3	Hull City	42	80	43	53
4	Oldham Athletic	42	67	46	51
5	Gateshead	42	84	59	51
6	Rotherham United	42	68	56	50
7	Lincoln City	42	66	50	46
8	Crewe Alexandra	42	71	53	45
9	Chester	42	77	72	44
10	Wrexham	42	58	63	43
11	York City	42	70	68	42
12	Carlisle United	42	57	67	39
13	New Brighton	42	60	61	38
14	Bradford City	42	66	69	38
15	Port Vale	42	65	73	38
16	Southport	42	53	82	38
17	Rochdale	42	67	78	37
18	Halifax Town	42	44	66	36
19	Darlington	42	54	79	32
20	Hartlepools United	42	53	80	32
21	Barrow	42	41	71	32
22	Accrington Stanley	42	45	75	29
		924	1401	1401	924

Tranmere Rovers were promoted to Division 2. *Accrington Stanley* (41 votes) and *Barrow* (35) were re-elected, having finished ahead of Shrewsbury Town (15), South Liverpool (5), Scunthorpe & Lindsey United (1) and Wigan Athletic (1) in the vote. Port Vale transferred to Division 3 (South).

1937-38 – DIVISION 3 (SOUTH)

MILLWALL

Division 3 (South) (top 6) at 01/01/38

1	Queen's Park Rangers	22	35-20	28
2	Notts County	22	32-16	27
3	Watford	22	39-20	27
4	Cardiff City	21	47-30	27
5	Brighton & Hove Albion	21	34-24	25
6	MILLWALL	21	37-23	24

FINAL PHASE ... AT THE TOP

April 16th ended with 5 teams in contention for the Division 3 (South) title. Watford and Queen's Park Rangers had the points, while Millwall and Bristol City had a game or more in hand. Brighton, lying fourth, seemed to lack advantages, but were still in the mix as the final stages began.

Top 5 at 16/04/38

1	Watford	38	67-40	47	1.68
2	Queen's Park Rangers	38	68-41	47	1.66
3	MILLWALL	37	67-35	46	1.91
4	Brighton & Hove Albion	38	60-40	46	1.50
5	Bristol City	35	55-32	45	1.72

(Figure in the right-hand column is goal average)

If the battle for the one promotion place was a question of whose nerve would crack, then results on the 18th and 19th of April provided little in the way of answers. The top four all had odd-goal victories on April 18th, meaning Bristol City lost ground by only drawing at Newport. When City lost 0-1 at Northampton a day later, the old 'points in the bag are much better' adage was trotted out. All the leading five won on April 23rd as nerves held all round.

On April 25th, Millwall won their match in hand and went top. Two days afterwards, Bristol City won again to go fourth, two points off the lead with a game less played. Q.P.R. and Brighton finally felt the pressure on April 30th when both lost, while City were held in the Bristol derby 0-0. All this worked in Millwall's favour and, having won their game on the 30th, they were able to go into the final day, May 7th, knowing victory would mean promotion. A 5-1 beating of Exeter City was enough.

Division 3 (South) (bottom 6) at 01/01/38

17	Torquay United	22	24-46	18
18	Bristol Rovers	21	23-36	17
19	Aldershot	20	19-31	17
20	Clapton Orient	21	21-32	16
21	Walsall	21	26-39	16
22	Gillingham	20	16-34	10

FINAL PHASE ... AT THE BOTTOM

The 4-point gap between 20th-placed Torquay and 21st-placed Gillingham at April 16th suggested the Gills would be facing re-election along with Walsall, who lay 2 points adrift at the foot of the table. The Saddlers had a game in hand, but their plight was looking ever more desperate.

Bottom 4 at 16/04/38

19	Clapton Orient	38	36-55	30	0.65
20	Torquay United	38	34-64	29	0.53
21	Gillingham	38	33-67	25	0.49
22	Walsall	37	45-82	23	0.55

(Figure in the right-hand column is goal average)

Only bottom club Walsall took a point in games played on 18th April, so when Clapton Orient beat Gillingham 3-0 on the 23rd the London side were able to go clear of a re-election threat. The Gills then failed to beat Torquay United at The Priestfield on April 30th, the match ending 1-1. With Walsall going down 1-3 at Notts County, this cleared up the situation at the foot of Division 3 (South). Torquay were safe and Gillingham and Walsall would have to seek re-election to the Football League.

August	28	Reading	0-1
	30	QUEEN'S PARK RANGERS	1-4
September	04	CRYSTAL PALACE	2-2
	09	Queen's Park Rangers	2-0
	11	Notts County	1-1
	13	EXETER CITY	2-1
	18	NEWPORT COUNTY	4-0
	20	WALSALL	4-0
	25	Bristol City	0-0
October	02	WATFORD	1-1
	09	Gillingham	3-2
	16	SOUTHEND UNITED	1-0
	23	Clapton Orient	1-2
	30	TORQUAY UNITED	7-0
November	06	Mansfield Town	1-1
	13	BRISTOL ROVERS	2-1
	20	Northampton Town	1-0
December	04	Cardiff City	2-3
	18	Brighton & Hove Albion	0-1
	27	Aldershot	1-2
January	01	READING	1-1
	15	Crystal Palace	0-0
	24	NOTTS COUNTY	5-0
	29	Newport County	1-3
February	05	BRISTOL CITY	0-3
	12	Watford	1-1
	19	GILLINGHAM	5-0
	26	Southend United	2-1
March	05	CLAPTON ORIENT	3-0
	12	Torquay United	1-1
	19	MANSFIELD TOWN	1-0
	26	Bristol Rovers	2-0
April	02	NORTHAMPTON TOWN	3-0
	04	ALDERSHOT	4-0
	09	Walsall	1-1
	15	SWINDON TOWN	0-2
	16	CARDIFF CITY	1-0
	18	Swindon Town	2-1
	23	Bournemouth & B.A.	3-0
	25	BOURNEMOUTH & B.A.	4-0
	30	BRIGHTON & HOVE ALBION	2-0
May	07	Exeter City	5-1

3rd Division (South) Final Table 1937-38

1	MILLWALL	42	83	37	56
2	Bristol City	42	68	40	55
3	Queen's Park Rangers	42	80	47	53
4	Watford	42	73	43	53
5	Brighton & Hove Albion	42	64	44	51
6	Reading	42	71	63	51
7	Crystal Palace	42	67	47	48
8	Swindon Town	42	49	49	44
9	Northampton Town	42	51	57	43
10	Cardiff City	42	67	54	42
11	Notts County	42	50	50	41
12	Southend United	42	70	68	40
13	Bournemouth & B.A.	42	56	57	40
14	Mansfield Town	42	62	67	39
15	Bristol Rovers	42	46	61	39
16	Newport County	42	43	52	38
17	Exeter City	42	57	70	38
18	Aldershot	42	39	59	35
19	Clapton Orient	42	42	61	33
20	Torquay United	42	38	73	30
21	Walsall	42	52	88	29
22	Gillingham	42	36	77	26
		924	1264	1264	924

Millwall were promoted to Division 2. *Walsall* (34 votes) were re-elected, but *Gillingham* (28) were replaced by *Ipswich Town* (36). Rather strangely, a preliminary vote had placed Gillingham first with 18 votes, with the other candidates both polling 11.

1938-39 – LEAGUE DIVISION 1

EVERTON

Division 1 (top 6) at 26/12/38

1	Derby County	22	42-25	31
2	EVERTON	21	45-22	30
3	Wolves	21	33-17	25
4	Charlton Athletic	20	30-26	24
5	Middlesbrough	21	44-34	23
6	Liverpool	21	36-33	23

Everton were homing in on the title as the second week in April began, with Wolves the only club left who could thwart Goodison ambitions. The Molineux side had a game in hand on the leaders, but there was a yawning 8-point gap between them.

Top 2 at 08/04/39

1	EVERTON	37	78-45	54	1.73
2	Wolves	36	79-35	46	2.26

(Figure in the right-hand column is goal average)

Everton took a big step towards ending the title race on April 10th by beating Sunderland 6-2. Wolves stayed just about in contention by beating Aston Villa 2-1, but time was running out. When the second-placed men drew at Villa the next day it simply moved Everton closer to championship success. On April 15th, the leaders gathered another point when drawing 0-0 with Preston and Wolves' cause was now almost hopeless, despite their 3-1 victory over Charlton Athletic. Decision day finally arrived on April 22nd. Everton lost 1-2 at Charlton, but Wolves could only draw at Bolton Wanderers and Everton could no longer be caught.

Division 1 (bottom 6) at 26/12/38

17	Chelsea	21	37-41	18
18	Preston North End	20	25-30	18
19	Huddersfield Town	22	28-36	17
20	Leicester City	22	26-40	17
21	Birmingham	22	33-38	16
22	Brentford	20	26-42	16

FINAL PHASE ... AT THE BOTTOM

After the games played on April 8th, four clubs were left in the battle to avoid relegation. The bottom two, Leicester City and Birmingham, were firm favourites to go down.

Bottom 4 at 08/04/39

19	Huddersfield Town	37	52-58	30	0.90
20	Chelsea	36	58-71	28	0.82
21	Leicester City	37	40-71	26	0.56
22	Birmingham	37	54-82	24	0.66

(Figure in the right-hand column is goal average)

Defeats for Chelsea and Leicester, plus Birmingham's draw with Liverpool, on April 10th improved the survival chances of Huddersfield Town, who produced a crucial piece of self-help by beating Grimsby Town 2-0 on the 11th, when Leicester won 5-3 over Middlesbrough to pull level with Chelsea. On April 15th, Leicester moved above the Londoners by drawing with Derby County, while Chelsea lost at Huddersfield, who were now safe. Birmingham won at Brentford to keep their hopes alive.

Results on April 22nd caused a shake-up at the foot of the 1st Division. Wins for Chelsea and Birmingham saw these two move above Leicester, who lost at home to Grimsby. Four days later the crunch clash between Birmingham and Chelsea at St. Andrew's ended 1-1, meaning the Stamford Bridge side stayed a point ahead of their rivals, who had one game left to Chelsea's two.

On April 29th, Leicester became the first relegation casualty after Chelsea drew at Preston North End. Birmingham beat Leeds United 4-0 to draw level with Chelsea on points, but inferior goal average left the Midlands club in 21st spot. Chelsea needed only to avoid a 7-goal defeat in their final game in order to survive and a 1-1 draw with Bolton Wanderers on May 6th was more than enough to send Birmingham down.

August	27	Blackpool	2-0
	31	GRIMSBY TOWN	3-0
September	03	BRENTFORD	2-1
	05	Aston Villa	3-0
	10	Arsenal	2-1
	17	PORTSMOUTH	5-1
	24	Huddersfield Town	0-3
October	01	LIVERPOOL	2-1
	08	WOLVES	1-0
	15	Bolton Wanderers	2-4
	22	LEEDS UNITED	4-0
	29	Leicester City	0-3
November	05	MIDDLESBROUGH	4-0
	12	Birmingham	0-1
	19	MANCHESTER UNITED	3-0
	26	Stoke City	0-0
December	03	CHELSEA	4-1
	10	Preston North End	1-0
	17	CHARLTON ATHLETIC	1-4
	24	BLACKPOOL	4-0
	26	DERBY COUNTY	2-2
	27	Derby County	1-2
	31	Brentford	0-2
January	14	ARSENAL	2-0
	28	HUDDERSFIELD TOWN	3-2
February	01	Portsmouth	1-0
	04	Liverpool	3-0
	18	BOLTON WANDERERS	2-1
	22	Wolves	0-7
	25	Leeds United	2-1
March	08	LEICESTER CITY	4-0
	11	Middlesbrough	4-4
	18	BIRMINGHAM	4-2
	29	Manchester United	2-0
April	01	STOKE CITY	1-1
	07	Sunderland	2-1
	08	Chelsea	2-0
	10	SUNDERLAND	6-2
	15	PRESTON NORTH END	0-0
	22	Charlton Athletic	1-2
	29	ASTON VILLA	3-0
May	06	Grimsby Town	0-3

1st Division Final Table 1938-39

1	EVERTON	42	88	52	59
2	Wolves	42	88	39	55
3	Charlton Athletic	42	75	59	50
4	Middlesbrough	42	93	74	49
5	Arsenal	42	55	41	47
6	Derby County	42	66	55	46
7	Stoke City	42	71	68	46
8	Bolton Wanderers	42	67	58	45
9	Preston North End	42	63	59	44
10	Grimsby Town	42	61	69	43
11	Liverpool	42	62	63	42
12	Aston Villa	42	71	60	41
13	Leeds United	42	59	67	41
14	Manchester United	42	57	65	38
15	Blackpool	42	56	68	38
16	Sunderland	42	54	67	38
17	Portsmouth	42	47	70	37
18	Brentford	42	53	74	36
19	Huddersfield Town	42	58	64	35
20	Chelsea	42	64	80	33
21	Birmingham	42	62	84	32
22	Leicester City	42	48	82	29
		924	1418	1418	924

Leicester City and Birmingham were relegated.

1938-39 – LEAGUE DIVISION 2

Division 2 (top 6) at 24/12/38

1	BLACKBURN ROVERS	21	49-28	27
2	Newcastle United	21	40-25	27
3	Sheffield United	20	33-21	26
4	West Bromwich Albion	21	55-42	26
5	Fulham	21	34-25	24
6	Coventry City	20	29-25	24

FINAL PHASE ... AT THE TOP

At the start of April 1939, Blackburn Rovers held a 5-point lead at the top of Division 2. 5 other clubs vied for the 2nd promotion spot, just 3 points separating 6th-placed West Bromwich Albion from Sheffield Wednesday, who lay 2nd.

Top 6 at 01/04/39

1	BLACKBURN ROVERS	36	86-52	48	1.65
2	Sheffield Wednesday	34	77-50	43	1.54
3	Newcastle United	37	57-41	43	1.39
4	Sheffield United	35	51-37	42	1.38
5	Chesterfield	35	56-43	42	1.30
6	West Bromwich Albion	35	84-64	40	1.31

(Figure in the right-hand column is goal average)

None of the top 6 teams finished the campaign with any great conviction. Blackburn had won 3 more matches by the time mid-April arrived, while below them Newcastle and West Brom failed to earn a win between them in 7 attempts and Chesterfield took 3 points from 3 games. This left the two Sheffield sides to emerge from the pack to contest 2nd spot, both clubs having 47 points from 38 games by April 15th. Blackburn completed their title-winning bid on April 26th with a 0-0 draw at Sheffield United, who trailed their neighbours Wednesday by 1 point after the Owls drew 1-1 at Manchester City on the same afternoon. United had a game in hand, however. On April 29th both Sheffield sides won, Owls beating Spurs and United defeating Coventry. Tottenham returned to Sheffield on May 6th to play United, whose 6-1 success gave them 2nd place and promotion.

Division 2 (bottom 6) at 24/12/38

17	Bury	20	29-39	18
18	Southampton	20	31-40	17
19	Nottingham Forest	20	25-44	15
20	Swansea Town	20	22-42	13
21	Norwich City	20	25-49	13
22	Tranmere Rovers	20	20-44	8

FINAL PHASE ... AT THE BOTTOM

Tranmere Rovers had looked doomed for some time by the time April 1st ended, but Norwich City and Forest were not so far ahead yet as to make Rovers' cause totally hopeless. In 19th spot, Swansea Town still had some work to do also.

Bottom 4 at 01/04/39

19	Swansea Town	34	42-68	26	0.62
20	Nottingham Forest	35	42-78	23	0.54
21	Norwich City	34	41-83	23	0.49
22	Tranmere Rovers	36	35-90	15	0.39

(Figure in the right-hand column is goal average)

Alarm bells began to sound for Swansea on Good Friday when they lost at Tranmere and Forest beat West Bromwich to move to within a point of the Vetch Field club. On the next day, April 8th, Tranmere were relegated because both Norwich and Nottingham Forest won. Swansea, beaten at home by Coventry, found themselves down to 20th and in the thick of the relegation dogfight. The wake-up call was at last loud enough and the Swans won their next two games, which was just as well because both their rivals picked up points as well. After drawing with West Brom, Swansea beat Newcastle 2-1 on April 22nd to pull 4 points clear of Forest and 5 ahead of Norwich, who had a game in hand. In their final home game Town drew 2-2 with Bradford Park Avenue and moved to safety at last. Forest beat Plymouth 2-1, while Norwich lost 2-4 at West Bromwich Albion to fall 3 points behind their Nottingham rivals. When the Canaries lost at Plymouth on May 3rd they were relegated and their 1-0 defeat of Forest on May 6th was little consolation.

BLACKBURN ROVERS

August	27	TRANMERE ROVERS	3-2
	29	West Ham United	2-1
September	03	Chesterfield	2-0
	08	Sheffield Wednesday	0-3
	10	SWANSEA TOWN	4-0
	17	Bradford Park Avenue	4-0
	19	WEST HAM UNITED	3-1
	24	MANCHESTER CITY	3-3
October	01	Millwall	1-4
	08	SHEFFIELD UNITED	1-2
	15	Burnley	2-3
	22	TOTTENHAM HOTSPUR	3-1
	29	Luton Town	1-1
November	05	COVENTRY CITY	0-2
	12	Nottingham Forest	3-1
	19	NEWCASTLE UNITED	3-0
	26	West Bromwich Albion	0-2
December	03	NORWICH CITY	6-0
	10	Southampton	3-1
	17	PLYMOUTH ARGYLE	4-0
	24	Tranmere Rovers	1-1
	26	BURY	1-0
	27	Bury	4-2
	31	CHESTERFIELD	3-0
January	02	SHEFFIELD WEDNESDAY	2-4
	14	Swansea Town	1-2
	23	BRADFORD PARK AVENUE	6-4
	28	Manchester City	2-3
February	04	MILLWALL	3-1
	18	BURNLEY	1-0
	25	Tottenham Hotspur	3-4
March	11	Coventry City	1-0
	16	LUTON TOWN	2-0
	18	NOTTINGHAM FOREST	3-2
	25	Newcastle United	2-2
April	01	WEST BROMWICH ALBION	3-0
	07	Fulham	3-2
	08	Norwich City	0-4
	10	FULHAM	2-1
	15	SOUTHAMPTON	3-0
	22	Plymouth Argyle	0-1
	26	Sheffield United	0-0

2nd Division Final Table 1938-39

1	BLACKBURN ROVERS	42	94	60	55
2	Sheffield United	42	69	41	54
3	Sheffield Wednesday	42	88	59	53
4	Coventry City	42	62	45	50
5	Manchester City	42	96	72	49
6	Chesterfield	42	69	52	49
7	Luton Town	42	82	66	49
8	Tottenham Hotspur	42	67	62	47
9	Newcastle United	42	61	48	46
10	West Bromwich Albion	42	89	72	45
11	West Ham United	42	70	52	44
12	Fulham	42	61	55	44
13	Millwall	42	64	53	42
14	Burnley	42	50	56	39
15	Plymouth Argyle	42	49	55	38
16	Bury	42	65	74	37
17	Bradford Park Avenue	42	61	82	35
18	Southampton	42	56	82	35
19	Swansea Town	42	50	83	34
20	Nottingham Forest	42	49	82	31
21	Norwich City	42	50	91	31
22	Tranmere Rovers	42	39	99	17
		924	1441	1441	924

Blackburn Rovers and Sheffield United were promoted. Norwich City (South) and Tranmere Rovers (North) were both relegated to Division 3.

1938-39 – DIVISION 3 (NORTH) — BARNSLEY

Division 3 (North) (top 6) at 24/12/38

1	BARNSLEY	21	46-21	31
2	Southport	18	43-19	26
3	Doncaster Rovers	19	42-25	26
4	Bradford City	20	42-24	25
5	Oldham Athletic	20	41-32	24
6	Crewe Alexandra	19	42-27	23

FINAL PHASE ... AT THE TOP

At March 24th, Barnsley led Division 3 (North) by 13 points. It seemed as if it was only going to be a matter of time before the title and promotion issues were settled in favour of the Oakwell club, who were in a different class to the rest.

Top 3 at 24/03/39

1	BARNSLEY	34	79-28	55	2.82
2	Bradford City	34	72-44	42	1.64
3	Doncaster Rovers	33	60-40	42	1.50

(Figure in the right-hand column is goal average)

Barnsley recorded another victory on March 25th, defeating Hartlepools United 2-0. Bradford City and Doncaster Rovers also won, but were playing for second place in reality. After drawing 1-1 at Gateshead on April 1st, Barnsley gathered a further point on Good Friday at Stockport County. Bradford City lost 1-2 at New Brighton, leaving only Doncaster, who beat Accrington Stanley 7-0, with a mathematical chance of catching the leaders. A day later, April 8th, Barnsley won the home game with Wrexham 2-1 and moved on to 61 points. This put the Colliers 'out of sight' and gave them the title.

Division 3 (North) (bottom 6) at 24/12/38

17	Carlisle United	19	29-42	16
18	York City	20	27-37	15
19	Lincoln City	19	33-47	15
20	Hartlepools United	19	23-34	15
21	Darlington	19	33-52	15
22	Accrington Stanley	20	17-48	6

FINAL PHASE ... AT THE BOTTOM

Accrington's shocking campaign meant they would face an application for re-election, barring a bizarre twist in form. The other spot looked likely to be filled by Hartlepools, York City or Darlington, even though plenty of games remained.

Bottom 6 at 24/03/39

17	Gateshead	32	58-56	29	1.04
18	Carlisle United	33	55-86	29	0.64
19	Darlington	34	53-80	26	0.66
20	York City	32	45-66	25	0.68
21	Hartlepools United	34	48-84	24	0.57
22	Accrington Stanley	34	38-85	12	0.45

(Figure in the right-hand column is goal average)

On April 1st Accrington followed a draw against Gateshead with a 0-2 defeat at Wrexham and were ensured of a finish in last place. Nine days later Gateshead beat Hartlepools United 2-0 and moved to safety from the re-election threat, leaving four teams looking to avoid 21st place. On April 15th, Darlington beat Barrow 2-0 and ended the day 2 points clear of the other three unwilling contenders.

None of the strugglers managed a win on the 22nd, but Darlington and Hartlepools both secured draws, to leave Carlisle United and York deeper in the mire. City lost again two days later and looked favourites to finish in the remaining re-election place. Strange game football - and things turned around dramatically on April 29th. Carlisle thrashed Rochdale 5-1 and York won 2-1 at Darlington, the Quakers' final match. This left Hartlepools next to bottom with one game to go. A 0-0 draw with Wrexham saw 'Pools' join York City, beaten at Southport on May 6th, on 32 points. York had a better goal average though and Hartlepools United were the ones forced to seek re-election.

Month	Date	Opponent	Result
August	27	Oldham Athletic	2-4
	29	Lincoln City	4-2
September	03	HALIFAX TOWN	1-0
	05	ROTHERHAM UNITED	2-0
	10	New Brighton	2-1
	12	Rotherham United	1-0
	17	BARROW	4-0
	24	Chester	1-2
October	01	BRADFORD CITY	5-2
	08	Hull City	1-0
	15	DONCASTER ROVERS	1-1
	22	Southport	0-0
	29	CREWE ALEXANDRA	5-2
November	05	Carlisle United	1-3
	12	DARLINGTON	7-1
	19	Hartlepools United	1-0
	26	YORK CITY	1-0
December	03	Wrexham	1-1
	10	GATESHEAD	2-0
	17	Rochdale	1-2
	24	OLDHAM ATHLETIC	3-0
	26	ACCRINGTON STANLEY	4-1
	27	Accrington Stanley	2-0
	31	Halifax Town	4-1
January	14	NEW BRIGHTON	1-1
	21	Barrow	2-1
	28	CHESTER	3-0
February	04	Bradford City	2-0
	11	HULL CITY	5-1
	18	Doncaster Rovers	3-1
	25	SOUTHPORT	3-1
March	04	Crewe Alexandra	0-0
	11	CARLISLE UNITED	3-0
	18	Darlington	1-0
	25	HARTLEPOOLS UNITED	2-0
April	01	Gateshead	1-1
	07	Stockport County	1-1
	08	WREXHAM	2-1
	10	STOCKPORT COUNTY	0-1
	15	York City	3-2
	22	ROCHDALE	2-0
	29	LINCOLN CITY	4-0

3rd Division (North) Final Table 1938-39

1	BARNSLEY	42	94	34	67
2	Doncaster Rovers	42	87	47	56
3	Bradford City	42	89	56	52
4	Southport	42	75	54	50
5	Oldham Athletic	42	76	59	49
6	Chester	42	88	70	49
7	Hull City	42	83	74	46
8	Crewe Alexandra	42	82	70	44
9	Stockport County	42	91	77	43
10	Gateshead	42	74	67	42
11	Rotherham United	42	64	64	42
12	Halifax Town	42	52	54	42
13	Barrow	42	66	65	41
14	Wrexham	42	66	79	41
15	Rochdale	42	92	82	39
16	New Brighton	42	68	73	39
17	Lincoln City	42	66	92	33
18	Darlington	42	62	92	33
19	Carlisle United	42	64	111	33
20	York City	42	66	92	32
21	Hartlepools United	42	55	94	31
22	Accrington Stanley	42	49	103	20
		924	1609	1609	924

Barnsley were promoted to Division 2. *Hartlepools United* (38 votes) and *Accrington Stanley* (28) were re-elected, having finished ahead of Shrewsbury Town (22), South Liverpool (5), Scunthorpe & Lindsey United (4) Burton Town (0) and Wigan Athletic (0) in the ballot.

1938-39 – DIVISION 3 (SOUTH)

Division 3 (South) (top 6) at 27/12/38

1	NEWPORT COUNTY	21	36-22	32
2	Crystal Palace	20	40-22	29
3	Aldershot	20	26-21	26
4	Northampton Town	21	36-29	25
5	Reading	22	34-29	24
6	Swindon Town	20	42-30	23

FINAL PHASE … AT THE TOP

A surprise package to many in football, Newport County held a 7-point lead by the close of April 1st. Crystal Palace's 2 matches in hand might well reduce this, but County were looking very well-placed to take the title.

Top 4 at 01/04/39

1	NEWPORT COUNTY	36	53-37	49	1.43
2	Crystal Palace	34	59-44	42	1.34
3	Brighton & Hove Albion	35	57-42	40	1.36
4	Reading	36	63-51	40	1.24

(Figure in the right-hand column is goal average)

Newport County defeated Torquay United 1-0 to move closer to promotion on Good Friday, April 7th. A day later, County's main challengers, Crystal Palace, lost at Reading, who ended the day out of contention, because Newport drew at Queen's Park Rangers.

Another draw, at Torquay, on Easter Monday, took Newport to within 3 points of the title with 3 games left, but, as it turned out, the club did not have to wait long to start celebrating. On April 15th, County beat Southend United 3-0 at Somerton Park. Palace were held at home by lowly Bristol Rovers and, as a result, Newport's 55 points total meant they were out of reach and on their way to Division 2.

Division 3 (South) (bottom 6) at 27/12/38

17	Ipswich Town	19	22-27	16
18	Clapton Orient	19	21-27	15
19	Bristol Rovers	20	21-25	14
20	Bournemouth & B.A.	19	17-26	14
21	Torquay United	19	20-32	14
22	Walsall	20	18-32	11

FINAL PHASE … AT THE BOTTOM

By the start of April, Walsall trailed the rest by 4 points and seemed destined for a re-election berth finish. Many clubs still harboured worries, however, and the whole of the lower half of the table were still in danger.

Bottom 5 at 01/04/39

18	Ipswich Town	32	43-46	29	0.93
19	Port Vale	34	44-50	29	0.88
20	Bristol Rovers	35	45-50	26	0.90
21	Clapton Orient	33	37-43	26	0.86
22	Walsall	34	41-60	22	0.68

(Figure in the right-hand column is goal average)

Each of the clubs played 3 Easter games. Ipswich Town took 5 points and pulled away from the danger zone, into which Torquay United drifted in their place. Bristol Rovers gained 4 points, while Clapton earned just one, meaning a gap opened up at the foot of Division 3 (South).

On the 15th, there were wins for Torquay, Port Vale, Orient and Walsall, while Bristol Rovers drew at high-flying Palace. Over the next 12 days, Ipswich moved to safety, but both Port Vale and Torquay faltered and remained on the outer edge of the 'problem zone'. Beneath them, Orient took 3 points from 3 games, Bristol Rovers managed 2 from 2 and Walsall won twice by 5-0 to leave nothing settled in terms of re-election. On April 29th, however, the various trends changed and things were finally settled. Clapton, Port Vale and Torquay all won, while Bristol Rovers and Walsall lost. All the winners were now in the clear and the 2 losers became the re-election pair.

NEWPORT COUNTY

August	27	Clapton Orient	3-1
	29	Port Vale	1-2
September	03	CARDIFF CITY	3-0
	08	WATFORD	1-0
	10	NORTHAMPTON TOWN	1-1
	14	Watford	1-1
	17	Notts County	0-2
	24	ALDERSHOT	1-0
October	01	Bristol City	2-0
	08	CRYSTAL PALACE	2-0
	15	Ipswich Town	4-1
	22	EXETER CITY	0-0
	29	Bristol Rovers	0-0
November	05	BRIGHTON & HOVE ALBION	2-0
	12	Bournemouth & B.A.	1-0
	19	WALSALL	2-1
December	03	QUEEN'S PARK RANGERS	2-0
	17	READING	2-0
	24	CLAPTON ORIENT	2-1
	26	Swindon Town	0-8
	27	SWINDON TOWN	6-4
	31	Cardiff City	2-1
January	11	Mansfield Town	2-0
	14	Northampton Town	0-1
	21	Reading	1-0
	28	Aldershot	0-1
February	02	NOTTS COUNTY	2-1
	04	BRISTOL CITY	0-2
	11	Crystal Palace	1-1
	18	IPSWICH TOWN	3-2
	25	Exeter City	1-3
March	04	BRISTOL ROVERS	2-0
	11	Brighton & Hove Albion	0-0
	18	BOURNEMOUTH & B.A.	2-2
	25	Walsall	1-1
April	01	MANSFIELD TOWN	0-0
	07	TORQUAY UNITED	1-0
	08	Queen's Park Rangers	0-0
	10	Torquay United	1-1
	15	SOUTHEND UNITED	3-0
	29	PORT VALE	0-2
May	02	Southend United	0-5

3rd Division (South) Final Table 1938-39

1	NEWPORT COUNTY	42	58	45	55
2	Crystal Palace	42	71	52	52
3	Brighton & Hove Albion	42	68	49	49
4	Watford	42	62	51	46
5	Reading	42	69	59	46
6	Queen's Park Rangers	42	68	49	44
7	Ipswich Town	42	62	52	44
8	Bristol City	42	61	63	44
9	Swindon Town	42	72	77	44
10	Aldershot	42	53	66	44
11	Notts County	42	59	54	43
12	Southend United	42	61	64	41
13	Cardiff City	42	61	65	41
14	Exeter City	42	65	82	40
15	Bournemouth & B.A.	42	52	58	39
16	Mansfield Town	42	44	62	39
17	Northampton Town	42	51	58	38
18	Port Vale	42	52	58	37
19	Torquay United	42	54	70	37
20	Clapton Orient	42	53	55	35
21	Walsall	42	68	69	33
22	Bristol Rovers	42	55	61	33
		924	1319	1319	924

Newport County were promoted to Division 2. *Bristol Rovers* (45 votes) and *Walsall* (36) were re-elected, having finished ahead of Gillingham (15), Chelmsford City (1) and Colchester United (1) in the ballot.

OTHER INFORMATION

1932-1939

GOALSCORING 1932-1939

GOALS PER GAME

FOOTBALL LEAGUE

1932-33 – 6,512 in 1,848 – 3.52 goals per game
1933-34 – 6,291 in 1,848 – 3.40 goals per game
1934-35 – 6,306 in 1,848 – 3.41 goals per game
1935-36 – 6,119 in 1,848 – 3.31 goals per game
1936-37 – 6,133 in 1,848 – 3.32 goals per game
1937-38 – 5,441 in 1,848 – 2.94 goals per game
1938-39 – 5,787 in 1,848 – 3.13 goals per game

DIVISION 1

1932-33 – 1,645 in 462 – 3.56
1933-34 – 1,524 in 462 – 3.30
1934-35 – 1,677 in 462 – 3.63
1935-36 – 1,556 in 462 – 3.37
1936-37 – 1,555 in 462 – 3.37
1937-38 – 1,430 in 462 – 3.10
1938-39 – 1,418 in 462 – 3.07

DIVISION 2

1932-33 – 1,542 in 462 – 3.34
1933-34 – 1,441 in 462 – 3.12
1934-35 – 1,502 in 462 – 3.25
1935-36 – 1,533 in 462 – 3.32
1936-37 – 1,479 in 462 – 3.20
1937-38 – 1,346 in 462 – 2.91
1938-39 – 1,441 in 462 – 3.12

DIVISION 3 NORTH

1932-33 – 1,691 in 462 – 3.66
1933-34 – 1,800 in 462 – 3.90
1934-35 – 1,593 in 462 – 3.45
1935-36 – 1,533 in 462 – 3.32
1936-37 – 1,602 in 462 – 3.47
1937-38 – 1,401 in 462 – 3.03
1938-39 – 1,609 in 462 – 3.48

DIVISION 3 SOUTH

1932-33 – 1,634 in 462 – 3.54
1933-34 – 1,526 in 462 – 3.30
1934-35 – 1,534 in 462 – 3.32
1935-36 – 1,497 in 462 – 3.24
1936-37 – 1,497 in 462 – 3.24
1937-38 – 1,264 in 462 – 2.74
1938-39 – 1,319 in 462 – 2.86

LOW SCORES ANALYSIS 1932-1939

Number of games in which fewer than 2 goals were scored in Football League matches and % of total games.

1932-33 – 280 out of 1,848 – 15.15%
1933-34 – 316 out of 1,848 – 18.10%
1934-35 – 288 out of 1,848 – 15.58%
1935-36 – 341 out of 1,848 – 18.44%
1936-37 – 300 out of 1,848 – 16.24%
1937-38 – 404 out of 1,848 – 21.66%
1938-39 – 362 out of 1,848 – 19.60%

DIVISIONAL HIGH SCORES 1932-1939

1932-33

Division 1
24/12 Arsenal   9-2 Sheffield United
Division 2
24/09 Port Vale   9-1 Chesterfield
Division 3 North
01/10 Crewe Alexandra   8-0 Rotherham United
07/01 Wrexham   8-1 Hartlepools United
19/01 Walsall   8-1 Mansfield Town
06/05 Stockport County   8-5 Chester
Division 3 South
03/09 Northampton Town   8-0 Newport County
10/09 Torquay United   8-1 Southend United
29/10 Luton Town   8-1 Cardiff City

DIVISIONAL HIGH SCORES (continued)

1933-34

Division 1
18/11 Middlesbrough   10-3 Sheffield United
Division 2
11/11 Nottingham Forest   7-2 Bury
26/12 Grimsby Town   7-3 Manchester United
28/04 Grimsby Town   7-0 Blackpool
28/04 Oldham Athletic   7-0 Hull City
Division 3 North
06/01 Stockport County   13-0 Halifax Town
Division 3 South
02/09 Luton Town   10-2 Torquay United

1934-35

Division 1
08/12 Derby County   9-3 West Bromwich A.
Division 2
15/12 Brentford   8-1 Barnsley
20/04 Brentford   8-1 Port Vale
Division 3 North
16/02 Doncaster Rovers   7-1 New Brighton
23/02 York City   7-3 Crewe Alexandra
27/04 York City   7-0 Carlisle United
Division 3 South
14/12 Watford   7-4 Swindon Town
25/12 Torquay United   7-1 Crystal Palace
26/12 Watford   7-0 Newport County
16/01 Bristol Rovers   7-1 Northampton Town
19/04 Crystal Palace   7-0 Swindon Town
22/04 Torquay United   7-0 Q.P.R.

1935-36

Division 1
30/11 Wolves   8-1 Blackburn Rovers
18/01 West Bromwich A.   8-1 Blackburn Rovers
Division 2
23/11 Nottingham Forest   9-2 Port Vale
Division 3 North
26/12 Tranmere Rovers   13-4 Oldham Athletic
Division 3 South
13/04 Luton Town   12-0 Bristol Rovers

1936-37

Division 1
04/02 Stoke City   10-3 West Bromwich A.
Division 2
10/04 Blackburn Rovers   9-1 Nottingham Forest
Division 3 North
23/01 Mansfield Town   8-2 Hartlepools United
Division 3 South
05/09 Southend United   9-2 Newport County

1937-38

Division 1
15/04 Wolves   10-1 Leicester City
Division 2
13/11 Chesterfield   1-7 Manchester United
11/12 Aston Villa   7-1 Stoke City
29/01 Bradford P.A.   7-1 Blackburn Rovers
Division 3 North
13/01 Hull City   10-1 Southport
Division 3 South
26/02 Walsall   2-8 Bristol City

1938-39

Division 1
10/12 Middlesbrough   9-2 Blackpool
Division 2
26/12 Tranmere Rovers   3-9 Manchester City
Division 3 North
27/12 Chester   8-2 Hartlepools United
27/12 Crewe Alexandra   8-2 York City
Division 3 South
26/12 Swindon Town   8-0 Newport County

OTHER INFORMATION

LEADING GOAL SCORERS 1932-1939

Division 1

1932-33	Jack Bowers (Derby County)	35
1933-34	Jack Bowers (Derby County)	34
1934-35	Ted Drake (Arsenal)	42
1935-36	Ginger Richardson (W.B.A.)	39
1936-37	Freddie Steele (Stoke City)	33
1937-38	Tommy Lawton (Everton)	28
1938-39	Tommy Lawton (Everton)	34

Division 2

1932-33	Ted Harper (Preston North End)	37
1933-34	Jack Glover (Grimsby Town)	42
1934-35	Jack Milsom (Bolton Wanderers)	31
1935-36	Jock Dodds (Sheffield United)	34
	Bob Finan (Blackpool)	34
1936-37	Jack Bowers (Leicester City)	33
1937-38	George Henson (Bradford P. A.)	27
1938-39	Hugh Billington (Luton Town)	28

Division 3 North

1932-33	Bill McNaughton (Hull City)	41
1933-34	Alf Lythgoe (Stockport County)	46
1934-35	Gilbert Alsop (Walsall)	39
1935-36	Bunny Bell (Tranmere Rovers)	33
1936-37	Ted Harston (Mansfield Town)	55
1937-38	John Roberts (Port Vale)	28
1938-39	Sam Hunt (Carlisle United)	32

Division 3 South

1932-33	Clarrie Bourton (Coventry City)	40
1933-34	Albert Dawes (Northampton Town and Crystal Palace)	27
1934-35	Ralph Allen (Charlton Athletic)	32
1935-36	Albert Dawes (Crystal Palace)	38
1936-37	Joe Payne (Luton Town)	55
1937-38	Harry Crawshaw (Mansfield Town)	25
1938-39	Ben Morton (Swindon Town)	28

ATTENDANCES 1932-1939

FOOTBALL LEAGUE

There were 1,848 matches played in each of the seven seasons covered. In the figures below, the total for each season is followed by the average crowd per game. Although the period started with crowds down slightly on the previous campaign because of further economic problems across the country, there was a steady rise in the numbers attending Football League matches, as Britain recovered from the worst effects of the Depression, until 1938. During the later stages of the 1938-1939 season, however, a new international crisis loomed and thousands were 'called up' for military service as the threat of war increased because of the actions of Adolf Hitler and Nazi Germany.

1932-33	21,393,046	11,576 per game
1933-34	22,486,739	12,168 per game
1934-35	23,103,179	12,502 per game
1935-36	24,670,558	13,350 per game
1936-37	26,430,675	14,302 per game
1937-38	27,901,189	15,098 per game
1938-39	27,015,883	14,619 per game

462 matches were played in each division in each of the 7 seasons. Arsenal, Aston Villa, Chelsea, Manchester City and Tottenham drew the largest crowds in Division 1, Spurs and Villa also boosting 2nd Division attendances when in that section. The same was true for Manchester United, both the Sheffield clubs, Newcastle United, and West Ham United, all of whom spent time at that level.

DIVISION 1

1932-33	9,543,588	20,657 per game
1933-34	10,452,617	22,624 per game
1934-35	10,804,468	23,386 per game
1935-36	11,376,232	24,624 per game
1936-37	11,367,598	24,605 per game
1937-38	11,624,004	25,160 per game
1938-39	11,466,718	24,820 per game

1932-1939 (CONTINUED)

DIVISION 2

1932-33	6,073,983	13,147 per game
1933-34	5,793,942	12,541 per game
1934-35	6,093,934	13,190 per game
1935-36	6,910,738	14,958 per game
1936-37	7,988,529	17,291 per game
1937-38	8,609,926	18,636 per game
1938-39	8,627,157	18,674 per game

The best-supported clubs in Division 3 tended to be the section winners, or, at least, those who went on to win promotion within 2-3 years. In the North, Barnsley, Hull City, Chesterfield and Stockport County were all prominent in the attendance figures. In the South, Coventry City, Luton Town and Norwich City had decent followings, as did Ipswich Town, who joined the League in 1938. London clubs were often at the top of the list, however, with Brentford, Charlton Athletic, Crystal Palace and Millwall all well-supported. After their revival in the late 1930s, Cardiff City also began to draw respectable crowds.

DIVISION 3 NORTH

1932-33	2,290,176	4,957 per game
1933-34	2,460,664	5,326 per game
1934-35	2,415,962	5,229 per game
1935-36	2,413,383	5,224 per game
1936-37	2,628,978	5,690 per game
1937-38	3,077,177	6,661 per game
1938-39	2,923,754	6,328 per game

DIVISION 3 SOUTH

1932-33	3,485,299	7,544 per game
1933-34	3,779,516	8,181 per game
1934-35	3,788,815	8,201 per game
1935-36	3,970,205	8,594 per game
1936-37	4,445,570	9,622 per game
1937-38	4,590,082	9,935 per game
1938-39	3,998,254	8,654 per game

F.A. CUP FINALS 1933-1939

April 29th, 1933 – Wembley

Everton 3-0 Manchester City (1-0)
Stein, Dean, Dunn
Crowd – 92,950   Referee – E. Wood

April 28th, 1934 – Wembley

Manchester City 2-1 Portsmouth (0-1)
Tilson (2)   Rutherford
Crowd – 93,258   Referee – S. F. Rous

April 27th, 1935 – Wembley

Sheffield Wednesday 4-2 West Bromwich Albion (1-1)
Palethorpe, Hooper,   Boyes, Sandford
Rimmer (2)
Crowd – 93,204   Referee – A.E. Fogg

April 25th, 1936 – Wembley

Arsenal 1-0 Sheffield United
Drake
Crowd – 93,384   Referee – H. Nattrass

May 1st, 1937 – Wembley

Sunderland 3-1 Preston North End (0-1)
Gurney, Carter,   F. O'Donnell
Burbanks
Crowd – 93,495   Referee – R.G. Rudd

April 30th, 1938 – Wembley

Preston North End 1-0 Huddersfield Town (0-0)
Mutch (pen.)   (after extra time)
Crowd – 93,497   Referee – A.J. Jewell

April 29th, 1939 – Wembley

Portsmouth 4-1 Wolverhampton Wanderers (2-0)
Barlow, Parker (2),   Dorsett
Anderson
Crowd – 99,370   Referee – T. Thompson

... AND ALSO 1932-1939

CLUBS

There were shocks in the F.A. Cup in the 1932-33 season, with **Arsenal** being beaten 0-2 at 3rd Division **Walsall** in Round 3 and **Tottenham Hotspur** suffering a similar fate at **Luton Town** in Round 4.

No 2nd Division side either scored or conceded 100 or more goals in the 1932-33 season – the first time this had been true for any Football League section for 4 years.

Arsenal's 118 goals in the 1932-33 season was the third highest total scored by the English champions.

Darlington and **New Brighton**, the bottom two clubs in the 3rd Division (North) both equalled records for the section in the 1932-33 season. The Quakers' 28 points total matched the highest for a club finishing bottom of the table, while the Rakers' 32 points was equal to the highest number obtained by a Division 3 (North) side having to seek re-election.

In 1935, **Arsenal** became the 2nd English team to complete a hat-trick of League titles.

In 1936 **Arsenal** were fined £250 by the Football League for fielding weakened teams in Division 1 games and saving their better players for F.A. Cup matches.

Millwall became the first 3rd Division (South) club to reach the F.A. Cup semi-finals when they achieved this in 1937.

At the end of the 1937-38 season **Manchester City** became the first reigning champions to be relegated from Division 1.

The 1938-39 season saw **Tranmere Rovers** lose 31 out of 42 Division 2 fixtures – a record for the section.

INDIVIDUALS

On January 6th, 1934, English football lost one of its all-time greats when Arsenal boss **Herbert Chapman** died in the early hours of the morning of pneumonia. Chapman had created the great Huddersfield Town side of the 1920s before moving to Arsenal and building the outstanding Highbury team of the 1930s.

At the close of the 1934-35 season, **Frederick Wall**, who had been F.A. Secretary since 1895, retired. He was replaced by **Stanley Rous**, who was to have a major effect on the English game.

On April 13th, 1936, Luton's reserve half-back **Joe Payne** was given a run as centre-forward against Bristol Rovers. He hit a League record 10 goals as the Hatters won 12-0. In the 1936-37 season Payne scored 55 League goals.

After 20 seconds of the Hull City v. Wrexham game on Christmas Day, 1936, the visitors' **Ambrose Brown** was sent off – the fastest dismissal in League history.

F.A. President **Sir Charles Clegg** died on June 26th, 1937.

Mass protests in the Potteries during the 1937-38 season led Stoke City's directors to make urgent the settling of a dispute between the club and star winger **Stanley Matthews**. Things were sorted out and Matthews withdrew his transfer request.

On August 4th, 1938, Arsenal paid Wolves a record £14,000 to buy **Bryn Jones**.

Reading manager **Johnny Cochrane** was sacked after just 13 days in charge during the 1938-39 season.

TELEVISION

Film of the August 29th fixture between Arsenal and Everton in 1936 was shown on television, making this game the first to be viewed in this way.

On September 16th, 1937 parts of a game between Arsenal's 1st and 2nd teams were shown live on television. The success of this led to a decision to allow the 1938 F.A. Cup Final to be televised live.

PENALTIES

During the 1934-35 season, 394 penalty-kicks were awarded in Football League games. Almost a third of these (131) were missed or saved.

POOLS COMPANIES

The ongoing wrangle between the Football League and the Football Pools Companies raised its head again during the 1933-34 season when a Royal Commission was set up to investigate matters. The Commission reported that, although they were 'small-scale businesses', the Pools Companies should be banned. There was disagreement about whether fixed-odds bets, which were restricted to credit betting, should be allowed to continue.

Government efforts to outlaw the Football Pools during the 1934-35 season failed. This was due to a massive wave of popular protest, with hundreds of 'punters' writing to their M.P.s (having been encouraged by the Pools Companies). The new Betting and Lotteries Act ended up not mentioning the Football Pools.

In February 1936, the Football League tried to make things difficult for the Pools Companies by keeping home teams' visitors secret until the day before games were played. This did not stop coupons being issued, however, and clubs began to complain that crowds were being affected by the lack of knowledge about the opposition, so the League dropped the idea.

During the 1936-37 season, the M.P. R.J. Russell introduced a Private Members' Bill in Parliament trying to ban Pools Companies, but this was defeated at its 2nd reading in the House of Commons by 287 votes to 24.

INTERNATIONAL

In 1934, Italy became the second winners of the World Cup by beating Czechoslovakia after extra time. The Italians retained the Jules Rimet Trophy 4 years later by defeating Hungary 4-2 in the World Cup Final.

The F.A. decided in 1938 to raise the match fee for playing in an international from £6 to £10.

NUMBERS

The 1933 F.A. Cup Final was the first in which players from the two teams wore numbered shirts. Everton wore numbers 1-11, while Manchester City used numbers 12-22.

In 1938, the Football League decided in favour of numbering players' shirts. The voting was close, however, being 24 for and 20 against.

RULES OF THE GAME

Experiments were carried out in the 1935-36 campaign on refereeing. In a number of 'friendlies' and amateur games, two referees were used instead of one. The F.A. and the Football League rejected the positive findings these produced.

During 1937, F.A. Secretary Stanley Rous began a major overhaul of the rules of the game. His first change was the introduction of a semi-circle on the front of the penalty area to ensure that all players were 10 yards away from the penalty spot when a kick was being taken.

It became a rule that a quarter circle was marked in each corner of the pitch and a corner kick had to be taken from within this.

CROWDS

The Manchester City v. Stoke City F.A. Cup quarter-final in 1934 was watched by 84,659 spectators – a record crowd for an English match, not counting Cup Finals.

The Manchester City-Arsenal match of February 23rd, 1935 was watched by 77,582 paying spectators + season-ticket holders – a record Football League crowd of over 80,000. A new League record attendance was set on October 12th, 1935 when 82,905 watched the Chelsea v. Arsenal game.

ENGLISH SOCCER DURING ... ... WORLD WAR II

1939-1940

The Football League season had barely started when the 2nd World War began in September 1939. Most clubs had only played three games, with the tables looking like this –

Division 1

1	Blackpool	3	5	2	6
2	Sheffield United	3	3	1	5
3	Arsenal	3	8	4	5
4	Liverpool	3	6	3	4
5	Everton	3	5	4	4
6	Bolton Wanderers	3	6	5	4
7	Derby County	3	3	3	4
8	Charlton Athletic	3	3	4	4
9	Stoke City	3	7	4	3
10	Manchester United	3	5	3	3
11	Brentford	3	3	3	3
12	Chelsea	3	4	4	3
13	Grimsby Town	3	2	4	3
14	Aston Villa	3	3	3	2
15	Sunderland	3	6	7	2
16	Wolves	3	3	4	2
17	Huddersfield Town	3	2	3	2
18	Portsmouth	3	3	5	2
19	Preston North End	3	0	2	2
20	Blackburn Rovers	3	3	5	1
21	Middlesbrough	3	3	8	1
22	Leeds United	3	0	2	1
		66	83	83	66

Division 2

1	Luton Town	3	7	1	5
2	Birmingham	3	5	1	5
3	Coventry City	3	8	6	4
	Plymouth Argyle	3	4	3	4
5	West Ham United	3	5	4	4
6	Leicester City	3	6	5	4
	Tottenham Hotspur	3	6	5	4
8	Nottingham Forest	3	5	5	4
9	Millwall	3	5	4	3
	Newport County	3	5	4	3
11	Manchester City	3	6	5	3
12	West Bromwich Albion	3	8	8	3
13	Bury	3	4	5	3
14	Newcastle United	3	8	6	2
15	Chesterfield	2	2	2	2
16	Barnsley	3	7	8	2
17	Southampton	3	5	6	2
18	Sheffield Wednesday	3	3	5	2
19	Swansea Town	3	5	11	2
20	Fulham	3	3	6	1
21	Burnley	2	1	3	1
22	Bradford Park Avenue	3	2	7	1
		64	110	110	64

Division 3 (North)

1	Accrington Stanley	3	6	1	6
2	Halifax Town	3	6	1	5
3	Chester	3	5	2	5
4	Darlington	3	5	2	5
5	New Brighton	3	6	5	4
6	Rochdale	3	2	2	4
7	Crewe Alexandra	2	3	0	3
8	Wrexham	3	3	2	3
9	Tranmere Rovers	3	6	6	3
10	Lincoln City	3	6	7	3
11	Rotherham United	3	5	6	3
12	Carlisle United	2	3	3	2
	Hull City	2	3	3	2
14	Gateshead	3	6	7	2
15	Barrow	3	4	5	2
	Doncaster Rovers	3	4	5	2
	Southport	3	4	5	2
18	Oldham Athletic	3	3	5	2
19	Hartlepools United	3	1	4	2
20	York City	3	3	5	1
21	Bradford City	3	3	6	1
22	Stockport County	2	0	5	0
		62	87	87	61

Division 3 (South)

1	Reading	3	8	2	5
2	Exeter City	3	5	3	5
3	Notts County	2	6	3	4
4	Ipswich Town	3	5	3	4
5	Brighton & Hove Albion	3	5	4	4
6	Cardiff City	3	5	5	4
7	Crystal Palace	3	8	9	4
8	Bournemouth & B.A.	3	13	4	3
9	Bristol City	3	5	5	3
	Mansfield Town	3	8	8	3
	Norwich City	3	4	4	3
	Clapton Orient	3	3	3	3
	Southend United	3	3	3	3
	Torquay United	3	4	4	3
	Walsall	3	3	3	3
16	Queen's Park Rangers	3	4	5	2
	Watford	3	4	5	2
18	Northampton Town	3	2	12	2
19	Aldershot	3	3	5	1
20	Swindon Town	3	2	4	1
21	Bristol Rovers	3	2	7	1
22	Port Vale	2	0	1	1
		64	102	102	64

The Football League programme was suspended before any more matches could be played. For Aston Villa, Exeter City, Derby County, Gateshead, Ipswich Town and Sunderland the season ended at this point. The other clubs, however, formed regional leagues, just as had happened during World War I.

1939-1940 – THE REGIONAL LEAGUES

As the conflict proved to be a 'Phoney War', most games in these competitions were completed and in the South two full rounds of matches were played, except for one fixture.

Two points were awarded for a win and one for a draw, with goal average used to separate teams finishing on the same number of points. There were 10 leagues across the country, the tops of which came out like this –

THE SOUTH

Note –
The 'A' and 'B' divisions were played first. After this there was some re-mixing after which divisions 'C' and 'D' played.

'A'

1	Arsenal	18	62-22	30
2	West Ham United	18	57-33	25
3	Millwall	18	46-38	21
4	Watford	18	44-38	21

'B'

1	Queen's Park Rangers	18	49-26	26
2	Bournemouth & B.A.	18	52-37	24
3	Chelsea	18	43-37	23
4	Reading	18	47-42	22

'C'

1	Tottenham Hotspur	18	43-30	26
2	West Ham United	18	53-28	24
3	Arsenal	18	41-26	23
4	Brentford	18	42-34	20

'D'

1	Crystal Palace	18	64-30	27
2	Queen's Park Rangers	18	38-28	23
3	Watford	18	41-29	21
4	Southend United	18	41-37	19

SOUTH WEST

1	Plymouth Argyle	28	72-41	36
2	Torquay United	28	73-62	34
3	Bristol Rovers	28	62-55	28
4	Newport County	28	70-63	28

MIDLANDS

1	Wolves	28	76-44	41
2	West Bromwich Albion	28	87-51	40
3	Coventry City	28	68-57	29
4	Birmingham	28	56-60	29

EAST MIDLANDS

1	Chesterfield	20	69-23	30
2	Sheffield United	20	46-34	25
3	Barnsley	20	43-39	25
4	Grimsby Town	20	40-44	22

WEST MIDLANDS

1	Stoke City	22	57-41	31
2	Liverpool	22	66-40	29
3	Everton	22	64-33	28
4	Manchester United	22	74-41	28

NORTH WEST

1	Bury	22	64-30	34
2	Preston North End	22	63-27	32
3	Blackpool	22	75-36	32
4	Bolton Wanderers	22	55-30	30

NORTH EAST

1	Huddersfield Town	20	54-22	34
2	Newcastle United	20	59-42	25
3	Bradford Park Avenue	19	47-38	22
4	Middlesbrough	20	49-42	22

1939-1940 (CONTINUED)

LEAGUE CUP

At the end of the season, between April 20th and June 8th, a League Cup competition was staged, in which 64 clubs took part. In the semi-finals Blackburn Rovers beat Newcastle United 1-0 and West Ham United defeated Fulham 4-3. A crowd of 42,399 watched at Wembley as a first-half goal from Small gave West Ham victory 1-0.

1940-1941

THINGS CHANGE

With the war hotting up in the Summer and Autumn of 1940, the regional leagues were abandoned. When, after the Battle of Britain, the threat of invasion subsided, soccer was able to start up again, though many clubs announced that they did not intend to take part, these being Aston Villa, Accrington Stanley, Barrow, Blackpool, Bolton Wanderers, Bristol Rovers, Carlisle United, Darlington, Derby County, Exeter City, Gateshead, Hartlepools United, Ipswich Town, Newport County, Plymouth Argyle, Port Vale, Sunderland, Swindon Town, Torquay United, and Wolves. Blackpool and Bolton were to have a change of mind and played in the second half of the season, during which Coventry City did not take part.

The participating clubs were divided into two sections – 36 in the North and 34 in the South. Games were played on an 'as and when possible' basis, so, in the North, Bury fitted in 38 games, while late-starters Bolton Wanderers completed just 16 matches. Swansea Town managed 10 fixtures in the Southern section compared with Stoke City's 36. The league placings in both sections were decided by goal average. The leading standings at the end of the season looked like this –

NORTH

1	Preston North End	29	81-37	2.19
2	Chesterfield	35	76-40	1.90
3	Manchester City	35	104-55	1.89
4	Barnsley	30	86-49	1.78
5	Everton	34	85-51	1.67
6	Blackpool	20	56-34	1.65

SOUTH

1	Crystal Palace	27	86-44	1.95
2	West Ham United	25	70-39	1.79
3	Coventry City	10	28-16	1.75
4	Arsenal	19	66-38	1.74
5	Cardiff City	24	75-50	1.50
6	Reading	26	73-51	1.43

In London, there was an additional 12-team competition and, between February 1st and May 31st, a League Cup was staged. For 'the London Cup' the teams were divided into 2 groups of six, who played each other home and away, with the top two going into semi-finals. Brentford and Crystal Palace finished first and second in Group 'A', with Reading winning Group 'B' and Tottenham Hotspur being runners-up. Brentford and Reading won the semi-finals, with the Berkshire side winning the Final 3-2.

The League Cup was played on a two-leg basis up to the Final, which took place at Wembley on May 10th, with 60,000 there to watch. Arsenal and Preston North End drew 1-1, so it was necessary to have a replay at Ewood Park, Blackburn, on May 31st. Beattie scored twice for Preston, who also contributed Arsenal's goal as the Lancashire club won 2-1 in front of a good crowd of 45,000.

CHANGES

Coventry City's continued absence for the next season was confirmed, with Birmingham, Crewe Alexandra, Hull City, Notts County and Southend United also opting out. On the other hand, Gateshead, Sunderland and Wolves declared their intention to field teams 1941-1942.

1941-1942

With Hitler's Germany more interested in conquests in Eastern and Southern Europe, plus North Africa, and German attack on Britain restricted to air raids, more organised football became possible. What players turned out for a club often depended, however, on where servicemen were stationed. The nation was united in the battle against Germany, but the 1941-42 season was marked by a clear division between the London area and the rest of the country.

The 'London area' ran its own 16-club league and cup, with 2 points for a win, 1 point for a draw and goal average to be used to separate teams on the same points. The top 4 ended like this -

1	Arsenal	30	108-43	48
2	Portsmouth	30	105-59	42
3	West Ham United	30	81-44	39
4	Aldershot	30	85-56	39

In the London Cup, the four section winners were Arsenal, Brentford, Charlton Athletic and Portsmouth, from which **Brentford** emerged victorious by beating Portsmouth 2-0 in the Final. Smith scored twice for the Bees in front of a 72,000 Wembley crowd.

Elsewhere in the country, 53 clubs played in two sections up to December 25th, before beginning a single, but dual-purpose league for the rest of the season, part of which was used to decide which 32 teams qualified for the League Cup.

Part 1 – ending December 25th

SOUTH (13 clubs – top 4. Points were worked out on a basis of 18 matches being completed.)

1	Leicester City	17	40-17	26.40
2	West Bromwich Albion	13	62-26	26.30
3	Cardiff City	15	43-28	22.80
4	Norwich City	8	20-13	22.50

NORTH (40 clubs – top 6. 2 points were awarded for a win, 1 point for a draw, and goal average was used to separate teams on the same points.)

1	Blackpool	18	75-19	29
2	Lincoln City	18	54-28	29
3	Preston North End	18	58-18	27
4	Manchester United	18	79-27	26
5	Stoke City	18	75-36	26
6	Everton	18	61-31	26

Part 2 – LEAGUE CUP QUALIFYING COMPETITION
(December 27th to March 28th – points based on 10 completed matches. Goal average was used to separate teams on the same points.)

1	Northampton Town	9	27-14	16.66
2	Blackburn Rovers	10	19-7	16.50
3	Manchester United	10	23-13	15.00
4	Blackpool	10	45-19	14.00
5	Barnsley	10	33-16	14.00
6	Liverpool	10	33-24	14.00

LEAGUE CUP (April 4th to May 30th)

The League Cup was played on a two-leg basis throughout. In the Final, Sunderland and Wolves drew 2-2 at Roker Park on May 23rd, with Wolves winning the 2nd leg at Molineux 4-1 on May 30th to complete a 6-3 win on aggregate. A total of 78,038 watched the 2 games. Wolves then drew a 'play-off', 1-1, with London Cup winners, Brentford, on June 6th, at Stamford Bridge.

1941-1942 (CONTINUED)

Part 3 – LEAGUE CHAMPIONSHIP COMPETITION
(December 27th to May 30th – points based on 23 completed matches, though only those having played 18 games or more qualified)

1	Manchester United	19	44-25	33.89
2	Blackpool	22	108-34	33.45
3	Northampton Town	21	70-31	32.85
4	Liverpool	21	57-39	32.85
5	Wolves	20	52-29	31.05
6	Huddersfield Town	20	42-33	27.60

CHANGES

4 sides opted out of the 1942-43 campaign – Bournemouth & Boscombe Athletic, New Brighton, Norwich City and Preston North End. Aston Villa, Birmingham, Coventry City, Crewe Alexandra, Derby County, Notts County and Swindon Town all announced an intention to play games. 3 new teams were to be involved – Aberaman, Bath City and Lovell's Athletic. The 2nd World War was still in full flow, of course, but the tide was beginning to turn in the Allies' favour and the chances for football improved accordingly. Things were not yet back to the point where the Football League could restart.

1942-1945

Over these 3 seasons there was a common format operating in English football. The London area had its own competitions – a championship in which 18 teams competed and a Cup, in which 4 group winners played in semi-finals, with the victors meeting in the Final. In the West, 6 teams had an 18-game league up to Christmas and in the North there was a similar 'championship' for 50+ sides, with as many matches fitted in by clubs as possible, up to an agreed number, which grew as the War turned further in Britain's favour. After Christmas, North and West combined in a single 'North (2nd Championship)' and a 'League North Cup Qualifying Competition' in which all clubs played nine or ten games, with the best 32 going on to the 2-legged, k.o. stages. Darlington and Hartlepools United returned to action in 1943, with Accrington Stanley, Hull City, Port Vale and Preston North End reappearing a year later. In league competitions the 2 points for a win, 1 for a draw and goal average rules applied.

THE SOUTH 1942-1945

League 1942-43

1	Arsenal	28	102-40	43
2	Tottenham Hotspur	28	68-28	38
3	Queen's Park Rangers	28	64-49	38
4	Portsmouth	28	66-52	35

League Cup 1942-43

Arsenal beat Charlton Athletic 7-1 at Wembley, watched by 75,000, on May 1st.

League 1943-44

1	Tottenham Hotspur	30	71-36	46
2	West Ham United	30	74-39	41
3	Queen's Park Rangers	30	69-54	40
4	Arsenal	30	72-42	38

League Cup 1943-44

Charlton Athletic beat Chelsea 3-1 on April 15th at Wembley. The crowd was 85,000.

League 1944-45

1	Tottenham Hotspur	30	81-30	52
2	West Ham United	30	96-47	47
3	Brentford	30	87-57	38
4	Chelsea	30	100-55	37

League Cup 1944-45

Chelsea beat Millwall 2-0, watched by 90,000. The game was played on April 7th at Wembley.

1942-1945 ...   ... (CONTINUED)

THE WEST 1942-1945

League 1942-43
1	Lovell's Athletic	18	59-21	30
2	Bath City	18	66-26	28

League 1943-44
1	Lovell's Athletic	18	62-30	24
2	Cardiff City	18	45-28	23

League 1944-45
1	Cardiff City	18	54-24	27
2	Bristol City	18	59-30	27

THE NORTH 1942-1945

1st Championship 1942-43
1	Blackpool	18	93-28	33
2	Liverpool	18	70-34	29
3	Sheffield Wednesday	18	61-26	27
4	Manchester United	18	58-26	26
5	Huddersfield Town	18	52-32	26
6	Stoke City	18	46-25	25

2nd Championship 1942-43
1	Liverpool	20	64-32	32
2	Lovell's Athletic	20	63-32	27
3	Manchester City	19	43-24	27
4	Aston Villa	20	44-30	27
5	Sheffield Wednesday	20	43-26	26
6	Manchester United	19	52-26	25

League Cup Qualifying 1942-43
1	Manchester City	10	30-15	16
2	Rochdale	10	31-16	16
3	Liverpool	10	27-14	16
4	Lovell's Athletic	10	32-10	15
5	Chesterfield	10	22-12	15
6	Huddersfield Town	9	31-14	14

League Cup 1942-43

Blackpool beat Sheffield Wednesday 3-2 on aggregate, watched by 70,657 spectators. In the Cup Winners' match, Blackpool defeated Arsenal 4-2 on May 15th.

1st Championship 1943-44
1	Blackpool	18	56-20	28
2	Manchester United	18	56-30	28
3	Liverpool	18	72-26	27
4	Doncaster Rovers	18	45-25	27
5	Bradford Park Avenue	18	65-28	26
6	Huddersfield Town	18	48-25	26

2nd Championship 1943-44
1	Bath City	21	78-26	34
2	Wrexham	21	62-29	34
3	Liverpool	21	71-38	30
4	Birmingham	20	47-19	29
5	Rotherham United	21	54-30	29
6	Aston Villa	21	50-34	29

League Cup Qualifying 1943-44
1	Wrexham	10	26-12	18
2	Bath City	10	30-11	17
3	Stoke City	10	43-19	17
4	Leicester City	10	22-9	15
5	Sheffield United	10	33-16	15
6	Bradford Park Avenue	10	23-14	15

League Cup 1943-44

Aston Villa beat Blackpool 5-4 on aggregate. 93,540 watched the two games. Villa then drew the Cup Winners' match with Charlton Athletic 1-1 on May 20th.

THE NORTH 1942-1945 (CONTINUED)

1st Championship 1944-45
1	Huddersfield Town	18	50-22	31
2	Derby County	18	54-19	29
3	Sunderland	18	52-25	28
4	Aston Villa	18	54-19	27
5	Everton	18	58-25	26
6	Wrexham	18	40-18	25

2nd Championship 1944-45
1	Derby County	26	78-28	41
2	Everton	27	79-43	37
3	Liverpool	24	67-26	35
4	Burnley	26	56-36	33
5	Newcastle United	23	71-38	31
6	Aston Villa	25	70-45	30

League Cup Qualifying 1944-45
1	Derby County	10	38-9	17
2	Aston Villa	10	31-13	17
3	Bristol City	10	27-10	16
4	Everton	10	39-15	16
5	Burnley	10	25-10	15
6	Cardiff City	10	26-11	15

League Cup 1944-45

Bolton Wanderers beat Manchester United 3-2 on aggregate. 97,395 watched the two games. Bolton then beat Chelsea 2-1 in the Cup Winners' match on June 27th.

BACK TO NORMAL ...   ... but not quite, 1945-1946

The war against Germany ended in May 1945, but fighting continued until August when Japan finally surrendered after the U.S.A. bombed Hiroshima and Nagasaki using nuclear weapons.

Although the Second World War was over it would be some time before normal life could resume. For one thing there was the question of getting troops back to Britain and then demobilising the majority of the armed forces.

In England things were complicated. Clubs from the top two divisions in 1939 played a full 42-match programme in North and South sections. For 3rd Division clubs, the northern and southern sections were each divided into two regional parts, with mini-leagues in the first half of the season and League Cup qualifying competitions in the second half, followed by a knock-out format.

TOP DIVISIONS COMBINED (NORTH)

1	SHEFFIELD UNITED	42	112	62	60
2	Everton	42	88	54	55
3	Bolton Wanderers	42	67	45	51
4	Manchester United	42	98	62	49
5	Sheffield Wednesday	42	67	60	48
6	Newcastle United	42	106	70	47
7	Chesterfield	42	68	49	46
8	Barnsley	42	76	68	45
9	Blackpool	42	94	92	45
10	Manchester City	42	78	75	44
11	Liverpool	42	80	70	43
12	Middlesbrough	42	75	87	43
13	Stoke City	42	88	79	42
14	Bradford Park Avenue	42	71	84	40
15	Huddersfield Town	42	90	89	38
16	Burnley	42	63	84	36
17	Grimsby Town	42	61	89	35
18	Sunderland	42	55	83	35
19	Preston North End	42	70	77	34
20	Bury	42	60	85	34
21	Blackburn Rovers	42	60	111	29
22	Leeds United	42	66	118	25
		924	1693	1693	924

TOP DIVISIONS COMBINED (SOUTH)

1	BIRMINGHAM	42	96	45	61
2	Aston Villa	42	106	58	61
3	Charlton Athletic	42	92	45	60
4	Derby County	42	101	62	55
5	West Bromwich Albion	42	104	69	52
6	Wolves	42	75	48	51
7	West Ham United	42	94	76	51
8	Fulham	42	93	73	50
9	Tottenham Hotspur	42	78	81	47
10	Chelsea	42	92	80	44
11	Arsenal	42	76	73	43
12	Millwall	42	79	105	42
13	Coventry City	42	70	69	40
14	Brentford	42	82	72	38
15	Nottingham Forest	42	72	73	37
16	Southampton	42	97	105	37
17	Swansea Town	42	90	112	37
18	Luton Town	42	60	92	33
19	Portsmouth	42	66	87	28
20	Leicester City	42	57	101	23
21	Newport County	42	52	125	20
22	Plymouth Argyle	42	39	120	14
		924	1771	1771	924

DIVISION 3 (NORTH) LEAGUE – WESTERN SECTION

1	ACCRINGTON STANLEY	18	37	19	24
2	Rochdale	18	43	35	22
3	Crewe Alexandra	18	43	31	21
4	Chester	18	44	38	21
5	Wrexham	18	30	25	20
6	Tranmere Rovers	18	33	31	20
7	Stockport County	18	38	38	15
8	Oldham Athletic	18	29	32	15
9	Barrow	18	21	44	12
10	Southport	18	22	47	10
		180	340	340	180

DIVISION 3 (NORTH) LEAGUE – EASTERN SECTION

1	ROTHERHAM UNITED	18	56	28	26
2	Darlington	18	61	36	26
3	Gateshead	18	51	34	24
4	Doncaster Rovers	18	34	35	20
5	York City	18	34	34	18
6	Halifax Town	18	39	46	18
7	Bradford City	18	45	40	16
8	Carlisle United	18	34	58	13
9	Lincoln City	18	34	54	10
10	Hartlepools United	18	22	45	9
		180	410	410	180

DIVISION 3 (SOUTH) LEAGUE – NORTHERN SECTION

1	QUEEN'S PARK RANGERS	20	50	15	32
2	Norwich City	20	54	31	26
3	Port Vale	20	34	25	24
4	Watford	20	42	47	22
5	Ipswich Town	20	33	36	20
6	Notts County	20	39	47	20
7	Northampton Town	20	37	34	19
8	Clapton Orient	20	28	42	16
9	Walsall	20	31	42	15
10	Southend United	20	33	49	15
11	Mansfield Town	20	29	42	11
		220	410	410	220

DIVISION 3 (SOUTH) LEAGUE – SOUTHERN SECTION

1	CRYSTAL PALACE	20	55	31	29
2	Cardiff City	20	69	31	28
3	Bristol City	20	51	40	24
4	Brighton & Hove Albion	20	49	50	21
5	Bristol Rovers	20	44	44	20
6	Swindon Town	20	35	47	19
7	Bournemouth & B.A.	20	52	50	17
8	Aldershot	20	38	56	17
9	Exeter City	20	33	41	16
10	Reading	20	43	49	15
11	Torquay United	20	22	52	14
		220	491	491	220

F.A. CUP 1945-1946

All ties were played on a two-legged, home and away basis, until the semi-finals, which were played on neutral grounds. Teams in the top two divisions were exempted until the 3rd Round, in which there were 64 teams involved, as is the case today.

5th Round

Aston Villa	1-0, 1-0	Chelsea
Barnsley	0-4, 1-6	Derby County
Birmingham	3-1, 0-1	Sunderland
Bolton Wanderers	1-0, 1-1	Middlesbrough
Brentford	3-1, 0-0	Q.P.R.
Brighton & Hove Albion	1-4, 0-6	Derby County
Charlton Athletic	6-0, 1-1	Preston North End
Sheffeld Wednesday	0-0, 0-2	Stoke City

Quarter-Finals

Aston Villa	3-4, 1-1	Derby County
Birmingham	6-0, 2-2	Bradford Park Avenue
Bolton Wanderers	2-0, 0-0	Stoke City
Brentford	3-6, 1-3	Charlton Athletic

Semi-Finals

Birmingham	1-1, 0-4	Derby County
Bolton Wanderers	0-2	Charlton Athletic

Final – April 27th – Wembley – Crowd : 98,215

Charlton Athletic	1-4	Derby County

Charlton's Bert Turner scored for both teams in the second half of normal time. Doherty and Stamps (2) got Derby's goals in extra time to win the trophy for the Rams.

1945-1946 ... ... (CONTINUED)

In the 2nd half of the season, 3rd Division clubs played regional 'League Cup' competitions. In the North, the top 8 from each league qualified for the knock-out stages, which were played over two legs.

In the South, the top 2 from each league qualified for the semi-finals, which were meant to be of the 'single game, knock-out' type. There are errors in the goal-scoring and points columns of the 3rd Division (South) tables shown below. It has proved impossible to correct these from information available to date.

DIVISION 3 (NORTH) League Cup Qualifying – Western

1	STOCKPORT COUNTY	10	26	15	15
2	Southport	10	20	13	14
3	Accrington Stanley	10	24	17	13
4	Oldham Athletic	10	18	15	12
5	Crewe Alexandra	10	23	27	10
6	Wrexham	10	21	20	9
7	Chester	10	26	25	9
8	Tranmere Rovers	10	17	25	9
9	Rochdale	10	18	20	6
10	Barrow	10	13	29	3
		100	206	206	100

DIVISION 3 (NORTH) League Cup Qualifying – Eastern

1	DONCASTER ROVERS	10	24	15	15
2	Carlisle United	10	30	17	14
3	Bradford City	10	27	22	11
4	Hartlepools United	10	25	21	11
5	Gateshead	10	21	23	10
6	Darlington	10	26	31	10
7	Rotherham United	10	24	26	8
8	York City	10	16	18	8
9	Halifax Town	10	15	18	8
10	Lincoln City	10	21	38	5
		100	229	229	100

Semi-Finals

Chester	3-0, 4-2	Southport
Gateshead	2-2, 1-3	Rotherham United

Final

Chester	2-2, 2-3	**Rotherham United**

DIVISION 3 (SOUTH) League Cup Qualifying – Northern

1	QUEEN'S PARK RANGERS	16	38	11	25
2	Walsall	16	34	18	24
3	Mansfield Town	16	24	15	20
4	Southend United	16	22	21	19
5	Norwich City	16	27	25	16
6	Ipswich Town	16	19	24	15
7	Clapton Orient	16	22	31	15
8	Port Vale	16	21	25	14
9	Northampton Town	16	27	29	12
10	Watford	16	23	35	11
11	Notts County	16	17	31	10
		176	274	265	181

DIVISION 3 (SOUTH) League Cup Qualifying – Southern

1	BOURNEMOUTH & B.A.	16	37	20	20
2	Bristol Rovers	16	27	19	19
3	Reading	16	46	29	18
4	Crystal Palace	16	37	30	18
5	Cardiff City	16	39	22	17
6	Bristol City	16	30	27	17
7	Torquay United	16	19	30	16
8	Exeter City	16	22	28	14
9	Swindon Town	16	21	35	14
10	Aldershot	16	23	48	10
11	Brighton & Hove Albion	16	23	45	8
		176	324	333	171

Semi-Finals

Bournemouth & B.A.	1-1, 1-0	Queen's Park Rangers
Bristol Rovers	1-3	Walsall

Final

Bournemouth & B.A.	1-0	Walsall